Living Letters

LIFE APPLICATION BIBLE

Living Letters

LIFE
APPLICATION™
BIBLE

Second printing, January 1989

*Life Application Bible, New Testa-
ment* © 1988 by Tyndale House Publishers, Inc., Wheaton, IL 60189.

The *Life Application Bible* is a trademark of Tyndale House Publishers,
Inc.

This special gift edition is
published by the Billy Graham
Evangelistic Association with
permission from the original
publisher. Tyndale House
Publishers. Inc.. Wheaton. Illinois.

The text of the *Life Application Bible,
New Testament* is from *The Living
Bible* © 1971 owned by assignment
to Illinois Regional Bank, N.A., Elm-
hurst, IL. All rights reserved.

Living History of Israel © 1970, *Liv-
ing Books of Moses* © 1969, *Living
Lessons of Life and Love* © 1968,
Living Psalms and Proverbs © 1967,
Living Gospels © 1966, *Living
Prophecies* © 1965, *Living Letters* ©
1962 owned by assignment to Illinois
Regional Bank, N.A. All rights
reserved.

New Testament Life Application
Notes and Bible Helps © 1986
owned by assignment to Tyndale
House Publishers, Inc., Wheaton, IL
60189. Harmony of the Gospels ©
1986 by James C. Galvin. Maps ©
1986 by Tyndale House Publishers,
Inc. All rights reserved.

ISBN 0-8423-2553-0 Cloth
ISBN 0-8423-2554-9 Kivar

Library of Congress
Catalog Card Number
87-50217

Printed in the United
States of America

Have you ever opened your Bible and asked the following:

- What does this passage really mean?
- How does it apply to my life?
- Why does some of the Bible seem irrelevant?
- What do these ancient cultures have to do with today?
- I love God; why can't I understand what he is saying to me through his Word?
- What's going on in the lives of these Bible people?

Many Christians do not read the Bible regularly. Why? Because in the pressures of daily living they cannot find a connection between the timeless principles of Scripture and the ever-present problems of day-by-day living.

God urges us to apply his Word (Isaiah 42:23; 1 Corinthians 10:11; 2 Thessalonians 3:4), but too often we stop at accumulating Bible knowledge. This is why the *Life Application Bible* was developed—to show how to put into practice what we have learned.

Applying God's Word is a vital part of one's relationship with God; it is the evidence that we are obeying him. The difficulty in applying the Bible is not with the Bible itself, but with the reader's inability to bridge the gap between the past and present, the conceptual and practical. When we don't or can't do this, spiritual dryness, shallowness, and indifference are the results.

The words of Scripture itself cry out to us, "Won't even one of you apply these lessons . . . ?" (Isaiah 42:23). The *Life Application Bible* does just that. Developed by an interdenominational team of pastors, scholars, family counselors, and a national organization dedicated to promoting God's Word and spreading the Gospel, the *Life Application Bible* took many years to complete, and all the work was reviewed by several renowned theologians under the directorship of Dr. Kenneth Kantzer.

The *Life Application Bible* does what a good resource Bible should—it helps you understand the context of a passage, gives important background and historical information, explains difficult words and phrases, and helps you see the interrelationship within Scripture. But it does much more. The *Life Application Bible* goes deeper into God's Word, helping you discover the timeless truth being communicated, see the relevance for your life, and make a personal application. While some study Bibles attempt application, over 75 percent of this Bible is application-oriented. The notes answer the questions, "So what?" and "What does this passage mean to me, my family, my friends, my job, my neighborhood, my church, my country?"

Imagine reading a familiar passage of Scripture and gaining fresh insight, as if it were the first time you had ever read it. How much richer your life would be if you left each Bible reading with a new perspective and a small change for the better. A small change every day adds up to a changed life—and that is the very purpose of Scripture.

The best way to define application is to first determine what it is *not*. Application is *not* just accumulating knowledge. This helps us discover and understand facts and concepts, but it stops there. History is filled with philosophers who knew what the Bible said, but failed to apply it to their lives, keeping them from believing and changing. Many think that understanding is the end goal of Bible study, but it is really only the beginning.

Application is *not* just illustration. Illustration only tells us how someone else handled a similar situation. While we may empathize with that person, we still have little direction for our personal situation.

Application is *not* just making a passage "relevant." Making the Bible relevant only helps us to see that the same lessons that were true in Bible times are true today; it does not show us how to apply them to the problems and pressures of our individual lives.

What, then, is application? Application begins by knowing and understanding God's Word and its timeless truths. *But you cannot stop there*. If you do, God's Word may not change your life, and it may become dull, difficult, tedious, and tiring. A good application focuses the truth of God's Word, shows the reader what to do about what is being read, and motivates the reader to respond to what God is teaching. All three are essential to application.

Application is putting into practice what we already know (Philippians 4:9; Hebrews 5:14) and answering the question, "So what?" by confronting us with the right questions and motivating us to take action (1 Timothy 4:8; James 2:20). Application is deeply personal—unique for each individual. It is making a relevant truth a personal truth, and involves developing a strategy and action plan to live your life in harmony with the Bible. It is the biblical "how to" of life.

You may ask, "How can your application notes be relevant to *my* life?" Each application note has three parts: (1) an *explanation* that ties the note directly to the Scripture passage and sets up the truth that is being taught, (2) the *bridge* which explains the timeless truth and makes it relevant for today, (3) the *application* which shows you how to take the timeless truth and apply it to your personal situation. No note, by itself, can apply Scripture directly to your life. It can only teach, direct, lead, guide, inspire, recommend, and urge. It can give you the resources and direction you need to apply the Bible; but only you can take these resources and put them into practice.

A good note, therefore, should not only give you knowledge and understanding, but point you to application. Before you buy any kind of resource Bible, you should evaluate the notes and ask the following questions: (1) Does the note contain enough information to help me understand the point of the Scripture passage? (2) Does the note assume I know too much? (3) Does the note avoid denominational bias? (4) Do the notes touch most of life's experiences? (5) Does the note help me *apply* God's Word?

NOTES

In addition to providing the reader with many application notes, the *Life Application Bible* offers several explanatory notes, which are notes that help the reader understand culture, history, context, difficult-to-understand passages, background, places, theological concepts, and the relationship of various passages in Scripture to other passages to which they relate. For an example of an application note, see Revelation 3:20. For an example of an explanatory note, see Romans 16:1.

BOOK INTRODUCTIONS

The Book Introductions are divided into several easy-to-find parts:

Timeline. This puts the Bible book into its historical setting. It lists the key events of each book and the date when they occurred.

Vital Statistics. This is a list of straight facts about the book—those pieces of information you need to know at a glance.

Overview. This is a summary of the book with general lessons and applications that can be learned from the book as a whole.

Blueprint. This is the outline of the book. It is printed in easy-to-understand language and is designed for easy memorization. To the right of each main heading is a key lesson that is taught in that particular section.

Megathemes. This section gives the main themes of the Bible book, explains their significance, and then tells why they are still important for us today.

Map. This shows the key places found in that book and retells the story of the book from a geographical point of view.

OUTLINE

The *Life Application Bible* has a new, custom-made outline that was designed specifically from an application point of view. Several unique features should be noted:

1. To avoid confusion and to aid memory work, each book outline has only three levels for headings. Main outline heads are marked with a capital letter. Subheads are marked by a number. Minor, explanatory heads have no letter or number.
2. Each main outline head marked by a letter also has a brief paragraph below it summarizing the Bible text and offering a general application.
3. Parallel passages are listed where they apply in the Gospels.

PROFILE NOTES

Another unique feature of this Bible is the profiles of many Bible people, including their strengths and weaknesses, greatest accomplishments and mistakes, and key lessons from their lives. The profiles of these people are found in the Bible books where their stories occur.

MAPS

The *Life Application Bible* has more maps than any other Bible. There are two kinds of maps: (1) A book introduction map, where applicable, telling the story of that Bible book. (2) Thumbnail maps in the notes, plotting most geographic movements in the Bible.

CHARTS AND DIAGRAMS

Over one hundred charts and diagrams are included to help the reader better visualize difficult concepts or relationships. Most charts not only present the needed information, but show the significance of the information as well.

CROSS REFERENCES

An updated, exhaustive cross reference system in the margins of the Bible text helps the reader find related passages quickly.

TEXTUAL NOTES

Directly related to *The Living Bible* text, the textual notes provide explanations on certain wording in the translation, alternate translations, and information about readings in the ancient manuscripts.

ROMANS

KNOWLEDGEABLE and experienced, the District Attorney makes his case. Calling key witnesses to the stand, he presents the evidence. He discredits the testimonies of witnesses for the defense by skillfully cross-examining them. Then he concludes with an airtight summary and stirring challenge for the jury. The announced verdict is no surprise. "Guilty" states the foreman; and justice is served.

The apostle Paul was intelligent, articulate, and committed to his calling. Like a skilled lawyer, he presents the case for the gospel clearly and forthrightly in his letter to the church at Rome.

Paul had heard of the church at Rome, but he had never been there, nor had any of the other apostles. Evidently the church was begun by Jews who had come to faith during Pentecost (Acts 2). They spread the faith on their return to Rome and the church grew.

Although many barriers separated them, Paul felt a bond with these Romans. They were his brothers and sisters in Christ, and he longed to see them face to face. He had never met most of the Christians in Rome, yet he loved them. He sent this letter to introduce himself and to make a clear declaration of the faith.

After a brief introduction, Paul presents the facts of the gospel (1:3) and declares his allegiance to it (1:16, 17). He continues by building an airtight case for the lostness of mankind and the necessity for God's intervention (1:18—3:20).

Then Paul presents the Good News—salvation is available to all, regardless of their identity, sin, or heritage. We are saved by *grace* (unearned, undeserved favor from God) through *faith* (complete trust) in Christ and his finished work. Through him we can stand before God justified, "not guilty" (3:21—5:21). With this foundation Paul moves directly into a discussion of the freedom that comes from being saved—freedom from the power of sin (6:1–23), freedom from the domination of the law (7:1–25), freedom to become like Christ and discover God's limitless love (8:1–39).

Speaking directly to his Jewish brothers and sisters, Paul shares his concern for them and explains how they fit into God's plan (9:1—11:12). God has made the way for Jews and Gentiles to be united in the body of Christ—both groups can praise God for his wisdom and love (11:13–36).

Paul explains what it means to live in complete submission to Christ—using spiritual gifts to serve others (12:3–8), genuinely loving others (12:9–21), and being good citizens (13:1–14). Freedom must be guided by love as we build each other up in the faith, being sensitive and helpful to those who are weak (14:1—15:4). Paul stresses unity, especially between Gentiles and Jews (15:5–13). He concludes by reviewing his reasons for writing, outlining his personal plans (15:22–33), greeting his friends, and giving a few final thoughts and greetings from his traveling companions (16:1–27).

As you read Romans, reexamine your commitment to Christ and reconfirm your relationships with other believers in Christ's body.

VITAL STATISTICS

PURPOSE:
To introduce Paul to the Romans and to give a sample of his message before he arrives in Rome

AUTHOR:
Paul

TO WHOM WRITTEN:
The Christians in Rome and believers everywhere

DATE WRITTEN:
About A.D. 57, from Corinth, as Paul was preparing for his visit to Jerusalem

SETTING:
Apparently Paul had finished his work in the east, and he planned to visit Rome on his way to Spain after first bringing a collection to Jerusalem for the poor Christians there (15:22–28). The Roman church was mostly Jewish but also contained a great number of Gentiles.

KEY VERSE:
"So now, since we have been made right in God's sight by faith in his promises, we can have real peace with him because of what Jesus Christ our Lord has done for us" (5:1).

KEY PEOPLE:
Paul, Phoebe

KEY PLACE:
Rome

SPECIAL FEATURES:
Paul writes Romans as an organized and carefully presented statement of his faith—it does not have the form of a typical letter. He does, however, spend considerable time greeting people in Rome at the end of the letter.

THE BLUEPRINT

A. WHAT TO BELIEVE (1:1—11:36)
   1. Sinfulness of mankind
   2. Forgiveness of sin through Christ
   3. Freedom from sin's grasp
   4. Israel's past, present, and future

Paul clearly sets forth the foundations of the Christian faith. All men are sinful; Christ died to forgive sin; we are made right with God through faith; this begins a new life with a new relationship with God. Like a sports team that constantly reviews the basics, we will be greatly helped in our faith by keeping close to these foundations. If we study Romans carefully, we will never be at a loss to know what to believe.

B. HOW TO BEHAVE (12:1—16:27)
   1. Personal responsibility
   2. Personal notes

Paul gives clear, practical guidelines for the believers in Rome. The Christian life is not abstract theology unconnected with life, but has practical implications which will affect how we choose to behave each day. It is not enough merely to know the gospel, we must let it transform our lives and let God impact every aspect of our lives.

MEGATHEMES

THEME	EXPLANATION	IMPORTANCE
Sin	Sin means refusing to do God's will and failing to do all that God wants. Since Adam's rebellion against God, our nature is to disobey him. Our sin cuts us off from God. Sin causes us to want to live our own way rather than God's way. Because God is morally perfect, just, and fair, he is right to condemn sin.	Each person has sinned, either by rebelling against God or by ignoring his will. No matter what our background or how hard we try to live good and moral lives, we cannot earn salvation or remove our sin. Only Christ can save us.
Salvation	Our sin points out our need to be forgiven and cleansed. Although we don't deserve it, God, in his kindness, reached out to love and forgive us. He provides the way for us to be saved. Christ's death paid the penalty for our sin.	It is good news that God saves us from our sin. But we must believe in Jesus Christ and that he forgave our sin in order to enter into a wonderful new relationship with God.
Growth	By God's power, believers are sanctified—made holy. This means we are set apart from sin, enabled to obey and to become more like Christ. When we are growing in our relationship with Christ, the Holy Spirit frees us from the demands of the law and from fear of judgment.	Because we are free from sin's control, the law's demands, and fear of God's punishment, we can grow in our relationship with Christ. By trusting in the Holy Spirit and allowing him to help us, we can overcome sin and temptation.
Sovereignty	God oversees and cares about his people—past, present, and future. God's ways of dealing with people are always fair. Because God is in charge of all creation, he can save whomever he wills.	Because of God's mercy, both Jews and Gentiles can be saved. We all must respond to his mercy and accept his gracious offer of forgiveness. Because he is sovereign, let him reign in your heart.
Service	When our purpose is to give credit to God for his love, power, and perfection in all we do, we can serve him properly. Serving him unifies all believers and enables them to show love and sensitivity to others.	Each one of us can't be fully Christlike by ourselves—it takes the entire body of Christ to fully express Christ. By actively and vigorously building up other believers, Christians can be a symphony of service to God.

A. WHAT TO BELIEVE (1:1—11:36)

Paul begins his message to the Romans by vividly portraying the sinfulness of all mankind, explaining how forgiveness is available through faith in Christ, and showing what believers experience in life through their new faith. In this section, we learn of the centrality of faith to becoming a Christian and to living the Christian life. Apart from faith, we have no hope in life.

1. Sinfulness of mankind

1:2
Rom 3:21
Tit 1:2
1:3
Mt 1:1-17
1:4
Rom 8:11

1 Dear friends in Rome: ¹This letter is from Paul, Jesus Christ's slave, chosen to be a missionary, and sent out to preach God's Good News. ²This Good News was promised long ago by God's prophets in the Old Testament. ³It is the Good News about his Son, Jesus Christ our Lord, who came as a human baby, born into King David's royal family line; ⁴and by being raised from the dead he was proved to be the mighty Son of God, with the holy nature of God himself.

THE GOSPEL GOES TO ROME
When Paul wrote his letter to the church in Rome, he had not yet been there, but he had taken the gospel "all the way from Jerusalem clear over into Illyricum" (15:19). He planned to visit and preach in Rome one day, and hoped to continue to take the gospel farther west—even to Spain.

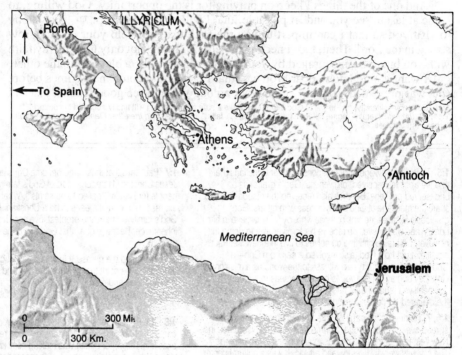

1:1 Paul wrote this letter to the church in Rome. None of the church leaders (James, Peter, Paul) had yet been to Rome; the Roman church was established by believers who had been at Jerusalem for Pentecost (Acts 2:10) and travelers who had heard the message in other places and brought it back to Rome (for example, Priscilla and Aquila, Acts 18:2; Romans 16:3–5). Paul wrote the letter to the Romans during his ministry in Corinth (at the end of his third missionary journey just before returning to Jerusalem; Acts 20:3; Romans 15:25; 16:1) to encourage the believers and to express his desire to visit them someday (within three years he would). The Roman church had no New Testament, since the Gospels were probably not yet being circulated in their final written form. Thus, this letter may well have been the first piece of Christian literature the Roman believers had seen. Written to both Jewish and Gentile Christians, the letter to the Romans is a systematic presentation of the Christian faith.

1:1 When Paul, a devout Jew who had at first persecuted the Christians, became a believer, God used him to spread the gospel throughout the world. Although he was a prisoner at the time, Paul did eventually preach in Rome (Acts 28), perhaps even to Caesar himself. Paul's Profile is found in Acts 9.

1:1 Paul humbly calls himself a slave to Jesus Christ. For a Roman citizen—which Paul was—to choose to be a slave was unthinkable, but Paul chose to be completely dependent on and obedient to his beloved master. What is your attitude toward Christ, your master? Our obedience to him enables us to be useful and usable servants to do work that really matters.

1:2 Some of the prophecies predicting the Good News of Jesus Christ are Genesis 12:3; Psalms 16:10; 40:6–10; 118:22; Isaiah 11:1ff; Zechariah 9:9–11; 12:1–10; Malachi 4:1–6.

1:3–5 Here Paul summarizes the Good News about Jesus Christ who (1) came as a human, (2) was part of the Jewish royal line, (3) died and was raised from the dead, and (4) opened the door for God's kindness to be poured out on us. The book of Romans is an expansion of these themes. As we read it we discover what Paul meant by Good News.

1:3 Paul believed that Jesus is the Son of God, the promised Messiah, and the resurrected Lord. Paul called Jesus a descendant of King David to emphasize that Jesus truly fulfilled the Old Testament Scriptures predicting that the Messiah would come from David's line. With this statement of faith, Paul declared his agreement with the teaching of all Scripture and of the apostles.

5And now, through Christ, all the kindness of God has been poured out upon us undeserving sinners; and now he is sending us out around the world to tell all people everywhere the great things God has done for them, so that they, too, will believe and obey him.

6, 7And you, dear friends in Rome, are among those he dearly loves; you, too, are invited by Jesus Christ to be God's very own—yes, his holy people. May all God's mercies and peace be yours from God our Father and from Jesus Christ our Lord.

Paul declares the power of the gospel

8Let me say first of all that wherever I go I hear you being talked about! For your faith in God is becoming known around the world. How I thank God through Jesus Christ for this good report, and for each one of you. 9God knows how often I pray for you. Day and night I bring you and your needs in prayer to the one I serve with all my might, telling others the Good News about his Son.

10And one of the things I keep on praying for is the opportunity, God willing, to come at last to see you and, if possible, that I will have a safe trip. 11, 12For I long to visit you so that I can impart to you the faith that will help your church grow strong in the Lord. Then, too, I need your help, for I want not only to share my faith with you but to be encouraged by yours: Each of us will be a blessing to the other.

13I want you to know, dear brothers, that I planned to come many times before (but was prevented) so that I could work among you and see good results, just as I

1:5
Acts 9:15
Rom 16:26
Gal 1:16
Eph 3:8,9

1:6
1 Cor 1:3
2 Cor 1:2
Gal 1:3
Eph 1:1,2

1:8
Rom 16:19
Phil 1:3
1 Thess 1:8

1:9
Eph 1:16
Phil 1:3
1 Thess 1:2
2 Tim 1:3
Philem 4-7

1:10
Rom 15:32
Jas 4:15

1:11
Rom 15:29

1:13
Rom 15:22,23

1:10 *God willing,* literally, "in the will of God." *that I will have a safe trip,* or, "that I will finally succeed in coming."
1:11, 12 *the faith,* literally, "some spiritual gift . . . that is, . . . faith." **1:13** *among the other Gentile churches,* literally, "among the Gentiles."

1:5 There is a privilege and a responsibility for Christians. Paul and the apostles received forgiveness (God's grace) as an undeserved privilege. But they also received the responsibility to share the message of God's forgiveness with others. God graciously forgives the sins of those who, by faith, believe in him as Lord. When we believe, we receive his forgiveness. In doing this, however, we are committing ourselves to live in a new life. Paul's new life, a gift from God, also involved a call from God—a God-given responsibility—to witness to the world as a missionary. God may or may not call you to be an overseas missionary, but he does call you (and all believers) to be a witness and an example of the changed life Jesus Christ has worked in you.

1:6, 7 Rome was the capital of the Roman empire, which had spread over most of Europe, North Africa, and the Near East. In New Testament times, Rome was experiencing a "golden age." The city was wealthy, literary, and artistic. It was a cultural center, but in terms of moral standards it was decadent in many respects. The Romans worshiped many pagan gods. Even some of the emperors were worshiped as deities. In stark contrast to the Romans, the followers of Christ believed in only one God and lived morally.

1:6, 7 Christianity was at odds with many elements in the Roman culture. (1) The Romans trusted in their strong military power to protect them against all enemies. Christians needed to be reminded that God was the only permanent source of their security and salvation. (2) Many Romans were naively pragmatic—that is, any means to accomplish the intended task was good. And for Romans, nothing worked better than physical might. Christians needed to learn the value of moral restraints in their new faith—restraints that often seemed foolish in the macho Roman society.

1:6–9 Paul showed his warm attitude toward the Roman church by expressing God's love for them and his own thanks and prayers for them. To have an effect on people's lives, you need to love them and believe in them. Paul's passion to teach these people and have fellowship with them began with his love for them. Thank God for your Christian brothers and sisters, and let them know how deeply you care for them (see, for example, Paul's commands to Philemon in Philemon 1:7).

1:7 Paul says that those who become Christians are invited by Jesus Christ to (1) become part of God's family, and (2) be holy people (or literally, "called to be saints"). What a wonderful expression of what it means to be a Christian. In being reborn into God's family we have the greatest love and the greatest inheritance. Because of all that God has done for us, we strive to be holy.

1:8 Paul used the phrase "I thank God through Jesus Christ" to emphasize the point that Christ is the one and only mediator between God and man. Through Christ, God sends his blessings to us; through Christ, we send our thanks to God (see 1 Timothy 2:5).

1:8 The Roman Christians, at the western world's political power center, were highly visible. Fortunately, their reputation was excellent: their strong faith was making itself known around the world. When people talk about your congregation or your denomination, what do they say? Are their comments accurate? Would you rather they noticed other features? What is the best way to get the public to recognize your faith?

1:9, 10 When you pray continually about a concern, don't be surprised at how God answers. Paul prayed to visit Rome so he could teach the Christians there. When he finally arrived in Rome, it was as a prisoner (see Acts 28:16). Paul prayed for a safe trip, and he did arrive safely—after getting arrested, slapped in the face, shipwrecked, and, among other things, bitten by a poisonous snake. God's ways of answering our prayers are often far from what we expect. When you pray, expect God to answer—although sometimes in ways you do not expect.

1:11, 12 Paul prayed for the chance to visit these Christians so that he could encourage them and be encouraged by them. As God's missionary, he could help them understand the meaning of the Good News about Jesus. As God's holy people, they could offer him fellowship and comfort. When Christians gather, everyone should give *and* receive.

1:13 By the end of his third missionary journey, Paul had traveled through Syria, Galatia, Asia, Macedonia, and Achaia. The churches in these areas were called Gentile churches because their members were mostly Gentiles.

1:14
Ps 40:9
1 Cor 9:16

1:15
Rom 15:20

1:16
Acts 3:26
1 Cor 1:18
2 Tim 1:8-12

1:17
Hab 2:4
Jn 3:36
Rom 3:21
Gal 3:11
Phil 3:9
Heb 10:38

have among the other Gentile churches. ¹⁴For I owe a great debt to you and to everyone else, both to civilized people and uncivilized alike; yes, to the educated and uneducated alike. ¹⁵So, to the fullest extent of my ability, I am ready to come also to you in Rome to preach God's Good News.

¹⁶For I am not ashamed of this Good News about Christ. It is God's powerful method of bringing all who believe it to heaven. This message was preached first to the Jews alone, but now everyone is invited to come to God in this same way. ¹⁷This Good News tells us that God makes us ready for heaven—makes us right in God's sight—when we put our faith and trust in Christ to save us. This is accomplished from start to finish by faith. As the Scripture says it, "The man who finds life will find it through trusting God."

1:17 *This is accomplished from start to finish by faith*, literally, " *this righteousness of God is revealed from faith to faith.*" *"The man who finds life will find it through trusting God"* (Hab 2:4).

FAITH

Faith is a word with many meanings. It can mean faithfulness (Matthew 24:45). It can mean absolute trust, as shown by some of the people who came to Jesus for healing (Luke 7:2–10). It can mean confident hope (Hebrews 11:1). Or, as James points out, it can even mean a barren belief that does not result in good works (James 2:14–26). What does Paul mean when, in Romans, he speaks of saving faith?

We must be very careful to understand faith as Paul uses the word, because he ties faith so closely to salvation. It is *not* something we must do in order to earn salvation— if that were true, then faith would be just one more work, and Paul clearly states that human works can never save us (Galatians 2:16). Instead, faith is a gift God gives us *because* he is saving us (Ephesians 2:8). It is God's grace, not our faith, that saves us. In his mercy, however, when he saves us he gives us faith—a relationship with his Son that helps us become like him. Through the faith he gives us, he carries us from death into life (John 5:24).

Even in Old Testament times grace, not works, was the basis of salvation. As Hebrews points out, "it is not possible for the blood of bulls and goats really to take away sins" (10:4). God intended for his people to look beyond the animal sacrifices to him, but all too often they, instead, put their confidence in fulfilling the requirements of the law—that is, performing the required sacrifices. When Jesus triumphed over death, he cancelled the charges against us and opened the way to the Father (Colossians 2:12–15). Because he is merciful, he offers us faith. How tragic if we turn faith into a work and try to develop it on our own! We can never come to God through our own faith, any more than his Old Testament people could come through their own sacrifices. Instead, we must accept his gracious offer with thanksgiving and allow him to plant the seed of faith within us.

1:14 What was Paul's debt? After his experience with Christ on the Damascus Road (Acts 9), his whole life was consumed with spreading the Good News of salvation. His debt was to Christ for being his Savior, and it was payable to the entire world. He paid his debt by proclaiming Christ's salvation to *all* people—both Jews and Gentiles, across all cultural, social, racial, and economic lines. We owe Christ this same debt because he took on the punishment we deserve for our sin. How will we begin to pay this "debt" back to him?

1:16 Jews and Christians alike stood against the idolatrous Roman religions, and Roman officials often confused the two groups. This was especially easy to do since the Christian church in Rome was originally composed of Jewish converts who attended the feast of Pentecost (see Acts 2:10ff). By the time Paul wrote Romans, however, many Gentiles had joined the church. The Jews and the Gentiles needed to know the relationship between Judaism and Christianity.

1:16, 17 Paul was not ashamed, because his message was *Good News.* It was powerful, it was for everyone, and it was part of God's revealed plan. When you are tempted to be ashamed, remember what the Good News is all about. If you focus on God and on what God is doing in the world rather than on your own inadequacy, your embarrassment will soon disappear.

1:16 Why did the message go to the Jews first? They had been God's special people for more than a thousand years, ever since God chose Abraham and promised great blessings to his descendants (Genesis 12:1–3). God did not choose them because they deserved to be chosen (Deuteronomy 7:7, 8; 9:4–6), but because he wanted to bless them, teach them, and prepare them to welcome his Messiah into the world. He chose them, not to play favorites, but to tell the world about his plan of salvation.

For centuries the Jews had been learning about God by obeying his laws, keeping his feasts, and living according to his moral principles. Often they forgot God's blessings; often they had to be disciplined; but still they had a precious heritage of belief in and obedience to the one true God. Of all the people on earth, the Jews should have been the most ready to welcome the Messiah and to understand his mission and message—and some of them were (see Luke 2:25, 36–38). Of course, the disciples and the great apostle Paul were faithful Jews who recognized in Jesus God's most precious gift to the human race.

1:17 Paul was quoting Habakkuk 2:4. When Habakkuk spoke of life, he may have meant this present life only, but Paul extends this to include eternal life. As we trust God, we are saved: we find life both now and forever.

God's anger at sin

18But God shows his anger from heaven against all sinful, evil men who push away the truth from them. 19For the truth about God is known to them instinctively; God has put this knowledge in their hearts. 20Since earliest times men have seen the earth and sky and all God made, and have known of his existence and great eternal power. So they will have no excuse [when they stand before God at Judgment Day].

21Yes, they knew about him all right, but they wouldn't admit it or worship him or even thank him for all his daily care. And after awhile they began to think up silly ideas of what God was like and what he wanted them to do. The result was that their foolish minds became dark and confused. 22Claiming themselves to be wise without God, they became utter fools instead. 23And then, instead of worshiping the glorious, ever-living God, they took wood and stone and made idols for themselves, carving them to look like mere birds and animals and snakes and puny men.

24So God let them go ahead into every sort of sex sin, and do whatever they wanted to—yes, vile and sinful things with each other's bodies. 25Instead of

1:18
Rom 5:9
Eph 5:6
Col 3:6

1:19
Jn 1:9
Acts 14:17

1:20
Ps 19:1
Acts 17:24

1:21
2 Kgs 17:15
Ps 106:13
Eph 4:17,18

1:22
Jer 10:14
1 Cor 1:20

1:23
Ps 106:20
Isa 40:18
Jer 2:11

1:24
Lev 18:22

1:19 *is known to them instinctively,* literally, "is manifest in them." **1:20** *when they stand before God at Judgment Day,* implied. Or, "They have no excuse for saying there is no God." **1:23** *puny,* literally, "mortal."

1:18ff Romans 1:18—3:20 develops Paul's argument that no one can claim to be good in God's sight—not the masses, not the Romans, not even the Jews. All people everywhere deserve God's condemnation.

1:18 Why is God angry at sinful people? Because even though God is holy and free of all evil, and even though he created people to love him and give glory to him, Adam and Eve rebelled and went their own way. Now all people are sinful. No one, except for Jesus, has ever been able to live perfectly. The holy God, who is the source of all life and hope, cannot live with sin, which brings death. He wants to remove the sin and restore the sinner—if the sinner does not push away the truth. But his anger erupts against those who insist and persist in living a sinful life.

1:18–20 In these verses, Paul answers a common objection: How could a loving God send anyone to hell, especially someone who has never heard the Good News of Jesus? In fact, says Paul, God has revealed himself plainly to *all* people. Everyone knows what God requires, but no one lives up to it. Put another way, our moral standards are always better than our behavior. If people suppress God's truth in order to live their own way, they have no excuse. They know the truth, and they will have to endure the consequences of ignoring it.

1:18–20 Does anyone have an excuse for not believing in God? The Bible answers an emphatic *no.* God has revealed his existence in his creation. Every person, therefore, either accepts or rejects God. Don't be fooled. When the day comes for God to judge your response to him, there will be no excuses. Begin today to give him what he deserves—your devotion and worship.

1:18–20 Some say, "Why do we need missionaries if people can know about God through nature (the things that have been made)?" (1) Although people know that God exists, they suppress that truth by their wickedness and thus deny him. (2) Although people may believe in God, they refuse to respond to him properly. (3) People who reject God need to be convinced of the consequences of their actions. (4) Most importantly, people need to hear about Jesus. Missionaries are needed to bring the Good News about Jesus. (5) Jesus commanded us to make disciples throughout the world (Matthew 28:19, 20). Missionaries are needed in order to help the church to be obedient to the great commission of our Lord.

Knowing that God exists is not enough. People must learn that God is loving. They must understand what he did to show that love to us. They must accept his forgiveness and live their lives in his service (see 10:14, 15).

1:20 What kind of God does nature reveal? Nature shows us a God of might, power, orderliness, and intricate detail; a God of love and beauty; a God who controls all things. But too often people try to create gods they can control rather than submit to the God who controls all things.

1:20 God reveals himself through nature, even though nature's testimony has been distorted by the Fall. Adam's sin resulted in a divine curse upon the whole natural order (Genesis 3:17–19); thorns and thistles were an immediate result, and natural disasters have been common from Adam's day to ours. If we want to know something *about* God, we can observe nature. But if we are to fully *understand* God and relate to him properly, we need more than nature—we also need his revelation in Scripture and in his Son. In Romans 8:19–21, Paul says that nature itself is eagerly awaiting its own redemption from the effects of sin (see Revelation 22:3).

1:21–24 How could intelligent people turn to idolatry? Idolatry begins when people reject what they know about God. Instead of looking to him as the Creator and sustainer of life, they see themselves as the center of the universe. They soon invent "gods" that are convenient projections of their own selfish plans and decrees. These gods may be wooden figures, but they may also be goals such as money, power, or comfort. They may even be misrepresentations of God himself—making God in our image, instead of the reverse. The common denominator is this—idolators worship the things God made rather than God himself. What are your priorities? Where are your dreams, your plans, your hopes? Do you worship God or idols of your own making?

1:21–32 Paul clearly portrays the inevitable downward spiral into sin. First people reject God; next they make up their own ideas of what a god should be and do; then they fall into sin—sexual sin, greed, hatred, envy, murder, fighting, lying, bitterness, gossip. Finally they grow to hate God and encourage others to do so. God does not cause this steady progression toward evil. Rather, when people reject him, he allows them to live as they choose. Once caught in the downward spiral, no one can pull himself out. Sinners must trust Christ alone to put them on the path of escape.

1:24–32 These people chose to reject God, and God allowed them to do it. God does not usually stop us from making choices against his will. He lets us declare our supposed independence from him, even though he knows that in time we will become slaves to our own rebellious choices—we will lose our freedom not to sin. Does life without God look like freedom to you? Look more closely. There is no worse slavery than slavery to sin.

1:25 People tend to believe lies that reinforce their own selfish, personal beliefs. Today more than ever we need to be careful about the input we allow to form our beliefs. With TV, music,

believing what they knew was the truth about God, they deliberately chose to believe lies. So they prayed to the things God made, but wouldn't obey the blessed God who made these things.

1:26
1 Thess 4:5
Jude 1
1:27
Lev 18:22; 20:13
1 Cor 6:9,10

26That is why God let go of them and let them do all these evil things, so that even their women turned against God's natural plan for them and indulged in sex sin with each other. 27And the men, instead of having a normal sex relationship with women, burned with lust for each other, men doing shameful things with other men and, as a result, getting paid within their own souls with the penalty they so richly deserved.

1:28
Eph 5:4

28So it was that when they gave God up and would not even acknowledge him, God gave them up to doing everything their evil minds could think of. 29Their lives became full of every kind of wickedness and sin, of greed and hate, envy, murder, fighting, lying, bitterness, and gossip.

1:30
2 Tim 3:2

30They were backbiters, haters of God, insolent, proud braggarts, always thinking of new ways of sinning and continually being disobedient to their parents.

1:31
2 Tim 3:3
1:32
Rom 6:21,23

31They tried to misunderstand, broke their promises, and were heartless—without pity. 32They were fully aware of God's death penalty for these crimes, yet they went right ahead and did them anyway, and encouraged others to do them, too.

God's judgment of sin

2:1
2 Sam 12:5-9
Mt 7:1
2:2
2 Thess 1:6
2:3
Prov 11:21

2 "Well," you may be saying, "what terrible people you have been talking about!" But wait a minute! You are just as bad. When you say they are wicked and should be punished, you are talking about yourselves, for you do these very same things. 2And we know that God, in justice, will punish anyone who does such things as these. 3Do you think that God will judge and condemn others for doing

1:31 *tried to misunderstand,* or "were confused fools."

---

movies, and the rest of the media often presenting something less than wholesome values, we find ourselves constantly bombarded by philosophies and assumptions that are in direct opposition to the Bible. Be careful about what you allow to form your opinions. The Bible is the only standard of truth. Look at all other opinions in light of its teachings.

1:26, 27 God's *natural* plan is God's ideal for his creation. Unfortunately, what comes *naturally* to human nature is sin. Sin often means not only denying God, but also denying the way we are made. When our society says that any sex act is acceptable so long as nobody gets hurt, it is fooling itself. In the long run (and often in the short run), sin hurts people—individuals, families, whole societies. How sad that people who worship the things God made instead of the Creator so often distort and destroy the very things they claim to value! But it is impossible to understand God's natural plan without knowing the Creator himself.

1:27 Homosexuality is strictly forbidden in Scripture (Leviticus 18:22). Homosexuality is considered an acceptable practice by many in our world today—even by some churches. Many homosexuals believe that their desires are normal and that they have a right to express them. But God does not obligate nor encourage us to fulfill all of our desires (even normal ones). Those desires that violate his laws are wrong and are to be avoided.

If you have this desire, you can and must resist acting upon it. Consciously avoid places or activities you know will kindle temptations of this kind. Don't underestimate the power of Satan to tempt you nor the potential for serious harm if you yield to these temptations. Remember, God can and will forgive sexual sins just as he forgives other sins. Surrender yourself to the grace and mercy of God, asking him to show you the way out of sin and into the light of his freedom and his love. Prayer, Bible study, and strong Christian fellowship in a Bible-believing church can help you to gain strength to resist these powerful temptations. If you are already deeply involved in this sin, you may need to seek help from a trustworthy, professional, pastoral counselor.

1:32 How were these people aware of God's death penalty?

Human beings, created in God's image, have a basic moral nature and a conscience. This truth is understood beyond religious circles. Psychologists, for example, say that the rare person who seems to have no conscience has a serious personality disorder, one that is extremely difficult to treat. Most people instinctively know when they do wrong—but they may not care. Some people will even trade an early death for the freedom to indulge their desires now. "I know it's wrong, but I really want it," they say; or, "I know it's dangerous, but it's worth the risk." For such people, part of the "fun" is going against God's law, the community's moral standards, common sense, or their own sense of right and wrong. But deep down inside they know that sin deserves the punishment of death (Romans 6:23).

2:1ff When Paul's letter was read in the Roman church, no doubt many heads nodded as he condemned idol worshipers, homosexual practices, and violent people. But what surprise his listeners must have felt when he turned on them and said, "You are just as bad!" Paul was emphatically making a point that is central to understanding the Good News—*nobody* is good enough to save himself. All of us in the entire human family, if we want to avoid punishment and live eternally with Christ, must depend totally on God's grace. This is true whether we have been murderers and child molesters or whether we have been honest, hardworking, solid citizens. Paul is not discussing whether some sins are worse than others. He is simply saying that *any* sin is enough to cause us to depend on Jesus Christ for salvation and eternal life. There is no way apart from Christ to be saved from sin, and we have all sinned repeatedly.

2:1 Whenever we find ourselves feeling justifiably angry about some sin we have observed in our community, we should be careful. We need to speak out against sin, but we must do so in a spirit of humility. Often the sins we see most clearly in others are the ones that have taken root in us. If we look closely at ourselves, we may find that we are committing the same sin in more socially acceptable forms. For example, one who gossips may be very critical of others who gossip about him.

them and overlook you when you do them, too? **4**Don't you realize how patient he is being with you? Or don't you care? Can't you see that he has been waiting all this time without punishing you, to give you time to turn from your sin? His kindness is meant to lead you to repentance.

5But no, you won't listen; and so you are saving up terrible punishment for yourselves because of your stubbornness in refusing to turn from your sin; for there is going to come a day of wrath when God will be the just Judge of all the world. **6**He will give each one whatever his deeds deserve. **7**He will give eternal life to those who patiently do the will of God, seeking for the unseen glory and honor and eternal life that he offers. **8**But he will terribly punish those who fight against the truth of God and walk in evil ways—God's anger will be poured out upon them. **9**There will be sorrow and suffering for Jews and Gentiles alike who keep on sinning. **10**But there will be glory and honor and peace from God for all who obey him, whether they are Jews or Gentiles. **11**For God treats everyone the same.

12-15 He will punish sin wherever it is found. He will punish the heathen when they sin, even though they never had God's written laws, for down in their hearts they know right from wrong. God's laws are written within them; their own conscience accuses them, or sometimes excuses them. And God will punish the Jews for sinning because they have his written laws but don't obey them. They know what is right but don't do it. After all, salvation is not given to those who know what to do, unless they do it. **16**The day will surely come when at God's command Jesus Christ will judge the secret lives of everyone, their inmost thoughts and motives; this is all part of God's great plan which I proclaim.

God's law is broken

17You Jews think all is well between yourselves and God because he gave his laws to you; you brag that you are his special friends. **18**Yes, you know what he wants; you know right from wrong and favor the right because you have been taught his laws from earliest youth. **19**You are so sure of the way to God that you

2:4
Ex 34:5,6
Rom 9:22,23
11:22
Eph 1:7
2 Pet 3:9

2:5
Ps 110:5
Jas 5:3

2:6
Mt 16:27

2:7
Mt 25:46
Lk 8:15
2 Cor 4:17
Heb 10:36
Jude 21
Rev 2:7

2:8
Isa 3:11
2 Thess 2:12

2:11
Job 34:19

2:12-15
Mt 7:21-26
Jn 13:17
Acts 10:35
Jas 1:22

2:16
Jn 5:22
Acts 10:42
Rom 16:25,26
Rev 20:12

2:17
Mic 3:11

2:18
Deut 4:8

2:7 *who patiently do the will of God,* literally, "who patiently do good." *seeking for the unseen glory and honor and eternal life that he offers,* implied.   **2:10** *all who obey him,* literally, "all who do good."   **2:17** *gave his laws to you,* or, "you rely upon the law for your salvation."

Romans 3:23	Everyone has sinned.	**SALVATION'S FREEWAY**
Romans 6:23	The penalty for our sin is death.	
Romans 5:8	Jesus Christ died for sin.	
Romans 10:8–10	To be forgiven for our sin, we must believe and confess that Jesus is Lord. Salvation comes through Jesus Christ.	

2:4 It is easy to mistake God's patience for approval of the wrong way we are living. Self-evaluation is difficult, and it is even more difficult to expose our lives to God and let him tell us where we need to change. But as Christians we must pray constantly that God will point out our sins, so that he can heal them. Unfortunately, we are more likely to be amazed at God's patience with others than humbled at his patience with us.

2:5–11 Although we usually are not punished immediately for each sin, God's eventual judgment is certain. We don't know exactly when it will happen, but we know that no one will escape that final encounter with the Creator. For more on judgment, see John 12:48 and Revelation 20:11–15.

2:7 Paul says that those who *do* God's will find eternal life. He is not contradicting his previous statement that salvation comes by faith alone (1:16, 17). We are not saved by good works, but when we commit our lives fully to God, we want to please him and do his will. As such, our good works are a grateful *response* to what God has done, not a prerequisite to earning his grace.

2:12–15 People are condemned not for what they don't know, but for what they do with what they know. Those who know God's

written Word and his law will be judged by them. Those who have never seen a Bible still know right from wrong, and they will be judged because they did not keep even those standards which they did know.

2:12–15 If you traveled around the world, you would find evidence in every society and culture of God's moral law. For example, all cultures prohibit murder, and yet in all societies that law has been broken. We belong to a stubborn race. We know what's right, but we insist on doing what's wrong. It is not enough to know what's right; we must also do it. Admit to yourself and to God that you fit the human pattern and frequently fail to live up to your own standards (much less to God's standards). That's the first step to forgiveness and healing.

2:17ff Paul continues to build his argument that all stand guilty before God. After describing the fate of the unbelieving, pagan Gentiles, he moves to that of the religiously privileged. Despite their knowledge of God's will, they are guilty because they too have refused to live by their beliefs. Those who have grown up in Christian families are the religiously privileged of today. Paul's condemnation applies to them if they do not live up to what they know.

2:20
2 Tim 3:5

2:21
Mt 23:3

2:22
Mal 3:8

2:23
Jn 5:45
Rom 9:4

2:24
2 Sam 12:14
Isa 52:5
Ezek 36:20

2:25
Gal 5:3

2:26
Acts 10:34

2:28
Mt 3:9
Jn 8:39
Gal 6:15
Rev 2:9

2:29
Jn 1:47
Rom 7:6
2 Cor 3:6
Phil 3:3
Col 2:11
1 Pet 3:4

3:2
Deut 4:8
Ps 147:19
Acts 7:38

3:3
Num 23:18,19

3:4
Ps 51:4; 62:9

could point it out to a blind man. You think of yourselves as beacon lights, directing men who are lost in darkness to God. 20You think that you can guide the simple and teach even children the affairs of God, for you really know his laws, which are full of all knowledge and truth.

21Yes, you teach others—then why don't you teach yourselves? You tell others not to steal—do *you* steal? 22You say it is wrong to commit adultery—do *you* do it? You say, "Don't pray to idols," and then make money your god instead.

23You are so proud of knowing God's laws, *but you dishonor him by breaking them*. 24No wonder the Scriptures say that the world speaks evil of God because of you.

25Being a Jew is worth something if you obey God's laws; but if you don't, then you are no better off than the heathen. 26And if the heathen obey God's laws, won't God give them all the rights and honors he planned to give the Jews? 27In fact, those heathen will be much better off than you Jews who know so much about God and have his promises but don't obey his laws.

28For you are not real Jews just because you were born of Jewish parents or because you have gone through the Jewish initiation ceremony of circumcision. 29No, a real Jew is anyone whose heart is right with God. For God is not looking for those who cut their bodies in actual body circumcision, but he is looking for those with changed hearts and minds. Whoever has that kind of change in his life will get his praise from God, even if not from you.

God remains faithful

3 Then what's the use of being a Jew? Are there any special benefits for them from God? Is there any value in the Jewish circumcision ceremony? 2Yes, being a Jew has many advantages.

First of all, God trusted them with his laws [so that they could know and do his will]. 3True, some of them were unfaithful, but just because they broke their promises to God, does that mean God will break his promises? 4Of course not!

2:22 *make money your god instead,* literally, "do you rob temples?" **2:27** *will be much better off,* literally, "will condemn you." **3:2** *so that they could know and do his will,* implied.

2:21–27 These verses are a scathing criticism of hypocrisy. It is much easier to tell others how to behave than to behave properly ourselves. It is easier to say the right words than to allow them to take root in our lives. Knowing God's will, however, is not the same as doing it. Do you ever tell others to do something you are unable to do yourself? Make sure your actions match your words.

2:21, 22 Paul explained to the Jews that they needed to judge *themselves,* not others, by their law. They knew the law so well that they had learned how to excuse their own actions while criticizing others. But the law is more than the "letter"—it is a guideline for living according to God's will, and it is also a reminder that we cannot live righteously without a relationship with God. As Jesus pointed out, even withholding what rightfully belongs to someone else is stealing (Mark 7:9–13), and looking on another person with lustful, adulterous intent is adultery (Matthew 5:27, 28). Before we accuse others, we must look at ourselves and see if that sin, in any form, exists within us.

2:24 If you claim to be one of God's people, your life should reflect what God is like. When you disobey God, you dishonor his name, and people may even speak evil of God because of you. What do people think about God from watching your life?

2:28, 29 To be a Jew meant you were in God's family, an heir to all his promises. Yet Paul made it clear that membership in God's family is based on internal, not external, qualities. All whose hearts are right with God are real Jews—that is, part of God's family (see also Galatians 3:7). Attending church or being baptized, confirmed, or accepted for membership are not enough, just as circumcision was not enough for the Jews.

3:1ff In this chapter Paul continues to build his case that all men stand guilty before God. Paul has dismantled the common excuses

of people who refuse to admit they are sinners: (1) "There is no God" or "I follow my conscience"—1:18–32; (2) "I'm not as bad as other people"—2:1–16; (3) "I'm a church member" or "I'm a religious person"—2:17–29. No one will be exempted from God's judgment on sin. Every person must accept that he or she is sinful and condemned by God. Only then can God's wonderful gift of salvation be understood and received.

3:1ff What a depressing picture Paul is painting! All of us—pagan Gentiles, humanitarians, or religious people—are condemned by our own actions. The law, which God gave to show the way to live, holds up our evil deeds to public view. Is there any hope for us? Yes, says Paul. The law condemns us, it is true, but the law is not the basis of our hope. God himself is. He, in his righteousness and wonderful love, offers us eternal life. We receive our salvation not through law but through faith in Jesus Christ.

3:2 The Jewish nation had many advantages. (1) They were entrusted with God's laws (Exodus 19, 20; Deuteronomy 4:8); (2) They were the race through whom the Messiah would come to earth (Isaiah 11:1–10). (3) They were the beneficiaries of covenants with God himself (Genesis 17:1–16; Exodus 19:3–6). But these privileges did not make them better than anyone else (see 3:9). In fact, because of them the Jews were even more responsible to live up to God's requirements.

3:4 This promise that God's words will always prove true, no matter what anyone says or does, is both a comfort and a challenge. It is a comfort to have something solid and unchanging on which to build our lives. It is a challenge to make the changes that God's words require. If you have been struggling with habits, attitudes, or ideas that do not agree with God's words, a fresh recognition of his unchanging truth will help you toward change.

Though everyone else in the world is a liar, God is not. Do you remember what the book of Psalms says about this? That God's words will always prove true and right, no matter who questions them.

5"But," some say, "our breaking faith with God is good, our sins serve a good purpose, for people will notice how good God is when they see how bad we are. Is it fair, then, for him to punish us when our sins are helping him?" (That is the way some people talk.) 6God forbid! Then what kind of God would he be, to overlook sin? How could he ever condemn anyone? 7For he could not judge and condemn me as a sinner if my dishonesty brought him glory by pointing up his honesty in contrast to my lies. 8If you follow through with that idea you come to this: the worse we are, the better God likes it! But the damnation of those who say such things is just. Yet some claim that this is what I preach!

All people are sinners

9Well, then, are we Jews *better* than others? No, not at all, for we have already shown that all men alike are sinners, whether Jews or Gentiles. 10As the Scriptures say,

"No one is good—no one in all the world is innocent."

11No one has ever really followed God's paths, or even truly wanted to.

12Every one has turned away; all have gone wrong. No one anywhere has kept on doing what is right; not one.

13Their talk is foul and filthy like the stench from an open grave. Their tongues are loaded with lies. Everything they say has in it the sting and poison of deadly snakes.

14Their mouths are full of cursing and bitterness.

15They are quick to kill, hating anyone who disagrees with them.

16Wherever they go they leave misery and trouble behind them, 17and they have never known what it is to feel secure or enjoy God's blessing.

18They care nothing about God nor what he thinks of them.

19So the judgment of God lies very heavily upon the Jews, for they are responsi-

3:5 Rom 5:8; 7:7 Gal 3:15

3:6 Job 34:17

3:7 Rom 9:19,20

3:8 Rom 5:20

3:9 Rom 1:18-32 2:1-29 Gal 3:21,22

3:10 Ps 14:1-3 53:1-4

3:13 Ps 5:9; 140:3

3:14 Ps 10:7

3:15 Prov 1:16 Isa 59:7

3:18 Ps 36:1

3:19 Rom 2:2,12

3:13 *Their talk is foul and filthy like the stench from an open grave,* literally, "Their throat is an open grave." Perhaps the meaning is "Their speech injures others." **3:15** *hating anyone who disagrees with them,* implied.

ELECTION Romans 9:10–13	God's choice of an individual or group for a specific purpose or destiny.	**CRUCIAL CONCEPTS IN ROMANS**
JUSTIFICATION Romans 4:25; 5:18	God's act of declaring us "not guilty" for our sins.	
PROPITIATION/EXPIATION Romans 3:25	The removal of God's punishment for sin through the perfect sacrifice of Jesus Christ.	
REDEMPTION Romans 3:24; 8:23	Jesus Christ has paid the price so we can go free. The price of sin is death; Jesus paid the price.	
SANCTIFICATION Romans 5:2; 15:16	Becoming more and more like Jesus Christ through the work of the Holy Spirit.	
GLORIFICATION Romans 8:18, 19	The ultimate state of the believer after death when he or she becomes like Christ (1 John 4:4).	

3:5 Some of us think we don't have to worry about sin because (1) it's God's job to forgive; (2) God is so loving, he won't judge us; (3) sin isn't so bad—it teaches us valuable lessons, or (4) we need to stay in touch with the culture around us. It is far too easy to take God's grace for granted. But God cannot overlook sin. Sinners, no matter how many excuses they make, will have to answer to God for their sin.

3:10–12 Paul is referring to Psalm 14:1–3. "No one is good" means "no one is innocent." Every person is valuable in God's eyes because God created us in his image and he loves us, but no one is righteous (that is, no one can earn right standing with God). Though valuable, we have fallen into sin. But God, through Jesus his Son, has redeemed us and offers to forgive us if we return to him in faith.

3:10–18 Paul uses these Old Testament references to show that humanity in general, in its present sinful condition, is unacceptable before God. Have you ever thought to yourself, "Well, I'm not too bad. I'm a pretty good person"? Look at these verses and see if any of them apply to you. Have you ever lied? Have you ever hurt someone's feelings by your words or tone of voice? Are you bitter toward anyone? Do you become angry with those who strongly disagree with you? In thought, word, and deed you, like everyone else in the world, stand guilty before God. We must remember who we are in his sight—alienated sinners. Don't deny that you are a sinner. Instead, allow that knowledge to point you toward Christ.

3:19 The last time someone accused you of wrongdoing, what was your reaction? Denial, argument, and defensiveness? The Bible tells us the world stands hushed and guilty before Almighty

ble to keep God's laws instead of doing all these evil things; not one of them has any excuse; in fact, all the world stands hushed and guilty before Almighty God.

3:20
Ps 143:2
Acts 13:39
Rom 4:15; 7:7
Gal 2:16; 3:11

20Now do you see it? No one can ever be made right in God's sight by doing what the law commands. For the more we know of God's laws, the clearer it becomes that we aren't obeying them; his laws serve only to make us see that we are sinners.

2. Forgiveness of sin through Christ
Christ took our punishment

3:21
Rom 1:2,17
9:30

3:22
Rom 4:16; 10:4,12
Gal 2:16
Col 3:11
Heb 11:4
1 Pet 1:10
2 Pet 1:1

21, 22But now God has shown us a different way to heaven—not by "being good enough" and trying to keep his laws, but by a new way (though not new, really, for the Scriptures told about it long ago). Now God says he will accept and acquit us—declare us "not guilty"—if we trust Jesus Christ to take away our sins. And we all can be saved in this same way, by coming to Christ, no matter who we are or what we have been like. 23Yes, all have sinned; all fall short of God's glorious ideal; 24yet now God declares us "not guilty" of offending him if we trust in Jesus Christ, who in his kindness freely takes away our sins.

3:23
Rom 3:9
Gal 3:21,22

3:24
Eph 1:7; 2:8
Heb 9:12
1 Pet 1:18,19

3:25
Lev 16:15
Acts 17:30
Heb 9:13,14
1 Pet 1:19
1 Jn 2:2; 4:10

25For God sent Christ Jesus to take the punishment for our sins and to end all God's anger against us. He used Christ's blood and our faith as the means of saving us from his wrath. In this way he was being entirely fair, even though he did not punish those who sinned in former times. For he was looking forward to the time when Christ would come and take away those sins. 26And now in these days also he can receive sinners in this same way, because Jesus took away their sins.

But isn't this unfair for God to let criminals go free, and say that they are innocent? No, for he does it on the basis of their trust in Jesus who took away their sins.

3:27
Rom 2:17; 4:2
1 Cor 1:29
Eph 2:9

3:28
Acts 13:39

3:29
Rom 9:24
10:12; 15:9
Gal 3:28

27Then what can we boast about doing, to earn our salvation? Nothing at all. Why? Because our acquittal is not based on our good deeds; it is based on what Christ has done and our faith in him. 28So it is that we are saved by faith in Christ and not by the good things we do.

29And does God save only the Jews in this way? No, the Gentiles, too, may come to him in this same manner. 30God treats us all the same; all, whether Jews or

3:21, 22 *God has shown us a different way to heaven,* literally, "A righteousness of God has been manifested." **3:25** *saving us from his wrath,* literally, "to be a propitiation." **3:28** *saved,* literally, "justified."

God. No excuses or arguments are left. Have you reached the point with God where you are ready to hang up your defenses and await his decision? If you haven't, stop now and admit your sin to him. If you have, the next five verses are truly good news for you!

3:20, 21 In these verses we see two purposes of God's law. First, it shows us where we go wrong. Because of the law, we know we are helpless sinners, and we are driven to Jesus Christ for mercy. Second, the moral code revealed in the law can serve to guide our actions by holding up God's moral standards. We do not earn salvation by keeping the law (no one except Christ ever kept or could keep the law perfectly), but we do please God when our lives conform to his revealed will for us.

3:21-29 After all this bad news about our sinfulness and God's condemnation, Paul now gives the wonderful news. There is a way to be declared not guilty—by trusting Jesus Christ to take away our sins. Trusting means putting our confidence in him to forgive our sins, to make us right with God, and to empower us to live the way he wants us to live. This is God's solution, and it is available to all of us regardless of our background or past behavior.

3:23 Some sins seem bigger than others because their obvious consequences are much more serious. Murder, for example, seems to us to be worse than hatred, and adultery seems worse than lust. But this does not mean we can get away with some sins and not with others. All sin makes us sinners, and all sin cuts us off from our holy God. All sin, therefore, leads to death (because it disqualifies us from living with God), regardless of how great or small it seems. Don't minimize "little" sins or overrate "big" sins. They all separate us from God, but they all can be forgiven.

3:24 When a judge in a court of law declares the defendant not guilty, all the charges are removed from his record. Legally, it is as if the person had never been accused. When God forgives our sins, our record is wiped clean. From his perspective, it is as though we had never sinned.

3:25 What happened to people who lived before Christ came and died for sin? If God condemned them, is he being unfair? If he saved them, was Christ's sacrifice unnecessary? Paul shows that God forgave all human sin at the cross of Jesus. Old Testament believers looked forward by faith to Christ's coming and were saved, even though they did not know Jesus' name or the details of his earthly life. New Testament believers look back in faith to their crucified Savior. Unlike the Old Testament believers, you know about the God who loved the world so much that he gave his own Son (John 3:16). Have you put your trust in him?

3:27, 28 Most religions prescribe specific duties that must be performed to make a person acceptable to God. Christianity is unique in teaching that the good things we do will not put us right with God. No amount of human achievement or progress in personal development will close the gap between God's moral perfection and our imperfect daily performance. Good deeds are fine, but they will not earn us eternal life. We are saved only by trusting in what God has done for us (see Ephesians 2:8–10).

3:28 Why does God save us by faith alone? (1) Faith eliminates human pride. (2) Faith exalts God, not people. (3) Faith makes salvation available to all. (4) Faith admits that we can't keep the law or measure up to God's standards—we need help. (5) Faith is based on a relationship with God, not on performance for God.

Gentiles, are acquitted if they have faith. ³¹Well then, if we are saved by faith, does this mean that we no longer need obey God's laws? Just the opposite! In fact, only when we trust Jesus can we truly obey him.

Abraham was justified by faith

4 Abraham was, humanly speaking, the founder of our Jewish nation. What were his experiences concerning this question of being saved by faith? Was it because of his good deeds that God accepted him? If so, then he would have something to boast about. But from God's point of view Abraham had no basis at all for pride. ³For the Scriptures tell us Abraham *believed God*, and that is why God canceled his sins and declared him "not guilty."

⁴, ⁵But didn't he earn his right to heaven by all the good things he did? No, for being saved is a gift; if a person could earn it by being good, then it wouldn't be free—but it is! It is *given* to those who do *not* work for it. For God declares sinners to be good in his sight if they have faith in Christ to save them from God's wrath.

⁶King David spoke of this, describing the happiness of an undeserving sinner who is declared "not guilty" by God. ⁷"Blessed, and to be envied," he said, "are those whose sins are forgiven and put out of sight. ⁸Yes, what joy there is for anyone whose sins are no longer counted against him by the Lord."

⁹Now then, the question: Is this blessing given only to those who have faith in Christ but also keep the Jewish laws, or is the blessing also given to those who do not keep the Jewish rules, but only trust in Christ? Well, what about Abraham? We say that he received these blessings through his faith. Was it by faith alone? Or because he also kept the Jewish rules?

¹⁰For the answer to that question, answer this one: *When* did God give this blessing to Abraham? It was *before he became a Jew*—before he went through the Jewish initiation ceremony of circumcision.

¹¹It wasn't until later on, *after* God had promised to bless him *because of his faith*, that he was circumcised. The circumcision ceremony was a sign that Abra-

4:2
1 Cor 1:31
4:3
Gen 15:6
Gal 3:6
Jas 2:23
4:4,5
Josh 24:2
Acts 13:38,39
Rom 11:6
Gal 2:16
4:6
1 Cor 1:30
2 Cor 5:19
4:7
Ps 32:1,2
4:8
Ps 32:1,2
2 Cor 5:19
4:9
Gen 15:6
Rom 3:30
4:10
Gen 15:6
17:10,11
4:11
Gen 17:1-11
Lk 19:9
Jn 8:39
Rom 4:16

4:5 *if they have faith in Christ to save them from God's wrath*, literally, "faith is reckoned for righteousness." **4:6** *"not guilty,"* literally "righteous." **4:8** *by the Lord*, see Psalm 32:1, 2.

3:31 This verse can also be translated: "Do we then overthrow the law by this faith? By no means! On the contrary, we uphold the law." There were some misunderstandings between Jewish and Gentile Christians at Rome. Worried Jewish Christians were asking Paul, "Does faith wipe out everything Judaism stands for? Does it cancel our Scriptures, put an end to our customs, declare that God is no longer working through us?" (This is essentially the question used to open chapter 3.) "Absolutely not!" says Paul. When we understand the way of salvation through faith, we understand the Jewish religion better. We know why Abraham was chosen, why the Mosiac law was given, why God worked patiently with Israel for centuries. Faith does not wipe out the Old Testament. Rather, it makes God's dealings with the Jewish people understandable. In chapter 4, Paul will expand on this theme (see also 5:20, 21; 8:3, 4; 13:9, 10; Galatians 3:24–29; and 1 Timothy 1:8 for more on this concept).

4:1 The Jews were proud to be called children of Abraham. Paul used Abraham as a good example of someone who was saved by faith. By emphasizing faith, Paul was not saying God's laws are unimportant (4:13), but that it is impossible to be saved simply by obeying them. For more about Abraham, see his Profile in Genesis 17.

4:5 Some people, when they learn that we are saved through faith, start to worry. "Do I have enough faith?" they wonder, "Is my faith strong enough to save me?" These people miss the point. It is Jesus Christ who saves us, not *our* feelings or actions, and he is strong enough to save us no matter how weak our faith is. Jesus

offers us salvation as a gift, because he loves us, not because we have earned it through our powerful faith. What, then, is the role of faith? Faith is believing and trusting in Jesus Christ, reaching out to accept his wonderful gift of salvation. Faith is effective whether it is great or small, timid or bold—because God loves us.

4:6 What can we do with guilt? King David was guilty of terrible sins—adultery, murder, lies—and yet he experienced the joy of forgiveness. We too can have this joy when we (1) quit denying our guilt and recognize we have sinned, (2) admit our guilt to God and ask his forgiveness, and (3) let go of our guilt and believe God has forgiven us. This can be difficult when a sin has taken root and grown over many years, when it is very serious, or when it involves others; but we must remember that Jesus is willing and able to forgive all possible sins. In view of the tremendous price he paid on the cross, it is arrogant to think any of our sins are too great for him to cover.

4:10 Circumcision was an outward sign for the Jews that they were a people special to God. Circumcision of all Jewish boys set the Jewish people apart from the nations who worshiped other gods; thus it was a very important ceremony. God gave the blessing and the command for this ceremony to Abraham (Genesis 17:9–14).

4:10–12 Rituals did not earn any blessings for Abraham; he was blessed long before the circumcision ceremony was introduced. Genesis 12:1–4 tells of God's call to Abraham when he was 75 years old; the circumcision ceremony was introduced when he was

ham already had faith and that God had already accepted him and declared him just and good in his sight—before the ceremony took place. So Abraham is the spiritual father of those who believe and are saved without obeying Jewish laws. We see, then, that those who do not keep these rules are justified by God through faith. 12And Abraham is also the spiritual father of those Jews who have been circumcised. They can see from his example that it is not this ceremony that saves them, for Abraham found favor with God by faith alone, *before he was circumcised.*

13It is clear, then, that God's promise to give the whole earth to Abraham and his descendants was not because Abraham obeyed God's laws but because he trusted God to keep his promise. 14So if you still claim that God's blessings go to those who are "good enough," then you are saying that God's promises to those who have faith are meaningless, and faith is foolish. 15But the fact of the matter is this: when we try to gain God's blessing and salvation by keeping his laws we always end up under his anger, for we always fail to keep them. The only way we can keep from breaking laws is not to have any to break!

16So God's blessings are given to us by faith, as a free gift; we are certain to get them whether or not we follow Jewish customs if we have faith like Abraham's, for Abraham is the father of us all when it comes to these matters of faith. 17That is what the Scriptures mean when they say that God made Abraham the father of many nations. God will accept all people in every nation who trust God as Abraham did. And this promise is from God himself, who makes the dead live again and speaks of future events with as much certainty as though they were already past.

18So, when God told Abraham that he would give him a son who would have many descendants and become a great nation, Abraham believed God even though such a promise just couldn't come to pass! 19And because his faith was strong, he didn't worry about the fact that he was too old to be a father, at the age of one hundred, and that Sarah his wife, at ninety, was also much too old to have a baby.

20But Abraham never doubted. He believed God, for his faith and trust grew ever stronger, and he praised God for this blessing even before it happened. 21He was completely sure that God was well able to do anything he promised. 22And because of Abraham's faith God forgave his sins and declared him "not guilty."

23Now this wonderful statement—that he was accepted and approved through his faith—wasn't just for Abraham's benefit. 24It was for us, too, assuring us that God will accept us in the same way he accepted Abraham—when we believe the promises of God who brought back Jesus our Lord from the dead. 25He died for our sins and rose again to make us right with God, filling us with God's goodness.

4:19 *at ninety, see Gen 17:17.*   **4:25** *rose again to make us right with God,* literally "raised for our justification."

4:13
Gen 12:3; 17:4-6
22:17,18
Rom 9:8
Gal 3:16,29

4:14
Gal 3:18

4:15
Rom 3:20; 7:7
1 Cor 15:55,56
Gal 3:10

4:16
Rom 9:8
Col 3:11

4:17
Gen 17:5
Isa 51:2
Jn 5:21
1 Cor 1:28-30

4:18
Gen 15:5

4:19
Gen 17:17; 18:11
Heb 11:11,12

4:22
Rom 4:3

4:23
Acts 13:30
Rom 15:4
1 Cor 10:11
2 Tim 3:16

4:25
Isa 53:5
Rom 8:32-34
1 Cor 15:12-20
2 Cor 5:15
Heb 9:28
1 Pet 1:21; 3:18

99 (Genesis 17:1–14). Ceremonies and rituals serve as reminders of our faith. They are not important in themselves, and we should not think that they give us any special merit before God. They are outward symbols that demonstrate an inner change of heart and attitude. The focus of our faith should be on Christ and his saving actions, not on our own actions.

4:16 Paul explains that Abraham was blessed through his faith alone, before he ever heard about the rituals that would become so important to the Jewish people. We too are saved by faith plus nothing. It is not by loving God and doing good that we are saved; neither is it by faith plus love or faith plus good works. We are saved only through faith in Christ, trusting him to forgive all our sins.

4:17 The promise (or covenant) God gave Abraham said that Abraham would be the father of many nations (Genesis 17:2–4) and that the entire world would be blessed through him (Genesis 12:3). This promise was fulfilled in Jesus Christ. Jesus was from Abraham's line, and truly the whole world was blessed through him. Paul points out that the promise to Abraham to be the father of

many nations extended beyond Israel to all nations of the world.

4:20–22 Abraham never doubted that God would fulfill his promise. His life was marked by mistakes, sins, and failures as well as by wisdom and goodness, but he consistently trusted God. His life is an example of faith in action. If he had looked only at his own resources for subduing Canaan and founding a nation, he would have given up in despair. But he looked to God, obeyed him, and waited for God to fulfill his word to him.

4:25 When we believe, an exchange takes place. We give Christ our sins, and he gives us his goodness and forgiveness (see 2 Corinthians 5:21). There is nothing we can do to earn this. Only through Christ can we receive God's goodness. What an incredible bargain for us, but many still choose to pass it up to continue "enjoying" their sin.

Faith brings joy

5 So now, since we have been made right in God's sight by faith in his promises, we can have real peace with him because of what Jesus Christ our Lord has done for us. 2For because of our faith, he has brought us into this place of highest privilege where we now stand, and we confidently and joyfully look forward to actually becoming all that God has had in mind for us to be.

3We can rejoice, too, when we run into problems and trials for we know that they are good for us—they help us learn to be patient. 4And patience develops strength of character in us and helps us trust God more each time we use it until finally our hope and faith are strong and steady. 5Then, when that happens, we are able to hold our heads high no matter what happens and know that all is well, for we know how dearly God loves us, and we feel this warm love everywhere within us because God has given us the Holy Spirit to fill our hearts with his love.

6When we were utterly helpless with no way of escape, Christ came at just the right time and died for us sinners who had no use for him. 7Even if we were good, we really wouldn't expect anyone to die for us, though, of course, that might be barely possible. 8But God showed his great love for us by sending Christ to die for us while we were still sinners. 9And since by his blood he did all this for us as sinners, how much more will he do for us now that he has declared us not guilty? Now he will save us from all of God's wrath to come. 10And since, when we were

5:1
Eph 2:14
Col 1:20

5:2
Eph 2:18; 3:12
Heb 3:6; 10:19

5:3
Mt 5:11
Phil 2:17

5:5
2 Cor 1:22
Gal 4:6
Eph 1:13
Phil 1:20

5:6
Gal 2:20; 4:4
Eph 5:2

5:8
Jn 3:16; 15:13
1 Pet 3:18

5:9
Rom 1:18
1 Thess 1:10
1 Jn 1:7

5:10
Rom 8:34
2 Cor 5:18
Eph 2:3

What we have as Adam's children	What we have as God's children	**WHAT WE HAVE AS CHILDREN**
Ruin 5:9	Rescue 5:8	
Sin 5:12, 15, 21	Righteousness 5:18	
Death 5:12, 16, 21	Eternal life 5:17, 21	
Separation from God 5:18	Relationship with God 5:11, 19	
Disobedience 5:12, 19	Obedience 5:19	
Judgment 5:18	Deliverance 5:10, 11	
Law 5:20	Grace 5:20	

5:1-5 These verses introduce a section that contains some difficult concepts. To understand the next four chapters, it helps to keep in mind the two-sided reality of the Christian life. On the one hand, we are complete in Christ (our acceptance with him is secure); on the other hand, we are growing in Christ (we are becoming more and more like him). At the same time we have the status of kings and the duties of slaves. We feel both the presence of Christ and the pressure of sin. We enjoy the peace that comes from being made right with God, but we still face daily problems that help us grow. If we remember these two sides of the Christian life, we will not grow discouraged as we face temptations and problems. Instead, we will learn to depend on the power available to us from Christ, who lives in us in the person of the Holy Spirit.

5:1 We now have peace *with* God, which differs from peaceful feelings such as assurance, security, and confidence. Peace with God means that we have been reconciled with him. There is no more hostility between us, no sin blocking our relationship with him. Peace with God is possible only because Jesus paid the price for our sins with his death on the cross.

5:2 Paul states that, as believers, we now stand in a place of highest privilege. Not only has God declared us not guilty; he has drawn us close to him. Instead of enemies, we have become his friends—in fact, his own children (John 15:15; Galatians 4:5).

5:2-5 As Paul states clearly in 1 Corinthians 13:13, faith, hope, and love are at the heart of the Christian life. Our relationship with God begins with *faith*, which helps us realize that we are delivered from our past by Christ's death. *Hope* grows as we learn all that God has in mind for us; it gives us the promise of the future. And God's *love* fills our lives and gives us the ability to reach out to others.

5:3, 4 Paul tells us that in the future we will *become*, but until then

we must *overcome*. This means we will experience difficulties that help us grow. Problems we run into will develop our patience—which in turn will strengthen our character, deepen our trust in God, and give us greater confidence about the future. You probably find your patience tested in some way every day. Thank God for these opportunities to grow, and deal with them in his strength (see also James 1:2-4; 1 Peter 1:6, 7).

5:5 All three members of the Trinity are involved in salvation. The Father loved us so much that he sent his Son to bridge the gap between us (John 3:16). The Father and the Son send the Holy Spirit to fill our lives with love and to enable us to live by his power (Acts 1:8).

5:6 We were helpless because we could do nothing on our own to save ourselves. Someone had to come and rescue us. Not only did Christ come at a good time in history; he came at exactly the right time—according to God's own schedule. God controls all history, and he controlled the timing, methods, and results of Jesus' death.

5:8 *While we were still sinners*—these are amazing words. God sent Jesus Christ to die for us, not because we were good enough, but because he loved us so much. Whenever you feel uncertain about God's love for you, remember that he loved you even before you turned to him.

5:9, 10 The love that caused Christ to die is the same love that sends the Holy Spirit to live in us and bless us every day. The power that raised Christ from the dead is the same power that saved you and is available to you in your daily life. Be assured that, having begun a life with Christ, you have a reserve of power and love to call on each day for help to meet every challenge or trial. Just as you can pray for forgiveness, you can pray for God's power and love as you need it.

his enemies, we were brought back to God by the death of his Son, what blessings he must have for us now that we are his friends, and he is living within us! ¹¹Now we rejoice in our wonderful new relationship with God—all because of what our Lord Jesus Christ has done in dying for our sins—making us friends of God.

Adam and Christ contrasted

5:12
Gen 2:17
Ezek 18:4
Rom 6:23
1 Cor 15:21,22,56

5:13
1 Jn 3:4

5:14
Hos 6:7
1 Cor 15:45

5:15
Isa 53:11

5:17
Gen 2:17
3:6,19
1 Cor 15:21

5:18
Rom 4:25
Heb 2:9

5:19
Rom 11:32
Phil 2:8

5:20
Lk 7:47
Jn 15:22
Rom 3:20; 4:15
7:8
Gal 3:19
1 Tim 1:14

5:21
Jn 1:17
Rom 6:23

¹²When Adam sinned, sin entered the entire human race. His sin spread death throughout all the world, so everything began to grow old and die, for all sinned. ¹³[We know that it was Adam's sin that caused this] because although, of course, people were sinning from the time of Adam until Moses, God did not in those days judge them guilty of death for breaking his laws—because he had not yet given his laws to them, nor told them what he wanted them to do. ¹⁴So when their bodies died it was not for their own sins since they themselves had never disobeyed God's special law against eating the forbidden fruit, as Adam had.

What a contrast between Adam and Christ who was yet to come! ¹⁵And what a difference between man's sin and God's forgiveness!

For this one man, Adam, brought death to many through his *sin*. But this one man, Jesus Christ, brought forgiveness to many through God's *mercy*. ¹⁶Adam's *one* sin brought the penalty of death to many, while Christ freely takes away *many* sins and gives glorious life instead. ¹⁷The sin of this one man, Adam, caused *death to be king over all*, but all who will take God's gift of forgiveness and acquittal are *kings of life* because of this one man, Jesus Christ. ¹⁸Yes, Adam's *sin* brought *punishment* to all, but Christ's *righteousness* makes men *right with God*, so that they can live. ¹⁹Adam caused many to be sinners because he *disobeyed* God, and Christ caused many to be made acceptable to God because he *obeyed*.

²⁰The Ten Commandments were given so that all could see the extent of their failure to obey God's laws. But the more we see our sinfulness, the more we see God's abounding grace forgiving us. ²¹Before, sin ruled over all men and brought them to death, but now God's kindness rules instead, giving us right standing with God and resulting in eternal life through Jesus Christ our Lord.

5:12 *grow old and die,* literally, "Sin entered into the world and death through sin." **5:13** *We know that it was Adam's sin that caused this,* implied. **5:14** *so when their bodies died it was not for their own sins,* implied. **5:17** *are kings of life,* literally, "reign in life."

5:11 How does Christ's death make us friends with God? God is holy, and he will not be associated with sin. All people are sinful, and all sin deserves punishment. Instead of punishing us with the death we deserve, however, Christ took our sins upon himself and paid the price for them with his own death. Now the way to friendship with God has been opened. Through faith in *his* work, we become his friends rather than enemies and outcasts.

5:12 How can we be declared guilty for something Adam did thousands of years ago? Many feel it isn't right for God to judge us because of Adam's sin, yet each of us confirms our solidarity with Adam by our sins. We are made of the same stuff, prone to rebel, and we are judged for the sins *we* commit. Because we are sinners, it isn't fairness we need—it's mercy.

5:13, 14 Paul has abundantly shown that keeping the law does not bring salvation. Now he adds that breaking the Mosiac law is not what brings death. Death is the result of Adam's sin and of the sins we all commit, even if they don't resemble Adam's. For thousands of years, he reminds his readers, the law had not yet been explicitly given, and yet people died. The law was added, he explains in 5:20, to help people see their sinfulness, to show them the seriousness of their offenses, and to drive them to God for mercy and pardon. This was true in Moses' day, and it is still true today. Sin is a profound rupture between who we are and who we were created to be. The law points out our sin and places the

responsibility for it squarely on our shoulders, but the law offers no remedy for it. When we're convicted of sin, we must turn to Jesus Christ for healing.

5:15–19 We are all born into Adam's physical family—the family line that leads to certain death. All of us reap the results of Adam's sin. We have inherited his guilt, the tendency to sin, and God's punishment. Because of Jesus, however, we can trade judgment for forgiveness. We can trade our sin for Jesus' goodness. Jesus offers us the opportunity to be born into his spiritual family—the family line that begins with forgiveness and leads to eternal life. If we do nothing, we have death through Adam; but if we come to God by faith, we have life through Christ. Which family line do you now belong to?

5:20 As a sinner, separated from God, you see his law from below, as a ladder to be climbed to get to God. Perhaps you have repeatedly tried to climb it, only to fall to the ground every time you have advanced one or two rungs. Or perhaps the sheer height of the ladder is so overwhelming that you have never even started up. In either case, what relief you should feel to see Jesus offering with open arms to lift you above the ladder of the law, to take you directly to God! Once Jesus lifts you into God's presence, you are free to obey—out of love, not necessity; through God's power, not your own. You know that if you stumble, you will not fall back to the ground. Instead, you will be caught and held in Jesus' loving arms.

3. Freedom from sin's grasp

Sin's power is broken

6 Well then, shall we keep on sinning so that God can keep on showing us more and more kindness and forgiveness?

2, 3Of course not! Should we keep on sinning when we don't have to? For sin's power over us was broken when we became Christians and were baptized to become a part of Jesus Christ; through his death the power of your sinful nature was shattered. 4Your old sin-loving nature was buried with him by baptism when he died, and when God the Father, with glorious power, brought him back to life again, you were given his wonderful new life to enjoy.

5For you have become a part of him, and so you died with him, so to speak, when he died; and now you share his new life, and shall rise as he did. 6Your old evil desires were nailed to the cross with him; that part of you that loves to sin was crushed and fatally wounded, so that your sin-loving body is no longer under sin's control, no longer needs to be a slave to sin; 7for when you are deadened to sin you are freed from all its allure and its power over you. 8And since your old sin-loving nature "died" with Christ, we know that you will share his new life. 9Christ rose from the dead and will never die again. Death no longer has any power over him. 10He died once for all to end sin's power, but now he lives forever in unbroken fellowship with God. 11So look upon your old sin nature as dead and unresponsive

6:1
Rom 3:5,8; 6:15

6:2
Col 2:20; 3:3

6:3
Gal 3:27

6:4
Eph 4:22
Col 2:12; 3:10

6:5
Jn 14:19,20

6:6
Rom 7:24
Gal 2:20
Col 2:11,12

6:7
1 Pet 4:1

6:8
Jn 14:19

6:9
Acts 2:24

6:11
Rom 7:4
Col 2:20; 3:3

6:5 *when he died*, literally, "united with him in the likeness of his death."

He has given us . . .				**WHAT HAS GOD DONE ABOUT SIN?**
New life	6:2, 3	Sin's power is broken.	We can be certain that sin's power is broken.	
	6:4	Sin-loving nature is buried.		
	6:6	You are no longer under sin's control.		
New nature	6:5	Now you share his new life.	We can see ourselves as unresponsive to the old power and alive to the new.	
	6:11	Look upon your old sin nature as dead and unresponsive, and instead be alive to God.		
New freedom	6:12	Do not let sin control you.	We can commit ourselves to obey Christ in perfect freedom.	
	6:13	Give yourselves completely to God.		
	6:14	You are free.		
	6:16	You can choose your own master.		

6:1—8:39 This section deals with *sanctification*—the change God makes in our lives when we become Christians. Chapter 6 explains that believers are free from sin's control. Chapter 7 discusses the continuing struggle believers have with sin. Chapter 8 describes how we can have victory over sin.

6:1 If God loves to forgive, why not give him more to forgive? If forgiveness is guaranteed, do we have the freedom to sin as much as we like? Paul's forceful answer is *no!* Such an attitude—deciding ahead of time to take advantage of God—would only make our sin worse. God's forgiveness does not make sin less serious. To the contrary, his Son's death for sin shows us how dreadfully serious sin is. We must never take lightly the price Jesus paid for our sin. Make it a regular habit to confess your sins to God and to ask his forgiveness.

6:1–4 In the church in Paul's day, immersion was the usual form of baptism—that is, new Christians were completely "buried" in water. They understood this form of baptism to symbolize the death and burial of the old way of life, followed by resurrection to life with Christ. If we think of our old, sinful life as dead and buried, we have a powerful motive to resist sin. Not wanting the ugly old life to come back to power again, we can consciously choose to treat it as if it were dead. Then we can continue to enjoy our wonderful new life with Jesus (see Galatians 3:27 and Colossians

3:1–4 for more on this concept).

6:5ff We can enjoy our new life in Christ because we have joined him in his death and resurrection. Our evil desires, our bondage to sin, and our love of sin died with him. Now, joining him in his resurrection life, we have unbroken fellowship with God and freedom from sin. For more on the difference between our new life in Christ and our old sinful nature read Ephesians 4:23, 24 and Colossians 3:3–15.

6:6 The penalty of sin and its power over our lives died with Christ on the cross. Paul has already stated that through faith in Christ we stand acquitted, "not guilty" before God. Here Paul emphasizes that we need no longer live under sin's power. God does not take us out of the world or make us robots—we will still feel like sinning, and sometimes we will sin. The difference is that before we were saved, we were slaves to our sinful nature, but now we can choose to live for Christ (see Galatians 2:20).

6:9–11 These verses offer wonderful assurances for your life as a believer in Jesus Christ. Because of him you need never fear death. This frees you to do his will, to be in unbroken fellowship with your Lord. This will affect all your activities—your work and your worship, your play and your Bible study, your quiet times and your times of caring for others. When you know you are free from death's power, you will experience a new vigor in life as a result.

to sin, and instead be alive to God, alert to him, through Jesus Christ our Lord.

6:12
Eph 4:22

¹²Do not let sin control your puny body any longer; do not give in to its sinful desires. ¹³Do not let any part of your bodies become tools of wickedness, to be used for sinning; but give yourselves completely to God—every part of you—for you are back from death and you want to be tools in the hands of God, to be used for his good purposes. ¹⁴Sin need never again be your master, for now you are no longer tied to the law where sin enslaves you, but you are free under God's favor and mercy.

6:13
Rom 12:1
2 Cor 5:14
Col 3:5

6:14
Rom 7:4,6
8:2,12
Gal 5:18
Tit 2:14

Slaves to righteousness

6:16
Jn 8:34
1 Cor 6:9,15
2 Pet 2:19

¹⁵Does this mean that now we can go ahead and sin and not worry about it? (For our salvation does not depend on keeping the law, but on receiving God's grace!) Of course not!

6:17
2 Tim 1:13

¹⁶Don't you realize that you can choose your own master? You can choose sin (with death) or else obedience (with acquittal). The one to whom you offer yourself—he will take you and be your master and you will be his slave. ¹⁷Thank God that though you once chose to be slaves of sin, now you have obeyed with all your heart the teaching to which God has committed you. ¹⁸And now you are free from your old master, sin; and you have become slaves to your new master, righteousness.

6:18
1 Cor 7:22
Gal 5:1
1 Pet 2:16

6:19
Mt 6:24

¹⁹I speak this way, using the illustration of slaves and masters, because it is easy to understand: just as you used to be slaves to all kinds of sin, so now you must let yourselves be slaves to all that is right and holy.

6:21
Jer 12:13
Rom 1:32; 8:6
Gal 6:8

²⁰In those days when you were slaves of sin you didn't bother much with goodness. ²¹And what was the result? Evidently not good, since you are ashamed now even to think about those things you used to do, for all of them end in eternal doom. ²²But now you are free from the power of sin and are slaves of God, and his benefits to you include holiness and everlasting life. ²³For the wages of sin is death, but the free gift of God is eternal life through Jesus Christ our Lord.

6:22
Jn 8:32
Rom 8:2
1 Cor 7:22
1 Pet 1:9; 2:16

6:23
Mt 25:46
Jn 3:16; 4:10
17:2
Rom 5:21
Gal 6:8

No longer bound to the law

7:2
Mt 19:5,6
1 Cor 7:39

7 Don't you understand yet, dear Jewish brothers in Christ, that when a person dies the law no longer holds him in its power?

²Let me illustrate: when a woman marries, the law binds her to her husband as long as he is alive. But if he dies, she is no longer bound to him; the laws of

6:14 *Sin need never again be your master,* literally, "Sin will never again be your master."   **7:1** *dear Jewish brothers,* implied. Literally, "men who know the law."

6:14, 15 If we're no longer tied to the law, are we now free to sin? Paul says, "Of course not." When we were tied to the law, sin was our master—the law does not justify us or help us overcome sin. But now that we are bound to Christ, he is our master, and he gives us power to do good rather than evil.

6:16–18 In certain skilled crafts, an apprentice trains under a "master," who trains, shapes, and molds his apprentice in the finer points of his craft. As spiritual people, we choose a master and pattern ourselves after him. Without Jesus, we would have no choice—we would have to apprentice ourselves to sin, and the results would be guilt, suffering, and separation from God. Thanks to Jesus, however, we can now choose God as our master. Following him, we can enjoy new life and learn the ways of the kingdom. Are you continuing with your first master, sin? Or have you apprenticed yourself to God?

6:17 To obey with all your heart means to give yourself fully to God, to love him "with all your heart, soul, and mind" (Matthew 22:37). And yet so often our efforts to know and obey God's commands can best be described as "half-hearted." How do you rate your heart's obedience? God is more than willing to give you the power to obey him with all your heart.

6:17 The "teaching" committed to them is the Good News that Jesus died for their sins and was raised to give them new life.

6:19–22 It is impossible to be neutral. Every person has a master—either God or sin. A Christian is not someone who cannot sin or who never sins, but someone who is no longer a slave to sin. He belongs to God, not to sin.

6:23 Each of the two masters pays with his own kind of currency. The currency of sin is death. Christ's currency is eternal life—new life with God that begins on earth and continues forever with God.

7:1ff There is a progression in chapter 7 that parallels the progression in the first three chapters. Paul shows that the law is powerless to save the pagan (7:7–14), the lawkeeper (7:15–22), and even the man with a new nature (7:23–25). The pagan is condemned by it; the lawkeeper can't live up to it; and the man with the new nature finds himself sabotaged by the remaining old nature. Thus this chapter summarizes everything that has gone before—and once again, Paul declares that salvation cannot be found by obeying the law. No matter who we are, only Jesus Christ can set us free.

marriage no longer apply to her. ³Then she can marry someone else if she wants to. That would be wrong while he was alive, but it is perfectly all right after he dies.

⁴Your "husband," your master, used to be the Jewish law; but you "died," as it were, with Christ on the cross; and since you are "dead," you are no longer "married to the law," and it has no more control over you. Then you came back to life again when Christ did, and are a new person. And now you are "married," so to speak, to the one who rose from the dead, so that you can produce good fruit, that is, good deeds for God. ⁵When your old nature was still active, sinful desires were at work within you, making you want to do whatever God said not to, and producing sinful deeds, the rotting fruit of death. ⁶But now you need no longer worry about the Jewish laws and customs because you "died" while in their captivity, and now you can really serve God; not in the old way, mechanically obeying a set of rules, but in the new way, [with all of your hearts and minds].

God's law reveals sin

⁷Well then, am I suggesting that these laws of God are evil? Of course not! No, the law is not sinful but it was the law that showed me my sin. I would never have known the sin in my heart—the evil desires that are hidden there—if the law had not said, "You must not have evil desires in your heart." ⁸But sin used this law against evil desires by reminding me that such desires are wrong and arousing all kinds of forbidden desires within me! Only if there were no laws to break would there be no sinning.

⁹That is why I felt fine so long as I did not understand what the law really demanded. But when I learned the truth, I realized that I had broken the law and was a sinner, doomed to die. ¹⁰So as far as I was concerned, the good law which

7:3
Mt 5:32
Mk 10:12
Lk 16:18
1 Cor 6:9
Heb 13:4

7:4
Rom 6:2
Gal 5:18
1 Pet 2:24

7:5
Rom 6:21; 8:8
Gal 5:19-21

7:6
2 Cor 3:6
Gal 5:22
Phil 3:3

7:7
Ex 20:17
Rom 3:20
4:15; 5:20

7:8
Rom 3:20; 4:15
1 Cor 15:56

7:10
Ezek 20:13
Rom 10:15
2 Cor 3:7
Gal 3:12

7:6 *But now you need no longer worry about the Jewish laws and customs,* literally, "But now we are delivered from the law." *with all of your hearts and minds,* implied.

7:3-6 Paul uses marriage to illustrate our relationship to the law. When a spouse dies, the law of marriage no longer applies. Because we have died with Christ, the law can no longer condemn us. The law gave us no power to live a righteous life, but the Spirit enables us to produce good fruit for God. As new people living new lives in the power of the Spirit, we are bound to Christ and will serve him with our hearts and minds.

7:4 What does it mean to be a "new person"? When you acknowledge Christ as your Lord, your life changes forever. An unbeliever's mindset is centered on his own personal gratification. His source of power is his own self-determination. By contrast, the center of a Christian's life is God. He supplies the power for the Christian's daily living. Many believers find that their whole way of looking at the world changes when they come to Christ.

7:6 Some people try to earn their way to God by keeping a set of rules. All they earn for their efforts, of course, is frustration and discouragement. What a relief when these people discover that, because of Christ's sacrifice, the way to God is already open, and they can become his children simply by putting their faith in him. Strangely enough, once they feel secure in God's love, their behavior improves. No longer trying to reach God by keeping rules, they nevertheless become more and more like Jesus as they live with him day by day. But perhaps it isn't so strange after all. When the Holy Spirit turns our eyes away from our own performance and toward Jesus' love, our lives can't help but reflect him.

7:6 A lot of Christians think the law means only "a set of rules for ethical behavior." But in Paul's day, *the law* often meant "the whole Jewish economy." Few of Paul's Jewish readers thought they would obtain eternal life because they kept the Sabbath, didn't murder, didn't bear false witness, etc. They thought they had already made it because they were part of the Jewish system—the men were circumcised, they all participated in the feasts, they kept away from ceremonial defilement, and men and women both

thought they were saved by the law; i.e., by their participation in Jewish religious and cultural life.

During Luther's day a parallel situation had developed: people thought they were saved by the sacramental system of the Catholic church. If they were baptized, took communion, and confessed to a priest, they thought they would be saved. But Luther, like Paul, knew in his heart that this was not enough. The church was not taking away sin any more than the Jewish sacrificial system was: only God could do this, and he would do it only in response to faith.

7:6 Keeping a set of rules is often not extremely difficult. How many times this week—this year—have you seriously considered bowing to an idol, murdering someone, or stealing something?

But, keeping the rules doesn't save us. Even if we could keep our actions pure (which we don't), we would still know we're doomed in God's eyes because our hearts aren't right. Like Paul, we can find no relief in the synagogue or church until we look to Jesus Christ himself for our salvation—which he gives us freely, whether we come from a Jewish, Muslim, or Christian background. But if we do come to Jesus, we are flooded with relief and gratitude. Will we keep the rules any better? We should want to try, especially if we need to improve our morals. But we may still have problems with some sins even when we're saved. But keeping the law is not the purpose of Christ—Christ is the purpose for the law. When we realize that *he* saves us and not the law, we can focus less on what we should and shouldn't be doing and more on how we can best serve him in love and service.

7:9-11 If people feel fine without the law, why did God give it? Because sin is real, and it is dangerous. Imagine a sunny day at the beach. You have just plunged into the surf, and you've never felt better. Suddenly you notice a sign on the pier: "No swimming: sharks in water." Your day is ruined. Is it the sign's fault? Are you angry with the people who put it up? The law is like the sign. It is essential, and we are grateful for it—but it doesn't get rid of the sharks.

7:11
Gen 3:13

7:12
Ps 19:8
1 Tim 1:8

was supposed to show me the way of life resulted instead in my being given the death penalty. ¹¹Sin fooled me by taking the good laws of God and using them to make me guilty of death. ¹²But still, you see, the law itself was wholly right and good.

¹³But how can that be? Didn't the law cause my doom? How then can it be good? No, it was sin, devilish stuff that it is, that used what was good to bring about my condemnation. So you can see how cunning and deadly and damnable it is. For it uses God's good laws for its own evil purposes.

The struggle within

7:14
Rom 3:9; 6:6

¹⁴The law is good, then, and the trouble is not there but with *me*, because I am sold into slavery with Sin as my owner.

7:15
1 Kgs 21:20-25
Gal 5:17

7:16
1 Tim 1:8

¹⁵I don't understand myself at all, for I really want to do what is right, but I can't. I do what I don't want to—what I hate. ¹⁶I know perfectly well that what I am doing is wrong, and my bad conscience proves that I agree with these laws I am breaking. ¹⁷But I can't help myself, because I'm no longer doing it. It is sin inside me that is stronger than I am that makes me do these evil things.

7:18
Gen 8:21
Jn 3:6
Rom 8:3

¹⁸I know I am rotten through and through so far as my old sinful nature is concerned. No matter which way I turn I can't make myself do right. I want to but I can't. ¹⁹When I want to do good, I don't; and when I try not to do wrong, I do it anyway. ²⁰Now if I am doing what I don't want to, it is plain where the trouble is: sin still has me in its evil grasp.

7:21
Rom 8:2

7:22
Ps 1:2

7:23-25
Rom 8:2
1 Cor 15:57
Gal 5:17
Col 2:11
Jas 4:1
1 Pet 2:11

²¹It seems to be a fact of life that when I want to do what is right, I inevitably do what is wrong. ²²I love to do God's will so far as my new nature is concerned; ²³, ²⁴, ²⁵but there is something else deep within me, in my lower nature, that is at war with my mind and wins the fight and makes me a slave to the sin that is still within me. In my mind I want to be God's willing servant but instead I find myself still enslaved to sin.

So you see how it is: my new life tells me to do right, but the old nature that is still inside me loves to sin. Oh, what a terrible predicament I'm in! Who will free

---

7:11 Sin has always fooled people by misusing the law. When Eve encountered the serpent in the Garden of Eden (Genesis 3), the serpent fooled her by taking her focus off the freedom God had given her and putting it on the one restriction he had made. Ever since then, we have all been rebels. Sin looks good to us precisely because God has said it is bad. Instead of paying attention to his warnings, we use them as a "to do" list. When we feel rebellious, we need to back off and look at the law from a wider perspective—in the light of God's grace and mercy. If we focus on his great love for us, we will understand why he asks us to restrict our behavior. He only restricts us from things that ultimately will harm us.

7:15 Paul gives three lessons he learned in trying to deal with his old sinful desires. (1) Knowledge is not the answer (7:9). Paul felt fine as long as he did not understand what the law demanded. When he learned the truth, he knew he was doomed. (2) Self-determination doesn't succeed (7:15). Paul found himself sinning in ways that weren't even attractive to him. (3) Even a profound Christian experience does not instantly stamp out all sin from the believer's life (7:22–25). Becoming like Christ is a lifelong process; Paul likens Christian growth to a strenuous race or fight (1 Corinthians 9:24–27; 2 Timothy 4:7). Thus, as Paul has been emphasizing since the beginning of his letter to the Romans, *no one* in the world is innocent; no one deserves to be saved—not the pagan who doesn't know God's laws, not the Christian or Jew who knows them and tries to keep them. All of us must depend totally on the work of Christ for our salvation. We cannot earn it by our good behavior.

7:15 This is more than the cry of one desperate man—it describes the experience of any Christian struggling against sin. We must never underestimate the power of sin. Satan is a crafty tempter, and we have a great ability to make excuses. Instead of trying to overcome sin with human willpower, we must take hold of the tremendous power of Christ that is available to us. This is God's provision for victory over sin; he sends the Holy Spirit to live in us and give us power. And when we fall, he lovingly reaches out to us and helps us up.

7:17 "The devil made me do it." It sounds like a lame excuse, but it may be true. Without Christ's help, sin is stronger than we are, and sometimes we are unable to defend ourselves against its attacks. That is why we should never stand up to sin all alone. Jesus Christ, who has conquered sin once and for all, promises to fight by our side. If we look to him for help, we will not have to give in to sin.

7:23–25 The sin deep within us is sometimes called the "flesh" or the "law of our members." This is our vulnerability to sin; it refers to everything within us that is more loyal to the world and self than to God.

7:23–25 The inward confusion about sin we sometimes feel was as real for Paul as it is for us. From Paul we learn what to do about it. Whenever he felt lost, he would return to the beginning of his spiritual life, remembering that he had already been freed by Jesus Christ. When you feel confused, follow his example: thank God he has given you freedom through Jesus Christ. Let the reality of Christ's power lift you up to real victory over sin.

me from my slavery to this deadly lower nature? Thank God! It has been done by Jesus Christ our Lord. He has set me free.

The Holy Spirit frees us from sin

8 So there is now no condemnation awaiting those who belong to Christ Jesus. ²For the power of the life-giving Spirit—and this power is mine through Christ Jesus—has freed me from the vicious circle of sin and death. ³We aren't saved from sin's grasp by knowing the commandments of God, because we can't and don't keep them, but God put into effect a different plan to save us. He sent his own Son in a human body like ours—except that ours are sinful—and destroyed sin's control over us by giving himself as a sacrifice for our sins. ⁴So now we can obey God's laws if we follow after the Holy Spirit and no longer obey the old evil nature within us.

⁵Those who let themselves be controlled by their lower natures live only to please themselves, but those who follow after the Holy Spirit find themselves doing those things that please God. ⁶Following after the Holy Spirit leads to life and peace, but following after the old nature leads to death, ⁷because the old sinful nature within us is against God. It never did obey God's laws and it never will. ⁸That's why those who are still under the control of their old sinful selves, bent on following their old evil desires, can never please God.

⁹But you are not like that. You are controlled by your new nature if you have the Spirit of God living in you. (And remember that if anyone doesn't have the Spirit of Christ living in him, he is not a Christian at all.) ¹⁰Yet, even though Christ lives within you, your body will die because of sin; but your spirit will live, for Christ has pardoned it. ¹¹And if the Spirit of God, who raised up Jesus from the dead, lives in you, he will make your dying bodies live again after you die, by means of this same Holy Spirit living within you.

¹²So, dear brothers, you have no obligations whatever to your old sinful nature to do what it begs you to do. ¹³For if you keep on following it you are lost and will perish, but if through the power of the Holy Spirit you crush it and its evil deeds, you shall live. ¹⁴For all who are led by the Spirit of God are sons of God.

8:1
Rom 8:30,34

8:2
Rom 8:11
2 Cor 3:6
Gal 2:19; 5:1

8:3
Acts 13:39
2 Cor 5:21
Phil 2:7
Heb 2:14; 4:15

8:4
Gal 5:16,25

8:5
Gal 5:19-22

8:6
Gal 6:8

8:9
Jn 14:17,18,23
15:5; 17:23,26
Gal 4:6
Phil 1:19
1 Pet 1:11

8:10
Jn 14:20;
15:5; 17:23,26
2 Cor 13:5
Col 1:26,27

8:11
Rom 6:4,5
1 Cor 6:14; 15:45

8:13
Gal 6:8
Col 3:5

8:14
Jn 1:12
Gal 3:26
Rev 21:7

7:25 *It has been done*, or, "It will be done," literally, "I thank God through Jesus Christ our Lord." **8:10** *for Christ has pardoned it*, or possibly, "but the Holy Spirit who lives in you will give you life, for he has already given you righteousness." Literally, "but the Spirit is life because of righteousness."

8:1 "Not guilty; let him go free"—what would those words mean to you if you were on death row? The fact is, of course, that the whole human race *is* on death row, justly condemned for repeatedly breaking God's holy law. Without Jesus we would have no hope at all. But thank God! He has declared us not guilty and has offered us freedom from sin and power to do his will.

8:2 This life-giving Spirit is the Holy Spirit. He was present at the creation of the world (Genesis 1:2), and he is the power behind the rebirth of every Christian. He gives us the power we need to live the Christian life. For more about the Holy Spirit read the notes on John 3:6; Acts 1:4; 1:5.

8:3 Jesus gave himself as a *sacrifice* for our sins. In Old Testament times, animal sacrifices were continually offered at the Temple. The sacrifices showed the Israelites the seriousness of sin: blood had to be shed before sins could be pardoned (see Leviticus 17:11). But animal blood could not really remove sins (Hebrews 10:4). The sacrifices could only point to Jesus' sacrifice, which paid the penalty for all sins.

8:5, 6 Paul divides people into two categories—those who let themselves be controlled by their lower natures, and those who follow after the Holy Spirit. All of us would be in the first category if Jesus hadn't offered us a way out. Once we have said yes to Jesus, we will want to continue following him, because his way brings life and peace. Daily we must consciously choose to center our lives on God. Use the Bible to discover God's guidelines, and then follow them. Ask yourself in every perplexing situation, "What would Jesus want me to do?" When the Holy Spirit points out what

is right, do it eagerly. For more on our lower natures versus our new life in Christ, see 6:6–8; Ephesians 4:23, 24; Colossians 3:3–15.

8:9 Have you ever worried about whether or not you really are a Christian? A Christian is anyone who has the Spirit of God living in him. If you have sincerely trusted Christ for your salvation and acknowledged him as Lord, then the Holy Spirit has come into your life, and you are a Christian. You won't know the Holy Spirit has come if you are waiting for a certain feeling; you will know he has come because Jesus promised he would. When the Holy Spirit is working within you, you will believe that Jesus Christ is God's Son and that eternal life comes through him (1 John 5:5–8); you will begin to act as Christ directs (Romans 8:5; Galatians 5:22, 23); you will find help in your daily problems and in your praying (Romans 8:26, 27); you will be empowered to serve God and do his will (Acts 1:8; Romans 12:6ff); and you will become part of God's plan to build up his church (Ephesians 4:12, 13).

8:14–17 Paul uses adoption to illustrate the believer's new relationship with God. In Roman culture, the adopted person lost all rights in his old family and gained all the rights of a legitimate child in his new family. He became a full heir to his new father's estate. Likewise, when a person becomes a Christian, he gains all the privileges and responsibilities of a child in God's family. One of these outstanding privileges is being led by the Spirit (see Galatians 4:5, 6).

8:14–17 We are no longer cringing and fearful slaves; instead, we are the Master's children. What a privilege! Because we are God's

8:15
Gal 4:5,6

8:16
2 Cor 1:22
Eph 1:13

8:17
Gal 3:29; 4:7
Tit 3:7

15And so we should not be like cringing, fearful slaves, but we should behave like God's very own children, adopted into the bosom of his family, and calling to him, "Father, Father." 16For his Holy Spirit speaks to us deep in our hearts, and tells us that we really are God's children. 17And since we are his children, we will share his treasures—for all God gives to his Son Jesus is now ours too. But if we are to share his glory, we must also share his suffering.

The future glory

8:18
2 Cor 4:17
Col 3:4
1 Pet 1:6.7

8:19
2 Pet 3:13
1 Jn 3:2

8:20
Gen 3:17-19

8:21
Acts 3:21
2 Pet 3:13
Rev 21:1

8:22
Jer 12:4,11

8:23
Lk 20:36
2 Cor 1:22; 5:3-6
Phil 3:21

8:24
2 Cor 5:7
1 Thess 5:8
Heb 11:1

8:25
1 Thess 1:3

8:26
Zech 12:10
Mt 20:22
Jn 14:16

8:27
1 Thess 2:4
1 Jn 5:14

18Yet what we suffer now is nothing compared to the glory he will give us later. 19For all creation is waiting patiently and hopefully for that future day when God will resurrect his children. 20, 21For on that day thorns and thistles, sin, death, and decay—the things that overcame the world against its will at God's command—will all disappear, and the world around us will share in the glorious freedom from sin which God's children enjoy.

22For we know that even the things of nature, like animals and plants, suffer in sickness and death as they await this great event. 23And even we Christians, although we have the Holy Spirit within us as a foretaste of future glory, also groan to be released from pain and suffering. We, too, wait anxiously for that day when God will give us our full rights as his children, including the new bodies he has promised us—bodies that will never be sick again and will never die.

24We are saved by trusting. And trusting means looking forward to getting something we don't yet have—for a man who already has something doesn't need to hope and trust that he will get it. 25But if we must keep trusting God for something that hasn't happened yet, it teaches us to wait patiently and confidently.

26And in the same way—by our faith—the Holy Spirit helps us with our daily problems and in our praying. For we don't even know what we should pray for, nor how to pray as we should; but the Holy Spirit prays for us with such feeling that it cannot be expressed in words. 27And the Father who knows all hearts knows, of course, what the Spirit is saying as he pleads for us in harmony with God's own

8:19 *waiting . . . for that future day,* literally, "waiting for the revelation of the sons of God." **8:20, 21** *thorns and thistles, sin, death, and decay,* implied. **8:22** *suffer in sickness and death as they await this great event,* literally, "the whole creation has been groaning in travail together until now." **8:26** *by our faith,* implied. Literally, "in like manner."

---

children, we share in great treasures. God has already given us his best gifts: his Son, forgiveness, and eternal life; and he encourages us to ask him for whatever we need.

8:17 There is a price for being identified with Jesus. Along with the great treasures, Paul mentions the suffering that Christians must face. What kinds of suffering are we to endure? For first-century believers, there were economic and social consequences, and many faced persecution and death. We too must pay a price for following Jesus. In many parts of today's world, Christians face pressures just as severe as those faced by Christ's first followers. Even in countries where Christianity is tolerated or encouraged, Christians must not become complacent. To live as Jesus did—serving others, giving up one's own rights, resisting pressures to conform to the world—always exacts a price. Nothing we suffer, however, can compare to the great price Jesus paid to save us.

8:19-22 All creation, not just humans, suffered when sin came into the world. By saying we live in a "fallen" world, we mean that sin has caused all creation to fall from the perfect state in which God created it.

8:19-22 Christians see the world as it is—physically decaying and spiritually infected with sin. But Christians do not need to be pessimistic, for they have hope. They look forward to the new heaven and new earth God has promised, and they wait for God's new order that will free the world of sin, sickness, and evil. In the meantime, they go with Christ into the world, where they heal people's bodies and souls and fight the evil effects of sin.

8:23 We will be resurrected with bodies, but they will be glorified bodies like the body Christ now has in heaven (see 1 Corinthians 15:25-53).

8:24, 25 It is natural for children to trust their parents, even though parents sometimes fail to keep their promises. Our heavenly Father, however, never makes promises he won't keep. Nevertheless, his plan may take more time than we expect. Rather than acting like impatient children as we wait for it to unfold, we should place our confidence in God's trustworthiness.

8:24, 25 In Romans, Paul presents the idea that salvation is both present and future. It is present because the moment we believe in Jesus Christ as Savior we *are* saved (3:21-26; 5:1-11; 6:1-11; 6:22, 23); our new life (eternal life) begins. But at the same time, we have not fully received all the benefits and blessings of salvation that will be ours when Christ's new kingdom is completely established. While we can be confident of our salvation, we still look ahead with hope and trust toward that which lies beyond this life, that which we cannot see but yet know is more wonderful than we can comprehend.

8:26, 27 Believers are not left to their own resources to cope with problems. Even when you don't have words to pray, the Holy Spirit prays with and for you, and God answers. With God helping you pray, you don't need to be afraid to come before him. Ask the Holy Spirit to plead for you "in harmony with God's own will." Then, when you bring your requests to God, trust that he will always do what is best.

will. 28And we know that all that happens to us is working for our good if we love God and are fitting into his plans.

29For from the very beginning God decided that those who came to him—and all along he knew who would—should become like his Son, so that his Son would be the First, with many brothers. 30And having chosen us, he called us to come to him; and when we came, he declared us "not guilty," filled us with Christ's goodness, gave us right standing with himself, and promised us his glory.

Nothing can separate us from God's love

31What can we ever say to such wonderful things as these? If God is on our side, who can ever be against us? 32Since he did not spare even his own Son for us but gave him up for us all, won't he also surely give us everything else?

33Who dares accuse us whom God has chosen for his own? Will God? No! He is the one who has forgiven us and given us right standing with himself.

34Who then will condemn us? Will Christ? *No!* For he is the one who died for us and came back to life again for us and is sitting at the place of highest honor next to God, pleading for us there in heaven.

35Who then can ever keep Christ's love from us? When we have trouble or calamity, when we are hunted down or destroyed, is it because he doesn't love us anymore? And if we are hungry, or penniless, or in danger, or threatened with death, has God deserted us?

36No, for the Scriptures tell us that for his sake we must be ready to face death at every moment of the day—we are like sheep awaiting slaughter; 37but despite all this, overwhelming victory is ours through Christ who loved us enough to die for us. 38For I am convinced that nothing can ever separate us from his love. Death can't, and life can't. The angels won't, and all the powers of hell itself cannot keep God's love away. Our fears for today, our worries about tomorrow, 39or where we are—high above the sky, or in the deepest ocean—nothing will ever be able to separate us from the love of God demonstrated by our Lord Jesus Christ when he died for us.

8:28
2 Cor 4:17
Eph 1:11
2 Tim 1:9

8:29
a) Eph 1:5
2 Tim 2:19
1 Pet 1:2
b) Heb 1:6

8:31
Ps 118:6

8:32
Jn 3:16
Rom 4:25; 5:8

8:33
Isa 50:8,9

8:34
Heb 7:25
1 Jn 2:1

8:35
2 Cor 4:7-12

8:36
Ps 44:22

8:37
Jn 16:33
1 Cor 15:57
1 Jn 5:4

8:38
Jn 10:28
Col 3:3

8:39
Rom 5:3-8

8:28 God works out all things—not just isolated incidents—for our good. This does not mean that all that happens to us is good. Evil is prevalent in our fallen world, but God is able to turn it around for our long-range good. Note that God is not working to make us happy, but to fulfill his purpose. Note also that this promise is not for everybody. It can be claimed only by those who love God and are fitting into God's plans. Such people have a new perspective, a new mindset on life. They trust in God, not life's treasures; they look to their security in heaven, not on earth; they learn to accept pain and persecution on earth, not resent it, because it brings them closer to God.

8:29 God's ultimate goal for us is to make us like Christ (1 John 3:2). As we become more and more like him, we discover our true selves, the persons we were created to be.

8:29, 30 Some say these verses mean that before the beginning of the world, God chose certain people to receive his gift of salvation. They point to verses like Ephesians 1:11, which says "we were chosen from the beginning to be his." Others say that God *knew* who would and would not be saved, but he did not specially *choose* some and condemn others. They point to verses like 2 Peter 3:9, which says God "is not willing that *any* should perish." What is clear is that God's *purpose* for man was not an afterthought; it was settled before the foundation of the world. Mankind is to serve and glorify God. God has always known who would and would not be saved. This sovereignty of God should be a reason for rejoicing and confidence, not of puzzlement or doubt.

8:31-34 Do you ever think that, because you aren't good enough

for God, he will not save you? Do you ever feel as if salvation is for everyone else but you? Then these verses are especially for you. If God gave his Son for you, he isn't going to hold back the gift of salvation! If Christ gave his life for you, he isn't going to turn around and condemn you! The book of Romans is more than a theological explanation of God's redeeming grace—it is a letter of comfort and confidence addressed to you.

8:34 Paul says that Jesus is pleading with God for us in heaven. For more on the concept of Christ as our advocate, see note in Hebrews 4:14.

8:35, 36 These words were written to a church that would soon undergo terrible persecution. In just a few years, Paul's hypothetical situations would turn into painful realities. This passage reaffirms God's profound love for his people. No matter what happens to us or where we are, we can never be lost to his love. When suffering comes, it should not drive us away from God, but help us to identify with him further and allow his love to reach us and heal us.

8:35-39 These verses contain one of the most comforting promises in all Scripture. Believers have always had to face hardships in many forms: persecution, illness, imprisonment, even death. These could cause them to fear that they have been abandoned by Christ. But Paul exclaims that it is *impossible* to be separated from Christ. His death for us is proof of his unconquerable love. Nothing can stop his constant presence with us. God tells us how great his love is so that we will feel totally secure in him. If we believe these overwhelming assurances, we will not be afraid.

4. Israel's past, present, and future
God's sovereignty

9:1-3
Ex 32:32
Rom 11:14

9 Oh, Israel, my people! Oh, my Jewish brothers! How I long for you to come to Christ. My heart is heavy within me and I grieve bitterly day and night because of you. Christ knows and the Holy Spirit knows that it is no mere pretense when I say that I would be willing to be forever damned if that would save you. 4God has given you so much, but still you will not listen to him. He took you as his own special, chosen people and led you along with a bright cloud of glory and told you how very much he wanted to bless you. He gave you his rules for daily life so you would know what he wanted you to do. He let you worship him, and gave you mighty promises. 5Great men of God were your fathers, and Christ himself was one of you, a Jew so far as his human nature is concerned, he who now rules over all things. Praise God forever!

9:4
Gen 17:2
Ex 4:22; 40:34
Deut 4:13; 7:6
Eph 2:12

9:5
a) Rom 11:28
b) Jn 1:1,14
Rom 1:3
Tit 2:13
2 Pet 1:1
1 Jn 5:20

9:6
Num 23:19
Rom 2:28
Gal 6:16

6Well then, has God failed to fulfill his promises to the Jews? No! [For these promises are only to those who are truly Jews.] And not everyone born into a Jewish family is truly a Jew! 7Just the fact that they come from Abraham doesn't make them truly Abraham's children. For the Scriptures say that the promises apply only to Abraham's son Isaac and Isaac's descendants, though Abraham had other children too. 8This means that not all of Abraham's children are children of God, but only those who believe the promise of salvation which he made to Abraham.

9:7
Gen 21:12
Gal 4:23
Heb 11:17,18

9:8
Rom 4:23; 8:14
Gal 3:29

9:9
Gen 18:10

9For God had promised, "Next year I will give you and Sarah a son." 10-13And years later, when this son, Isaac, was grown up and married, and Rebecca his wife was about to bear him twin children, God told her that Esau, the child born first, would be a servant to Jacob, his twin brother. In the words of the Scripture, "I chose to bless Jacob, but not Esau." And God said this before the children were even born, before they had done anything either good or bad. This proves that God was doing what he had decided from the beginning; it was not because of what the children did but because of what God wanted and chose.

9:10-13
Gen 25:21-23
Deut 21:15
Mal 1:2,3
Eph 1:4

9:14
Deut 32:4
2 Chron 19:7

14Was God being unfair? Of course not. 15For God had said to Moses, "If I want to be kind to someone, I will. And I will take pity on anyone I want to." 16And so God's blessings are not given just because someone decides to have them or works hard to get them. They are given because God takes pity on those he wants to.

9:15
Ex 33:19

9:16
Ps 115:3
Eph 2:8

9:17
Ex 9:16
Prov 16:4

17Pharaoh, king of Egypt, was an example of this fact. For God told him he had given him the kingdom of Egypt for the very purpose of displaying the awesome power of God against him: so that all the world would hear about God's glorious name. 18So you see, God is kind to some just because he wants to be, and he makes some refuse to listen.

9:18
Ex 4:21; 14:4
Josh 11:20
Jn 12:40
Rom 11:7,22-25

9:19
Job 9:12

19Well then, why does God blame them for not listening? Haven't they done what he made them do?

9:20
Isa 29:16; 45:9
64:8

20No, don't say that. Who are you to criticize God? Should the thing made say to the one who made it, "Why have you made me like this?" 21When a man makes a jar out of clay, doesn't he have a right to use the same lump of clay to make one jar

9:21
Jer 18:6
2 Tim 2:20

9:6 *For these promises are only to those who are truly Jews,* implied.   **9:17** *that all the world would hear about God's glorious name,* literally, "that my name might be published abroad in all the earth."

9:1–3 Paul expressed concern for his people Israel by saying he would willingly take their punishment if that could save them. While the only one who can save us is Christ, Paul showed a rare depth of love. Like Jesus, he was willing to sacrifice for others. How concerned are you for those who don't know Christ? Are you willing to sacrifice your time, money, energy, comfort, and safety to see them come to faith in Jesus?

9:6 God's promises were made to Abraham. Covenant people, the true children of Abraham, are not just his biological descendants. They are all those who trust in God and in what Jesus Christ has done for them. (See also 2:29; Galatians 3:7.)

9:14 Was it right for God to choose Jacob, the younger, to be over Esau? Keep in mind the kind of God we worship: he is

sovereign; he works for our good in everything; he is trustworthy; he will save all who believe in him. When we understand these qualities of God, we know his choices are good even if we don't understand all his reasons. Besides, if we wanted what was right, we would deserve death for our sins; it is not "fair" for God to punish Christ in our place. But would you think of asking God to take back his offer of salvation because you don't deserve it?

9:21 Paul is not saying that some of us are worth more than others, but simply that the Creator has control over the created object. The created object, therefore, has no right to demand anything from its Creator—its very existence depends on him. Keeping this perspective removes any temptation to have pride in personal achievement.

beautiful, to be used for holding flowers, and another to throw garbage into? 22Does not God have a perfect right to show his fury and power against those who are fit only for destruction, those he has been patient with for all this time? 23, 24And he has a right to take others such as ourselves, who have been made for pouring the riches of his glory into, whether we are Jews or Gentiles, and to be kind to us so that everyone can see how very great his glory is.

25Remember what the prophecy of Hosea says? There God says that he will find other children for himself (who are not from his Jewish family) and will love them, though no one had ever loved them before. 26And the heathen, of whom it once was said, "You are not my people," shall be called "sons of the Living God."

27Isaiah the prophet cried out concerning the Jews that though there would be millions of them, only a small number would ever be saved. 28"For the Lord will execute his sentence upon the earth, quickly ending his dealings, justly cutting them short."

29And Isaiah says in another place that except for God's mercy all the Jews would be destroyed—all of them—just as everyone in the cities of Sodom and Gomorrah perished.

9:22 Prov 16:4 Rom 2:4 1 Thess 5:9
9:23 Acts 9:15 Rom 8:29
9:24 Rom 3:29
9:25 Hos 2:23
9:26 Hos 1:10 1 Pet 2:10
9:27 Isa 10:22 Rom 11:5
9:28 Isa 28:22
9:29 Isa 1:9; 13:19 Lam 3:22

Israel's unbelief of the gospel

30Well then, what shall we say about these things? Just this, that God has given the Gentiles the opportunity to be acquitted by faith, even though they had not been really seeking God. 31But the Jews, who tried so hard to get right with God by keeping his laws, never succeeded. 32Why not? Because they were trying to be saved by keeping the law and being good instead of by depending on faith. They have stumbled over the great stumbling stone. 33God warned them of this in the Scriptures when he said, "I have put a Rock in the path of the Jews, and many will stumble over him (Jesus). Those who believe in him will never be disappointed."

9:30 Gal 2:16 Heb 11:7
9:31 Isa 51:1 Gal 5:4
9:32 Isa 8:14,15
9:33 Ps 118:22 Isa 28:16

10 Dear brothers, the longing of my heart and my prayer is that the Jewish people might be saved. 2I know what enthusiasm they have for the honor of God, but it is misdirected zeal. 3For they don't understand that Christ has died to

10:3 Rom 1:17 Phil 3:9

9:27 *millions,* literally, "as the sand of the sea," i.e., numberless. **9:29** *perished,* see Isa 1:9. **9:33** *never be disappointed,* see Isa 28:16.

9:25, 26 Seven hundred years before Jesus' birth, Hosea told of God's intention to bring Gentiles into his family after the Jews rejected his plan. Verse 25 is a quotation from Hosea 2:23 and verse 26 is from Hosea 1:10.

9:27–29 Isaiah prophesied that only a small number—a remnant—of God's original people, the Jews, would be saved. Paul saw this happening in every city where he preached. Even though he went to the Jews first, relatively few ever accepted the message. Verses 27 and 28 are based on Isaiah 10:22, 23; and 9:29 is from Isaiah 1:9.

9:31–33 Sometimes we are like these people, trying "hard to get right with God by keeping his laws." We may think church attendance, church work, giving offerings, and being nice will be enough. After all, we've played by the rules, haven't we? But Paul's words sting—this approach never succeeds. Paul explains that God's plan is not for those who try to earn his favor by being good; it is for those who realize they can never be good enough and so must depend on Christ. Only by putting our faith in what Jesus Christ has done will we be saved. If we do that, we will "never be disappointed."

9:32 The Jews had a worthy goal—to honor God. But they tried to achieve it the wrong way—by rigid and painstaking obedience to the law. Thus some of them became more dedicated to the law than to God. They thought that if they kept the law, God would have to accept them as his people. But God cannot be controlled. The Jews did not see that their Scriptures, the Old Testament, taught salvation by faith, and not by human effort (see Genesis 15:6).

9:32 The stumbling stone was Jesus. The Jews did not believe in

him because he didn't meet their expectations for the Messiah. Some people still stumble over Christ because salvation by faith doesn't make sense to them. They would rather try to work their way to God, or else they expect him simply to overlook their shortcomings. Others stumble over Christ because his values are the opposite of the world's. He asks for humility, not success; and many are unwilling to humble themselves before him. Some simply refuse to acknowledge any authority over them, and thus they stumble over the Lordship of Christ.

10:1 What will happen to the Jewish people who believe in God but not in Christ? Since they believe in the same God, won't they be saved? If that were true, Paul would not have worked so hard and sacrificed so much to teach them about Christ. Since Jesus is the most complete revelation of God, and we cannot fully know God apart from Christ; and since God appointed Jesus to bring God and man together, we cannot come to God by another path. The Jews, like everyone else, can find salvation only through Jesus Christ (John 14:6; Acts 4:12). Like Paul, we should wish that all Jews might be saved. We should pray for them and lovingly share the Good News with them.

10:3, 4 Why did God give the law when he knew people couldn't keep it? According to Paul, one reason the law was given was to show men how guilty they are (Galatians 3:19). The law was a shadow of Christ—that is, the sacrificial system educated the people so that when the true sacrifice came, they would be able to understand his work. The system of ceremonial laws was to last until the coming of Christ. The law points to Christ, the reason for all those animal sacrifices.

10:3–5 Rather than living by faith in God, the Jews established

10:4
Gal 3:24

10:5
Lev 18:4,5
Ezek 20:11,
13,21
Rom 7:10

10:6
Deut 30:11-14

10:7
1 Cor 15:3,4

10:8
Deut 30:14

10:9
Mt 10:32
Lk 12:8
Acts 2:24; 16:31
Rom 4:24

10:11
Isa 28:16

10:12
Acts 15:9
Eph 2:4-7

10:13
Joel 2:32
Acts 2:21

10:14
Acts 8:28-31
Tit 1:3

10:15
Isa 52:7
Rom 1:15; 15:20

10:16
Isa 53:1
Jn 12:38
Heb 4:2

10:17
Gal 3:2,5
Col 3:16

10:18
Ps 19:4
Mt 24:14

10:19
Deut 32:21

10:20
Isa 65:1,2

10:21
1 Sam 12:22
Jer 31:37

make them right with God. Instead they are trying to make themselves good enough to gain God's favor by keeping the Jewish laws and customs, but that is not God's way of salvation. 4They don't understand that Christ gives to those who trust in him everything they are trying to get by keeping his laws. He ends all of that.

5For Moses wrote that if a person could be perfectly good and hold out against temptation all his life and never sin once, only then could he be pardoned and saved. 6But the salvation that comes through faith says, "You don't need to search the heavens to find Christ and bring him down to help you," and, 7"You don't need to go among the dead to bring Christ back to life again."

8For salvation that comes from trusting Christ—which is what we preach—is already within easy reach of each of us; in fact, it is as near as our own hearts and mouths. 9For if you tell others with your own mouth that Jesus Christ is your Lord, and believe in your own heart that God has raised him from the dead, you will be saved. 10For it is by believing in his heart that a man becomes right with God; and with his mouth he tells others of his faith, confirming his salvation.

11For the Scriptures tell us that no one who believes in Christ will ever be disappointed. 12Jew and Gentile are the same in this respect: they all have the same Lord who generously gives his riches to all those who ask him for them. 13Anyone who calls upon the name of the Lord will be saved.

14But how shall they ask him to save them unless they believe in him? And how can they believe in him if they have never heard about him? And how can they hear about him unless someone tells them? 15And how will anyone go and tell them unless someone sends him? That is what the Scriptures are talking about when they say, "How beautiful are the feet of those who preach the Gospel of peace with God and bring glad tidings of good things." In other words, how welcome are those who come preaching God's Good News!

16But not everyone who hears the Good News has welcomed it, for Isaiah the prophet said, "Lord, who has believed me when I told them?" 17Yet faith comes from listening to this Good News—the Good News about Christ.

18But what about the Jews? Have they heard God's Word? Yes, for it has gone wherever they are; the Good News has been told to the ends of the earth. 19And did they understand [that God would give his salvation to others if they refused to take it]? Yes, for even back in the time of Moses, God had said that he would make his people jealous and try to wake them up by giving his salvation to the foolish heathen nations. 20And later on Isaiah said boldly that God would be found by people who weren't even looking for him. 21In the meantime, he keeps on reaching out his hands to the Jews, but they keep arguing and refusing to come.

10:10 *confirming his salvation*, literally, "confession is made unto salvation."   **10:15** *good things*, see Isa 52:7.
10:16 *When I told them?*, see Isa 53:1.   **10:19** *that God would give his salvation to others if they refused to take it*, implied.   **10:20** *looking for him*, see Isa 65:1.   **10:21** *arguing*, literally, "disobedient, obstinate."

---

customs and traditions (in addition to God's law) to try to make themselves acceptable in God's sight. But human effort, no matter how sincere, can never substitute for the goodness God offers us by faith. The only way to *earn* salvation is to be perfect—and that is impossible. We can only hold out our empty hands and receive it as a gift.

10:6–8 People have always looked for God through dramatic experiences. Hoping for a life-changing encounter, some travel across the world to meet a spiritual leader. But God's salvation is right in front of us. He will come to us wherever we are. All we need to do is to respond and accept his gift of salvation.

10:8–12 Have you ever been asked, "How do I become a Christian?" These verses give you the beautiful answer—salvation is as close as your own heart and mouth. People think it must be a complicated process, but it is not. If they believe in their hearts and say with their mouths that Christ is the risen Lord, they will be saved.

10:11 This verse must be read in context. Paul is not saying Christians will be free of all disappointments. There will be times when people will let us down and when circumstances will take a turn for the worse. Paul is saying that God's offer of salvation will never disappoint us. Jesus Christ will never let us down: *everyone* who believes in him will be saved.

10:14, 15 God's great message of salvation must be taken to others, so they can have the chance to respond to the Good News. How will your loved ones and neighbors hear it unless someone tells them? Is God calling you to take a part in making his message known in your community? Think of one person who needs to hear the Good News, and think of something you can do to help him or her hear it. Then do that act as soon as possible.

10:20 Many Jews who were looking for the Messiah missed him. Many Gentiles who didn't even know about a Messiah found him. Today some of the most spiritually blind people are religious, and those who have never set foot in a church are sometimes the most responsive. Since appearances are deceiving and we can't see into people's hearts, beware of judging beforehand who will respond to the gospel and who will not.

God's mercy on Israel

11 I ask then, has God rejected and deserted his people the Jews? Oh no, not at all. Remember that I myself am a Jew, a descendant of Abraham and a member of Benjamin's family.

11:1
1 Sam 12:22
Jer 31:36,37
2 Cor 11:22
Phil 3:5

2, 3No, God has not discarded his own people whom he chose from the very beginning. Do you remember what the Scriptures say about this? Elijah the prophet was complaining to God about the Jews, telling God how they had killed the prophets and torn down God's altars; Elijah claimed that he was the only one left in all the land who still loved God, and now they were trying to kill him too.

11:2
1 Kgs 19:10

4And do you remember how God replied? God said, "No, you are not the only one left. I have seven thousand others besides you who still love me and have not bowed down to idols!"

11:4
1 Kgs 19:18

5It is the same today. Not all the Jews have turned away from God; there are a few being saved as a result of God's kindness in choosing them. 6And if it is by God's kindness, then it is not by their being good enough. For in that case the free gift would no longer be free—it isn't free when it is earned.

11:5
2 Kgs 19:4
Rom 9:27

11:6
Rom 4:4,5

7So this is the situation: Most of the Jews have not found the favor of God they are looking for. A few have—the ones God has picked out—but the eyes of the others have been blinded. 8This is what our Scriptures refer to when they say that God has put them to sleep, shutting their eyes and ears so that they do not understand what we are talking about when we tell them of Christ. And so it is to this very day.

11:7
Mk 6:52
2 Cor 3:14,15

11:8
Deut 29:4
Isa 6:9-13
29:10
Mt 13:14
Jn 12:40
Acts 28:26,27

9King David spoke of this same thing when he said, "Let their good food and other blessings trap them into thinking all is well between themselves and God. Let these good things boomerang on them and fall back upon their heads to justly crush them. 10Let their eyes be dim," he said, "so that they cannot see, and let them walk bent-backed forever with a heavy load."

11:9
Ps 69:22

11:10
Ps 69:23

11Does this mean that God has rejected his Jewish people forever? Of course not! His purpose was to make his salvation available to the Gentiles, and then the Jews would be jealous and begin to want God's salvation for themselves. 12Now if the whole world became rich as a result of God's offer of salvation, when the Jews stumbled over it and turned it down, think how much greater a blessing the world will share in later on when the Jews, too, come to Christ.

11:11
Ezek 18:23
33:11
Acts 18:6

11:12
Jer 30:3-9,11
Zech 2:11

13As you know, God has appointed me as a special messenger to you Gentiles. I lay great stress on this and remind the Jews about it as often as I can, 14so that if

11:13
Acts 9:15

11:14
Rom 9:3
1 Cor 9:20
2 Tim 1:9

11:1ff In this chapter Paul points out that not *all* Jews have rejected God's message of salvation. Paul himself, after all, was a Jew, and so were Jesus' disciples and nearly all of the early Christian missionaries.

11:2, 3 God chose the Jews to be the people through whom the rest of the world could find salvation. But this did not mean the entire Jewish nation would be saved; only those who were faithful to God were considered true Jews. People are saved through faith in Christ, not because they are part of a nation, religion, or family. On what are you depending for salvation?

11:6 This great truth can be hard to grasp. Do you think it's easier for God to love you when you're good? Do you secretly suspect God chose you because you deserved to be chosen? Do you think some people's behavior is so bad that God couldn't possibly save them? If you ever think this way, you don't entirely understand the Good News that salvation is a free gift. It cannot be earned, in whole or in part; it can only be accepted with thankfulness and praise.

11:8-10 These verses describe the punishment for hardened hearts predicted by the prophet Isaiah (Isaiah 6:9–13). If people refuse to hear God's Good News, they eventually will be unable to understand it. Paul saw this happening in the synagogues he visited. (Verse 8 is based on Deuteronomy 29:4 and Isaiah 29:10.

Verses 9 and 10 are from Psalm 69:22, 23.)

11:11ff Paul had a vision for a church in which all Jews and Gentiles were united in their love of God and obedience to Christ. While respecting God's law, this ideal church would look to Christ alone for salvation and eternal life. One's ethnic background and social status would be irrelevant (see Galatians 3:28)—what mattered would be one's faith in Christ.

But Paul's vision has not yet come true. In his day many Jewish people rejected the Good News. They looked to their heritage for salvation, and they did not have the "heart religion" that was so important to the Old Testament prophets and to Paul.

Soon after Paul's day, once Gentiles were in control of most Christian churches, another obstacle to Jewish/Christian unity arose. Rather than loving those Jews who wanted to come into the church and yearning for their salvation, as Paul did, many Gentile Christians began rejecting them and even persecuting them. Unfortunately, this has often been continued through the centuries.

True Christians—those who follow Jesus from the heart—should not do such things, of course. But both Christians and Jews have done so much damage to the cause of the God they claim to serve that Paul's vision often seems impossible to fulfill.

Yet the truth remains—God chose the Jews, just as he chose the Christians, and he is still working to unite Jew and Gentile in a new Israel, a new Jerusalem, ruled by his Son.

11:15
Lk 15:24,32
Rom 5:11

possible I can make them want what you Gentiles have and in that way save some of them. 15And how wonderful it will be when they become Christians! When God turned away from them it meant that he turned to the rest of the world to offer his salvation; and now it is even more wonderful when the Jews come to Christ. It will be like dead people coming back to life. 16And since Abraham and the prophets are God's people, their children will be too. For if the roots of the tree are holy, the branches will be too.

11:17
Jer 11:16
Eph 2:11-16

17But some of these branches from Abraham's tree, some of the Jews, have been broken off. And you Gentiles who were branches from, we might say, a wild olive tree, were grafted in. So now you, too, receive the blessing God has promised Abraham and his children, sharing in God's rich nourishment of his own special olive tree.

11:18
Jn 4:22
1 Cor 10:12

18But you must be careful not to brag about being put in to replace the branches that were broken off. Remember that you are important only because you are now a part of God's tree; you are just a branch, not a root.

19"Well," you may be saying, "those branches were broken off to make room for me so I must be pretty good."

11:20
Rom 12:16
Phil 2:12

20Watch out! Remember that those branches, the Jews, were broken off because they didn't believe God, and you are there only because you do. Do not be proud; be humble and grateful—and careful. 21For if God did not spare the branches he put there in the first place, he won't spare you either.

11:22
Jn 15:2
Heb 3:6
11:23
2 Cor 3:14-16

22Notice how God is both kind and severe. He is very hard on those who disobey, but very good to you if you continue to love and trust him. But if you don't, you too will be cut off. 23On the other hand, if the Jews leave their unbelief behind them and come back to God, God will graft them back into the tree again. He has the power to do it.

24For if God was willing to take you who were so far away from him—being part of a wild olive tree—and graft you into his own good tree—a very unusual thing to do—don't you see that he will be far more ready to put the Jews back again, who were there in the first place?

God's mercy on all

11:25
Lk 21:24
Rom 11:12; 16:25
Eph 3:3-6

25I want you to know about this truth from God, dear brothers, so that you will not feel proud and start bragging. Yes, it is true that some of the Jews have set themselves against the Gospel now, but this will last only until all of you Gentiles have come to Christ—those of you who will. 26And then all Israel will be saved.

11:26
Ps 14:7
Isa 59:20
Jer 3:18
11:27
Jer 31:31
Heb 8:8; 10:16

Do you remember what the prophets said about this? "There shall come out of Zion a Deliverer, and he shall turn the Jews from all ungodliness. 27At that time I will take away their sins, just as I promised."

28Now many of the Jews are enemies of the Gospel. They hate it. But this has been a benefit to you, for it has resulted in God's giving his gifts to you Gentiles.

11:15 In the early days following Pentecost, the Christian church was predominantly Jewish, and Gentiles were the exception. But because of the missionary efforts of Peter, Philip, Paul, and others, Gentiles became believers and soon became the majority in the church. However, this does not mean there is no longer any place in the church for Jews. When a Jew comes to Christ, there is great rejoicing, as if a dead person had come back to life.

11:17–21 Paul, speaking to Gentile Christians, is warning them not to feel superior because God rejected some Jews. The Jewish religion, he says, is like the root of a tree, and the Jewish people are the tree's natural branches. Gentile believers have been grafted into the tree, and now Jews and Gentiles share its nourishment. Both Jews and Gentiles depend on Christ for life; neither can rest on heritage, culture, or theological beliefs for salvation.

11:26 Some say the phrase "And then all Israel will be saved" means that the majority of Jews in the final generation before Christ's return will turn to Christ for salvation. Others say that Paul

is using the term "Israel" in the sense of the "spiritual" nation of Israel made up of everyone—Jew and Gentile—who has received salvation through faith in Christ. Thus "all Israel" (or all believers) will receive God's promised gift of salvation. God chose the nation of Israel, and he has never rejected it. He also chose the church, through Jesus Christ, and he will never reject it either. This does not mean, of course, that all Jews or all church members will be saved. It is possible to belong to a nation or to an organization without ever responding in faith to Jesus.

11:28–32 In this passage Paul shows how the Jews and the Gentiles benefit each other. Whenever God shows mercy on one group, the other shares the blessing. In God's original plan, the Jews would freely share their blessings with the Gentiles (see Genesis 12:3). When the Jews neglected to do this, God blessed the Gentiles anyway through the Jewish Messiah. Now it is the Gentiles' turn to bless the Jews. God's plans will not be thwarted: he will "have mercy upon all alike." For a beautiful picture of Jews and Gentiles being blessed together, see Isaiah 60.

Yet the Jews are still beloved of God because of his promises to Abraham, Isaac, and Jacob. 29For God's gifts and his call can never be withdrawn; he will never go back on his promises. 30Once you were rebels against God, but when the Jews refused his gifts God was merciful to you instead. 31And now the Jews are the rebels, but some day they, too, will share in God's mercy upon you. 32For God has given them all up to sin so that he could have mercy upon all alike.

33Oh, what a wonderful God we have! How great are his wisdom and knowledge and riches! How impossible it is for us to understand his decisions and his methods! 34For who among us can know the mind of the Lord? Who knows enough to be his counselor and guide? 35And who could ever offer to the Lord enough to induce him to act? 36For everything comes from God alone. Everything lives by his power, and everything is for his glory. To him be glory evermore.

11:29
Num 23:18-24
Heb 7:21

11:32
Rom 3:9
Gal 3:22

11:33
Job 11:7; 15:8
Eph 3:8,10

11:34
Isa 40:13
1 Cor 2:16

11:35
Job 35:7; 41:11
Col 1:16

11:36
1 Cor 8:6

B. HOW TO BEHAVE (12:1—16:27)
Moving from theological to practical, Paul gives guidelines for living as a redeemed people in a fallen world. We are to give ourselves to Christ as living sacrifices, obey the government, love our neighbors, and take special care of those who are weak in the faith. He closes with personal remarks. Throughout this section, we learn how to live our faith each day.

1. Personal responsibility
A living sacrifice to God

12 And so, dear brothers, I plead with you to give your bodies to God. Let them be a living sacrifice, holy—the kind he can accept. When you think of what he has done for you, is this too much to ask? 2Don't copy the behavior and customs of this world, but be a new and different person with a fresh newness in all you do and think. Then you will learn from your own experience how his ways will really satisfy you.

3As God's messenger I give each of you God's warning: Be honest in your estimate of yourselves, measuring your value by how much faith God has given you. 4, 5Just as there are many parts to our bodies, so it is with Christ's body. We are all parts of it, and it takes every one of us to make it complete, for we each have different work to do. So we belong to each other, and each needs all the others.

6God has given each of us the ability to do certain things well. So if God has

12:1
Rom 6:12,13
12:2
Gal 1:4
Eph 4:23
Col 3:10

12:3
1 Cor 12:7
Phil 2:3-5
Eph 4:7
12:4,5
1 Cor 10:17
12:12-14
Eph 4:4,12,25
12:6
1 Pet 4:10,11

11:32 *has given them all up to sin,* literally, "shut up all unto disobedience."

12:1 When sacrificing an animal according to God's law, a priest killed the animal, cut it in pieces, and placed it on the altar. Sacrifice was important, but even in the Old Testament God made it clear that obedience from the heart was much more important (see 1 Samuel 15:22; Psalm 40:6; Amos 5:21–24). God wants us to offer ourselves, not animals, as *living* sacrifices—daily laying aside our own desires to follow him. We do this out of gratitude that our sins have been forgiven.

12:1, 2 God has good, pleasing, and perfect plans for his children. He wants us to be new people with freshness of thought, alive to glorify him. Since he wants only what is best for us, and since he gave his Son to make our new lives possible, we should joyfully offer ourselves as living sacrifices for him.

12:2 "The behavior and customs of this world" are usually selfish and often corrupting, and many Christians wisely decide that much worldly behavior is off-limits for them. Our refusal to conform to the world, however, must go even deeper than the level of behavior and customs—it must be firmly founded in our minds. This verse is also translated "Do not be conformed to this world, but be transformed by the renewal of your mind." It is possible to avoid most worldly customs and still be proud, covetous, selfish, stubborn, and arrogant. Only when our minds are renewed by the new attitude Christ gives us are we truly transformed. If our character is like Christ's, we can be sure our behavior will honor God.

12:3 We hear a lot about the importance of healthy self-esteem.

Paul warns us, however, not to go too far in self-love—another translation says that no one should "think of himself more highly than he ought to think." Some of us think too little of ourselves; some think too much. The key to an honest and accurate evaluation is knowing the basis of our self-worth—our new identity in Christ. Apart from him, we aren't worth very much by eternal standards; in him, our worth as a creation of God is infinite. Evaluating yourself by the worldly standards of success and achievement can cause you to think too much about your worth in the eyes of others and miss your true value in God's eyes.

12:4, 5 Paul uses the concept of the human body to teach how Christians should live and work together. Just as the parts of the body function under the direction of the brain, so Christians are to work under the command and authority of Jesus Christ (see 1 Corinthians 12:12–31; Ephesians 4:1–16).

12:4–8 God gives us gifts so we can build up his church. To use them effectively, we must (1) realize that all gifts and abilities come from God; (2) understand that not everyone has the same gifts; (3) know who we are and what we do best; (4) dedicate our gifts to God's service and not to our personal success; (5) be willing to spend our gifts generously, not holding back anything from God's service.

12:6 *Prophecy* in Scripture is not always predicting the future. Often it means preaching God's messages (1 Corinthians 14:1).

12:6–8 Look at this list of gifts and imagine the kinds of people who would have each gift. Prophets are often bold and articulate.

12:7
1 Cor 12:8,28

12:8
Acts 15:32
20:27,28
1 Cor 14:3,4
1 Pet 5:2

12:9
Amos 5:15
1 Tim 1:5

12:10
Jn 13:34
Phil 2:3,4
1 Thess 4:9
2 Pet 1:7

12:11
Acts 18:25
20:19
Rev 3:15

12:12
Rom 5:2,3
Heb 3:6; 10:32

12:13
Heb 6:10
13:1-3

12:14
1 Pet 3:9

12:15
Job 30:25
Heb 13:3

12:16
2 Cor 13:11
Phil 2:2; 4:2

12:17
Prov 20:22

given you the ability to prophesy, then prophesy whenever you can—as often as your faith is strong enough to receive a message from God. 7If your gift is that of serving others, serve them well. If you are a teacher, do a good job of teaching. 8If you are a preacher, see to it that your sermons are strong and helpful. If God has given you money, be generous in helping others with it. If God has given you administrative ability and put you in charge of the work of others, take the responsibility seriously. Those who offer comfort to the sorrowing should do so with Christian cheer.

9Don't just pretend that you love others: really love them. Hate what is wrong. Stand on the side of the good. 10Love each other with brotherly affection and take delight in honoring each other. 11Never be lazy in your work but serve the Lord enthusiastically.

12Be glad for all God is planning for you. Be patient in trouble, and prayerful always. 13When God's children are in need, you be the one to help them out. And get into the habit of inviting guests home for dinner or, if they need lodging, for the night.

14If someone mistreats you because you are a Christian, don't curse him; pray that God will bless him. 15When others are happy, be happy with them. If they are sad, share their sorrow. 16Work happily together. Don't try to act big. Don't try to get into the good graces of important people, but enjoy the company of ordinary folks. And don't think you know it all!

17Never pay back evil for evil. Do things in such a way that everyone can see you are honest clear through. 18Don't quarrel with anyone. Be at peace with everyone, just as much as possible.

19Dear friends, never avenge yourselves. Leave that to God, for he has said that

---

Servers are faithful and loyal. Teachers are clear thinkers. Preachers know how to motivate others. Givers are generous and trusting. Administrators are good organizers and managers. Comforters are caring people who are happy to give their time to others. It would be difficult for one person to embody all these gifts. An assertive prophet would not usually make a good counselor, and a generous giver might fail as an administrator. When you identify your own gifts (and you don't have to stop with this list—it is far from complete), ask how you can use them to God's glory. At the same time, realize that your gifts can't do the work of the church all alone. Be thankful for people whose gifts are completely different from yours. Let your strengths balance their weaknesses, and be grateful that their abilities make up for your deficiencies. Together you can build the church.

12:9 Most of us have learned how to pretend to love others—how to speak kindly, avoid hurting their feelings, and appear to take an interest in them. We may even be skilled in pretending to ourselves—we feel moved with compassion when we hear of others' needs, or we become indignant when we learn of injustice. But God calls us to real love that goes far beyond surface behaviors and emotions. Real love requires work. It means doing something for the people we love so that they will be better people. It demands our time, our money, and our personal involvement. No individual has the resources to love a whole community, but a church—the body of Christ in your town—can do this. Look for people who need your active love, and look for ways you and your fellow believers can get together and love your community in the name of Christ.

12:10 We can honor others two ways. The world's way has an ulterior motive. In the world, we honor our bosses so they will reward us, our employees so they will work harder, the wealthy so they will contribute to our cause, the powerful so they will use their power for us and not against us. God's way of honoring others is different. As Christians, we honor people because they have been created in God's image, because they are our brothers and sisters in Christ, because we are grateful for the ways they are building up the body of Christ.

12:13 Christian hospitality is different from the world's way of entertaining. Entertaining focuses on the host family—their home must be spotless; their food must be well prepared and abundant; they must appear relaxed and good natured. Hospitality, by contrast, focuses on the guests. Their needs—whether for a place to stay, nourishing food, a listening ear, acceptance—are of first importance. Hospitality can happen in a messy home. It can happen around a dinner table where the main dish is canned soup. It can even happen while the host and the guest are doing chores together. Don't be afraid to offer hospitality just because you are too tired, too busy, or too poor to entertain.

12:17–21 These verses summarize the real core of Christian living. If we love someone the way Christ loves us, we will be willing to forgive. If we have experienced God's grace, we will want to pass it on to others. And remember, grace is *undeserved* favor. By giving an enemy a drink, we're not excusing his misdeeds. We're recognizing them, forgiving them, and loving the individual in spite of them—just as Christ did in our case.

12:19–21 In this day of constant lawsuits and incessant demands for legal rights, Paul's command sounds almost impossible. When someone hurts you deeply, instead of giving him what he deserves, Paul says to befriend him. Why does Paul tell us to forgive our enemies? (1) Forgiveness may break a cycle of retaliation and lead to mutual reconciliation. (2) It may make the enemy feel ashamed and change his ways. (3) By contrast, returning evil for evil hurts you just as much as it hurts your enemy. Even if your enemy never repents, forgiving him will free you of a heavy load of bitterness.

12:19–21 Forgiveness involves both attitudes and action. If you find it hard to *feel* forgiving of someone who has hurt you, try *acting* forgiving. If appropriate, tell this person you would like to heal your relationship. Give him a helping hand. Send him a gift. Smile at him. Many times you will discover that right actions lead to right feelings.

he will repay those who deserve it. [Don't take the law into your own hands.] 20Instead, feed your enemy if he is hungry. If he is thirsty give him something to drink and you will be "heaping coals of fire on his head." In other words, he will feel ashamed of himself for what he has done to you. 21Don't let evil get the upper hand but conquer evil by doing good.

12:20
Prov 25:21
Mt 5:44

12:21
1 Pet 2:21

Obedience to the government

13 Obey the government, for God is the one who has put it there. There is no government anywhere that God has not placed in power. 2So those who refuse to obey the laws of the land are refusing to obey God, and punishment will follow. 3For the policeman does not frighten people who are doing right; but those doing evil will always fear him. So if you don't want to be afraid, keep the laws and you will get along well. 4The policeman is sent by God to help you. But if you are doing something wrong, of course you should be afraid, for he will have you punished. He is sent by God for that very purpose. 5Obey the laws, then, for two reasons: first, to keep from being punished, and second, just because you know you should.

13:1
Dan 2:21; 4:32
Jn 19:11
Tit 3:1

13:3
1 Pet 2:14

13:5
Eccles 8:2
1 Pet 2:13

6Pay your taxes too, for these same two reasons. For government workers need to be paid so that they can keep on doing God's work, serving you. 7Pay everyone whatever he ought to have: pay your taxes and import duties gladly, obey those over you, and give honor and respect to all those to whom it is due.

13:7
Mt 17:24,25
22:21
Lk 20:25

Love fulfills God's requirements

8Pay all your debts except the debt of love for others—never finish paying that! For if you love them, you will be obeying all of God's laws, fulfilling all his requirements. 9If you love your neighbor as much as you love yourself you will not want to harm or cheat him, or kill him or steal from him. And you won't sin with his wife or want what is his, or do anything else the Ten Commandments say is wrong. All ten are wrapped up in this one, to love your neighbor as you love yourself. 10Love does no wrong to anyone. That's why it fully satisfies all of God's requirements. It is the only law you need.

13:8
Mt 7:12; 22:39
Jn 13:34
Jas 2:8

13:9
Ex 20:13-17
Lev 19:18

13:10
Mt 22:39
Jn 13:34,35
Gal 5:13,14

12:19 *Don't take the law into your own hands,* implied.

13:1ff Christians understand Romans 13 in different ways. All Christians agree that we are to live at peace with the state as long as the state allows us to live by our religious convictions. For hundreds of years, however, there have been at least three interpretations of how we are to do this. (1) Some Christians believe that the state is so corrupt that Christians should have as little to do with it as possible. Although they should be good citizens as long as they can do so without compromising their beliefs, they should not work for the government, vote, or serve in the military. (2) Others believe God has given the state authority in certain areas and the church authority in others. Christians can be loyal to both and can work for either. They should not, however, confuse the two. In this view, church and state are concerned with two totally different spheres—the spiritual and the physical—and thus complement each other but do not work together. (3) Still others believe that Christians have a responsibility to make the state better. They can do this politically, by electing Christian or other high-principled leaders. They can also do this morally, by serving as an influence for good in society. In this view, church and state ideally work together for the good of all.

None of these views advocate rebelling against or refusing to obey the government's laws or regulations unless they clearly require you to violate the moral standards revealed by God. Wherever we find ourselves, we must be responsible citizens, as well as responsible Christians.

13:1 Are there times when we should not obey the government? We can never allow government to force us to disobey God. Jesus and his apostles never disobeyed the government for personal reasons; when they disobeyed, it was in order to follow their higher loyalty to God. Their disobedience was not cheap: they were threatened, beaten, thrown into jail, tortured, and executed for their convictions. Like them, if we are compelled to disobey, we must be ready to accept the consequences.

13:3 When the police are unjust, good people are afraid. In this verse, Paul is talking about police who are doing their duty. When the police are just, people who are doing right have nothing to fear.

13:8 Why is love for others called a debt? We are permanently in debt to Christ for the lavish love he has poured out on us. The only way we can even begin to repay this debt is by loving others in turn. Since Christ's love will always be infinitely greater than ours, we will always have the obligation to love our neighbors.

13:9 Somehow many of us have gotten the idea that self-love is wrong. But if this were the case, it would be pointless to love our neighbors as ourselves. But Paul explains what he means by self-love. Even if you have low self-esteem, you probably don't willingly let yourself go hungry. You clothe yourself reasonably well. You make sure there's a roof over your head if you can. You try not to let yourself be cheated or injured. And you get angry if someone tries to ruin your marriage. This is the kind of love we need to have for our neighbors. Do we see that others are fed, clothed, and housed as well as they can be? Are we concerned about issues of social justice? Are our morals above reproach? Loving others as ourselves means to be actively working to see that their needs are met. Interestingly, people who focus on others rather than on themselves rarely suffer from low self-esteem.

13:11
1 Cor 7:29
1 Thess 5:6
Jas 5:8
1 Pet 4:7
Rev 1:3

13:12,13
Eph 5:11; 6:13
Phil 4:8
Col 3:5-10
1 Thess 5:8
Jas 3:14

[11]Another reason for right living is this: you know how late it is; time is running out. Wake up, for the coming of the Lord is nearer now than when we first believed. [12, 13]The night is far gone, the day of his return will soon be here. So quit the evil deeds of darkness and put on the armor of right living, as we who live in the daylight should! Be decent and true in everything you do so that all can approve your behavior. Don't spend your time in wild parties and getting drunk or in adultery and lust, or fighting, or jealousy. [14]But ask the Lord Jesus Christ to help you live as you should, and don't make plans to enjoy evil.

Weak and strong believers

14:1
1 Cor 9:22
14:2
1 Cor 10:25

14:3
Col 2:16

14 Give a warm welcome to any brother who wants to join you, even though his faith is weak. Don't criticize him for having different ideas from yours about what is right and wrong. [2]For instance, don't argue with him about whether or not to eat meat that has been offered to idols. You may believe there is no harm in this, but the faith of others is weaker; they think it is wrong, and will go without any meat at all and eat vegetables rather than eat that kind of meat. [3]Those who think it is all right to eat such meat must not look down on those who won't. And if you are one of those who won't, don't find fault with those who do. For God has

13:12, 13 *his return,* literally, "our salvation."   **14:1** *Don't criticize him . . . about what is right and wrong,* literally, "Receive him that is weak in faith, not for decisions of scruples." Perhaps the meaning is, "Receive those whose consciences hurt them when they do things others have no doubts about." Accepting them might cause discord in the church, but Paul says to welcome them anyway.

13:10 Christians must obey the law of love, which supersedes both religious and civil laws. How easy it is to excuse our indifference to others merely because we have no legal obligation to help them, even to justify harming them if our actions are technically legal! But Jesus does not leave loopholes in the law of love. Whenever love demands it, we are to go beyond human legal requirements and imitate the God of love. See James 2:8, 9; 4:11 and 1 Peter 2:16, 17 for more about this law of love.

13:12, 13 Some people are surprised that Paul lists jealousy and lust with the gross and obvious sins of drunkenness, adultery, and fighting. Like Jesus in his Sermon on the Mount (Matthew 5—7), Paul considers attitudes as important as actions. Just as hatred leads to murder, so jealousy leads to fighting and lust to adultery. When Christ returns, he wants to find his people clean on the inside as well as on the outside.

14:1 This verse assumes there will be differences of opinion in the church. These differences should not be feared or avoided, but accepted and handled with love. Don't expect everyone, even in the best church, to agree on every subject. Through sharing ideas we can come to a fuller understanding of what the Bible teaches. Accept, listen to, and respect others. Differences of opinion need not cause division. They can be a source of learning and richness in our relationships.

14:1ff What is weak faith? It is not faith mixed with works. In all his letters, Paul is violently opposed to any attempt to gain salvation through works of the law. Rather, Paul is speaking about immature faith, faith that has not yet developed the muscle it needs to stand against external pressures. For example, if a person who once worshiped idols became a Christian, he might understand perfectly well that Christ saved him through faith and that idols have no real power. Still, because of his past associations, he might be badly shaken if he knowingly ate meat that had been used in idol worship as part of a heathen ritual. If a person who once worshiped God on the required Jewish holy days became a Christian, he might well know that Christ saved him through faith, not through his keeping of the law. Still, when the feast days came, he might feel empty and unfaithful if he didn't dedicate them to God.

Paul responds to both weak brothers in love. Both are acting according to their consciences, but their honest scruples do not need to be made into rules for the church. Certainly some issues are central to the faith and worth fighting for—but many are based on individual differences and should not be legislated. Someone has said that a general principle in these matters is this: "In essentials, unity; in nonessentials, liberty; in everything, love."

14:1 Who is weak in faith and who is strong? We are all weak in some areas and strong in others. Our faith is strong in an area if we can survive contact with sin without falling into it. It is weak if we must avoid certain activities or places in order to protect our spiritual life. It is important to take a self-inventory in order to find out where we are weak and where we are strong. Whenever we feel called to go into the world in whatever capacity, we should ask, "Can I do that without sinning? Can I influence others for good, rather than being influenced by them for evil?" Our answer will show whether our faith is weak or strong in that area, at that time.

In areas of strength, we should not fear that we will be defiled by the world. Rather, from our position of strength we should lead the world. In areas of weakness, however, we need to play it safe. If we have a strong faith but shelter it, we are not doing Christ's work in the world. If we have a weak faith but expose it, we are being extremely foolish. Strength and weakness are not permanent conditions. Strength may diminish if it is not put to the test, and areas of weakness may develop by God's power into areas of strength.

14:2 How would Christians end up eating meat that had been offered to idols? The ancient system of sacrifice was at the center of the religious, social, and domestic life of the Roman world. After a sacrifice was presented to a god in a heathen temple, only part of it was burned. The remainder was often sent to the market to be sold. Thus a Christian might easily—even unknowingly—buy such meat in the marketplace or eat it at the home of a friend. Should a Christian question the source of his meat? Some thought there was nothing wrong with eating meat that had been offered to idols, since idols were not real gods. Others carefully checked the source of their meat, or else gave up meat altogether, in order to avoid a guilty conscience. The problem was especially acute for Christians who had once been idol worshipers. For them, such a strong reminder of their pagan days might weaken their newfound faith. Paul also deals with this problem in 1 Corinthians 8.

accepted them to be his children. 4They are God's servants, not yours. They are responsible to him, not to you. Let him tell them whether they are right or wrong. And God is able to make them do as they should.

5Some think that Christians should observe the Jewish holidays as special days to worship God, but others say it is wrong and foolish to go to all that trouble, for every day alike belongs to God. On questions of this kind everyone must decide for himself. 6If you have special days for worshiping the Lord, you are trying to honor him; you are doing a good thing. So is the person who eats meat that has been offered to idols; he is thankful to the Lord for it; he is doing right. And the person who won't touch such meat, he, too, is anxious to please the Lord, and is thankful. 7We are not our own bosses to live or die as we ourselves might choose. 8Living or dying we follow the Lord. Either way we are his. 9Christ died and rose again for this very purpose, so that he can be our Lord both while we live and when we die.

10You have no right to criticize your brother or look down on him. Remember, each of us will stand personally before the Judgment Seat of God. 11For it is written, "As I live," says the Lord, "every knee shall bow to me and every tongue confess to God." 12Yes, each of us will give an account of himself to God.

13So don't criticize each other any more. Try instead to live in such a way that you will never make your brother stumble by letting him see you doing something he thinks is wrong.

14As for myself, I am perfectly sure on the authority of the Lord Jesus that there is nothing really wrong with eating meat that has been offered to idols. But if someone believes it is wrong, then he shouldn't do it because for him it is wrong. 15And if your brother is bothered by what you eat, you are not acting in love if you go ahead and eat it. Don't let your eating ruin someone for whom Christ died. 16Don't do anything that will cause criticism against yourself even though you know that what you do is right.

17For, after all, the important thing for us as Christians is not what we eat or drink but stirring up goodness and peace and joy from the Holy Spirit. 18If you let Christ be Lord in these affairs, God will be glad; and so will others. 19In this way aim for harmony in the church and try to build each other up.

20Don't undo the work of God for a chunk of meat. Remember, there is nothing wrong with the meat, but it is wrong to eat it if it makes another stumble. 21The right thing to do is to quit eating meat or drinking wine or doing anything else that offends your brother or makes him sin. 22You may know that there is nothing wrong with what you do, even from God's point of view, but keep it to yourself; don't flaunt your faith in front of others who might be hurt by it. In this situation, happy is the man who does not sin by doing what he knows is right. 23But anyone

14:5
Rom 14:23
Gal 4:10

14:6
1 Cor 10:31
1 Tim 4:3

14:7
1 Cor 6:19
2 Cor 5:15
Gal 2:20

14:8
Phil 1:20
1 Thess 5:10

14:9
Phil 2:11
Rev 1:18

14:10
Mt 25:31,32
Rom 2:16
2 Cor 5:10

14:11
Isa 45:23

14:12
Mt 12:36

14:13
Mt 7:1
1 Cor 8:9

14:14
1 Cor 8:7

14:15
1 Cor 8:11

14:16
1 Cor 10:29,30
Tit 2:5

14:17
Rom 15:13
Gal 5:22

14:19
Ps 34:14

14:20
Acts 10:15
1 Cor 8:9

14:21
1 Cor 8:13

14:22
1 Jn 3:21

14:4 Each person is accountable to Christ, not to others. While the church must be uncompromising in its stand against activities expressly forbidden by Scripture (adultery, homosexuality, murder, theft), it should not create additional rules and regulations and give them equal standing with God's law. Many times Christians base their moral judgments on opinion, personal dislikes, or cultural bias rather than on the Word of God. When they do this, they show that their own faith is weak. They do not think God is powerful enough to guide his children.

14:10–15 Both "strong" and "weak" Christians can cause their brothers to stumble. The strong but insensitive Christian may flaunt his freedom and intentionally offend others' consciences. The scrupulous but weak Christian may fence in others with petty rules and regulations until they can't take it any longer. Paul wants his readers to be both strong in the faith and sensitive to others' needs. Since we are all strong in some areas and weak in others, we need constantly to monitor the effect of our behavior on others.

14:13ff Some Christians use an invisible weaker brother to support their own opinions, prejudices, or standards. "You must live by these standards," they say, "or you will be offending the weaker brother." In truth, you will often be offending no one but the speaker. While Paul urges us to be sensitive to those whose faith may be harmed by our actions, we should not sacrifice our liberty in Christ just to satisfy the selfish motives of those who are trying to force their opinion on us. Neither fear them nor criticize them, but follow Christ as closely as you are able.

14:14 At the Jerusalem council (Acts 15), the Jewish church in Jerusalem asked the Gentile church in Antioch not to eat meat offered to idols. Paul was at the Jerusalem council, and he accepted this request not because he felt this practice was wrong in itself, but because this practice would deeply offend many Jewish believers. Paul did not think the issue was worth dividing the church; his desire was to promote unity.

14:22 Sin is not just a private matter. Everything we do affects others, and we have to think of them constantly. God created us to be interdependent, not independent.

14:23 We try to steer clear of actions forbidden by Scripture, of course; but sometimes Scripture is silent. Then we should follow our conscience. When God shows us something is wrong for us, we should avoid it. But we should not look down on other Christians who exercise their freedom in those areas.

who believes that something he wants to do is wrong shouldn't do it. He sins if he does, for he thinks it is wrong, and so for him it *is* wrong. Anything that is done apart from what he feels is right is sin.

Live to please others

15 Even if we believe that it makes no difference to the Lord whether we do these things, still we cannot just go ahead and do them to please ourselves; for we must bear the "burden" of being considerate of the doubts and fears of others—of those who feel these things are wrong. Let's please the other fellow, not ourselves, and do what is for his good and thus build him up in the Lord. ³Christ didn't please himself. As the Psalmist said, "He came for the very purpose of suffering under the insults of those who were against the Lord." ⁴These things that were written in the Scriptures so long ago are to teach us patience and to encourage us, so that we will look forward expectantly to the time when God will conquer sin and death.

⁵May God who gives patience, steadiness, and encouragement help you to live in complete harmony with each other—each with the attitude of Christ toward the other. ⁶And then all of us can praise the Lord together with one voice, giving glory to God, the Father of our Lord Jesus Christ.

Fellowship among believers

⁷So, warmly welcome each other into the church, just as Christ has warmly welcomed you; then God will be glorified. ⁸Remember that Jesus Christ came to show that God is true to his promises and to help the Jews. ⁹And remember that he came also that the Gentiles might be saved and give glory to God for his mercies to them. That is what the Psalmist meant when he wrote: "I will praise you among the Gentiles, and sing to your name."

¹⁰And in another place, "Be glad, O you Gentiles, along with his people the Jews."

¹¹And yet again, "Praise the Lord, O you Gentiles, let everyone praise him."

¹²And the prophet Isaiah said, "There shall be an Heir in the house of Jesse, and he will be King over the Gentiles; they will pin their hopes on him alone."

¹³So I pray for you Gentiles that God who gives you hope will keep you happy and full of peace as you believe in him. I pray that God will help you overflow with hope in him through the Holy Spirit's power within you.

2. Personal notes

Paul explains his reason for writing

¹⁴I know that you are wise and good, my brothers, and that you know these things so well that you are able to teach others all about them. ¹⁵, ¹⁶But even so I have been bold enough to emphasize some of these points, knowing that all you need is this reminder from me; for I am, by God's grace, a special messenger from Jesus Christ to you Gentiles, bringing you the Gospel and offering you up as a fragrant sacrifice to God; for you have been made pure and pleasing to him by the Holy Spirit. ¹⁷So it is right for me to be a little proud of all Christ Jesus has done through me. ¹⁸I dare not judge how effectively he has used others, but I know this:

15:1,2
Rom 14:1
1 Cor 9:19,22
10:23,24
Gal 6:2
Phil 2:4,5

15:3
Ps 69:9

15:4
Rom 4:23
2 Tim 3:16

15:5
1 Cor 1:10
2 Cor 1:3,4
15:6
Rev 1:6

15:7
Rom 5:2
15:8
Mt 15:24
Jn 1:11
Acts 3:25,26
Rom 3:3,4
2 Cor 1:20
15:9
Ps 18:49
Jn 10:16
Rom 9:23
15:10
Deut 32:43
15:11
Ps 117:1
15:12
Isa 11:10
Rev 5:5; 22:16

15:14
2 Pet 1:12
1 Jn 2:21

15:15,16
Acts 9:15
Gal 1:15; 2:7-9
1 Tim 2:7

15:17
Phil 3:3

15:18
Rom 1:5

15:4 The knowledge of the Scriptures affects our attitude toward the present and the future. The more we know about what God has done in years past, the greater the confidence we have about what he will do in the days ahead. We should read our Bibles diligently to increase our trust that God's will is the best choice for us.

15:5, 6 To accept Jesus' lordship in all areas of life means to share his values and his perspective. Just as we take Jesus' view on the authority of Scripture, the nature of heaven, and the resurrection, we are to have his attitude of love toward other Christians as well. As we grow in faith and come to know Jesus better, we become more capable of maintaining this attitude throughout each day. Christ's attitude is explained in more detail in Philippians 2.

15:17 Paul was not proud of what he had done, but of what God had done through him. Being proud of God's work is not a sin—it is worship. If you are not sure whether your pride is selfish or holy, ask yourself this question: Are you just as proud of what God is doing through other people as of what he is doing through you?

he has used me to win the Gentiles to God. 19I have won them by my message and by the good way I have lived before them, and by the miracles done through me as signs from God—all by the Holy Spirit's power. In this way I have preached the full Gospel of Christ all the way from Jerusalem clear over into Illyricum.

20But all the while my ambition has been to go still farther, preaching where the name of Christ has never yet been heard, rather than where a church has already been started by someone else. 21I have been following the plan spoken of in the Scriptures where Isaiah says that those who have never heard the name of Christ before will see and understand. 22In fact that is the very reason I have been so long in coming to visit you.

Paul explains his travel plans

23But now at last I am through with my work here, and I am ready to come after all these long years of waiting. 24For I am planning to take a trip to Spain, and when I do, I will stop off there in Rome; and after we have had a good time together for a little while, you can send me on my way again.

25But before I come, I must go down to Jerusalem to take a gift to the Jewish Christians there. 26For you see, the Christians in Macedonia and Achaia have taken up an offering for those in Jerusalem who are going through such hard times. 27They were very glad to do this, for they feel that they owe a real debt to the Jerusalem Christians. Why? Because the news about Christ came to these Gentiles from the church in Jerusalem. And since they received this wonderful spiritual gift of the Gospel from there, they feel that the least they can do in return is to give some material aid. 28As soon as I have delivered this money and completed this good deed of theirs, I will come to see you on my way to Spain. 29And I am sure that when I come the Lord will give me a great blessing for you.

30Will you be my prayer partners? For the Lord Jesus Christ's sake, and because of your love for me—given to you by the Holy Spirit—pray much with me for my work. 31Pray that I will be protected in Jerusalem from those who are not Christians. Pray also that the Christians there will be willing to accept the money I am bringing them. 32Then I will be able to come to you with a happy heart by the will of God, and we can refresh each other.

33And now may our God, who gives peace, be with you all. Amen.

Paul greets his friends

16 Phoebe, a dear Christian woman from the town of Cenchreae, will be coming to see you soon. She has worked hard in the church there. Receive her as your sister in the Lord, giving her a warm Christian welcome. Help her in every way you can, for she has helped many in their needs, including me.

15:19 *I have preached the full Gospel,* or, "I have fully accomplished my gospel ministry." **15:27** *the least they can do in return is to give some material aid,* literally, "For if the Gentiles have come to share in their spiritual blessings, they ought also to be of service to them in material blessings."

15:19
Acts 19:11
1 Cor 2:4
1 Thess 1:5

15:20
Rom 1:15
1 Cor 3:10
2 Cor 10:13,15

15:21
Isa 52:14,15

15:22
Rom 1:13
1 Thess 2:18

15:23
Acts 19:21
Rom 1:10

15:24
Acts 15:3
Rom 1:12

15:25
Acts 19:21; 24:17

15:26
1 Cor 16:1,5
2 Cor 8:1; 9:2

15:27
1 Cor 9:11

15:29
Acts 19:21
Rom 1:10,11

15:30
2 Cor 1:11
Col 1:8; 4:12

15:31
2 Cor 8:4
2 Thess 3:2

15:32
2 Cor 7:13
2 Tim 1:16
Philem 7

15:33
Rom 16:20
Heb 13:20

16:1
Acts 18:18

16:2
Phil 2:29
3 Jn 5,6

15:19 Illyricum was a Roman territory on the Adriatic Sea between present-day Italy and Greece. It covers much the same territory as present-day Yugoslavia. See map in Romans 1 for its location.

15:22 Paul wanted to visit the church at Rome, but he had delayed his visit because he had heard many good reports about the believers there and he knew they were doing well on their own. It was more important for him to preach in areas that had not yet heard the Good News.

15:23, 24 Paul was referring to his work in Corinth, the city from which he most likely wrote this letter. Most of Paul's three-month stay in Achaia (see Acts 20:3) was probably spent in Corinth. He believed he had done what God wanted him to do there—he was now looking forward to taking the gospel to new lands west of Rome. When Paul eventually went to Rome, however, it was as a prisoner under house arrest (see Acts 28). Tradition holds that Paul

was released for a time, and that he used this opportunity to go to Spain to preach the Good News. This journey is not mentioned in the book of Acts.

15:31 Because of several prophecies he had received en route, Paul knew trouble awaited him in Jerusalem. See Acts 21:4, 10–14 for the story.

15:33 This phrase sounds like the end of the book, and it does signal the end of Paul's teaching. He concludes his letter, then, with personal greetings and remarks.

16:1 Phoebe was known as a servant (the Greek word used here is often translated "deacon") and a helper. She apparently was wealthy and helped support Paul's ministry financially. She was highly regarded in the church, and she may have delivered this letter from Corinth to Rome. This provides evidence that women

³Tell Priscilla and Aquila "hello." They have been my fellow workers in the affairs of Christ Jesus. ⁴In fact, they risked their lives for me; and I am not the only one who is thankful to them: so are all the Gentile churches.

16:5
1 Cor 16:15,19
Col 4:15
Philem 1,2

⁵Please give my greetings to all those who meet to worship in their home. Greet my good friend Epaenetus. He was the very first person to become a Christian in Asia. ⁶Remember me to Mary, too, who has worked so hard to help us. ⁷Then there are Andronicus and Junias, my relatives who were in prison with me. They are respected by the apostles, and became Christians before I did. Please give them my greetings. ⁸Say "hello" to Ampliatus, whom I love as one of God's own children, ⁹and Urbanus, our fellow worker, and beloved Stachys.

16:7
Rom 16:11,21
2 Cor 11:23
Col 4:10
Philem 23

16:10
1 Cor 1:11

16:11
Rom 16:7,21

¹⁰Then there is Apelles, a good man whom the Lord approves; greet him for me. And give my best regards to those working at the house of Aristobulus. ¹¹Remember me to Herodion my relative. Remember me to the Christian slaves over at Narcissus House. ¹²Say "hello" to Tryphaena and Tryphosa, the Lord's workers, and to dear Persis, who has worked so hard for the Lord. ¹³Greet Rufus for me, whom the Lord picked out to be his very own; and also his dear mother who has been such a mother to me. ¹⁴And please give my greetings to Asyncritus, Phlegon, Hermes, Patrobas, Hermas, and the other brothers who are with them. ¹⁵Give my love to Philologus, Julia, Nereus and his sister, and to Olympas, and all the Christians who are with them. ¹⁶Shake hands warmly with each other. All the churches here send you their greetings.

16:13
Mk 15:21
Eph 1:4
2 Jn 1

16:16
1 Thess 5:26
1 Pet 5:14

Paul gives final instructions

16:17
Acts 15:1-29
1 Cor 5:9
2 Thess 3:6
1 Tim 6:3
2 Tim 3:5,6
Tit 3:10
2 Jn 10

¹⁷And now there is one more thing to say before I end this letter. Stay away from those who cause divisions and are upsetting people's faith, teaching things about Christ that are contrary to what you have been taught. ¹⁸Such teachers are not working for our Lord Jesus, but only want gain for themselves. They are good speakers, and simple-minded people are often fooled by them. ¹⁹But everyone knows that you stand loyal and true. This makes me very happy. I want you always to remain very clear about what is right, and to stay innocent of any wrong. ²⁰The God of peace will soon crush Satan under your feet. The blessings from our Lord Jesus Christ be upon you.

16:18
Phil 3:19
Col 2:4
2 Pet 2:3

16:19
Mt 10:16

16:20
Gen 3:15

16:21
Acts 13:1; 16:1
17:5
1 Tim 1:2

²¹Timothy my fellow-worker, and Lucius and Jason and Sosipater, my relatives, send you their good wishes. ²²I, Tertius, the one who is writing this letter for Paul, send my greetings too, as a Christian brother. ²³Gaius says to say "hello" to you for him. I am his guest, and the church meets here in his home. Erastus, the city treasurer, sends you his greetings and so does Quartus, a Christian brother. ²⁴Goodbye. May the grace of our Lord Jesus Christ be with you all.

---

had important roles in the early church. Cenchreae, the town where Phoebe lived, was the eastern port of Corinth, six miles from the city center.

16:3 Priscilla and Aquila were a married couple who became Paul's close friends. They, along with all other Jews, had been expelled from Rome by the emperor (Acts 18:2, 3), and they had moved to Corinth. There they met Paul and invited him to live with them. They were Christians before they met Paul, and probably told him much about the Roman church. Like Paul, Priscilla and Aquila were missionaries. They helped believers in Ephesus (Acts 18:18–28), in Rome when they were allowed to return, and again at Ephesus (2 Timothy 4:19).

16:5ff Paul's personal greetings went to Romans and Greeks, Jews and Gentiles, men and women, prisoners and prominent citizens. The church's base was broad: it crossed cultural, social, and economic lines. From this list we learn that the Christian community was mobile. Though Paul had not yet been to Rome, he had met these people in other places on his journeys.

16:7 Some translations say that Andronicus and Junias were "of note among the apostles"—very likely they had distinguished themselves as missionaries. Scholars are not sure whether the second name should be Junias (masculine) or Junia (feminine). If Junia is correct, some suggest she was Andronicus' wife.

16:17–20 When we read books or listen to sermons, we should check the content of what is written or said and not be fooled by smooth style. Christians who study God's Word do not need to be fooled, even if superficial listeners are easily taken in. For an example of believers who carefully checked God's Word, see Acts 17:10–12.

16:21 Timothy was a key person in the growth of the early church, traveling with Paul on his second missionary journey (Acts 16:1–3). Later Paul wrote two letters to him as he worked to strengthen the churches in Ephesus—1 and 2 Timothy. See his Profile in the book of 1 Timothy.

25, 26, 27I commit you to God, who is able to make you strong and steady in the Lord, just as the Gospel says, and just as I have told you. This is God's plan of salvation for you Gentiles, kept secret from the beginning of time. But now as the prophets foretold and as God commands, this message is being preached everywhere, so that people all around the world will have faith in Christ and obey him. To God, who alone is wise, be the glory forever through Jesus Christ our Lord. Amen.

16:25
1 Cor 2:1,7; 4:1
Eph 3:3-5
1 Col 1:27; 2:2
2 Tim 1:10
1 Pet 1:20

16:26
Rom 1:2,5

16:27
Rom 11:36

Sincerely, Paul

16:25–27 Paul exclaims that it is wonderful to be alive when God's secret—his way of saving the Gentiles—is becoming known throughout the world! All the Old Testament prophecies were coming true, and God was using Paul as his instrument to tell this Good News.

16:25–27 As Jerusalem was the center of Jewish life, Rome was the world's political, religious, social, and economic center. There the major governmental decisions were made, and from there the gospel spread to the ends of the earth. The church in Rome was a cosmopolitan mixture of Jews, Gentiles, slaves, free people, men, women, Roman citizens, and world travelers; therefore, it had potential for both great influence and great conflict.

Paul had not yet been to Rome to meet all the Christians there, and, of course, he has not yet met us. We too live in a cosmopolitan setting with the entire world open to us. We also have the potential for both widespread influence and wrenching conflict. We should listen carefully to Paul's teaching about unity, service, and love.

1 CORINTHIANS

ON A BED of grass, a chameleon's skin turns green. On the earth, it becomes brown. The animal changes to match the environment. Many creatures blend into nature with God-given camouflage suits to aid their survival. It's natural to fit in and adapt to the environment. But followers of Christ are *new creations*, born from above and changed from within, with values and life-styles which confront the world and clash with accepted morals. True believers don't blend in very well.

The Christians in Corinth were struggling with their environment. Surrounded by corruption and every conceivable sin, they felt the pressure to adapt to their environment. They knew they were free in Christ, but what did this freedom mean? How should they view idols or sexuality? What should they do about marriage, women in the church, and the gifts of the Spirit? These were more than theoretical questions—the church was being undermined by immorality and spiritual immaturity. Their faith was being tried in the crucible of immoral Corinth, and some of them were failing the test.

Paul heard of their struggles and wrote this letter to address their problems, heal their divisions, and answer their questions. Paul confronted them with their sin and their need for corrective action and clear commitment to Christ.

After a brief introduction (1:1–9), Paul immediately turns to the question of unity (1:10—4:21). He emphasizes the clear and simple gospel message around which all believers should rally; he explains the role of church leaders; and he urges them to grow up in their faith.

Paul then deals with the immorality of certain church members and lawsuits among Christians (5:1—6:8). He tells them to exercise church discipline and to settle their internal matters themselves. Because so many of the problems in the Corinthian church involved sex, Paul denounces sexual sin in the strongest possible terms (6:9–20).

Next Paul answers some questions which the Corinthians had. Because prostitution and immorality were pervasive, marriages in Corinth were in shambles, and Christians weren't sure how to react. Paul gives pointed and practical answers (7:1–40). Concerning the question of meat sacrificed to idols, Paul suggests that we show complete commitment to Christ and sensitivity to other believers, especially weaker brothers and sisters (8:1—11:2).

Paul goes on to talk about worship, and he carefully explains the role of women, the Lord's supper, and spiritual gifts (11:3—14:39). Sandwiched in the middle of this section is his magnificent description of the greatest gift—love (chapter 13). Then Paul concludes with a discussion of the resurrection (15:1–58), some final thoughts, greetings, and a benediction (16:1–24).

In this letter Paul confronts the Corinthians about their sins and shortcomings. And 1 Corinthians calls all Christians to be careful not to blend in with the world, accepting its values and life-styles. We must live Christ-centered, blameless, loving lives that make a difference for God. As you read 1 Corinthians, examine your values in light of complete commitment to Christ.

VITAL STATISTICS

PURPOSE:
To identify problems in the Corinthian church, to offer solutions, and to teach the believers how to live for Christ in a corrupt society

AUTHOR:
Paul

TO WHOM WRITTEN:
The church in Corinth

DATE WRITTEN:
About A.D. 55 near the end of Paul's three-year ministry in Ephesus during his third missionary journey

SETTING:
Corinth was a major cosmopolitan city, a seaport and major trade center—the most important city in Achaia. It was also filled with idolatry and immorality. The church was largely made up of Gentiles. Paul had established this church on his second missionary journey.

KEY VERSE:
"But, dear brothers, I beg you in the name of the Lord Jesus Christ to stop arguing among yourselves. Let there be real harmony so there won't be splits in the church. I plead with you to be of one mind, united in thought and purpose" (1:10).

KEY PEOPLE:
Paul, Timothy, members of Chloe's household

KEY PLACES:
Worship meetings in Corinth

SPECIAL FEATURES:
This is a strong, straightforward letter.

THE BLUEPRINT

A. PAUL ADDRESSES CHURCH
PROBLEMS (1:1—6:20)
  1. Divisions in the church
  2. Disorders in the church

Without Paul's presence, the Corinthian church had fallen into divisiveness and disorder. This resulted in many problems which Paul addressed squarely. We must be concerned for unity and order in our local churches, but we should not mistake inactivity for order and cordiality for unity. We too must squarely address problems in our churches.

B. PAUL ANSWERS CHURCH
QUESTIONS (7:1—16:24)
  1. Instruction on Christian marriage
  2. Instruction on Christian freedom
  3. Instruction on public worship
  4. Instruction on the resurrection

The Corinthians had sent Paul a list of questions, and he answered them in a way to correct abuses in the church and to show how important it is that they live what they believe. Paul gives us a Christian approach to problem-solving. He analyzed the problem thoroughly to uncover the underlying issue, and then highlighted the biblical values that should guide our actions.

MEGATHEMES

THEME	EXPLANATION	IMPORTANCE
Loyalties	The Corinthians were rallying around various church leaders and teachers—Peter, Paul, and Apollos. These loyalties led to intellectual pride and created a spirit of division in the church.	Our loyalty to human leaders or human wisdom must never divide Christians into camps. We must care for our fellow believers, not strive with them. Your allegiance must be to Christ. Let him lead you.
Immorality	Paul received a report of uncorrected sexual sin in the church at Corinth. The people had grown indifferent to immorality. Others had misconceptions about marriage. We are to live morally because our bodies are to be ready to serve God.	Christians must never compromise with sinful ideas and practices. We should not blend in with people around us. You must live up to God's standard of morality and not condone immoral behavior.
Freedom	Paul taught freedom of choice on practices not expressly forbidden in Scripture. Some believers felt certain actions—like buying meat from animals used in pagan rituals—were corrupt by association. Others felt free from the law to do such actions without sin.	We are free in Christ, yet we must not abuse our Christian freedom by being inconsiderate and insensitive to others. We must never encourage others to do wrong by anything we do. Let love guide your behavior.
Worship	Paul addressed disorder in worship. People were taking the Lord's Supper without first confessing sin. There was misuse of spiritual gifts and confusion over women's role in the church.	Worship must be carried out properly and in an orderly manner. Everything we do to worship God should be done in a manner worthy of his high honor. Make sure that worship is harmonious, useful, and builds up all believers.
Resurrection	Some people denied that Christ rose from the dead. Others felt that people would not physically be resurrected. Christ's resurrection assures us that we will have new, living bodies after we die. The hope of the resurrection forms the secret of Christian confidence.	Since we will be raised again to life after we die, our life is not in vain. We must stay faithful to God in our morality and our service. We are to live today knowing we will spend eternity with Christ.

A. PAUL ADDRESSES CHURCH PROBLEMS (1:1—6:20)

Through various sources, Paul had received reports of problems in the Corinthian church, including jealousy, divisiveness, sexual immorality, and failure to discipline members. Churches today must also address the problems they face. We can learn a great deal by observing how Paul handled these delicate situations.

1:1
Acts 18:17
Rom 1:1

1:2
Rom 8:28
Rom 10:12,13
2 Tim 2:22

1 *From:* Paul, chosen by God to be Jesus Christ's missionary, and from brother Sosthenes.

²*To:* The Christians in Corinth, invited by God to be his people and made acceptable to him by Christ Jesus. *And to:* All Christians everywhere—whoever calls upon the name of Jesus Christ, our Lord and theirs.

1:2 *made acceptable to him by Christ Jesus,* or "chosen by Christ Jesus," literally, "sanctified in Christ Jesus."

CORINTH AND EPHESUS
Paul wrote this letter to Corinth during his three-year visit in Ephesus during his third missionary journey. The two cities sat across from each other on the Aegean Sea—both were busy and important ports. Titus may have carried this letter from Ephesus to Corinth (2 Corinthians 12:18).

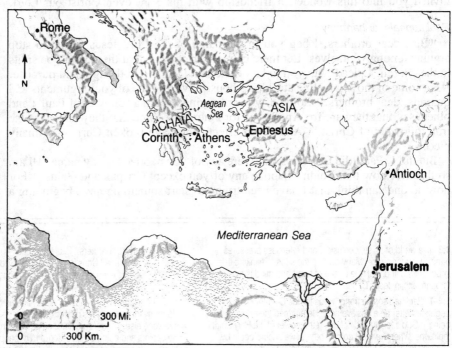

1:1 Paul, visiting Ephesus, was in the middle of his third missionary journey (Acts 19:1—20:1) when he wrote this letter to the church in Corinth. Corinth and Ephesus faced each other across the Aegean Sea. Paul knew the Corinthian church well because he had spent 18 months in Corinth during his second missionary journey (Acts 18:1–18). While in Ephesus, he heard about problems in Corinth (1:11). About the same time, a delegation from the Corinthian church visited Paul to ask his advice about their divisions (16:17). Paul wrote this letter to help correct those problems as well as to answer questions church members had asked in a previous letter (7:1).

1:1 Paul was specially selected by God to preach about Jesus Christ. Each Christian has a job to do. One may seem more spectacular than another, but all are necessary to carry out God's greater plans for the world (12:12–27). Be useful to God by using your gifts in his service. As you discover what he wants, be ready to serve.

1:1 Sosthenes may have been Paul's secretary who wrote this letter as Paul dictated it. He was probably the Jewish synagogue leader in Corinth (Acts 18:17) who was beaten during an attack on Paul. If so, he later became a believer. Sosthenes was well known to the members of the Corinthian church; therefore, Paul included his familiar name in the opening of his letter.

1:2 Corinth was a giant cultural melting pot with great diversion of wealth, religions, intellect, and moral standards. It had a reputation for being fiercely independent and as decadent as any city in the world. The Romans destroyed Corinth in 146 B.C. after a rebellion, but in 46 B.C. the Roman emperor Julius Caesar rebuilt it because of its strategic seaport. By Paul's day (A.D. 50), the Romans had made Corinth the capital of Achaia (present-day Greece). It was a large city, offering Rome great profits through trade as well as the military protection of its ports. But the city's prosperity made it ripe for all sorts of corruption. Idolatry flourished, and there were more than a dozen pagan temples employing at least a thousand prostitutes. Prostitutes in other cities were called "Corinthian girls."

1:2 By including a salutation to "all Christians everywhere," Paul made it clear that this was not a private letter. Although it dealt with specific issues facing the church at Corinth, all believers could learn from it. The Corinthian church must have included a great cross-section of believers—wealthy merchants, common laborers, former temple prostitutes, middle-class families. Because there was such a wide diversity of people and backgrounds, Paul took great pains to stress unity in his letter.

1:2 A personal invitation makes a person feel wanted and welcome. Through his Word, God has personally invited us to become citizens of his eternal Kingdom. But Jesus Christ, God's Son, is the only one who can bring us into this glorious Kingdom, because he removes our sins. Accepting God's invitation means accepting his Son, Jesus Christ, and trusting in the work he did on the cross to forgive our sins.

³May God our Father and the Lord Jesus Christ give you all of his blessings, and great peace of heart and mind.

1:3
Rom 1:7

1. Divisions in the church
Paul thanks God

⁴I can never stop thanking God for all the wonderful gifts he has given you, now that you are Christ's: ⁵he has enriched your whole life. He has helped you speak out for him and has given you a full understanding of the truth; ⁶what I told you Christ could do for you has happened! ⁷Now you have every grace and blessing; every spiritual gift and power for doing his will are yours during this time of waiting for the return of our Lord Jesus Christ. ⁸And he guarantees right up to the end that you will be counted free from all sin and guilt on that day when he returns. ⁹God will surely do this for you, for he always does just what he says, and he is the one who invited you into this wonderful friendship with his Son, even Christ our Lord.

1:4,5
Rom 15:14
2 Cor 8:7; 9:11

1:7
Rom 8:19,23
Phil 3:20
2 Pet 3:12

1:8
Phil 1:6
1 Thess 5:23
2 Thess 3:3

1:9
1 Jn 1:3

Paul appeals for harmony

¹⁰But, dear brothers, I beg you in the name of the Lord Jesus Christ to stop arguing among yourselves. Let there be real harmony so that there won't be splits in the church. I plead with you to be of one mind, united in thought and purpose. ¹¹For some of those who live at Chloe's house have told me of your arguments and quarrels, dear brothers. ¹²Some of you are saying, "I am a follower of Paul"; and others say that they are for Apollos or for Peter; and some that they alone are the true followers of Christ. ¹³And so, in effect, you have broken Christ into many pieces.

But did I, Paul, die for your sins? Were any of you baptized in my name? ¹⁴I am so thankful now that I didn't baptize any of you except Crispus and Gaius. ¹⁵For now no one can think that I have been trying to start something new, beginning a

1:10
Rom 12:16
1 Cor 11:18
Phil 1:27

1:12
Jn 1:42
Acts 18:24
1 Cor 3:4

1:13
Acts 2:38
Eph 4:5

1:14
Acts 18:8
Rom 16:23

1:3 In a world of noise, confusion, and relentless pressures, people long for peace. Many give up the search, thinking it impossible to find, but true peace of heart and mind is available through faith in Jesus Christ.

1:4–7 Paul had some strong words for the Corinthians, but he began his letter on a positive note. He affirmed their privilege of being in God's family and of having the power of the Holy Spirit in their lives. When we must correct others, we should begin by affirming what God has already accomplished in them.

1:7 The Corinthian church members had all the spiritual gifts they needed to live the Christian life, to witness for Christ, and to stand against the paganism and immorality of Corinth. But instead of using what God had given them, they were arguing over which gifts were more important. Paul addresses this issue in depth in chapters 12—14.

1:7–9 The Corinthian believers were guaranteed that they would be counted free from sin when Christ returned (see Ephesians 1:7–10). This was not because of their great gifts (1:4) or performance, but because of what Jesus Christ accomplished through his death and resurrection (see Colossians 2:15). A guarantee is a promise. God says he will count *all* who obey his Word free from sin when Jesus Christ returns (1 Thessalonians 3:13; Hebrews 9:28); and God does what he says (1 Thessalonians 5:24). If you have faith in Christ, you *are* and *will be* saved.

1:10 Paul founded the church in Corinth on his second missionary journey. After he left, 18 months later, the church began to slip toward the immoral lifestyle prevalent in the city. Paul wrote this letter to recommend that immediate corrective action be taken to clear up their confusion about right and wrong and to remove the immorality among them. Corinthians had a reputation for jumping from fad to fad; Paul wanted to keep Christianity from degenerating into another fad.

1:10 By saying "brothers," Paul was speaking to all believers, male and female. All Christians are part of God's family and share a unity that runs even deeper than that of blood brothers and sisters.

1:10, 11 Harmony is beautiful—in families, in friendships, at work. Harmony, however, does not require everyone to believe just like everyone else. There is a difference between having opposing viewpoints and being divisive. A group of people will not completely agree on every issue, but they can work together harmoniously if they agree on what truly matters—Jesus Christ as Lord of all. In your church, talk and behave in a way that will reduce arguments and increase harmony. Petty differences should never divide Christians.

1:12ff In this large and diverse Corinthian church, the believers favored different preachers. Because there was as yet no written New Testament, the believers depended heavily on preaching and teaching for spiritual insight into the meaning of the Old Testament. Some followed Paul, who had founded their church; some who had heard Peter in Jerusalem followed him; while others listened only to Apollos, an eloquent and popular preacher who had had a dynamic ministry in Corinth (Acts 18:24; 19:1). Although these three preachers were united in their message, their personalities attracted different people. Now the church was in danger of dividing. By mentioning Jesus Christ ten times in the first ten verses, Paul makes it clear what all preachers and teachers should emphasize. The message is more important than the messenger.

1:12, 13 The Corinthians' arguing had "broken Christ into many pieces," a graphic picture of what happens when the church (the body of Christ) is divided. With the many opportunities for worship available today, we could get caught up in the same game of "my preacher is better than yours!" But this would divide Christ once more. Make sure your teachers are helping you learn more about Christ, and not merely trying to bring recognition and glory to themselves.

1:16
1 Cor 16:15

1:17
Acts 26:17
2 Cor 10:10
11:16

"Church of Paul." 16Oh, yes, and I baptized the family of Stephanas. I don't remember ever baptizing anyone else. 17For Christ didn't send me to baptize, but to preach the Gospel; and even my preaching sounds poor, for I do not fill my sermons with profound words and high sounding ideas, for fear of diluting the mighty power there is in the simple message of the cross of Christ.

Christ brings us life from God

1:18
Acts 17:18
Rom 1:16
1 Cor 2:14
2 Cor 2:15,16

1:19
Isa 29:14

1:20
Job 12:17
Isa 44:25
1 Cor 2:6

1:21
Lk 10:21

1:22
Mt 12:38
Lk 11:16

1:23
Isa 8:14,15
Mt 11:6

1:24
Rom 1:4

1:25
2 Cor 4:7; 13:4

1:26
Mt 11:25
Jn 7:48
1 Cor 2:8

1:27
Ps 8:2

1:28
Job 34:19
Rom 4:17
1 Cor 2:6

18I know very well how foolish it sounds to those who are lost, when they hear that Jesus died to save them. But we who are saved recognize this message as the very power of God. 19For God says, "I will destroy all human plans of salvation no matter how wise they seem to be, and ignore the best ideas of men, even the most brilliant of them."

20So what about these wise men, these scholars, these brilliant debaters of this world's great affairs? God has made them all look foolish, and shown their wisdom to be useless nonsense. 21For God in his wisdom saw to it that the world would never find God through human brilliance, and then he stepped in and saved all those who believed his message, which the world calls foolish and silly. 22It seems foolish to the Jews because they want a sign from heaven as proof that what is preached is true; and it is foolish to the Gentiles because they believe only what agrees with their philosophy and seems wise to them. 23So when we preach about Christ dying to save them, the Jews are offended and the Gentiles say it's all nonsense. 24But God has opened the eyes of those called to salvation, both Jews and Gentiles, to see that Christ is the mighty power of God to save them; Christ himself is the center of God's wise plan for their salvation. 25This so-called "foolish" plan of God is far wiser than the wisest plan of the wisest man, and God in his weakness—Christ dying on the cross—is far stronger than any man.

26Notice among yourselves, dear brothers, that few of you who follow Christ have big names or power or wealth. 27Instead, God has deliberately chosen to use ideas the world considers foolish and of little worth in order to shame those people considered by the world as wise and great. 28He has chosen a plan despised by the world, counted as nothing at all, and used it to bring down to nothing those the

1:18 *are lost,* or "are being lost." *are saved,* or "are being saved."

1:17 When Paul said Christ didn't send him to baptize, he wasn't putting down baptism. Baptism was commanded by Jesus himself (Matthew 28:19) and practiced by the early church (Acts 2:41). Paul was emphasizing that he couldn't do everything; he needed others to use their gifts to help him. Paul's gift was preaching, and that's what he did.

This is a model for us. Christian ministry should be a team effort; no preacher or teacher is a complete link between God and people, and no individual should think he can do everything the apostles did. We must be content with the job God has given us.

1:17 Some speakers are big on words but small on content. Paul wanted to make sure he was big on content and practical help for his listeners. He wanted them to be impressed with his *message,* not just his style (see 2:1–5). You don't need to be a great speaker with a large vocabulary to share the gospel effectively. The persuasive power is in the story, not the storyteller. Paul was not speaking against those who carefully prepare what they say (see 2:6), but against those who try to impress others only with their knowledge or speaking ability.

1:18–25 The message of Christ's death for sins sounds foolish to those who don't believe. Death seems to be the end of the road, the ultimate weakness. But Jesus did not stay dead. His resurrection shows his power even over death, and he will save us from eternal death and give us everlasting life if we trust him as Savior and Lord. This sounds so simple that many people won't accept it. They try other ways to obtain eternal life (being good, being wise, etc.). But their attempts will not work. The "foolish" people who simply accept Christ's offer are actually the wisest of all, because they alone will live eternally with God.

1:19 In this verse Paul summarizes Isaiah 29:14 to emphasize a point Jesus often made during his ministry on earth: God's way is not like the world's way, but God offers eternal life while the world cannot.

1:22 Many Jews thought the Good News of Jesus Christ was foolish because they had been taught the Messiah would be a conquering king, not a suffering servant. Jesus had not restored David's throne as they expected. Besides, he was executed as a common criminal, and how could a common criminal be a savior? Greeks, too, considered the gospel foolish: they did not believe in a bodily resurrection; they did not see in Jesus the powerful characteristics of their mythological gods; and they thought no reputable person would be crucified. Death was defeat, not victory.

The Good News of Jesus Christ still sounds foolish to many. Our society worships power, influence, and wealth. Jesus came as a humble, poor servant, and he offers his Kingdom to those with faith, not works. This looks backward to the world, but it is the way God has chosen to save it.

1:28–31 Paul continues to emphasize that the way to receive salvation is so ordinary and simple that *any* person who wants to can understand it. Skill does not get you into God's Kingdom—simple faith does. God planned it this way so no one could boast that his achievements helped him secure eternal life. Salvation is totally from God through Jesus' death, which allowed us to become perfect in God's eyes. There is *nothing* we can do to become acceptable to God; we need only accept what Jesus has already done for us. He has done the work; we acknowledge that work; we acknowledge his position as God.

world considers great, 29so that no one anywhere can ever brag in the presence of God.

1:29
Eph 2:8-10

30For it is from God alone that you have your life through Christ Jesus. He showed us God's plan of salvation; he was the one who made us acceptable to God; he made us pure and holy and gave himself to purchase our salvation. 31As it says in the Scriptures, "If anyone is going to boast, let him boast only of what the Lord has done."

1:30
Rom 3:24; 8:1,2
2 Cor 5:21
Eph 1:7

1:31
Jer 9:23,24
2 Cor 10:17

The Spirit gives wisdom

2 Dear brothers, even when I first came to you I didn't use lofty words and brilliant ideas to tell you God's message. 2For I decided that I would speak only of Jesus Christ and his death on the cross. 3I came to you in weakness—timid and trembling. 4And my preaching was very plain, not with a lot of oratory and human wisdom, but the Holy Spirit's power was in my words, proving to those who heard them that the message was from God. 5I did this because I wanted your faith to stand firmly upon God, not on man's great ideas.

2:1
1 Cor 1:17
2:2
Gal 6:14
Phil 3:8
2:3
2 Cor 10:1
Gal 4:13
2:4
1 Cor 4:20
2:5
2 Cor 4:7; 6:7

6Yet when I am among mature Christians I do speak with words of great wisdom, but not the kind that comes from here on earth, and not the kind that appeals to the great men of this world, who are doomed to fall. 7Our words are wise because they are from God, telling of God's wise plan to bring us into the glories of heaven. This plan was hidden in former times, though it was made for our benefit before the world began. 8But the great men of the world have not understood it; if they had, they never would have crucified the Lord of Glory.

2:6
Eph 4:13
Heb 5:14
2:7
Rom 8:29; 16:25
Eph 3:3-5
2:8
Acts 13:27

9That is what is meant by the Scriptures which say that no mere man has ever seen, heard or even imagined what wonderful things God has ready for those who

2:9
Isa 64:4; 65:17

1:30 *he made us pure and holy,* or, "he brought us near to God." *to purchase our salvation,* or, "to free us from slavery to sin."

The Meaning of the Cross 1:18—2:16	Be considerate of one another because of what Christ has done for us. There is no place for pride or a know-it-all attitude. We are to have the mind of Christ.	**HIGHLIGHTS OF 1 CORINTHIANS**
The Story of the Last Supper 11:23–29	The Last Supper is a time of reflection on Christ's final words to his disciples before he died on the cross; we must celebrate this in an orderly and correct manner.	
The Poem of Love 13:1–13	Love is to guide all we do. We have different gifts, abilities, likes, dislikes—but we are called, without exception, to love.	
The Christian's Destiny 15:42–58	We are promised by Christ who died for us that, as he came back to life after death, so our perishable bodies will be exchanged for heavenly bodies. Then we will live and reign with Christ.	

2:1 Paul is referring to his first visit to Corinth (A.D. 51), when he founded the church during his second missionary journey (Acts 18:1ff).

2:1–5 A brilliant scholar, Paul could have overwhelmed his listeners with intellectual arguments and persuasive oratory. Instead he shared the simple message of Jesus Christ by allowing the Holy Spirit to guide his words. In sharing the gospel with others, we should follow Paul's example and keep our message simple and basic. The Holy Spirit will give power to our words and use them to bring glory to Jesus.

2:4 Paul's confidence was not in his keen intellect or speaking ability, but in his knowledge that the Holy Spirit was helping and guiding him. Paul is not writing off the importance of study and preparation for preaching—he had a thorough education in the Scriptures. Effective preaching must combine studious preparation with the work of the Holy Spirit.

2:7 God's "wise plan" was his offer of salvation to all people. Originally unknown to mankind, this plan became crystal clear

when Jesus rose from the dead. His resurrection proved that he had power over sin and death and could now offer us this power as well (see 1 Peter 1:10, 11 and the note on Romans 16:25–27 for more about God's plan). God's plan, however, is still hidden to unbelievers because they either refuse to accept it, choose to ignore it, or simply haven't heard about it.

2:8 Jesus was misunderstood and rejected by those whom the world considered wise and great. He was put to death by the leaders in Palestine—the High Priest, King Herod, Pilate, and the Pharisees and Sadducees. Jesus' rejection by these leaders was predicted in Isaiah 53:3 and Zechariah 12:10, 11.

2:9 We cannot imagine all that God has in store for us both in this life and for eternity. He will create a new heaven and a new earth (Isaiah 65:17; Revelation 21:1), and we will live with him forever. Until then, his Holy Spirit comforts and guides us. Knowing the future that awaits us should give us hope and courage to press on in this life, to endure hardship, and to avoid giving in to temptation. This world is not all there is.

2:10
Mt 11:25; 16:17
Jn 14:26;
15:26; 16:13-15
1 Jn 2:27

2:11
Prov 20:27
Jer 17:9
Rom 11:33

2:12
Rom 8:15
1 Cor 1:27

2:13
Mt 16:23
Rom 8:5
2 Pet 1:20,21

2:14
Jn 14:17
Jude 19

2:15
Prov 28:5

2:16
Ps 25:14
Jn 15:15
Rom 11:34

love the Lord. ¹⁰But we know about these things because God has sent his Spirit to tell us, and his Spirit searches out and shows us all of God's deepest secrets. ¹¹No one can really know what anyone else is thinking, or what he is really like, except that person himself. And no one can know God's thoughts except God's own Spirit. ¹²And God has actually given us his Spirit (not the world's spirit) to tell us about the wonderful free gifts of grace and blessing that God has given us. ¹³In telling you about these gifts we have even used the very words given to us by the Holy Spirit, not words that we as men might choose. So we use the Holy Spirit's words to explain the Holy Spirit's facts. ¹⁴But the man who isn't a Christian can't understand and can't accept these thoughts from God, which the Holy Spirit teaches us. They sound foolish to him, because only those who have the Holy Spirit within them can understand what the Holy Spirit means. Others just can't take it in. ¹⁵But the spiritual man has insight into everything, and that bothers and baffles the man of the world, who can't understand him at all. ¹⁶How could he? For certainly he has never been one to know the Lord's thoughts, or to discuss them with him, or to move the hands of God by prayer. But, strange as it seems, we Christians actually do have within us a portion of the very thoughts and mind of Christ.

Paul condemns division in the church

3:1
Gal 6:1
Eph 4:14

3 Dear brothers, I have been talking to you as though you were still just babies in the Christian life, who are not following the Lord, but your own desires; I cannot talk to you as I would to healthy Christians, who are filled with the Spirit.

3:2
Heb 5:12-13
1 Pet 2:2,3

²I have had to feed you with milk and not with solid food, because you couldn't digest anything stronger. And even now you still have to be fed on milk. ³For you

3:3
Rom 13:12-13
1 Cor 1:10; 11:18

are still only baby Christians, controlled by your own desires, not God's. When you are jealous of one another and divide up into quarreling groups, doesn't that prove you are still babies, wanting your own way? In fact, you are acting like people who don't belong to the Lord at all. ⁴There you are, quarreling about whether I am greater than Apollos, and dividing the church. Doesn't this show how little you have grown in the Lord?

3:4
1 Cor 1:12

3:5
Rom 12:3,6
2 Cor 6:4

⁵Who am I, and who is Apollos, that we should be the cause of a quarrel? Why, we're just God's servants, each of us with certain special abilities, and with our help you believed. ⁶My work was to plant the seed in your hearts, and Apollos'

3:6
Isa 55:10
Acts 18:4; 19:1

work was to water it, but it was God, not we, who made the garden grow in your

2:13 *to explain the Holy Spirit's facts,* or, "interpreting spiritual truth in spiritual language." **2:16** *to move the hands of God by prayer,* or, "who can advise him?" **3:4** *Doesn't this show how little you have grown in the Lord?* Literally, "Are you not mere men?"

2:10 These secrets are Jesus' resurrection and God's plan of salvation, revealed only to those who believe that what God says is true. Those who believe in the resurrection and put their faith in Christ will know all they need to know to be saved. This knowledge, however, can't be grasped by even the wisest people unless they accept God's message. All who reject God's message are foolish, no matter how wise the world thinks they are.

2:13 Paul's words are authoritative because their source is the Holy Spirit. In one sense, every believer has the ability to interpret Scripture because of the illuminating work of the Holy Spirit. In a unique sense, however, Paul was writing directly under the inspiration of the Holy Spirit. His words are the very words of God.

2:14, 15 Just as a tone-deaf person cannot appreciate fine music, the person who rejects God cannot understand God's beautiful message. The lines of communication are broken, and he cannot hear what God is saying to him.

2:14 Non-Christians cannot comprehend God, and they cannot grasp the concept that God's Spirit lives in believers. Don't expect most people to approve of or understand your decision to follow Christ. It all seems silly to them.

2:15, 16 No one can comprehend God by human effort (Romans 11:34), but by his Spirit many of his thoughts are revealed to us.

Believers are spiritual people having insight into some of God's plans, thoughts, and actions. By his Holy Spirit we can begin to know his thoughts, discuss them with him, and expect his answers to our prayers. Are you spending enough time with Christ to have his very mind in you? An intimate relationship with Christ comes only from consistent time spent in his presence and in his Word. Read Philippians 2:5ff for more on the mind of Christ.

3:1-3 Paul called the Corinthians babies in the Christian life because they were not yet spiritually healthy and mature. The proof was that they quarreled like children. Baby Christians are controlled by their own desires; mature believers by God's desires. How much influence do your own desires have on your life? Our goal is to let God's desires be our own.

3:6 Paul's work was to plant the seed of God's Word in people's hearts. He was a missionary pioneer, one who brought the message of salvation. Apollos' role was to water—to help the believers grow stronger in the faith Paul had helped them discover. Paul founded the church in Corinth, and Apollos built on that foundation. Tragically, the believers in Corinth had split into factions, pledging loyalty to different teachers (see 1:11-13). Paul wanted them to see that the preachers were merely their guides to point them to God.

hearts. 7The person who does the planting or watering isn't very important, but God is important because he is the one who makes things grow. 8Apollos and I are working as a team, with the same aim, though each of us will be rewarded for his own hard work. 9We are only God's co-workers. You are *God's* garden, not ours; you are *God's* building, not ours.

10God, in his kindness, has taught me how to be an expert builder. I have laid the foundation and Apollos has built on it. But he who builds on the foundation must be very careful. 11And no one can ever lay any other real foundation than that one we already have—Jesus Christ. 12But there are various kinds of materials that can be used to build on that foundation. Some use gold and silver and jewels; and some build with sticks, and hay, or even straw! 13There is going to come a time of testing at Christ's Judgment Day to see what kind of material each builder has used. Everyone's work will be put through the fire so that all can see whether or not it keeps its value, and what was really accomplished. 14Then every workman who has built on the foundation with the right materials, and whose work still stands, will get his pay. 15But if the house he has built burns up, he will have a great loss. He himself will be saved, but like a man escaping through a wall of flames.

16Don't you realize that all of you together are the house of God, and that the Spirit of God lives among you in his house? 17If anyone defiles and spoils God's home, God will destroy him. For God's home is holy and clean, and you are that home.

18Stop fooling yourselves. If you count yourself above average in intelligence, as judged by this world's standards, you had better put this all aside and be a fool rather than let it hold you back from the true wisdom from above. 19For the wisdom of this world is foolishness to God. As it says in the book of Job, God uses man's own brilliance to trap him; he stumbles over his own "wisdom" and falls. 20And again, in the book of Psalms, we are told that the Lord knows full well how the human mind reasons, and how foolish and futile it is.

21So don't be proud of following the wise men of this world. For God has already given you everything you need. 22He has given you Paul and Apollos and Peter as your helpers. He has given you the whole world to use, and life and even death are

3:8
Ps 62:12
Rom 2:6
Rev 2:23; 22:12

3:9
Isa 61:3
Jn 15:1-5
Eph 2:20
Col 2:7
1 Pet 2:5

3:10
Rom 15:20
1 Pet 4:11

3:11
Isa 28:16
Mt 16:18
1 Pet 2:4

3:13
2 Tim 1:12,18
4:8

3:14
1 Cor 9:25
Gal 6:4

3:15
Jude 23

3:16
2 Cor 6:16
Eph 2:21

3:17
Heb 3:1

3:18
Isa 5:21
1 Cor 8:2
Gal 6:3

3:19
Job 5:13
1 Cor 1:20

3:20
Ps 94:11

3:21
Rom 8:28,32

3:22
Rom 8:38

3:21 *So don't be proud of following the wise men of this world,* literally, "Let no one glory in men."

3:7–9 God's work in the world involves many different individuals with a variety of gifts and abilities. There are no superstars in this task, only team members performing their own special roles. We become useful members of God's team by setting aside the desire to receive glory for what we do. The praise that comes from people is comparatively worthless; invaluable approval comes from God.

3:10, 11 The foundation of the church—of all believers—is Jesus Christ, and this is the foundation Paul laid when he began the church at Corinth. Whoever builds on the foundation—teachers, preachers, parents, and others—must build with high quality materials (3:12ff) that match God's standards, including right doctrine as taught in the Bible and right living as taught by Christ.

3:10 Those who build the church have a great responsibility. Paul was not criticizing Apollos, but challenging future church leaders to realize the heavy responsibility of preaching and teaching.

3:10–17 The foundation of the church is Jesus Christ, and ideally each church member will be mature, spiritually sensitive, and doctrinally sound. The Corinthian church was filled with "wood, hay, and straw," members who were immature, insensitive to each other, and eagerly accepting wrong doctrine (3:1–4). No wonder they had so many problems. Local churches must be built on Christ, and their members should be those who know him well and are deeply committed to him.

3:11 A building is only as solid as its foundation. The foundation of our lives is Jesus Christ; he is our base, our reason for being. Everything we are and do must fit into the pattern provided by Jesus Christ. Are you building your life on the only real and lasting foundation, or are you building on another foundation such as

wealth, security, or success? What is your reason for living?

3:13 Two ways to destroy a building are to tamper with the foundation or to build with inferior materials. You cannot build a true church on any person or principle except Jesus Christ. Christ will evaluate each minister's contribution to the life of the church. The day of judgment will reveal the sincerity of each person's work. God will determine whether or not he or she has been faithful to Jesus' instructions.

3:16 Paul not only said that our bodies are the home of the Holy Spirit (6:19), but that the local church or Christian community is the house of God. Just as the Temple was not to be defiled, the church is not to be spoiled and ruined by divisions, controversy, or other sins as its members come together to worship God.

3:18, 19 Paul is not telling the Corinthian believers to neglect the pursuit of knowledge, but if one has to choose between earthly knowledge and heavenly wisdom, choose heavenly wisdom even though you may look foolish to the world. Worldly wisdom, if it holds you back from God, is no wisdom at all. The Corinthians were using so-called worldly wisdom to evaluate their leaders and teachers. Their pride made them value the presentation of the message more than its content.

3:22 Paul said that both life and death are our servants. How can this be? While nonbelievers are victims of life, swept along by its current and wondering if there is meaning to it, believers use life well because they understand its true purpose. Nonbelievers can only fear death. For believers, however, death holds no terrors, because Christ has conquered them all. Through him, they will live eternally in God's presence.

3:23
1 Cor 11:3

your servants. He has given you all of the present and all of the future. All are yours, 23and you belong to Christ, and Christ is God's.

Paul counsels his beloved children

4:1
Rom 16:25-27
1 Cor 2:1,7
Eph 3:3-5

4 So Apollos and I should be looked upon as Christ's servants who distribute God's blessings by explaining God's secrets. 2Now the most important thing about a servant is that he does just what his master tells him to. 3What about me? Have I been a good servant? Well, I don't worry over what you think about this, or what anyone else thinks. I don't even trust my own judgment on this point. 4My conscience is clear, but even that isn't final proof. It is the Lord himself who must examine me and decide.

4:2
Ps 143:1,2
Lk 12:42-45
Acts 23:1
Rom 2:12,13
2 Cor 1:12

4:5
Mt 7:1
Rom 2:16,29
2 Cor 5:10
Rev 20:12

5So be careful not to jump to conclusions before the Lord returns as to whether someone is a good servant or not. When the Lord comes, he will turn on the light so that everyone can see exactly what each one of us is really like, deep down in our hearts. Then everyone will know why we have been doing the Lord's work. At that time God will give to each one whatever praise is coming to him.

4:6
1 Cor 1:12,31
4:18

4:7
Jn 3:27
Rom 12:3,6
1 Pet 4:10

6I have used Apollos and myself as examples to illustrate what I have been saying: that you must not have favorites. You must not be proud of one of God's teachers more than another. 7What are you so puffed up about? What do you have that God hasn't given you? And if all you have is from God, why act as though you are so great, and as though you have accomplished something on your own?

4:8
Rev 3:17

4:9
Ps 44:22
Rom 8:36
2 Cor 4:11

8You seem to think you already have all the spiritual food you need. You are full and spiritually contented, rich kings on your thrones, leaving us far behind! I wish you really were already on your thrones, for when that time comes you can be sure that we will be there, too, reigning with you. 9Sometimes I think God has put us apostles at the very end of the line, like prisoners soon to be killed, put on display at the end of a victor's parade, to be stared at by men and angels alike.

4:10
1 Cor 1:18,19
2 Cor 11:19,20
13:9

4:11
Acts 23:2
Rom 8:35
2 Cor 11:23-27

10Religion has made us foolish, you say, but of course you are all such wise and sensible Christians! We are weak, but not you! You are well thought of, while we are laughed at. 11To this very hour we have gone hungry and thirsty, without even enough clothes to keep us warm. We have been kicked around without homes of our own. 12We have worked wearily with our hands to earn our living. We have blessed those who cursed us. We have been patient with those who injured us. 13We have replied quietly when evil things have been said about us. Yet right up to the present moment we are like dirt under foot, like garbage.

4:12
Mt 5:44
Acts 18:2,3
1 Tim 4:9,10
1 Pet 3:9

4:14
1 Cor 6:5; 15:34
2 Cor 6:13
12:14

14I am not writing about these things to make you ashamed, but to warn and counsel you as beloved children. 15For although you may have ten thousand others to teach you about Christ, remember that you have only me as your father. For I

4:15
Rom 15:20
Gal 4:19

4:1, 2 Paul urged the Corinthians to think of him, Peter, and Apollos not as leaders of parties, but as servants of Christ. A servant does what his master tells him to do. We must do what God tells us to do in the Bible and through his Holy Spirit. Daily God confronts us with needs and opportunities that challenge us to do what we know is right.

4:5 It is tempting to judge a fellow Christian, evaluating whether or not he or she is a good follower of Christ. But only God knows a person's heart, and he is the only one with the right to judge. Paul's warning to the Corinthians should also warn us. We are to help those who are sinning (see 5:12, 13), but we must not judge who is a better servant for Christ. When you judge someone, you automatically consider yourself better, and this is pride.

4:6-13 The Corinthians had split into various cliques, each following its own superstar preacher (Paul, Apollos, Peter, etc.). Each clique really believed it was the only one who had the whole truth, and thus felt spiritually proud. But Paul told the groups not to boast about being tied to a particular preacher because even the

superstars were simply humble servants who had each suffered many things for the same message of salvation in Jesus Christ. No preacher of God has more authority than another.

4:6, 7 How easy it is for us to become attached to a spiritual leader. When someone has helped us, it's natural to feel loyalty. But Paul warns against having such pride in our favorite leaders that we cause divisions in the church. Any true spiritual leader is a representative of Christ and has nothing to offer that God hasn't given him. Don't let your loyalty cause fighting, slander, or broken relationships. Make sure your deepest loyalties are to Christ and not to his human agents. Those who spend more time debating church leadership than declaring Christ's message don't have Christ as their top priority.

4:15 In an attempt to unify the church, Paul appealed to his relationship with them. By "father," he meant he was the church's founder. Because he started the church, he could be trusted to have its best interests at heart. Paul's tough words were motivated by love—like the love a good father has for his children.

was the one who brought you to Christ when I preached the Gospel to you. [16]So I beg you to follow my example, and do as I do.

[17]That is the very reason why I am sending Timothy—to help you do this. For he is one of those I won to Christ, a beloved and trustworthy child in the Lord. He will remind you of what I teach in all the churches wherever I go.

[18]I know that some of you will have become proud, thinking that I am afraid to come to deal with you. [19]But I will come, and soon, if the Lord will let me, and then I'll find out whether these proud men are just big talkers or whether they really have God's power. [20]The Kingdom of God is not just talking; it is living by God's power. [21]Which do you choose? Shall I come with punishment and scolding, or shall I come with quiet love and gentleness?

2. Disorders in the church
Paul condemns immorality in the church

5 Everyone is talking about the terrible thing that has happened there among you, something so evil that even the heathen don't do it: you have a man in your church who is living in sin with his father's wife. [2]And are you still so conceited, so "spiritual"? Why aren't you mourning in sorrow and shame, and seeing to it that this man is removed from your membership?

[3, 4]Although I am not there with you, I have been thinking a lot about this, and in the name of the Lord Jesus Christ I have already decided what to do, just as though I were there. You are to call a meeting of the church—and the power of the Lord Jesus will be with you as you meet, and I will be there in spirit— [5]and cast out this

5:1 *his father's wife,* possibly his stepmother.

4:16
1 Cor 11:1
Phil 3:17

4:17
Acts 16:1; 19:22
1 Tim 1:2

4:19
Acts 19:21
1 Cor 11:34; 16:5
2 Cor 1:15

4:20
1 Thess 1:5

4:21
2 Cor 1:23; 2:1

5:1
Lev 18:7,8
Deut 27:20
2 Cor 7:12
Eph 5:3

5:3,4
Mt 18:15-18
Jn 20:23
2 Cor 2:5-10
13:3,4

5:5
Acts 26:18
1 Tim 1:20

Situations	Steps (Matthew 18:15–17)	**CHURCH DISCIPLINE**
Unintentional error and/or private sin	1. Go to the brother or sister, reprove him or her in private.	The church, at times, must exercise discipline toward members who have sinned. But church discipline must be handled carefully, straightforwardly, and in love.
Public sin and/or those done with prior knowledge and flagrantly	2. If he/she does not listen, go with one or two witnesses.	
	3. If he/she refuses to listen, take the matter before the church.	

After these steps have been carried out, the next steps are:
1. Remove the one in error from the fellowship (1 Corinthians 5:2–13).
2. The church gives united disapproval, but forgiveness and comfort is in order if he/she chooses to repent (2 Corinthians 2:5–7).
3. Do not associate with the disobedient person; and if you must, speak to him/her as one who needs a warning (2 Thessalonians 3:14, 15.)
4. After two warnings, reject the person from the fellowship (Titus 3:10).

4:16 Paul told the Corinthians to follow his example. He was able to make this statement because he walked close to God, spent time in God's Word and in prayer, and was aware of God's presence in his life at all times. God was his example, therefore, his life could be an example to other Christians. Paul wasn't expecting others to copy everything he did, because people are all different. But they should copy those aspects of his life that modeled Christ's way of living.

4:17 Timothy had traveled with Paul on his second missionary journey (see Acts 16:1–3) and was a key person in the growth of the early church. Timothy may have delivered this letter to Corinth, but more likely he arrived there shortly after the letter (see 16:10). His role was to see that Paul's advice was received, read, and implemented. He was then to return to Paul and report on the church's progress.

4:18–20 Some people talk a lot about faith, but that's all it is—talk. They may know all the right words to say, but their lives are not examples of Christian living. Paul says the Kingdom of God is to be *lived,* not just discussed. There is a big difference between knowing the right words and living them out. Don't be content to have the right answers about Christ. Let your life put flesh on your words.

4:19 It is not known whether Paul ever returned to Corinth, but it is likely. In 2 Corinthians 2:1, he says he decided not to make *another* painful visit, implying that he had had a previous painful confrontation with the Corinthian believers.

5:1ff The church must discipline flagrant sin among its members—such actions, left unchecked, can polarize and paralyze a church. The correction, however, is never to be vengeful. Instead, it is intended to bring about a cure. The Corinthian church had a specific sin in their midst, but they had refused to deal with it. In this case, a man was having an affair with his mother (or stepmother), and the church members were trying to ignore the situation. Paul was telling the church that they had a responsibility to maintain standards of morality found in God's Word. God tells us not to judge others, but he also tells us not to tolerate flagrant sin that opposes his holiness and has a dangerous influence on the lives of other believers (5:6).

man from the fellowship of the church and into Satan's hands, to punish him, in the hope that his soul will be saved when our Lord Jesus Christ returns.

5:6
Mt 13:33; 16:6,11
Gal 5:9

5:7
Ex 12:21
Isa 53:7
Jn 1:29; 19:14
1 Pet 1:19
Rev 5:6

5:8
Ex 12:15-19
Deut 16:3

5:9
2 Cor 6:14

5:10
Jn 17:15

5:11
Mt 18:17
Rom 16:17
2 Thess 3:6
2 Jn 1:10

5:12
1 Tim 3:7

5:13
Eccles 12:14
Heb 13:4

6What a terrible thing it is that you are boasting about your purity, and yet you let this sort of thing go on. Don't you realize that if even one person is allowed to go on sinning, soon all will be affected? 7Remove this evil cancer—this wicked person—from among you, so that you can stay pure. Christ, God's Lamb, has been slain for us. 8So let us feast upon him and grow strong in the Christian life, leaving entirely behind us the cancerous old life with all its hatreds and wickedness. Let us feast instead upon the pure bread of honor and sincerity and truth.

9When I wrote to you before I said not to mix with evil people. 10But when I said that I wasn't talking about unbelievers who live in sexual sin, or are greedy cheats and thieves and idol worshipers. For you can't live in this world without being with people like that. 11What I meant was that you are not to keep company with anyone who claims to be a brother Christian but indulges in sexual sins, or is greedy, or is a swindler, or worships idols, or is a drunkard, or abusive. Don't even eat lunch with such a person.

12It isn't our job to judge outsiders. But it certainly is our job to judge and deal strongly with those who are members of the church, and who are sinning in these ways. 13God alone is the Judge of those on the outside. But you yourselves must deal with this man and put him out of your church.

Believers should not sue each other

6:1
Mt 18:15-17

6:2
Dan 7:18,22
Lk 22:30
Rev 2:26; 20:4

6:3
2 Pet 2:4
Jude 6

6:5
1 Cor 4:14; 15:34

6 How is it that when you have something against another Christian, you "go to law" and ask a heathen court to decide the matter instead of taking it to other Christians to decide which of you is right? 2Don't you know that some day we Christians are going to judge and govern the world? So why can't you decide even these little things among yourselves? 3Don't you realize that we Christians will judge and reward the very angels in heaven? So you should be able to decide your problems down here on earth easily enough. 4Why then go to outside judges who are not even Christians? 5I am trying to make you ashamed. Isn't there anyone in

6:4 *Why then go to outside judges who are not even Christians?* Or, "Even the least capable people in the church should be able to decide these things for you." Both interpretations are possible.

5:5 Why was it necessary to cast this man out of the church? To cast this man into Satan's hands meant to exclude him from the fellowship of believers. Without the spiritual support of Christians, he would be left alone with his sin and Satan, and perhaps this emptiness would drive him to repentance. Putting someone out of the church should be a last resort in disciplinary action. It should not be done out of vengeance, but out of love, just as parents punish children to correct them. The church's role is to help the offender, not to hurt him, motivating him to repent of his sins and to return to the fellowship of the church.

5:6 Paul was talking to those who wanted to ignore this church problem, not realizing that allowing blatant sin to exist in the church body affects all its members. Paul was not expecting anyone to be sinless—all believers struggle with sin on a daily basis. Instead, he was speaking against those who deliberately sinned, felt no guilt, and would not repent. This kind of sin cannot be tolerated in the church because it affects others. We have a responsibility to other believers. Blatant sins, left uncorrected, confuse and divide the congregation. While believers should encourage, pray for, and build up one another, they must also be intolerant of sin when it jeopardizes the spiritual health of the church.

5:9 Paul was referring to an earlier letter to the Corinthian church, often called the lost letter because it has not been preserved.

5:10, 11 Paul makes it clear that we should not dissociate ourselves from unbelievers—otherwise, we could not carry out Christ's command to tell them about salvation (Matthew 28:18–20). But we are to distance ourselves from the person who claims to be a Christian, yet indulges in sins explicitly forbidden in Scripture

and then rationalizes his actions. By sinning, a person harms others for whom Christ died and dims the image of God in himself. A church that includes greedy people and sexual sinners is hardly fit to be the light of the world. It is distorting the picture of Christ it presents to the world. Instead of joining Christ's Kingdom with its constant fight to replace darkness with light, it is adding to the darkness.

5:12 The Bible consistently tells us not to criticize others by gossiping or making rash judgments. At the same time, however, we are to judge and deal with sin that can hurt others. Paul's instructions are not to be used to handle trivial matters or to take revenge; nor are they to be applied to individual problems between believers. These verses are instructions for dealing with open sin in the church, with a person who claims to be a Christian and yet who sins without remorse. The church's responsibility is to confront and discipline such a person in love. Also see the notes on 4:5 and 5:1ff.

6:1–6 In chapter 5 Paul discussed what to do with blatant sinners in the congregation. In chapter 6 he discusses how the congregation should handle smaller problems between believers. Society has set up a legal system where disagreements can be solved in courts. But Paul says that disagreeing Christians should not have to go to a secular court to resolve their differences. As Christians we have the Holy Spirit and the mind of Christ, so why should we turn to those who lack God's wisdom? With all that we have been given as believers, and the power that we will have in the future to judge the world and the angels, we should be able to deal with the disputes between ourselves.

all the church who is wise enough to decide these arguments? 6But, instead, one Christian sues another and accuses his Christian brother in front of unbelievers.

7To have such lawsuits at all is a real defeat for you as Christians. Why not just accept mistreatment and leave it at that? It would be far more honoring to the Lord to let yourselves be cheated. 8But, instead, you yourselves are the ones who do wrong, cheating others, even your own brothers.

6:7
Prov 20:22
Mt 5:39
Rom 12:17
1 Thess 5:15

6:8
1 Thess 4:6

Use your body to give God glory

9, 10Don't you know that those doing such things have no share in the Kingdom of God? Don't fool yourselves. Those who live immoral lives, who are idol worshipers, adulterers or homosexuals—will have no share in his Kingdom. Neither will thieves or greedy people, drunkards, slanderers, or robbers. 11There was a time when some of you were just like that but now your sins are washed away, and you are set apart for God, and he has accepted you because of what the Lord Jesus Christ and the Spirit of our God have done for you.

6:9,10
Isa 3:11
Acts 20:32
Gal 5:21
Eph 5:5

6:11
Acts 22:16
Rom 8:30
1 Cor 1:2,30
Heb 10:22

12I can do anything I want to if Christ has not said no, but some of these things aren't good for me. Even if I am allowed to do them, I'll refuse to if I think they might get such a grip on me that I can't easily stop when I want to. 13For instance, take the matter of eating. God has given us an appetite for food and stomachs to digest it. But that doesn't mean we should eat more than we need. Don't think of eating as important, because some day God will do away with both stomachs and food.

6:12
1 Cor 10:23

6:13
Mt 5:17
Col 2:22
1 Thess 4:3

But sexual sin is never right: our bodies were not made for that, but for the Lord, and the Lord wants to fill our bodies with himself. 14And God is going to raise our bodies from the dead by his power just as he raised up the Lord Jesus Christ. 15Don't you realize that your bodies are actually parts and members of Christ? So

6:14
Acts 2:24
Rom 6:5
1 Cor 15:23
Eph 1:19,20

6:6 Why does Paul say it isn't good to sue another Christian? (1) If the judge and jury are not Christians, they are unlikely to be sensitive to Christian values. (2) The basis for going to court is often revenge; this should never be a Christian's motive. (3) Lawsuits make the church look bad, causing unbelievers to focus on its problems rather than its purpose.

6:9–11 Paul is describing characteristics of unbelievers. He doesn't mean that adulterers, homosexuals, thieves, or greedy people are automatically and irrevocably excluded from heaven. Christians come from all backgrounds, including these. They may still struggle with evil desires, but they should not continue in these practices. In 6:11, Paul clearly states that even those who sin in these ways can have their lives changed by Christ. However, those who say they are Christians but persist in these practices with no remorse should reevaluate their lives to see if they truly believe in Christ.

6:9–11 In a permissive society it is easy for Christians to overlook or accept immoral behavior (sexual sins, greed, drunkenness, gossip, etc.) because it is so widespread. Although it surrounds us, we cannot take part in it or condone it in any way. Staying away from generally accepted sin is difficult, but it is no harder for us than it was for the Corinthians. God expects his followers in any age to have high standards.

6:12 "I can do anything if Christ has not said no" is literally translated, "All things are lawful for me." Apparently the church was quoting and misapplying this line frequently. Some Christians in Corinth were excusing many of their sins by saying that (1) Christ had taken away all sin, and so they had complete freedom to live as they pleased, or (2) what they were doing was not strictly forbidden by Scripture. Paul answered both these excuses. (1) While Christ has taken away our sin, this does not give us freedom to go on doing what we know is wrong. Scripture specifically forbids many sins (see 6:9, 10). (2) Some actions are not sinful in themselves, but they are not appropriate because they can control our lives and lead us away from God. (3) Anything we do that hurts rather than helps others is not right.

6:12, 13 Many of the world's religions think the soul is important and the body is not, and Christianity has sometimes been influenced by them. In truth, however, Christianity is a very physical religion. We worship a God who created a physical world and pronounced it good. He promises us a new earth where real people continue to live physical lives—not a pink cloud where disembodied souls listen to harp music. At the heart of Christianity is the story of God himself taking on flesh and blood and coming to live with us, offering both physical healing and spiritual restoration.

We humans, like Adam, are a combination of dust and spirit. Just as our spiritual lives affect our bodies, so our physical lives affect our souls. We cannot commit sin with our bodies without damaging our souls, because our bodies and souls are inseparably joined. In the new earth we will have resurrection bodies that are not corrupted by sin. Then we will enjoy the fullness of our salvation.

6:12, 13 Freedom is a mark of the Christian faith—freedom from sin and guilt, and freedom to use and enjoy anything that comes from God. But Christians should not abuse this freedom and hurt themselves or others. Drinking too much leads to alcoholism, gluttony leads to obesity. Be careful that what God has allowed you to enjoy doesn't grow into a bad habit that controls you. For more about Christian freedom and everyday behavior, read chapter 8.

6:13 Sexual sin is a temptation we cannot escape. In movies and on television, sex outside marriage is treated as a normal, even desirable, part of life, while marriage is often shown as confining and joyless. We can even be looked down upon by others if suspected of being pure. But God does not forbid sexual sin just to be difficult. He knows its power to destroy us physically and spiritually. No one should underestimate the power of sexual sin. It has devastated countless lives and destroyed families, communities, and even nations. God wants to protect us from damaging ourselves and others, and so he offers to fill us—our loneliness, our desires—with himself.

6:16
Gen 2:24
Mt 19:5,6

6:17
Jn 17:21
Rom 8:16
2 Cor 3:17
Eph 5:30

6:18
Rom 1:24
1 Thess 4:3,4

6:19
Rom 14:7,8
2 Cor 6:16

6:20
1 Pet 1:18,19

should I take part of Christ and join him to a prostitute? Never! 16And don't you know that if a man joins himself to a prostitute she becomes a part of him and he becomes a part of her? For God tells us in the Scripture that in his sight the two become one person. 17But if you give yourself to the Lord, you and Christ are joined together as one person.

18That is why I say to run from sex sin. No other sin affects the body as this one does. When you sin this sin it is against your own body. 19Haven't you yet learned that your body is the home of the Holy Spirit God gave you, and that he lives within you? Your own body does not belong to you. 20For God has bought you with a great price. So use every part of your body to give glory back to God, because he owns it.

B. PAUL ANSWERS CHURCH QUESTIONS (7:1—16:24)
After discussing disorders in the church, Paul moves to the list of questions which the Corinthians had sent him, including subjects of marriage, singleness, eating meat offered to idols, clothing in worship, orderliness in the Lord's Supper, spiritual gifts, and the resurrection. Questions which plague churches today are remarkably similar to these, so we can receive specific guidance in these areas.

1. Instruction on Christian marriage
Questions about marriage

7:1
1 Cor 7:8,26

7:2
Prov 5:19

7:3
Ex 21:10
1 Pet 3:7

7:5
1 Thess 3:5

7 Now about those questions you asked in your last letter: my answer is that if you do not marry, it is good. 2But usually it is best to be married, each man having his own wife, and each woman having her own husband, because otherwise you might fall back into sin.

3The man should give his wife all that is her right as a married woman, and the wife should do the same for her husband: 4for a girl who marries no longer has full right to her own body, for her husband then has his rights to it, too; and in the same way the husband no longer has full right to his own body, for it belongs also to his wife. 5So do not refuse these rights to each other. The only exception to this rule would be the agreement of both husband and wife to refrain from the rights of

---

6:15–17 This teaching about sexual sin and prostitutes was especially important for the Corinthian church because the temple of the goddess Aphrodite was in Corinth. It employed more than a thousand prostitutes, and sex was part of the worship ritual. Paul clearly states that Christians are to have no part in sexual sin, even if it is acceptable and popular in our culture.

6:18 As Christians we are free to be all we can be for God; we are not free *from* God. God created sex to be a beautiful and essential ingredient of marriage, but sexual sin—sex outside the marriage relationship—*always* hurts someone. It hurts God because it shows we prefer following our own desires instead of the leading of the Holy Spirit. It hurts others because it violates the commitment so necessary to a relationship. It often brings disease to our bodies, and it deeply affects our personalities, which respond in anguish when we harm ourselves physically and spiritually.

6:19, 20 What did Paul mean when he said that God owns our bodies? Many people say they have the right to do whatever they want with their own bodies. Although they think this is freedom, they are really enslaved to their own desires. When we become Christians, the Holy Spirit fills our lives and lives in us. Therefore, we no longer own our bodies. If you live in a building owned by someone else, you don't violate the building rules. Since your body belongs to God, you must not violate his standards for living.

7:1 The Corinthians had written to Paul asking him several questions relating to the Christian life and problems in the church. Paul gives his answers to these questions in the remainder of this book.

7:1ff Christians in Corinth were surrounded by sexual temptation. The city had a reputation even among pagans for sexual immorality and religious prostitution. It was to this kind of society that Paul delivered these instructions on sex and marriage. The

Corinthians needed special, specific instructions because of their culture's immoral standards. Paul was especially careful with this teaching to the Corinthians because their culture was so contrary to God's plan. For more on Paul's teaching on marriage, see Ephesians 5.

7:3–5 Sexual temptations are difficult to withstand because they appeal to the normal and natural desires God has given us. Marriage is meant, in part, to satisfy these natural sexual desires and to strengthen the partners against temptation. Married couples have the responsibility to care for each other. Therefore, husbands and wives should not withhold themselves from one another, but should fulfill each other's needs and desires. (See also the note on 10:13.)

7:3–11 The Corinthian church was in turmoil because of the immorality of the culture around them. Some Greeks, in rejecting immorality, rejected sex and marriage altogether. The Corinthian Christians wondered if this was what they were to do also, so they asked Paul several questions: "Because sex is perverted, shouldn't we also abstain in marriage?" "If my spouse is unsaved, should I seek a divorce?" "Should unmarried people and widows not marry?" Paul answered many of these questions by saying, "For now, stay put. Be content in the situation in which God has placed you. Don't seek to be married or single. Live God's way one day at a time, and he will show you what to do." He then proceeded to answer the specific questions by clarifying people's responsibilities in each of these situations.

7:4 Spiritually, our bodies belong to God when we become Christians, because Jesus Christ bought us by paying the price to release us from sin (see 6:19, 20). Physically, our bodies belong to our spouses, because God designed marriage so that through the union of husband and wife, the two become one (Genesis 2:24).

marriage for a limited time, so that they can give themselves more completely to prayer. Afterwards, they should come together again so that Satan won't be able to tempt them because of their lack of self-control.

6I'm not saying you *must* marry; but you certainly *may* if you wish. 7I wish everyone could get along without marrying, just as I do. But we are not all the same. God gives some the gift of a husband or wife, and others he gives the gift of being able to stay happily unmarried. 8So I say to those who aren't married, and to widows—better to stay unmarried if you can, just as I am. 9But if you can't control yourselves, go ahead and marry. It is better to marry than to burn with lust.

10Now, for those who are married I have a command, not just a suggestion. And it is not a command from me, for this is what the Lord himself has said: A wife must not leave her husband. 11But if she is separated from him, let her remain single or else go back to him. And the husband must not divorce his wife.

12Here I want to add some suggestions of my own. These are not direct commands from the Lord, but they seem right to me: If a Christian has a wife who is not a Christian, but she wants to stay with him anyway, he must not leave her or divorce her. 13And if a Christian woman has a husband who isn't a Christian, and he wants her to stay with him, she must not leave him. 14For perhaps the husband who isn't a Christian may become a Christian with the help of his Christian wife. And the wife who isn't a Christian may become a Christian with the help of her Christian husband. Otherwise, if the family separates, the children might never come to know the Lord; whereas a united family may, in God's plan, result in the children's salvation.

15But if the husband or wife who isn't a Christian is eager to leave, it is permitted. In such cases the Christian husband or wife should not insist that the other stay, for God wants his children to live in peace and harmony. 16For, after all, there is no assurance to you wives that your husbands will be converted if they stay; and the same may be said to you husbands concerning your wives.

Believers should be content where they are

17But be sure in deciding these matters that you are living as God intended, marrying or not marrying in accordance with God's direction and help, and

7:6
2 Cor 8:8; 11:17

7:7
Mt 19:12
1 Cor 9:5; 12:11

7:9
1 Tim 5:14

7:10
Mal 2:14,16
Mt 5:32; 19:5,6
Mk 10:10-12
Lk 16:18

7:12
2 Cor 11:17

7:14
Ezra 9:2
Mal 2:15

7:16
1 Pet 3:1

7:17
1 Cor 4:17
11:16; 14:33

7:6, 7 Both marriage and singleness are gifts from God. One is not better than the other, and both are valuable to accomplishing God's purposes. It is important, therefore, to accept one's present situation. When Paul said he wished more could get along without marrying, he was expressing his desire that more people would devote themselves *completely* to the ministry without the added concerns of spouse and family, as he had done. He was not criticizing marriage—after all, it is God's created way of providing companionship and populating the earth.

7:9 Sexual pressure is not the best motive for getting married, but it is better to marry the right person than to burn with lust. Many new believers in Corinth thought that all sex was wrong, and so engaged couples were deciding not to get married. In this passage, Paul is telling couples who wanted to marry that they should not deny their normal sexual drives by avoiding marriage. This does not mean, however, that people who have trouble controlling their thoughts should marry the first person who comes along. It is better to deal with the pressure of desire than to deal with an unhappy marriage.

7:11 Because of their desire to serve Christ, some people in the Corinthian church thought they ought to divorce their pagan spouses and marry Christians. But Paul affirmed the marriage commitment. God's ideal is for marriages to stay together—even when one spouse is not a believer. The Christian spouse should try to win the other to Christ. It would be easy to rationalize leaving; however, Paul makes a strong case for staying with the unbelieving spouse and being a positive influence on the marriage. Paul, like

Jesus, believed marriage is permanent (see Mark 10:1–9).

7:12 Paul's *command* about the permanence of marriage comes from the Old Testament and from Jesus. His *suggestion* is based on God's command and he applies it to the situation the Corinthians were facing. Paul ranks the command above the suggestion because one is an eternal principle, whereas the other is a specific application. Nevertheless, for people in similar situations, Paul's suggestion is the best advice they will get. Paul was a man of God, an apostle; and he had the mind of Christ.

7:15, 16 This verse is misused by some as a loophole to get out of marriage. But Paul's statements were given to encourage the Christian spouse to try to get along with the unbeliever and make the marriage work. If, however, the unbelieving spouse insists on leaving, Paul says to let him or her go. The only alternative would be for the Christian to deny his faith to preserve his marriage, and this would be the one thing worse than dissolving the marriage. It cannot be stressed enough that Paul's purpose in writing this was to urge the married couples to seek unity, not separation (see 7:17; 1 Peter 3:1, 2).

7:17 Apparently the Corinthians were ready to make wholesale changes without thinking through the ramifications. Paul was writing to say that people should be Christians where they are. You can do God's work and demonstrate your faith *anywhere*. You don't have to be married to a Christian to live for Christ. Don't assume that you are in the wrong place, stuck with the wrong person. You may be just where God wants you (see 7:20).

accepting whatever situation God has put you into. This is my rule for all the churches.

7:18
Acts 15:4-19
Gal 5:2

7:19
Rom 2:25
Gal 5:6; 6:15
Col 3:11
1 Jn 2:3; 3:24

18For instance, a man who already has gone through the Jewish ceremony of circumcision before he became a Christian shouldn't worry about it; and if he hasn't been circumcised, he shouldn't do it now. 19For it doesn't make any difference at all whether a Christian has gone through this ceremony or not. But it makes a lot of difference whether he is pleasing God and keeping God's commandments. That is the important thing.

7:21
Gal 3:28

7:22
Gal 5:13
Eph 6:6
1 Pet 2:16

7:23
Lev 25:42
1 Cor 6:20
1 Pet 1:18

20Usually a person should keep on with the work he was doing when God called him. 21Are you a slave? Don't let that worry you—but of course, if you get a chance to be free, take it. 22If the Lord calls you, and you are a slave, remember that Christ has set you free from the awful power of sin; and if he has called you and you are free, remember that you are now a slave of Christ. 23You have been bought and paid for by Christ, so you belong to him—be free now from all these earthly prides and fears. 24So, dear brothers, whatever situation a person is in when he becomes a Christian, let him stay there, for now the Lord is there to help him.

Questions about singleness

7:25
2 Cor 4:1

25Now I will try to answer your other question. What about girls who are not yet married? Should they be permitted to do so? In answer to this question, I have no special command for them from the Lord. But the Lord in his kindness has given me wisdom that can be trusted, and I will be glad to tell you what I think.

7:26
Lk 21:23

26Here is the problem: We Christians are facing great dangers to our lives at present. In times like these I think it is best for a person to remain unmarried. 27Of course, if you already are married, don't separate because of this. But if you aren't, don't rush into it at this time. 28But if you men decide to go ahead anyway and get married now, it is all right; and if a girl gets married in times like these, it is no sin. However, marriage will bring extra problems that I wish you didn't have to face right now.

7:29
Rom 13:11
1 Cor 7:31
1 Pet 4:7

29The important thing to remember is that our remaining time is very short, [and so are our opportunities for doing the Lord's work]. For that reason those who have

7:23 *be free now from all these earthly prides and fears,* literally, "Become not bondservants of men."   **7:29** *and so are our opportunities for doing the Lord's work,* implied. *those who have wives should stay as free as possible for the Lord,* literally, "[that] those who have wives may be as though they didn't."

7:18, 19 The ceremony of circumcision was an important part of the Jews' relationship with God. In fact, before Christ came, circumcision was commanded by God for all who claimed to follow him (Genesis 17:9-14). But after Christ's death, circumcision was no longer necessary (Acts 15; Romans 2:28, 29; 4:9-11; Galatians 5:2-4; Colossians 2:11). More important than ceremonies, says Paul, is pleasing God and obeying him.

7:20 Often we are so concerned about what we *could* be doing for God somewhere else that we miss great opportunities right where we are. Paul says that when someone becomes a Christian, he should usually continue with the work he has previously been doing—provided it isn't immoral or unethical. Every job can become Christian work when you realize that the purpose of your life is to honor, serve, and speak out for Christ. Because God has placed you where you are, look carefully for opportunities to serve him there.

7:23 Slavery was common throughout the Roman empire. Some Christians in the Corinthian church were slaves. Paul said that although they were slaves to men, they were free from the power of sin in their lives. People today are slaves to sin until they commit their lives to Christ, who alone can conquer sin's power. Sin, pride, and fear no longer have claim over us, just as a slaveowner no longer has power over slaves he has sold. The Bible says we become Christ's slaves when we become Christians, but this actually means we gain our freedom, because sin no longer controls us.

7:26 Paul saw the impending persecution that the Roman

government would soon bring upon Christians. He gave this practical advice because being unmarried would mean less suffering and more freedom to throw one's life into the cause of Christ (7:29), even to the point of fearlessly dying for him. Paul's advice reveals his singleminded devotion to spreading the Good News.

7:28 Many people naively think that marriage will solve all their problems. Here are some problems marriage won't solve: (1) loneliness, (2) sexual temptation, (3) satisfaction of one's deepest emotional needs, (4) elimination of life's difficulties. Marriage alone does not hold two people together, but commitment does—commitment to Christ and to each other despite conflicts and problems. As wonderful as it is, marriage does not solve problems. Whether married or single, we must be content with our situation and focus on Christ, not humans, to solve our problems.

7:29 Paul urges all believers to make the most of their time before Christ's return. Every person in every generation should have this sense of urgency about telling the Good News to others. Life is short no matter how long we live.

7:29-31 Paul urged the believers to "stay as free as possible for the Lord." This means that we should not regard marriage, home, or financial security as the ultimate goal of life. As far as possible, we should live unhindered by the cares of this world, not getting involved with mortgages, budgets, investments, or bills that will keep us from doing God's work. A married man, as Paul points out (7:33), has to think about his earthly responsibilities—but he should be careful to keep them modest and manageable.

wives should stay as free as possible for the Lord; 30happiness or sadness or wealth should not keep anyone from doing God's work. 31Those in frequent contact with the exciting things the world offers should make good use of their opportunities without stopping to enjoy them; for the world in its present form will soon be gone.

7:31
Ps 39:6
Jas 4:14
1 Jn 2:17

32In all you do, I want you to be free from worry. An unmarried man can spend his time doing the Lord's work and thinking how to please him. 33But a married man can't do that so well; he has to think about his earthly responsibilities and how to please his wife. 34His interests are divided. It is the same with a girl who marries. She faces the same problem. A girl who is not married is anxious to please the Lord in all she is and does. But a married woman must consider other things such as housekeeping and the likes and dislikes of her husband.

7:34
Lk 10:40
1 Tim 5:5

35I am saying this to help you, not to try to keep you from marrying. I want you to do whatever will help you serve the Lord best, with as few other things as possible to distract your attention from him.

36But if anyone feels he ought to marry because he has trouble controlling his passions, it is all right, it is not a sin; let him marry. 37But if a man has the willpower not to marry and decides that he doesn't need to and won't, he has made a wise decision. 38So the person who marries does well, and the person who doesn't marry does even better.

7:38
Heb 13:4

39The wife is part of her husband as long as he lives; if her husband dies, then she may marry again, but only if she marries a Christian. 40But in my opinion she will be happier if she doesn't marry again; and I think I am giving you counsel from God's Spirit when I say this.

7:39
Rom 7:2
2 Cor 6:14

7:40
1 Cor 7:6,25

2. Instruction on Christian freedom
Questions about food offered to idols

8 Next is your question about eating food that has been sacrificed to idols. On this question everyone feels that only his answer is the right one! But although being a "know-it-all" makes us feel important, what is really needed to build the church is love. 2If anyone thinks he knows all the answers, he is just showing his ignorance. 3But the person who truly loves God is the one who is open to God's knowledge.

8:1
Acts 15:20
Rom 14:19

8:2
1 Cor 3:18
13:8,9

8:3
Gal 4:9
2 Tim 2:19

4So now, what about it? Should we eat meat that has been sacrificed to idols? Well, we all know that an idol is not really a god, and that there is only one God, and no other. 5According to some people, there are a great many gods, both in heaven and on earth. 6But we know that there is only one God, the Father, who created all things and made us to be his own; and one Lord Jesus Christ, who made everything and gives us life.

8:4
Deut 4:39
Isa 44:8
Acts 15:20

8:5
Jn 10:34

8:6
Jn 1:3
Acts 17:28
Eph 4:6
Col 1:16

7However, some Christians don't realize this. All their lives they have been used to thinking of idols as alive, and have believed that food offered to the idols is really being offered to actual gods. So when they eat such food it bothers them and hurts

8:7
Rom 14:14,22
1 Cor 8:4

7:34 *in all she is and does,* literally, "pure in body and in spirit."   **8:6** *who created all things,* literally, "of whom are all things."

7:32–34 Some single people feel tremendous pressure to be married. They think their lives can be complete only with a spouse. But Paul underlines one advantage of being single—the potential of a greater focus on Christ and his work. If you are unmarried, use your special opportunity to serve Christ wholeheartedly.

7:38 When Paul said the unmarried person does better, he was talking about the potential time available for service to God because the single person has fewer responsibilities related to raising a family. Singleness, however, does not insure service to God—that is up to the commitment of the individual.

8:1 Meat bought in the marketplace was likely to have been symbolically offered to an idol in one of the many pagan temples. Animals were brought to a temple, killed before an idol as part of a pagan religious ceremony, then taken to butchers who sold the meat in a temple restaurant or in the marketplace. Believers

wondered if by eating such meat they were somehow participating in the worship of pagan idols.

8:1–3 Love is more important than knowledge. Knowledge makes us look good and feel important, but one can easily develop a prideful, know-it-all attitude. Many people with strong opinions are unwilling to listen and learn from God and others. Paul says that God's knowledge, the kind needed to build the church, can be obtained only by loving him.

8:4–9 Paul addressed these words to believers who weren't bothered by eating meat that had been sacrificed to idols. Although idols were not real, and the pagan ritual of sacrificing to them was meaningless, eating such meat offended Christians with more sensitive consciences. Paul said, therefore, that if a **weaker** or less mature believer misunderstood their actions, they should, out of consideration, avoid eating meat offered to idols.

8:8
Rom 14:17

8:9
Rom 14:1,13,21
1 Cor 8:10
10:28
Gal 5:13

8:10
Acts 15:20

8:11
Rom 14:15,20
1 Cor 8:4

8:12
Mt 18:6
Rom 14:20

8:13
Rom 14:21
1 Cor 10:32
2 Cor 6:3; 11:29

9:1
Acts 9:3; 18:9
1 Cor 3:6;
4:15; 15:8
1 Tim 2:7
2 Tim 1:11

9:2
2 Cor 3:2

their tender consciences. 8Just remember that God doesn't care whether we eat it or not. We are no worse off if we don't eat it, and no better off if we do. 9But be careful not to use your freedom to eat it, lest you cause some Christian brother to sin whose conscience is weaker than yours.

10You see, this is what may happen: Someone who thinks it is wrong to eat this food will see you eating at a temple restaurant, for you know there is no harm in it. Then he will become bold enough to do it too, although all the time he still feels it is wrong. 11So because you "know it is all right to do it," you will be responsible for causing great spiritual damage to a brother with a tender conscience for whom Christ died. 12And it is a sin against Christ to sin against your brother by encouraging him to do something he thinks is wrong. 13So if eating meat offered to idols is going to make my brother sin, I'll not eat any of it as long as I live, because I don't want to do this to him.

The rights of apostles

9 I am an apostle, God's messenger, responsible to no mere man. I am one who has actually seen Jesus our Lord with my own eyes. And your changed lives are the result of my hard work for him. 2If in the opinion of others, I am not an apostle, I certainly am to you, for you have been won to Christ through me. 3This is my answer to those who question my rights.

4Or don't I have any rights at all? Can't I claim the same privilege the other

8:9 *conscience*, implied. Literally, "faith."

STRONGER, WEAKER BROTHERS	*Advice to:*	
	Stronger brother	Don't be proud of your maturity; don't flaunt your freedom. Act in love so you do not cause a weaker brother to stumble.
	Weaker brother	Although you may not feel the same freedom in some areas as in others, take your time, pray to God, but do not force others to adhere to your stipulations. You would hinder other believers by making up rules and standards for how everyone ought to behave. Make sure your convictions are based on God's Word, not your opinions.
	Pastors and leaders	Teach correctly from God's Word, helping Christians understand what is right and wrong in God's eyes, and helping them see that they can have varied opinions on other issues and still be unified. Don't allow potential problems to get out of hand, causing splits and divisions.

Paul advises those who are more mature in the faith about how they must care about their brothers and sisters in Christ who have more tender consciences; those "weaker" brothers and sisters are advised concerning their growth; and pastors and leaders are instructed on how to deal with the conflicts that easily could arise between these groups.

8:10–13 Christian freedom does not mean "anything goes." It means that our salvation is not determined by legalism, good works, or rules, but by the free gift of God (Ephesians 2:8, 9). Christian freedom, then, is inseparably tied to Christian responsibility. New believers are often very sensitive to what is right or wrong, what they should or shouldn't do. Some actions may be perfectly all right for us to do, but may harm a Christian brother or sister who is still young in the faith and learning what the Christian life is all about. We must be careful not to offend a sensitive or younger Christian or, by our example, to cause him or her to sin. When we love others, our freedom to do certain things won't be as important to us as strengthening the faith of a brother or sister in Christ.

9:1 Some Corinthians were questioning Paul's authority as an apostle. Paul gives his credentials as an apostle—he actually saw and talked with the resurrected Christ, who called him to be an apostle (see Acts 9:3–18). Such credentials make the advice he gives in this letter more persuasive. In 2 Corinthians 10—13, Paul defends his apostleship in greater detail.

9:1 Paul's hard work had visible results at Corinth—changed lives were the evidence that God was using him. Does your faith have an impact on others? You can be a life-changer, helping others grow spiritually, if you dedicate yourself to be used by God and let him make you effective.

9:4ff Paul uses himself as an illustration of giving up personal rights. Paul had the right to hospitality, to be married, to bring guests, to be paid for his work; but he willingly gave up these rights to win people to Christ. When your focus is on living for Christ, your rights become comparatively unimportant.

9:4–10 Jesus said that workers are worthy of their pay (Luke 10:7). Paul echoes this thought and urges the church to be sure to pay their Christian workers. We have the responsibility to care for our pastors, teachers, and other spiritual leaders. It is our duty to see that those who serve us in the ministry are fairly and adequately compensated.

apostles have of being a guest in your homes? 5If I had a wife, and if she were a believer, couldn't I bring her along on these trips just as the other disciples do, and as the Lord's brothers do, and as Peter does? 6And must Barnabas and I alone keep working for our living, while you supply these others? 7What soldier in the army has to pay his own expenses? And have you ever heard of a farmer who harvests his crop and doesn't have the right to eat some of it? What shepherd takes care of a flock of sheep and goats and isn't allowed to drink some of the milk? 8And I'm not merely quoting the opinions of men as to what is right. I'm telling you what God's law says. 9For in the law God gave to Moses he said that you must not put a muzzle on an ox to keep it from eating when it is treading out the wheat. Do you suppose God was thinking only about oxen when he said this? 10Wasn't he also thinking about us? Of course he was. He said this to show us that Christian workers should be paid by those they help. Those who do the plowing and threshing should expect some share of the harvest.

11We have planted good spiritual seed in your souls. Is it too much to ask, in return, for mere food and clothing? 12You give them to others who preach to you, and you should. But shouldn't we have an even greater right to them? Yet we have *never* used this right, but supply our own needs without your help. We have never demanded payment of any kind for fear that, if we did, you might be less interested in our message to you from Christ.

13Don't you realize that God told those working in his temple to take for their own needs some of the food brought there as gifts to him? And those who work at the altar of God get a share of the food that is brought by those offering it to the Lord. 14In the same way the Lord has given orders that those who preach the Gospel should be supported by those who accept it.

15Yet I have never asked you for one penny. And I am not writing this to hint that I would like to start now. In fact, I would rather die of hunger than lose the satisfaction I get from preaching to you without charge. 16For just preaching the Gospel isn't any special credit to me—I couldn't keep from preaching it if I wanted to. I would be utterly miserable. Woe unto me if I don't.

17If I were volunteering my services of my own free will, then the Lord would give me a special reward; but that is not the situation, for God has picked me out and given me this sacred trust and I have no choice. 18Under this circumstance, what is my pay? It is the special joy I get from preaching the Good News without expense to anyone, never demanding my rights.

19And this has a real advantage: I am not bound to obey anyone just because he pays my salary; yet I have freely and happily become a servant of any and all so that I can win them to Christ. 20When I am with the Jews I seem as one of them so that they will listen to the Gospel and I can win them to Christ. When I am with Gentiles who follow Jewish customs and ceremonies I don't argue, even though I don't agree, because I want to help them. 21When with the heathen I agree with them as much as I can, except of course that I must always do what is right as a Christian. And so, by agreeing, I can win their confidence and help them too.

22When I am with those whose consciences bother them easily, I don't act as though I know it all and don't say they are foolish; the result is that they are willing

9:5
Mt 8:14; 12:46
Mk 6:2,3
Lk 6:15

9:6
2 Thess 3:8

9:7
Deut 20:6
Prov 27:18
1 Cor 3:6
2 Cor 10:4
2 Tim 4:7
1 Pet 5:2

9:9
Deut 25:4
1 Tim 5:18

9:10
Rom 4:23
2 Tim 2:6

9:11
Rom 15:27

9:12
2 Cor 6:3; 11:7,12

9:13
Lev 6:16
Num 5:9,10

9:14
Mt 10:10
Lk 10:7
Gal 6:6
1 Tim 5:17

9:15
Acts 18:3; 20:33
2 Cor 11:8-10

9:16
Acts 9:15
Rom 1:14

9:17
Gal 2:7
Eph 3:1-8
Phil 1:16,17
Col 1:25

9:18
2 Cor 11:7
12:13

9:19
Gal 5:13

9:20
Acts 16:3
21:20-27
Rom 11:14

9:21
Rom 2:8-11
Gal 3:2

9:22
Rom 14:1; 15:1
1 Cor 10:33
2 Cor 11:29

9:5 *If I had a wife, and if,* implied. Literally, "Have we no right to lead about a wife that is a believer?"   **9:21** *I can win their confidence,* implied.

9:13 As part of their pay, priests in the Temple received a portion of the offerings as their food (see Numbers 18:8–24).

9:16 Preaching the gospel was Paul's gift and calling, and he said he couldn't stop preaching if he wanted to. He was driven by the desire to do what God wanted, using his gifts for God's glory. What special gifts has God given you? Are you motivated, like Paul, to glorify God with your gifts?

9:19–27 In 9:19–22 Paul says that he has freedom to do anything; in 9:24–27 he emphasizes a life of strict discipline. The Christian life involves both freedom and discipline. The goal of Paul's life was to glorify God and bring people to Christ. Thus he stayed free

of any philosophical position or material entanglement that could sidetrack him, while he strictly disciplined himself to carry out his goal and not get sidetracked by life's enticements. For Paul, both freedom and discipline were important tools to be used in God's service.

9:22, 23 Paul gives several important principles for ministry: (1) find common ground with those you contact; (2) avoid a know-it-all attitude; (3) make others feel accepted; (4) be sensitive to their needs and concerns; and (5) look for opportunities to tell them about Christ. These principles are just as valid for us as they were for Paul.

to let me help them. Yes, whatever a person is like, I try to find common ground with him so that he will let me tell him about Christ and let Christ save him. 23I do this to get the Gospel to them and also for the blessing I myself receive when I see them come to Christ.

24In a race, everyone runs but only one person gets first prize. So run your race to win. 25To win the contest you must deny yourselves many things that would keep you from doing your best. An athlete goes to all this trouble just to win a blue ribbon or a silver cup, but we do it for a heavenly reward that never disappears. 26So I run straight to the goal with purpose in every step. I fight to win. I'm not just shadow-boxing or playing around. 27Like an athlete I punish my body, treating it roughly, training it to do what it should, not what it wants to. Otherwise I fear that after enlisting others for the race, I myself might be declared unfit and ordered to stand aside.

Avoiding idol worship

10 For we must never forget, dear brothers, what happened to our people in the wilderness long ago. God guided them by sending a cloud that moved along ahead of them; and he brought them all safely through the waters of the Red Sea. 2This might be called their "baptism"—baptized both in sea and cloud!—as

9:24
Heb 12:1

9:25
1 Tim 6:12
2 Tim 2:5
Jas 1:12
1 Pet 5:4
Rev 2:10; 3:11

9:26
2 Tim 4:7,8
Heb 12:1

9:27
2 Cor 13:5

10:1
Ex 13:21,22
14:15-22

10:2
Rom 6:2,3

9:25 a silver cup, literally, "a wreath that quickly fades," given to the winners of the original Olympic races of Paul's time.

WHY WE DON'T GIVE UP
Perseverance, persistence, the prize!! The Christian life was never promised as an easy way to live; instead, Paul constantly reminds us that we must have a purpose and a plan because times will be difficult and Satan will attack. But we never persevere without the promise of a prize—a promise God will keep.

Reference	The Purpose	The Plan	The Prize
1 Corinthians 9:24–27	• Run your race to win • Run straight to the goal	• Deny yourself whatever is potentially harmful • Discipline your body, training it	• A heavenly reward that never disappears
Galatians 6:7–10	• Don't get tired of doing right • Don't get discouraged and give up • Be kind to everyone	• Plant the good things of the Spirit	• Reap everlasting life
Ephesians 6:10–20	• Put on all of God's armor • Pray all the time	• Use all the pieces of God's armor provided for you	• Standing safe against all the strategies and tricks of Satan
Philippians 3:12–14	• Keep working for the day when you will be all God wants you to be	• Forget the past, look forward to what lies ahead	• The heavenly prize to which God calls us
2 Timothy 2:3–13	• Teach these great truths to people who will pass them on • Hold on to your faith, even when you feel too weak to have any left	• Take your suffering as a soldier, and don't get tied up in worldly affairs • Follow the Lord's rules, as an athlete must do in order to win • Work hard, like a farmer who tends his fields for the harvest	• We will live with Christ; we will sit and rule with him • He always remains faithful to us and always carries out his promises

---

9:24–27 Winning a race requires purpose and discipline. Paul used this illustration to explain that the Christian life takes hard work, self-denial, and grueling preparation. As Christians, we are running toward our heavenly reward. The essential disciplines of prayer, Bible study, and worship equip us to run with vigor and stamina. Don't merely observe from the grandstand; don't just turn out to jog a couple of laps each morning. Train diligently, because the Christian life truly is important.

9:25 At times we must give up doing something we want in order to do what God wants. Each individual's goal determines the discipline and denial he must accept. Without a goal, discipline is nothing but self-punishment. With the goal of pleasing God, our

denial seems like nothing compared to the eternal reward that is ours.

9:27 When Paul said he might be declared unfit and ordered to stand aside, he did not mean he could lose his salvation, but rather that he could lose his privilege to tell others about Christ. It is easy to tell others how to live and then not to take our own advice. We must be careful to practice what we preach.

10:1ff In chapter 9 Paul uses himself as an example of a mature Christian who disciplines himself to better serve God. In chapter 10, he uses Israel as an example of spiritual immaturity shown by their overconfidence and lack of self-discipline.

followers of Moses—their commitment to hm as their leader. ³, ⁴And by a miracle God sent them food to eat and water to drink there in the desert; they drank the water that Christ gave them. He was there with them as a mighty Rock of spiritual refreshment. ⁵Yet after all this most of them did not obey God, and he destroyed them in the wilderness.

⁶From this lesson we are warned that we must not desire evil things as they did, ⁷nor worship idols as they did. (The Scriptures tell us, "The people sat down to eat and drink and then got up to dance" in worship of the golden calf.)

⁸Another lesson for us is what happened when some of them sinned with other men's wives, and 23,000 fell dead in one day. ⁹And don't try the Lord's patience—they did, and died from snake bites. ¹⁰And don't murmur against God and his dealings with you, as some of them did, for that is why God sent his Angel to destroy them.

¹¹All these things happened to them as examples—as object lessons to us—to warn us against doing the same things; they were written down so that we could read about them and learn from them in these last days as the world nears its end.

¹²So be careful. If you are thinking, "Oh, I would never behave like that"—let this be a warning to you. For you too may fall into sin. ¹³But remember this—the wrong desires that come into your life aren't anything new and different. Many others have faced exactly the same problems before you. And no temptation is irresistible. You can trust God to keep the temptation from becoming so strong that you can't stand up against it, for he has promised this and will do what he says. He will show you how to escape temptation's power so that you can bear up patiently against it.

¹⁴So, dear friends, carefully avoid idol-worship of every kind.

10:3,4 Ex 16:4,13-15
17:5,6
Num 20:11
Ps 78:15
Jn 4:10
6:32-58; 7:37
Rev 22:17

10:5 Num 14:29,37
26:65
Heb 3:17
Jude 5

10:6 Num 11:4,5,34
Ps 106:14

10:7 Ex 32:4-19

10:8 Num 25:1-9

10:9 Ex 17:2,7
Num 21:6

10:10 Num 16:3,32,41
Rom 13:11; 15:4
Heb 10:25

10:11 Rom 4:23

10:12 Rom 11:20
2 Pet 3:17

10:13 2 Pet 2:9

10:14 1 Jn 5:21

10:3, 4 *and by a miracle,* implied. Literally, "all ate the same supernatural food and drink." *they drank the water that Christ gave them,* literally, "For they drank of a spiritual Rock that followed them, and the Rock was Christ."

If I choose one course of action:	. . . does it help my witness for Christ? (9:19–22)	**MAKING CHOICES IN SENSITIVE ISSUES**

. . . am I motivated by a desire to help others to know Christ? (9:23; 10:33)

. . . does it help me do my best? (9:25)

. . . is it against a specific command in Scripture and thus cause me to sin? (10:12)

. . . is it best and helpful? (10:23, 33)

. . . am I thinking only of myself, or do I truly care about the other person? (10:24)

. . . am I acting lovingly or selfishly? (10:28–31)

. . . does it glorify God? (10:31)

. . . will it encourage someone else to sin? (10:32)

All of us make hundreds of choices every day. Most choices have no right or wrong attached to them—like what you wear or what you eat. But we always face decisions that carry a little more weight. We don't want to do wrong, and we don't want to cause others to do wrong, so how can we make such decisions?

10:10, 11 Today's pressures make it easy to ignore or forget the lessons of the past. But Paul cautions us to remember the lessons the Israelites learned about God so we can avoid repeating their errors. The key to remembering is to study the Bible regularly so that these lessons become continual reminders of how God wants us to live. We need not repeat their mistakes!

10:11 Did Paul think the world was going to end soon? Neither Paul nor even Jesus himself knew when the end of the world would come—God alone knows (Mark 13:32). For all practical purposes, however, we have been living in the last days since Christ's ascension. We are to be ready for Christ's return at any moment. Anyone close to Christ feels, with Paul, the urgency of spreading the gospel.

10:13 In a culture filled with moral depravity and pressures, Paul gave strong encouragement to the Corinthians about temptation.

He said: (1) wrong desires and temptations happen to everyone, so don't feel you've been singled out; (2) others have resisted temptation, and so can you; (3) any temptation can be resisted, because God will help you resist it. God helps you resist temptation by helping you (1) recognize those people and situations that give you trouble, (2) run from anything you know is wrong, (3) choose to do only what is right, (4) pray for God's help, and (5) seek friends who love God and can offer help in times of temptation. Running from a tempting situation is the first step to victory (see 2 Timothy 2:22).

10:14 Idol worship was a serious problem in Corinth. There were several pagan temples in the city, and they were very popular. The statues of wood or stone were not bad in themselves, but people gave them credit for what only God could do, such as provide good weather, crops, and children. Idolatry is still a serious

10:16
Mt 26:26-29
Acts 2:42
1 Cor 11:25-27

10:17
Rom 12:4,5
1 Cor 12:12,13

10:18
Deut 12:17
Lev 7:15

10:19
1 Cor 8:4

10:20
Deut 32:16,17
Ps 106:36,37
Gal 4:8
Rev 9:20

10:21
Deut 32:38
Isa 65:11
2 Cor 6:15

10:22
Deut 32:21
Ezek 22:14

10:23
Rom 14:19
1 Cor 6:12

10:24
Rom 15:1,2

10:25
Acts 10:15
1 Cor 8:7
1 Tim 4:4

10:26
Ps 24:1; 105:12

10:27
Lk 10:8,9

10:28
Rom 14:16
1 Cor 8:7,10

10:31
Mt 5:15,16
Jn 15:8
Rom 14:6
Phil 1:11

10:32
Acts 24:16
1 Cor 8:13

¹⁵You are intelligent people. Look now and see for yourselves whether what I am about to say is true. ¹⁶When we ask the Lord's blessing upon our drinking from the cup of wine at the Lord's Table, this means, doesn't it, that all who drink it are sharing together the blessing of Christ's blood? And when we break off pieces of the bread from the loaf to eat there together, this shows that we are sharing together in the benefits of his body. ¹⁷No matter how many of us there are, we all eat from the same loaf, showing that we are all parts of the one body of Christ. ¹⁸And the Jewish people, all who eat the sacrifices, are united by that act.

¹⁹What am I trying to say? Am I saying that the idols to whom the heathen bring sacrifices are really alive and are real gods, and that these sacrifices are of some value? No, not at all. ²⁰What I am saying is that those who offer food to these idols are united together in sacrificing to demons, certainly not to God. And I don't want any of you to be partners with demons when you eat the same food, along with the heathen, that has been offered to these idols. ²¹You cannot drink from the cup at the Lord's Table and at Satan's table, too. You cannot eat bread both at the Lord's Table and at Satan's table.

²²What? Are you tempting the Lord to be angry with you? Are you stronger than he is?

²³You are certainly free to eat food offered to idols if you want to; it's not against God's laws to eat such meat, but that doesn't mean that you should go ahead and do it. It may be perfectly legal, but it may not be best and helpful. ²⁴Don't think only of yourself. Try to think of the other fellow, too, and what is best for him.

²⁵Here's what you should do. Take any meat you want that is sold at the market. Don't ask whether or not it was offered to idols, lest the answer hurt your conscience. ²⁶For the earth and every good thing in it belongs to the Lord and is yours to enjoy.

²⁷If someone who isn't a Christian asks you out to dinner, go ahead; accept the invitation if you want to. Eat whatever is on the table and don't ask any questions about it. Then you won't know whether or not it has been used as a sacrifice to idols, and you won't risk having a bad conscience over eating it. ²⁸But if someone warns you that this meat has been offered to idols, then don't eat it for the sake of the man who told you, and of his conscience. ²⁹In this case *his* feeling about it is the important thing, not yours.

But why, you may ask, must I be guided and limited by what someone else thinks? ³⁰If I can thank God for the food and enjoy it, why let someone spoil everything just because he thinks I am wrong? ³¹Well, I'll tell you why. It is because you must do everything for the glory of God, even your eating and drinking. ³²So don't be a stumbling block to anyone, whether they are Jews or

---

problem today. We don't put our trust in statues of wood and stone, but in paper money and plastic cards. Thanking anything for what God alone provides is idolatry. When we understand contemporary parallels to idolatry, Paul's words to "avoid idol-worship of every kind" become much more meaningful.

10:16–21 The idea of unity with God through eating a sacrifice was strong in Judaism and Christianity as well as paganism. In Old Testament days, when a Jew offered a sacrifice, he ate a part of that sacrifice as a way of restoring his unity with God, against whom he had sinned (Deuteronomy 12:17, 18). Similarly, Christians participate in Christ's once-for-all sacrifice when they eat the bread and drink the wine symbolizing his body and blood. Recent converts from paganism could not help being affected if they knowingly ate meat offered to idols.

10:21 As followers of Christ we must give him our total allegiance. We cannot, as Paul explains, eat "both at the Lord's table and at Satan's." Eating at the Lord's table means communing with Christ and identifying with his death. Eating at Satan's table means identifying with Satan by participating in actions that worship or promote heathen (or evil) activities. Are you trying to lead two lives, following the desires of both Christ and the crowd? The Bible says you can't do both at the same time.

10:22–24 Sometimes it's hard to know when to defer to the weaker brother. Paul gives a simple rule of thumb to help in making the decision—we should be sensitive and gracious. While we have freedom in Christ, we shouldn't exercise our freedom at the cost of hurting a Christian brother or sister. For more on the proper attitude toward the weaker brother, see the notes in 8:10–13 and Romans 14.

10:25 When we become too worried about our every action, we become legalistic and cannot enjoy life. God has given us all things richly to enjoy (10:26). If you know something is a problem, then deal with it, but don't go looking for problems. When we focus on the law, we worry only about protecting ourselves. When we focus on love, our concern is to help others.

10:31 God must so permeate our lives that all we do is for his glory. Keep this as a guiding principle by asking, "Is this glorifying God?" or "How can I glorify God through this?"

Gentiles or Christians. 33That is the plan I follow, too. I try to please everyone in everything I do, not doing what I like or what is best for me, but what is best for them, so that they may be saved.

10:33
Rom 11:14
15:1-2
1 Cor 9:22
13:1-8

3. Instruction on public worship

Questions about covering the head in worship

11 And you should follow my example, just as I follow Christ's.

2I am so glad, dear brothers, that you have been remembering and doing everything I taught you. 3But there is one matter I want to remind you about: that a wife is responsible to her husband, her husband is responsible to Christ, and Christ is responsible to God. 4That is why, if a man refuses to remove his hat while praying or preaching, he dishonors Christ. 5And that is why a woman who publicly prays or prophesies without a covering on her head dishonors her husband [for her covering is a sign of her subjection to him]. 6Yes, if she refuses to wear a head covering, then she should cut off all her hair. And if it is shameful for a woman to have her head shaved, then she should wear a covering. 7But a man should not wear anything on his head [when worshiping, for his hat is a sign of subjection to men].

God's glory is man made in his image, and man's glory is the woman. 8The first man didn't come from woman, but the first woman came out of man. 9And Adam, the first man, was not made for Eve's benefit, but Eve was made for Adam. 10So a woman should wear a covering on her head as a sign that she is under man's authority, a fact for all the angels to notice and rejoice in.

11But remember that in God's plan men and women need each other. 12For

11:1
1 Cor 4:16

11:3
Gen 3:16
1 Cor 3:23; 7:17
Gal 4:4
Eph 5:23
Phil 2:7

11:5
Lk 2:36
Acts 21:9

11:6
Num 5:18

11:7
Gen 1:26
Jas 3:9

11:8
Gen 2:21
1 Tim 2:13

11:9
Gen 2:18

11:12
Rom 11:36

11:5 *for her covering is a sign of her subjection to him,* implied in vss 7, 10. **11:7** *when worshiping, for his hat is a sign of subjection to men,* implied. **11:8** *the first woman came out of man,* Gen 2:21, 22. **11:10** *as a sign that she is under man's authority,* literally, "For this cause ought the woman to have power on her head." *a fact for all the angels to notice and rejoice in,* literally, "because of the angels."

10:33 Paul's criterion was not what he liked best, but what was best for those around him. There are several hurtful attitudes toward others: (1) being insensitive and doing what we want, no matter who is hurt by it; (2) being oversensitive and doing nothing, for fear someone may be displeased; (3) being a "yes person" by going along with everything, trying to gain approval from people rather than from God. In this age of "me first" and "looking out for number one," Paul's startling statement is a good standard. When we make the good of others one of our primary goals, we develop a servant heart.

11:1ff In this section Paul's main concern is irreverence in worship. We need to read it in the context of the situation in Corinth. The matter of wearing hats or head coverings, although seemingly insignificant, had become a big problem because two cultural backgrounds were colliding. Jewish women always covered their heads in worship. For a woman to uncover her head in public was a sign of loose morals. On the other hand, Greek women were used to worshiping without head coverings.

In this letter Paul has already spoken about divisions in the church and scruples. Both are involved in this issue. Paul's solution comes from his desire for unity among church members and appropriateness in the worship service. He accepts God's sovereignty in creating the rules for relationships.

11:1 Why did Paul say, "You should follow my example"? Paul wasn't being proud—he did not think of himself as sinless. At this time, however, the Corinthian believers did not know much about the life and ministry of Christ. Paul could not tell them to imitate Jesus, because the Gospels had not yet been written, so they did not know what Jesus was like. The best way to point these new Christians to Christ was to point them to a Christian whom they trusted (see also Galatians 4:12; Philippians 3:17; 1 Thessalonians 1:6; 2:14; 2 Thessalonians 3:7, 9). Paul had been in Corinth almost two years and had built up a relationship of trust with many of these people.

11:2–16 This section focuses on attitudes toward worship, not on

marriage or the role of women in the church. While Paul's specific instructions may be cultural (women wearing hats in worship), the principles behind his specific instructions are timeless, including respect for spouse, reverence and appropriateness in worship, and focusing all of life on God. If anything you do can easily offend members and divide the church, then change your ways to promote church unity. Thus Paul told the women who were not wearing head coverings to wear them; not because it was a Scriptural command, but because it kept the congregation from dividing over a petty issue that served only to take people's minds off Christ.

11:3, 4 Submission is a key element in the smooth functioning of any business, government, or family. God ordained submission in certain relationships to prevent chaos. It is essential to understand that submission is not surrender, withdrawal, or apathy. And it does not mean inferiority, because God created all people in his image and all have equal value. Submission is mutual commitment and cooperation.

Thus God calls for submission among *equals*. He did not make the man superior; he made a way for the man and woman to work together. Jesus Christ, although equal with God the Father, submitted to him to carrry out the plan for salvation. Likewise, although equal to man under God, the wife should submit to her husband for the sake of their marriage and family. Submission between equals is submission by choice, not force. We serve God in these relationships by willing submission to others in our church, to our spouses, and to our government leaders.

11:9–11 By referring to Adam and Eve, the first man and woman, Paul was saying that God created lines of authority in order for his created world to function smoothly. Although there must be lines of authority, even in marriage, there should *not* be lines of superiority. God created men and women with unique and complementary characteristics. One sex is not better than the other. We must not let the issue of authority and submission become a wedge to destroy oneness in marriage. Instead, we should use our unique gifts to strengthen our marriages and glorify God.

although the first woman came out of man, all men have been born from women ever since, and both men and women come from God their Creator.

11:13
Lk 12:57
¹³What do you yourselves really think about this? Is it right for a woman to pray in public without covering her head? ¹⁴, ¹⁵Doesn't even instinct itself teach us that women's heads should be covered? For women are proud of their long hair, while a man with long hair tends to be ashamed. ¹⁶But if anyone wants to argue about

11:16
1 Tim 6:4
this, all I can say is that we never teach anything else than this—that a woman should wear a covering when prophesying or praying publicly in the church, and all the churches feel the same way about it.

Order at the Lord's Supper

¹⁷Next on my list of items to write you about is something else I cannot agree with. For it sounds as if more harm than good is done when you meet together for your communion services. ¹⁸Everyone keeps telling me about the arguing that goes

11:18,19
1 Cor 1:10
2 Pet 2:1
1 Tim 4:1
1 Jn 2:19
on in these meetings, and the divisions developing among you, and I can just about believe it. ¹⁹But I suppose you feel this is necessary so that you who are always right will become known and recognized!

11:21
Jude 12
²⁰When you come together to eat, it isn't the Lord's Supper you are eating, ²¹but your own. For I am told that everyone hastily gobbles all the food he can without waiting to share with the others, so that one doesn't get enough and goes hungry

11:22
Lev 19:30
1 Cor 10:32
Jas 2:6
while another has too much to drink and gets drunk. ²²What? Is this really true? Can't you do your eating and drinking at home, to avoid disgracing the church and shaming those who are poor and can bring no food? What am I supposed to say about these things? Do you want me to praise you? Well, I certainly do not!

11:23
Mt 26:26-28
Mk 14:22-24
Lk 22:17-20
1 Cor 10:16
Gal 1:12
²³For this is what the Lord himself has said about his Table, and I have passed it on to you before: That on the night when Judas betrayed him, the Lord Jesus took bread, ²⁴and when he had given thanks to God for it, he broke it and gave it to his disciples and said, "Take this and eat it. This is my body, which is given for you. Do this to remember me." ²⁵In the same way, he took the cup of wine after supper,

11:25
Lk 22:20
1 Cor 10:16
2 Cor 3:6
saying, "This cup is the new agreement between God and you that has been

11:24 *given.* Some ancient manuscripts read, "broken."

11:14, 15 In talking about head coverings and length of hair, Paul is saying that believers should look and behave in ways that are honorable within their own culture. In many cultures long hair on men is considered appropriate and masculine. In Corinth, it was thought to be a sign of sexual perversion. And women with short hair were labeled prostitutes. Paul was saying that in the Corinthian culture, women should keep their long hair. If short hair on women was a sign of prostitution, then a Christian woman with short hair would find it even more difficult to be a believable witness for Jesus Christ. The issue is similar with head coverings, considered a sign of rebellion in Jewish culture. Paul isn't saying we should adopt all the practices of our culture, but that we should avoid appearances and behavior that detract from our goal of being believable witnesses for Jesus Christ and demonstrating our Christian faith.

11:17–34 The Lord's Supper is a visible representation of the gospel, the death of Christ for our sins. It focuses on the remembrance of Christ's death and the glorious hope of his return. It is an act of fellowship among believers. And it strengthens our faith through fellowship with Christ and with other believers.

11:21 When the Lord's Supper was celebrated in the early church, it included a feast or fellowship meal followed by communion. In Corinth the fellowship meal had become a time of gluttony and excessive drinking rather than a time of preparation for communion. Although the feast was similar to a potluck, there was little sharing and caring. This certainly did not demonstrate the unity and love that should characterize the church, nor was it a preparation for communion. Paul condemned these actions and reminded the church of the real purpose of the Lord's Supper.

11:24, 25 What does the Lord's Supper mean? The early church

remembered that Jesus taught about the Lord's Supper on the night of the Passover (Luke 22:13–20). Just as Passover celebrated deliverance from slavery in Egypt, so the Lord's Supper celebrates deliverance from sin by Christ's death.

Christians have several options about what Christ meant when he said, "This is my body." Some believe that the wine and bread actually become Christ's physical blood and body. Others believe that the bread and wine remain unchanged, but Christ is spiritually present with the bread and wine. Still others believe that the bread and wine symbolize Christ's body and blood. Christians agree, however, that the important point to remember is that God is a part of the communion experience, blessing us as we remember Christ's death until he comes again.

11:25 What is this new agreement (covenant)? With the old agreement, people could approach God only through the priests and the sacrificial system. Jesus' death on the cross brought in the new agreement between God and us. Now all people can personally approach God and communicate with him. The old agreement was first made on Mount Sinai between God and the Israelites (Exodus 19, 20) and was designed to point to the day when Jesus Christ would come. The new agreement completes, rather than replaces, the old agreement, fulfilling everything the old agreement looked forward to. Eating the bread and drinking the cup shows we are regularly recommitting ourselves to this new agreement. See Jeremiah 31:31–34 for a prediction of it.

11:25 Jesus said, "Do this to remember me." How do we remember Christ in the Lord's Supper? By thinking about what he did and why he did it. If the Lord's Supper becomes just a ritual or pious habit, it no longer remembers Christ.

established and set in motion by my blood. Do this in remembrance of me whenever you drink it." 26For every time you eat this bread and drink this cup you are re-telling the message of the Lord's death, that he has died for you. Do this until he comes again.

27So if anyone eats this bread and drinks from this cup of the Lord in an unworthy manner, he is guilty of sin against the body and the blood of the Lord. 28That is why a man should examine himself carefully before eating the bread and drinking from the cup. 29For if he eats the bread and drinks from the cup unworthily, not thinking about the body of Christ and what it means, he is eating and drinking God's judgment upon himself; for he is trifling with the death of Christ. 30That is why many of you are weak and sick, and some have even died.

31But if you carefully examine yourselves before eating you will not need to be judged and punished. 32Yet, when we are judged and punished by the Lord, it is so that we will not be condemned with the rest of the world. 33So, dear brothers, when you gather for the Lord's Supper—the communion service—wait for each other; 34if anyone is really hungry he should eat at home so that he won't bring punishment upon himself when you meet together.

I'll talk to you about the other matters after I arrive.

Paul teaches about spiritual gifts

12 And now, brothers, I want to write about the special abilities the Holy Spirit gives to each of you, for I don't want any misunderstanding about them. 2You will remember that before you became Christians you went around from one idol to another, not one of which could speak a single word. 3But now you are meeting people who claim to speak messages from the Spirit of God. How can you know whether they are really inspired by God or whether they are fakes? Here is the test: no one speaking by the power of the Spirit of God can curse Jesus, and no one can say, "Jesus is Lord," and really mean it, unless the Holy Spirit is helping him.

4Now God gives us many kinds of special abilities, but it is the same Holy Spirit who is the source of them all. 5There are different kinds of service to God, but it is the same Lord we are serving. 6There are many ways in which God works in our lives, but it is the same God who does the work in and through all of us who are his. 7The Holy Spirit displays God's power through each of us as a means of helping the entire church.

8To one person the Spirit gives the ability to give wise advice; someone else may be especially good at studying and teaching, and this is his gift from the same Spirit. 9He gives special faith to another, and to someone else the power to heal the

11:26
Acts 1:11
Rev 1:7

11:27
Heb 10:29

11:28
Mt 26:20-22
2 Cor 13:5
Gal 6:4

11:31
1 Jn 1:9
Rev 3:19

11:32
2 Sam 7:14
Job 5:17
Ps 94:12
Amos 3:2
Heb 12:5-7

11:34
1 Cor 4:19

12:1
1 Cor 14:1

12:2
Isa 46:7
Hab 1:18,19
1 Thess 1:9
1 Pet 4:3

12:3
Jn 13:13
Rom 10:9
1 Jn 4:2

12:4
Rom 12:6
Eph 4:4
Heb 2:4

12:6
Eph 1:23

12:7
Rom 12:6
1 Cor 14:26
Eph 4:12

12:8
1 Cor 2:6,11

12:9
Mt 17:19,20

11:27 Paul gives specific instructions on how the Lord's Supper should be observed. (1) We should take the Lord's Supper with a repentant attitude because we are remembering that Christ died for our sins (11:26). (2) We should take it after self-examination (11:28). We are to be prepared and ready, doing it only through our belief in and love for Christ. (3) We should take it in recognition of Jesus' act of love in taking away the punishment we deserve for our sins (11:29). (4) We should take it with mutual consideration (11:33), waiting until everyone is present and eating in an orderly and unified manner.

11:27 When Paul said no one should take the Lord's Supper in an unworthy manner, he was speaking to the church members who were rushing into it without thinking of its meaning. *No one* is worthy to take the Lord's Supper. We are all sinners saved by grace. This is why we should prepare ourselves for communion through healthy introspection, confession of sin, and resolution of differences with others, removing the barriers to our relationship with Christ and with other believers. Don't let awareness of your sin keep you away from communion, but drive you to it.

11:30 This may have been a special supernatural judgment on the Corinthian church. It highlights the seriousness of the communion service. The Lord's Supper is not to be taken lightly;

this new agreement cost Jesus his life. It is not a meaningless ritual, but a sacrament given by Christ to help strengthen our faith.

12:1ff The special abilities given to each person by the Holy Spirit are called *spiritual gifts*. They enable us to minister to the needs of the body of believers. This chapter is not an exhaustive list of spiritual gifts (see Romans 12; Ephesians 4; 1 Peter 4:10, 11 for more examples). There are many gifts, people have different gifts, and one gift is not superior to another. They all come from the Holy Spirit, and their purpose is to build up Christ's body, the church.

12:1ff Instead of building and unifying the Corinthian church, spiritual gifts were splitting it. They had become symbols of spiritual power, causing rivalries and setting up hierarchies of supposedly spiritual and unspiritual people. This was a terrible misuse of spiritual gifts, because their purpose is always to help the church function more effectively, not to divide it.

12:3 Anyone can claim to speak for God, and the world is full of false teachers. Paul gives us a test to help us discern whether or not a messenger is really from God: does he or she confess Christ as Lord? Don't naively accept the words of all who claim to speak for God; test their credentials by finding what they teach about Christ.

12:9 All Christians have faith. Some, however, have the spiritual

12:10
Acts 2:4
Rom 12:6
1 Cor 14:26-32
Gal 3:5
1 Jn 4:1

12:11
Rom 12:6-8
Eph 4:7
Heb 2:4

12:12
Rom 12:4
1 Cor 10:17
12:27

12:13
Jn 6:63; 7:37-39
Rom 6:5
Gal 3:27,28
Eph 2:13-16,18
Col 3:11

12:18
Rom 12:6
1 Cor 12:28

12:27
Rom 12:4,5
1 Cor 12:12
Eph 1:22,23
4:12; 5:23,30
Col 1:24

12:28
Num 11:16,17
Acts 13:1
Rom 12:6-8
Eph 2:20; 3:5
4:11
1 Tim 5:17
Heb 13:17

sick. 10He gives power for doing miracles to some, and to others power to prophesy and preach. He gives someone else the power to know whether evil spirits are speaking through those who claim to be giving God's messages—or whether it is really the Spirit of God who is speaking. Still another person is able to speak in languages he never learned; and others, who do not know the language either, are given power to understand what he is saying. 11It is the same and only Holy Spirit who gives all these gifts and powers, deciding which each one of us should have.

Believers are the body of Christ

12Our bodies have many parts, but the many parts make up only one body when they are all put together. So it is with the "body" of Christ. 13Each of us is a part of the one body of Christ. Some of us are Jews, some are Gentiles, some are slaves and some are free. But the Holy Spirit has fitted us all together into one body. We have been baptized into Christ's body by the one Spirit, and have all been given that same Holy Spirit.

14Yes, the body has many parts, not just one part. 15If the foot says, "I am not a part of the body because I am not a hand," that does not make it any less a part of the body. 16And what would you think if you heard an ear say, "I am not part of the body because I am only an ear, and not an eye"? Would that make it any less a part of the body? 17Suppose the whole body were an eye—then how would you hear? Or if your whole body were just one big ear, how could you smell anything?

18But that isn't the way God has made us. He has made many parts for our bodies and has put each part just where he wants it. 19What a strange thing a body would be if it had only one part! 20So he has made many parts, but still there is only one body.

21The eye can never say to the hand, "I don't need you." The head can't say to the feet, "I don't need you."

22And some of the parts that seem weakest and least important are really the most necessary. 23Yes, we are especially glad to have some parts that seem rather odd! And we carefully protect from the eyes of others those parts that should not be seen, 24while of course the parts that may be seen do not require this special care. So God has put the body together in such a way that extra honor and care are given to those parts that might otherwise seem less important. 25This makes for happiness among the parts, so that the parts have the same care for each other that they do for themselves. 26If one part suffers, all parts suffer with it, and if one part is honored, all the parts are glad.

27Now here is what I am trying to say: All of you together are the one body of Christ and each one of you is a separate and necessary part of it. 28Here is a list of some of the parts he has placed in his Church, which is his body:

---

gift of faith which is an unusual measure of trust in the Holy Spirit's power.

12:12 Paul compares the body of Christ to a human body. Each part has a specific function that is necessary to the body as a whole. The parts are different for a purpose, and in their differences they must work together. Christians must avoid two common errors: (1) being too proud of their abilities, or (2) thinking they have nothing to give to the body of believers. Instead of comparing ourselves to one another, we must use our different gifts, together, to spread the Good News of salvation.

12:13 The church is composed of many types of people from a variety of backgrounds with a multitude of gifts and abilities. It is easy for these differences to divide people, as was the case in Corinth. But despite the differences, all believers have one thing in common—faith in Christ. On this essential truth the church finds unity. All believers are baptized by one Holy Spirit into one body of believers, the church. We don't lose our individual identities, but we have an overriding oneness in Christ. When a person becomes a Christian, the Holy Spirit takes up residence and he or she is born into God's family. As members of God's family, we may have

different interests and gifts, but we have a common goal.

12:14–17 Using the analogy of the body, Paul emphasizes the importance of each church member (see the note on 12:12). If a seemingly insignificant part is taken away, the whole body becomes less effective (12:22). Thinking that your gift is more important than someone else's is spiritual pride. We should not look down on those who seem unimportant, and we should not be jealous of others who have impressive gifts. Instead, we must use the gifts we have been given and encourage others to use theirs. If we don't, the body of believers will be less effective.

12:25, 26 What is your response when a fellow Christian is honored? When someone is suffering? We are called to rejoice with those who rejoice and weep with those who weep (Romans 12:15). Too often, unfortunately, we are jealous of those who rejoice and separate ourselves from those who weep. Believers are in the world together—there is no such thing as individualistic Christianity. We can't concern ourselves only with our own relationship with God; we need to get involved in the lives of others.

Apostles,
Prophets—those who preach God's Word,
Teachers,
Those who do miracles,
Those who have the gift of healing,
Those who can help others,
Those who can get others to work together,
Those who speak in languages they have never learned.

29Is everyone an apostle? Of course not. Is everyone a preacher? No. Are all teachers? Does everyone have the power to do miracles? 30Can everyone heal the sick? Of course not. Does God give all of us the ability to speak in languages we've never learned? Can just anyone understand and translate what those are saying who have that gift of foreign speech? 31No, but try your best to have the more important of these gifts.

First, however, let me tell you about something else that is better than any of them!

12:31
1 Cor 14:1-39

The characteristics of love

13 If I had the gift of being able to speak in other languages without learning them, and could speak in every language there is in all of heaven and earth, but didn't love others, I would only be making noise. 2If I had the gift of prophecy and knew all about what is going to happen in the future, knew everything about *everything*, but didn't love others, what good would it do? Even if I had the gift of faith so that I could speak to a mountain and make it move, I would still be worth nothing at all without love. 3If I gave everything I have to poor people, and if I were burned alive for preaching the Gospel but didn't love others, it would be of no value whatever.

4Love is very patient and kind, never jealous or envious, never boastful or proud, 5never haughty or selfish or rude. Love does not demand its own way. It is not irritable or touchy. It does not hold grudges and will hardly even notice when others do it wrong. 6It is never glad about injustice, but rejoices whenever truth wins out. 7If you love someone you will be loyal to him no matter what the cost. You will always believe in him, always expect the best of him, and always stand your ground in defending him.

8All the special gifts and powers from God will someday come to an end, but love goes on forever. Someday prophecy, and speaking in unknown languages, and special knowledge—these gifts will disappear. 9Now we know so little, even with our special gifts, and the preaching of those most gifted is still so poor. 10But when we have been made perfect and complete, then the need for these inadequate special gifts will come to an end, and they will disappear.

11It's like this: when I was a child I spoke and thought and reasoned as a child does. But when I became a man my thoughts grew far beyond those of my childhood, and now I have put away the childish things. 12In the same way, we can

13:1
1 Tim 1:5

13:2
Mk 17:20
Lk 17:6
1 Cor 12:8-10

13:3
Mt 6:1,2

13:4
1 Cor 4:6
1 Pet 4:8

13:5
1 Cor 10:24
Phil 2:4; 4:8

13:6
Ps 10:3
Prov 10:12
Rom 1:32
2 Thess 2:12
2 Jn 4

13:7
Gal 6:2

13:8
1 Cor 13:1,2

13:9
1 Cor 8:2

13:10
Isa 60:19
Jer 31:34

13:12
2 Cor 3:18; 5:7
Phil 3:12
1 Jn 3:2

12:30 Paul discusses the subject of speaking in tongues in more detail in chapter 14.

12:31 The more important gifts are those that are more beneficial to the body of Christ. Paul has already made it clear that one gift is not superior to another, but he urges the believers to discover how they can serve Christ's body best with the gifts God has given them. Your spiritual gifts are not for your own self-advancement. They were given for serving God and enhancing the spiritual growth of the body.

13:1ff In chapter 12 Paul gives evidence of the Corinthians' lack of love, chapter 13 explains what real love is, and chapter 14 shows how love works. Love is more important than all the spiritual gifts exercised in the church body. Great faith and miracle-working power produce very little without love. Love makes our actions and

gifts useful. Although people have different gifts, love is available to everyone.

13:4-7 Our society confuses love and lust. Unlike lust, God's kind of love is directed outward toward others, not inward toward ourselves. It is utterly unselfish.

13:4-7 This love is not natural. It is possible only if God supernaturally helps us set aside our own desires and instincts, so we can give love while expecting nothing in return. Thus the closer we come to Christ, the more love we will show to others.

13:10 God gives us spiritual gifts for life on earth in order to build up, serve, and strengthen fellow Christians. The spiritual gifts are for the church. In eternity, we will be made perfect and complete and will be in the very presence of God. We will no longer need the spiritual gifts, so they will come to an end.

see and understand only a little about God now, as if we were peering at his reflection in a poor mirror; but someday we are going to see him in his completeness, face to face. Now all that I know is hazy and blurred, but then I will see everything clearly, just as clearly as God sees into my heart right now.

13:13
Mt 22:37-39
Gal 5:6

13There are three things that remain—faith, hope, and love—and the greatest of these is love.

Paul teaches about the gifts of prophecy and tongues

14:1
Lev 19:18
Num 11:25
Mt 22:37-40
Mk 12:29-31
Rom 12:6
13:8-10
1 Cor 12:1
Gal 5:14
Eph 5:2
Col 3:14
1 Tim 1:5
Jas 2:8

14 Let love be your greatest aim; nevertheless, ask also for the special abilities the Holy Spirit gives, and especially the gift of prophecy, being able to preach the messages of God.

14:2
Mk 16:17
Acts 2:4
10:46,47; 19:6

2But if your gift is that of being able to "speak in tongues," that is, to speak in languages you haven't learned, you will be talking to God but not to others, since they won't be able to understand you. You will be speaking by the power of the Spirit but it will all be a secret. 3But one who prophesies, preaching the messages of God, is helping others grow in the Lord, encouraging and comforting them. 4So a person "speaking in tongues" helps himself grow spiritually, but one who prophesies, preaching messages from God, helps the entire church grow in holiness and happiness.

14:3
Rom 14:19

14:4
1 Cor 12:10,30
14:18,19,26-28

5I wish you all had the gift of "speaking in tongues" but, even more, I wish you were all able to prophesy, preaching God's messages, for that is a greater and more useful power than to speak in unknown languages—unless, of course, you can tell everyone afterwards what you were saying, so that they can get some good out of it too.

14:6
Rom 6:17
1 Cor 12:8; 13:2
Eph 1:16,17

6Dear friends, even if I myself should come to you talking in some language you don't understand, how would that help you? But if I speak plainly what God has revealed to me, and tell you the things I know, and what is going to happen, and the great truths of God's Word—that is what you need; that is what will help you. 7Even musical instruments—the flute, for instance, or the harp—are examples of the need for speaking in plain, simple English rather than in unknown languages. For no one will recognize the tune the flute is playing unless each note is sounded clearly. 8And if the army bugler doesn't play the right notes, how will the soldiers know that they are being called to battle? 9In the same way, if you talk to a person in some language he doesn't understand, how will he know what you mean? You might as well be talking to an empty room.

14:8
Num 10:9
Jer 4:19
Ezek 33:2-6
Joel 2:1

10I suppose that there are hundreds of different languages in the world, and all are excellent for those who understand them, 11but to me they mean nothing. A person talking to me in one of these languages will be a stranger to me and I will be a stranger to him. 12Since you are so anxious to have special gifts from the Holy

14:12
Rom 14:19

14:7 *simple English.* The local language, whatever it is.

13:12 Paul offers a glimpse into the future to give us hope that one day we will be complete when we see God face to face. This truth should strengthen our faith—we don't have all the answers now, but then we will. Someday we will see Christ in person and be able to see with God's perspective.

13:13 In the morally corrupt society of Corinth, love had become a mixed-up term with little meaning. Today people are still confused about love. Love is the greatest of all human qualities. It involves unselfish service to others; therefore, it gives evidence that you care. Faith is the foundation and content of God's message, hope is the attitude and focus, love is the action. When faith and hope are in line, you are free to truly love because you understand how God loved. Love is an attribute of God himself (1 John 4:8).

14:1 Prophecy may involve predicting future events, but its main purpose is to communicate God's Word to people, providing insight, warning, correction, and encouragement.

14:2 The gift of speaking in tongues was a concern of the Corinthian church because it had caused disorder in worship. Speaking in tongues is a legitimate gift of the Holy Spirit, but the Corinthian believers were using it as a sign of spiritual superiority rather than as a means to spiritual unity. Do you want God's special gifts to build up the church or to use for yourself? Spiritual gifts are beneficial only when they are properly used to help everyone in the church. We do not exercise them to make *ourselves* feel good.

14:2ff Paul makes several points about speaking in tongues: (1) it is a spiritual gift from God (14:2); (2) it is a desirable gift even though it isn't a requirement of faith (12:28–31); (3) it is less important than prophecy and teaching (14:4). Although Paul himself spoke in tongues, he stresses prophecy (preaching) because it benefits the whole church, while speaking in tongues primarily benefits the speaker. Public worship must be understandable and beneficial to the whole church.

Spirit, ask him for the very best, for those that will be of real help to the whole church.

13If someone is given the gift of speaking in unknown tongues, he should pray also for the gift of knowing what he has said, so that he can tell people afterwards, plainly. 14For if I pray in a language I don't understand, my spirit is praying but I don't know what I am saying.

14:13
1 Cor 12:10

15Well, then, what shall I do? I will do both. I will pray in unknown tongues and also in ordinary language that everyone understands. I will sing in unknown tongues and also in ordinary language, so that I can understand the praise I am giving; 16for if you praise and thank God with the spirit alone, speaking in another language, how can those who don't understand you be praising God along with you? How can they join you in giving thanks when they don't know what you are saying? 17You will be giving thanks very nicely, no doubt, but the other people present won't be helped.

14:15
Ps 47:6,7
Eph 5:19
Col 3:16

14:16
1 Chron 16:36
Neh 5:13; 8:6
Ps 106:48

14:17
Rom 14:19

18I thank God that I "speak in tongues" privately more than any of the rest of you. 19But in public worship I would much rather speak five words that people can understand and be helped by, than ten thousand words while "speaking in tongues" in an unknown language.

20Dear brothers, don't be childish in your understanding of these things. Be innocent babies when it comes to planning evil, but be men of intelligence in understanding matters of this kind. 21We are told in the ancient Scriptures that God would send men from other lands to speak in foreign languages to his people, but even then they would not listen. 22So you see that being able to "speak in tongues" is not a sign to God's children concerning his power, but is a sign to the unsaved. However, prophecy (preaching the deep truths of God) is what the Christians need, and unbelievers aren't yet ready for it. 23Even so, if an unsaved person, or someone who doesn't have these gifts, comes to church and hears you all talking in other languages, he is likely to think you are crazy. 24But if you prophesy, preaching God's Word, [even though such preaching is mostly for believers] and an unsaved person or a new Christian comes in who does not understand about these things, all these sermons will convince him of the fact that he is a sinner, and his conscience will be pricked by everything he hears. 25As he listens, his secret thoughts will be laid bare and he will fall down on his knees and worship God, declaring that God is really there among you.

14:20
Mt 11:25
Rom 16:19
Eph 4:14
Heb 5:12

14:21
Isa 28:11
Jn 10:34

14:22
1 Cor 14:1

14:23
Acts 2:12,13

14:24
1 Cor 14:1

14:25
Isa 45:14
Zech 8:23
Heb 4:12,13

Worship in an orderly way

26Well, my brothers, let's add up what I am saying. When you meet together some will sing, another will teach, or tell some special information God has given him, or speak in an unknown language, or tell what someone else is saying who is speaking in the unknown language, but everything that is done must be useful to all, and build them up in the Lord. 27No more than two or three should speak in an unknown language, and they must speak one at a time, and someone must be ready to interpret what they are saying. 28But if no one is present who can interpret, they must not speak out loud. They must talk silently to themselves and to God in the unknown language but not publicly.

14:26
Rom 14:19
1 Cor 12:8-10
14:2-6
Eph 4:12-13
5:19

14:27
1 Cor 12:10
14:2,5,13
1 Thess 5:20,21

29, 30Two or three may prophesy, one at a time, if they have the gift, while all the others listen. But if, while someone is prophesying, someone else receives a message or idea from the Lord, the one who is speaking should stop. 31In this way

14:31
Rom 12:6

14:18 *privately*, implied. See vss 19, 28.　　14:24 *even though such preaching is mostly for believers*, implied.

14:22, 23 The way the Corinthians were speaking in tongues was helping no one because believers did not understand what was being said and unbelievers thought the people speaking in tongues were crazy. Speaking in tongues was supposed to be a *sign* to unbelievers (as it was in Acts 2). After speaking in tongues, believers were supposed to explain what was said and give the credit to God. The unsaved people would then be convinced of a spiritual reality and motivated to search the Christian faith further.

While this is one way to reach unbelievers, Paul says that clear preaching is usually better (14:5).

14:26ff Everything done in worship services must be beneficial to the worshipers. This principle touches every aspect—singing, preaching, and the exercise of spiritual gifts. Those contributing to the service (singers, speakers, readers) must have love as their chief motivation, giving useful words or help that will strengthen the faith of other believers.

14:32
1 Jn 4:1

14:33
1 Cor 4:17; 7:17

14:34
Gen 3:16
1 Cor 11:3,16
Eph 5:22
Col 3:18
1 Tim 2:11
Tit 2:5
1 Pet 3:1

14:36
Isa 2:3

14:37
Lk 10:16
1 Cor 2:15
2 Cor 10:7
1 Jn 4:6

14:39
1 Cor 12:31
1 Thess 5:20

15:3
Isa 53:5
Lk 24:25-27
1 Pet 2:24

15:4
Lk 24:25-27

15:5
Mk 16:14
Lk 24:34,35
Jn 20:19

15:6
Lk 24:13-31,36
Jn 20:19,26,30
21:1

15:8
Acts 9:3-12

all who have the gift of prophecy can speak, one after the other, and everyone will learn and be encouraged and helped. 32Remember that a person who has a message from God has the power to stop himself or wait his turn. 33God is not one who likes things to be disorderly and upset. He likes harmony, and he finds it in all the other churches.

34Women should be silent during the church meetings. They are not to take part in the discussion, for they are subordinate to men as the Scriptures also declare. 35If they have any questions to ask, let them ask their husbands at home, for it is improper for women to express their opinions in church meetings.

36You disagree? And do you think that the knowledge of God's will begins and ends with you Corinthians? Well, you are mistaken! 37You who claim to have the gift of prophecy or any other special ability from the Holy Spirit should be the first to realize that what I am saying is a commandment from the Lord himself. 38But if anyone still disagrees—well, we will leave him in his ignorance.

39So, my fellow believers, long to be prophets so that you can preach God's message plainly; and never say it is wrong to "speak in tongues"; 40however, be sure that everything is done properly in a good and orderly way.

4. Instruction on the resurrection
The resurrection of Christ

15 Now let me remind you, brothers, of what the Gospel really is, for it has not changed—it is the same Good News I preached to you before. You welcomed it then and still do now, for your faith is squarely built upon this wonderful message; 2and it is this Good News that saves you if you still firmly believe it, unless of course you never really believed it in the first place.

3I passed on to you right from the first what had been told to me, that Christ died for our sins just as the Scriptures said he would, 4and that he was buried, and that three days afterwards he arose from the grave just as the prophets foretold. 5He was seen by Peter and later by the rest of "the Twelve." 6After that he was seen by more than five hundred Christian brothers at one time, most of whom are still alive, though some have died by now. 7Then James saw him and later all the apostles. 8Last of all I saw him too, long after the others, as though I had been born almost

14:32 *has the power to stop himself or wait his turn,* literally, "The spirits of the prophets are subject to the prophets." **14:34** *they are subordinate to men,* literally, "They are not authorized to speak." They are permitted to pray and prophesy (1 Cor 11:5), apparently in public meetings, but not to teach men (1 Tim 2:12). **14:38** *we will leave him in his ignorance,* or, "If he disagrees, ignore his opinion." **15:5** *the Twelve,* the name given to Jesus' twelve disciples, and still used after Judas was gone from among them.

14:33 In worship, everything must be done in harmony and with order. Even when the gifts of the Holy Spirit are being exercised, there is no excuse for disorder. When there is chaos, the church is not allowing God to work among the believers as he would like.

14:33 What did Paul mean when he said he found harmony "in all the other churches"? Some other translations end the sentence after the word, "harmony," reading, "God likes harmony." The following phrase, "As in all the [other] churches . . ." then relates to the next verse.

14:34, 35 Does this mean that women should not speak in church services today? It is clear from 11:5 that women can pray and prophesy in the church, apparently in public meetings. It is also clear in chapters 12—14 that women have spiritual gifts, and they are encouraged to exercise them in the body of Christ. Women have much to contribute and can participate in worship services.

In the Corinthian culture, women were not allowed to confront men in public. Apparently some of the women who had become Christians thought their Christian freedom gave them the right to speak up in public worship and question the men. This was causing division in the church. In addition, women of that day did not receive formal religious education as did the men. Women may have been raising questions in the worship service which could have more easily been answered at home without disrupting the church service. To promote unity, Paul was asking the women not to flaunt their Christian freedom during the worship service. The purpose of Paul's words here was to promote unity, not to teach about women's role in the church.

14:40 Worship is vital to the life of an individual and to the whole church. Our church services should be conducted in a good and orderly way so that we can worship, be taught, and be prepared to serve God. Those who are responsible for planning worship should make sure it has order and direction.

15:2 All churches have people who do not yet believe. Some are moving in the direction of belief, and others are simply pretending. Imposters, however, are not to be removed (see Matthew 13:29), for that is the Lord's work alone. The Good News saves us *if* we believe it.

15:5–8 There will always be people who say Jesus didn't rise from the dead. Paul assures us that many people saw Jesus after his resurrection, including more than 500 Christian believers. The resurrection is a historical fact. Don't be discouraged by doubters who deny the resurrection.

15:7 This is probably James, Jesus' brother, who at first did not believe Jesus was the Messiah (John 7:5). But after seeing the resurrected Christ, he became a believer and ultimately a leader of the church in Jerusalem (Acts 15:3). He also wrote the New Testament book of James.

15:8, 9 Paul's most important credential to be an apostle was that he was an eyewitness of the risen Christ (see Acts 9:3–6).

too late for this. 9For I am the least worthy of all the apostles, and I shouldn't even be called an apostle at all after the way I treated the church of God.

10But whatever I am now it is all because God poured out such kindness and grace upon me—and not without results: for I have worked harder than all the other apostles, yet actually I wasn't doing it, but God working in me, to bless me. 11It makes no difference who worked the hardest, I or they; the important thing is that we preached the Gospel to you, and you believed it.

The resurrection of the dead

12But tell me this! Since you believe what we preach, that *Christ* rose from the dead, why are some of you saying that dead people will never come back to life again? 13For if there is no resurrection of the dead, then Christ must still be dead. 14And if he is still dead, then all our preaching is useless and your trust in God is empty, worthless, hopeless; 15and we apostles are all liars because we have said that God raised Christ from the grave, and of course that isn't true if the dead do not come back to life again. 16If they don't, then Christ is still dead, 17and you are very foolish to keep on trusting God to save you, and you are still under condemnation for your sins; 18in that case all Christians who have died are lost! 19And if being a Christian is of value to us only now in this life, we are the most miserable of creatures.

20But the fact is that Christ did actually rise from the dead, and has become the first of millions who will come back to life again some day.

21Death came into the world because of what one man (Adam) did, and it is because of what this other man (Christ) has done that now there is the resurrection from the dead. 22Everyone dies because all of us are related to Adam, being members of his sinful race, and wherever there is sin, death results. But all who are related to Christ will rise again. 23Each, however, in his own turn: Christ rose first; then when Christ comes back, all his people will become alive again.

24After that the end will come when he will turn the Kingdom over to God the Father, having put down all enemies of every kind. 25For Christ will be King until

15:9
Acts 8:3
2 Cor 12:11
Eph 3:8

15:10
2 Cor 11:23
Gal 2:8
Eph 2:7
1 Tim 4:10

15:12
Acts 17:32
2 Tim 2:18

15:13
1 Thess 4:14

15:17
Rom 4:25

15:18
1 Thess 4:16
Rev 14:13

15:19
2 Tim 3:12

15:20
Col 1:18
1 Pet 1:3
Rev 1:5

15:21
Rom 5:12

15:22
Rom 5:14-18

15:23
1 Thess 4:15-17

15:24
Dan 7:14
2 Cor 4:14

15:25
Ps 110:1
Heb 1:13

15:20 *the first of millions,* literally, "the first-fruits of them that are asleep."

15:9 As a zealous Pharisee, Paul had been an enemy of the Christian church—even to the point of capturing and persecuting believers (see Acts 9:1–3). This is why he said he was unworthy to be called an apostle (a chosen messenger) of Christ. Though the most influential of the apostles, Paul was deeply humble. He knew he had worked hard and accomplished much, but only because God had poured kindness and grace upon him. True humility is not convincing yourself that you are worthless, but recognizing God's work in you. It is having God's perspective on who you are and acknowledging his grace in developing your abilities.

15:10 Paul speaks of working harder than the other apostles. This is not a prideful statement because he knew that his power came from God (15:9) and that it didn't matter who worked hardest (15:11). Because of his prominent position as a Pharisee, Paul's conversion made him the object of even greater persecution than the other apostles, thus he had to work harder to preach the same message.

15:12ff Most Greeks did not believe that people's bodies would be resurrected after death. They saw the afterlife as something that happened only to the soul. According to Greek philosophers, the soul was the real person, imprisoned in a physical body, and at death the soul was released. There was no immortality for the body, but the soul entered an eternal state. In Scripture, by contrast, the body and soul will be united after resurrection. The church at Corinth was in the heart of Greek culture. Thus many believers had a difficult time believing in a bodily resurrection. Paul wrote this part of his letter to solve this confusion about resurrection.

15:13, 14 The resurrection of Christ is the center of the Christian

faith. Because Christ rose from the dead, we know that what he said is true—he is God. Because he rose, his death for our sins was validated and we can be forgiven. Because he rose, he lives and makes intercession for us. Because he rose and defeated death, we know we will also rise.

15:19 Why did Paul say people would be miserable if there were only earthly value to Christianity? In Paul's day, Christianity often brought a person persecution, ostracism from family, and, in many cases, poverty. There were few tangible benefits for being a Christian in that society. It was certainly not a step up the social or career ladder. Even more important, however, is the fact that if Christ had not been resurrected from death, Christians could not be forgiven for their sins and would have no hope of eternal life.

15:21 Death came into the world as a result of Adam and Eve's sin. In Romans 5:12–21, Paul explains why Adam's sin brought sin to all people, how death and sin spread to all humans because of this first sin, and the parallel between Adam's death and Christ's death.

15:23 Those related to Christ are Christians, who by faith become Christ's brothers and sisters and share in his resurrection. Because Christ *did* rise from the dead, we now have the certainty that we who are believers will be resurrected as well.

15:24–28 This is not a chronological sequence of events, and no specific time for these events is given. Paul's point is that the resurrected Christ will conquer all evil, including death.

15:25–28 Although God the Father and God the Son are equal, each has special roles (15:28). Christ is not inferior to the Father, but his role is to defeat all evil on earth. First he defeated sin and death on the cross, and in the final days he will defeat Satan and

15:26
1 Cor 15:54,55
2 Tim 1:10
Heb 2:14
Rev 1:18; 20:14
21:4

15:27
Ps 8:6
Mt 28:18
Eph 1:22
Heb 2:8
1 Pet 3:22

15:28
Jn 14:28
1 Cor 3:23; 11:3
Eph 1:10
Phil 3:21

15:30
Rom 8:36
2 Cor 11:26

15:31
2 Cor 4:10

15:32
Isa 22:13
Lk 12:19-21
1 Cor 16:8
2 Cor 1:8

15:34
Eph 5:14
1 Cor 6:5
1 Thess 4:5

he has defeated all his enemies, 26including the last enemy—death. This too must be defeated and ended. 27For the rule and authority over all things has been given to Christ by his Father; except, of course, Christ does not rule over the Father himself, who gave him this power to rule. 28When Christ has finally won the battle against all his enemies, then he, the Son of God, will put himself also under his Father's orders, so that God who has given him the victory over everything else will be utterly supreme.

29If the dead will not come back to life again, then what point is there in people being baptized for those who are gone? Why do it unless you believe that the dead will some day rise again?

30And why should we ourselves be continually risking our lives, facing death hour by hour? 31For it is a fact that I face death daily; that is as true as my pride in your growth in the Lord. 32And what value was there in fighting wild beasts—those men of Ephesus—if it was only for what I gain in this life down here? If we will never live again after we die, then we might as well go and have ourselves a good time: let us eat, drink, and be merry. What's the difference? For tomorrow we die, and that ends everything!

33Don't be fooled by those who say such things. If you listen to them you will start acting like them. 34Get some sense and quit your sinning. For to your shame I say it, some of you are not even Christians at all and have never really known God.

The resurrection body

15:35
Ezek 37:3

15:36
Jn 12:23,24

15:38
Gen 1:11
Ps 104:14

15:42
Dan 12:3
Mt 13:43
1 Cor 15:50

15:43
Phil 3:21
Col 3:4

35But someone may ask, "How will the dead be brought back to life again? What kind of bodies will they have?" 36What a foolish question! You will find the answer in your own garden! When you put a seed into the ground it doesn't grow into a plant unless it "dies" first. 37And when the green shoot comes up out of the seed, it is very different from the seed you first planted. For all you put into the ground is a dry little seed of wheat, or whatever it is you are planting, 38then God gives it a beautiful new body—just the kind he wants it to have; a different kind of plant grows from each kind of seed. 39And just as there are different kinds of seeds and plants, so also there are different kinds of flesh. Humans, animals, fish, and birds are all different.

40The angels in heaven have bodies far different from ours, and the beauty and the glory of their bodies is different from the beauty and the glory of ours. 41The sun has one kind of glory while the moon and stars have another kind. And the stars differ from each other in their beauty and brightness.

42In the same way, our earthly bodies which die and decay are different from the bodies we shall have when we come back to life again, for they will never die. 43The bodies we have now embarrass us for they become sick and die; but they will be full of glory when we come back to life again. Yes, they are weak, dying bodies now, but when we live again they will be full of strength. 44They are just human bodies at death, but when they come back to life they will be superhuman bodies.

15:34 *have never really known God,* or, "There are some who know nothing of God." **15:40** *The angels,* literally, "There are celestial bodies." But perhaps this may refer to the sun, moon, planets, and stars.

---

all evil. World events may seem out of control and justice may seem scarce, but God is in control, allowing evil to remain for a time until he sends Jesus to earth again. Then Jesus will present to God a perfect new world.

15:29 Some believers were baptized on behalf of others who had died unbaptized. Nothing more is known about this practice, but it obviously affirms a belief in resurrection. Paul was not necessarily approving of baptism for the dead, but was using it as an illustration to reinforce his argument that the resurrection is a reality.

15:30-34 If death ended it all, enjoying the moment would be all that matters. But Christians know that there is life *beyond* the grave and that our life on earth is only a preparation for that life.

15:35ff Paul launches into a discussion about what our resurrected bodies will be like. If you could select your own body, what kind would you choose—strong, athletic, beautiful? Paul explains that we will be recognized in our resurrected bodies, yet they will be better than we can imagine, for they will be made to live forever. We will still have our own personalities and individualities, but these will be perfected through Christ's work. Scripture does not say what our resurrected bodies will be able to do, but we know they will be perfect, without sickness or disease.

15:44 *Supernatural* means "more than natural." Thus our spiritual bodies will be above and not limited to the laws of nature. This does not necessarily mean we'll be superpeople, but our bodies will be different and more capable than our present earthly bodies.

For just as there are natural, human bodies, there are also supernatural, spiritual bodies.

45The Scriptures tell us that the first man, Adam, was given a natural, human body but Christ is more than that, for he was life-giving Spirit.

46First, then, we have these human bodies and later on God gives us spiritual, heavenly bodies. 47Adam was made from the dust of the earth, but Christ came from heaven above. 48Every human being has a body just like Adam's, made of dust, but all who become Christ's will have the same kind of body as his—a body from heaven. 49Just as each of us now has a body like Adam's, so we shall some day have a body like Christ's.

50I tell you this, my brothers: an earthly body made of flesh and blood cannot get into God's Kingdom. These perishable bodies of ours are not the right kind to live forever.

51But I am telling you this strange and wonderful secret: we shall not all die, but we shall all be given new bodies! 52It will all happen in a moment, in the twinkling of an eye, when the last trumpet is blown. For there will be a trumpet blast from the sky and all the Christians who have died will suddenly become alive, with new bodies that will never, never die; and then we who are still alive shall suddenly have new bodies too. 53For our earthly bodies, the ones we have now that can die, must be transformed into heavenly bodies that cannot perish but will live forever.

54When this happens, then at last this Scripture will come true—"Death is swallowed up in victory." 55, 56O death, where then your victory? Where then your sting? For sin—the sting that causes death—will all be gone; and the law, which reveals our sins, will no longer be our judge. 57How we thank God for all of this! It is he who makes us victorious through Jesus Christ our Lord!

58So, my dear brothers, since future victory is sure, be strong and steady, always

15:45 *human body*, literally, "was made a living soul." *but Christ*, literally, "the last Adam." *is more*, implied.
15:52 *from the sky*, implied.

15:45
Gen 2:7
Jn 5:21
Rom 8:2
2 Cor 3:17
Col 3:4
1 Pet 3:18

15:47
Gen 3:19
Jn 3:13,31

15:48
Phil 3:20,21

15:49
Gen 5:3
Rom 8:29
Phil 3:21
1 Jn 3:2

15:50
Mt 16:17
Jn 3:3,5

15:51
2 Cor 5:2-4
Phil 3:21
1 Thess 4:15,16

15:52
Mt 24:31

15:53
2 Cor 5:4

15:54
Isa 25:8

15:55
Hos 13:14
Rom 4:15

15:57
Rom 7:23-25
1 Jn 5:4

Physical Bodies	Resurrection Bodies	**PHYSICAL AND RESURRECTION BODIES**
Die and decay	Never die	
Embarrassing	Full of glory	
Weak and sick	Full of strength	
Human	Superhuman	
Natural	Spiritual	
From the dust	From heaven	

We all have bodies—each looks different, each has different abilities and weaknesses. But as physical, earthly bodies, they are all alike. All believers are promised life after death and bodies like Christ's (15:49), resurrection bodies.

15:45 When Christ rose from the dead, he became "life-giving Spirit." This means he entered into a new form of existence (see note on 2 Corinthians 3:17). Christ's new glorified human body now suits his new glorified life—just as Adam's human body was suitable to his natural life. When we will be resurrected, God will give us a glorified body suited to our new eternal life.

15:50-53 We all face limitations. Those who have physical, mental, or emotional handicaps are especially aware of this. Some may be blind, but they can see a new way to live. Some may be deaf, but they can hear God's Good News. Some may be lame, but they can walk in God's love. In addition, they have the encouragement that those handicaps are only temporary. Paul tells us we shall all be given new bodies when Jesus returns, and these bodies will be without handicaps, never to die or become sick. This can give us hope in our suffering.

15:52 A trumpet blast will usher in the new heaven and earth. The Jews would understand the significance of this because trumpets were always blown to signal the start of great feasts and other extraordinary events (Numbers 10:10).

15:54-56 Satan seemed to be victorious in the Garden of Eden (Genesis 3) and when Jesus died on the cross (Mark 15:22-24). But God turned Satan's apparent victory into defeat when Jesus Christ rose from the dead (Colossians 2:15; Hebrews 2:14, 15). Thus death is no longer a source of dread or fear. Christ overcame it, and one day we will also. Death has been defeated, and we have hope beyond the grave.

15:58 Paul said that because of the resurrection, nothing we do is wasted. Sometimes we hesitate to do good because we don't see any results. But if we can maintain a heavenly perspective, we understand that we don't often see the good that results from our efforts. If we truly believe that Christ has won the ultimate victory, it must affect the way we live right now. Don't let discouragement over an apparent lack of results keep you from working. Do the good that you have opportunity to do, knowing your work will have eternal results.

abounding in the Lord's work, for you know that nothing you do for the Lord is ever wasted as it would be if there were no resurrection.

Directions for the offering

16:1
Acts 11:29
24:17
Rom 15:26
2 Cor 8:4; 9:1
Gal 2:10

16:2
Lk 24:1
Acts 20:7
Rev 1:10

16:3
2 Cor 8:19-21

16 Now here are the directions about the money you are collecting to send to the Christians in Jerusalem (and, by the way, these are the same directions I gave to the churches in Galatia). 2On every Lord's Day each of you should put aside something from what you have earned during the week, and use it for this offering. The amount depends on how much the Lord has helped you earn. Don't wait until I get there and then try to collect it all at once. 3When I come I will send your loving gift with a letter to Jerusalem, to be taken there by trustworthy messengers you yourselves will choose. 4And if it seems wise for me to go along too, then we can travel together.

Paul's final instructions

16:5
Acts 19:21
1 Cor 4:19
2 Cor 1:15,16

16:6
Acts 15:3; 17:5
21:5

16:7
Acts 18:21

16:8
Acts 2:1

16:9
Acts 14:27
19:8-10
2 Cor 2:12

16:10
Acts 16:1
Rom 16:21

16:11
1 Tim 4:12,13

16:12
Acts 18:24
1 Cor 1:12
Tit 3:13

16:13
Mt 24:42
Phil 1:27; 4:1
1 Thess 3:7,8
2 Thess 2:15

16:14
1 Cor 14:1

16:15
1 Cor 14:16

16:16
1 Thess 5:12,13

5I am coming to visit you after I have been to Macedonia first, but I will be staying there only for a little while. 6It could be that I will stay longer with you, perhaps all winter, and then you can send me on to my next destination. 7This time I don't want to make just a passing visit and then go right on; I want to come and stay awhile, if the Lord will let me. 8I will be staying here at Ephesus until the holiday of Pentecost, 9for there is a wide open door for me to preach and teach here. So much is happening, but there are many enemies.

10If Timothy comes make him feel at home, for he is doing the Lord's work just as I am. 11Don't let anyone despise or ignore him [because he is young], but send him back to me happy with his time among you; I am looking forward to seeing him soon, along with the others who are returning.

12I begged Apollos to visit you along with the others, but he thought that it was not at all God's will for him to go now; he will be seeing you later on when he has the opportunity.

13Keep your eyes open for spiritual danger; stand true to the Lord; act like men; be strong; 14and whatever you do, do it with kindness and love.

15Do you remember Stephanas and his family? They were the first to become Christians in Greece and they are spending their lives helping and serving Christians everywhere. 16Please follow their instructions and do everything you can to help them as well as all others like them who work hard at your side with such real devotion. 17I am so glad that Stephanas, Fortunatus, and Achaicus have arrived here for a visit. They have been making up for the help you aren't here to give me. 18They have cheered me greatly and have been a wonderful encouragement to me, as I am sure they were to you, too. I hope you properly appreciate the work of such men as these.

16:1 *Christians in Jerusalem,* implied.   **16:11** *because he is young,* implied in 1 Tim 4:12.

16:1ff Paul had just said that no good work is ever wasted (15:58). Now he mentions some practical works that have value for all Christians.

16:1–4 The Christians in Jerusalem were suffering from poverty and famine, and so Paul was collecting money for them. Although the Jerusalem church was where Christianity began, it was experiencing hard times (see Romans 15:25–31; 2 Corinthians 8:4; 9:1ff). Paul suggested that believers set aside a certain amount each week and give it to the church until he arrived to take it on to Jerusalem. Paul had planned to go straight to Corinth from Ephesus, but he changed his mind (2 Corinthians 1, 2). When he finally arrived, he took the gift and delivered it to the Jerusalem church (Acts 21:18; 24:17).

16:10, 11 Paul was sending Timothy ahead to Corinth. Paul respected Timothy and had worked closely with him (Philippians 2:20–22; 1 Timothy 1:2). Although Timothy was young, Paul

encouraged the Corinthian church to welcome him because he was doing the Lord's work. God's work is not limited by age. Paul wrote two personal letters to Timothy that have been preserved in the Bible (1 and 2 Timothy). See also the note on 4:17.

16:12 Apollos, who had preached in Corinth, was doing evangelistic work in Greece (see Acts 18:24–28; 1 Corinthians 3:3, 4). Apollos didn't go to Corinth right away, partly because he knew of the factions there and didn't want to cause any more divisions. Paul probably had the authority to send Apollos to Corinth, but he did not force him to go, because Apollos didn't feel it was God's will for him.

16:13, 14 As the Corinthians awaited Paul's next visit, they were directed to (1) be alert to spiritual dangers, (2) stand true to the Lord, (3) behave maturely, (4) be strong, and (5) do all things with kindness and love. Today, as we wait the return of Christ, we should follow the same instructions.

¹⁹The churches here in Asia send you their loving greetings. Aquila and Priscilla send you their love and so do all the others who meet in their home for their church service. ²⁰All the friends here have asked me to say "hello" to you for them. And give each other a loving handshake when you meet.

²¹I will write these final words of this letter with my own hand: ²²if anyone does not love the Lord, that person is cursed. Lord Jesus, come! ²³May the love and favor of the Lord Jesus Christ rest upon you. ²⁴My love to all of you, for we all belong to Christ Jesus.

Sincerely, Paul

16:19
Rom 16:5
Philem 2
Rev 1:4,11

16:21
Rom 16:22
Gal 6:11
Col 4:18
2 Thess 3:17
Philem 19

16:22
Gal 1:8,9
Heb 10:26

16:19 Aquila and Priscilla were tentmakers (or leather workers) whom Paul met in Corinth (Acts 18:1–3). They followed Paul to Ephesus and lived there with him, helping to teach others about Jesus (Romans 16:3–5). Many in the Corinthian church would have known this Christian couple. They are also mentioned in Acts 18:18, 26; Romans 16:3; 2 Timothy 4:19.

16:21 Paul had a helper, or secretary, who wrote this letter while he dictated. Paul wrote the final words, however, in his own handwriting. This is similar to adding a handwritten postscript (P.S.) to a typewritten letter. It also served to verify that this was a genuine letter from the apostle, not a forgery.

16:22 The Lord Jesus Christ is coming back to earth again. To Paul, this was a glad hope, the best he could look forward to. He

was not afraid of seeing Christ—he could hardly wait! Do you share Paul's eager anticipation? Those who love Christ are looking forward to that wonderful time of his return (Titus 2:13).

16:24 The church at Corinth was a church in trouble. Paul lovingly and forcefully confronted their problems and pointed them back to Christ. He dealt with divisions and conflicts, selfishness, inconsiderate use of freedom, disorder in worship, misuse of spiritual gifts, and wrong attitudes about the resurrection.

In every church, there are enough problems to split it. We should not ignore or gloss over problems in our church or in our lives. Instead, like Paul, we should deal with problems head on as they arise. The lesson for us in 1 Corinthians is that unity and love in a church are far more important than leaders and labels.

2 CORINTHIANS

SLITHERING through the centuries, the serpent whispers his silver-lined promises, beguiling, deceiving, and tempting—urging men and women to reject God and to follow him. Satan's emmissaries have been many—false prophets contradicting God's ancient spokesmen, "pious" leaders hurling blasphemous accusations, and heretical teachers infiltrating churches. And the deception continues. Our world is filled with cults, "isms," and ideologies, all claiming to be the way to God.

Paul constantly struggled with those who would mislead God's people, and poured his life into spreading the Good News to the uttermost parts of the world. During three missionary trips and other travels, he proclaimed Christ, made converts, and established churches. But often young believers were easy prey for false teachers. False teachers were a constant threat to the gospel and the early church. So Paul had to spend much time warning and correcting them.

The church at Corinth was weak. Surrounded by idolatry and immorality, they struggled with their Christian faith and life-style. Through personal visits and letters, Paul tried to instruct them in the faith, resolve their conflicts, and solve some of their problems. First Corinthians was sent to deal with specific moral issues in the church and to answer questions about sex, marriage, and tender consciences. That letter confronted the issues directly and was well received by most. But there were false teachers who denied Paul's authority and slandered him. Paul then wrote 2 Corinthians to defend his position and to denounce those who were twisting the truth.

Second Corinthians was a difficult letter for Paul to write because he had to list his credentials as an apostle. Paul was reluctant to do so because he was a humble servant of Christ, but he knew it was necessary. Paul also knew that most of the believers in Corinth had taken his previous words to heart and were beginning to mature in their faith. He affirmed their commitment to Christ.

Second Corinthians begins with Paul reminding his readers of (1) their relationship to him—Paul had always been honest and straightforward with them (1:12–14), (2) his itinerary—he was planning to visit them again (1:15—2:3), and (3) his previous letter (2:4–11). Paul then moves directly to the subject of false teachers (2:17), and he reviews his ministry among them to demonstrate the validity of his message, and to urge them not to turn away from the truth (3:1—7:16).

Paul next turns to the issue of collecting money for the poor Christians in Jerusalem. He tells them how others have given, and he urges them to show their love in a tangible way as well (8:1—9:15). Paul then gives a strong defense for his authority as a genuine apostle while pointing out the deception of the false apostles (10:1—13:14).

As you read this intensely personal letter, listen to Paul's words of love and exhortation, and be committed to the truth of God's Word, prepared to reject all false teaching.

VITAL STATISTICS

PURPOSE:
To affirm his own ministry, defend his authority as an apostle, and refute the false teachers in Corinth

AUTHOR:
Paul

TO WHOM WRITTEN:
The church in Corinth, and Christians everywhere

DATE WRITTEN:
About A.D. 55–57, from Macedonia

SETTING:
Paul had already written three letters to the Corinthians (two are now lost). In 1 Corinthians (the second of these letters), he used strong words to correct and teach. Most of the church had responded in the right spirit; there were, however, those who were denying Paul's authority and questioning his motives.

KEY VERSE:
"We are Christ's ambassadors. God is using us to speak to you: we beg you, as though Christ himself were here pleading with you, receive the love he offers you—be reconciled to God" (5:20).

KEY PEOPLE:
Paul, Timothy, Titus, false teachers

KEY PLACES:
Corinth, Jerusalem

SPECIAL FEATURES:
This is an intensely personal and autobiographical letter.

THE BLUEPRINT

1. Paul explains his actions (1:1—2:13)
2. Paul defends his ministry (2:14—7:16)
3. Paul defends the collection (8:1—9:15)
4. Paul defends his authority (10:1—13:14)

In responding to the attacks on his character and authority, Paul explains the nature of Christian ministry and, as an example, openly shares about his ministry. This is an important letter for all who wish to be involved in any kind of Christian ministry, because it has much to teach us about how we should handle our ministries today. Like Paul, those involved in ministry should be blameless, sincere, confident, caring, open, and willing to suffer for the sake of Christ.

MEGATHEMES

THEME	EXPLANATION	IMPORTANCE
Trials	Paul experienced great suffering, persecution, and opposition in his ministry. He even struggled with a personal weakness—a "thorn in the flesh." Through it all, Paul affirmed God's faithfulness.	God is faithful. His strength is sufficient for any trial. When trials come, they keep us from pride and teach us dependence on God. He comforts us so we can comfort others.
Church discipline	Paul defends his role in church discipline. Neither immorality nor false teaching could be ignored. The church was to be neither lax nor too severe in administering discipline. The church was to restore the corrected person when he or she repented.	The goal of all discipline in the church should be correction, not vengeance. For churches to be effective, they must confront and solve problems, not ignore them. In everything, we must act in love.
Hope	To encourage the Corinthians as they faced trials, Paul reminded them that they would receive new bodies in heaven. This would be a great victory in contrast to their present suffering.	To know we will receive new bodies offers us hope. No matter what adversity we face, we can keep going. Our faithful service will result in triumph.
Giving	Paul organized a collection of funds for the poor in the Jerusalem church. Many of the Asian churches gave money. Paul explains and defends his beliefs about giving, and he urges the Corinthians to follow through on their previous commitment.	Like the Corinthians, we should follow through on our financial commitments. Our giving must be generous, sacrificial, according to a plan, and based on need. Our generosity not only helps those in need, but enables them to thank God.
Sound doctrine	False teachers were challenging Paul's ministry and authority as an apostle. Paul asserts his authority in order to preserve correct Christian doctrine. His sincerity, his love for Christ, and his concern for the people were his defense.	We should share Paul's concern for correct teaching in our churches. But in so doing, we must share his motivation—love for Christ and people—and be sincere.

1. Paul explains his actions

1:1
1 Cor 1:1
2 Cor 1:19
Eph 1:1
1:2
Rom 1:7

1 Dear friends, This letter is from me, Paul, appointed by God to be Jesus Christ's messenger; and from our dear brother Timothy. We are writing to all of you Christians there in Corinth and throughout Greece. ²May God our Father and the Lord Jesus Christ mightily bless each one of you, and give you peace.

We pass on God's comfort to others

1:3
Eph 1:3
1 Pet 1:3
1:4
Isa 51:12; 66:13
2 Cor 7:6
1:5
2 Cor 4:10
Phil 3:10
Col 1:24
1:6
2 Cor 4:15
2 Tim 2:10; 4:10
1:7
Rom 8:17
2 Tim 2:12

³, ⁴What a wonderful God we have—he is the Father of our Lord Jesus Christ, the source of every mercy, and the one who so wonderfully comforts and strengthens us in our hardships and trials. And why does he do this? So that when others are troubled, needing our sympathy and encouragement, we can pass on to them this same help and comfort God has given us. ⁵You can be sure that the more we undergo sufferings for Christ, the more he will shower us with his comfort and encouragement. ⁶, ⁷We are in deep trouble for bringing you God's comfort and salvation. But in our trouble God has comforted us—and this, too, to help you: to show you from our personal experience how God will tenderly comfort you when you undergo these same sufferings. He will give you the strength to endure.

⁸I think you ought to know, dear brothers, about the hard time we went through

1:1 *throughout Greece*, or, "throughout Achaia."

DIFFERENCES BETWEEN 1 AND 2 CORINTHIANS
The two letters to the Corinthian church found in the Bible are very different, with different tones and focuses.

1 Corinthians	2 Corinthians
Practical	Personal
Focuses on the character of the Corinthian church	Focuses on Paul as he bares his soul and tells of his love for the Corinthian church
Deals with questions on marriage, freedom, spiritual gifts, and order in the church	Deals with the problem of false teachers, whereby Paul defends his authority and the truth of his message
Paul instructs in matters concerning the church's well-being	Paul gives his testimony because he knows they trust him and that acceptance of his advice is vital to the church's well-being
Contains advice to help the church against the pagan influences in the wicked city of Corinth	Contains testimony to help the church against the havoc caused by false teachers

---

1:1 Paul visited Corinth on his second missionary journey and founded a church (Acts 18:1ff). He later wrote several letters to the church there, two of which are included in the Bible. Paul's first letter to the Corinthians is lost (1 Corinthians 5:9–11), his second letter to them is our book of 1 Corinthians, his third letter is lost as well (2:6–9; 7:12), and his fourth letter is our book of 2 Corinthians. Second Corinthians was written about a year after 1 Corinthians.

Paul wrote 1 Corinthians to deal with divisions in the church, but when his advice was not taken and their problems weren't solved, he visited Corinth a second time (called "another painful visit" in 2:1). He then planned a third visit, but delayed it and wrote 2 Corinthians instead. After writing 2 Corinthians, he visited Corinth once more (Acts 20:2).

1:1 Paul had great respect for Timothy (see Philippians 2:20; 1 Timothy 1:2; 6:11), one of his traveling companions (Acts 16:1–3). Timothy had accompanied Paul to Corinth on his second missionary journey, and Paul had recently sent him there to minister (1 Corinthians 4:17; 16:10). Timothy's report to Paul about the crisis in the Corinthian church prompted Paul to make an unplanned visit to the church to deal with the problem in person (see 2:1). For more information on Timothy, see his Profile in 1 Timothy.

1:2 The Romans had made Corinth the capital of Achaia (the southern half of present-day Greece). The city was a flourishing trade center because of its seaport, and with the thousands of sailors who disembarked there each year, it had become a center

of prostitution. Corinth had a reputation as one of the most immoral cities in the ancient world. Many heathen temples had sprung up with all forms of sexual immorality and idol worship. In fact, the Greek word for practicing sexual immorality was "to Corinthianize." A Christian church in the city would face great temptations. For more information on Corinth, see the note in 1 Corinthians 1:2.

1:3, 4 Many think that when God comforts us, our hardships should go away. But if that were always so, people would turn to God only to be relieved of pain and not out of love for him. We must understand that *comfort* can also mean receiving strength, encouragement, and hope to deal with our hardships. The more we suffer, the more comfort God gives us (1:5). If you are feeling overwhelmed, allow God to comfort you as he can. Remember that every trial you endure will later become an opportunity to minister to other people suffering similar hardships.

1:8 Paul does not say what happened to him during this "hard time" in Asia, although his accounts of all three missionary journeys record many difficult trials he faced (Acts 13:2—14:28; Acts 15:40—21:17).

1:8–10 We often depend on our own skills and abilities when life seems easy, but when we feel powerless to help ourselves, we turn to God. Dependence is not defeat, but constant contact. It is realizing that our source of truth and power is God and then keeping in touch with him. With this attitude, problems drive us to God rather than away from him. Learn how to depend on God daily.

in Asia. We were really crushed and overwhelmed, and feared we would never live through it. 9We felt we were doomed to die and saw how powerless we were to help ourselves; but that was good, for then we put everything into the hands of God, who alone could save us, for he can even raise the dead. 10And he did help us, and saved us from a terrible death; yes, and we expect him to do it again and again. 11But you must help us too, by praying for us. For much thanks and praise will go to God from you who see his wonderful answers to your prayers for our safety!

1:9
Jer 17:5,7

1:10
2 Pet 2:9

1:11
Rom 15:30
2 Cor 4:15
Phil 1:19
Philem 22

Paul's change of plans

12We are so glad that we can say with utter honesty that in all our dealings we have been pure and sincere, quietly depending upon the Lord for his help, and not on our own skills. And that is even more true, if possible, about the way we have acted toward you. 13, 14My letters have been straightforward and sincere; nothing is written between the lines! And even though you don't know me very well (I hope someday you will), I want you to try to accept me and be proud of me, as you already are to some extent; just as I shall be of you on that day when our Lord Jesus comes back again.

1:12
Acts 23:1
1 Cor 2:4
2 Cor 2:17; 4:15

1:14
2 Cor 5:12
Phil 4:1
1 Thess 2:19

15, 16It was because I was so sure of your understanding and trust that I planned to stop and see you on my way to Macedonia, as well as afterwards when I returned, so that I could be a double blessing to you and so that you could send me on my way to Judea.

1:15
Rom 1:11,12
1 Cor 4:19

1:16
1 Cor 16:5

1:17
2 Cor 10:2

17Then why, you may be asking, did I change my plan? Hadn't I really made up my mind yet? Or am I like a man of the world who says "yes" when he really means "no"? 18Never! As surely as God is true, I am not that sort of person. My "yes" means "yes."

1:19
Ex 3:14
Mt 16:16; 26:63
Lk 1:35
Acts 9:20; 18:5
Heb 13:8

19Timothy and Silvanus and I have been telling you about Jesus Christ the Son of God. He isn't one to say "yes" when he means "no." He always does exactly what he says. 20He carries out and fulfills all of God's promises, no matter how many of them there are; and we have told everyone how faithful he is, giving glory to his name. 21It is this God who has made you and me into faithful Christians and commissioned us apostles to preach the Good News. 22He has put his brand upon us—his mark of ownership—and given us his Holy Spirit in our hearts as guarantee

1:20
Rom 15:8,9
Rev 3:14

1:21
1 Jn 2:20,27

1:22
2 Cor 5:5
Eph 1:13,14
4:30
2 Tim 2:19
Rev 2:17

1:11 Pray for pastors, teachers, missionaries, and others who are on the "front lines" of spreading the gospel. Anyone making a real difference for God will be challenged by Satan.

1:12–14 Paul knew the importance of honesty in writing and speaking, especially in a situation where constructive criticism was necessary. God wants us to be real and transparent in all our relationships. If we aren't, we will give in to rumors, gossip, and second-guessing.

1:13, 14 Paul had ministered in Corinth for a year and a half (Acts 18:11), and he had visited a second time. Why then did he say they didn't know him very well? Many new believers had been added to the church, and in his letters Paul often focused on those who were wavering in their faith and who did not see Paul as a God-ordained apostle. These people did not know him or understand what he was saying about Jesus Christ.

1:15–17 Paul had recently made a brief, unscheduled visit to Corinth which was very painful for him and the church (see 2:1). After that visit, he told the church when he would come again. But Paul changed his original travel plans. Instead of sailing from Ephesus to Corinth before going to Macedonia, he traveled from Ephesus directly to Macedonia, where he wrote a letter that caused him much anguish (7:8, 9). He had made his original plans thinking the church would have solved its problems. When the time came for Paul's scheduled trip to Corinth, however, the crisis had not been fully resolved (although progress was being made in some areas; 7:11–16). So he wrote a letter instead (2:3, 4; 7:8), because another visit would only have made matters worse. Thus

Paul stayed away from Corinth because he was concerned over the church's unity, not because he was fickle.

1:17 Paul's change of plans caused some of his accusers to say he couldn't be trusted, hoping to undermine his authority. Paul explained that not indecision but concern for their feelings forced him to change his plans. The reason for his trip—to bring joy (1:24)—could not be accomplished with the present crisis. He didn't want to visit them only to rebuke them severely (1:23). Just as the Corinthians could trust God to keep his promises, they could trust Paul as God's representative to keep his. He would still visit them, but at a better time.

1:19, 20 Jesus faithfully obeyed God and never sinned (1 Peter 3:18); faithfully died for us (Hebrews 2:9); and now faithfully intercedes for us (Romans 8:34; Hebrews 4:14, 15). Because Jesus Christ is faithful, Paul was faithful in his ministry.

1:21, 22 Paul mentions two gifts God gives when we become believers: a "mark of ownership" to show who our master is, and the Holy Spirit as a guarantee that we belong to him (Ephesians 1:13, 14). With the privilege of belonging to God comes the responsibility of identifying ourselves as faithful representatives and servants of our master. Don't be ashamed to let others know you are his.

1:22 Paul calls the Holy Spirit the "first installment" for two reasons: he guarantees that salvation is ours, and yet we will receive so much more, both now and when Christ returns. The great comfort and power the Holy Spirit gives in this life is a foretaste of the benefits and blessings of our eternal life in God's presence.

that we belong to him, and as the first installment of all that he is going to give us.
²³I call upon this God to witness against me if I am not telling the absolute truth: the reason I haven't come to visit you yet is that I don't want to sadden you with a severe rebuke. ²⁴When I come, although I can't do much to help your faith, for it is strong already, I want to be able to do something about your joy: I want to make you happy, not sad.

2 "No," I said to myself, "I won't do it. I'll not make them unhappy with another painful visit." ²For if I make you sad, who is going to make me happy? You are the ones to do it, and how can you if I cause you pain? ³That is why I wrote as I did in my last letter, so that you will get things straightened out before I come. Then, when I do come, I will not be made sad by the very ones who ought to give me greatest joy. I felt sure that your happiness was so bound up in mine that you would not be happy either, unless I came with joy.

⁴Oh, how I hated to write that letter! It almost broke my heart and I tell you honestly that I cried over it. I didn't want to hurt you, but I had to show you how very much I loved you and cared about what was happening to you.

Reinstate the repentant sinner

⁵, ⁶Remember that the man I wrote about, who caused all the trouble, has not caused sorrow to me as much as to all the rest of you—though I certainly have my share in it too. I don't want to be harder on him than I should. He has been punished enough by your united disapproval. ⁷Now it is time to forgive him and comfort him. Otherwise he may become so bitter and discouraged that he won't be able to recover. ⁸Please show him now that you still do love him very much.

⁹I wrote to you as I did so that I could find out how far you would go in obeying me. ¹⁰When you forgive anyone, I do too. And whatever I have forgiven (to the extent that this affected me too) has been by Christ's authority, and for your good. ¹¹A further reason for forgiveness is to keep from being outsmarted by Satan; for we know what he is trying to do.

¹²Well, when I got as far as the city of Troas, the Lord gave me tremendous opportunities to preach the Gospel. ¹³But Titus, my dear brother, wasn't there to

2:3 *so that you will get things straightened out before I come,* implied.

1:23
1 Cor 4:21

1:24
Rom 11:20
1 Cor 15:1,2

2:1
1 Cor 4:21
2 Cor 12:20

2:2
2 Cor 7:8

2:4
2 Cor 2:9; 7:8,9

2:5,6
1 Cor 5:1-5
2 Cor 7:11

2:7
Gal 6:1
Eph 4:32

2:10
1 Cor 5:4

2:11
2 Cor 4:4; 11:3
1 Pet 5:8

2:12
Acts 14:27
2 Cor 4:3; 10:14

2:13
2 Cor 7:5,6

1:23 The Corinthian church had written to Paul with questions about their faith (see 1 Corinthians 7:1). In response, Paul wrote 1 Corinthians. But they did not follow Paul's instructions. Paul had planned to visit them again, but instead wrote a sorrowful letter (7:8, 9) to give them another chance to change their ways. He didn't want to visit and repeat the same advice for the same problems. He wrote that emotional letter to encourage them to follow the advice he had already given in previous letters and visits.

2:1 Paul's phrase "another painful visit" indicates he had already made one difficult trip to Corinth (see notes on 1:1; 1:15–17) since founding the church. He went there to deal with those in the church who were attacking and undermining his authority as an apostle of Jesus Christ, thus confusing other believers.

2:3 Paul's "last letter" was not the book of 1 Corinthians, but a letter written between 1 and 2 Corinthians, just after his unplanned, painful visit (2:1). Paul refers to this letter again in 7:8.

2:4 Paul did not enjoy reprimanding his friends and fellow believers, but he cared enough for the Corinthians to confront them about their wrongdoing. Proverbs 27:6 says that "wounds from a friend are better than kisses from an enemy." Sometimes our friends make choices that we know are wrong. If we ignore their behavior and let them continue, we aren't showing love to them. Love means honestly sharing our concerns with those we love. When we don't move to help, we show that we are more concerned about what will happen to us than what will happen to them.

2:5–11 It was time to forgive the man who had been punished by the church and had subsequently repented. He now needed

friendship and comfort. This may have been the man who required the disciplinary action described in 1 Corinthians 5 or the chief opponent of Paul who had caused Paul the anguish described in 2:1–11. The sorrowful letter taken by Titus had finally brought about the repentance of the Corinthians (7:8–14), and their discipline of the man had led to his repentance. Church discipline should always allow for restoration. Two mistakes can be made in church discipline—being too lenient with sin and not correcting mistakes, or being too harsh and not forgiving.

2:11 We use church discipline in order to keep the church pure and to help wayward people to repent. But Satan tries to harm the church by tempting it to use discipline in an unforgiving way. This causes those exercising discipline to become proud of their purity and it causes the one being disciplined to become bitter and perhaps to leave the church entirely. We must remember that our purpose in discipline is to *restore* a person to the fellowship, not to destroy him or her. We must be cautious that personal anger is not vented under the guise of church discipline.

2:13 Titus was a Greek convert whom Paul greatly loved and trusted (the book of Titus is a letter Paul wrote to him). Titus was one of the men responsible for collecting the money for the poverty-stricken Jerusalem church (8:6). Paul had also sent Titus with the sorrowful letter. On his way to Macedonia, Paul was supposed to meet Titus in Troas. When he didn't find him there, he was worried for Titus' safety, and left Troas to search for him in Macedonia. There Paul found him (7:6), and the good news he received (7:8–16) led to this epistle. Paul would send Titus back to Corinth with this letter (8:16, 17).

meet me and I couldn't rest, wondering where he was and what had happened to him. So I said good-bye and went right on to Macedonia to try to find him.

2. Paul defends his ministry
The fragrance of Christ

¹⁴But thanks be to God! For through what Christ has done, he has triumphed over us so that now wherever we go he uses us to tell others about the Lord and to spread the Gospel like a sweet perfume. ¹⁵As far as God is concerned there is a sweet, wholesome fragrance in our lives. It is the fragrance of Christ within us, an aroma to both the saved and the unsaved all around us. ¹⁶To those who are not being saved, we seem a fearful smell of death and doom, while to those who know Christ we are a life-giving perfume. But who is adequate for such a task as this? ¹⁷Only those who, like ourselves, are men of integrity, sent by God, speaking with Christ's power, with God's eye upon us. We are not like those hucksters—and

2:14
Col 2:15

2:15
Eph 5:2

2:16
Lk 2:34
Jn 9:39
2 Cor 3:5

2:17
2 Cor 4:2

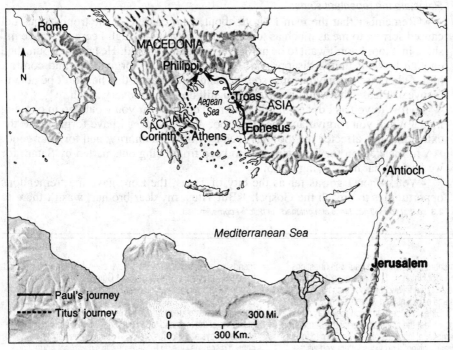

PAUL SEARCHES FOR TITUS
Paul had searched for Titus, hoping to meet him in Troas and receive news about the Corinthian church. When he did not find Titus in Troas, he went on to Macedonia (2:13), most likely to Philippi, where he found Titus.

———— Paul's journey
------- Titus' journey

0   300 Mi.
0   300 Km.

2:14ff In the middle of discussing his unscheduled trip to Macedonia, Paul breaks off into a discussion about his ministry, his relationship with the Corinthian believers, and the way God has used him to help others wherever he went (2:14—7:4). In 7:5, Paul resumes the story of his trip to Macedonia.

2:14–16 Believers are to be like a sweet perfume whose fragrance others can't help noticing. Just as we cannot control a person's opinion about a perfume's fragrance, we cannot control a person's reaction to our Christian message and actions. But if we remain true to Christ, his Spirit working in us will attract others.

2:16 In a Roman victory procession, the Roman general would display his treasures and captives amidst a cloud of incense. To the victors, the smell was sweet; to the captives in the parade, it was the stench of death. When Christians preach the gospel, it is good news to some and repulsive to others. Believers recognize the life-giving fragrance of this news. To nonbelievers, however, it smells foul, like death—their own.

2:16, 17 When we face the task of representing Christ, we never feel adequate. Perhaps we shouldn't, for to do so would be the

basis for pride. Our adequacy is always from God (1 Corinthians 15:10; 2 Corinthians 3:5). He has already commissioned and sent us (see Matthew 28:18–20). He has given us the Holy Spirit to speak with Christ's power. He keeps his eye upon us, protecting us as we work for him. Thus, if we realize that God makes us adequate and useful for him, there is no such thing as an inadequate believer. Serving him, therefore, requires that we focus on what he can do through us, not on what we can't do by ourselves.

2:17 A huckster is a salesman who has no concern for the customers or the quality of the product—he just wants to make as much money as possible. Some preachers in Paul's day were hucksters, preaching without understanding God's message or caring about what happened to their listeners. They weren't concerned about furthering God's Kingdom—they just wanted money. Today there are still religious hucksters who care only about money, not about truth. Those who truly speak for God should have integrity and avoid preaching for profit or self-gain (1 Timothy 6:5–10).

there are many of them—whose idea in getting out the Gospel is to make a good living out of it.

God's great new covenant

3:1
Acts 18:27
2 Cor 5:12; 10:12

3:2
1 Cor 9:2

3:3
Ex 24:12
Ps 40:8
Prov 3:3
Jer 31:33
Ezek 36:26
1 Cor 3:5

3:5
Jn 15:5
1 Cor 15:10

3:6
Jer 31:31
Lk 22:20
Jn 6:63
Rom 2:27; 7:6
8:2
Gal 3:10
Heb 8:6

3:7
Ex 34:29-35
Deut 9:10

3:8
Gal 3:5

3:9
Rom 1:17; 3:21

3:10,11
Jn 17:10,22
Heb 2:10

3:12
Eph 6:19
1 Thess 2:2

3:13
Ex 34:33
Rom 10:4
Gal 3:23

3:14
Isa 6:10
Jn 12:40
Acts 13:15
Rom 11:7
2 Cor 4:4

3 Are we beginning to be like those false teachers of yours who must tell you all about themselves and bring long letters of recommendation with them? I think you hardly need someone's letter to tell you about us, do you? And we don't need a recommendation from you, either! 2The only letter I need is you yourselves! By looking at the good change in your hearts, everyone can see that we have done a good work among you. 3They can see that you are a letter from Christ, written by us. It is not a letter written with pen and ink, but by the Spirit of the living God; not one carved on stone, but in human hearts.

4We dare to say these good things about ourselves only because of our great trust in God through Christ, that he will help us to be true to what we say, 5and not because we think we can do anything of lasting value by ourselves. Our only power and success comes from God. 6He is the one who has helped us tell others about his new agreement to save them. We do not tell them that they must obey every law of God or die; but we tell them there is life for them from the Holy Spirit. The old way, trying to be saved by keeping the Ten Commandments, ends in death; in the new way, the Holy Spirit gives them life.

7Yet that old system of law that led to death began with such glory that people could not bear to look at Moses' face. For as he gave them God's law to obey, his face shone out with the very glory of God—though the brightness was already fading away. 8Shall we not expect far greater glory in these days when the Holy Spirit is giving life? 9If the plan that leads to doom was glorious, much more glorious is the plan that makes men right with God. 10In fact, that first glory as it shone from Moses' face is worth nothing at all in comparison with the overwhelming glory of the new agreement. 11So if the old system that faded into nothing was full of heavenly glory, the glory of God's new plan for our salvation is certainly far greater, for it is eternal.

12Since we know that this new glory will never go away, we can preach with great boldness, 13and not as Moses did, who put a veil over his face so that the Israelis could not see the glory fade away.

14Not only Moses' face was veiled, but his people's minds and understanding were veiled and blinded too. Even now when the Scripture is read it seems as

---

3:1-3 Some false teachers had started carrying forged letters of recommendation to increase their authority. In no uncertain terms, Paul states that he needs no such letters. The lives of the believers whom he and his companions had converted were enough of a recommendation. Paul used letters of introduction, however, many times. For example, he wrote them for Phoebe (Romans 16:1, 2) and Timothy (1 Corinthians 16:10, 11). These letters helped Paul's trusted companions and friends find a welcome in various churches.

3:3 Paul uses powerful imagery from famous Old Testament passages predicting the promised day of new beginnings (see Jeremiah 31:33; Ezekiel 11:19; 36:26). This process of conversion isn't one for which any human minister can take credit; it is the work of God's Spirit. We do not become believers by following some manual or using some technique. Our conversion is a result of God's branding his Spirit on our hearts, guaranteeing his presence in us.

3:4, 5 Paul is not boasting; he gives God the credit for all his accomplishments. While the false teachers boasted of their own power and prestige, Paul expressed his humility before God. No one can claim to be adequate without God's help. No one is competent to carry out the responsibilities to which God has called him or her. Without the Holy Spirit's enabling, natural talent can carry us only so far. As Christ's witnesses, we need the character and special strength that only God gives.

3:6 The last sentence of this verse is literally translated "the letter kills, but the Spirit gives life." No one but Jesus has ever fulfilled the written law perfectly, and thus the whole world is condemned to death. The law makes people realize their sin, but it cannot give life. Eternal life comes from the Holy Spirit, who gives new life to all who believe in Christ. The moral law is still helpful to point out sin and show us how to live a life pleasing to God, but forgiveness comes only through the grace and mercy of Christ (see Romans 7:10—8:2).

3:7-11 Jesus Christ is far superior to the Old Testament ceremonial order (see Hebrews 8, 10 for a more complete discussion). That is saying a lot, because God himself gave the law amidst dazzling splendor. The law served its purpose until it could be translated into each person's heart by the Holy Spirit.

3:14-18 When Moses came down Mount Sinai with the Ten Commandments, his face glowed from being in God's presence (Exodus 34:29–35). He put on a veil to keep the people from being terrified by the brightness of his face. Paul adds that his veil kept them from seeing the glory fade away. Moses and his veil illustrate the fading of the old system and the veiling of the people's minds and hearts. The Jews' heritage was like a veil of pride that kept them from understanding the references to Christ in the Scriptures. When anyone becomes a Christian, Christ must remove his or her veil of pride (3:16). Don't let pride in your past keep you from eternity.

though Jewish hearts and minds are covered by a thick veil, because they cannot see and understand the real meaning of the Scriptures. For this veil of misunderstanding can be removed only by believing in Christ. 15Yes, even today when they read Moses' writings their hearts are blind and they think that obeying the Ten Commandments is the way to be saved.

16But whenever anyone turns to the Lord from his sins, then the veil is taken away. 17The Lord is the Spirit who gives them life, and where he is there is freedom [from trying to be saved by keeping the laws of God]. 18But we Christians have no veil over our faces; we can be mirrors that brightly reflect the glory of the Lord. And as the Spirit of the Lord works within us, we become more and more like him.

Satan blinds, but God gives light

4 It is God himself, in his mercy, who has given us this wonderful work [of telling his Good News to others], and so we never give up. 2We do not try to trick people into believing—we are not interested in fooling anyone. We never try to get anyone to believe that the Bible teaches what it doesn't. All such shameful methods we forego. We stand in the presence of God as we speak and so we tell the truth, as all who know us will agree.

3If the Good News we preach is hidden to anyone, it is hidden from the one who is on the road to eternal death. 4Satan, who is the god of this evil world, has made him blind, unable to see the glorious light of the Gospel that is shining upon him, or to understand the amazing message we preach about the glory of Christ, who is God. 5We don't go around preaching about ourselves, but about Christ Jesus as Lord. All we say of ourselves is that we are your slaves because of what Jesus has done for us. 6For God, who said, "Let there be light in the darkness," has made us understand that it is the brightness of his glory that is seen in the face of Jesus Christ.

7But this precious treasure—this light and power that now shine within us—is held in a perishable container, that is, in our weak bodies. Everyone can see that the glorious power within must be from God and is not our own.

8We are pressed on every side by troubles, but not crushed and broken. We are perplexed because we don't know why things happen as they do, but we don't give up and quit. 9We are hunted down, but God never abandons us. We get knocked

3:16
Isa 25:7
Rom 11:23
1 Cor 2:10

3:17
Rom 8:9
1 Cor 15:45
Gal 4:6
Phil 1:19

3:18
Rom 8:29
2 Cor 4:4,6
Col 3:10

4:2
2 Cor 2:17
1 Thess 2:3,5

4:3
Isa 6:9
1 Cor 1:18
2 Cor 3:14

4:4
Isa 6:10
Jn 1:18
12:31,40,45
2 Cor 3:14
Eph 6:12
Col 1:15
Heb 1:3

4:5
1 Cor 9:19

4:6
Gen 1:3
Ps 36:9
Jn 8:12; 12:46
Eph 5:8,14
1 Pet 2:9
2 Pet 1:19

4:7
2 Cor 5:1
2 Tim 2:20

4:8
2 Cor 7:5

4:9
Rom 8:35,36

3:17 *from trying to be saved by keeping the laws of God,* implied.   **4:1** *of telling his Good News to others,* implied.
4:4 *who is God,* literally, "who is the image of God."   **4:7** *this light and power that now shine within us,* implied.

3:17 When the Lord Jesus rose from the dead, he became life-giving Spirit (1 Corinthians 15:45). This does not mean that Jesus is now without a body or that he became the Holy Spirit; it means that he entered into a new form of existence when he was glorified. As such, he can live in heaven and in the hearts of the believers at the same time. Admittedly, this is a mystery; but those who know that Christ lives within them appreciate the reality of his presence.

3:17, 18 The glory that the Spirit imparts to the believer is greater both in quality and longevity than that which Moses experienced. The glory gradually transforms the believer into Christlikeness. Becoming Christlike is a progressive experience (see Romans 8:29; Galatians 4:19; Philippians 3:21; 1 John 3:2). The more closely we relate to him, the more we will be like him.

4:2 Preachers, teachers, and anyone who talks about Jesus Christ must remember that they stand in God's presence—he hears every word. When you tell people about Christ, be careful not to distort the message to please the audience. Proclaim the truth of God's Word.

4:3, 4 The Good News is open and revealed to everyone, except to those who refuse to believe. Satan's work is to deceive, and those who don't believe have been blinded by him (see 11:14, 15). The allure of money, power, and pleasure makes God's offer seem irrelevant. But those who refuse Christ, preferring their worldly lives, have made Satan their god.

4:5 The focus of Paul's preaching was Christ, not himself. When you witness, tell people about what Christ has done, and not about your abilities and accomplishments. People must be introduced to Christ, not to you. And if you hear someone preaching himself or his own ideas rather than Christ, beware—he is a false teacher.

4:5 Paul willingly served the Corinthian church despite the disappointments the people brought him. Any service requires a sacrifice of time and personal desires. Being Christ's follower means serving others, even when they do not measure up to our expectations.

4:7 The supremely valuable message of salvation in Jesus Christ has been entrusted by God to frail and fallible human beings. Paul's focus, however, is not on the perishable container but on its priceless contents—God's power dwelling in us. Though we are weak, God uses us to spread his Good News and gives us power to do his work. Knowing that the power is his, not ours, keeps us from pride and motivates us to keep daily contact with God, our power source. Our responsibility is to let people see God through us.

4:8–12 Paul reminds us that though we may be at the end of our rope, we are never at the end of hope. Our perishable bodies are subject to sin and suffering, but God never abandons us. Because Christ won victory over death, we have eternal life. All our risks, humiliations, and trials are opportunities to demonstrate Christ's power and presence in us.

4:10
Rom 8:17
1 Cor 15:31
Gal 6:17
Phil 3:10
Col 1:24
2 Tim 2:11
1 Pet 4:13

4:13
Ps 116:10

4:14
Acts 2:24
1 Thess 2:19

4:15
2 Cor 1:6,11

4:16
Eph 3:16
Col 3:10

4:17
Rom 8:18
1 Pet 1:6,7

4:18
Rom 8:24
2 Cor 5:7

down, but we get up again and keep going. ¹⁰These bodies of ours are constantly facing death just as Jesus did; so it is clear to all that it is only the living Christ within [who keeps us safe].

¹¹Yes, we live under constant danger to our lives because we serve the Lord, but this gives us constant opportunities to show forth the power of Jesus Christ within our dying bodies. ¹²Because of our preaching we face death, but it has resulted in eternal life for you.

¹³We boldly say what we believe [trusting God to care for us], just as the Psalm writer did when he said, "I believe and therefore I speak." ¹⁴We know that the same God who brought the Lord Jesus back from death will also bring us back to life again with Jesus, and present us to him along with you. ¹⁵These sufferings of ours are for your benefit. And the more of you who are won to Christ, the more there are to thank him for his great kindness, and the more the Lord is glorified.

¹⁶That is why we never give up. Though our bodies are dying, our inner strength in the Lord is growing every day. ¹⁷These troubles and sufferings of ours are, after all, quite small and won't last very long. Yet this short time of distress will result in God's richest blessing upon us forever and ever! ¹⁸So we do not look at what we can see right now, the troubles all around us, but we look forward to the joys in heaven which we have not yet seen. The troubles will soon be over, but the joys to come will last forever.

Earthly bodies are weak

5:1
1 Cor 15:47
2 Cor 4:7
Phil 3:21
Heb 11:10
2 Pet 1:13

5:2
Rom 8:23
1 Cor 15:53

5:3
Rom 3:18

5:4
1 Cor 15:53,54

5:5
Rom 8:23
2 Cor 1:22
Eph 1:14

5 For we know that when this tent we live in now is taken down—when we die and leave these bodies—we will have wonderful new bodies in heaven, homes that will be ours forevermore, made for us by God himself, and not by human hands. ²How weary we grow of our present bodies. That is why we look forward eagerly to the day when we shall have heavenly bodies which we shall put on like new clothes. ³For we shall not be merely spirits without bodies. ⁴These earthly bodies make us groan and sigh, but we wouldn't like to think of dying and having no bodies at all. We want to slip into our new bodies so that these dying bodies will, as it were, be swallowed up by everlasting life. ⁵This is what God has prepared for us and, as a guarantee, he has given us his Holy Spirit.

⁶Now we look forward with confidence to our heavenly bodies, realizing that every moment we spend in these earthly bodies is time spent away from our eternal

4:10 *who keeps us safe,* implied.   **4:13** *trusting God to care for us,* implied.

4:15–18 Paul faced sufferings, trials, and distress as he preached the Good News, but he knew that they would one day be over and he would obtain God's great blessings. As we face great troubles, it's easy to focus on the pain rather than on our ultimate goal. Just as athletes concentrate on the finish line and ignore their discomfort, we too must focus on the reward for our faith and the joy that lasts forever. No matter what happens to us in this life, we have the assurance of eternal life where all suffering will end.

4:16 It is easy to quit. We all have faced problems in our relationships or work that caused us to want to lay down the tools and walk away. Rather than giving up, however, Paul concentrated on developing his inner strength. Don't let fatigue, pain, or criticism force you off the job. Renew your commitment to serving Christ. Don't forsake your eternal reward because of the intensity of today's pain. Your very weakness allows the resurrection power of Christ to strengthen you moment by moment.

4:18 Our troubles should not diminish our faith or disillusion us. Instead, we should realize that there is a purpose in our suffering. Problems and human limitations have several benefits: (1) they help us remember Christ's suffering for us; (2) they help keep us from pride; (3) they help us look beyond this brief life; (4) they prove our faith to others; and (5) they give God the opportunity to demonstrate his great power. Don't resent your troubles—see them as opportunities!

5:1–10 Greeks did not believe in a bodily resurrection. Most saw the afterlife as something that happened only to the soul—the real person, imprisoned in a physical body. At death the soul was released. There was no immortality for the body, but the soul entered an eternal state. But the Bible teaches that the body and soul are ultimately inseparable. The church at Corinth was in the heart of Greek culture, and many believers had difficulty with the concept of bodily resurrection.

Paul describes our resurrected bodies in more detail in 1 Corinthians 15:46–58. We will still have our own personalities and individualities in our resurrected bodies, but they will be made better than we can imagine through Christ's work. Scripture is unclear about what our resurrected bodies will be like, but we know they will be perfect, without sickness or disease (see Philippians 3:21).

5:1–5 The Holy Spirit within us is our guarantee that God has reserved for us brand-new everlasting bodies that he will give us at the resurrection (1:22). We have eternity in us now! Such hope should give us great courage and patience to endure anything we might experience.

5:6–8 Death is frightening for many people because it is mysterious and unknown. Paul was not afraid to die because he was confident of spending eternity with Christ. Of course, facing the unknown is cause for anxiety and leaving loved ones hurts deeply, but if we believe in Jesus Christ, we can share Paul's hope and confidence of eternal life with Christ.

home in heaven with Jesus. 7We know these things are true by believing, not by seeing. 8And we are not afraid, but are quite content to die, for then we will be at home with the Lord. 9So our aim is to please him always in everything we do, whether we are here in this body or away from this body and with him in heaven. 10For we must all stand before Christ to be judged and have our lives laid bare—before him. Each of us will receive whatever he deserves for the good or bad things he has done in his earthly body.

5:7
1 Cor 13:12

5:8
Phil 1:23

5:10
Mt 16:27
Acts 10:42
1 Cor 3:13-15
Rev 22:12

Be reconciled to God

11It is because of this solemn fear of the Lord, which is ever present in our minds, that we work so hard to win others. God knows our hearts, that they are pure in this matter, and I hope that, deep within, you really know it too.

12Are we trying to pat ourselves on the back again? No, I am giving you some good ammunition! You can use this on those preachers of yours who brag about how well they look and preach, but don't have true and honest hearts. You can boast about us that we, at least, are well intentioned and honest.

5:12
2 Cor 1:14; 3:1

13, 14Are we insane [to say such things about ourselves]? If so, it is to bring glory to God. And if we are in our right minds, it is for your benefit. Whatever we do, it is certainly not for our own profit, but because Christ's love controls us now. Since we believe that Christ died for all of us, we should also believe that we have died to the old life we used to live. 15He died for all so that all who live—having received eternal life from him—might live no longer for themselves, to please themselves, but to spend their lives pleasing Christ who died and rose again for them. 16So stop evaluating Christians by what the world thinks about them or by what they seem to be like on the outside. Once I mistakenly thought of Christ that way, merely as a human being like myself. How differently I feel now! 17When someone becomes a Christian he becomes a brand new person inside. He is not the same any more. A new life has begun!

5:14
Rom 5:15
Gal 2:20

5:15
Rom 14:7-9
1 Pet 4:2

5:16
Mt 12:50

5:17
Isa 65:17
Gal 6:15
Eph 4:24
Rev 21:5

18All these new things are from God who brought us back to himself through what Christ Jesus did. And God has given us the privilege of urging everyone to come into his favor and be reconciled to him. 19For God was in Christ, restoring the world to himself, no longer counting men's sins against them but blotting them out. This is the wonderful message he has given us to tell others. 20We are Christ's ambassadors. God is using us to speak to you: we beg you, as though Christ himself were here pleading with you, receive the love he offers you—be reconciled to God. 21For God took the sinless Christ and poured into him our sins. Then, in exchange, he poured God's goodness into us!

5:18
Rom 5:10
Col 1:20-22

5:19
Isa 43:25
Rom 3:24; 4:28

5:20
Rom 5:10

5:21
Isa 53:6,9
Jer 23:6
Dan 9:24
Rom 1:17
Gal 3:13
Heb 4:15; 7:26
1 Pet 2:22

5:13, 14 *to say such things about ourselves,* implied.   **5:21** *he poured God's goodness into us,* literally, "Him who knew no sin, he made sin on our behalf, that we might become the righteousness of God in him."

5:8 Death is not the last word. For those who believe in Christ, death is only a prelude to eternal life with God. Our lives will continue, both in body and in spirit. Let this confident hope inspire you to faithful service.

5:9, 10 While eternal life is a free gift given on the basis of God's grace (Ephesians 2:8, 9), our lives will still be judged by Christ. This judgment is for rewards for how we have lived. Faith does not free us from obedience. We must never use God's grace as an excuse for laziness. All Christians must give account for how they have lived (see Matthew 16:27; Romans 14:10–12; 1 Corinthians 3:10–15).

5:12 The false preachers or hucksters (see 2:17) were concerned only about getting ahead in this world. They were preaching the gospel for money, while Paul and his companions were preaching out of concern for eternity. You can tell who false preachers are by noticing what really motivates them. If they are more concerned about themselves than Christ, they are false. Avoid them and their message.

5:16, 17 Christians are brand new people on the *inside.* The Holy Spirit gives them new life, and they are not the same any more. We

are not reformed, rehabilitated, or reeducated—we are new creations, living in vital union with Christ (Colossians 2:6, 7). We are not merely turning over a new leaf; we are beginning a new life under a new Master.

5:18–21 God brings us back to himself (reconciles us) by blotting out our sins (see also Ephesians 2:13–18) and making us righteous. We are no longer strangers, foreigners, or enemies to God when we trust in Christ. Because we have been reconciled to God, he now gives us the privilege of encouraging others to do the same.

5:20 An ambassador is an official representative from one country to another. As believers, we are Christ's ambassadors, sent with his message of reconciliation to the world. An ambassador of reconciliation has an important responsibility. We dare not take this responsibility lightly. How well are you fulfilling your commission as Christ's ambassador?

5:21 When we trust in Christ, we make a trade—our sin for his goodness. Our sin was poured into Christ at his crucifixion. His righteousness is poured into us at our conversion. This is what Christians mean by Christ's atonement for sin. In the world,

6:1
1 Cor 3:9
2 Cor 5:20
Heb 12:15

6:2
Isa 49:8

6 As God's partners we beg you not to toss aside this marvelous message of God's great kindness. ²For God says, "Your cry came to me at a favorable time, when the doors of welcome were wide open. I helped you on a day when salvation was being offered." Right now God is ready to welcome you. Today he is ready to save you.

Paul patiently endures hardship

6:3
1 Cor 8:9; 9:12

6:4
2 Cor 4:8
11:23-28

6:5
Acts 16:23
1 Cor 4:11

6:6
2 Cor 11:6

6:7
1 Cor 2:4
2 Cor 2:17; 4:2
10:4

6:8
Mt 27:63
Rom 3:8
1 Cor 4:10,13
2 Cor 4:2

6:9
Ps 118:18
Rom 8:36
1 Cor 4:9
2 Cor 1:8; 4:11

6:10
Acts 3:6
Rom 8:32
1 Cor 3:21
2 Cor 8:9

6:11
2 Cor 7:3

6:12
2 Cor 12:15

³We try to live in such a way that no one will ever be offended or kept back from finding the Lord by the way we act, so that no one can find fault with us and blame it on the Lord. ⁴In fact, in everything we do we try to show that we are true ministers of God.

We patiently endure suffering and hardship and trouble of every kind. ⁵We have been beaten, put in jail, faced angry mobs, worked to exhaustion, stayed awake through sleepless nights of watching, and gone without food. ⁶We have proved ourselves to be what we claim by our wholesome lives and by our understanding of the Gospel and by our patience. We have been kind and truly loving and filled with the Holy Spirit. ⁷We have been truthful, with God's power helping us in all we do. All of the godly man's arsenal—weapons of defense, and weapons of attack—have been ours.

⁸We stand true to the Lord whether others honor us or despise us, whether they criticize us or commend us. We are honest, but they call us liars.

⁹The world ignores us, but we are known to God; we live close to death, but here we are, still very much alive. We have been injured but kept from death. ¹⁰Our hearts ache, but at the same time we have the joy of the Lord. We are poor, but we give rich spiritual gifts to others. We own nothing, and yet we enjoy everything.

¹¹Oh, my dear Corinthian friends! I have told you all my feelings; I love you with all my heart. ¹²Any coldness still between us is not because of any lack of love on my part, but because your love is too small and does not reach out to me and draw me in. ¹³I am talking to you now as if you truly were my very own children. Open your hearts to us! Return our love!

Be separate from unbelievers

6:14
Deut 7:3; 22:10
Eph 5:6,7
1 Jn 1:6,7

¹⁴Don't be teamed with those who do not love the Lord, for what do the people of God have in common with the people of sin? How can light live with darkness? ¹⁵And what harmony can there be between Christ and the devil? How can a

---

bartering works only when two people exchange goods of relatively equal value. But God offers to trade righteousness for sin—something of immeasurable worth for something worthless. How grateful we should be for his goodness to us.

6:1 How could the Corinthian believers toss aside God's message? Perhaps they were doubting Paul and his words, confused by the false teachers who taught a different message. "To toss aside this message" can also be translated "to receive the grace of God in vain." The people heard God's message, but did not let it affect what they said and did. How often does God's message reach you in vain?

6:2 God is now offering salvation to all people. Sometimes we put off a decision for Christ, thinking there will be a better time—but we could easily miss our opportunity altogether. There is no time like the present to receive God's forgiveness. Don't let anything hold you back from God.

6:3, 4 In everything he did, Paul always considered what his actions communicated about Jesus Christ. If you are a believer, you are a minister for God. In the course of each day, non-Christians observe you. Consider whether your actions will keep anyone from God. Don't let your careless or undisciplined actions be another's excuse for rejecting God.

6:7 See Ephesians 6:10-18 for more about the weapons of faith.

6:8-10 What a difference knowing Jesus can make! He turns

everything around, caring for us in spite of what the world thinks. Christians don't have to give in to public opinion and pressure. Paul stood true to God whether people praised him or condemned him. He remained active, joyous, and content in the most difficult conditions. Don't let circumstances or people's expectations control you. Be firm as you stand true to God, and refuse to compromise on his standards for living.

6:12, 13 It is easy to react against those whom God has placed over us in leadership rather than to accept their exhortations as a sign of their love for us. We need an open heart rather than a hardened heart toward God's messengers.

6:14-17 Paul urged believers not to form binding relationships with nonbelievers, because this might weaken their Christian commitment, integrity, or standards. Earlier, Paul had explained that this did not mean isolating themselves from nonbelievers (see 1 Corinthians 5:9, 10). Paul even told Christians to stay with their nonbelieving spouses (1 Corinthians 7:12, 13). Paul wanted believers to be active in their witness for Christ to nonbelievers, but they should not lock themselves into personal or business relationships which could cause them to compromise their faith. Just as those in business should avoid conflicts of interest, believers should avoid situations that would force them to divide their loyalties.

Christian be a partner with one who doesn't believe? 16And what union can there be between God's temple and idols? For you are God's temple, the home of the living God, and God has said of you, "I will live in them and walk among them, and I will be their God and they shall be my people." 17That is why the Lord has said, "Leave them; separate yourselves from them; don't touch their filthy things, and I will welcome you, 18and be a Father to you, and you will be my sons and daughters."

6:16
Ex 25:8; 29:45
Jer 31:33
Ezek 36:28
6:17
Isa 52:11
6:18
Jer 31:1,9
Hos 1:10

7 Having such great promises as these, dear friends, let us turn away from everything wrong, whether of body or spirit, and purify ourselves, living in the wholesome fear of God, giving ourselves to him alone.

7:1
1 Pet 1:22
1 Jn 3:3

The church's repentance gives Paul joy

2Please open your hearts to us again, for not one of you has suffered any wrong from us. Not one of you was led astray. We have cheated no one nor taken advantage of anyone. 3I'm not saying this to scold or blame you, for, as I have said before, you are in my heart forever and I live and die with you. 4I have the highest confidence in you, and my pride in you is great. You have greatly encouraged me; you have made me so happy in spite of all my suffering.

7:2
2 Cor 6:12
7:3
2 Cor 6:11
7:4
1 Cor 1:4
2 Cor 7:14; 8:24
10:8
Phil 2:17

5When we arrived in Macedonia there was no rest for us; outside, trouble was on every hand and all around us; within us, our hearts were full of dread and fear. 6Then God who cheers those who are discouraged refreshed us by the arrival of Titus. 7Not only was his presence a joy, but also the news that he brought of the wonderful time he had with you. When he told me how much you were looking forward to my visit, and how sorry you were about what had happened, and about your loyalty and warm love for me, well, I overflowed with joy!

7:5
2 Cor 2:13; 4:8
7:6
2 Cor 2:13; 7:13
2 Thess 2:16

8I am no longer sorry that I sent that letter to you, though I was very sorry for a time, realizing how painful it would be to you. But it hurt you only for a little while. 9Now I am glad I sent it, not because it hurt you, but because the pain turned you to God. It was a good kind of sorrow you felt, the kind of sorrow God wants his people to have, so that I need not come to you with harshness. 10For God sometimes uses sorrow in our lives to help us turn away from sin and seek eternal life. We should never regret his sending it. But the sorrow of the man who is not a Christian is not the sorrow of true repentance and does not prevent eternal death.

7:8
2 Cor 2:2-4

7:10
2 Sam 12:13
Jer 31:18-20
Mt 26:75
27:4,5

Method	Reference	PRINCIPLES OF CONFRONTATION IN 2 CORINTHIANS
Be firm	7:9; 10:2	
Affirm all you see that is good	7:4	
Be accurate and honest	7:14; 8:21	
Know the facts	11:22–27	
Follow up after the confrontation	7:13; 12:14	
Be gentle after being firm	7:15; 13:11–13	
Speak words that reflect Christ's message, not your own ideas	10:3; 10:12, 13; 12:19	
Use discipline only when all else fails	13:2	

Sometimes rebuke is necessary, but it must be used with caution. The purpose of any rebuke, confrontation, or discipline is to help people, not hurt them.

6:17 Separation from the world involves more than keeping our distance from sinners; it means staying close to God (see 7:1, 2). It involves more than avoiding entertainment that leads to sin; it extends as well into how we spend our time and money. In this fallen world, there is no way to separate ourselves totally from all effects of sin. Nevertheless, we are to resist the sin around us, not give up and give in.

7:1 Purifying ourselves is a twofold action: turning *away* from sin, and turning *toward* God.

7:5 Here Paul resumes the story he left off in 2:13, where he says he went to Macedonia to look for Titus.

7:8ff "That letter" refers to the third letter (now lost) that Paul wrote the Corinthians. Apparently it had caused the people to begin to change. For an explanation of the chronology of Paul's letters to Corinth, see the note on 1:1.

7:10 True repentance means being sorry for our sins and changing our behavior. Many people are sorry only for the effects of their sins or for being caught. Compare Peter's remorse and repentance with Judas' bitterness and suicide. Both denied Christ. One repented and was restored to faith and service; the other took his own life.

7:11
Jer 50:4,5
Zech 12:10
2 Cor 2:6

11Just see how much good this grief from the Lord did for you! You no longer shrugged your shoulders, but became earnest and sincere, and very anxious to get rid of the sin that I wrote you about. You became frightened about what had happened, and longed for me to come and help. You went right to work on the problem and cleared it up [punishing the man who sinned]. You have done everything you could to make it right.

7:12
1 Cor 5:1-5

12I wrote as I did so the Lord could show how much you really do care for us. That was my purpose even more than to help the man who sinned, or his father to whom he did the wrong.

7:13
Rom 15:32
2 Cor 2:13; 7:6

13In addition to the encouragement you gave us by your love, we were made happier still by Titus' joy when you gave him such a fine welcome and set his mind at ease. 14I told him how it would be—told him before he left me of my pride in you—and you didn't disappoint me. I have always told you the truth and now my boasting to Titus has also proved true! 15He loves you more than ever when he remembers the way you listened to him so willingly and received him so anxiously and with such deep concern. 16How happy this makes me, now that I am sure all is well between us again. Once again I can have perfect confidence in you.

7:15
2 Cor 2:9
Phil 2:12

7:16
2 Cor 2:3
2 Thess 3:4
Philem 21

3. Paul defends the collection
Generous giving glorifies the Lord

8:1
Acts 16:9

8 Now I want to tell you what God in his grace has done for the churches in Macedonia.

2Though they have been going through much trouble and hard times, they have mixed their wonderful joy with their deep poverty, and the result has been an overflow of giving to others. 3They gave not only what they could afford, but far more; and I can testify that they did it because they wanted to, and not because of nagging on my part. 4They begged us to take the money so they could share in the joy of helping the Christians in Jerusalem. 5Best of all, they went beyond our

8:4
Acts 24:17
Rom 15:25
1 Cor 16:1,3

8:5
Mt 25:40
Heb 13:16

7:11 *punishing the man who sinned,* implied. So also in vs 12.

NEEDS FOR A FUNDRAISING PROJECT

Information	8:4
Definite purpose	8:4
Readiness and willingness	9:7
Dedication	8:5
Leadership	8:7
Enthusiasm	8:7, 8, 11
Persistence	8:2ff
Honesty and integrity	8:21
Accountability	9:3
Someone to keep it moving	8:18–22

The topic of fundraising is not one to be avoided or one that should embarrass us, but all fundraising efforts should be planned and conducted responsibly.

7:11 It is difficult to hear that we have sinned, and even more difficult to get rid of sin. Paul praised the Corinthians for clearing up an especially troublesome situation (see note on 2:5–11). Do you tend to be defensive when confronted? Don't let pride keep you from admitting your sins. Accept confrontation as a tool for growth, and do all you can to correct problems that are pointed out to you.

8:1ff Paul, writing from Macedonia, hoped that news of the generosity of these churches would encourage the Corinthian believers and motivate them to solve their problems and unite in fellowship.

8:2 While making his third missionary journey, Paul was collecting money for the impoverished believers in Jerusalem. The churches in Macedonia—Philippi, Thessalonica, and Beroea—gave money even though they were poor, and they gave more than Paul

expected. This was sacrificial giving—they were poor themselves, but they wanted to help. The point of giving is not so much the amount we give, but why and how we give. God does not want gifts given grudgingly. Instead, he wants us to give as these churches did—out of dedication to him, love for fellow believers, the joy of helping those in need, and because it was right to do so. How well does your giving measure up to the standards set by the Macedonian churches?

8:3–6 Through believers' concern and eagerness to help others, the Kingdom of God spreads. Here we see several churches joining to help others beyond their own circle of friends and their own city. Explore ways you might link up with a ministry outside your city, either through your church or through a Christian organization. By joining with other believers to do God's work, you increase Christian unity and help the Kingdom to grow.

highest hopes, for their first action was to dedicate themselves to the Lord and to us, for whatever directions God might give to them through us. 6They were so enthusiastic about it that we have urged Titus, who encouraged your giving in the first place, to visit you and encourage you to complete your share in this ministry of giving. 7You people there are leaders in so many ways—you have so much faith, so many good preachers, so much learning, so much enthusiasm, so much love for us. Now I want you to be leaders also in the spirit of cheerful giving.

8I am not giving you an order; I am not saying you must do it, but others are eager for it. This is one way to prove that your love is real, that it goes beyond mere words.

9You know how full of love and kindness our Lord Jesus was: though he was so very rich, yet to help you he became so very poor, so that by being poor he could make you rich.

10I want to suggest that you finish what you started to do a year ago, for you were not only the first to propose this idea, but the first to begin doing something about it. 11Having started the ball rolling so enthusiastically, you should carry this project through to completion just as gladly, giving whatever you can out of whatever you have. Let your enthusiastic idea at the start be equalled by your realistic action now. 12If you are really eager to give, then it isn't important how much you have to give. God wants you to give what you have, not what you haven't.

13Of course, I don't mean that those who receive your gifts should have an easy time of it at your expense, 14but you should divide with them. Right now you have plenty and can help them; then at some other time they can share with you when you need it. In this way each will have as much as he needs. 15Do you remember what the Scriptures say about this? "He that gathered much had nothing left over, and he that gathered little had enough." So you also should share with those in need.

16I am thankful to God that he has given Titus the same real concern for you that I have. 17He is glad to follow my suggestion that he visit you again—but I think he would have come anyway, for he is very eager to see you! 18I am sending another well-known brother with him, who is highly praised as a preacher of the Good News in all the churches. 19In fact, this man was elected by the churches to travel with me to take the gift to Jerusalem. This will glorify the Lord and show our

8:6
2 Cor 12:18

8:7
Prov 22:9; 28:27
Mt 19:21
Mk 10:21
Lk 18:22
1 Cor 1:5; 12:13
2 Cor 9:8

8:9
Mt 8:20
Lk 9:58
Phil 2:6,7

8:10
Prov 19:17
Mt 10:42
1 Tim 6:18
Heb 13:16

8:12
Mk 12:43
2 Cor 9:7

8:14
Acts 4:34,35

8:15
Ex 16:18

8:16
2 Cor 2:13,14

8:17
2 Cor 12:18

8:18
2 Cor 12:18

8:19
Acts 14:23
1 Cor 16:3

8:7, 8 Giving is a natural response of love. Paul did not order the Corinthians to give, but he encouraged them to prove that their love was real. When you love someone, you want to give him your time and attention and to provide for his needs. If you refuse to help, your love may not be as genuine as you say.

8:9 Jesus became poor by giving up his rights as God and becoming human. Incarnation means God voluntarily becoming man—the wholly human person, Jesus of Nazareth. As a man, Jesus was subject to place, time, and all other human attributes. He did not give up his eternal power to become human, but he did set aside his glory and his rights. In response to the Father's will, he limited his power and knowledge. What made Jesus' humanity unique was his freedom from sin. In his full humanity, we can see everything about God's character which can be conveyed in human terms. The incarnation is explained further in these Bible passages: John 1:1–14; Romans 1:2–5; Philippians 2:6–11; 1 Timothy 3:16; Hebrews 2:14; 1 John 1:1–3.

8:10–15 The Corinthian church had money, and Paul challenged them to share with the Jerusalem Christians just as the Macedonian churches had done. Four principles of giving emerge here: (1) your willingness to give cheerfully is more important than the amount you give; (2) you should strive to fulfill your financial commitments; (3) if you give to others in need, they will in turn help you when you are in need. (4) Nevertheless, you should give as a response to Christ, not for anything you can get out of it. How you give reflects your devotion to Christ. These principles apply regardless of your financial condition.

8:11 How do you decide how much to give? Paul gave the Corinthian church several principles to follow: (1) each person should follow through on previous promises (8:10; 9:3); (2) each person should give as much as he is able (8:12; 9:6); (3) each person must make up his own mind how much to give (9:7); and (4) each person should give in proportion to what God has given (9:10). God gives to us so we can give to others.

8:12 The attitude with which we give is more important than the amount we give. We don't have to be embarrassed if we can give only a small gift. God is concerned about *how* we give from the resources we have (see Mark 12:41–44). According to this standard, the giving of the Macedonian churches was difficult to match.

8:12 Paul says, "God wants you to give what you have, not what you haven't." Sacrificial giving must be responsible. Paul wants believers to give generously, but not to the point where those who depend on the givers must go without having their basic needs met. Give until it hurts, but don't give so that it hurts those people who depend on you (i.e., your family and/or relatives needing your financial support).

8:18–21 Paul chose more than one person to carry the gift so there would be no suspicion over the way the money was handled. The people whom Paul sent were well recommended. The church did not need to worry that these were false teachers or that they would misuse the money.

eagerness to help each other. 20By traveling together we will guard against any suspicion, for we are anxious that no one should find fault with the way we are handling this large gift. 21God knows we are honest, but I want everyone else to know it too. That is why we have made this arrangement.

22And I am sending you still another brother, whom we know from experience to be an earnest Christian. He is especially interested, as he looks forward to this trip, because I have told him all about your eagerness to help.

23If anyone asks who Titus is, say that he is my partner, my helper in helping you, and you can also say that the other two brothers represent the assemblies here and are splendid examples of those who belong to the Lord.

24Please show your love for me to these men and do for them all that I have publicly boasted you would.

God prizes cheerful givers

9 I realize that I really don't even need to mention this to you, about helping God's people. 2For I know how eager you are to do it, and I have boasted to the friends in Macedonia that you were ready to send an offering a year ago. In fact, it was this enthusiasm of yours that stirred up many of them to begin helping. 3But I am sending these men just to be sure that you really are ready, as I told them you would be, with your money all collected; I don't want it to turn out that this time I was wrong in my boasting about you. 4I would be very much ashamed—and so would you—if some of these Macedonian people come with me, only to find that you still aren't ready after all I have told them!

5So I have asked these other brothers to arrive ahead of me to see that the gift you promised is on hand and waiting. I want it to be a real gift and not look as if it were being given under pressure.

6But remember this—if you give little, you will get little. A farmer who plants just a few seeds will get only a small crop, but if he plants much, he will reap much. 7Every one must make up his own mind as to how much he should give. Don't force anyone to give more than he really wants to, for cheerful givers are the ones God prizes. 8God is able to make it up to you by giving you everything you need and more, so that there will not only be enough for your own needs, but plenty left over to give joyfully to others. 9It is as the Scriptures say: "The godly man gives generously to the poor. His good deeds will be an honor to him forever."

10For God, who gives seed to the farmer to plant, and later on, good crops to harvest and eat, will give you more and more seed to plant and will make it grow so that you can give away more and more fruit from your harvest.

11Yes, God will give you much so that you can give away much, and when we take your gifts to those who need them they will break out into thanksgiving and praise to God for your help. 12So, two good things happen as a result of your gifts—those in need are helped, and they overflow with thanks to God. 13Those you help will be glad not only because of your generous gifts to themselves and to others, but they will praise God for this proof that your deeds are as good as your

8:21
Prov 3:4
Rom 12:17
Phil 4:8
1 Pet 2:12

8:23
Phil 2:25

8:24
2 Cor 7:4

9:1
Rom 15:26
1 Cor 16:1
Gal 2:10
1 Thess 4:9

9:2
2 Cor 8:6,17

9:3
1 Cor 16:2

9:5
Gen 33:11

9:6
Prov 11:24
19:17
Lk 6:38
Gal 6:7,9

9:7
Ex 35:5
Deut 15:7-10
Rom 12:8
2 Cor 8:12

9:8
Prov 28:27
Phil 4:19

9:9
Ps 112:9

9:10
Hos 10:12
Mt 6:1

9:11
2 Cor 1:11; 4:16

9:12
2 Cor 8:14

9:13
Mt 5:16
Heb 13:16

9:1 The example of giving here was at the heart of Jewish piety—for they showed their godliness by sharing with the poor. Christians today have forgotten this central idea of true godly living, largely because it is not tax-deductible! Of course, giving to organizations is still important, but we are urged to fulfill this biblical mandate by helping the poor, whether or not it is tax-deductible.

9:3, 4 Paul was reminding the Corinthians to fulfill the commitment they had already made (see also 8:10-12). He was holding them accountable to keep their promise.

9:6-8 People may hesitate to give generously to God if they worry about having enough money left over to meet their own needs. Paul assured the Corinthians that God is able to meet their needs. The person who gives only a little will receive only a little in return. Don't let a lack of faith keep you from giving freely and generously.

9:10 God gives us resources to use and invest for him. Paul used the illustration of seeds to explain that the resources God gives us are not to be hidden, foolishly devoured, or thrown away, but cultivated in order to produce more crops. When we invest what God has given us in his work, he will provide us with even more to give.

9:12 Paul emphasizes the spiritual rewards for those who give generously to God's work. We should not expect to become wealthy through giving; the rewards about which Paul speaks are treasures in heaven (see Matthew 6:19-21 for Jesus' teaching on this).

9:13, 14 Paul notes that those who receive your gifts will be glad and will pray for you. This is the unexpected result of giving—as you bless others, you yourself are blessed. Giving is a wonderful experience that only the generous fully enter into.

doctrine. 14And they will pray for you with deep fervor and feeling because of the wonderful grace of God shown through you.

15Thank God for his Son—his Gift too wonderful for words.

9:15
Jas 1:17

4. Paul defends his authority
Paul's authority is discredited

10 I plead with you—yes, I, Paul—and I plead gently, as Christ himself would do. Yet some of you are saying, "Paul's letters are bold enough when he is far away, but when he gets here he will be afraid to raise his voice!"

10:1
1 Cor 2:3
2 Cor 10:10

2I hope I won't need to show you when I come how harsh and rough I can be. I don't want to carry out my present plans against some of you who seem to think my deeds and words are merely those of an ordinary man. 3It is true that I am an ordinary, weak human being, but I don't use human plans and methods to win my battles. 4I use God's mighty weapons, not those made by men, to knock down the devil's strongholds. 5These weapons can break down every proud argument against God and every wall that can be built to keep men from finding him. With these weapons I can capture rebels and bring them back to God, and change them into men whose hearts' desire is obedience to Christ. 6I will use these weapons against every rebel who remains after I have first used them on you yourselves, and you surrender to Christ.

10:2
1 Cor 4:18,21
2 Cor 1:17; 13:2

10:4
Jer 1:10
1 Cor 9:7
Eph 6:13-17
1 Thess 5:8

10:5
Isa 2:11
1 Cor 1:19; 3:19

10:6
2 Cor 2:9; 7:15
13:2

7The trouble with you is that you look at me and I seem weak and powerless, but you don't look beneath the surface. Yet if anyone can claim the power and authority of Christ, I certainly can. 8I may seem to be boasting more than I should about my authority over you—authority to help you, not to hurt you—but I shall make good every claim. 9I say this so that you will not think I am just blustering when I scold you in my letters.

10:7
Jn 7:24
1 Cor 9:1; 14:37
2 Cor 11:23
1 Jn 4:6

10"Don't bother about his letters," some say. "He sounds big, but it's all noise. When he gets here you will see that there is nothing great about him, and you have never heard a worse preacher!" 11This time my personal presence is going to be just as rough on you as my letters are!

10:10
1 Cor 1:17; 2:3
2 Cor 11:6
Gal 4:13

12Oh, don't worry, I wouldn't dare say that I am as wonderful as these other men who tell you how good they are! Their trouble is that they are only comparing themselves with each other, and measuring themselves against their own little ideas. What stupidity!

10:12
2 Cor 3:1; 5:12

13But we will not boast of authority we do not have. Our goal is to measure up to God's plan for us, and this plan includes our working there with you. 14We are not going too far when we claim authority over you, for we were the first to come to you with the Good News concerning Christ. 15It is not as though we were trying to claim credit for the work someone else has done among you. Instead, we hope that your faith will grow and that, still within the limits set for us, our work among you will be greatly enlarged.

10:13
Rom 12:3

10:14
1 Cor 9:1

10:15
Rom 15:20
2 Thess 1:3

16After that, we will be able to preach the Good News to other cities that are far beyond you, where no one else is working; then there will be no question about

10:16
Acts 19:21

10:1 From 7:8–16 we know that the majority of Corinthian believers sided with Paul. However, a minority continued to slander him, saying that he was bold in his letters but had no authority in person. Chapters 10–13 are Paul's response to this charge.

10:3–6 The Christian must choose whose methods to use, God's or man's. Paul assures us that God's mighty weapons—prayer, faith, hope, love, God's Word, the Holy Spirit—are powerful and effective (see Ephesians 6:13–18)! When dealing with the pride that keeps people from a relationship with Christ, we may be tempted to use our own methods. But nothing can break down these barriers like God's weapons.

10:7–9 Paul reminded the Corinthians of his authority because of the opposition he was receiving from various people in their church. False teachers were encouraging them to ignore Paul, and

he wanted to protect the Corinthians from heresy.

10:10 Apparently Paul was not a powerful preacher (although he was an excellent debater). But he responded obediently to God's call, and he introduced Christianity to the Roman Empire. (Moses also had problems with speaking. Apparently preaching ability is not the first prerequisite of a powerful leader!)

10:12, 13 Paul criticized the false teachers who tried to prove their goodness by comparing themselves with others rather than with God. When we compare ourselves with others, we may feel proud because we think we're better. But when we measure ourselves against God's standards, it becomes obvious that we're not nearly good enough. Don't worry about how other people live. Instead, continually ask how your life measures up to what God wants you to be and how your life compares to that of Jesus Christ.

10:17
Jer 9:24
1 Cor 1:31

10:18
Prov 27:2

being in someone else's field. [17]As the Scriptures say, "If anyone is going to boast, let him boast about what the Lord has done and not about himself." [18]When someone boasts about himself and how well he has done, it doesn't count for much. But when the Lord commends him, that's different!

Paul and the false apostles

11:1
2 Cor 5:13

11:2
Hos 2:19
1 Cor 4:15

11 I hope you will be patient with me as I keep on talking like a fool. Do bear with me and let me say what is on my heart. [2]I am anxious for you with the deep concern of God himself—anxious that your love should be for Christ alone, just as a pure maiden saves her love for one man only, for the one who will be her

---

PAUL'S CREDENTIALS
One of Paul's biggest problems with the church in Corinth was his concern that they viewed him as no more than a blustering preacher; thus, they were not taking seriously his advice in his letters and on his visits. Paul addressed this attitude in the letter of 2 Corinthians, pointing out his credentials as an apostle of Christ and why they should take his advice.

1:1; 1:21; 4:1	Commissioned by God
1:18; 4:2	Spoke truthfully
1:12	Acted with purity, sincerity, and dependence on God alone in his dealings with them
1:13, 14	Was straightforward and sincere in his letters
1:22	Had God's Holy Spirit
2:4; 6:11; 11:11	Loved the Corinthian believers
2:17	Spoke with integrity and Christ's power
3:2, 3	Worked among them and changed their lives
3:4; 12:6	Lived as an example to the believers
4:1, 16	Never gave up
4:2	Taught the Bible with integrity
4:5	Had Christ as the center of his message
4:8–12; 6:4, 5, 9, 10	Endured persecution as he taught the Good News
5:11	Worked to win others and to please God
5:12	Was well-intentioned and honest
5:18–20	Was Christ's ambassador, called to tell the Good News
6:3, 4	Tried to live a blameless life so others would not be kept from God because of his actions
6:6	Led a wholesome life, understood the gospel, and displayed patience with the Corinthians
6:7	Was truthful and filled with God's power
6:8	Stood true to God first and always
7:2; 11:7–9	Never cheated, wronged, or took advantage of anyone
8:20, 21	Handled their money offering to be sent to Jerusalem in a responsible, blameless manner
10:1–6	Used God's weapons, not his own, for God's work
10:7, 8	Had the power and authority of Christ
10:12, 13	Wanted to measure up to God's plan, not glorify himself
10:14, 15	Had authority because he taught them the Good News
11:23–33	Endured pain and danger as he fulfilled his calling
12:2–4	Was blessed with an astounding vision
12:7–10	Was constantly humbled by a "thorn in the flesh" that God refused to take away
12:12	Did miracles among them
12:19	Was always motivated to build up others spiritually
13:4	Was filled with God's power
13:5, 6	Stood the test
13:9	Was always concerned that his spiritual children become mature believers

---

10:17, 18 When we do something well, we want to tell others and be recognized. But recognition is dangerous—it can lead to inflated pride. How much better to seek the praise of God rather than men. Interestingly, these two are usually opposites. To earn God's praise means giving up the praise of others. How should you live differently to receive God's commendation?

husband. 3But I am frightened, fearing that in some way you will be led away from
your pure and simple devotion to our Lord, just as Eve was deceived by Satan in the
Garden of Eden. 4You seem so gullible: you believe whatever anyone tells you
even if he is preaching about another Jesus than the one we preach, or a different
spirit than the Holy Spirit you received, or shows you a different way to be saved.
You swallow it all.

5Yet I don't feel that these marvelous "messengers from God," as they call
themselves, are any better than I am. 6If I am a poor speaker, at least I know what
I am talking about, as I think you realize by now, for we have proved it again and
again.

7Did I do wrong and cheapen myself and make you look down on me because I
preached God's Good News to you without charging you anything? 8, 9Instead I
"robbed" other churches by taking what they sent me, and using it up while I was
with you, so that I could serve you without cost. And when that was gone and I was
getting hungry I still didn't ask you for anything, for the Christians from Macedonia brought me another gift. I have never yet asked you for one cent, and I never
will. 10I promise this with every ounce of truth I possess—that I will tell everyone
in Greece about it! 11Why? Because I don't love you? God knows I do. 12But I will
do it to cut out the ground from under the feet of those who boast that they are doing
God's work in just the same way we are.

13God never sent those men at all; they are "phonies" who have fooled you into
thinking they are Christ's apostles. 14Yet I am not surprised! Satan can change
himself into an angel of light, 15so it is no wonder his servants can do it too, and
seem like godly ministers. In the end they will get every bit of punishment their
wicked deeds deserve.

11:8, 9 *And when that was gone,* implied.

11:3
Gen 3:4
Jn 8:44
1 Thess 3:5
1 Tim 1:3; 4:1
2 Pet 3:17
Jude 4
Rev 12:9

11:4
Rom 8:15
Gal 1:6-8

11:5
2 Cor 12:11
Gal 2:6

11:6
2 Cor 10:10
Eph 3:4

11:7
Acts 18:3
2 Cor 12:13

11:9
2 Cor 12:14

11:11
2 Cor 7:3; 12:15

11:12
1 Cor 9:12

11:13
Gal 1:7
Rev 2:2

11:14
Rev 12:9

11:15
Rom 2:6; 3:8
Phil 3:19

11:3 The Corinthians' pure and simple devotion to Christ was
being threatened by false teaching. Paul did not want the believers
to lose their single-minded love for Christ. Keeping Christ first in
our lives can be very difficult when we have so many distractions
threatening to sidetrack our faith. As Eve lost her focus by listening
to the serpent, we too can lose our focus by letting our lives
become overcrowded and confused. Is there anything that
threatens your ability to keep Christ first in your life? How can you
minimize the distractions that threaten your devotion to Christ?

11:3, 4 The Corinthian believers fell for smooth talk and messages
that sounded good and seemed to make sense. Today there are
many false teachings that seem to make sense. Don't believe
anyone simply because he sounds like an authority or says things
you like to hear. Search the Bible and check people's words
against God's Word. The Bible should be your authoritative guide
to all teaching.

11:4 The false teachers distorted the truth about Christ and
ended up preaching a different Christ, a different Spirit, and a
different way of salvation. Because the Bible is God's infallible
Word, those who teach anything different from what it says are
both mistaken and misleading.

11:6 Paul, a brilliant thinker, may not have been a spellbinding
speaker. Although his ministry was effective (see Acts 17), he was
not trained in the Greek schools of oratory and speech making, as
many of the false teachers probably were. Paul believed in a
simple presentation of the gospel (see 1 Corinthians 1:17), and
some people thought this showed simplemindedness. Thus his
speaking performance was often used against him by false
teachers. In all our teaching and preaching, we must make sure
that the content is far more important than the presentation. Unless
speaking methods help to make the message clear, they are
useless. A simple, clear presentation that helps listeners
understand, however, is of great value.

11:7 The Corinthians may have thought that preachers could be
judged by how much money they demanded. A good speaker
would charge a large sum, a fair speaker would be a little cheaper,
and a poor speaker would speak for free. The false teachers may
have argued that because Paul asked no fee for his preaching, he
must be an amateur, with little authority. Believers today must be
careful not to assume that every speaker who is well known and
receives a large sum of money has something good to say.

11:7–12 Paul could have asked the Corinthian church for financial
support. Jesus himself taught that those who minister for God
should be supported by the people to whom they minister
(Matthew 10:10). But Paul thought that asking for support in
Corinth could be misunderstood. There were many false teachers
who hoped to make a good profit from preaching (2:17), and Paul
might look like one of them. Paul separated himself completely
from these false teachers.

11:14 In one popular version of the story of Eve's temptation,
Satan masqueraded as an angel. Paul may have been thinking of
this story. In either case, nothing is farther from the truth than
Satan, the prince of darkness (Ephesians 6:12; Colossians 1:13),
pretending to represent the light. By the same token, when the
false teachers claimed to represent Christ, they were lying
shamelessly.

11:14, 15 Satan and his servants can deceive us by appearing
attractive, good, and moral. Many unsuspecting people follow
smooth-talking, Bible-quoting leaders into cults which alienate
them from their families and practice immorality and deceit. Don't
be fooled by external appearances. Our impressions alone are not
an accurate indicator of who is or isn't a true follower of Christ; so it
helps to ask these questions: (1) Do their teachings confirm
Scripture (Acts 17:11)? (2) Do the teachers affirm and proclaim
that Jesus Christ is God who came into the world as a man to save
people from their sins (1 John 4:1–3)? (3) Is their lifestyle
consistent with biblical morality (Matthew 12:33–37)?

Paul's many trials

16Again I plead, don't think that I have lost my wits to talk like this; but even if you do, listen to me anyway—a witless man, a fool—while I also boast a little as they do. 17Such bragging isn't something the Lord commanded me to do, for I am acting like a brainless fool. 18Yet those other men keep telling you how wonderful they are, so here I go: 19, 20(You think you are so wise—yet you listen gladly to those fools; you don't mind at all when they make you their slaves and take everything you have, and take advantage of you, and put on airs, and slap you in the face. 21I'm ashamed to say that I'm not strong and daring like that!

But whatever they can boast about—I'm talking like a fool again—I can boast about it, too.)

22They brag that they are Hebrews, do they? Well, so am I. And they say that they are Israelites, God's chosen people? So am I. And they are descendants of Abraham? Well, I am too.

23They say they serve Christ? But I have served him far more! (Have I gone mad to boast like this?) I have worked harder, been put in jail oftener, been whipped times without number, and faced death again and again and again. 24Five different times the Jews gave me their terrible thirty-nine lashes. 25Three times I was beaten with rods. Once I was stoned. Three times I was shipwrecked. Once I was in the open sea all night and the whole next day. 26I have traveled many weary miles and have been often in great danger from flooded rivers, and from robbers, and from my own people, the Jews, as well as from the hands of the Gentiles. I have faced grave dangers from mobs in the cities and from death in the deserts and in the stormy seas and from men who claim to be brothers in Christ but are not. 27I have lived with weariness and pain and sleepless nights. Often I have been hungry and thirsty and have gone without food; often I have shivered with cold, without enough clothing to keep me warm.

28Then, besides all this, I have the constant worry of how the churches are getting along: 29Who makes a mistake and I do not feel his sadness? Who falls without my longing to help him? Who is spiritually hurt without my fury rising against the one who hurt him?

30But if I must brag, I would rather brag about the things that show how weak I am. 31God, the Father of our Lord Jesus Christ, who is to be praised forever and ever, knows I tell the truth. 32For instance, in Damascus the governor under King Aretas kept guards at the city gates to catch me; 33but I was let down by rope and basket from a hole in the city wall, and so I got away! [What popularity!]

Paul's vision and his thorn

12 This boasting is all so foolish, but let me go on. Let me tell about the visions I've had, and revelations from the Lord.

11:33 *What popularity!* Implied.

11:17
2 Cor 7:4

11:18
Phil 3:3

11:20
Gal 2:4; 4:9

11:21
2 Cor 10:10

11:22
Acts 22:3
Rom 11:1
Phil 3:5

11:23
Rom 8:36
1 Cor 15:10
16:23
2 Cor 6:4,5

11:24
Deut 25:3

11:25
Acts 14:19
16:22; 27:41

11:26
Acts 9:23
13:50; 14:5
17:5; 19:23
21:31; 23:10
Gal 2:4

11:27
1 Cor 4:11
2 Cor 6:5
1 Thess 2:9

11:28
Acts 20:18
Rom 1:14

11:29
1 Cor 9:22

11:31
Rom 9:5

11:32
Acts 9:24

11:33
Acts 9:25

12:1
Gal 1:12

11:22, 23 Paul presented his credentials to counteract charges the false teachers were making against him. He felt awkward speaking like this, but if the believers turned against him, they might begin to turn against the gospel he was preaching. Paul also gave a list of his credentials in his letter to the Philippians (see Philippians 3:4–8).

11:23-29 Paul was angry that the false teachers had impressed and deceived the Corinthians (11:13–15). Therefore, he had to reestablish his credibility and authority by listing the trials he had endured in his service for Christ. Some of these trials are recorded in the book of Acts (Acts 14:19; 16:22–24). Because Paul wrote this letter during his third missionary journey (Acts 18:23—21:17), he would experience yet further trials and humiliations for the cause of Christ (see Acts 21:30–33; 22:24–30). These trials showed he was sacrificing his life for the gospel, something the false teachers would never do. The trials and hurts you have experienced for Christ's sake have built your character, demonstrated your faith, and prepared you to work for the Lord.

11:25 The seaways were not as safe as they are today. Paul had been shipwrecked three times, and he would face another accident on his voyage to Rome (see Acts 27). By this time, Paul had probably made at least eight or nine voyages.

11:28, 29 Though an apostle with God's authority to preach the gospel, Paul showed enormous personal concern for individuals in the churches he served. If God has placed you in a position of leadership and authority, treat people with Paul's kind of empathy and concern.

11:32 King Aretas, king of the Nabateans (Edomites) from A.D. 9 to 40, appointed a governor to oversee the Nabatean segment of the population in Damascus. Somehow the Jews in Damascus were able to enlist this governor to help them try to capture Paul (see Acts 9:22–25). Paul recounted this incident to show what he had endured for Christ. The false teachers couldn't make such a claim.

2, 3Fourteen years ago I was taken up to heaven for a visit. Don't ask me whether my body was there or just my spirit, for I don't know; only God can answer that. But anyway, there I was in paradise, 4and heard things so astounding that they are beyond a man's power to describe or put in words (and anyway I am not allowed to tell them to others). 5That experience is something worth bragging about, but I am not going to do it. I am going to boast only about how weak I am and how great God is to use such weakness for his glory. 6I have plenty to boast about and would be no fool in doing it, but I don't want anyone to think more highly of me than he should from what he can actually see in my life and my message.

7I will say this: because these experiences I had were so tremendous, God was afraid I might be puffed up by them; so I was given a physical condition which has been a thorn in my flesh, a messenger from Satan to hurt and bother me, and prick my pride. 8Three different times I begged God to make me well again.

9Each time he said, "No. But I am with you; that is all you need. My power shows up best in weak people." Now I am glad to boast about how weak I am; I am glad to be a living demonstration of Christ's power, instead of showing off my own power and abilities. 10Since I know it is all for Christ's good, I am quite happy about "the thorn," and about insults and hardships, persecutions and difficulties; for when I am weak, then I am strong—the less I have, the more I depend on him.

Paul's concern for the Corinthians

11You have made me act like a fool—boasting like this—for you people ought to be writing about me and not making me write about myself. There isn't a single thing these other marvelous fellows have that I don't have too, even though I am really worth nothing at all. 12When I was there I certainly gave you every proof that I was truly an apostle, sent to you by God himself: for I patiently did many wonders and signs and mighty works among you. 13The only thing I didn't do for you, that I do everywhere else in all other churches, was to become a burden to you—I didn't ask you to give me food to eat and a place to stay. Please forgive me for this wrong!

14Now I am coming to you again, the third time; and it is still not going to cost you anything, for I don't want your money. I want *you!* And anyway, you are my children, and little children don't pay for their father's and mother's food—it's the other way around; parents supply food for their children. 15I am glad to give you myself and all I have for your spiritual good, even though it seems that the more I love you, the less you love me.

16Some of you are saying, "It's true that his visits didn't seem to cost us

12:2, 3 *I*, literally, "A man in Christ." *heaven*, literally, "the third heaven."

12:2
Deut 10:14
Acts 22:17
Rom 16:7
2 Cor 5:17
Gal 1:22

12:4
Lk 23:43
Rev 2:7

12:5
1 Cor 2:3
2 Cor 11:30

12:6
2 Cor 10:8

12:7
Job 2:7
Lk 13:16
Gal 4:13

12:8
Mt 26:44

12:9
Eccles 7:18
Isa 40:29; 42:10
1 Cor 10:13
Eph 3:16
Phil 4:13
Heb 2:18
1 Pet 4:14
2 Pet 2:9

12:11
1 Cor 15:9,10
2 Cor 11:15,16
Gal 2:6

12:12
Rom 15:18,19
1 Cor 9:1,2

12:13
1 Cor 1:7; 9:12, 18
2 Cor 11:7

12:14
1 Cor 4:14
9:19; 10:33
2 Cor 13:1

12:15
2 Cor 1:6; 6:12
11:11
1 Thess 2:8
Phil 2:17

12:16
2 Cor 11:9

12:2, 3 This incident cannot be positively matched with a recorded event in Paul's career. Paul tells about this incident to show that he had been uniquely touched by God.

12:7, 8 We don't know what Paul's "thorn in the flesh" was, because he doesn't tell us. Some have suggested that it was malaria, epilepsy, or a disease of the eyes (see Galatians 4:13–15). Whatever it was, it was a chronic and debilitating physical problem, which at times kept him from working. This thorn was a hindrance to his ministry, and he prayed for its removal; but God refused. It kept Paul humble, reminded him of his need for constant contact with God, and benefited those around him as they saw God at work in his life.

12:9 Although God did not remove Paul's physical affliction, he promised to demonstrate his power in Paul. The fact that God's power shows up in weak people should give us courage. If we recognize our limitations, we will not congratulate ourselves. Instead, we will turn to God to seek pathways for effectiveness. We must rely on God for our effectiveness rather than on simple energy, effort, or talent. Our weakness not only helps develop Christian character; it also deepens our worship, for in admitting our weakness, we affirm God's strength.

12:10 When we are strong in abilities or resources, we are tempted to do God's work on our own, and that leads to pride. When we are weak, when we allow God to fill us with *his* power, then we are stronger than we could ever be on our own. We must depend on God—only work done in his power makes us effective for him and has lasting value.

12:11–15 Paul is not merely revealing his feelings but defending his authority as an apostle of Jesus Christ. He was hurt that the church in Corinth was doubting and questioning him, but he was defending himself for the cause of the gospel, not to satisfy his ego. When you are "put on trial," do you think only about saving your reputation or are you more concerned about what people will think about Christ?

12:13 When Paul says, "Please forgive me for this wrong," he is using irony. He actually did more for the Corinthians than for any other church, and still they misunderstood him.

12:14 Paul had founded the church in Corinth on his first visit there (Acts 18:1). He subsequently made a second, "painful" visit (2:1). Thus, this would be his third visit (see also 13:1).

anything, but he is a sneaky fellow, that Paul, and he fooled us. As sure as anything he must have made money from us some way."

12:17
2 Cor 7:2; 9:5

12:18
2 Cor 8:6,18

17But how? Did any of the men I sent to you take advantage of you? 18When I urged Titus to visit you, and sent our other brother with him, did they make any profit? No, of course not. For we have the same Holy Spirit, and walk in each other's steps, doing things the same way.

12:19
Rom 9:1
1 Cor 10:33
2 Cor 5:12
11:31

12:20
1 Cor 4:21

19I suppose you think I am saying all this to get back into your good graces. That isn't it at all. I tell you, with God listening as I say it, that I have said this to help *you*, dear friends—to build you up spiritually and not to help myself. 20For I am afraid that when I come to visit you I won't like what I find, and then you won't like the way I will have to act. I am afraid that I will find you quarreling, and envying each other, and being angry with each other, and acting big, and saying wicked things about each other and whispering behind each other's backs, filled with conceit and disunity. 21Yes, I am afraid that when I come God will humble me before you and I will be sad and mourn because many of you have sinned before and don't even care about the wicked, impure things you have done: your lust and immorality, and the taking of other men's wives.

12:21
1 Cor 5:1
2 Cor 2:1,4
Gal 5:19
Phil 3:18

Paul's final advice

13:1
Num 35:30
Deut 19:15
Acts 18:1
2 Cor 2:1; 12:14

13 This is the third time I am coming to visit you. The Scriptures tell us that if two or three have seen a wrong, it must be punished. [Well, this is my third warning, as I come now for this visit.] 2I have already warned those who had been sinning when I was there last; now I warn them again, and all others, just as I did then, that this time I come ready to punish severely and I will not spare them.

13:2
2 Cor 1:23; 10:2
12:21

13:3
Mt 10:20
1 Cor 7:40; 9:2

3I will give you all the proof you want that Christ speaks through me. Christ is not weak in his dealings with you, but is a mighty power within you. 4His weak, human body died on the cross, but now he lives by the mighty power of God. We, too, are weak in our bodies, as he was, but now we live and are strong, as he is, and have all of God's power to use in dealing with you.

13:4
2 Cor 10:3,4
Rom 1:4; 6:4
Phil 2:7,8
1 Pet 3:18

13:5
Jn 14:20; 17:23,
26
Rom 8:10
1 Cor 9:27; 11:28
Gal 4:19
Col 1:27

5Check up on yourselves. Are you really Christians? Do you pass the test? Do you feel Christ's presence and power more and more within you? Or are you just pretending to be Christians when actually you aren't at all? 6I hope you can agree that I have stood that test and truly belong to the Lord.

13:7
2 Cor 6:9

13:9
1 Cor 4:10
Eph 4:12-16
1 Thess 3:10

7I pray that you will live good lives, not because that will be a feather in our caps, proving that what we teach is right; no, for we want you to do right even if we ourselves are despised. 8Our responsibility is to encourage the right at all times, not to hope for evil. 9We are glad to be weak and despised if you are really strong. Our greatest wish and prayer is that you will become mature Christians.

13:10
Tit 1:13

10I am writing this to you now in the hope that I won't need to scold and punish when I come; for I want to use the Lord's authority which he has given me, not to punish you but to make you strong.

13:1 *Well, this is my third warning, as I come now for this visit,* implied.   **13:7** *a feather in our caps,* literally, "not that we may appear approved."   **13:8** *not to hope for evil,* literally, "For we can do nothing against the truth, but for the truth."

12:20, 21 After reading this catalog of sins, it is hard to believe that these are the people Paul said were enriched with "every spiritual gift and power for doing his will" (1 Corinthians 1:7). Paul feared that the practices of wicked Corinth had invaded the congregation, and he wrote sternly in hope that they would straighten up their lives before he arrived. We must live differently than unbelievers, not letting secular society dictate how we are to treat others. Don't let culture invade your practices at church.

13:2 How would Paul punish unrepentant sinners? (1) He could confront and publicly denounce their behavior. (2) He could exercise church discipline by calling them before the church leaders. (3) He could excommunicate them from the church.

13:5 Just as we get physical check-ups, Paul urges us to give ourselves spiritual check-ups. We should look for a growing awareness of Christ's presence and power in our lives. Only then will we know if we are true Christians or imposters. If we're not taking active steps to grow closer to God, we are growing farther away from him.

13:8, 9 Just as parents want their children to grow into mature adults, so Paul wanted the Corinthians to grow into mature believers. As we share the Good News, our goal should be not merely to see others profess faith or begin attending church, but to see them become mature in their faith. Don't set your sights too short.

¹¹I close my letter with these last words: Be happy. Grow in Christ. Pay attention to what I have said. Live in harmony and peace. And may the God of love and peace be with you.

¹²Greet each other warmly in the Lord. ¹³All the Christians here send you their best regards. ¹⁴May the grace of our Lord Jesus Christ be with you all. May God's love and the Holy Spirit's friendship be yours.

Paul

13:11
Rom 12:16
15:33
1 Cor 1:10
1 Pet 3:8
13:13
Rom 5:5; 16:20
Phil 2:1

13:11 Paul's closing words—what he wants the Corinthians to remember about the needs for their church—are still fitting for the church today. When these qualities are not present, there are problems to be dealt with in the church. These traits do not come to a church by glossing over problems, conflicts, and difficulties. They are not produced by neglect, denial, withdrawal, or bitterness. They are the by-products of the extremely hard work of solving problems. Just as Paul and the Corinthians had to hammer out difficulties to bring peace, so we must receive and obey the principles of God's Word and not just hear them.

13:14 Paul's farewell blessing invokes all three members of the Godhead—Father, Son, and Holy Spirit. Although the doctrine of the Trinity is not explicitly taught in Scripture, verses such as this one show that it was believed.

13:14 Paul was dealing with an ongoing problem in the Corinthian church. He could have refused to communicate until they cleared up their problems, but he loved them and reached out to them again with the love of Christ. Love, however, means that sometimes we must confront those we care about. Authority and personal concern are both needed in dealing with people who are ruining their lives with sin. But there are several wrong approaches in confronting others, and these can further break relationships rather than heal them. We can be legalistic and blast people with the laws they should be obeying. We can turn away from them because we don't want to face the situation. We can isolate them by gossiping about their problem and turning others against them as well. Or, like Paul, we can seek to build relationships by taking a better approach—sharing, communicating, and caring. This is a difficult approach that can drain us emotionally; but it is best for the other person, and it is the only Christlike way to deal with others' sin.

GALATIANS

A FAMILY, executing their carefully planned escape at midnight, dashing for the border . . . a man standing outside prison walls, gulping fresh air, awash in the new sun . . . a young woman with every trace of the ravaging drug gone from her system . . . they are FREE! With fresh anticipation, they can begin life anew.

Whether fleeing oppression, stepping out of prison, or breaking a strangling habit, freedom means life. There is nothing so exhilarating as knowing that the past is forgotten and that new options await. People yearn to be free.

The book of Galatians is the charter of Christian freedom. In this profound letter, Paul proclaims the reality of our liberty in Christ—freedom from the Law and the power of sin, to serve our living Lord.

Most of the first converts and early leaders in the church were Jewish Christians who proclaimed Jesus as their Messiah. As Jewish Christians, they struggled with a dual identity: their Jewishness constrained them to be strict followers of the law; their newfound faith in Christ invited them to celebrate a holy liberty. They wondered how Gentiles (non-Jews) could be part of the Kingdom of Heaven.

This controversy wracked the early church. Judaizers—an extremist Jewish faction within the church—taught that Gentile Christians had to submit to Jewish laws and traditions *in addition to* believing in Christ. As a missionary to the Gentiles, Paul had to confront this issue many times.

Galatians was written, therefore, to refute the Judaizers and to call believers back to the pure gospel. The Good News is for all people—Jews and Gentiles alike. Salvation is by God's grace through faith in Christ Jesus *and nothing else*. Faith in Christ means true freedom.

After a brief introduction (1:1–5), Paul addresses those who were accepting the Judaizers' twisted gospel (1:6–9). He summarizes the controversy including his personal confrontation with Peter and other church leaders (1:10—2:16). He then demonstrates that salvation is by faith alone by alluding to his conversion (2:17–21), appealing to his readers' own experience of the Good News (3:1–5), and showing how the Old Testament teaches grace (3:6–20). Next, he explains the purpose of God's laws and the relationship between law, God's promises, and Christ (3:21—4:31).

Having laid the foundation, Paul builds his case for Christian liberty. We are saved by faith, not by works (5:1–12); our freedom means we are free to love and serve one another, not to do wrong (5:13–26); and Christians should bear one another's burdens and be kind to one another (6:1–10). In 6:11–18, Paul shares his final thoughts by taking the pen into his own hand.

As you read Galatians, try to understand this first-century conflict between law and grace, faith and works, but also be aware of modern parallels. Like Paul, defend the truth of the gospel and reject all those who would add to or twist this truth. You are *free* in Christ—step into the light and celebrate!

VITAL STATISTICS

PURPOSE:
To refute the Judaizers (who taught that Gentile believers must obey the Jewish law in order to be saved), and to call Christians to faith and freedom in Christ

AUTHOR:
Paul

TO WHOM WRITTEN:
The churches in southern Galatia founded on Paul's first missionary journey (including Iconium, Lystra, Derbe)

DATE WRITTEN:
About A.D. 49, from Antioch, prior to the Jerusalem council (A.D. 50)

SETTING:
The most pressing controversy of the early church was the relationship of new believers, especially Gentiles, to the Jewish laws. This was especially a problem for the converts and young churches Paul founded on his first missionary journey. Paul writes to correct this problem. Later, at the council in Jerusalem, the conflict was officially resolved by the church leaders.

KEY VERSE:
"So Christ has made us free" (5:1).

KEY PEOPLE:
Paul, Peter, Barnabas, Titus, Abraham, false teachers

KEY PLACES:
Galatia, Jerusalem

SPECIAL FEATURES:
This letter is not addressed to any specific body of believers and was probably circulated to several churches.

THE BLUEPRINT

1. Authenticity of the gospel (1:1—2:21)
2. Superiority of the gospel (3:1—4:31)
3. Freedom of the gospel (5:1—6:18)

In response to attacks from false teachers, Paul wrote to defend his apostleship and to defend the authority of the gospel. The Galatians were beginning to turn from faith to legalism. The struggle between the gospel and legalism is still a crisis. Many today would have us return to trying to earn God's favor through following rituals or obeying a set of rules. As Christians, we are not boxed in, but set free. To preserve our freedom, we must stay close to Christ and resist any who promote subtle ways of trying to earn our salvation.

MEGATHEMES

THEME	EXPLANATION	IMPORTANCE
Law	A group of Jewish teachers insisted that non-Jewish believers must obey Jewish law and traditional rules. They believed a person was saved by following the law of Moses (with emphasis on circumcision, the sign of the covenant), in addition to faith in Christ. Paul opposed them by showing that the law can't save anyone.	We can't be saved by keeping the Old Testament law, even the Ten Commandments. The law served as a guide to point out our need to be forgiven. Christ fulfilled the obligations of the law for us. We must turn to him to be saved. He alone can make us right with God.
Faith	We are saved from God's judgment and penalty for sin by God's gracious gift to us. We receive salvation by faith—trusting in him—not in anything else. Becoming a Christian is in no way based on our initiative, wise choice, or good character. We can only be right with God by believing in him.	Your acceptance with God comes by believing in Christ alone. You must never add to or twist this truth. We are saved by faith, not by the good that we do. Have you placed your whole trust and confidence in Christ? He alone can forgive you and bring you into relationship with God.
Freedom	Galatians is our charter of Christian freedom. We are not under the jurisdiction of Jewish laws and traditions, nor under the authority of Jerusalem. Faith in Christ brings true freedom from sin and from the futile attempt to be right with God by keeping the law.	We are free in Christ, and yet freedom is a privilege. We are not free to disobey Christ or be immoral, but we are free to serve the risen Christ. Let us use our freedom to love and to serve, not to do wrong.
Holy Spirit	We become Christians through the work of the Holy Spirit. He brings new life; even our faith to believe is a gift from him. The Holy Spirit instructs, guides, leads, and gives us power. He ends our bondage to evil desires, and he creates in us love, joy, peace, and many other wonderful changes.	When the Holy Spirit leads us, he produces his fruit in us. Just as we are saved by faith, not works, we also grow by faith. By believing, we can have the Holy Spirit within us, helping us live our lives. Obey Christ by following the Holy Spirit's leading.

1. Authenticity of the gospel

1 *From:* Paul the missionary and all the other Christians here.
To: The churches of Galatia. I was not called to be a missionary by any group or agency. My call is from Jesus Christ himself, and from God the Father who

---

1:1 Paul and Barnabas had just completed their first missionary journey (Acts 13:2–14:28), during which they visited Iconium, Lystra, and Derbe, cities in the Roman province of Galatia (present-day Turkey). Upon returning to Antioch, Paul was accused by some Jewish Christians of diluting Christianity to make it more appealing to Gentiles. These Jewish Christians disagreed

1:4
Jn 15:19; 17:14
Rom 4:25
1:5
Rom 11:36

raised him from the dead. ³May peace and blessing be yours from God the Father and from the Lord Jesus Christ. ⁴He died for our sins just as God our Father planned, and rescued us from this evil world in which we live. ⁵All glory to God through all the ages of eternity. Amen.

There is no other gospel

1:6
2 Cor 11:4

⁶I am amazed that you are turning away so soon from God who, in his love and mercy, invited you to share the eternal life he gives through Christ; you are already following a different "way to heaven," which really doesn't go to heaven at all.

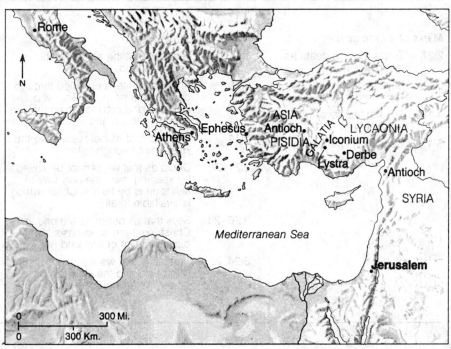

CITIES IN GALATIA
Paul visited several cities in Galatia on each of his three missionary journeys. On his first journey he went through Antioch in Pisidia, Iconium, Lystra, and Derbe, then retraced his steps; on his second journey he went by land from Antioch in Syria through the four cities in Galatia; on his third journey he also went through those cities on the main route to Ephesus.

with Paul's statements that Gentiles did not have to follow many of the religious laws which the Jews had obeyed for centuries. Some of Paul's accusers had even followed him to those Galatian cities and told the Gentile converts that they had to be circumcised and follow all the Jewish laws and customs in order to be saved. In short, according to these men, Gentiles had to become Jews in order to become Christians.

In response to this threat, Paul wrote this letter to the Galatian churches. In it, he explains that following the Old Testament laws or the Jewish laws will not bring salvation. A person is saved by grace through faith. The Jewish law is not a condition for salvation. Paul wrote this letter about A.D. 49, shortly before the meeting of the Jerusalem council, which also dealt with the law versus grace controversy (Acts 15).

1:1 For more information about Paul's life, see his Profile in Acts 9. Paul had been a Christian for about 15 years at this time.

1:2 In Paul's time *Galatia* was the Roman province located in the center section of present-day Turkey. Much of the region rests on a large and fertile plateau and large numbers of people had moved to the region because of its favorable geography. One of Paul's goals during his missionary journeys was to visit regions with large population centers in order to reach as many people as possible.

1:2 Paul was called by Jesus Christ himself. He presented his apostolic credentials at the very outset of this letter, because some people in Galatia were questioning his authority.

1:3-5 God's plan all along was to save us by Jesus' death. We have been rescued from the power of this evil world—a world ruled by Satan, full of cruelty, tragedy, temptation, and deception. Being rescued from this evil world doesn't mean we are taken out of it, but that we are no longer enslaved to it. We have been saved to live righteous lives for God, and we have been promised eternity with him.

1:6 The different "way to heaven" was preached by people who wanted Gentile believers to follow Jewish laws in order to obtain salvation. Those proclaiming this different way believed that faith in Christ was not enough; a Christian must also follow the Jewish laws and customs, especially the rite of circumcision, in order to be saved. This message undermined the truth of the Good News that salvation is a gift, not a reward. Jesus Christ has made this gift available to all people, not just to those who are Jewish in orientation. Beware of people who say that more is needed for salvation than faith in Christ. When people set up additional requirements for salvation, they deny the power of Christ's redemptive work on the cross (see 3:1-5).

7For there is no other way than the one we showed you; you are being fooled by those who twist and change the truth concerning Christ.

8Let God's curses fall on anyone, including myself, who preaches any other way to be saved than the one we told you about; yes, if an angel comes from heaven and preaches any other message, let him be forever cursed. 9I will say it again: if anyone preaches any other Gospel than the one you welcomed, let God's curse fall upon him.

10You can see that I am not trying to please you by sweet talk and flattery; no, I am trying to please God. If I were still trying to please men I could not be Christ's servant.

1:7
Acts 15:1
Gal 5:10

1:8
2 Cor 11:14

1:9
Deut 4:2; 12:32
Prov 30:6
Rev 22:18

1:10
1 Thess 2:4

Marks of a false gospel		Marks of the true gospel		THE MARKS OF THE TRUE GOSPEL AND OF FALSE GOSPELS
2:21	Treats Christ's death as meaningless	1:11, 12	Teaches that the source of the gospel is God	
3:12	Says people must obey the law in order to be saved	2:20	Knows that life is obtained through death; we trust in the God who loved us and died for us so that we might die to sin and live for him	
4:10	Tries to find favor with God by observing certain rituals			
5:4	Counts on keeping laws to erase sin	3:14	Explains that all believers have the Holy Spirit through faith	
		3:21, 22	Declares that we cannot be saved by keeping laws; the only way of salvation is by faith in Christ, which is available to all	
		3:26–28	Says that all believers are one in Christ, so there is no basis for discrimination of any kind	
		5:24, 25	Proclaims that we are free from the grip of sin and the Holy Spirit's power fills and guides us	

1:7 No other person, method, or ritual can give eternal life. There is only one way to spend eternity with God—through believing in Jesus Christ as Savior and Lord. Some people think all religions are equally valid paths to God. But that is not what God says. He has provided just one way—Jesus Christ (John 14:6).

1:7 Those who fooled the Galatian believers were zealous Jewish Christians who believed that the Old Testament practices such as circumcision and dietary restrictions were required of all believers in Christ. Because these teachers wanted to turn the Gentile Christians into Jews, they were called *Judaizers.* Some time after the letter to the Galatians was sent, Paul met with the apostles in Jerusalem to discuss this matter further (see Acts 15).

1:7 The Galatian Christians were mainly Greek, unfamiliar with Jewish laws and customs. The Judaizers were an extreme faction of Jewish Christians. Both groups believed in Christ, but their lifestyles differed considerably. We do not know why the Judaizers traveled to teach their mistaken notions to the new Gentile converts. They may have been motivated by (1) a sincere wish to integrate Judaism with the new Christian faith, (2) a sincere love for their Jewish heritage, or (3) a jealous desire to destroy Paul's authority. Whether or not these Judaizers were sincere, their teaching threatened these new churches and had to be countered. Paul was not rejecting everything Jewish. He himself was a Jew who worshiped in the Temple and attended the religious festivals.

But he was concerned that *nothing* get in the way of the simple truth of his message—that salvation, to Jews and Gentiles alike, is by faith in Jesus Christ alone.

1:7 Twisted truth is sometimes more difficult to spot than outright lies. The Judaizers were twisting the truth about Christ. They claimed to follow him, but they denied that Jesus' work on the cross was sufficient for salvation. There will always be people who twist the Good News. Either they do not understand what the Bible teaches, or they are uncomfortable with the truth as it stands. How can we tell when people are twisting the truth? Before accepting the teachings of any group, find out what the group teaches about Jesus Christ. If their teaching does not match the truth in God's Word, then it is twisted.

1:8, 9 What these Judaizers were doing was so bad that Paul used strong words to denounce their actions. He said that even if an angel from heaven comes preaching another message, let that angel be cursed forever. If an angel came preaching another message, he would not be from heaven, no matter how he looked. In 2 Corinthians 11:14,15, Paul warns that Satan and his angels can turn themselves into angels of light. Here he invokes a curse on an angel who spreads a false gospel—a fitting response to an emissary of hell. Paul extended that curse to himself. His message must never change, for the truth of the gospel never changes. Paul uses strong language because he is dealing with a life-and-death issue.

Paul received the gospel from God

1:11
1 Cor 15:1-3

1:12
1 Cor 2:10
Gal 1:15,16
Eph 3:3

1:13
Acts 8:3; 9:21
22:3-5; 26:4-11

1:14
Acts 26:3

1:15
Acts 9:15; 15:10
Eph 2:3

1:16
Rom 1:17; 8:3,
10
Gal 2:9,20
Col 1:27

1:17
1 Jn 3:8

1:18
Acts 9:26

1:19
Mt 13:55
Acts 12:17; 15:13
21:18
1 Cor 15:7
Gal 2:9,12

1:23
Acts 9:20

11Dear friends, I solemnly swear that the way to heaven which I preach is not based on some mere human whim or dream. 12For my message comes from no less a person than Jesus Christ himself, who told me what to say. No one else has taught me.

13You know what I was like when I followed the Jewish religion—how I went after the Christians mercilessly, hunting them down and doing my best to get rid of them all. 14I was one of the most religious Jews of my own age in the whole country, and tried as hard as I possibly could to follow all the old, traditional rules of my religion.

15But then something happened! For even before I was born God had chosen me to be his, and called me—what kindness and grace— 16to reveal his Son within me so that I could go to the Gentiles and show them the Good News about Jesus.

When all this happened to me I didn't go at once and talk it over with anyone else; 17I didn't go up to Jerusalem to consult with those who were apostles before I was. No, I went away into the deserts of Arabia, and then came back to the city of Damascus. 18It was not until three years later that I finally went to Jerusalem for a visit with Peter, and stayed there with him for fifteen days. 19And the only other apostle I met at that time was James, our Lord's brother. 20(Listen to what I am saying, for I am telling you this in the very presence of God. This is exactly what happened—I am not lying to you.) 21Then after this visit I went to Syria and Cilicia. 22And still the Christians in Judea didn't even know what I looked like. 23All they knew was what people were saying, that "our former enemy is now preaching the very faith he tried to wreck." 24And they gave glory to God because of me.

1:10 Paul had to speak harshly to the Christians in Galatia because they were in serious danger. He did not apologize for his straightforward words; he knew he could not serve Christ faithfully if he allowed the Galatian Christians to remain on the wrong track. Whom are you trying to please—other people or God? Pray for the courage to put God's approval first.

1:11ff Why should the Galatians listen to Paul instead of the Judaizers? Paul answers this implicit question by furnishing his credentials: his message was directly from Christ (1:12); he had been an exemplary Jew (1:13, 14); he had a special conversion experience (1:15, 16; see also Acts 9:1–9); he was confirmed in his ministry by the other apostles (1:18, 19; 2:1–9). Paul also presented his credentials to the Corinthian and Philippian churches (2 Corinthians 11, 12; Philippians 3:4–9).

1:12 Paul did not choose to become an apostle, Christ appointed him to that task. Mere human wisdom was not the ultimate source or authority for Paul's preaching. The Good News which Paul preached rests upon the authority of Jesus Christ himself. Since Jesus appointed the apostles to be his official messengers, let us obey Christ by submitting to the apostolic teaching in the New Testament.

1:13, 14 Paul had been one of the most religious Jews of his day, scrupulously keeping the law and relentlessly persecuting Christians (see Acts 9:1, 2). Before his conversion he had been even more zealous for the law than the Judaizers were. He was sincere in his zeal—but wrong. When he met Jesus Christ, his life changed. Now he directed all his energies toward building up the Christian church.

1:15, 16 Because God was guiding his ministry, Paul wasn't doing anything God hadn't already planned and given him power to do. The great prophets Isaiah and Jeremiah knew that God had called them, even before they were born, to do special work for him (see Isaiah 49:1; Jeremiah 1:5). God knows you intimately as well, and he chose you to be his even before you were born (see Psalm 139). He wants you to draw close to him, and fulfill the job he has given you to do.

1:16 The word *Jew* refers not only to nationality but also to religion. To be fully Jewish, a person must have descended from Abraham. In addition, a faithful Jew adheres to the Jewish laws. *Gentiles* are non-Jews, whether in nationality or religion. In Paul's day, Jews thought of all Gentiles as pagans. Jews avoided Gentiles because they believed that contact with Gentiles brought spiritual corruption. Although Gentiles by nationality could become Jews in religion by undergoing circumcision and by following Jewish laws and customs, they were never fully accepted.

Many Jews had difficulty understanding that God's message is for Jews and Gentiles alike. Some Jews thought Gentiles had to become Jews before they could become Christians. But God planned to bless both Jews and Gentiles. He had revealed this plan through Old Testament prophets (see, for example, Genesis 12:3; Isaiah 42:6; 66:19), he fulfilled it through Jesus Christ, and he was proclaiming it to the Gentiles through Paul.

1:15–24 Paul tells of his conversion to show that his message came directly from God. God commissioned him to preach the Good News to the Gentiles (1:15, 16). After his call, Paul did not consult with the apostles until he had spent three years in the desert. Then he spoke with Peter and James, but he had no other contact with Jewish Christians for several more years. During those years, he was preaching to the Gentiles the message God gave him. His Good News did not come from man; it came from God.

1:18 Most believe that Paul is talking about his first visit to Jerusalem as a Christian, as recorded in Acts 9:26–30.

1:24 Paul's changed life caused many comments from people who saw or heard of him. His new life astonished them, and they glorified God because only he could have turned this zealous persecutor of Christians into a Christian himself. We may not have had as dramatic a change as Paul had, but even so our new lives should glorify our Savior. When people look at us, do they recognize that God has made changes in us? If not, perhaps we are not living our new lives as we should.

The apostles accepted Paul

2 Then fourteen years later I went back to Jerusalem again, this time with Barnabas; and Titus came along too. 2I went there with definite orders from God to confer with the brothers there about the message I was preaching to the Gentiles. I talked privately to the leaders of the church so that they would all understand just what I had been teaching and, I hoped, agree that it was right. 3And they did agree; they did not even demand that Titus, my companion, should be circumcised, though he was a Gentile.

4Even that question wouldn't have come up except for some so-called "Christians" there—false ones, really—who came to spy on us and see what freedom we enjoyed in Christ Jesus, as to whether we obeyed the Jewish laws or not. They tried to get us all tied up in their rules, like slaves in chains. 5But we did not listen to them for a single moment, for we did not want to confuse you into thinking that salvation can be earned by being circumcised and by obeying Jewish laws.

6And the great leaders of the church who were there had nothing to add to what

2:1
Acts 15:2-29
2:2
Gal 1:6
2:3
Acts 16:3
2:4
Gal 1:7; 4:3,9
5:1
2:5
Gal 1:6; 2:14
2:6
Acts 10:34
Rom 2:11
2 Cor 12:11
Gal 6:3

What the Judaizers said about Paul	Paul's defense	**JUDAIZERS VS. PAUL**
They said he was perverting the truth.	He received his message from Christ himself (1:11, 12).	
They said he was a traitor to the Jewish faith.	Paul was one of the most dedicated Jews of his time. Yet, in the midst of one of his most zealous acts, God transformed him through a revelation of the Good News about Jesus (1:13–16; Acts 9:1–30).	
They said he compromised and watered down his message for the Gentiles.	The other apostles declared that the message Paul preached was the true gospel (2:1–10).	
They said he was disregarding the law of Moses.	Far from downgrading the law, Paul puts the law in its proper place. He says it shows people where they have sinned and it points them to Christ (3:19–29).	

As the debate raged between the Gentile Christians and the Judaizers, Paul found it necessary to write to the churches in Galatia. The Judaizers were trying to undermine Paul's authority and taught a false gospel. In reply, Paul defended his authority as an apostle and the truth of his message. The debate over Jewish laws and Gentile Christians was officially resolved at the Jerusalem council (Acts 15) yet, it continued to be a point of contention after that time.

2:1 Paul was converted around A.D. 35. The 14 years he mentions are probably calculated from the time of his conversion. Therefore, this trip to Jerusalem was not his first. He made his first trip to Jerusalem around A.D. 38 (see Acts 9:26–30); and other trips to Jerusalem in approximately A.D. 44 (Acts 11:30; Galatians 2:1–10); A.D. 49/50 (Acts 15); A.D. 52 (Acts 18:22); A.D. 57 (Acts 21:15ff). Paul probably visited Jerusalem on several other occasions as well.

2:1 Barnabas and Titus were two of Paul's close friends. Barnabas and Paul visited Galatia together on their first missionary journey. Paul wrote a personal letter to Titus, a faithful believer and church leader serving on the island of Crete (see the book of Titus). For more information on Barnabas, see his Profile in Acts 13. For more information on Titus, see the letter Paul wrote to him in the New Testament.

2:1 After his conversion Paul spent many years preparing for the ministry to which God had called him. This preparation period included time alone with God (1:16, 17) as well as time conferring with other Christians. Often new Christians, in their zeal, want to begin a full-time ministry without investing the necessary time studying the Bible and learning from qualified teachers. We need not wait to share Christ with our friends, but we may need more preparation before embarking on a special ministry, whether volunteer or full-time. While we wait for God's timing, we should continue to study, learn, and grow.

2:2 The essence of Paul's message to both Jews and Gentiles

was that God's salvation is offered to all people regardless of race, sex, nationality, wealth, social standing, education, or anything else. Forgiveness comes through trusting in Christ (see Romans 10:8–13).

2:2, 3 This issue threatened to divide the church. Even though God had specifically sent Paul to the Gentiles (Acts 9:15,16), Paul was willing to discuss his gospel message with the leaders of the Jerusalem church (Acts 15). This meeting prevented a major split in the church, and it formally acknowledged the apostles' approval of Paul's preaching. Sometimes we avoid conferring with others because we fear that problems or arguments may develop. Instead, we should openly discuss our plans and actions with others. This helps everyone understand the situation better, it reduces gossip, and builds unity in the church.

2:3–5 When Paul took Titus, a Greek Christian, to Jerusalem, the Judaizers said he should be circumcised. Paul adamantly refused to give in to their demands. The apostles agreed that circumcision was an unnecessary rite for Gentile converts. Several years later, Paul personally circumcised Timothy, another Greek Christian (Acts 16:3). Unlike Titus, Timothy was half Jewish. Paul did not deny Jews the right to be circumcised; he was simply saying that Gentiles should not be asked to become Jews before becoming Christians.

2:6 It's easy to rate people on the basis of their official status and to be intimidated by the "great leaders of the church." As Paul points out, however, all believers are brothers and sisters in Christ.

2:7
Acts 13:46
1 Thess 2:4

2:8
Acts 9:15; 13:2
22:21; 26:17
1 Cor 15:10

2:9
Rom 1:5

2:10
Acts 11:30
24:17

I was preaching. (By the way, their being great leaders made no difference to me, for all are the same to God.) 7, 8, 9In fact, when Peter, James, and John, who were known as the pillars of the church, saw how greatly God had used me in winning the Gentiles, just as Peter had been blessed so greatly in his preaching to the Jews—for the same God gave us each our special gifts—they shook hands with Barnabas and me and encouraged us to keep right on with our preaching to the Gentiles while they continued their work with the Jews. 10The only thing they did suggest was that we must always remember to help the poor, and I, too, was eager for that.

Paul publicly opposed Peter

2:12
Acts 10:28
11:2,3

2:14
Acts 11:3

2:15
Acts 15:10
Eph 2:3
Phil 3:4

2:16
Acts 13:39
Rom 1:17; 3:20
8:3
Heb 7:18

11But when Peter came to Antioch I had to oppose him publicly, speaking strongly against what he was doing for it was very wrong. 12For when he first arrived he ate with the Gentile Christians [who don't bother with circumcision and the many other Jewish laws]. But afterwards when some Jewish friends of James came, he wouldn't eat with the Gentiles anymore because he was afraid of what these Jewish legalists, who insisted that circumcision was necessary for salvation, would say; 13and then all the other Jewish Christians and even Barnabas became hypocrites too, following Peter's example, though they certainly knew better. 14When I saw what was happening and that they weren't being honest about what they really believed, and weren't following the truth of the Gospel, I said to Peter in front of all the others, "Though you are a Jew by birth, you have long since discarded the Jewish laws; so why, all of a sudden, are you trying to make these Gentiles obey them? 15You and I are Jews by birth, not mere Gentile sinners, 16and yet we Jewish Christians know very well that we cannot become right with God by obeying our Jewish laws, but only by faith in Jesus Christ to take away our sins. And so we, too, have trusted Jesus Christ, that we might be accepted by God because of faith—and not because we have obeyed the Jewish laws. For no one will ever be saved by obeying them."

2:12 who don't bother with circumcision and the many other Jewish laws, implied.

We should show respect for our spiritual leaders, but our ultimate allegiance must be to Christ. We are to serve him with our whole being. He doesn't rate us according to our status; he looks at the attitude of our hearts (1 Samuel 16:7).

2:10 Here the apostles were referring to the poor of Jerusalem. While many Gentile converts were financially comfortable, the Jerusalem church was suffering from a severe famine in Palestine (see Acts 11:28–30). Much of Paul's time was spent gathering funds for the Jewish Christians (Acts 24:17; Romans 15:25–29; 1 Corinthians 16:1–4; 2 Corinthians 8). The need for believers to care for the poor is a constant theme of Scripture, but often we do nothing about it. We get caught up in meeting our own needs and desires, or we just don't see enough poor people to remember their needs. Both in your own city and across the oceans, there are people who need help. What can you do to show them tangible evidence of God's love?

2:11 Antioch in Syria (distinguished from Antioch in Pisidia) was a major trade center in the ancient world. Heavily populated by Greeks, it eventually became a strong Christian center. In Antioch the believers were first called Christians (Acts 11:26). Antioch in Syria became the headquarters for the Gentile church and Paul's base of operations.

2:11ff The Judaizers accused Paul of watering down the gospel to make it easier for Gentiles to accept, while Paul accused the Judaizers of nullifying the truth of the gospel by adding conditions to it. The basis of salvation was the issue—is salvation through Christ alone, or does it come through Christ and adherence to the law? The argument came to a head when Peter, Paul, the Judaizers, and some Gentile Christians all gathered together in Antioch to share a meal. Peter probably thought that by staying aloof from the Gentiles, he was promoting harmony—he did not

want to offend the friends of James. But Paul charged that Peter's action violated the gospel. By joining the Judaizers, Peter implicitly supported their claim that Christ was not sufficient for salvation. Compromise is an important element in getting along with others, but we should never compromise the truth of God's Word. If we feel we have to change our Christian beliefs to match those of our companions, we are on dangerous ground.

2:11 Although Peter was a "pillar of the church" (2:7), he was acting like a hypocrite. Paul knew he had to confront Peter before his actions damaged the church. Therefore, Paul publicly confronted Peter. Note, however, that Paul did not go to the other "pillars," nor did he write letters to the churches telling them not to follow Peter's example. Instead, he confronted Peter face to face. Sometimes sincere Christians, even Christian leaders, make mistakes; it may take other sincere Christians to get them back on track. If you are convinced that someone is doing harm to himself or the church, a direct approach is usually the best one to take. There is no place for backstabbing in the body of Christ.

2:15,16 If the Jewish laws cannot save us, why should we still obey the Ten Commandments and other Old Testament laws? Paul was not saying the law was bad, for in another letter he wrote, "the law itself was wholly right and good" (Romans 7:12). Instead, he was saying that the law can never make us acceptable to God. The law still has an important role to play in the life of a Christian. The law: (1) guards us from sin by giving us standards for behavior; (2) convicts us of sin, leaving us the opportunity to get in tune with God by asking his forgiveness; (3) drives us to trust in the sufficiency of Christ because we can never keep the commandments perfectly. The law cannot possibly save us, but after we have become Christians, the law can be a valuable guide for living a life pleasing to God.

17But what if we trust Christ to save us and then find that we are wrong, and that we cannot be saved without being circumcised and obeying all the other Jewish laws? Wouldn't we need to say that faith in Christ had ruined us? God forbid that anyone should dare to think such things about our Lord. 18Rather, we are sinners if we start rebuilding the old systems I have been destroying, of trying to be saved by keeping Jewish laws, 19for it was through reading the Scripture that I came to realize that I could never find God's favor by trying—and failing—to obey the laws. I came to realize that acceptance with God comes by believing in Christ.

20I have been crucified with Christ: and I myself no longer live, but Christ lives in me. And the real life I now have within this body is a result of my trusting in the Son of God, who loved me and gave himself for me. 21I am not one of those who treats Christ's death as meaningless. For if we could be saved by keeping Jewish laws, then there was no need for Christ to die.

2:17 1 Jn 3:8

2:19 Rom 6:2,14; 7:4 8:2 Heb 9:14

2:20 Rom 6:6 2 Cor 5:15

2:21 Heb 7:11

2. Superiority of the gospel
The law and faith

3 Oh, foolish Galatians! What magician has hypnotized you and cast an evil spell upon you? For you used to see the meaning of Jesus Christ's death as clearly as though I had waved a placard before you with a picture on it of Christ dying on the cross. 2Let me ask you this one question: Did you receive the Holy Spirit by trying to keep the Jewish laws? Of course not, for the Holy Spirit came upon you only after you heard about Christ and trusted him to save you. 3Then have you gone completely crazy? For if trying to obey the Jewish laws never gave you spiritual life in the first place, why do you think that trying to obey them now will make you stronger Christians? 4You have suffered so much for the Gospel. Now are you going to just throw it all overboard? I can hardly believe it!

5I ask you again, does God give you the power of the Holy Spirit and work

3:1 1 Cor 1:23 Gal 5:7

3:2 Acts 2:38 Rom 10:17

3:3 Gal 4:9 Heb 7:16

3:4 2 Jn 8

3:5 Phil 1:19

2:19 *acceptance with God comes by believing in Christ,* literally, "For I through the law died unto the law, that I might live unto God."

2:17-19 Through studying the Old Testament Scripture, Paul realized he could not be saved by obeying God's laws. The prophets knew that God's plan of salvation did not rest upon keeping the law. Because we have all been infected by sin, we cannot keep God's laws perfectly. Fortunately, God has provided a way of salvation that depends on Jesus Christ, not on our own efforts. We ignore God's system and try to earn our salvation whenever we think God accepts us because we do good things or because we are better than other people. In truth, only by trusting Christ to take away our sin will we be acceptable to God.

2:20 In what senses have I been crucified with Christ? *Legally,* God looks at me as if I had died with Christ. Because my sins died with him, I am no longer condemned (Colossians 2:13–15). *Relationally,* I have become one with Christ, and his experiences are mine. My Christian life began when, in unity with him, I died to my old life (see Romans 6:5–11). *In my daily life,* I have had repeatedly to crucify sinful desires that have tried to keep me from following Christ. This too is a kind of dying with him (Luke 9:23–25).

And yet the focus of Christianity is not dying, but living. Because I have been crucified with Christ, I have also been raised with him (Romans 6:5). *Legally,* I have been reconciled with God (2 Corinthians 5:19) and am free to grow into Christ's likeness (Romans 8:29). And *in my daily life,* as I continue to fight sin, Christ's resurrection power is abundantly available to me (Ephesians 1:19, 20). Christ lives in me—this is my reason for living and my hope for the future (Colossians 1:27).

2:21 Believers today are still in danger of treating Christ's death as meaningless. How? (1) By replacing Jewish legalism with their own brand of Christian legalism, giving people extra laws to obey before accepting them into fellowship; (2) by believing they can earn acceptability with God by what they do rather than by trusting

completely in Christ's work on the cross; (3) by focusing only on God's power to change us (sanctification) rather than giving equal time to God's power to save us (justification). If we could be saved by being good, then Christ did not need to die. But the cross is the only way to salvation.

3:1 The Galatian believers had become fascinated by the false teachers' arguments, almost as though they had fallen under a magician's spell. Magic was common in Paul's day (Acts 8:9–11; 13:6, 7). Magicians used both illusions and Satan's power to perform miracles. People were drawn into the magician's mysterious rites, not recognizing their dangerous source.

3:2, 3 The believers in Galatia, many of whom may have been in Jerusalem at Pentecost and received the Holy Spirit there, knew they didn't receive God's Spirit by obeying the Jewish law. Paul stresses that just as we were saved by faith in Christ, so also we grow by faith in Christ. The Galatians took a step backward when they decided to insist on keeping the Jewish laws. We must realize that we grow spiritually because of God's work in our lives, not by following special rules.

3:4 The Galatians were about to throw away their faith in Christ by attempting to find Christian perfection through keeping the law (see 1:6). Paul shouts that they need to *remember* what Christ has done for them, how they have suffered for their faith, and what salvation is all about! When you feel confused about your faith, seeing different options and not knowing what is right, *remember* your old life, *remember* how Christ has changed you, and *remember* his forgiveness. Then stay true to him.

3:5 This is a rhetorical question. The Galatians knew they received the Holy Spirit when they believed, not when they obeyed the law. People still feel insecure in their faith because faith alone seems too easy; people still try to become close to God by

miracles among you as a result of your trying to obey the Jewish laws? No, of course not. It is when you believe in Christ and fully trust him.

3:6
Gen 15:6
Rom 4:3

6Abraham had the same experience—God declared him fit for heaven only because he believed God's promises. 7You can see from this that the real children of Abraham are all the men of faith who truly trust in God.

3:7
Jn 8:39

8, 9What's more, the Scriptures looked forward to this time when God would save the Gentiles also, through their faith. God told Abraham about this long ago when he said, "I will bless those in every nation who trust in me as you do." And so it is: all who trust in Christ share the same blessing Abraham received.

3:8
Gen 12:3

3:10
Deut 27:26
Jer 11:3

10Yes, and those who depend on the Jewish laws to save them are under God's curse, for the Scriptures point out very clearly, "Cursed is everyone who at any time breaks a single one of these laws that are written in God's Book of the Law."

3:11
Hab 2:4

11Consequently, it is clear that no one can ever win God's favor by trying to keep the Jewish laws, because God has said that the only way we can be right in his sight is by faith. As the prophet Habakkuk says it, "The man who finds life will find it through trusting God." 12How different from this way of faith is the way of law which says that a man is saved by obeying every law of God, without one slip.

3:12
Lev 18:5
Rom 4:4; 11:6

3:13
Deut 21:23

13But Christ has bought us out from under the doom of that impossible system by taking the curse for our wrongdoing upon himself. For it is written in the Scripture,

3:13 *as Jesus was hung upon a wooden cross,* implied.

WHAT IS THE LAW? Part of the Jewish law included those laws found in the Old Testament. When Paul says that non-Jews (Gentiles) are no longer bound by these laws, he is not saying that the Old Testament laws do not apply to us today. He is saying certain types of laws may not apply to us. In the Old Testament there were three categories of laws:	Ceremonial law	This kind of law relates specifically to Israel's worship (see for example, Leviticus 1:1–13). Its primary purpose was to point forward to Jesus Christ. Therefore, these laws were no longer necessary after Jesus' death and resurrection. While we are no longer bound by ceremonial laws, the principles behind them—to worship and love a holy God—still apply. The Jewish Christians often accused the Gentile Christians of violating the ceremonial law.
	Civil law	This type of law dictated Israel's daily living (see Deuteronomy 24:10, 11, for example). Because modern society and culture are so radically different, some of these guidelines cannot be followed specifically. But the principles behind the commands should guide our conduct. At times, Paul asked Gentile Christians to follow some of these laws, not because they had to, but to promote unity.
	Moral law	This sort of law is the direct command of God—for example, the Ten Commandments (Exodus 20:1–17). It requires strict obedience. It reveals the nature and will of God and it still applies to us today. We are to obey this moral law, not to obtain salvation, but to live in ways pleasing to God.

---

following rules. By asking these questions, Paul hoped to get the Galatians to focus again on Christ as the center of their faith.

3:5 The Holy Spirit gives Christians great power to live their lives for God. Some Christians want more than this. They think that if the Holy Spirit is working in their lives, they will live in a state of perpetual excitement. The tedium of everyday living seems to say that something is wrong spiritually. These Christians may have missed the point. Often the Holy Spirit's greatest work in us is teaching us to persist, to keep on doing what is right even when it no longer seems new and interesting. The Galatians quickly turned from Paul's Good News to the teachings of the newest teachers in town; they needed the Holy Spirit's gift of persistence. If we get bored with the Christian life, we may not need the Spirit to stir us up—we may need him to settle us down and get us to see the challenge of the ordinary.

3:6–9 The main argument of the Judaizers was that Gentiles had to become Jews in order to become Christians. Paul exposed the flaw in this argument by showing that real children of Abraham are those who have faith, not those who keep the law. Abraham himself was saved by his faith (Genesis 15:6). All believers of all time and

from every nation share Abraham's blessing. This is a comforting promise, a great heritage, and a solid foundation for living.

3:10 Paul quotes Deuteronomy 27:26 to prove that, contrary to what the Judaizers claimed, the law cannot justify and save—it can only condemn. Breaking even one commandment brings a person under condemnation. Because everyone has broken the commandments, everyone is condemned, and the law can do nothing to reverse the condemnation (Romans 3:20–24). But Christ took the curse of the law upon himself when he hung on the cross (3:13). He did this so we wouldn't have to bear our own punishment and so we could be saved through him. The only condition is that we accept Christ's work on the cross (Colossians 1:20–23).

3:11 Trying to be righteous in our own power doesn't work. Good intentions such as "I'll do better next time" or "I'll never do that again" usually end in failure. Paul pointed to Habakkuk's declaration (Habakkuk 2:4) that by trusting God—believing in his provision for our sins and living each day in the power of his Spirit—we can break this cycle of failure.

"Anyone who is hanged on a tree is cursed" [as Jesus was hung upon a wooden cross].

14Now God can bless the Gentiles, too, with this same blessing he promised to Abraham; and all of us as Christians can have the promised Holy Spirit through this faith.

3:14
Isa 44:3
Joel 2:28
Acts 2:33
Eph 1:13

The law and the promise

15Dear brothers, even in everyday life a promise made by one man to another, if it is written down and signed, cannot be changed. He cannot decide afterward to do something else instead.

3:15
Heb 9:17

16Now, God gave some promises to Abraham and his Child. And notice that it doesn't say the promises were to his *children*, as it would if all his sons—all the Jews—were being spoken of, but to his *Child*—and that, of course, means Christ. 17Here's what I am trying to say: God's promise to save through faith—and God wrote this promise down and signed it—could not be canceled or changed four hundred and thirty years later when God gave the Ten Commandments. 18If *obeying those laws* could save us, then it is obvious that this would be a different way of gaining God's favor than Abraham's way, for he simply accepted God's promise.

3:16
Gen 22:17,18

3:17
Ex 12:40
Rom 4:13,14

3:18
Rom 4:14
Heb 6:14

19Well then, why were the laws given? They were added after the promise was given, to show men how guilty they are of breaking God's laws. But this system of law was to last only until the coming of Christ, the Child to whom God's promise was made. (And there is this further difference. God gave his laws to angels to give to Moses, who then gave them to the people; 20but when God gave his promise to Abraham, he did it by himself alone, without angels or Moses as go-betweens.)

3:19
Ex 20:19
Deut 5:5; 33:2
Jn 15:22
Acts 7:53
1 Tim 1:9
Heb 2:2

3:20
1 Tim 2:5

21, 22Well then, are God's laws and God's promises against each other? Of course not! If we could be saved by his laws, then God would not have had to give us a different way to get out of the grip of sin—for the Scriptures insist we are all its prisoners. The only way out is through faith in Jesus Christ; the way of escape is open to all who believe him.

3:22
Rom 11:32

23Until Christ came we were guarded by the law, kept in protective custody, so to speak, until we could believe in the coming Savior.

24Let me put it another way. The Jewish laws were our teacher and guide until Christ came to give us right standing with God through our faith. 25But now that Christ has come, we don't need those laws any longer to guard us and lead us to him.

3:24
Mt 5:17

Sons of God through faith

26For now we are all children of God through faith in Jesus Christ, 27and we who

---

3:17 God kept his promise to Abraham (Genesis 17:7, 8)—he has not revoked it, though thousands of years have passed. He saved Abraham through his faith, and he has blessed the world through Abraham by sending the Messiah as one of his descendants. Circumstances may change, but God remains constant and does not break his promises. He has promised to forgive our sins through Jesus Christ, and we can be sure he will do so.

3:18, 19 The law has two functions. On the positive side, it reveals the nature and will of God and shows people how to live. On the negative side, it points out people's sins and shows them that it is impossible to please God by obeying all his laws completely. God's promise to Abraham dealt with his faith; the law focuses on actions. The covenant with Abraham shows that faith is the only way to be saved; the law then shows how to live out our salvation. Faith does not annul the law, but the more we know God, the more we see how sinful we are. Then we are driven to depend on our faith in Christ alone for our salvation.

3:20 This is yet another reason Paul gives for the superiority of Abraham's covenant (faith) over Moses' laws (works) for salvation. The Judaizers had it backwards: the laws flowed *from* faith; they

were not a prerequisite for it. Similarly, right living is not the condition for faith, but the result of it. When we understand the transforming power of faith we will want to live in a way that demonstrates this transformation.

3:21, 22 The iron grip of sin is a reality for all people. We are trapped in sin, beaten down by past mistakes, and choked by desires for things we know are wrong. God knows we are sin's prisoners, and he has provided a way of escape: faith in Jesus Christ. All are caught in sin's grasp, and only those who place their faith in Christ ever get out of it. Look to him—he is reaching out to set you free.

3:25 The law shows the *need* for salvation; God's grace *gives* us that salvation. The Old Testament still applies today. In it, God reveals his nature, his will for man, his moral laws, and guidelines for living.

3:27 In Roman society, a youth coming of age laid aside the robe of childhood and put on a new toga. This represented his move into adult citizenship with full rights and responsibilies. Paul is saying, "You have laid aside the old clothes of the law, and now you are putting on Christ's new robe of righteousness" (see

3:28
Jn 10:16; 17:21
1 Cor 12:13
Col 3:10,11

3:29
Gen 21:10
Rom 8:17; 9:7
Gal 3:16; 4:28
Heb 11:18

have been baptized into union with Christ are enveloped by him. 28We are no longer Jews or Greeks or slaves or free men or even merely men or women, but we are all the same—we are Christians; we are one in Christ Jesus. 29And now that we are Christ's we are the true descendants of Abraham, and all of God's promises to him belong to us.

4 But remember this, that if a father dies and leaves great wealth for his little son, that child is not much better off than a slave until he grows up, even though he

THREE DISTORTIONS OF CHRISTIANITY:	Group	Their definition of a Christian	Their genuine concern	The danger	Application question
Almost from the beginning there were forces at work within Christianity which could have destroyed or sidetracked the movement. Of these, three created many problems then and have continued to reappear in other forms even today. The three aberrations are contrasted to true Christianity:	Judaized Christianity	Christians are Jews who have recognized Jesus as the promised Savior. Therefore any Gentile desiring to become a Christian must first become a Jew.	Having a high regard for God's word and his choice of Jews as his people, they did not want to see God's commands overlooked or broken.	Tends to add human traditions and standards to God's law. Also subtracts from the Scriptures God's clear concern for all nations.	Do you appreciate God's choice of a unique people through which he offered forgiveness and eternal life to all peoples?
	Legalized Christianity	Christians are those who live by a long list of "don'ts." God's favor is earned by good behavior.	Recognized that real change brought about by God should lead to changes in behavior.	Tends to make God's love something to earn rather than to accept freely. Would reduce Christianity to a set of impossible rules and transform the Good News into bad news.	As important as change in action is, can you see that God may be desiring different changes in you than in others?
	Law-less Christianity	Christians live above the law. They need no guidelines. God's word is not as important as our personal sense of God's guidance.	Recognized that forgiveness from God cannot be based on our ability to live up to his perfect standards. It must be received by faith as a gift made possible by Christ's death on the cross.	Forgets that Christians are still human and fail consistently when trying to live only by what they "feel" God wants.	Do you recognize the ongoing need for God's expressed commands as you live out your gratitude for his great salvation?
	True Christianity	Christians are those who believe inwardly and outwardly that Jesus' death has allowed God to offer them forgiveness and eternal life as a gift. They have accepted that gift by faith and are seeking to live a life of obedient gratitude for what God has done for them.	Christianity is both private and public; heart-belief and mouth-confession. Our relationship to God and the power he provides result in obedience. Having received the gift of forgiveness and eternal life, we are now daily challenged to live that life with his help.	Avoids the above dangers.	How would those closest to you describe your Christianity? Do they think you live *so* that God will accept you or do they know that you live *because* God has accepted you in Christ?

2 Corinthians 5:21; Ephesians 4:23, 24).

3:28 Jewish males greeted each new day by praying, "Lord, I thank you that I am not a Gentile, a slave, or a woman." This prayer should no longer be said, because faith in Christ transcends these differences and makes all believers one in Christ.

3:28 It's our natural inclination to feel uncomfortable around those who are different from us and to gravitate toward those who resemble us. But when we allow our differences to separate us

from our fellow believers, we are disregarding clear biblical teaching. Make a point of seeking out and appreciating people who are not just like you and your friends. You may find that you and they have a lot in common.

3:29 The original covenant with Abraham was intended for the whole world, not just for his descendants (see Genesis 12:3). All believers partake of this covenant and are blessed as children of Abraham.

actually owns everything his father had. ²He has to do what his guardians and managers tell him to, until he reaches whatever age his father set.

³And that is the way it was with us before Christ came. We were slaves to Jewish laws and rituals for we thought they could save us. ⁴But when the right time came, the time God decided on, he sent his Son, born of a woman, born as a Jew, ⁵to buy freedom for us who were slaves to the law so that he could adopt us as his very own sons. ⁶And because we are his sons God has sent the Spirit of his Son into our hearts, so now we can rightly speak of God as our dear Father. ⁷Now we are no longer slaves, but God's own sons. And since we are his sons, everything he has belongs to us, for that is the way God planned.

Paul's concern for the Galatians

⁸Before you Gentiles knew God you were slaves to so-called gods that did not even exist. ⁹And now that you have found God (or I should say, now that God has found you) how can it be that you want to go back again and become slaves once more to another poor, weak, useless religion of trying to get to heaven by obeying God's laws? ¹⁰You are trying to find favor with God by what you do or don't do on certain days or months or seasons or years. ¹¹I fear for you. I am afraid that all my hard work for you was worth nothing.

¹²Dear brothers, please feel as I do about these things, for I am as free from these chains as you used to be. You did not despise me then when I first preached to you, ¹³even though I was sick when I first brought you the Good News of Christ. ¹⁴But even though my sickness was revolting to you, you didn't reject me and turn me away. No, you took me in and cared for me as though I were an angel from God, or even Jesus Christ himself.

¹⁵Where is that happy spirit that we felt together then? For in those days I know you would gladly have taken out your own eyes and given them to replace mine if that would have helped me.

¹⁶And now have I become your enemy because I tell you the truth?

¹⁷Those false teachers who are so anxious to win your favor are not doing it for your good. What they are trying to do is to shut you off from me so that you will pay more attention to them. ¹⁸It is a fine thing when people are nice to you with good

4:3
Col 2:8
Heb 9:10

4:4
Mk 1:15
Jn 1:14
Eph 1:10
Heb 2:14

4:5
Mt 20:28
Rom 8:14,15
Eph 1:5

4:7
Rom 8:16,17

4:8
2 Chron 13:9
Rom 1:25
1 Cor 8:4
Eph 2:12
1 Thess 1:9

4:9
Col 2:20

4:10
Rom 14:5
Col 2:16

4:12
Gal 6:14

4:13
1 Cor 2:3
Gal 1:6

4:14
Mt 10:40
1 Thess 2:13

4:16
Amos 5:10

4:17
Rom 10:2

4:3–7 Paul uses the illustration of slavery to show that before Christ came and died for sins, people were in bondage to the law. Thinking they could be saved by it, they became enslaved to trying—and failing—to keep it. But the Good News is that we who were once slaves are now God's very own children with an intimate relationship with him. Because of Christ, there is no reason to be afraid of God. We can come boldly into his presence, knowing he will welcome us as members of his family.

4:4 "At just the right time" God sent Jesus to earth to die for our sins. For centuries the Jews were wondering when their Messiah would come—but God's timing was perfect. We may sometimes wonder if God will ever respond to our prayers. But we must never stop trusting him or give up hope. At the right time he will respond. Are you waiting for his timing? Trust his judgment for your best interests.

4:4, 5 Jesus was born of a woman—he was human. He was born as a Jew—he was subject to God's law and fulfilled it perfectly. Thus Jesus was the perfect sacrifice because, although he was fully human, he never sinned. His death bought freedom for us who were enslaved to sin so we could be adopted into God's family.

4:5–7 Under Roman law, an adopted child was guaranteed all legal rights to his father's property. He was not a second-class son; he was equal to any other sons, biological or adopted, in his father's family. As adopted children of God, we share with Jesus all rights to God's resources. As God's heirs, we can claim what he has provided for us—our full identity as his children (see Romans 8:15–17).

4:14 The world is often callous to people's pain and misery. Paul

commended the Galatians for not rejecting him, even though his condition was revolting (he doesn't explain what was wrong with him). Such caring was what Jesus meant when he called us to serve the homeless, hungry, sick, and imprisoned as if they were Jesus himself (Matthew 25:40). Do you avoid those in pain or facing difficulty—or are you willing to care for them as if they were Jesus Christ himself?

4:15 Paul sensed that the Galatians had lost the joy of their salvation because of legalism. How does legalism take away "that happy spirit"? (1) It makes people feel guilty rather than loved; (2) it produces self-hatred rather than humility; (3) it stresses performance over relationship; (4) it points out how far short we fall rather than how far we've come because of what Christ did for us. If you feel guilty and inadequate, check your focus. Are you putting your faith in Christ or in rule-keeping?

4:16 Paul did not gain great popularity when he rebuked the Galatians for turning away from their first faith in Christ. Human nature hasn't changed much—we still get angry when we're scolded. But don't write off someone who challenges you. There may be truth in what he says. Receive his words with humility; carefully think them over. If you discover you need to change an attitude or action, take steps to do it.

4:17 These false teachers claimed to be religious authorities, experts in Judaism and Christianity. Appealing to the believers' desire to do what is right, they drew quite a following. Paul said, however, that they were wrong and that their motives were selfish. False teachers are often respectable and persuasive. That is why all teachings need to be checked with the Bible.

motives and sincere hearts, especially if they aren't doing it just when I am with you! 19Oh, my children, how you are hurting me! I am once again suffering for you the pains of a mother waiting for her child to be born—longing for the time when you will finally be filled with Christ. 20How I wish I could be there with you right now and not have to reason with you like this, for at this distance I frankly don't know what to do.

Abraham's two children

21Listen to me, you friends who think you have to obey the Jewish laws to be saved: Why don't you find out what those laws really mean? 22For it is written that Abraham had two sons, one from his slavewife and one from his freeborn wife. 23There was nothing unusual about the birth of the slave-wife's baby. But the baby of the freeborn wife was born only after God had especially promised he would come.

24, 25Now this true story is an illustration of God's two ways of helping people. One way was by giving them his laws to obey. He did this on Mount Sinai, when he gave the Ten Commandments to Moses. Mount Sinai, by the way, is called "Mount Hagar" by the Arabs—and in my illustration Abraham's slave-wife Hagar represents Jerusalem, the mother-city of the Jews, the center of that system of trying to please God by trying to obey the Commandments; and the Jews, who try to follow that system, are her slave children. 26But our mother-city is the heavenly Jerusalem, and she is not a slave to Jewish laws.

27That is what Isaiah meant when he prophesied, "Now you can rejoice, O childless woman; you can shout with joy though you never before had a child. For I am going to give you many children—more children than the slave-wife has."

28You and I, dear brothers, are the children that God promised, just as Isaac was. 29And so we who are born of the Holy Spirit are persecuted now by those who want us to keep the Jewish laws, just as Isaac the child of promise was persecuted by Ishmael the slave-wife's son.

30But the Scriptures say that God told Abraham to send away the slave-wife and her son, for the slave-wife's son could not inherit Abraham's home and lands along with the free woman's son. 31Dear brothers, we are not slave children, obligated to the Jewish laws, but children of the free woman, acceptable to God because of our faith.

3. Freedom of the gospel

Living in the freedom of Christ

5 So Christ has made us free. Now make sure that you stay free and don't get all tied up again in the chains of slavery to Jewish laws and ceremonies. 2Listen to me, for this is serious: *if you are counting on circumcision and keeping the Jewish laws to make you right with God, then Christ cannot save you.* 3I'll say it again. Anyone trying to find favor with God by being circumcised must always obey every other Jewish law or perish. 4Christ is useless to you if you are counting on

4:19
1 Cor 4:15
Eph 3:17; 4:13

4:22
Gen 16:15; 21:2

4:23
Gen 18:10
Rom 9:7,8

4:24
Deut 32:2-4

4:26
Heb 12:22
Rev 3:12; 21:2

4:27
Isa 54:1

4:28
Rom 4:16
Gal 3:29

4:29
Gen 21:9

4:30
Gen 21:10
Jn 8:35
Gal 3:8

5:1
Jn 8:32
Acts 15:10
Gal 2:4

5:2
Acts 15:1

5:3
Gal 3:10

4:19 Paul led many people to Christ and helped them mature spiritually. Perhaps one reason for his success as a spiritual father was the deep concern he felt for his spiritual children; he compared his pain over their faithlessness to the pain of childbirth. We should have the same intense care for those to whom we are spiritual parents. When you lead people to Christ, remember to stay by to help them grow.

4:21ff People are saved because of their faith in Christ, not because of what they do. Paul contrasts those who are enslaved to the law (represented by Hagar, the slave woman) with those who are free from the law (represented by Sarah, the free woman). Hagar's abuse of Sarah (Genesis 16:4) was like the persecution Gentile Christians were getting from the Judaizers, who insisted on keeping the law in order to be saved. Eventually Sarah triumphed because her son was promised by God, just as those who worship Christ in faith will also triumph.

5:1 Christ died to set us free from sin and from a long list of laws and regulations. Christ came to set us free—not free to do whatever we want, for that would lead back into slavery to our selfish desires. Rather, thanks to Christ, we are now free and able to do what was impossible before—to live unselfishly. Those who appeal to their freedom so they can have their own way or indulge their desires are falling back into sin. Do you use your freedom for yourself or for others?

5:2 "Christ cannot save you" is literally "Christ will be of no advantage to you." Trying to be saved by keeping the law and being saved by grace are two entirely different approaches. Christ's provision for our salvation will not help us if we are trying to save ourselves. We cannot make it any easier for God to save us. All we can do is accept his grace through faith.

clearing your debt to God by keeping those laws; you are lost from God's grace.

5But we by the help of the Holy Spirit are counting on Christ's death to clear away our sins and make us right with God. 6And we to whom Christ has given eternal life don't need to worry about whether we have been circumcised or not, or whether we are obeying the Jewish ceremonies or not; for all we need is faith working through love.

7You were getting along so well. Who has interfered with you to hold you back from following the truth? 8It certainly isn't God who has done it, for he is the one who has called you to freedom in Christ. 9But it takes only one wrong person among you to infect all the others.

10I am trusting the Lord to bring you back to believing as I do about these things. God will deal with that person, whoever he is, who has been troubling and confusing you.

11Some people even say that I myself am preaching that circumcision and Jewish laws are necessary to the plan of salvation. Well, if I preached that, I would be persecuted no more—for that message doesn't offend anyone. The fact that I am still being persecuted proves that I am still preaching salvation through faith in the cross of Christ alone.

12I only wish these teachers who want you to cut yourselves by being circumcised would cut themselves off from you and leave you alone!

13For, dear brothers, you have been given freedom: not freedom to do wrong, but freedom to love and serve each other. 14For the whole Law can be summed up in

5:5
Rom 8:23
5:6
Col 3:11
1 Thess 1:3
Jas 2:18
5:7
1 Cor 9:24
5:8
Rom 8:28
5:9
1 Cor 5:6
5:10
Gal 1:7
5:11
1 Cor 1:23
15:30
5:12
Acts 15:1
1 Cor 5:13
5:13
1 Pet 2:16
5:14
Lev 19:18
Jn 13:34
Rom 13:8

5:12 *would cut themselves off from you and leave you alone,* or "would that those disturbing you would go and castrate themselves."

Vices
(Neglecting God and others)

Impure thoughts (Galatians 5:19)
Lust (Galatians 5:19)
Hatred (Galatians 5:20)
Fighting (Galatians 5:20)
Jealousy (Galatians 5:20)
Anger (Galatians 5:20)
Trying to be first (Galatians 5:20)
Complaining (Galatians 5:20)
Criticizing (Galatians 5:20)
Thinking you're always right (Galatians 5:20)
Envy (Galatians 5:21)
Murder (Galatians 5:21; Revelation 22:12–16)
Idolatry (Galatians 5:20; Ephesians 5:5)
Spiritism (Galatians 5:20)
Drunkenness (Galatians 5:21)
Wild parties (Galatians 5:21)
Cheating (1 Corinthians 6:8)
Adultery (1 Corinthians 6:9, 10)
Homosexuality (1 Corinthians 6:9, 10)
Greed (1 Corinthians 6:9, 10; Ephesians 5:5)
Stealing (1 Corinthians 6:9, 10)
Lying (Revelation 22:12–16)

Virtues
(The by-products of living for God)

Love (Galatians 5:22)
Joy (Galatians 5:22)
Peace (Galatians 5:22)
Patience (Galatians 5:22)
Kindness (Galatians 5:22)
Goodness (Galatians 5:22)
Faithfulness (Galatians 5:22)
Gentleness (Galatians 5:23)
Self-control (Galatians 5:23)

VICES AND VIRTUES
The Bible mentions many specific actions and attitudes that are either right or wrong. Look at the list included here. Are there too many characteristics from the wrong column that are influencing you?

5:6 We are saved by faith, not works, but love for others and for God is the response of those whom God has forgiven. God's forgiveness is complete, and Jesus said that those who are forgiven much love much (Luke 7:47). Since faith expresses itself through love, you can check up on your love to monitor your faith.

5:11 Persecution proved that Paul was preaching the gospel. If he taught what the false teachers taught, no one would be offended; but because he taught the truth, he was persecuted by both Jews and Judaizers. Have friends or loved ones rejected you because you have taken a stand for Christ? Paul's experience reminds us that this is to be expected. Jesus said not to be surprised if the world hates you, because it hated him (John 15:18,

19). Just as Paul continued faithfully proclaiming the message about Christ, you should continue doing the work God has given you to do—in spite of the obstacles others may put in your way.

5:13 Paul distinguished between freedom to sin and freedom to serve. Freedom to sin is no freedom at all, because it enslaves you to Satan, others, or your own evil desires. People who are slaves to sin are not free to live a righteous life. Christians, by contrast, should not be slaves to sin because they are free to do right and glorify God through their actions.

5:14, 15 When we are not motivated by love, we become critical of others. We stop looking for good in them and see only their faults. Soon the unity of believers is broken. Have you talked

this one command: "Love others as you love yourself." [15]But if instead of showing love among yourselves you are always critical and catty, watch out! Beware of ruining each other.

Living by the Holy Spirit's power

5:16
Rom 6:12; 8:4-6

5:17
Rom 7:15,23

[16]I advise you to obey only the Holy Spirit's instructions. He will tell you where to go and what to do, and then you won't always be doing the wrong things your evil nature wants you to. [17]For we naturally love to do evil things that are just the opposite from the things that the Holy Spirit tells us to do; and the good things we want to do when the Spirit has his way with us are just the opposite of our natural desires. These two forces within us are constantly fighting each other to win control over us, and our wishes are never free from their pressures. [18]When you are guided

5:18
Rom 6:14; 8:14

by the Holy Spirit you need no longer force yourself to obey Jewish laws.

5:19
Rom 13:12,13
1 Cor 3:3
Jas 3:14

[19]But when you follow your own wrong inclinations your lives will produce these evil results: impure thoughts, eagerness for lustful pleasure, [20]idolatry, spiritism (that is, encouraging the activity of demons), hatred and fighting, jealousy and anger, constant effort to get the best for yourself, complaints and criticisms, the feeling that everyone else is wrong except those in your own little group—and

5:21
1 Cor 6:9
Eph 5:5
Rev 22:15

there will be wrong doctrine, [21]envy, murder, drunkenness, wild parties, and all that sort of thing. Let me tell you again as I have before, that anyone living that sort of life will not inherit the Kingdom of God.

5:22
Jas 3:17

[22]But when the Holy Spirit controls our lives he will produce this kind of fruit in us: love, joy, peace, patience, kindness, goodness, faithfulness, [23]gentleness and self-control; and here there is no conflict with Jewish laws.

OUR WRONG DESIRES VS. THE FRUIT OF THE SPIRIT The will of the Holy Spirit is in constant opposition to our sinful desires. The two are on opposite sides of the spiritual battle.	*Our wrong desires are:*	*The fruit of the Spirit is:*
	Evil	Good
	Destructive	Productive
	Easy to ignite	Difficult to ignite
	Difficult to stifle	Easy to stifle
	Self-centered	Self-giving
	Oppressive and possessive	Liberating and nurturing
	Decadent	Uplifting
	Sinful	Holy
	Deadly	Abundant life

---

behind someone's back? Have you focused on others' shortcomings instead of their strengths? Remind yourself of Jesus' command to love others as we love ourselves (Matthew 22:39). When you begin to feel critical of someone, make a list of that person's positive qualities. And don't say anything behind his back that you wouldn't say to his face.

5:16-18 If your desires would lead to the qualities listed in 5:22, then you know the Holy Spirit is leading you. At the same time, you must beware of confusing your feelings with the Spirit's leading. Thus, being led by the Holy Spirit involves the desire to hear, and the readiness to obey, and the sensitivity to discern between your feelings and his promptings.

5:17 Paul describes the two forces at work within us—the Holy Spirit and our evil inclinations. Paul is not saying that these forces are equal. The Holy Spirit is infinitely stronger, but *we* are weak. Left to our sin, we will make wrong choices. Our only way to freedom from our natural evil desires is through the empowering of the Holy Spirit (see Romans 8:9; Ephesians 4:23, 24; Colossians 3:3-8).

5:19-21 We all have natural evil desires, and we can't ignore them. In order for us to follow the Holy Spirit's guidance, we must deal with them decisively (nail them to Christ's cross—5:24). These desires include obvious sins such as sexual immorality and

witchcraft. They also include less obvious sins such as ambition, anger, and envy. Ignoring our sins or refusing to deal with them prevents us from inheriting the Kingdom of God.

5:22 We are all controlled by some outside force. If we are controlled by the law, we are condemned by our inability to keep it. If we are controlled by sin, we are destroyed by our own evil actions. If we are controlled by the Holy Spirit, we produce the kind of fruit listed here. We do not need to fear the Spirit's control. He does not possess us against our wills or treat us as robots.

5:22 The Spirit produces character traits, not specific actions. We can't go out and *do* these things, and we can't obtain them by trying to get them. If we want the fruit of the Spirit to develop in our lives, we must recognize that all of these characteristics are found in Christ. Thus the way to grow them is to join our lives to his (see John 15:4, 5). We must know him, love him, remember him, imitate him. The result will be that we will fulfill the intended purpose of the law—loving God and man. Which of these qualities most needs further development in your life?

5:23 Because the God who sent the law also sent the Spirit, the by-products of the Spirit-filled life are in perfect harmony with the intent of God's law. A person who is rich in the fruit of the Spirit fulfills the law far better than a person who observes the rituals but has little love in his heart.

24Those who belong to Christ have nailed their natural evil desires to his cross and crucified them there.

5:24
Rom 6:6

25If we are living now by the Holy Spirit's power, let us follow the Holy Spirit's leading in every part of our lives. 26Then we won't need to look for honors and popularity, which lead to jealousy and hard feelings.

5:25
Gal 5:16

5:26
Phil 2:3

We will reap what we sow

6 Dear brothers, if a Christian is overcome by some sin, you who are godly should gently and humbly help him back onto the right path, remembering that next time it might be one of you who is in the wrong. 2Share each other's troubles and problems, and so obey our Lord's command. 3If anyone thinks he is too great to stoop to this, he is fooling himself. He is really a nobody.

6:1
1 Cor 2:15; 7:5
Jas 5:19,20
1 Jn 5:16

6:2
Rom 15:1

6:3
Rom 12:3
1 Cor 3:18
2 Cor 3:5; 12:11

4Let everyone be sure that he is doing his very best, for then he will have the personal satisfaction of work well done, and won't need to compare himself with someone else. 5Each of us must bear some faults and burdens of his own. For none of us is perfect!

6:6
Rom 15:27
1 Cor 9:11,14

6Those who are taught the Word of God should help their teachers by paying them.

6:7
1 Cor 6:9
2 Cor 9:6

7Don't be misled; remember that you can't ignore God and get away with it: a man will always reap just the kind of crop he sows! 8If he sows to please his own wrong desires, he will be planting seeds of evil and he will surely reap a harvest of spiritual decay and death; but if he plants the good things of the Spirit, he will reap the everlasting life which the Holy Spirit gives him. 9And let us not get tired of doing what is right, for after a while we will reap a harvest of blessing if we don't get discouraged and give up. 10That's why whenever we can we should always be kind to everyone, and especially to our Christian brothers.

6:8
Job 4:8
Rom 8:9-14
Jas 3:18

6:9
Mt 24:13
2 Thess 3:13

6:10
Jn 9:4
Eph 2:19
1 Tim 6:18
Heb 3:6

Paul's final warning

11I will write these closing words in my own handwriting. See how large I have to make the letters! 12Those teachers of yours who are trying to convince you to be

6:11
1 Cor 16:21

5:24 In order to accept Christ as Savior, we need to turn from our sins and willingly nail our natural evil desires to the cross. This doesn't mean, however, that we will never see traces of those desires again. As Christians we still have the capacity to sin, but we have been set free from sin's power over us and no longer have to give in to it. We must daily commit our sinful tendencies to God's control, daily nail them to Christ's cross, and moment by moment draw on the Spirit's power to overcome them (see 2:20; 6:14).

5:25 God is interested in every part of our lives, not just the spiritual part. As we live by the Holy Spirit's power, we need to submit every aspect of our lives to God—emotional, physical, social, intellectual, vocational. Paul says, "You're saved, so live like it!" The Holy Spirit is the source of your new life, so walk with him. Don't let anything or anyone else determine your values and standards in any area of your life.

5:26 We all need a certain amount of approval from others. But those who go out of their way to secure honors or to win popularity with a lot of people show they are not following the Holy Spirit's leading. Those who look to God for approval won't need to seek it from others.

6:1-3 No one should ever think he or she is totally independent and doesn't need help from others, and no one should feel excused from the task of helping. The body of Christ—the universal church—functions only when the members work together for the common good. Is there someone near you who needs help in a task of daily living? Is there a Christian brother or sister who needs correction or encouragement? Humbly and gently reach out to that person (John 13:34, 35). Any who feel they are too busy to help others take their work far too seriously.

6:4 When you do your very best, you feel good about the results and there is no need to compare yourself with others. People make comparisons for many reasons. Some point out others' flaws in order to feel better about themselves. Others simply want reassurance that they are doing well. When you are tempted to compare, look at Jesus Christ. His example will inspire you to do your very best, and his loving acceptance will comfort you when you fall short of your goals.

6:6 Paul insisted that we fulfill our responsibility to take care of the material needs of those who teach us (1 Corinthians 9:7–12). It is easy to take the benefit of good Bible teaching and take our spiritual leaders for granted, ignoring their financial and physical needs. We should care for them, not grudgingly or reluctantly, but with a generous spirit, showing honor and appreciation for their service (1 Timothy 5:17, 18).

6:7, 8 It would certainly be a surprise if you planted corn in the ground and pumpkins came up. But it probably would not be a surprise if you gossiped about your friends and soon found you had no friends. It's a law of life—both physical and spiritual—that you reap what you sow. Every action has results. If you plant to please your own desires, you'll reap a crop of sorrow and evil; if you plant to please God, you'll reap joy and everlasting life. What kind of seeds are you sowing in the soil of your life?

6:9, 10 It is discouraging to continue to do right and receive no word of thanks or see no tangible results. But Paul challenges the Galatians and us to keep on doing what is right and to trust God for the results. In due time, we will reap a harvest of blessing.

6:11 Up to this point, Paul had dictated the letter to a scribe. Now he took the pen into his own hands to write his final, personal greetings. He did this in other letters as well, to add emphasis to his words and validate that the letter was genuine.

circumcised are doing it for just one reason: so that they can be popular and avoid the persecution they would get if they admitted that the cross of Christ alone can save. 13And even those teachers who submit to circumcision don't try to keep the other Jewish laws; but they want you to be circumcised in order that they can boast that you are their disciples.

14As for me, God forbid that I should boast about anything except the cross of our Lord Jesus Christ. Because of that cross my interest in all the attractive things of the world was killed long ago, and the world's interest in me is also long dead. 15It doesn't make any difference now whether we have been circumcised or not; what counts is whether we really have been changed into new and different people.

16May God's mercy and peace be upon all of you who live by this principle and upon those everywhere who are really God's own.

17From now on please don't argue with me about these things, for I carry on my body the scars of the whippings and wounds from Jesus' enemies that mark me as his slave.

18Dear brothers, may the grace of our Lord Jesus Christ be with you all.

Sincerely, Paul

6:13
Rom 2:25

6:14
Rom 6:2,3,6
1 Cor 2:2
Gal 2:20
Col 2:20

6:15
2 Cor 5:17
Gal 5:6

6:16
Gal 3:7
Phil 3:3

6:17
2 Cor 1:5; 4:10
Col 1:24

6:18
Rom 16:20
2 Tim 4:22

6:13 Some of the Judaizers emphasized circumcision as proof of holiness—but ignored the other Jewish laws. People often choose a certain principle or prohibition and make it the measuring rod of faith. Some may abhor drunkenness but ignore gluttony. Others despise promiscuity but tolerate prejudice. The Bible in its entirety is our rule of faith and practice. We cannot pick and choose the mandates we will follow.

6:14 The world is full of enticements. We are daily confronted with both subtle cultural pressures and overt propaganda. The only way to escape these destructive influences is to ask God to help us die to them, just as Paul did. How much do the interests of this world matter to you? (See 2:20 and 5:24 for more on this concept.)

6:15 It is easy to get caught in the externals. Beware of those who emphasize things we should or shouldn't do, with no concern for the inward condition of the heart. Living a "good" life without an inward change leads to a spiritual walk that is shallow and empty.

What matters to God is that we be completely changed from the inside out (2 Corinthians 5:17).

6:18 The Epistle of Paul to the Galatians boldly declares the freedom of the Christian. Doubtless these early Christians in Galatia wanted to grow in the Christian life, but they were being misled by those who said this could be done only by keeping certain Jewish laws.

How strange it would be for a prisoner who had been set free to walk back into his cell and refuse to leave! How strange for an animal, released from a trap, to go back inside it! How sad for a believer to be set free from the bondage of sin, only to return to rigid conformity to a set of rules and regulations! If you believe in Jesus Christ, you have been set free. Instead of going back into some form of slavery, whether legalism or sin, use your freedom to live for Christ and serve him as he desires.

EPHESIANS

VITAL STATISTICS

PURPOSE:
To strengthen the believers in Ephesus in their Christian faith by explaining the nature and purpose of the church, the body of Christ

AUTHOR:
Paul

TO WHOM WRITTEN:
The church at Ephesus, and all believers everywhere

DATE WRITTEN:
About A.D. 60, from Rome during Paul's imprisonment there

SETTING:
The letter was not written to confront any heresy or problem in the churches. It was sent with Tychicus to strengthen and encourage the churches in the area. Paul spent over three years with the Ephesian church. As a result, Paul was very close to this church. Paul met with the elders of the Ephesian church for the last time at Miletus (Acts 20:17-38)—a meeting that was filled with great sadness because Paul was leaving them for the last time. Because there are no specific references to people or problems in the Ephesian church and because the words "at Ephesus" (1:1) are not present in the earliest manuscripts, Paul may have intended this to be a circular letter—read to all the churches in the area.

KEY VERSE:
"We are all parts of one body, we have the same Spirit, and we have all been called to the same glorious future" (4:4).

KEY PEOPLE:
Paul, Tychicus

SPECIAL FEATURES:
Several pictures of the church are presented: body, temple, mystery, new man, bride, and soldier. This epistle became a circular letter distributed to many of the early churches.

OUR churches come in all styles and shapes— the secret meetings in homes; the wide-open gatherings in amphitheaters; the worship services packing thousands into the sanctuary while the overflow crowd watches on closed circuit television; the handful who kneel in an urban storefront. Buildings will vary, but the church is not confined to four walls. The church of Jesus Christ is *people,* his people, of every race and nation who love Christ and are committed to serving him.

The "church age" began at Pentecost (Acts 2). Born in Jerusalem, the church spread rapidly through the ministry of the apostles and the early believers. Fanned by persecution, the gospel flame then spread to other cities and nations. On three courageous journeys, Paul and his associates established local assemblies in scores of Gentile cities.

One of the most prominent of those churches was at Ephesus. It was established in A.D. 53 on Paul's homeward journey to Jerusalem. But he returned a year later, on his third missionary trip, and stayed there for three years, preaching and teaching with great effectiveness (Acts 19:1-20). At another time, he met with the Ephesian elders, and he sent Timothy to serve as their leader (1 Timothy 1:3). Just a few years later, Paul was sent as a prisoner to Rome. There he was visited by messengers from various churches. Among these was Tychicus of Ephesus. Paul wrote this letter to the church and sent it with Tychicus. Not written to counteract heresy or to confront any specific problem, Ephesians is a letter of encouragement. In it Paul describes the nature and appearance of the church, and he challenges believers to function as the living body of Christ on earth.

After a warm greeting (1:1, 2), Paul affirms the nature of the church— the glorious fact that believers in Christ have been showered with God's kindness (1:3-8), chosen for greatness (1:9-12), marked by the Holy Spirit (1:13, 14), filled with his power (1:15-23), freed from sin's curse and bondage (2:1-10), and brought near to God (2:11-19). As part of God's "house," we stand with the prophets, apostles, Jews, Gentiles, and Christ himself (2:20—3:11). Then, as though overcome with emotion by remembering all that God has done, Paul challenges them to live close to Christ—breaking into spontaneous praise (3:12-21).

Paul then turns his attention to the implications of being in the body of Christ, the church. Believers should have unity in their commitment to Christ and their use of spiritual gifts (4:1-16). They should have the highest moral standards (4:17—6:9)— for the individual, this means rejecting heathen practices (4:17—5:20), and for the family, this means mutual submission and love (5:21—6:9).

Paul then reminds them that the church is in a constant battle with the forces of darkness, and that they should use every spiritual weapon at their disposal (6:10-17). He concludes by asking for their prayers, commissioning Tychicus, and giving a benediction (6:18-24).

As you read this masterful description of the church, thank God for the diversity and unity in his family, pray for your brothers and sisters across the world, and draw close to those in the local church.

THE BLUEPRINT

1. Unity in Christ (1:1—3:21)
2. Unity in the church (4:1—6:24)

In this letter, Paul explains the wonderful things that we have received through Christ and refers to the church as a body, a temple, a bride, and a soldier. These all illustrate unity of purpose and show how each individual member is a part which must work together with all the other parts. In our own lives, we should work to eradicate all backbiting, gossip, criticism, jealousy, anger, and bitterness, because these are barriers to unity in the church.

MEGATHEMES

THEME	EXPLANATION	IMPORTANCE
God's purpose	According to God's eternal, loving plan, he directs, carries out, and sustains our salvation.	When we respond to Christ's love by trusting in him, his purpose becomes our mission. Have you committed yourself to fulfilling God's purpose?
Christ the center	Christ is exalted as the central meaning of the universe and the focus of history. He is the head of the body, the church.	Because Christ is central to everything, his power must be central in us. Begin by placing all your priorities in his control.
Living Church	The nature of the church is presented. The church, under Christ's control, is a living body, a family, a dwelling. God gives believers special abilities by his Holy Spirit to build the church.	We are part of Christ's body, and we must live in vital union with him. Our conduct must be consistent with this living relationship. Use your God-given abilities to equip believers for service. Fulfill your role in the living church.
New family	Because God through Christ paid our penalty for sin and forgave us, we have been reconciled—brought near to him. We are a new society, a new family. United with Christ means we are to treat one another as family members.	We are one family in Christ; so there should be no barriers, no divisions, no basis for discrimination. We all belong to him, so we should live in harmony with one another.
Christian conduct	Paul encourages all Christians to wise, dynamic Christian living, for with privileges goes family responsibility. As a new community, we are to have Christ's new standards.	God provides his Holy Spirit to enable us to live his way. To utilize his power, we must lay aside our evil desires and draw upon the power of his new life. Submit your will to Christ, and seek to love others.

1. Unity in Christ

1 Dear Christian friends at Ephesus, ever loyal to the Lord: This is Paul writing to you, chosen by God to be Jesus Christ's messenger. ²May his blessings and peace be yours, sent to you from God our Father and Jesus Christ our Lord.

1:2
Rom 1:7
Tit 1:4

God's overflowing kindness

³How we praise God, the Father of our Lord Jesus Christ, who has blessed us with every blessing in heaven because we belong to Christ.

1:3
Eph 1:20; 2:6

⁴Long ago, even before he made the world, God chose us to be his very own, through what Christ would do for us; he decided then to make us holy in his eyes, without a single fault—we who stand before him covered with his love. ⁵His

1:4
2 Thess 2:13
1 Pet 1:2,20
1:5
Rom 8:15,29

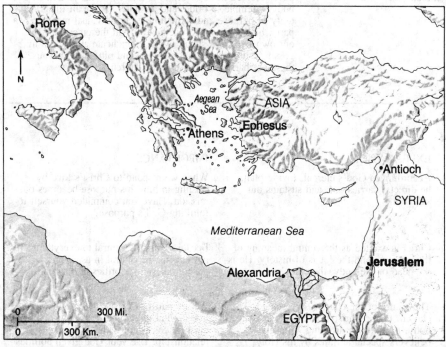

LOCATION OF EPHESUS
Ephesus was a strategic city, ranking in importance with Alexandria in Egypt and Antioch in Syria as a port. It lay on the most western edge of Asia Minor (modern-day Turkey), the most important port on the Aegean Sea on the main route from Rome to the east.

1:1 From inside the walls of a Roman prison, Paul wrote this letter to the church at Ephesus, in order to give them in-depth teaching about how to nurture and maintain the unity of the church. He wanted to circulate this important information in written form because he was in prison and could not visit the churches himself. Paul mentions no particular problems or local situations, and he offers no personal greetings. This was probably a circular letter—one sent to Ephesus and to neighboring local churches.

1:1 Paul had been a Christian for nearly 30 years. He had taken three missionary trips and established churches all around the Mediterranean Sea. When he wrote Ephesians, he was under house arrest in Rome (See Acts 28:16ff). Though a prisoner, he was free to have visitors and write letters. For more information on Paul, see his Profile in Acts 9.

1:1 Ephesus was one of the five major cities in the Roman Empire, along with Rome, Corinth, Antioch, and Alexandria. Paul first visited Ephesus on his second missionary journey (Acts 18:19–21) and, during his third missionary journey, stayed there almost three years (Acts 19). He later met again with the elders of the Ephesian church at Miletus (Acts 20:16–38). Ephesus was a commercial, political, and religious center for all of Asia Minor. The temple to the goddess Artemis (Diana) was located there.

1:1 "Ever loyal to the Lord"—what an excellent reputation! Such a label would be an honor for any believer. What would it take for others to characterize you this way? Hold fast to your faith one day

at a time; faithfully obey God even in the details of life; and like the Ephesians you will be known as loyal to the Lord.

1:3 What is heaven? Heaven is where God is. "Every blessing in heaven" means all the good things God gives us— salvation, the gifts of the Spirit, power to do God's will, the hope of eternity with Christ. Because we live in an intimate relationship with Christ, we can enjoy these blessings now. Other references to heaven in this letter include 1:20; 2:6; 3:10. They show Christ in his victorious, exalted role as ruler of all.

1:4 Paul said, "God chose us," to emphasize that salvation depends totally on God. We are not saved because we deserve it, but because he is gracious and freely gives it. We did not influence God's decision to save us; he did it according to his plan. Thus there is no way to take credit for your salvation, or to find room for pride. The mystery of salvation originated in the timeless mind of God long before we existed. It is hard to understand how God could accept us, but because of Christ we are holy and blameless in his eyes. God chose you, and when you belong to him through Jesus Christ, he looks at you as if you had never sinned.

1:5 God has adopted us as his own children. Through Jesus' sacrifice, he has brought us into his family and made us heirs along with Jesus (Romans 8:17). In Roman law, adopted children had the same rights and privileges as natural children. Paul uses this term to show how strong our relationship to God is. For more

1:6
Rom 3:24
Col 1:13

1:7
1 Cor 6:20
Col 1:14
Heb 9:12
Rev 5:9

1:9
Col 1:26,27; 2:2

1:10
Mk 1:15
Gal 4:4
Col 1:20

1:11
Rom 9:11
Eph 3:11

unchanging plan has always been to adopt us into his own family by sending Jesus Christ to die for us. And he did this because he wanted to!

6Now all praise to God for his wonderful kindness to us and his favor that he has poured out upon us, because we belong to his dearly loved Son. 7So overflowing is his kindness toward us that he took away all our sins through the blood of his Son, by whom we are saved; 8and he has showered down upon us the richness of his grace—for how well he understands us and knows what is best for us at all times.

9God has told us his secret reason for sending Christ, a plan he decided on in mercy long ago; 10and this was his purpose: that when the time is ripe he will gather us all together from wherever we are—in heaven or on earth—to be with him in Christ, forever. 11Moreover, because of what Christ has done we have become gifts to God that he delights in, for as part of God's sovereign plan we were chosen from

OUR TRUE IDENTITY IN CHRIST		
	Romans 3:24	We are declared "not guilty" of sin.
	Romans 8:1	No condemnation awaits us.
	Romans 8:2	We are free from the vicious circle of sin and death.
	1 Corinthians 1:2	We are acceptable to God through Jesus Christ.
	1 Corinthians 1:30	We are pure and holy.
	1 Corinthians 15:22	We will rise again.
	2 Corinthians 3:17	We are free from trying to be saved by being good enough.
	2 Corinthians 5:17	We are brand new people inside.
	2 Corinthians 5:21	We are full of God's goodness.
	Galatians 3:28	We are one in Christ with all other believers.
	Ephesians 1:3	We are blessed with every spiritual blessing in heaven.
	Ephesians 1:4	We are holy, faultless, and covered with God's love.
	Ephesians 1:5, 6	We belong to Christ.
	Ephesians 1:7	Our sins are taken away and we are forgiven.
	Ephesians 1:10, 11	We will live with Christ forever; we are gifts to God.
	Ephesians 1:13	We are marked as belonging to God by the Holy Spirit.
	Ephesians 2:6	We have been lifted from the grave to sit with Christ in glory.
	Ephesians 2:10	We have been given new lives.
	Ephesians 2:13	We have been brought near to God.
	Ephesians 3:6	We will receive great blessings.
	Ephesians 3:12	We can come fearlessly into God's presence.
	Ephesians 5:29, 30	We are part of Christ's body, the church.
	Colossians 2:10	We have everything because we have Christ; we are filled with God.
	Colossians 2:11	We are set free from our evil desires.
	2 Timothy 2:10	We will have eternal glory.

on the meaning of adoption, see Galatians 4:5–7.

1:7 To speak of Jesus' blood was an important first-century way of speaking of Christ's death. His death points to two wonderful truths—redemption and forgiveness. *Redemption* was the price paid to gain freedom for a slave (Leviticus 25:47–54). Through his death, Jesus paid the price to release us from our slavery to sin. *Forgiveness* was granted in Old Testament times on the basis of the shedding of animals' blood (Leviticus 17:11, the death of the animal). Now we are forgiven on the basis of the shedding of Jesus' blood, because he died and was the perfect and final sacrifice. (See also Romans 5:9; Ephesians 2:13; Colossians 1:20; Hebrews 9:22; 1 Peter 1:19.)

1:8 Grace is God's voluntary and loving favor given to those he saves. We can't earn it, nor do we deserve it. No religious or moral effort can gain it, for it comes only from God's mercy and love. Without grace, no person can be saved.

1:9, 10 God was not intentionally keeping a secret, but his plan for the world could not be fully understood until Christ rose from the dead. His secret purpose for sending Christ was to unite Jews and Gentiles in one body with Christ as the head. Many people still do not understand God's plan, but "when the time is ripe" he will gather us to be with him forever and then everyone will understand. On that day, all people will bow to Jesus as Lord, either because they love him or because they fear his power (see Philippians 2:10, 11).

1:11 What delight youngsters display when given a special gift. Joy radiates from their eyes, spreading across their faces in big, happy smiles. As adults, we rarely experience such pure delight. Yet we ourselves are gifts that inspire an infinitely higher and greater delight in the heart of God. He accepts us with joy because of what Christ did for us. When you feel that your life isn't worth much to anyone, remember that you are a special gift in God's eyes, a precious present that brings him great joy.

1:11 God has offered salvation to the world just as he planned to do long ago. God is sovereign; he is in charge. When your life seems chaotic, rest in this truth: Jesus is Lord, and God is in control. His purpose to save you cannot be thwarted, no matter what evil Satan may bring.

the beginning to be his, and all things happen just as he decided long ago. 12God's purpose in this was that we should praise God and give glory to him for doing these mighty things for us, who were the first to trust in Christ.

1:12
Eph 1:6,14
Jas 1:18

13And because of what Christ did, all you others too, who heard the Good News about how to be saved, and trusted Christ, were marked as belonging to Christ by the Holy Spirit, who long ago had been promised to all of us Christians. 14His presence within us is God's guarantee that he really will give us all that he promised; and the Spirit's seal upon us means that God has already purchased us and that he guarantees to bring us to himself. This is just one more reason for us to praise our glorious God.

1:13
2 Cor 1:22
Eph 4:30
Col 1:5

1:14
Rom 8:23
2 Cor 1:22; 5:5

Paul's prayer for the Ephesian believers

15That is why, ever since I heard of your strong faith in the Lord Jesus and of the love you have for Christians everywhere, 16, 17I have never stopped thanking God for you. I pray for you constantly, asking God, the glorious Father of our Lord Jesus Christ, to give you wisdom to see clearly and really understand who Christ is and all that he has done for you. 18I pray that your hearts will be flooded with light so that you can see something of the future he has called you to share. I want you to realize that God has been made rich because we who are Christ's have been given to him! 19I pray that you will begin to understand how incredibly great his power is to help those who believe him. It is that same mighty power 20that raised Christ from the dead and seated him in the place of honor at God's right hand in heaven, 21far, far above any other king or ruler or dictator or leader. Yes, his honor is far more glorious than that of anyone else either in this world or in the world to come. 22And God has put all things under his feet and made him the supreme Head of the Church— 23which is his body, filled with himself, the Author and Giver of everything everywhere.

1:16
Col 1:9

1:17
1 Cor 2:9-12

1:18
Acts 26:18
Eph 1:11; 4:4

1:19
Eph 3:7,16; 6:10
Phil 3:21

1:20
Acts 2:24

1:21
Phil 2:9

1:22
Col 2:19

1:23
Eph 3:19; 4:10
3:11

The spiritually dead are made alive

2 Once you were under God's curse, doomed forever for your sins. 2You went along with the crowd and were just like all the others, full of sin, obeying Satan, the mighty prince of the power of the air, who is at work right now in the hearts of those who are against the Lord. 3All of us used to be just as they are, our lives expressing the evil within us, doing every wicked thing that our passions or

2:1
Eph 2:5

2:2
Eph 5:6,8; 6:10

2:3
Gal 5:16
Tit 3:3

1:14 The Holy Spirit is God's guarantee to us that he will do what he has promised. He is like a down payment, a deposit, a validating signature on the contract. The presence of the Holy Spirit in our lives is our assurance of eternal life with all its blessings. His power at work in us now is transforming our lives, and is a taste of the total change we will experience in eternity (see 2 Corinthians 1:22).

1:16, 17 Paul's prayer for the Ephesians was that they might really understand who Christ is. Christ is our goal and our model, and the more we know of him, the more we will be like him. Study Jesus' life in the Bible to see what he was like on earth 2,000 years ago, and get to know him in prayer now. Personal knowledge of Christ is life-changing!

1:19, 20 The world fears the power of the atom, yet we belong to the God of the universe who not only created that atomic power but also raised Jesus Christ from the dead. We don't need to feel inadequate. God's incomparable power is for us who believe.

1:20–22 Having been raised from the dead, Christ is now the supreme head of the church, the ultimate authority over the world. Christ is the Messiah, God's anointed One, the One Israel longed for, the One who would set their broken world right. As Christians we can be confident that God has won the final victory and is in control of everything. We need not fear any dictator, nation, death, or Satan himself. The contract has been signed and sealed; we are waiting just a short while for delivery. Paul says, in Romans 8:37–39, that nothing can separate us from God and his love.

1:22, 23 When reading Ephesians, it is important to remember that it was written not to an individual but to the church. Christ is the head and we are the body of his church (Paul uses this metaphor in Romans 12:4, 5; 1 Corinthians 12:12- 27; and Colossians 3:15 as well as throughout the book of Ephesians). The image of the body shows the church's unity. Each member is involved with all the others as they go about doing Christ's work on earth.

2:2 "Mighty prince of the power of the air" was understood by Paul's readers to mean Satan and the evil spiritual forces they thought inhabited the region between earth and sky. Satan is thus pictured as ruling the evil spiritual world—the demons and those who are against Christ. "Satan" means "the Adversary." He is also called the devil (4:27) and the king of demons (Mark 3:22). In his resurrection, Christ was victorious over Satan and his power. Therefore Jesus Christ is the permanent ruler of the whole world; Satan is only the temporary ruler of the part of the world that chooses to follow him.

2:3 The fact that all people, without exception, commit sin proves that they share in the sinful nature. Does this mean there are no good people who are not Christians? Of course not— many people do good to others. On a relative scale, many are moral, kind, keep the laws, and so on. Comparing these people to criminals, we would say they are very good indeed. But on God's absolute scale, *no one* is good. Only through uniting our lives to Christ's perfect life can we become good in God's sight.

our evil thoughts might lead us into. We started out bad, being born with evil natures, and were under God's anger just like everyone else.

2:4
Jn 3:16
Rom 10:12
Eph 1:7

⁴But God is so rich in mercy; he loved us so much ⁵that even though we were spiritually dead and doomed by our sins, he gave us back our lives again when he raised Christ from the dead—only by his undeserved favor have we ever been saved— ⁶and lifted us up from the grave into glory along with Christ, where we sit with him in the heavenly realms—all because of what Christ Jesus did. ⁷And now God can always point to us as examples of how very, very rich his kindness is, as shown in all he has done for us through Jesus Christ.

2:5
Rom 5:6; 6:4

2:6
Eph 1:3,20
Col 2:12

2:7
Tit 3:4

⁸Because of his kindness you have been saved through trusting Christ. And even trusting is not of yourselves; it too is a gift from God. ⁹Salvation is not a reward for the good we have done, so none of us can take any credit for it. ¹⁰It is God himself who has made us what we are and given us new lives from Christ Jesus; and long ages ago he planned that we should spend these lives in helping others.

2:8
Jn 4:10
Rom 4:16

2:9
Rom 3:20
2 Tim 1:9
Tit 3:5

Christ is the way to peace

2:11
Rom 2:28
Col 2:11

¹¹Never forget that once you were heathen, and that you were called godless and "unclean" by the Jews. (But their hearts, too, were still unclean, even though they were going through the ceremonies and rituals of the godly, for they circumcised themselves as a sign of godliness.) ¹²Remember that in those days you were living

2:12
Rom 9:4,8
Gal 4:8

2:5 *gave us back our lives again,* literally, "he made us alive."   **2:8** *And even trusting is not of yourselves,* or, "Salvation is not of yourselves."

OUR LIVES BEFORE AND AFTER CHRIST	Before	After
	Under God's curse	Loved by God
	Doomed because of our sins	Shown God's mercy and given salvation
	Went along with the crowd	Stand for Christ and truth
	God's enemies	God's children
	Enslaved to Satan	Free in Christ to love, serve, and sit with him
	Followed our evil thoughts and passions	Taken from the grave to glory
	Under God's anger	Given undeserved favor
	Spiritually dead	Given new spiritual life

2:4, 5 In the previous verses Paul is talking about our old sinful nature (2:1–3). Here Paul emphasizes that we do not need to live any longer under sin's power. The penalty of sin and its power over our lives was destroyed by Christ on the cross. Paul has already stated that through faith in Christ we stand acquitted, "not guilty" before God (Romans 3:21, 22). God does not take us out of the world or make us robots—we will still feel like sinning, and sometimes we will sin. The difference is that before we became Christians we were slaves to our sinful nature, but now we can choose to live for Christ (see also Galatians 2:20).

2:6 Because of Christ's resurrection, we know that our bodies will also be raised from the dead (1 Corinthians 15:2–23) and that we have been given the power to live the Christian life now (Ephesians 1:19). These ideas are combined in Paul's image of sitting with Christ in glory. Our eternal life in Christ is certain, because we are united in his powerful victory.

2:8, 9 When someone gives you a gift, do you say, "That's very nice—now how much do I owe you?" No, the appropriate response to a gift is "Thank you." Yet how often Christians, even after they have been given the gift of salvation, feel obligated to try to work their way to God. Because our salvation and even our faith are gifts, we should respond with gratitude, praise, and joyfulness.

2:8–10 We become Christians through God's unmerited gift to us (called "grace" in Ephesians 1:8), not as the result of any effort, ability, intelligent choice, or act of service to others on our part. However, out of gratitude for this free gift, we will seek to help and serve others with kindness, charity, and goodness, and not merely please ourselves. While no action or "work" we do can help us obtain salvation, God's intention is that our salvation will result in works of service. We are not saved merely for our own benefit but for his—to glorify him and build up the church (Ephesians 4:12).

2:11 Pious Jews considered all non-Jews ceremonially unclean. They thought of themselves as pure and clean because of their national heritage and religious ceremonies. Paul points out that Jews and Gentiles alike are unclean before God and need to be cleansed by Christ. In order to realize how great a gift salvation is, we need to remember our natural, unclean condition.

2:11, 12 Before Christ's coming, Gentiles and Jews kept apart from each other. Jews considered Gentiles beyond God's saving power and therefore without hope. Gentiles resented Jewish claims. Christ revealed the total sinfulness of both Jews and Gentiles, and then he offered his salvation equally to both. Only Christ breaks down the walls of prejudice, reconciles all believers to God, and unifies us in one body.

2:11–13 Jews and Gentiles alike could be guilty of spiritual pride—Jews for thinking their ceremonies elevated them above everyone else, Gentiles for forgetting the hopelessness of their condition apart from Christ. Spiritual pride blinds us to our own faults and magnifies the faults of others. Be careful not to become proud of your salvation. Instead, humbly thank God for what he has done, and encourage others who might be struggling in their faith.

utterly apart from Christ; you were enemies of God's children and he had promised you no help. You were lost, without God, without hope.

13But now you belong to Christ Jesus, and though you once were far away from God, now you have been brought very near to him because of what Jesus Christ has done for you with his blood.

14For Christ himself is our way of peace. He has made peace between us Jews and you Gentiles by making us all one family, breaking down the wall of contempt that used to separate us. 15By his death he ended the angry resentment between us, caused by the Jewish laws which favored the Jews and excluded the Gentiles, for he died to annul that whole system of Jewish laws. Then he took the two groups that had been opposed to each other and made them parts of himself; thus he fused us together to become one new person, and at last there was peace. 16As parts of the same body, our anger against each other has disappeared, for both of us have been reconciled to God. And so the feud ended at last at the cross. 17And he has brought this Good News of peace to you Gentiles who were very far away from him, and to us Jews who were near. 18Now all of us, whether Jews or Gentiles, may come to God the Father with the Holy Spirit's help because of what Christ has done for us.

19Now you are no longer strangers to God and foreigners to heaven, but you are members of God's very own family, citizens of God's country, and you belong in God's household with every other Christian.

20What a foundation you stand on now: the apostles and the prophets; and the cornerstone of the building is Jesus Christ himself! 21We who believe are carefully joined together with Christ as parts of a beautiful, constantly growing temple for God. 22And you also are joined with him and with each other by the Spirit, and are part of this dwelling place of God.

Paul's special mission to Gentiles

3 I Paul, the servant of Christ, am here in jail because of you—for preaching that you Gentiles are a part of God's house. 2, 3No doubt you already know that God has given me this special work of showing God's favor to you Gentiles, as I briefly mentioned before in one of my letters. God himself showed me this secret plan of his, that the Gentiles, too, are included in his kindness. 4I say this to explain to you how I know about these things. 5In olden times God did not share this plan

2:13
Acts 2:39
Col 1:20

2:14
Mic 5:5
1 Cor 12:13

2:15
2 Cor 5:17
Gal 3:28
Col 1:22; 2:14

2:16
Eph 4:4
Col 1:20

2:17
Isa 57:19
Zech 9:10
Acts 10:36

2:18
Jn 14:6,17-20
Eph 3:12; 4:4

2:19
Eph 2:12

2:20
Ps 118:22
Isa 28:16
Mt 16:18; 21:42
1 Cor 3:11
Rev 21:14

2:21
1 Cor 3:16
Eph 4:15,16

2:22
Jn 17:23
1 Pet 2:5

3:1
2 Tim 2:10

3:2
Rom 16:25

3:3
Eph 1:9; 3:4-9
Col 1:25-27

3:5
Eph 1:17

2:14 *by making us all one family*, literally, "by making us one." *breaking down the wall of contempt*, implied.

2:14ff Christ has broken down the walls people build between themselves. Since these walls have been removed, we can come to real unity with people who are not like us. This is true reconciliation. Because of Christ's death, we are all one family (2:14); our anger against each other has disappeared (2:16); we can all approach God through the Holy Spirit (2:18); we are no longer strangers to God (2:19); and we are all part of a beautiful temple with Christ as our cornerstone (2:20, 21).

2:14 There are many barriers that can divide us from other Christians: age, appearance, intelligence, political persuasion, economic status, race, theological perspective. One of the best ways to stifle Christ's love is to cater only to those for whom we have natural affinity. Fortunately, Christ has knocked down the barriers and unified all believers in one family. His cross should be the focus of our unity. The Holy Spirit helps us look beyond the barriers to the unity we are called to enjoy.

2:17, 18 The Jews were "near" to God because they already knew of him through the Scriptures and worshiped him in their religious ceremonies. The Gentiles were "far away" because they knew little or nothing about God. Because neither group could be saved by good works or sincerity, both Jews and Gentiles needed to hear about the salvation available through Jesus Christ. Both Jews and Gentiles are now free to come to God through Christ.

2:19–21 A church building is sometimes called God's house. In reality, God's house is not a building, but a group of people. He lives in us and shows himself to a watching world through us.

People can see that God is love and that Jesus is Lord as we live in harmony with each other and with what God says in his Word.

2:20 What does it mean to stand on the foundation of the apostles and the prophets? It means that the church is not built on modern ideas, but rather on the spiritual heritage given to us in the Old and New Testaments.

3:1 Paul was under house arrest in Rome for preaching about Christ. The religious leaders, who felt threatened by Christ's teachings and didn't believe he was the Messiah, pressured the Romans to arrest Paul and bring him to trial for treason and for causing rebellion among the Jews. Paul had appealed that his case be heard by the emperor, and he was awaiting trial (see Acts 28:16–31). Even though he was under arrest, Paul maintained his firm belief that God was in control of all that happened to him. Do you let circumstances convince you that God has lost control of this world? Like Paul, remember that no matter what happens, God is directing the world's affairs.

3:2, 3 "In one of my letters" is literally, "as I wrote before in brief." This could refer to a previous letter which was not preserved by the church, or it could refer to an earlier part of this letter (especially 1:9ff; 2:11ff).

3:5, 6 God's plan was hidden from previous generations, not because God wanted to keep something from his people, but because he would reveal it to everyone in his perfect timing. God planned to have Jews and Gentiles comprise one body, the church. It was known in the Old Testament that the Gentiles would

with his people, but now he has revealed it by the Holy Spirit to his apostles and prophets.

3:6
Gal 3:14
Eph 2:14-16

6And this is the secret: that the Gentiles will have their full share with the Jews in all the riches inherited by God's sons; both are invited to belong to his Church, and all of God's promises of mighty blessings through Christ apply to them both when they accept the Good News about Christ and what he has done for them. 7God

3:7
Rom 15:18
Col 1:23

has given me the wonderful privilege of telling everyone about this plan of his; and he has given me his power and special ability to do it well.

3:8
1 Cor 15:9
Col 2:2,3,9,10

8Just think! Though I did nothing to deserve it, and though I am the most useless Christian there is, yet I was the one chosen for this special joy of telling the Gentiles

3:9
1 Cor 2:7

the Glad News of the endless treasures available to them in Christ; 9and to explain to everyone that God is the Savior of the Gentiles too, just as he who made all things had secretly planned from the very beginning.

3:10
Rom 11:33
1 Cor 2:7
Eph 1:21; 6:12
1 Pet 3:22

10And his reason? To show to all the rulers in heaven how perfectly wise he is when all of his family—Jews and Gentiles alike—are seen to be joined together in his Church, 11in just the way he had always planned it through Jesus Christ our

3:11
Eph 1:11

Lord.

3:12
Eph 2:18
Heb 4:16

12Now we can come fearlessly right into God's presence, assured of his glad welcome when we come with Christ and trust in him.

13So please don't lose heart at what they are doing to me here. It is for you I am suffering and you should feel honored and encouraged.

The magnitude of God's love

3:14
Phil 2:9,10

14, 15When I think of the wisdom and scope of his plan I fall down on my knees and pray to the Father of all the great family of God—some of them already in

3:16
Phil 4:13,19
Col 1:11

heaven and some down here on earth— 16that out of his glorious, unlimited resources he will give you the mighty inner strengthening of his Holy Spirit. 17And

3:17
Jn 14:23
Col 1:27; 2:7

I pray that Christ will be more and more at home in your hearts, living within you as you trust in him. May your roots go down deep into the soil of God's marvelous

3:18
Jn 1:16
Col 2:9,10

love; 18, 19and may you be able to feel and understand, as all God's children should, how long, how wide, how deep, and how high his love really is; and to experience

---

receive salvation (Isaiah 49:6; 56:3), but it was never revealed in the Old Testament that all Gentile and Jewish believers would become equal in the body of Christ. Yet this equality was accomplished when Jesus broke down the "wall of contempt" and created the "one new person" (2:14,15).

3:7 God gave the apostle Paul the ability to share effectively the gospel of Christ. You may not be an apostle or even an evangelist, but God will also give you opportunities to tell others about Christ—and with the opportunity he will provide the ability, courage, and power. Whenever an opportunity presents itself, make yourself available to God. As you focus on the other person and his or her needs, God will communicate your caring attitude, and your words will be natural, loving, and compelling.

3:8 When Paul describes himself as a useless Christian, he is saying that without God's help, he would never be able to do God's work. Yet God chose him to share the gospel with the Gentiles and gave him the power to do this. If we feel useless, we may be right—except that we have forgotten what a difference God makes. How does God want to use you? Do your part and faithfully perform the special role you play in God's plan.

3:10 The rulers in heaven are either angels (see 1 Peter 1:12), or perhaps hostile forces opposed to God (2:2; 6:12).

3:12 It is an awesome privilege to be admitted into God's presence. Most of us would be apprehensive in the presence of a powerful ruler, but thanks to Christ, we can enter directly into God's presence through prayer. We know we'll be welcomed with open arms because we are God's children through our unity with Christ. Don't be afraid of God. Talk with him about everything. He is waiting to hear from you.

3:13 Why should Paul's suffering make the Ephesians feel honored? If Paul had not preached the gospel, he would not be in jail—but then the Ephesians would not have heard the Good News and been converted either. As a mother endures the pain of childbirth in order to bring new life into the world, Paul endured the pain of persecution in order to bring new believers to Christ. Obeying Christ is never easy. He calls us to take up our crosses and follow him (Matthew 16:24)—that is, to be willing to endure pain so that God's message of salvation can reach the entire world. We should feel honored that others have suffered and sacrificed for us so that we might be blessed.

3:14, 15 The great family of God includes all who have believed in him in the past, all who believe in the present, and all who will believe in the future. We are all a family because we have the same Father. He is the source of all creation, the rightful owner of everything. God promises his love and power to his family, the church (3:16–21); if we want to receive his blessings, it is important that we stay in living contact with other believers in the body of Christ. Those who isolate themselves from God's family and try to go it alone are cutting themselves off from God's power.

3:17-19 God's love is total, says Paul. It reaches every corner of our experience. It is *long*—it continues the length of our lives. It is *deep*—it reaches to the depths of discouragement, despair, and even death. It is *wide*—it covers the breadth of our own experience, and it reaches out to the whole world. It is *high*—it rises to the heights of our celebration and elation. When you feel shut out or isolated, remember that you can never be lost to God's love. For another hymn to God's immeasurable and inexhaustible love, see Paul's words in Romans 8:38, 39.

this love for yourselves, though it is so great that you will never see the end of it or fully know or understand it. And so at last you will be filled up with God himself.

20Now glory be to God who by his mighty power at work within us is able to do far more than we would ever dare to ask or even dream of—infinitely beyond our highest prayers, desires, thoughts, or hopes. 21May he be given glory forever and ever through endless ages because of his master plan of salvation for the Church through Jesus Christ.

3:19
Eph 1:23
Col 2:10

3:20
Eph 1:19,20

3:21
1 Tim 1:17

2. Unity in the church
We are one body in Christ

4 I beg you—I, a prisoner here in jail for serving the Lord—to live and act in a way worthy of those who have been chosen for such wonderful blessings as these. 2Be humble and gentle. Be patient with each other, making allowance for each other's faults because of your love. 3Try always to be led along together by the Holy Spirit, and so be at peace with one another.

4We are all parts of one body, we have the same Spirit, and we have all been called to the same glorious future. 5For us there is only one Lord, one faith, one baptism, 6and we all have the same God and Father who is over us all and in us all, and living through every part of us. 7However, Christ has given each of us special abilities—whatever he wants us to have out of his rich storehouse of gifts.

8The Psalmist tells about this, for he says that when Christ returned triumphantly

4:2
Col 3:12,13

4:3
Col 3:14

4:4
Rom 12:5
1 Cor 12:12,13

4:5
1 Cor 8:6

4:6
Rom 11:36

4:7
Rom 12:3
1 Cor 12:7

4:8
Ps 68:18

Believers are one in:	Our unity is experienced in:	**THE ONENESS OF ALL BELIEVERS**
Body	The fellowship of believers—the church	
Spirit	The Holy Spirit who activates the fellowship	
Hope	That glorious future to which we are all called	
Lord	Christ, to whom we all belong	
Faith	Our singular commitment to Christ	
Baptism	Baptism—the sign of entry into the church	
God	God, who is our Father and keeps us for eternity	

Too often believers are separated because of minor differences in doctrine. But Paul here shows those areas where Christians must agree to attain true unity. When believers have this unity of Spirit, petty differences should never be allowed to dissolve that unity.

3:21 This *doxology*—hymn of praise to God—ends Part One of Ephesians, in which Paul describes the timeless role of the church. In Part Two (chapters 4—6), he will explain how church members should live in order to bring about the unity God wants. As in most of his books, Paul first lays a doctrinal foundation, then makes practical applications of the truths he has presented.

4:1–6 "We are all parts of one body," says Paul, and we have been given many gifts and abilities. Unity does not just happen; we have to work at it. Often differences among people can lead to division, but this should not be true in the church. Instead of concentrating on what divides us, we should remember what unites us: *one* body, *one* Spirit, *one* future, *one* Lord, *one* faith, *one* baptism, *one* God! Have you learned to appreciate people who are different from you? Can you see how their differing gifts and viewpoints can help the church as it does God's work? Learn to enjoy the way we members of Christ's body complement one another (see 1 Corinthians 12:12, 13 for more on this thought).

4:1, 2 God has chosen us to be Christ's representatives on earth. In light of this truth, Paul challenges us to live worthy of the name "Christian," meaning *Christ's one*. This includes being humble, gentle, patient, understanding, and peaceful. People are watching your life. Can they see Christ in you? How well are you doing as his representative?

4:2 No one is ever going to be perfect here on earth, so we must accept and love other Christians in spite of their faults. When we

see faults in fellow believers, we should be patient and gentle. Is there someone whose actions or personality really annoys you? Rather than dwelling on that person's weaknesses, or looking for faults, pray for that person. Then do even more—spend time together and see if you can learn to like him or her.

4:3 Unity is one of the Holy Spirit's important roles. He leads, but we have to be willing to be led. We do that by focusing on God, not on ourselves. For more about who the Holy Spirit is and what he does, see the notes on John 3:6; Acts 1:5; and Ephesians 1:14.

4:4–7 All believers in Christ belong to one body; all are united under one Head, who is Christ himself (see 1 Corinthians 12:12–26). Each believer has God-given abilities that can strengthen the whole body. Your special ability may be seemingly small or large, but it is yours to use in God's service. Ask God to use your unique gifts to contribute to the strength and health of the body of believers.

4:6 God is *over us all*—this shows his overruling care (transcendence). He is *in us all*—this shows his active presence in the world and in the lives of believers (immanence). Any view of God that violates either his transcendence or his immanence is not a true picture of him.

4:8 In Psalm 68:18, God is pictured as a conqueror marching to the gates and taking tribute from the fallen city. Paul uses that picture to teach that Christ, in his crucifixion and resurrection, was victorious over Satan. When he ascended to heaven, he gave gifts

4:9
Jn 3:13
Acts 2:27
1 Pet 3:18

4:10
Eph 1:23
1 Tim 3:16
Heb 4:14; 8:1
1 Pet 3:22

4:11
1 Cor 12:28

4:12
1 Cor 14:26

4:13
Eph 1:17
Col 2:2

4:14
Mt 11:7
1 Cor 14:20
Eph 6:11

4:15,16
Col 2:19

4:17
Jn 1:4,5
Acts 17:30; 26:18
Eph 2:2

to heaven after his resurrection and victory over Satan, he gave generous gifts to men. 9Notice that it says he returned to heaven. This means that he had first come down from the heights of heaven, far down to the lowest parts of the earth. 10The same one who came down is the one who went back up, that he might fill all things everywhere with himself, from the very lowest to the very highest.

11Some of us have been given special ability as apostles; to others he has given the gift of being able to preach well; some have special ability in winning people to Christ, helping them to trust him as their Savior; still others have a gift for caring for God's people as a shepherd does his sheep, leading and teaching them in the ways of God.

12Why is it that he gives us these special abilities to do certain things best? It is that God's people will be equipped to do better work for him, building up the Church, the body of Christ, to a position of strength and maturity; 13until finally we all believe alike about our salvation and about our Savior, God's Son, and all become full-grown in the Lord—yes, to the point of being filled full with Christ.

14Then we will no longer be like children, forever changing our minds about what we believe because someone has told us something different, or has cleverly lied to us and made the lie sound like the truth. 15, 16Instead, we will lovingly follow the truth at all times—speaking truly, dealing truly, living truly—and so become more and more in every way like Christ who is the Head of his body, the Church. Under his direction the whole body is fitted together perfectly, and each part in its own special way helps the other parts, so that the whole body is healthy and growing and full of love.

Living as a new person

17, 18Let me say this, then, speaking for the Lord: Live no longer as the unsaved do, for they are blinded and confused. Their closed hearts are full of darkness; they are far away from the life of God because they have shut their minds against him,

4:10 *from the very lowest to the very highest,* literally, "that he might fill all things." **4:15, 16** *speaking truly, dealing truly, living truly,* Amplified New Testament.

---

to the church, some of which he discusses in verses 11–13.

4:9 The "lowest parts of the earth" may be (1) the earth itself, (2) the grave, or (3) Hades (which many believe is the resting place of souls between death and resurrection). Whichever way you understand it, Christ is Lord of the whole universe, past, present, and future. Nothing or no one is hidden from him. The Lord of all came to earth and went down into death to rescue all people. No one is beyond his reach.

4:11 Our oneness in Christ does not destroy our individuality. The Holy Spirit has given each Christian special gifts for building up the church. Now that we have these gifts, it is crucial to use them. Are you spiritually mature, exercising the gifts God has given you? If you know what your gifts are, look for opportunities to serve. If you don't know, ask God to show you, perhaps through Christian friends. Then, as you begin to recognize your special area of service, use your gifts to strengthen and encourage the church.

4:12 God has given his church an enormous responsibility— to make disciples in every nation (Matthew 28:18–20). This involves preaching, teaching, healing, nurturing, giving, administering, building, and many other tasks. If we had to fulfill this command as individuals, we might as well give up without trying—it would be impossible. But God calls us as members of his body. Some of us can do one task; some can do another. Together we can obey him more fully than any of us could do alone. It is a human tendency to overestimate what we can do by ourselves and to underestimate what we can do as a group. The truth is just the opposite. Alone, we are quite ineffective. Together, as the body of Christ, we can do far more than we would ever dream possible.

4:14–16 Christ is the Truth (John 14:6), and the Holy Spirit who guides the church is the Spirit of truth (John 16:13). Satan, by contrast, is the father of liars (John 8:44). As followers of Christ, we

must be committed to the truth. This means both that our words will be honest and that our actions will reflect Christ's integrity. "Living truly" is not always easy, convenient, or pleasant; but it is necessary if the church is going to do Christ's work in the world.

4:15, 16 Some Christians fear that any mistake will destroy their witness for the Lord. They see their own weaknesses, and they know that many non-Christians seem to have stronger character than they do. How can they be new and different persons, holy and good? The Good News is that Jesus forms us into a body—into a group of individuals who are united in their purpose and in their love for one another and for Christ. If an individual stumbles, the rest of the group is there to pick him up and help him walk with his Lord again. If an individual sins, he can find restoration through the church (Galatians 6:1) even as the rest of the body continues to witness to God's truth. As part of Christ's body, you will reflect part of Christ's character and do part of his work. As you grow to be more and more like him, you will be able to give more and more thanks for your brothers and sisters in Christ, without whom you could not adequately represent the Lord.

4:17–24 People should be able to see a difference between Christians and non-Christians because of the way Christians live. Paul tells the Ephesians to leave behind the old life of sin now that they are followers of Christ. The Christian life is a process. Although we have a new nature, we don't automatically have all good thoughts and attitudes when we become new people in Christ. But if we keep listening to God, we will be changing all the time. As you look over the last year, do you see a process of change for the better in your thoughts, attitudes, and actions? Although change may be slow, it comes about if you trust God to change you. For more about our new nature as believers see Romans 6:6; 8:9; Galatians 5:16–26; Colossians 3:3–8.

and they cannot understand his ways. 19They don't care anymore about right and wrong and have given themselves over to impure ways. They stop at nothing, being driven by their evil minds and reckless lusts.

20But that isn't the way Christ taught you! 21If you have really heard his voice and learned from him the truths concerning himself, 22then throw off your old evil nature—the old you that was a partner in your evil ways—rotten through and through, full of lust and sham.

23Now your attitudes and thoughts must all be constantly changing for the better. 24Yes, you must be a new and different person, holy and good. Clothe yourself with this new nature.

25Stop lying to each other; tell the truth, for we are parts of each other and when we lie to each other we are hurting ourselves. 26If you are angry, don't sin by nursing your grudge. Don't let the sun go down with you still angry—get over it quickly; 27for when you are angry you give a mighty foothold to the devil.

28If anyone is stealing he must stop it and begin using those hands of his for honest work so he can give to others in need. 29Don't use bad language. Say only what is good and helpful to those you are talking to, and what will give them a blessing.

30Don't cause the Holy Spirit sorrow by the way you live. Remember, he is the one who marks you to be present on that day when salvation from sin will be complete.

31Stop being mean, bad-tempered and angry. Quarreling, harsh words, and dislike of others should have no place in your lives. 32Instead, be kind to each other, tenderhearted, forgiving one another, just as God has forgiven you because you belong to Christ.

4:19
Rom 1:24
Col 3:5

4:22
Rom 6:6
Col 3:8
Jas 1:21

4:23
Rom 12:2

4:24
2 Cor 5:17
Col 3:10

4:25
Zech 8:16
Rom 12:5
Col 3:9

4:27
Rom 12:19
Jas 4:7

4:28
1 Thess 4:11

4:29
Mt 12:34
Rom 14:19
Col 4:6

4:30
Isa 63:10
Eph 1:13
1 Thess 5:19

4:31
Col 3:8
1 Pet 2:1

4:32
Col 3:12,13

Living as a child of the light

5 Follow God's example in everything you do just as a much loved child imitates his father. 2Be full of love for others, following the example of Christ who loved you and gave himself to God as a sacrifice to take away your sins. And God was pleased, for Christ's love for you was like sweet perfume to him.

3Let there be no sex sin, impurity or greed among you. Let no one be able to accuse you of any such things. 4Dirty stories, foul talk and coarse jokes—these are not for you. Instead, remind each other of God's goodness and be thankful.

5:1
Mt 5:45

5:2
Gen 8:21
Jn 13:34
2 Cor 2:15

5:3
Col 3:5

5:4
Rom 1:28

4:30 *he is the one who marks you to be present,* literally, "in whom you were sealed unto the day of redemption."

4:25 Lying to each other disrupts unity by creating conflicts and destroying trust. It tears down relationships and leads to open war in a church.

4:26, 27 The Bible doesn't tell us we shouldn't feel angry, but it points out that it is important to handle our anger properly. If ventilated thoughtlessly, anger can hurt others and destroy relationships. If bottled up inside, it can cause us to become bitter and destroy us from within. Paul tells us to deal with our anger immediately in a way that builds relationships rather than destroying them. If we nurse our anger, we will give Satan a foothold from which he can divide us. Are you angry with someone right now? What can you do to resolve your differences? Don't let the day end before you begin to work on the conflict and mend your relationship.

4:28–32 We can cause the Holy Spirit sorrow by the way we live.

Paul warns us against bad language, meanness, improper use of anger, quarrels, harsh words, and bad attitudes toward others. Instead of acting that way, we should be forgiving, just as God has forgiven us. Are you grieving or pleasing God with your attitudes and actions? Act in love toward your brothers and sisters in Christ, just as God acted in love by sending his Son to die for your sins.

4:30 God's Spirit within us is a sign that we belong to him. For more information on this thought, see the note on 1:14.

4:32 This is Christ's law of forgiveness as taught in the Gospels (Matthew 6:14, 15; 18:35; Mark 11:25). We also see it in the Lord's prayer—"Forgive us our debts, as we forgive our debtors." God does not forgive us because we forgive others, but out of his great mercy. As we come to understand his mercy, however, we will want to be like him. Having received forgiveness, we will pass it on to others. Those who are unwilling to forgive have not become one with Christ, who was willing to forgive even those who crucified him (Luke 23:34).

5:5
1 Cor 6:9
Gal 5:21

5:8
Isa 9:2
Jn 8:12
Eph 2:2
1 Jn 2:9

5:11
Lev 19:17
1 Cor 5:9

5:13
Jn 3:20
Heb 4:13

5:14
Isa 26:19; 51:17
52:1; 60:1
Jn 5:25
Rom 6:4,5; 13:11

5:15
Col 4:5

5:17
1 Thess 4:3

5:18
Prov 20:1; 23:31
Jn 7:37-39
1 Cor 12:13

5:19
1 Cor 14:26
Col 3:16
Jas 5:13

⁵You can be sure of this: The Kingdom of Christ and of God will never belong to anyone who is impure or greedy, for a greedy person is really an idol worshiper—he loves and worships the good things of this life more than God. ⁶Don't be fooled by those who try to excuse these sins, for the terrible wrath of God is upon all those who do them. ⁷Don't even associate with such people. ⁸For though once your heart was full of darkness, now it is full of light from the Lord, and your behavior should show it! ⁹Because of this light within you, you should do only what is good and right and true.

¹⁰Learn as you go along what pleases the Lord. ¹¹Take no part in the worthless pleasures of evil and darkness, but instead, rebuke and expose them. ¹²It would be shameful even to mention here those pleasures of darkness which the ungodly do. ¹³But when you expose them, the light shines in upon their sin and shows it up, and when they see how wrong they really are, some of them may even become children of light! ¹⁴That is why God says in the Scriptures, "Awake, O sleeper, and rise up from the dead; and Christ shall give you light."

¹⁵, ¹⁶So be careful how you act; these are difficult days. Don't be fools; be wise: make the most of every opportunity you have for doing good. ¹⁷Don't act thoughtlessly, but try to find out and do whatever the Lord wants you to. ¹⁸Don't drink too much wine, for many evils lie along that path; be filled instead with the Holy Spirit, and controlled by him.

¹⁹Talk with each other much about the Lord, quoting psalms and hymns and singing sacred songs, making music in your hearts to the Lord. ²⁰Always give thanks for everything to our God and Father in the name of our Lord Jesus Christ.

5:10 *Learn as you go along what pleases the Lord,* or "Your lives should be an example."

5:1, 2 Just as children imitate their parents, we should imitate Christ. His great love for us led him to sacrifice himself so that we might live. Our love for others should be of the same kind—a love that goes beyond affection to self-sacrificing service.

5:4 Foul language or talk about shameful things is so common that we begin to take it for granted. Paul cautions, however, that vulgar speech should have no place in the Christian's conversation because it does not reflect God's gracious presence in us. How can we praise God and remind others of his goodness when we are speaking coarsely (see Colossians 3:15)?

5:7 Paul is not saying that believers should keep away from all unbelievers. Jesus taught his followers to befriend sinners and lead them to him (Luke 5:30–32). Instead, Paul is speaking against condoning or adopting the lifestyles of people who excuse, love, and recommend bad behavior—whether they are in the church or outside of it. Such people can quickly pollute the church, and endanger its unity and purpose. We must befriend unbelievers if we are to lead them to Christ, but we must be wary of those who are viciously evil, immoral, or opposed to all that Christianity stands for. Such people are more likely to influence us for evil than we are likely to influence them for good.

5:8 Your actions should reflect your faith. We should live moral lives so that we can reflect God's goodness to others. Jesus stressed this in the Sermon on the Mount (Matthew 5:15, 16).

5:10–14 It is important to avoid evil pleasures, but we must go even further. Paul instructs us to rebuke and expose them, for often our silence is interpreted as approval. God needs people who will take a stand for what is right. Wherever you are, lovingly speak out for what is true and right.

5:14 This is not a direct quote from Scripture but was probably taken from a hymn well-known to the Ephesians. The hymn seems

to have been based on Isaiah 26:19; 51:17; 52:1; 60:1; and Malachi 4:2. Paul was appealing to the Ephesians to wake up and realize the dangerous condition into which some of them had been slipping.

5:15, 16 By saying, "these are difficult days," Paul communicates his sense of urgency because of evil's pervasiveness. We need the same sense of urgency because our days are also difficult. We must keep our standards high, act wisely, and do good whenever we can.

5:17 It is not enough to *know* what God wants us to do; we must also *do* it. We must follow our beliefs with actions.

5:18 Paul contrasted being filled with wine, which can produce harmful effects, to being filled with the Spirit, which produces positive effects. What matters is not how much of the Holy Spirit we have, but how much of us the Holy Spirit has. We need to submit daily to his leading and draw on his power. Some effects of being filled with the Holy Spirit are mentioned in 5:19–21.

5:19 In the meetings of the early church, the Christians enjoyed speaking to one another. The content of their speech was drawn from the Old Testament Scriptures (particularly the Psalms). They not only spoke the Psalms, they sung them; and they composed other hymns and songs. Throughout the ages Christians have enjoyed singing hymns full of Scripture and praise.

5:20 When you feel down, you may find it difficult to give thanks. Take heart—God works all things out for good if we love him and are fitting into his plans (Romans 8:28). Thank God, not for your problems, but for the strength he is building in you through the difficult experiences of your life. You can be sure that God's perfect love will see you through.

Wives and husbands

21Honor Christ by submitting to each other. 22You wives must submit to your husbands' leadership in the same way you submit to the Lord. 23For a husband is in charge of his wife in the same way Christ is in charge of his body the Church. (He gave his very life to take care of it and be its Savior!) 24So you wives must willingly obey your husbands in everything, just as the Church obeys Christ.

25And you husbands, show the same kind of love to your wives as Christ showed to the Church when he died for her, 26to make her holy and clean, washed by baptism and God's Word; 27so that he could give her to himself as a glorious Church without a single spot or wrinkle or any other blemish, being holy and without a single fault. 28That is how husbands should treat their wives, loving them as parts of themselves. For since a man and his wife are now one, a man is really doing himself a favor and loving himself when he loves his wife! 29, 30No one hates his own body but lovingly cares for it, just as Christ cares for his body the Church, of which we are parts.

31(That the husband and wife are one body is proved by the Scripture which says, "A man must leave his father and mother when he marries, so that he can be perfectly joined to his wife, and the two shall be one.") 32I know this is hard to understand, but it is an illustration of the way we are parts of the body of Christ.

33So again I say, a man must love his wife as a part of himself; and the wife must see to it that she deeply respects her husband—obeying, praising and honoring him.

5:21 1 Pet 5:5
5:22 Gen 3:16
5:23 1 Cor 11:3
5:24 Eph 5:2
5:26 Jn 15:3; 17:17 Tit 3:5 Heb 10:22
5:27 Eph 1:4 Col 1:22 Rev 21:2
5:28 1 Pet 3:7
5:29 1 Cor 12:27
5:30 1 Cor 6:15
5:31 Gen 2:24
5:33 1 Pet 3:1,2,5

5:26 *washed by baptism,* literally, "having cleansed it by washing of water with the word."

5:21, 22 *Submission* is an often misused word. It does not mean becoming a doormat. Christ—at whose name "every knee shall bow in heaven and on earth and under the earth" (Philippians 2:10)—submitted his will to the Father, and we honor Christ by following his example. When we submit to God, we become more willing to obey his command to submit to others; that is, to subordinate our rights to theirs. In a marriage relationship both husband and wife are called to submit. For the wife this means willingly following her husband's leadership in Christ. For the husband it means putting aside his own interests in order to care for his wife. Submission is rarely a problem in homes where both spouses are in a strong relationship with Christ and where each is concerned for the happiness of the other.

5:22–26 Why did Paul tell wives to submit and husbands to love? Perhaps Christian women, newly freed in Christ, found submission difficult; and Christian men, used to the Roman custom of giving unlimited power to the head of the family, were not used to treating their wives with respect and love. Of course both husbands and wives should submit to each other (5:21), just as both should love each other.

5:22–24 In Paul's day, the lot of women, children, and slaves was to submit to the head of the family—slaves until they were freed, male children until they grew up, and women and girls their whole lives. Paul emphasized the equality of all believers in Christ (Galatians 3:28), but he did not suggest overthrowing Roman society to achieve it. Instead, he counseled all believers to submit to one another by choice—wives to husbands and also husbands to wives; slaves to masters and also masters to slaves; children to parents and also parents to children. This kind of mutual submission preserves order and harmony in the family while it increases love and respect among family members.

5:22–24 Although some people have distorted Paul's teaching on submission by giving unlimited authority to husbands, we cannot get around it—Paul told wives to submit to their husbands. The fact that a teaching is not popular is no reason to discard it. According to the Bible, the man is the spiritual head of the family and his wife goes along with his leadership. But real spiritual leadership is service. Just as Christ served the disciples, even to the point of washing their feet, so the husband is to serve his wife. A wise and

Christ-honoring husband will not take advantage of his role, and a wise and Christ-honoring wife will not try to undermine her husband's leadership. Either approach causes disunity and friction in marriage.

5:25ff Some Christians have thought Paul was negative about marriage because of the counsel he gave in 1 Corinthians 7:32–38. These verses in Ephesians, however, show a high view of marriage. Here marriage is not a practical necessity or a cure for lust, but a picture of the relationship between Christ and his church! Why the apparent difference? Paul's counsel in 1 Corinthians was designed for a state of emergency during a time of persecution and crisis. Paul's counsel to the Ephesians was more a theology of marriage. Marriage, for Paul, is a holy union, a living symbol, a precious relationship that needs tender, self-sacrificing care.

5:25–30 Paul devotes twice as many words to telling husbands to love their wives as to telling wives to submit to their husbands. How should a man love his wife? (1) He should be willing to sacrifice everything for her. (2) He should make her well-being of primary importance. (3) He should care for her as he cares for his body. No wife needs to fear submitting to a man who treats her in this way.

5:26 Jesus Christ purifies the church through the work of the Holy Spirit, who draws people to Christ. In this case, Paul is using the water of baptism to mean the washing away of sin. The believer is making a commitment to be part of this purification process. Then the Spirit, who inspired the Bible, works through his people in order to build up Christ's church. Just as Christ draws his church to him and then builds her up, so a loving husband will care for his wife in ways that make her strong.

5:31–33 The union of husband and wife merges two persons in such a way that little can affect one without also affecting the other. Oneness in marriage does not mean losing your personality in the personality of the other. Instead, it means caring for your spouse as you care for yourself, learning to anticipate the other person's needs, helping the other person become all he or she can be. The creation story tells of God's plan that husband and wife should be one (Genesis 2:24), and Jesus also referred to this plan (Matthew 19:4–6).

Children and parents

6:1
Prov 23:22
Col 3:20

6:2
Ex 20:12
Mt 15:4

6:4
Col 3:21

6 Children, obey your parents; this is the right thing to do because God has placed them in authority over you. 2Honor your father and mother. This is the first of God's Ten Commandments that ends with a promise. 3And this is the promise: that if you honor your father and mother, yours will be a long life, full of blessing.

4And now a word to you parents. Don't keep on scolding and nagging your children, making them angry and resentful. Rather, bring them up with the loving discipline the Lord himself approves, with suggestions and godly advice.

Slaves and masters

6:5
Col 3:22

6:6
Col 3:22,23

6:8
Rom 2:6
2 Cor 5:10
Col 3:24

6:9
Job 31:13,14
Col 4:1

5Slaves, obey your masters; be eager to give them your very best. Serve them as you would Christ. 6, 7Don't work hard only when your master is watching and then shirk when he isn't looking; work hard and with gladness all the time, as though working for Christ, doing the will of God with all your hearts. 8Remember, the Lord will pay you for each good thing you do, whether you are slave or free.

9And you slave owners must treat your slaves right, just as I have told them to treat you. Don't keep threatening them; remember, you yourselves are slaves to Christ; you have the same Master they do, and he has no favorites.

Wearing the whole armor of God

6:11
Rom 13:12
1 Thess 5:8

6:12
Eph 3:10

10Last of all I want to remind you that your strength must come from the Lord's mighty power within you. 11Put on all of God's armor so that you will be able to stand safe against all strategies and tricks of Satan. 12For we are not fighting against people made of flesh and blood, but against persons without bodies—the evil rulers

---

6:1–4 If our faith in Christ is real, it will usually prove itself at home, in our relationships with those who know us best. Children and parents have a responsibility to each other. Children should honor their parents even if the parents are demanding and unfair. Parents should care gently for their children, even if the children are disobedient and unpleasant. Ideally, of course, Christian parents and Christian children will relate to each other with thoughtfulness and love. This will happen if both parents and children put the others' interests above their own—that is, if they submit to one another.

6:1, 2 There is a difference between obeying and honoring. To obey means to do as one is told; to honor means to show respect and love. Children are to obey until they are no longer under their parents' care, but the responsibility to honor parents continues for a lifetime.

6:3 Some societies honor their elders. They respect their wisdom, they defer to their authority, and they pay attention to their comfort and happiness. This is how Christians should act. Where elders are respected, long life is a blessing, not a burden to them.

6:4 The purpose of parental discipline is to help children grow, not to hurt or discourage them (see also Colossians 3:21). Parenting is not easy—it takes lots of patience to raise children in a loving, Christ-honoring manner. But frustration and anger should not be causes for discipline. Instead, parents should act in love, treating their children as Jesus treats the people he loves. This is vital to children's development and to their concept of the Lord.

6:5 Slaves played a significant part in Roman culture. It is estimated that there were several million slaves in the Roman Empire at this time. Since many slave owners and slaves became Christians, the early church had to deal straightforwardly with the question of master/slave relations. Paul's statement neither condemns nor condones the institution of slavery. Instead, it tells masters and slaves how to live together in Christian households. In Paul's day, women, children, and slaves had few rights. In the church, however, they had freedoms that society denied them. Paul gave firm directions to those responsible for these groups: husbands, parents, and masters.

6:6, 7 Paul's instructions encourage responsibility and integrity on the job. Christian employees should do their jobs as if Jesus Christ were their supervisor, and Christian employers should treat their employees fairly and with respect. Are you trusted in any job to do your best, whether or not the boss is around? Do you work hard and with enthusiasm? Do you treat your employees as people, not machines? Remember that no matter whom you work for, and no matter who works for you, the One you ultimately want to please is your Father in heaven.

6:9 Although Christians may be at different levels in earthly society, we are all equal before God. He does not play favorites; no one is more important than anyone else. Paul's letter to Philemon stresses the same point: Philemon, the master, and Onesimus, his slave, were brothers before God.

6:10–17 In the Christian life we battle against powerful evil forces, headed by Satan, a vicious fighter (see 1 Peter 5:8). To withstand his attacks, we must depend on God's strength and use every piece of his armor. Paul is not only giving this counsel to the church, the body of Christ, but to all individuals within the church. The whole body needs to be armed. As you do battle against "the evil rulers of the unseen world," fight in the strength of the church, whose power comes from the Holy Spirit.

6:12 These evil rulers, satanic beings, and evil princes of darkness are not people, but fallen angels over whom Satan has control. They are not mere fantasies—they are very real. We face a powerful army whose goal is to defeat Christ's church. When we believe in Christ and join his church, these beings become our enemies, and they try every device to turn us away from Christ and back to sin. Although we are assured of victory, we must engage in the struggle until Christ comes, because Satan is constantly battling against all who are on the Lord's side. We need supernatural power to defeat Satan, and God has provided that in his Holy Spirit within us and his armor surrounding us. If you feel discouraged, remember Jesus' words to Peter: "Upon this rock I will build my church; and all the powers of hell shall not prevail against it" (Matthew 16:18).

of the unseen world, those mighty satanic beings and great evil princes of darkness who rule this world; and against huge numbers of wicked spirits in the spirit world. 13So use every piece of God's armor to resist the enemy whenever he attacks, and when it is all over, you will still be standing up.

14But to do this, you will need the strong belt of truth and the breastplate of God's approval. 15Wear shoes that are able to speed you on as you preach the Good News of peace with God. 16In every battle you will need faith as your shield to stop the fiery arrows aimed at you by Satan. 17And you will need the helmet of salvation and the sword of the Spirit—which is the Word of God.

18Pray all the time. Ask God for anything in line with the Holy Spirit's wishes. Plead with him, reminding him of your needs, and keep praying earnestly for all Christians everywhere. 19Pray for me, too, and ask God to give me the right words as I boldly tell others about the Lord, and as I explain to them that his salvation is for the Gentiles too. 20I am in chains now for preaching this message from God. But pray that I will keep on speaking out boldly for him even here in prison, as I should.

6:13
Jas 4:7
6:14
Isa 11:5; 59:17
1 Thess 5:8
6:15
Isa 52:7
6:16
1 Jn 5:4
6:17
Isa 59:17
Jn 6:63
1 Thess 5:8
Heb 4:12
6:18
Rom 8:26
Phil 4:6
Col 4:2
6:19
Col 4:3,4

Piece of Armor	Use	Application	
Strong Belt	Truth	Satan fights with lies, and sometimes his lies *sound* like truth; but only believers have God's truth which can defeat Satan's lies.	**GOD'S ARMOR FOR US** We are engaged in a spiritual battle—all believers find themselves subject to Satan's attacks because they are no longer on Satan's side. Thus, Paul tells us to use *every piece* of God's armor to resist Satan's attacks and to stand true to God in the midst of them.
Breastplate	God's approval	Satan often attacks our hearts—the seat of our emotions, self-worth, and trust. God's approval is the breastplate that protects our hearts. He approves of us because he loves us and sent his Son to die for us.	
Shoes	Readiness to spread the Good News	Satan wants us to think that telling others the Good News is a worthless and hopeless task—the size of the task is too big and the negative responses are too much to handle. But the "shoes" God gives us are the motivation to continue to proclaim the true peace which is available in God—news everyone needs to hear.	
Shield	Faith	What *we* see are Satan's attacks in the form of insults, setbacks, and temptations. But the shield of faith protects us from Satan's flaming arrows. With God's perspective, we can see beyond our circumstances and know that ultimate victory is ours.	
Helmet	Salvation	Satan wants to make us doubt God, Jesus, and our salvation. The helmet protects our minds from doubting God's saving work for us.	
Sword	The Spirit, the Word of God	The sword is the only weapon of *offense* in this list of armor. There are times when we need to take the offensive against Satan. When we are tempted, we need to trust in the truth of God's Word.	

6:18 How can anyone pray all the time? One way to pray constantly is to make quick, brief prayers your habitual response to every situation you meet throughout the day. Another way is to order your life around God's desires and teachings so that your very life becomes a prayer. You don't have to isolate yourself from other people and from daily work in order to pray constantly. You can make prayer your life and your life a prayer while living in a world that needs God's powerful influence.

6:20 Undiscouraged and undefeated, Paul wrote powerful letters of encouragement from prison. Paul did not ask the Ephesians to pray that his chains would be removed, but that he would continue to speak boldly for Christ in spite of them. God can use us in any circumstances to do his will. Even as we pray for a change in our circumstances, we should also pray that God will accomplish his plan through us right where we are. Knowing God's eternal purpose for our lives helps us through the difficult times.

Paul's final greetings

6:21
Acts 20:4
2 Tim 4:12
Tit 3:12

²¹Tychicus, who is a much loved brother and faithful helper in the Lord's work, will tell you all about how I am getting along. ²²I am sending him to you for just this purpose, to let you know how we are and be encouraged by his report.

6:22
Col 4:7,8

²³May God give peace to you, my Christian brothers, and love, with faith from God the Father and the Lord Jesus Christ. ²⁴May God's grace and blessing be upon all who sincerely love our Lord Jesus Christ.

6:23
2 Thess 3:16

Sincerely, Paul

6:21 Tychicus is also mentioned in Acts 20:4, Colossians 4:7, 2 Timothy 4:12, and Titus 3:12.

6:24 This letter was written to the church at Ephesus, but it was also meant for circulation among other churches. In this epistle, Paul presents the supremacy of Christ, gives information on both the nature of the church and on how church members should live, and stresses the unity of all believers—male, female, parent, child, master, slave—regardless of sex, nationality, or social rank. The home and the church are difficult places to live the Christian life, because our real self comes through to those who know us well. Close relationships between imperfect people can lead to trouble—or to increased faith and deepened dependence on God. We can build unity in our churches through willing submission to Christ's leadership and humble service to one another.

PHILIPPIANS

VITAL STATISTICS

PURPOSE:
To thank the Philippians for the gift they had sent him and to strengthen these believers by showing them that true joy comes from Jesus Christ alone

AUTHOR:
Paul

TO WHOM WRITTEN:
All the Christians at Philippi and all believers everywhere

DATE WRITTEN:
About A.D. 61, from Rome during Paul's imprisonment there

SETTING:
Paul and his companions founded the church at Philippi on his second missionary journey (Acts 16:11–40). This was the first church established on the European continent. The Philippian church had sent a gift with Epaphroditus (one of their members) to be delivered to Paul (4:18). Paul was in a Roman prison at the time. He writes this letter to thank them for their gift and to encourage them in their faith.

KEY VERSE:
"Always be full of joy in the Lord; I say it again, rejoice!" (4:4)

KEY PEOPLE:
Paul, Timothy, Epaphroditus, Euodias and Syntyche

KEY PLACE:
Philippi

THE word *happiness* evokes visions of unwrapping gifts on Christmas morning, strolling hand in hand with the one you love, being surprised on your birthday, responding with unbridled laughter to a comedian, or vacationing in an exotic locale. Everyone wants to be happy; we make chasing this elusive ideal a lifelong pursuit: spending money, collecting things, and searching for new experiences. But if happiness depends upon our circumstances, what happens when the toys rust, loved ones die, health deteriorates, money is stolen, and the party's over? Often happiness flees and despair sets in.

In contrast to *happiness* stands *joy*. Running deeper and stronger, joy is the quiet, confident assurance of God's love and work in our lives, that he will be there no matter what! Happiness depends on happenings, but joy depends on Christ.

Philippians is Paul's joy letter. The church in that Macedonian city had been a great encouragement to Paul. The Philippian believers had enjoyed a very special relationship with Paul, so he wrote them a personal expression of his love and affection. They had brought him great joy (4:1). Philippians is also a joyful book because it emphasizes the real joy of the Christian life. The concept of *rejoicing* or *joy* appears 16 times, and the pages radiate this positive message, culminating in the exhortation to "Always be full of joy in the Lord; I say it again, rejoice!" (4:4).

In a life dedicated to serving Christ, Paul had faced excruciating poverty, abundant wealth, and everything in-between. He even wrote this joyful letter from prison. Whatever the circumstances, Paul had learned to be content (4:11, 12), finding real joy as he focused all of his attention and energy on knowing Christ (3:8) and obeying him (3:12, 13).

Paul's desire to know Christ above all else is wonderfully expressed in the following words: "Everything else is worthless when compared with the priceless gain of knowing Christ Jesus my Lord. I have put aside all else, counting it worth less than nothing, in order that I can have Christ, and become one with him. . . . Now I have given up everything else—I have found it to be the only way to really know Christ and to experience the mighty power that brought him back to life again, and to find out what it means to suffer and to die with him" (3:8–10). May we share Paul's aspiration and seek to know Jesus Christ more and more. This is the secret of a joyful Christian life.

THE BLUEPRINT

1. Joy in suffering (1:1–30)
2. Joy in serving (2:1–30)
3. Joy in believing (3:1–21)
4. Joy in giving (4:1–23)

Although Paul was writing from prison, joy is a dominant theme in this letter. The secret of his joy is grounded in his relationship with Christ. People today desperately want to be happy but are tossed and turned by daily successes, failures, and inconveniences. Christians are to be joyful in every circumstance, even when things are going badly, even when we feel like complaining, even when no one else is joyful. Christ still reigns and we still know him, so we can rejoice at all times.

MEGATHEMES

THEME	EXPLANATION	IMPORTANCE
Humility	Christ showed true humility when he laid aside his rights and privileges as God to become human. He poured out his life to pay the penalty we deserve. Laying aside self-interest is essential to all our relationships.	We are to take Christ's attitude in serving others. We must renounce personal recognition and merit. When we give up our self-interest, we can serve with joy, love, and kindness.
Self-sacrifice	Christ suffered and died so we might have eternal life. With courage and faithfulness, Paul sacrificed himself for the ministry. He preached the gospel even while he was in prison.	Christ gives us power to lay aside our personal needs and concerns. To utilize his power, we must imitate those leaders who show self-denying concern for others. We dare not be self-centered.
Unity	In every church, in every generation, there are divisive influences (issues, loyalties, and conflicts). In the midst of hardships, it is easy to turn on one another. Paul encouraged the Philippians to agree with one another, stop complaining, and work together.	As believers, we should contend against a common enemy, not against one another. When we are unified in love, Christ's strength is most abundant. Keep before you the ideals of teamwork, consideration of others, and unselfishness.
Christian living	Paul shows us how to live successful Christian lives. We can become mature by being so identified with Christ that his attitude of humility and sacrifice rules us. Christ is both our source of power and our guide.	Developing our character begins with God's work in us. But growth also requires discipline, obedience, and relentless concentration on our part.
Joy	Believers can have profound contentment, serenity, and peace no matter what happens. This joy comes from knowing Christ personally and from depending on his strength rather than our own.	We can have joy, even in hardship. Joy does not come from outward circumstances but from inward strength. As Christians, we must not rely on what we have or what we experience to give us joy, but on Christ within us.

1. Joy in suffering

1 *From:* Paul and Timothy, slaves of Jesus Christ.
 To: The pastors and deacons and all the Christians in the city of Philippi. ²May God bless you all. Yes, I pray that God our Father and the Lord Jesus Christ will give each of you his fullest blessings, and his peace in your hearts and your lives.

1:1
Acts 16:1,12
2 Cor 1:1
Col 1:1
Philem 1
1:2
Rom 1:7

Paul's prayer for the Philippian believers

³All my prayers for you are full of praise to God! ⁴When I pray for you, my heart is full of joy, ⁵because of all your wonderful help in making known the Good News about Christ from the time you first heard it until now. ⁶And I am sure that God who

1:3
Col 1:3
1:6
1 Cor 1:8

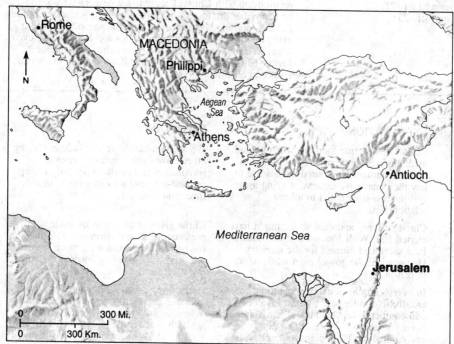

LOCATION OF PHILIPPI
Philippi sat on the Egnatian Way, the main transportation route in Macedonia, an extension of the Appian Way, which joined the eastern empire with Italy.

1:1 This is a personal letter to the Philippians, not intended for general circulation as was the letter to the Ephesians. Paul wanted to thank the believers for helping him when he had a need. He also wanted to tell them why he could be full of joy despite his imprisonment and coming trial. This is an uplifting letter in which Paul devotes only a small space to correcting the Philippians and warning them about potential problems.

1:1 On Paul's first missionary journey, he visited towns close to his headquarters in Antioch of Syria. On his second and third journeys, his travels extended even farther. Because of the great distance between the congregations which Paul had founded, he could no longer personally oversee them all. Thus he was compelled to write letters to teach and encourage the believers. Fortunately, Paul had a staff of volunteers (including Timothy, Mark, and Epaphras) who personally delivered these letters and often remained with the congregations for a while to teach and encourage them.

1:1 For more information on Paul, see his Profile in Acts 9. Timothy's Profile is found in 1 Timothy.

1:1 Pastors and deacons led the early Christian churches. "Pastors" were the "overseers" or "elders"; their qualifications and duties are explained in detail in 1 Timothy 3:1–7; Titus 1:5–9. The qualifications and duties of deacons are spelled out in 1 Timothy 3:8–13.

1:1 The Roman colony of Philippi was located in northern Greece (called Macedonia in Paul's day). This thriving commercial center sat at the crossroads between Europe and Asia. In about A.D. 50, Paul, Silas, Timothy, and Luke crossed the Aegean Sea from Asia Minor and landed at Philippi (Acts 16:11–40). The church in Philippi consisted mostly of Gentile (non-Jewish) believers. Since they were not familar with the Old Testament, Paul did not specifically quote any Old Testament passages in this letter.

1:4 This is the first of many times Paul used the word *joy* in his letter. Here he says that the Philippians were a source of joy when he prayed. By helping Paul, they were helping Christ's cause. The Philippians were willing to be used by God for whatever task he had in store for them. When others think about you, are you a source of joy for them?

1:4, 5 The Philippians first heard the Good News about ten years earlier when Paul and his companions visited Philippi (during Paul's second missionary journey) and founded the church there.

1:6 The God who begins his good work in us continues it through our lives and will finish it when we meet him face to face. God's work *for* us began when Christ died on the cross to forgive our sins. His work *in* us begins when the Holy Spirit comes into our hearts, enabling us to be more like Christ every day. Paul is describing the process of Christian growth and maturity that begins when we accept Jesus and continues until Christ returns.

began the good work within you will keep right on helping you grow in his grace until his task within you is finally finished on that day when Jesus Christ returns. [7]How natural it is that I should feel as I do about you, for you have a very special place in my heart. We have shared together the blessings of God, both when I was in prison and when I was out, defending the truth and telling others about Christ. [8]Only God knows how deep is my love and longing for you—with the tenderness of Jesus Christ. [9]My prayer for you is that you will overflow more and more with love for others, and at the same time keep on growing in spiritual knowledge and insight, [10]for I want you always to see clearly the difference between right and wrong, and to be inwardly clean, no one being able to criticize you from now until our Lord returns. [11]May you always be doing those good, kind things which show that you are a child of God, for this will bring much praise and glory to the Lord.

Honor Christ by life or death

[12]And I want you to know this, dear brothers: Everything that has happened to me here has been a great boost in getting out the Good News concerning Christ. [13]For everyone around here, including all the soldiers at the barracks, knows that I am in chains simply because I am a Christian. [14]And because of my imprisonment many of the Christians here seem to have lost their fear of chains! Somehow my patience has encouraged them and they have become more and more bold in telling others about Christ.

[15]Some, of course, are preaching the Good News because they are jealous of the way God has used me. They want reputations as fearless preachers! But others have purer motives, [16, 17]preaching because they love me, for they know that the Lord has brought me here to use me to defend the Truth. And some preach to make me jealous, thinking that their success will add to my sorrows here in jail! [18]But whatever their motive for doing it, the fact remains that the Good News about Christ is being preached and I am glad.

[19]I am going to keep on being glad, for I know that as you pray for me, and as the

1:7
2 Cor 7:3
Eph 3:1; 6:20
Col 4:3
2 Tim 1:8

1:8
Rom 1:9

1:9
Col 1:9
1 Thess 3:12
Philem 6

1:10
Rom 12:2
1 Cor 1:8

1:11
Jn 15:4

1:12
Lk 21:12,13

1:13
Acts 28:30,31

1:14
Phil 1:20

1:15
Phil 2:3

1:17
1 Cor 9:17

1:19
Acts 16:7
Rom 8:9
2 Cor 1:11

1:6 Do you sometimes feel as if you'll never make progress in your spiritual life? When God starts a project, he finishes it! As with the Philippians, God will work in your life and help you grow in grace until he has completed his work in your life. When you are discouraged, remember that God won't give up on you. He promises to finish the work he has begun. Let him do it!

1:7 Paul is probably referring to his imprisonment in Philippi, recorded in Acts 16:22–36. In verses 13 and 14, Paul speaks of his Roman imprisonment. Wherever Paul was, even in prison, he faithfully preached the Good News.

1:7, 8 Have you ever longed to see a friend with whom you share fond memories? Paul had such a longing to see the Christians at Philippi. His love and affection for them was based not merely on past experiences, but upon the unity that comes when believers draw upon Christ's love. All Christians are part of God's family and thus share equally in the transforming power of his love. Do you feel a deep love for fellow Christians, friends and strangers alike? Let Christ's love for you motivate you to love other Christians, and feel free to express that love.

1:10 Paul calls for discernment—the ability to differentiate between right and wrong, good and bad, vital and trivial. This is to help us avoid the criticism of unbelievers and to keep us from compromising our Christian morals and values (Hebrews 5:14).

1:12–14 Being imprisoned would cause many people to become bitter or to give up, but Paul saw it as one more opportunity to spread the Good News of Christ. Paul realized that his current circumstances weren't as important as what he did with them. Turning a bad situation into a good one, he reached out to the Roman soldiers and encouraged those Christians who were afraid of persecution. We may not be in prison, but we still have plenty of

opportunities to be discouraged—times of indecision, financial burdens, family conflict, church conflict, or the loss of our jobs. How we act in such situations reflects what we believe. Like Paul, look for opportunities to demonstrate your faith even in bad situations. Whether or not the situation improves, your faith will grow stronger.

1:13 How did Paul end up in a Roman prison? While he was visiting Jerusalem, some Jews had him arrested for preaching the gospel, but he appealed to Caesar to hear his case (Acts 21:15—25:12). He was then escorted by soldiers to Rome, where he was placed under house arrest while awaiting trial—not a trial for breaking civil law, but for proclaiming the Good News of Christ. At that time, the Roman authorities did not consider "proclaiming the Good News" to be a serious charge. A few years later, however, Rome took a different view of Christianity and made every effort to stamp it out of existence. Paul's house arrest allowed him some degree of freedom. He could have visitors, continue to preach, and write letters such as this one. A brief record of Paul's time in Rome is found in Acts 28:11–31.

1:15–18 Paul had an amazingly selfless attitude. He knew that some were preaching to build their own reputations, but he was glad the gospel was being preached, regardless of the motives of these preachers. Many Christians serve for the wrong reasons. God doesn't excuse their motives, but, like Paul, we should be glad if God uses their message, regardless of their motives.

1:19–21 This was not Paul's final imprisonment in Rome. Awaiting trial, he knew he could either be released or executed. As it turned out, he was released from this imprisonment but arrested again two or three years later.

Holy Spirit helps me, this is all going to turn out for my good. 20For I live in eager expectation and hope that I will never do anything that will cause me to be ashamed of myself but that I will always be ready to speak out boldly for Christ while I am going through all these trials here, just as I have in the past; and that I will always be an honor to Christ, whether I live or whether I must die. 21For to me, living means opportunities for Christ, and dying—well, that's better yet! 22But if living will give me more opportunities to win people to Christ, then I really don't know which is better, to live or die! 23Sometimes I want to live and at other times I don't, for I long to go and be with Christ. How much happier for *me* than being here! 24But the fact is that I can be of more help to *you* by staying!

1:20
Rom 5:5; 14:8
1 Cor 6:20
Eph 6:19

1:21
Gal 2:20
Col 1:27

1:22
Rom 1:13

1:23
2 Cor 5:8
2 Tim 4:6

25Yes, I am still needed down here and so I feel certain I will be staying on earth a little longer, to help you grow and become happy in your faith; 26my staying will make you glad and give you reason to glorify Christ Jesus for keeping me safe, when I return to visit you again.

1:25
Phil 2:24

27But whatever happens to me, remember always to live as Christians should, so that, whether I ever see you again or not, I will keep on hearing good reports that you are standing side by side with one strong purpose—to tell the Good News 28fearlessly, no matter what your enemies may do. They will see this as a sign of their downfall, but for you it will be a clear sign from God that he is with you, and that he has given you eternal life with him. 29For to you has been given the privilege not only of trusting him but also of suffering for him. 30We are in this fight together. You have seen me suffer for him in the past; and I am still in the midst of a great and terrible struggle now, as you know so well.

1:27
Acts 4:32
Phil 4:1,2

1:28
Mt 10:28
Rom 8:17
2 Tim 2:11
Heb 13:6

1:29
Mt 5:11,12
Acts 5:41

1:30
Acts 16:19
Col 2:1
1 Thess 2:2

2. Joy in serving

Be humble like Christ

2 Is there any such thing as Christians cheering each other up? Do you love me enough to want to help me? Does it mean anything to you that we are brothers in the Lord, sharing the same Spirit? Are your hearts tender and sympathetic at all? 2Then make me truly happy by loving each other and agreeing wholeheartedly with each other, working together with one heart and mind and purpose.

2:1
2 Cor 13:14
Col 3:12

2:2
1 Pet 3:8

3Don't be selfish; don't live to make a good impression on others. Be humble, thinking of others as better than yourself. 4Don't just think about your own affairs, but be interested in others, too, and in what they are doing.

2:3
Rom 12:10,16
1 Pet 5:5

2:4
Rom 15:1,2
1 Cor 10:24

1:20, 21 To those who don't believe in God, life on earth is all there is, and so it is natural for them to strive for the things that this world values—money, popularity, power, and prestige. For Paul, however, life meant developing eternal values and telling others about Christ, who alone can help us see life from an eternal perspective. Paul's whole purpose in life was to speak out boldly for Christ and to become more like him. Thus Paul could confidently say that dying would be even better than living, because in death he would be spared from the troubles of the world and see Christ face to face (1 John 3:2, 3). If you're not ready to die, then you're not ready to live. Once you know your eternal purpose, then you're free to serve—devoting your life to what really counts without fear of dying.

1:29 Suffering, in and of itself, is not a privilege. But when we suffer because we faithfully represent Christ, we know that our message and example are having an effect and that God considers us worthy to represent him (see Acts 5:41). Suffering has these additional benefits: (1) it takes our eyes off of earthly comforts; (2) it weeds out superficial believers; (3) it strengthens the faith of those who endure; (4) it serves as an example to others who may follow us. Suffering for our faith doesn't mean we have done something wrong. In fact, the opposite is often true—it verifies that we have been faithful.

1:30 Throughout his life Paul suffered for spreading the Good News. Like the Philippians, we struggle against the forces of evil that would discredit the saving message of Christ. All true believers are in this fight together, uniting against the same enemy for the same cause.

2:1–5 Many people—even Christians—live only to make a good impression on others or to please themselves. This is self-centered living; if people are concerned only for themselves, seeds of discord are sown. Paul therefore stresses spiritual unity, asking the Philippians to love one another and to work together with one heart and purpose. When we work together, caring for the problems of others as if they were our own, we are demonstrating Christ's example of putting others first. This brings unity. Don't be concerned about making a good impression or pleasing yourself to the point where you strain your relationship to others in God's family. Let the Spirit of God work through you to attract fellow believers to himself.

2:3 Being humble means having a true perspective on ourselves (see Romans 12:3). It does not mean that we should put ourselves down. We see that we are sinners, saved only by God's grace; but we *are* saved and therefore have great worth in God's Kingdom. We should place ourselves in his hands to be used as he wants in order to spread his Word and share his love with others.

2:3, 4 Immediately after Paul calls for unity among the believers (2:2), he urges the Philippians to avoid selfishness. The cure for selfishness is servanthood, which is being like Christ (2:5). Selfish ambitions destroy church unity by pitting one Christian against another.

2:6
Isa 9:6
Jn 1:1,2
2:7
Jn 1:14
Gal 4:4
2:8
Heb 5:8; 12:2
2:9
Eph 1:20,21
Heb 1:4
2:10
Rom 14:11

5Your attitude should be the kind that was shown us by Jesus Christ, 6who, though he was God, did not demand and cling to his rights as God, 7but laid aside his mighty power and glory, taking the disguise of a slave and becoming like men. 8And he humbled himself even further, going so far as actually to die a criminal's death on a cross.

9Yet it was because of this that God raised him up to the heights of heaven and gave him a name which is above every other name, 10that at the name of Jesus every knee shall bow in heaven and on earth and under the earth, 11and every tongue shall confess that Jesus Christ is Lord, to the glory of God the Father.

Shine like lights in a dark world

2:12
Phil 1:5
2:13
Rom 8:28
1 Cor 12:6
Heb 13:20,21

12Dearest friends, when I was there with you, you were always so careful to follow my instructions. And now that I am away you must be even more careful to do the good things that result from being saved, obeying God with deep reverence, shrinking back from all that might displease him. 13For God is at work within you, helping you want to obey him, and then helping you do what he wants.

2:7 *becoming like men,* literally, "was made in the likeness of men." **2:8** *to die a criminal's death on a cross,* literally, "became obedient to death, even the death of the cross."

2:4 Philippi was a cosmopolitan city. The composition of the church reflected this with its people from a variety of backgrounds and walks of life. Acts 16 gives us some indication of the diverse makeup of this church. For example, Lydia was a Jewish convert from Asia, a wealthy merchant (Acts 16:14), the slave girl in Acts 16:16, 17 was probably a native Greek and the jailer serving this colony of the empire was probably Roman (Acts 16:25–36). With so many different backgrounds among the members, unity must have been difficult to achieve. Although there is no evidence of widespread division in the church, its unity had to be safeguarded (3:2; 4:2). Paul encourages us to guard against any selfishness, prejudice, or jealousy that might lead to dissension. Showing genuine interest in others is one way to strive actively for unity among believers.

2:5–11 These verses were probably from a hymn which was sung in the early Christian church. The passage holds many parallels to the prophecy of the suffering servant in Isaiah 53. As a hymn, it was not meant to be a complete statement about the nature and work of Christ. Several key characteristics of Jesus Christ, however, are inferred from this passage: (1) he has always existed with God; (2) he is equal to God because he *is* God (John 1:1ff; Colossians 1:15–19); (3) though he is God, he became a man in order to fulfill God's plan of salvation for all people; (4) he did not just pretend to have a man's body; he actually became a man to identify with man's sins; (5) he voluntarily laid aside his divine rights, privileges, and position, out of love for his Father; (6) he died on the cross for our sins, so we wouldn't have to face eternal death; (7) God glorified him because of his obedience; (8) God raised him to his original position at the Father's right hand where he will reign forever as our Lord and Judge.

Jesus Christ was humble, willing to give up his rights in order to obey God and serve people. Like Christ, we must serve out of love for God and for others, not out of guilt or fear.

2:5–11 Often people excuse selfishness, pride, or evil by claiming their "rights." They think, "I can cheat on this test; after all, I deserve to pass this class," or "I can spend all this money on myself—I worked for it," or "I can get an abortion; I have a right to control my own body." But as believers, we should have a different attitude, an attitude that enables us to give up our rights for the good of others—in order to serve others. If we say we follow Christ, we must also say we want to live as he lived. We should develop his attitude of humble service, even when we are not likely to get

recognition for our efforts. Are you selfishly clinging to your rights, or are you willing to serve?

2:5–7 The *incarnation* was the act of the preexistent Son of God voluntarily assuming a human body and human nature. Without ceasing to be God, he became a human being, the man called Jesus. He did not give up his deity to become human, but he set aside the right to his glory and power. In submission to the Father's will, he limited his power and knowledge. Jesus of Nazareth was subject to place, time, and many other human limitations. What made his humanity unique was his freedom from sin. In his full humanity, Jesus showed us everything about God's character that can be conveyed in human terms. The incarnation is explained further in these passages: John 1:1–14; Romans 1:2–5; 2 Corinthians 8:9; 1 Timothy 3:16; Hebrews 2:14; and 1 John 1:1–3.

2:8 Crucifixion was the form of capital punishment Romans used for notorious criminals. It was excruciatingly painful, humiliating, and could last for several days. Prisoners were nailed or tied to a cross and left to die. Death usually came by suffocation when the weight of the weakened body made breathing more and more difficult. Jesus died as one who was cursed (Galatians 3:13). How amazing that the perfect man should die this most shameful death so that we would not have to face eternal punishment!

2:9–11 At the last judgment, even those who are condemned will recognize Jesus' authority and right to rule.

2:12 The Philippian Christians needed to be especially careful to obey Christ, now that Paul wasn't there to continually remind them about what was right. We too must be careful about how we live, especially when we are on our own. In the absence of cherished Christian leaders, we must focus our attention and devotion even more on Christ so that we won't be sidetracked.

2:13 God has not left us alone in our struggles to do his will. He wants to come alongside us and within us to help. He helps us want to obey him and then gives us the power to do it. The secret to changing our lives is to submit to his control and let him work in us.

2:13 To be like Christ, we must condition ourselves to think like Christ. To change our desires to be more like Christ's, we need the power of the indwelling Spirit (1:19), the influence of faithful Christians, obedience to God's Word (not just exposure to it), and sacrificial service. Often it is in *doing* God's will that we gain the *desire* for it (see 4:8, 9).

14In everything you do, stay away from complaining and arguing, 15so that no one can speak a word of blame against you. You are to live clean, innocent lives as children of God in a dark world full of people who are crooked and stubborn. Shine out among them like beacon lights, 16holding out to them the Word of Life.

Then when Christ returns how glad I will be that my work among you was so worthwhile. 17And if my lifeblood is, so to speak, to be poured out over your faith which I am offering up to God as a sacrifice—that is, if I am to die for you—even then I will be glad, and will share my joy with each of you. 18For you should be happy about this, too, and rejoice with me for having this privilege of dying for you.

2:14
Rom 14:1
1 Cor 10:10

2:15
Mt 5:45
Jn 12:36
Eph 5:1

2:16
Jn 6:63,68
1 Thess 2:19,20

2:17
Rom 15:16
Col 1:24

Those who will soon come to you

19If the Lord is willing, I will send Timothy to see you soon. Then when he comes back he can cheer me up by telling me all about you and how you are getting along. 20There is no one like Timothy for having a real interest in you; 21everyone else seems to be worrying about his own plans and not those of Jesus Christ. 22But you know Timothy. He has been just like a son to me in helping me preach the Good News. 23I hope to send him to you just as soon as I find out what is going to happen to me here. 24And I am trusting the Lord that soon I myself may come to see you.

2:20
1 Cor 16:10

2:21
1 Cor 10:24
13:5

2:22
1 Cor 4:17
1 Tim 1:2

2:24
Phil 1:25

25Meanwhile, I thought I ought to send Epaphroditus back to you. You sent him to help me in my need; well, he and I have been real brothers, working and battling side by side. 26Now I am sending him home again, for he has been homesick for all of you and upset because you heard that he was ill. 27And he surely was; in fact, he almost died. But God had mercy on him, and on me too, not allowing me to have this sorrow on top of everything else.

2:25
Phil 4:18

28So I am all the more anxious to get him back to you again, for I know how thankful you will be to see him, and that will make me happy and lighten all my cares. 29Welcome him in the Lord with great joy, and show your appreciation, 30for he risked his life for the work of Christ and was at the point of death while trying to do for me the things you couldn't do because you were far away.

2:29
Rom 16:2
1 Cor 16:18
1 Thess 5:12
1 Tim 5:17

2:30
1 Cor 16:17

3. Joy in believing

All is worthless compared to knowing Christ

3 Whatever happens, dear friends, be glad in the Lord. I never get tired of telling you this and it is good for you to hear it again and again.

2Watch out for those wicked men—dangerous dogs, I call them—who say you

3:1
Phil 4:4

3:2
Gal 5:2

2:14–16 Why are complaining and arguing so harmful? If all that people know about a church is that its members constantly argue, complain, and gossip, they get a false impression of the gospel. Belief in Christ should unite those who trust him. If our church is always complaining and arguing, it lacks the unifying power of Jesus Christ. Stop arguing with other Christians or complaining about conditions within the church and let the world see Christ.

2:14–16 Our lives should be characterized by purity, patience, and peacefulness, so that we will shine out "like beacon lights." A transformed life is an effective witness to the power of God's Word. Is your light shining brightly, or is it clouded by complaints and arguing? Be a clean, radiant light shining out for God.

2:17 Even if he had to die, Paul was content, knowing he had helped the Philippians live for Christ. When you're totally committed to serving Christ, sacrifice is more rewarding than painful.

2:19 Timothy was with Paul in Rome at the time Paul wrote this letter. He was also with Paul on his second missionary journey when the church at Philippi was founded. For more information on Timothy, see his Profile in 1 Timothy.

2:23 Paul was in prison (either awaiting his trial or its verdict), for preaching the message of Jesus Christ. He was telling the

Philippians that when he learned of the court's decision, he would send Timothy to them with the news, but that he was ready to accept whatever came (1:21–26).

2:25 Epaphroditus delivered money from the Philippians to Paul; then he returned with this thank-you letter to Philippi. Epaphroditus may have been an elder in Philippi (2:25–30; 4:18) who, while staying with Paul, became ill (2:27, 30). After his recovery, he returned home. He is mentioned only in Philippians.

3:2, 3 These wicked men to whom Paul refers are Judaizers—Jewish Christians who wrongly believed it was essential for Gentiles to follow all the Old Testament Jewish laws, especially the rite of circumcision, in order to receive salvation. Many Judaizers were motivated by spiritual pride. Because they had invested so much time and effort in keeping their laws, they couldn't accept the fact that all their efforts wouldn't bring them a step closer to salvation.

Paul criticized the Judaizers because they looked at Christianity backwards—thinking that what they *did* made them believers rather than the free gift of grace given by Christ. What believers do is a *result* of faith, not a *prerequisite* to faith. This had been confirmed by the early church leaders at the Jerusalem council 11 years earlier (Acts 15). No person should try to add anything to

3:3
Deut 30:6
Jn 4:21-24
Rom 2:29; 7:6
Col 2:11

3:5
Acts 22:3; 23:6
Rom 11:1
2 Cor 11:22

3:6
Acts 8:3; 22:4
Rom 10:5
Gal 1:13

3:7
Mt 13:44
Lk 14:33

3:8
Isa 53:11
Jn 17:3
Eph 4:13
2 Pet 3:18

3:9
Isa 64:6
Rom 1:17;
9:30; 10:3
Gal 2:16
2 Pet 1:1

3:10
Jn 17:3
Rom 8:17,29
Eph 1:19,20
1 Pet 4:13

3:11
Acts 26:8
1 Cor 15:23

must be circumcised to be saved. ³For it isn't the *cutting of our bodies* that makes us children of God; it is *worshiping him with our spirits*. That is the only true "circumcision." We Christians glory in what Christ Jesus has done for us and realize that we are helpless to save ourselves.

⁴Yet if anyone ever had reason to hope that he could save himself, it would be I. If others could be saved by what they are, certainly I could! ⁵For I went through the Jewish initiation ceremony when I was eight days old, having been born into a pure-blooded Jewish home that was a branch of the old original Benjamin family. So I was a real Jew if there ever was one! What's more, I was a member of the Pharisees who demand the strictest obedience to every Jewish law and custom. ⁶And sincere? Yes, so much so that I greatly persecuted the Church; and I tried to obey every Jewish rule and regulation right down to the very last point.

⁷But all these things that I once thought very worthwhile—now I've thrown them all away so that I can put my trust and hope in Christ alone. ⁸Yes, everything else is worthless when compared with the priceless gain of knowing Christ Jesus my Lord. I have put aside all else, counting it worth less than nothing, in order that I can have Christ, ⁹and become one with him, no longer counting on being saved by being good enough or by obeying God's laws, but by trusting Christ to save me; for God's way of making us right with himself depends on faith—counting on Christ alone. ¹⁰Now I have given up everything else—I have found it to be the only way to really know Christ and to experience the mighty power that brought him back to life again, and to find out what it means to suffer and to die with him. ¹¹So, whatever it takes, I will be one who lives in the fresh newness of life of those who are alive from the dead.

Forget the past and reach to the goal

¹²I don't mean to say I am perfect. I haven't learned all I should even yet, but I

Christ's offer of salvation by grace through faith.

3:2, 3 It is easy to place more emphasis on religious effort than on internal faith; but God values the attitude of our hearts above all else. Don't judge people's spirituality by their fulfillment of rituals or level of human activity. And don't think you will satisfy God by feverishly doing his work. God notices all you do for him and will reward you for it, but only if you first accept his free gift of salvation.

3:4–6 At first glance, it seems that Paul is boasting about his achievements. But he is actually doing the opposite, showing that human achievements, no matter how impressive, cannot earn a person salvation and eternal life with God. Paul had impressive credentials: upbringing, nationality, family background, inheritance, orthodoxy, activity, and morality (see 2 Corinthians 11; Galatians 1:13, 24, for more of his credentials). But when he was converted to faith in Christ (Acts 9), it wasn't based upon his credentials, but upon the grace of Christ. Paul did not depend on his credentials to please God, because even the most impressive credentials fall short of God's holy standards. Are you depending on Christian parents, church affiliation, or just being good to make you right with God? Credentials, accomplishments, or reputation cannot earn salvation. Like Paul, you must realize that salvation comes only through faith in Christ.

3:5 Paul belonged to the tribe of Benjamin, a heritage greatly esteemed among the Jews. From this tribe came Israel's first king, Saul (1 Samuel 10:20–24). When the kingdom was divided after Solomon's death, only the tribes of Benjamin and Judah remained loyal to David's line (1 Kings 12:20, 21). In addition, Benjamin and Judah were the only two tribes to return to Israel after the exile (Ezra 4:1). Paul was also a Pharisee, a very devout Jewish sect, which scrupulously kept its own numerous rules in addition to the laws of Moses. Jewish listeners would have been impressed by both of these facts on Paul's resumé.

3:6 Why did Paul, a devout Jewish leader, persecute the church?

In harmony with the leaders of the religious establishment, Paul thought Christianity was heretical and blasphemous. Because Jesus did not meet his expectations of what the Messiah would be like, Paul assumed Jesus' claims were false—and therefore wicked. In addition, he saw Christianity as a political menace because it threatened to disrupt the fragile harmony between the Jews and the Roman establishment.

3:8 After Paul considered everything he had accomplished in his life, he said that it was all worthless when compared with knowing Christ. This is a profound statement about values: a person's relationship with Christ is more important than anything else. To know Christ should be our ultimate goal. Consider your values. Do you place anything above your relationship with Christ? If your priorities are wrong, how can you reorder them?

3:10 Paul gave up everything—family, friendship, and political freedom—in order to know Christ and his resurrection power. We too have access to this knowledge and this power, but we may have to make sacrifices to enjoy it fully. What are you willing to give up in order to know Christ—a few minutes each day for prayer and Bible study? Your friend's approval? Some of your plans or pleasures? Whatever it is, knowing Christ is more than worth the sacrifice.

3:11 The last part of verse 11 literally reads, "if somehow I may attain to the resurrection of the dead." Just as Christ was exalted after his resurrection, so we will one day share Christ's glory (Revelation 22:1–7). Paul knew that he might die soon, but he had faith that he would be raised to life again.

3:12–14 Paul said his goal was to know Christ, to be like Christ, and to be all Christ has in mind for him. This goal absorbed all his energy. This is an example for us. We should not let anything take our eyes off our goal—Christ. With the singlemindedness of an athlete in training, we must lay aside everything harmful and forsake even the good things that may distract us from being effective Christians.

keep working toward that day when I will finally be all that Christ saved me for and wants me to be.

13No, dear brothers, I am still not all I should be but I am bringing all my energies to bear on this one thing: Forgetting the past and looking forward to what lies ahead, 14I strain to reach the end of the race and receive the prize for which God is calling us up to heaven because of what Christ Jesus did for us.

15I hope all of you who are mature Christians will see eye-to-eye with me on these things, and if you disagree on some point, I believe that God will make it plain to you— 16if you fully obey the truth you have.

17Dear brothers, pattern your lives after mine and notice who else lives up to my example. 18For I have told you often before, and I say it again now with tears in my eyes, there are many who walk along the Christian road who are really enemies of the cross of Christ. 19Their future is eternal loss, for their god is their appetite: they are proud of what they should be ashamed of; and all they think about is this life here on earth. 20But our homeland is in heaven, where our Savior the Lord Jesus Christ is; and we are looking forward to his return from there. 21When he comes back he will take these dying bodies of ours and change them into glorious bodies like his own, using the same mighty power that he will use to conquer all else everywhere.

3:13
Lk 9:62
1 Cor 9:24
Heb 6:1

3:14
2 Tim 4:7,8
Heb 12:1

3:15
1 Cor 2:6; 14:20
Gal 5:10
Phil 1:9,10

3:16
Gal 6:16

3:17
1 Cor 4:16
1 Pet 5:3

3:18
Gal 6:14

3:20
Eph 2:16,19
Col 3:1,3

3:21
Mt 17:2; 28:18
1 Cor 15:43-53
Col 3:4
Heb 7:25
1 Jn 3:2

		THREE STAGES OF PERFECTION
1. *Perfect Relationship*	We are perfect because of our eternal union with the infinitely perfect Christ. When we become his children, we are declared "not guilty," thus righteous, because of what Christ, God's beloved Son, has done for us. This perfection is absolute and unchangeable, and it is this perfect relationship that guarantees that we will one day be "completely perfect" (below). See Colossians 2:8–10; Hebrews 10:8–14.	
2. *Perfect Progress*	We can grow and mature spiritually as we continue to trust Christ, learn more about him, draw closer to him, and obey him. Our progress is changeable (in contrast to our relationship, above) because it depends on our daily walk— at times in life we mature more than at other times. But we are growing toward perfection if we "work toward it" (3:12). These good works do not perfect us; rather, as God perfects us, we do good works for him. See Philippians 3:1–15.	
3. *Completely Perfect*	When Christ returns to take us into his eternal Kingdom, we will be glorified and made completely perfect. See Philippians 3:20, 21.	

All phases of perfection are grounded in faith in Christ and what he has done, not what we can do for him. We cannot perfect ourselves; only God can work in and through us until his task is "finally finished on that day when Jesus Christ returns" (1:6).

3:13, 14 Paul had reason to feel guilty—he held the coats of those who stoned Stephen, the first Christian martyr (Acts 7:57, 58). We have all done things for which we are ashamed, and we all live in the tension of what we have been and what we want to be. Because our hope is in Christ, however, we can let go of past guilt and look forward to what he will help us become. Don't dwell on your past. Instead, grow in the knowledge of God by concentrating on your relationship with him *now*. Know you are forgiven, and then move on to a life of faith and obedience. Look forward to a fuller and more meaningful life because of your hope in Christ.

3:17 Paul challenged the Philippians to pursue Christlikeness by telling them to follow his example. This did not mean, of course, that they should copy everything he did; he had just stated that he was not perfect (3:12). But as he focused his life on being like Christ, so should they. It is likely that none of the Gospels had yet been written, so Paul could not tell them to read the Bible to see what Christ was like. Therefore he urged them to imitate him. That Paul could tell people to follow his example is a testimony to his

character. Can you do the same? What kind of follower would a new Christian become if he or she imitated you?

3:17–21 Paul criticized not only the Judaizers (see the note on 3:2, 3), but also the self-indulgent Christians. These are people who claim to be Christians but don't live up to Christ's model of servanthood and sacrifice. They satisfy their own desires before even thinking about the needs of others. Freedom in Christ does not mean freedom to be selfish. It means the opportunity to serve and to become the best person you can be.

3:20 Citizens of Philippi had the same rights and privileges as the citizens of Rome because Philippi was a Roman colony. Likewise we Christians will one day experience all the special privileges of our heavenly citizenship because we belong to Christ.

3:21 The bodies we receive when we are raised from the dead will be like Christ's resurrected body. For a more detailed discussion of our new bodies, see 1 Corinthians 15:35ff and 2 Corinthians 5:1–10.

4. Joy in giving

Think about pure and lovely things

4:2
Phil 2:2

4 Dear brother Christians, I love you and long to see you, for you are my joy and my reward for my work. My beloved friends, stay true to the Lord.

²And now I want to plead with those two dear women, Euodias and Syntyche. Please, please, with the Lord's help, quarrel no more—be friends again. ³And I ask you, my true teammate, to help these women, for they worked side by side with me in telling the Good News to others; and they worked with Clement, too, and the rest of my fellow workers whose names are written in the Book of Life.

4:3
Rev 3:5; 20:12
21:27

4:4
Phil 3:1

4:5
Heb 10:25,37
1 Pet 4:7

⁴Always be full of joy in the Lord; I say it again, rejoice! ⁵Let everyone see that you are unselfish and considerate in all you do. Remember that the Lord is coming soon. ⁶Don't worry about anything; instead, pray about everything; tell God your needs and don't forget to thank him for his answers. ⁷If you do this you will

4:6
Mt 6:25
1 Pet 5:7

TRAINING FOR THE CHRISTIAN LIFE

As a great amount of training is needed for athletic activities, so we must train diligently for the Christian life. Such training takes time, dedication, energy, continued practice, and vision. We must all commit ourselves to the Christian life, but we must first know the rules as prescribed in God's Word (2 Timothy 2:5).

Reference	Metaphors	Training	Our Goal as Believers
1 Corinthians 9:24–27	Race	Deny yourself many things in order to do your best.	We train ourselves to run the race of life. So we keep our eyes on Christ—the goal—and don't get sidetracked or slowed down. When we do this, we will win a reward in Christ's Kingdom.
Philippians 3:13, 14	Race	Put all your energies toward winning the race.	Living the Christian life demands all of our energy. We can forget the past and strain for the goal because we know Christ promises eternity with him at the race's end.
2 Timothy 4:7, 8	Fight	Fighting long and hard without giving up.	The Christian life is a fight against evil forces from without and temptation from within. If we stay true to God through it all, he promises an end, a rest, and a crown.
1 Timothy 4:7–10	Exercise	Spiritual exercise will help you grow in faith and character.	As we must repeat exercises to tone our bodies, so we must steadily repeat spiritual exercises to be spiritually fit. When we do this, we will be better Christians, living in accordance with God's will. Such a life will attract others to Christ and pay dividends in this present life and the next.

4:2, 3 Paul did not warn the Philippian church of doctrinal errors, but they did have some relational problems. These two women had been workers for Christ in the church. Their broken relationship was no small matter, because many had become believers through their efforts. It is possible to believe in Christ, work hard for his Kingdom, and yet have broken relationships with others who are committed to the same cause. But there is no excuse for remaining unreconciled. Do you need to be reconciled to someone today?

4:3 Those whose names are written in the Book of Life are all who are marked out for salvation through their faith in Christ (see Luke 10:17–20; Revelation 20:11–15, for more on this concept).

4:4 It seems strange that a man in prison would be telling a church to be joyful. But Paul's attitude serves to teach us an important lesson—our inner attitudes do not have to reflect our outward circumstances. Paul was full of joy because he knew that no matter what happened to him, Jesus Christ was with him. Several times in this letter, Paul urges the Philippians to be joyful,

probably because they needed to hear this. It's easy to get discouraged about unpleasant circumstances or to take unimportant events too seriously. If you haven't been joyful lately, you may not be looking at life from the right perspective.

4:4, 5 Ultimate joy comes from Christ dwelling within us. At Christ's Second Coming we will fully realize this ultimate joy, because he who dwells within us will fulfill his final purposes for us.

4:6, 7 Imagine never having to worry about anything! It seems like an impossibility—we all have worries on the job, in our homes, at school. But Paul's advice is to turn your worries into prayers. Do you want to worry less? Then pray more! Whenever you start to worry, stop and pray.

4:7 God's peace is different from the world's peace (see John 14:27). It is not found in positive thinking, in absence of conflict, or in good feelings. Real peace comes from knowing that because God is in control, our citizenship in Christ's Kingdom is sure, our destiny is set, and our victory over sin is certain.

experience God's peace, which is far more wonderful than the human mind can understand. His peace will keep your thoughts and your hearts quiet and at rest as you trust in Christ Jesus.

8And now, brothers, as I close this letter let me say this one more thing: Fix your thoughts on what is true and good and right. Think about things that are pure and lovely, and dwell on the fine, good things in others. Think about all you can praise God for and be glad about. 9Keep putting into practice all you learned from me and saw me doing, and the God of peace will be with you.

4:8
1 Thess 5:22

4:9
Rom 15:33

Paul is grateful for their gift

10How grateful I am and how I praise the Lord that you are helping me again. I know you have always been anxious to send what you could, but for a while you didn't have the chance. 11Not that I was ever in need, for I have learned how to get along happily whether I have much or little. 12I know how to live on almost nothing or with everything. I have learned the secret of contentment in every situation, whether it be a full stomach or hunger, plenty or want; 13for I can do everything God asks me to with the help of Christ who gives me the strength and power. 14But even so, you have done right in helping me in my present difficulty.

15As you well know, when I first brought the Gospel to you and then went on my way, leaving Macedonia, only you Philippians became my partners in giving and receiving. No other church did this. 16Even when I was over in Thessalonica you sent help twice. 17But though I appreciate your gifts, what makes me happiest is the well-earned reward you will have because of your kindness.

18At the moment I have all I need—more than I need! I am generously supplied with the gifts you sent me when Epaphroditus came. They are a sweet-smelling sacrifice that pleases God well. 19And it is he who will supply all your needs from his riches in glory, because of what Christ Jesus has done for us. 20Now unto God our Father be glory forever and ever. Amen.

Sincerely, Paul

4:10
2 Cor 11:9

4:11
1 Tim 6:6

4:12
1 Cor 4:11
2 Cor 11:9

4:13
Jn 15:5
2 Cor 12:9

4:14
Phil 1:7
Heb 10:33,34

4:15
Rom 15:26
2 Cor 11:8,9
Phil 1:5

4:17
Tit 3:14

4:18
2 Cor 9:12
Phil 2:25
Heb 13:16

4:19
Ps 23:1
Prov 8:21
2 Cor 9:8

4:8 What we put into our minds determines what comes out in our words and actions. Paul tells us to fill our minds with thoughts that are "true and good and right." Do you have problems with impure thoughts and daydreams? Examine what you are putting into your mind through television, books, movies, and magazines. Replace harmful input with wholesome material. Above all, read God's Word and pray. Ask him to help you focus your mind on what is good and pure. It takes practice, but it can be done.

4:10 In 1 Corinthians 9:11–18, Paul said he didn't accept gifts from the Corinthian church because he didn't want to be accused of preaching only to get money. But Paul maintained that it was a church's responsibility to support God's ministers (1 Corinthians 9:14). Here he accepted the Philippians' gift because they gave it willingly and he was in need.

4:10–14 Are you content in any situation you face? Paul knew how to be content whether he had much or little. The secret was Christ's power in his life. Do you have great needs, or are you discontented because you don't have what you want? Learn to rely on God's promises and Christ's power to help you be content. If you always want more, ask God to remove that desire and teach you contentment in every situation. He will supply all your needs, but in a way that he knows is best for you (see note on 4:19 for more on God supplying our needs).

4:12, 13 Paul was content because he could see life from God's point of view. He focused on what he was supposed to *do*, not what he felt he should *have*. He had his priorities straight and was grateful for everything God had given him. Often the desire for more or better possessions is really a longing to fill an empty place in one's life. To what are you drawn when you feel empty inside? How can you find true contentment? The answer lies in your perspective, your priorities, and your source of power.

4:17 When we give to those in need, there is not only benefit to the receiver, but we are benefited as well. It was not the Philippians' gift, but their spirit of love and devotion that Paul appreciated most.

4:18 Paul was not referring to a sin offering but to a thank offering (Leviticus 7:12–15 contains the instructions for thank offerings). Although the Greek and Roman Christians were not Jews and had not offered sacrifices according to the Old Testament laws, they were well acquainted with the custom of offering sacrifices.

4:19 We can trust that God will always meet our needs, but we must remember that he may not supply them all in this life. Christians suffer and die (tradition says Paul himself was beheaded), and God does not always intervene to spare them. In the new earth, however, when sin has been permanently destroyed, our wants and needs will be abundantly supplied for eternity.

Paul's final greetings

4:22
2 Cor 13:13
4:23
2 Tim 4:22

21Say "hello" for me to all the Christians there; the brothers with me send their greetings too. 22And all the other Christians here want to be remembered to you, especially those who work in Caesar's palace. 23The blessings of our Lord Jesus Christ be upon your spirits.

4:22 There were many Christians in Rome; some were even in Caesar's palace. Perhaps Paul, while awaiting trial, was making converts of the Roman civil service! Paul sent greetings from these Roman Christians to the believers at Philippi. The gospel had spread to all strata of society, linking people who had no other bond but Christ. The Roman Christians and the Philippian Christians were brothers and sisters because of their unity in Christ. Believers today are also linked to others across cultural, economic, and social barriers. We are family—all believers truly are our brothers and sisters in Christ.

4:23 In many ways the Philippian church was a model

congregation. It was made up of many different kinds of people who were learning to work together in unity. But Paul recognized that problems could arise, so in his thank-you letter, he prepared the Philippians for difficulties that could crop up within a body of believers. Though a prisoner in Rome, Paul had learned the true secret of joy and peace—imitating Christ and serving others. By focusing our minds on Christ we will learn unity, humility, joy, and peace. We will also be motivated to live for him. We can live confidently for him because we have "the blessings of our Lord Jesus Christ" (4:23) upon us.

COLOSSIANS

VITAL STATISTICS

PURPOSE:
To combat errors in the church and to show that believers have everything they need in Christ

AUTHOR:
Paul

TO WHOM WRITTEN:
The church at Colosse, a city in Asia Minor, and all believers everywhere

DATE WRITTEN:
About A.D. 60, during Paul's imprisonment in Rome

SETTING:
Paul had never visited Colosse—evidently the church had been founded by Epaphras and other converts from Paul's missionary travels. The church, however, had been infiltrated by religious relativism with some believers attempting to combine elements of paganism and secular philosophy with Christian doctrine. Paul confronts these false teachings and affirms the sufficiency of Christ.

KEY VERSES:
"For in Christ there is all of God in human body; so you have everything when you have Christ, and you are filled with God through your union with Christ. He is the highest Ruler, with authority over every other power" (2:9, 10).

KEY PEOPLE:
Paul, Timothy, Tychicus, Onesimus, Aristarchus, Mark, Epaphras

KEY PLACES:
Colosse, Laodicea (4:15, 16)

SPECIAL FEATURES:
Christ is presented as having absolute supremacy and sole sufficiency. Colossians has similarities to Ephesians, probably because it was written at about the same time, but it has a different emphasis.

REMOVE the head coach, and the team flounders; break the fuel line, and the car won't run; unplugged the electrical appliance has no power; without the head, the body dies. Whether for leadership, power, or life, connections are vital!

Colossians is a book of connections. Writing from prison in Rome, Paul combatted false teachings which had infiltrated the Colossian church. The problem was "syncretism," combining ideas from other philosophies and religions (such as paganism, strains of Judaism, and Greek thought) with Christian truth. The resulting heresy later became known as "gnosticism," emphasizing special knowledge (*gnosis* in Greek) and denying Christ as God and Savior. To combat this devious error, Paul stressed Christ's deity and his sacrificial death on the cross for sin. Only by being connected with Christ through faith can anyone have eternal life and only through a continuing connection with him can anyone have power for living. Christ is God incarnate and the *only* way to peace with God the Father. Paul also emphasized believers' connections with each other as Christ's body on earth.

Paul's introduction to the Colossians includes a greeting, a note of thanksgiving, and a prayer for spiritual wisdom and strength for these brothers and sisters in Christ (1:1–12). He then moves into a doctrinal discussion of the person and work of Christ (1:13–23), stating that Christ is the "exact likeness of the unseen God" (1:15), the "Creator" (1:16), the "Head of the body . . . his Church" (1:18), and the "Leader of all those who arise from the dead" (1:18). His death on the cross makes it possible for us to stand in the presence of God (1:22).

Paul then explains how the world's teachings are totally empty when compared with God's plan, and he challenges the Colossians to reject shallow answers and to live in union with Christ (1:23—2:23).

Against this theological backdrop, Paul turns to practical considerations—what the divinity, death, and resurrection of Jesus should mean to all believers (3:1—4:6). Because our eternal destiny is sure, heaven should fill our thoughts (3:1–4), sexual impurity and other worldly lusts should not be named among us (3:5–8), and truth, love, and peace should mark our lives (3:9–15). Our love for Christ should also translate into love for others—friends, fellow believers, spouses, children, and parents (3:16—4:1). Furthermore, we should constantly communicate with God through prayer (4:2–4), and we should take every opportunity to tell others the Good News (4:5, 6). In Christ we have everything we need for salvation and for living the Christian life.

Paul had probably never visited Colosse, so he concludes this epistle with personal comments about their common Christian associations, providing a living lesson of the connectedness of the body of Christ.

Read Colossians as a book for an embattled church in the first century, but read it also for its timeless truths. Gain a fresh appreciation for Christ as the *fullness* of God and the *only* source for living the Christian life.

THE BLUEPRINT

1. What Christ has done (1:1—2:23)
2. What Christians should do (3:1—4:18)

In this letter Paul clearly teaches that Christ has paid for sin, that Christ has reconciled us to God, and that Christ gives us the pattern and the power to grow spiritually. Since Christ is the exact likeness of God, when we learn what he is like, we see what we need to become. Since Christ is Lord over all creation, we should crown him Lord over our lives. Since Christ is the Head of the body, his church, we should nurture our vital connection to him.

MEGATHEMES

THEME	EXPLANATION	IMPORTANCE
Christ is God	Jesus Christ is God in the flesh, Lord of all creation, and Lord of the new creation. He is the express reflection of the invisible God. He is eternal, preexistent, omnipotent, equal with the Father. He is supreme and complete.	Because Christ is supreme, our lives must be Christ centered. To recognize him as God means to regard our relationship with him most vital and to make his interests our top priority.
Christ is head of the Church	Because Christ is God, he is the head of the church, his true believers. Christ is the founder, the leader, and the highest authority on earth. He requires first place in all our thoughts and activities.	To acknowledge him as our head, we must welcome his leadership in all we do or think. No person, group, or church can regard any loyalty as more critical than that of loyalty to Christ.
Union with Christ	Because our sin has been forgiven and we have been reconciled to God, we have a union with Christ that can never be broken. In our faith connection with him, we identify with his death, burial, and resurrection.	We should live in constant contact and communication with God. When we do, we all will be unified with Christ and with one another.
Man-made religion	False teachers were promoting a heresy that stressed man-made rules (legalism). They also sought spiritual growth by asceticism and mysticism. This search created pride in their self-centered efforts.	We must not cling to our own ideas and try to blend them into Christianity. Nor should we let our hunger for a more fulfilling Christian experience cause us to trust in a teacher, a group, or a system of thought more than in Christ himself. Christ is our hope and our true source of wisdom.

1. What Christ has done

1 *From:* Paul, chosen by God to be Jesus Christ's messenger, and from Brother Timothy.   **1:1** Eph 1:1

²*To:* The faithful Christian brothers—God's people—in the city of Colosse. May God our Father shower you with blessings and fill you with his great peace.   **1:2** Rom 1:7

Paul's prayer for the Colossian believers

³Whenever we pray for you we always begin by giving thanks to God the Father of our Lord Jesus Christ, ⁴for we have heard how much you trust the Lord, and how much you love his people. ⁵And you are looking forward to the joys of heaven, and have been ever since the Gospel first was preached to you. ⁶The same Good News   **1:4** Eph 1:15   **1:5** Eph 1:13 1 Pet 1:4

The Heresy	Reference	Paul's Answer
Spirit is good; matter is evil.	1:15–20	God created heaven and earth for his glory.
One must follow ceremonies, rituals, and restrictions in order to be saved or perfected.	2:11, 16–23; 3:11	These were only shadows that ended when Christ came. He is all you need to be saved.
One must deny the body and live in strict asceticism.	2:20–23	This is no help in conquering evil thoughts and desires, instead it leads to pride.
Angels must be worshiped.	2:18	Angels are not to be worshiped; Christ alone is worthy of worship.
Christ could not be both human and divine.	1:15–20; 2:2, 3	Christ is God in the flesh; he is the eternal One, Head of the body, first in everything, supreme.
One must obtain "secret knowledge" in order to be saved or perfected—and this was not available to everyone.	2:2, 18	God's secret is Christ, and he has been revealed to all.
One must adhere to human wisdom, tradition, and philosophies.	2:4, 8–10; 3:15–17	By themselves, these can be misleading and shallow because they have human origin; instead, we should remember what Christ taught and follow his words as our ultimate authority.
It is even better to combine aspects of several religions.	2:10	You have everything when you have Christ; he is all-sufficient.
There is nothing wrong with immorality.	3:1–11	Get rid of sin and evil because you have been chosen by God and must live a new life as a representative of the Lord Jesus.

THE COLOSSIAN HERESY
Paul answered the various tenets of the Colossian heresy that threatened the church. This heresy was a "mixed bag," containing elements from several different heresies, some of which contradicted each other (as the chart shows).

1:1 Colossians, along with Philippians, Ephesians, and Philemon, is called a *prison epistle* because Paul wrote it from prison in Rome. This prison was actually a house where Paul was kept under close guard at all times (probably chained to a soldier) but given certain freedoms not offered to most prisoners: he was allowed to write letters and to see any visitors he wanted to see.

1:1 Paul and Timothy worked together on other New Testament letters: 2 Corinthians, Philippians, 1 and 2 Thessalonians, and Philemon. Paul also wrote two letters to Timothy (1 and 2 Timothy). For more information on these men, two of the greatest missionaries of the early church, see Paul's Profile in Acts 9 and Timothy's Profile in 1 Timothy.

1:1 The city of Colosse was 100 miles east of Ephesus on the Lycus River. It was not as influential as the nearby city of Laodicea, but as a trading center it was a crossroads for ideas and religions. Colosse had a large Jewish population—many Jews fled there when they were forced out of Jerusalem under the persecutions of Antiochus III and IV, almost 200 years before Christ. The church in Colosse was founded by Epaphras (1:7), one of Paul's converts.

Paul had not yet visited this church. His purpose in writing was to refute a heretical teaching about Christ, which had been causing confusion among the Christians there.

1:2, 3 Letters in Paul's day frequently began with the writer's name, followed by a blessing. Paul usually added Christian elements to his greetings, reminding his readers of his call by God to spread the gospel, emphasizing that the authority for his words came from God, and giving thanks for God's blessings.

1:4, 5 Throughout this letter Paul combats a heresy related to *gnosticism* (see note on 2:4). Gnostics believed it took special knowledge to be accepted by God; for them, even if they claimed to be Christians, Christ alone was not the way of salvation (1:20). In his introductory comments, therefore, Paul commends the Colossians for their faith, hope, and love—three main emphases of Christianity (1 Corinthians 13:13). He deliberately omits any mention of knowledge because of the heresy. It is not *what* one knows that makes him a Christian, but *whom* he knows. Knowing Christ is knowing God.

1:6 Wherever Paul went, he preached the gospel—to Gentile

that came to you is going out all over the world and changing lives everywhere, just as it changed yours that very first day you heard it and understood about God's great kindness to sinners.

1:7
Col 4:12,13
Philem 23

7Epaphras, our much-loved fellow worker, was the one who brought you this Good News. He is Jesus Christ's faithful slave, here to help us in your place. 8And he is the one who has told us about the great love for others which the Holy Spirit has given you.

1:9
Rom 12:2
Eph 1:15-17

1:10
Jn 15:16
Eph 4:1
1 Thess 2:12
4:1

9So ever since we first heard about you we have kept on praying and asking God to help you understand what he wants you to do; asking him to make you wise about spiritual things; 10and asking that the way you live will always please the Lord and

LOCATION OF COLOSSE
Paul had no doubt been through Laodicea on his third missionary journey, as it lay on the main route to Ephesus, but he had never been to Colosse. Though a large city with a significant population, Colosse was smaller and less important than the nearby cities of Laodicea and Hieropolis.

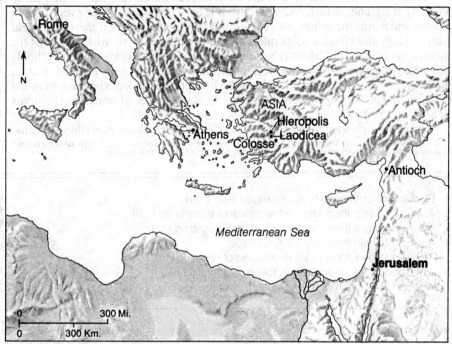

audiences, to hostile Jewish leaders, and even to his Roman guards. Whenever people believed in the message he spoke, they were changed. God's Word is not just for our information, it is for our transformation! Becoming a Christian means beginning a whole new relationship with God, not just turning over a new leaf or determining to do right. New believers have a changed purpose, direction, attitude, and behavior. They no longer seek to serve themselves, but to serve God. Can you point to any areas where hearing God's Word has changed your life, or where it should do so?

1:7 Epaphras probably founded the church at Colosse while Paul was living in Ephesus (Acts 19:10). He may have been converted in Ephesus, then returned to Colosse, his hometown. For some reason, Epaphras visited Rome and, while there, told Paul about the problem with the Colossian heresy. This prompted Paul to write this letter. Epaphras is also mentioned in Philemon 1:23 (the Colossian church met in Philemon's house).

1:8 Because of their love for one another, Christians can have an impact that goes far beyond their neighborhoods and communities. Christian love for others comes from the Holy Spirit (see Galatians 5:22). The Bible speaks of it as an action and attitude, not just an emotion. It is a by-product of our new life in Christ (see Romans 5:5; 1 Corinthians 13). Christians have no excuse for not loving others, because Christian love is not a feeling but a decision to *act* in the best interests of others.

1:9-14 Paul was exposing a heresy in the Colossian church that was a forerunner of *gnosticism* (see the note on 2:4 for more information). Gnostics valued the accumulation of knowledge, but Paul pointed out that knowledge in itself is empty. To be worth anything, it must lead to a changed life and right living. His prayer for the Colossians (1:9-14) has two dimensions—that they might *understand* what God wants, and that they might also have the power *to do* God's will. Knowledge is not merely to be accumulated; it should give us direction for living. Paul wanted the Colossians to be wise, but to *use* their knowledge. Knowledge of God is not a secret that only a few can discover; it is open to everyone. God wants us not only to learn more about him, but also to live for him and do his will.

1:9-14 Sometimes we wonder how to pray for missionaries and other leaders we have never met. Paul had never met the Colossians, but he faithfully prayed for them. His prayers teach us how to pray for others, whether we know them or not. We can request that they (1) understand God's will, (2) gain spiritual wisdom, (3) live lives pleasing and honoring to God, (4) do kind things for others, (5) know God better and better, (6) be filled with God's strength, (7) endure in faith, (8) stay full of Christ's joy, and (9) always be thankful. All believers have these same basic needs. When you don't know how to pray for someone, remember Paul's prayer pattern for the Colossians.

honor him, so that you will always be doing good, kind things for others, while all the time you are learning to know God better and better.

¹¹We are praying, too, that you will be filled with his mighty, glorious strength so that you can keep going no matter what happens—always full of the joy of the Lord, ¹²and always thankful to the Father who has made us fit to share all the wonderful things that belong to those who live in the Kingdom of light. ¹³For he has rescued us out of the darkness and gloom of Satan's kingdom and brought us into the Kingdom of his dear Son, ¹⁴who bought our freedom with his blood and forgave us all our sins.

1:11
Acts 5:41
Eph 3:16,20
1:12
Acts 26:18
Eph 1:11; 5:20
1:13
Acts 26:18
Heb 2:14,15
1:14
Eph 1:7

Person and work of Christ

¹⁵Christ is the exact likeness of the unseen God. He existed before God made anything at all, and, in fact, ¹⁶Christ himself is the Creator who made everything in heaven and earth, the things we can see and the things we can't; the spirit world with its kings and kingdoms, its rulers and authorities; all were made by Christ for his own use and glory. ¹⁷He was before all else began and it is his power that holds everything together. ¹⁸He is the Head of the body made up of his people—that is, his Church—which he began; and he is the Leader of all those who arise from the dead, so that he is first in everything; ¹⁹for God wanted all of himself to be in his Son.

²⁰It was through what his Son did that God cleared a path for everything to come

1:15
Jn 1:1,18; 14:9
2 Cor 4:4
Rev 3:14
1:16
Jn 1:3
Heb 1:2
1:17
Jn 1:1,2; 8:58
1:18
Eph 1:22,23
1:19
Jn 1:16
Col 2:9

1:15 *He existed before God made anything at all,* literally, "He is the firstborn of all creation." **1:18** *he is the Leader of all those who arise from the dead,* literally, "he is the Beginning, the firstborn from the dead."

---

1. Be thankful for their faith and changed lives (1:3)
2. Ask God to help them know what he wants them to do (1:9)
3. Ask God to give them deep spiritual understanding (1:9)
4. Ask God to help them live for him (1:10)
5. Ask God to give them more knowledge of himself (1:10)
6. Ask God to give them strength for endurance (1:11)
7. Ask God to fill them with joy, strength, and thankfulness (1:11)

HOW TO PRAY FOR OTHER CHRISTIANS How many people in your life could be touched if you prayed in this way?

1:13 The Colossians feared the unseen forces of darkness, but Paul says that true believers have been transferred from darkness to light, from slavery to freedom, from guilt to forgiveness, and from the power of Satan to the power of God. We have been rescued from a rebel kingdom to serve the rightful King.

1:14 In verses 12–14, Paul lists five benefits God secured for us when Christ died on the cross: (1) he made us fit to be part of his Kingdom (see also 2 Corinthians 5:21); (2) he rescued us from Satan's domination and made us his children (see also 2:15); (3) he brought us into his eternal Kingdom (see also Ephesians 1:5, 6); (4) he bought our freedom from sin and judgment (see also Hebrews 9:12); and (5) he forgave all our sins (see also Ephesians 1:7).

1:15–23 The Colossian church had several misconceptions about Christ, which Paul directly refutes: (1) They believed that matter is evil, so they said God would not have come to earth as a true human being in bodily form. Paul states that Christ is the exact likeness of God, is himself God, and yet died on the cross as a human being. (2) They believed God did not create the world because he would not have created evil. Paul says that Jesus Christ, who was also God in the flesh, is the Creator of both heaven and earth. (3) They said Christ was not the unique Son of God, but rather one of many intermediaries between God and people. Paul explains that Christ existed before anything else and is the firstborn of those resurrected. (4) They refused to see Christ as the source of salvation, insisting that people could find God through special and secret knowledge. Paul affirms that a person can be saved through Christ alone.

1:15, 16 This is one of the strongest statements about the divine

nature of Christ found anywhere in the Bible. Jesus is not only equal to God (Philippians 2:6), he is God (John 10:30, 38; 12:45; 14:1–11). He not only reflects God, but he reveals God to us (John 1:18; 14:9). He came from heaven, not from the dust of the ground (1 Corinthians 15:47), and is Lord of all (Romans 9:5; 10:11–13; Revelation 1:5; 17:14). He is completely holy (Hebrews 7:26–28; 1 Peter 1:19; 2:22; 1 John 3:5), and he has authority to judge the world (Romans 2:16; 2 Corinthians 5:10; 2 Timothy 4:1). Therefore, he is supreme over all creation, including the spirit world. We, like the Colossian believers, must believe in the deity of Jesus Christ (that Jesus is God), or our Christian faith is hollow, misdirected, and meaningless. This is a central truth of Christianity.

1:16 Because the false teachers believed the physical world was evil, they thought God himself could not have created it. If Christ were God, they reasoned, he would be in charge only of the spiritual world. But Paul explains that both the spiritual and physical worlds were created by and are under the authority of Christ himself. He has no equal and no rival. For more on the connection between our spiritual and physical selves, see the note on 1 Corinthians 6:12, 13.

1:18 The resurrection proves Christ's lordship over the material world. All who trust in Christ will also defeat death and rise again to live eternally with him (1 Corinthians 15:20; 1 Thessalonians 4:14). See the note on Luke 24:6, 7 for more about the significance of Christ's resurrection.

1:19 Christ is fully divine (see the note on Philippians 2:5–7). Christ has always been God and will always be God.

1:20 Christ's death provided a way for all people to come to God. It cleared away the sin that keeps us from having a right

to him—all things in heaven and on earth—for Christ's death on the cross has made peace with God for all by his blood. 21This includes you who were once so far away from God. You were his enemies and hated him and were separated from him by your evil thoughts and actions, yet now he has brought you back as his friends. 22He has done this through the death on the cross of his own human body, and now as a result Christ has brought you into the very presence of God, and you are standing there before him with nothing left against you—nothing left that he could even chide you for; 23the only condition is that you fully believe the Truth, standing in it steadfast and firm, strong in the Lord, convinced of the Good News that Jesus died for you, and never shifting from trusting him to save you. This is the wonderful news that came to each of you and is now spreading all over the world. And I, Paul, have the joy of telling it to others.

Paul's mission and concern

24But part of my work is to suffer for you; and I am glad, for I am helping to finish up the remainder of Christ's sufferings for his body, the Church.

25God has sent me to help his Church and to tell his secret plan to you Gentiles. 26, 27He has kept this secret for centuries and generations past, but now at last it has pleased him to tell it to those who love him and live for him, and the riches and glory of his plan are for you Gentiles too. And this is the secret: *that Christ in your hearts is your only hope of glory.*

28So everywhere we go we talk about Christ to all who will listen, warning them and teaching them as well as we know how. We want to be able to present each one to God, perfect because of what Christ has done for each of them. 29This is my work, and I can do it only because Christ's mighty energy is at work within me.

2 I wish you could know how much I have struggled in prayer for you and for the church at Laodicea, and for my many other friends who have never known me personally. 2This is what I have asked of God for you: that you will be encouraged and knit together by strong ties of love, and that you will have the rich experience of knowing Christ with real certainty and clear understanding. *For God's secret*

1:21
Rom 5:10
2 Cor 5:18,19
Eph 2:3,12

1:22
Rom 7:4
Eph 1:4; 5:27

1:23
Eph 3:17
Col 1:5,6

1:24
Phil 2:17; 3:10
2 Tim 1:8

1:25
Eph 3:2

1:26
Eph 3:3

1:27
Rom 8:10; 9:23,24
Eph 3:8,9,16

1:28
Eph 4:13

1:29
Eph 1:19
Col 4:12

2:1
Col 4:12,13

2:2
Mt 11:25-27
Eph 1:18,19
Phil 3:8
Col 2:19

---

relationship with our Creator. This does not mean that everyone has been saved, but that the way has been cleared for anyone who will trust Christ to be saved. God gives salvation to all those who by faith accept Christ's death for themselves.

1:21, 22 *No one* is good enough to save himself. If we want to live eternally with Christ, we must depend totally on God's grace. This is true whether we have been murderers or honest, hardworking citizens. We have all sinned repeatedly, and *any* sin is enough to cause us to depend on Jesus Christ for salvation and eternal life. Apart from Christ, there is no way to be saved from sin.

1:22, 23 The way to be declared not guilty for our sins is to trust Jesus Christ to take them away. Trusting means putting our confidence in him to forgive our sins, to make us right with God, and to empower us to live the way he wants us to live. When a judge in a court of law declares the defendant "not guilty," he has been acquitted of all the charges. Legally, it is as if the person had never been accused. When God forgives our sins, our record is wiped clean. From his perspective, it is as though we had never sinned. This is God's solution, and it is available to all of us regardless of our background or past behavior.

1:24 When Paul says he is finishing up the remainder of Christ's suffering, he does not mean Christ's suffering was inadequate to save us, nor does he mean that there is a predetermined amount of suffering that must be paid by all believers. Paul is simply saying that suffering is unavoidable in bringing the Good News of Christ to the world. It is called Christ's suffering because of our relationship to Christ. When we suffer, Christ feels it with us. But this suffering can be endured joyfully because it changes lives and brings people into God's Kingdom (see 1 Peter 4:1, 2, 12–19). For more about how Paul could be glad despite his suffering, see the note on Philippians 1:29.

1:26, 27 The false teachers in the Colossian church believed spiritual perfection was a secret and hidden plan that only a few privileged people would discover. Their secret plan was meant to be exclusive. Paul calls God's plan a secret, not in the sense that only a few would understand, but because it was hidden until Christ came. Who could have imagined that God's secret plan was to have his Son, Jesus Christ, live in the hearts of all who believe in him.

1:28 The word *perfect* means mature or complete, not flawless. Paul wanted to see each believer mature spiritually. To mature, we must grow daily in our faith.

1:28, 29 Christ's message is for everyone; so everywhere Paul and Timothy went they brought the Good News to all who would listen. An effective presentation of the gospel includes warning and teaching. The warning is that without Christ, people are doomed to eternal separation from God. The teaching is that salvation is available through faith in Christ. As Christ works in you, tell others about him, warning and teaching them in love. Do you know someone who needs to hear this message?

2:1 Laodicea was located a few miles northwest of Colosse. Like the church at Colosse, the Laodicean church was probably founded by one of Paul's converts while Paul was staying in Ephesus (Acts 19:10). The city was wealthy, a center of trade and commerce, but later the apostle John would criticize the believers for their lukewarm commitment to Christ (Revelation 3:14–22). The fact that Paul wanted this letter to be passed on to the Laodicean church (4:16) indicates that false teaching had spread there as well. Paul was counting on ties of love to bring the churches together to stand against this heresy and to encourage each other to remain true to God's plan of salvation in Christ.

plan, now at last made known, is Christ himself. ³In him lie hidden all the mighty, untapped treasures of wisdom and knowledge.

2:3
Isa 11:2
Rom 11:33
Eph 3:8

⁴I am saying this because I am afraid that someone may fool you with smooth talk. ⁵For though I am far away from you my heart is with you, happy because you are getting along so well, happy because of your strong faith in Christ.

2:5
1 Cor 5:7

New life in Christ

⁶And now just as you trusted Christ to save you, trust him, too, for each day's problems; live in vital union with him. ⁷Let your roots grow down into him and draw up nourishment from him. See that you go on growing in the Lord, and become strong and vigorous in the truth you were taught. Let your lives overflow with joy and thanksgiving for all he has done.

2:6
Jn 1:12
Col 1:10

2:7
Eph 2:20; 3:17

⁸Don't let others spoil your faith and joy with their philosophies, their wrong and shallow answers built on men's thoughts and ideas, instead of on what Christ has said. ⁹For in Christ there is all of God in a human body; ¹⁰*so you have everything when you have Christ,* and you are filled with God through your union with Christ. He is the highest Ruler, with authority over every other power.

2:8
Jer 29:8
Mt 15:2,3
Col 2:20,23
Heb 13:9

2:9
Isa 7:14; 9:6
Jn 1:14
Col 1:19

¹¹When you came to Christ he set you free from your evil desires, not by a bodily operation of circumcision but by a spiritual operation, the baptism of your souls.

2:10
Eph 1:21; 3:19
1 Pet 3:22

	Religion by Self-effort	Salvation by Faith	
Goal	Please God by our own good works	Trust in Christ and then live to please God	**SALVATION BY FAITH**
Means	Practice diligent service, discipline, and obedience, in hope of reward	Confess, submit, and commit yourself to Christ's control	
Power	Good, honest effort through self-determination	The Holy Spirit in us helps us do good work for Christ's Kingdom	
Control	Self-motivation; self-control	Christ in me; I in Christ	
Results	Chronic decision-making, apathy, depression, failure, constant desire for approval	Joy, thankfulness, love, guidance, service, forgiveness	

Salvation by faith in Christ sounds too easy for many people. They would rather think that they have done something to save themselves. Their religion becomes one of self-effort that leads either to disappointment or pride, but finally to eternal death. Christ's simple way is the only way, and it alone leads to eternal life.

2:4ff The problem Paul was combatting in the Colossian church was similar to *gnosticism* (from the Greek word for "knowledge"). This *heresy* (a teaching contrary to biblical doctrine) attacked Christianity in several basic ways: (1) It insisted that important hidden knowledge was secret from most believers; Paul, however, said that in Christ we see all we need to see of God's provision for us. (2) It taught that the body was evil; Paul countered that God himself dwelt in a body—that is, he was embodied in Jesus Christ. (3) It said that Christ seemed to be human, but was not. Paul insisted that in Jesus we see one who is fully human and fully God.

Gnosticism became fashionable in the second century. Even in Paul's day, these ideas sounded attractive to many and could easily seduce a church that didn't know Christian doctrine well. Aspects of this early heresy still pose significant problems for many in the church today. The antidote for heretical ideas is a thorough acquaintance with God's Word through personal study and sound Bible teaching.

2:6, 7 Accepting Christ as Lord of your life is the beginning of life with Christ. But you must continue to follow his leadership. Every day he desires to guide you and help you with your daily problems. You can live for Christ by (1) committing your life and submitting your will to him (Romans 12:1, 2); (2) seeking to learn from him, his life, and his teachings (3:16); and (3) recognizing the Holy Spirit's power in you (Acts 1:8; Galatians 5:22).

2:7 Paul used the illustration of our being rooted in or connected to Christ. As plants draw nourishment from the soil through their roots, so we draw our life-giving strength from Christ. The more we draw our life from him, the less we will be fooled by those who falsely claim to have life's answers (2:8).

2:8 Paul writes against any philosophy of life based only on human ideas and experiences. Paul himself was a gifted philosopher, so he is not condemning philosophy. He was condemning teaching that credits humanity, not Christ, with being the answer to life's problems and thus becomes a false religion. The way to resist heresy is not to quit using your mind and retreat, but to focus on Christ's words as the foundation for your faith.

2:9 Again Paul asserts Christ's deity. The totality of God is embodied in Christ. See the note on 1:15, 16.

2:10 When we know Jesus Christ, we don't need to investigate other religions, cults, or unbiblical philosophies as the Colossians were doing. Christ alone holds the answers to the true meaning of life, because Christ *is* life. He is the unique source for the Christian life; therefore, no Christian needs anything he has not provided.

2:11, 12 Jewish males were circumcised as a sign of the Jews' covenant with God (Genesis 17:9-14; Deuteronomy 10:16). With the death of Christ, circumcision was no longer necessary. Now our commitment to God is written on our souls, not our bodies. In baptism we let God operate on our souls to put off the old nature and to make room for the new nature.

2:12 In the church in Paul's day, immersion was the usual form of baptism—that is, new Christians were completely "buried" in water. They understood this form of baptism to symbolize the

2:12
Rom 6:4,5
Eph 2:6

12For in baptism you see how your old, evil nature died with him and was buried with him; and then you came up out of death with him into a new life because you trusted the Word of the mighty God who raised Christ from the dead.

2:13
Eph 2:1,5

13You were dead in sins, and your sinful desires were not yet cut away. Then he gave you a share in the very life of Christ, for he forgave all your sins, 14and blotted out the charges proved against you, the list of his commandments which you had not obeyed. He took this list of sins and destroyed it by nailing it to Christ's cross. 15In this way God took away Satan's power to accuse you of sin, and God openly displayed to the whole world Christ's triumph at the cross where your sins were all taken away.

2:14
Eph 2:15
1 Pet 2:24

2:15
Isa 53:12
Jn 12:31
2 Cor 2:14
Eph 4:8

Freedom from legalism

2:16
1 Chron 23:31
Rom 14:3,5
Gal 4:10

16So don't let anyone criticize you for what you eat or drink, or for not celebrating Jewish holidays and feasts or new moon ceremonies or Sabbaths. 17For these were only temporary rules that ended when Christ came. They were only shadows of the real thing—of Christ himself. 18Don't let anyone declare you lost when you refuse to worship angels, as they say you must. They have seen a vision, they say,

2:17
Heb 8:5; 10:1

TRUST: YESTERDAY, TODAY, AND TOMORROW!
Living the lordship of Christ means realizing that each day brings new opportunities to trust Christ and experience his powerful work in us. Have you trusted this day to Christ?

1. Trusting Christ = living in vital union with Christ day by day (Colossians 2:2–7)

2. Accepting Christ as Head or Lord = he is in control (Colossians 1:15–18; 2:19; 3:10, 17)

3. Experiencing the power of the Holy Spirit = God's mighty energy at work in us (Colossians 1:11, 28, 29)

4. Inward and outward results =
   ● assurance of forgiveness (Colossians 2:15)
   ● freedom from evil desires (Colossians 2:11)
   ● happiness (joy) (Colossians 2:7)
   ● personal growth (Colossians 1:28)
   ● opportunities to tell others the gospel (Colossians 1:4, 28)
   ● thankfulness to God (Colossians 2:7)

5. Direction = God becoming involved in our decisions (Colossians 3:1, 16)

---

death and burial of the old way of life, followed by resurrection to life with Christ. If we think of our old, sinful life as dead and buried, we have a powerful motive to resist sin. Not wanting the ugly old life to come back to power again, we can consciously choose to treat it as if it were dead. Then we continue to enjoy our wonderful new life with Jesus (see Galatians 3:27 and Colossians 3:1–4 for more on this concept).

2:12-15 Before we believed in Christ, our nature was evil. The Christian, however, has a new nature. God has crucified the old rebellious nature (Romans 6:6) and replaced it with a new loving nature (Colossians 3:9, 10). The penalty of sin died with Christ on the cross. God has declared us not guilty, and we need no longer live under sin's power. God does not take us out of the world or make us robots—we will still feel like sinning, and sometimes we will sin. The difference is that before we were saved, we were slaves to our sinful nature, but now we can choose to live for Christ (see Galatians 2:20).

2:15 We can enjoy our new life in Christ because we have joined him in his death and resurrection. Our evil desires, our bondage to sin, and our love of sin died with him. Now, joining him in his resurrection life, we may have unbroken fellowship with God and freedom from sin. Our debt for sin has been paid in full; our sins are swept away and forgotten by God; and we can be clean and new. For more on the difference between our new life in Christ and our old sinful nature, read Ephesians 4:23, 24 and Colossians 3:3–15.

2:16, 17 Paul told the Colossian Christians not to let others criticize their diet or their religious ceremonies. Instead of outward observance, they should focus on Christ alone. In our worship,

traditions and ceremonies can help bring us close to God, but we should never criticize fellow Christians whose traditions and ceremonies differ from ours. The Bible does not define how we should worship, only *whom*.

2:17 The purpose of the Old Testament laws, holidays, and feasts was simply to point toward Christ. Paul calls them shadows of the real thing—Christ himself. Once Christ came, he dispelled the shadows.

2:18 The false teachers claimed that God was remote and could be approached only through various levels of angels. They taught that people had to worship angels in order eventually to reach God. This is unscriptural; the Bible teaches that angels are inferior to God, and it forbids worshiping them (Exodus 20:3, 4; Revelation 22:8, 9).

2:18 The false teachers were proud of their humility! This false humility brought attention and praise to themselves rather than to God. True humility is viewing ourselves as we really are from God's perspective and acting accordingly. People today practice false humility when they talk themselves down so that others will think they are spiritual. False humility is self-centered; true humility is God centered.

2:18 The expression "clever imagination" has also been translated "fleshly minds," which is another way of saying that these men had a man-made religion. Paul pointed out that the false teachers were trying to deny the body by saying it was evil, but their desire for attention from others showed they were actually obsessed by it. Their philosophy that the flesh was evil came from the flesh itself—they made it up (2:8).

and know you should. These proud men (though they claim to be so humble) have a very clever imagination. [19]But they are not connected to Christ, the Head to which all of us who are his body are joined; for we are joined together by his strong sinews and we grow only as we get our nourishment and strength from God.

2:19
Eph 1:22,23
4:15,16

[20]Since you died, as it were, with Christ and this has set you free from following the world's ideas of how to be saved—by doing good and obeying various rules—why do you keep right on following them anyway, still bound by such rules as [21]not eating, tasting, or even touching certain foods? [22]Such rules are mere human teachings, for food was made to be eaten and used up. [23]These rules may seem good, for rules of this kind require strong devotion and are humiliating and hard on the body, but they have no effect when it comes to conquering a person's evil thoughts and desires. They only make him proud.

2:20
Rom 6:2
Gal 2:20; 4:9

2:22
Mt 15:9
1 Cor 6:13

2:23
1 Tim 4:3

2. What Christians should do
Principles of Christian living

3 Since you became alive again, so to speak, when Christ arose from the dead, now set your sights on the rich treasures and joys of heaven where he sits

3:1
Mt 6:33
Eph 2:6

2:20 *obeying various rules*, literally, "by the rudiments of the world."

The Bible uses many illustrations to teach what happens when we choose to let Jesus be Lord of our lives. Following are some of the most vivid pictures:

FROM DEATH TO LIFE

1. Because Christ died for us, we have been crucified with him.

Romans 6:2–13; 7:4–6
2 Corinthians 5:14
Galatians 2:20; 5:24; 6:14
Colossians 2:20; 3:3–5
1 Peter 2:24

2. Our old, rebellious nature died with Christ.

Romans 6:6; 7:4–6
Colossians 3:9, 10

3. Christ's resurrection guarantees our new life now and eternal life with him later.

Romans 6:4, 11
Colossians 2:12, 13; 3:1, 3

This process is acted out in baptism (Colossians 2:12), based on our faith in Christ: (1) The old evil nature dies (crucified); (2) We are ready to receive a new life (buried); (3) Christ gives us new life (resurrected).

2:19 The fundamental problem with the false teachers is that they were not connected to Christ. If they had been joined to him, they could not have taught false doctrine or lived evil lives. Anyone who teaches about God without being connected to him by faith is going to speak falsely about him.

2:20; 3:1 How do we die with Christ, and how are we raised with him? When a person becomes a Christian, he is given new life through the power of the Holy Spirit. See the notes on 2:12 and 2:12–15 for further information.

2:20–23 People should be able to see a difference between the way Christians and non-Christians live. Still, we should not expect instant maturity of new Christians. The Christian life is a process. Although we have a new nature, we don't automatically have all good thoughts and attitudes when we become new people in Christ. But if we keep listening to God, we will be changing all the time. As you look over the last year, what changes for the better have you seen in your thoughts and attitudes? Change may be slow, but your life will change significantly if you trust God to change you.

2:20–24 We cannot reach up to God by following rules and rituals or by practicing religion. Paul isn't saying all rules are bad (see the note on Galatians 2:16). But no keeping of laws or rules will earn salvation. The Good News is that God reaches down to man, and we respond. Man-made religions focus on human effort; Christianity focuses on Christ's work. Paul agrees that believers must put aside sinful desires, but that is the by-product of our new

life in Christ, not the cause of it. Our salvation does not depend on our own discipline and rule keeping, but on the power of Christ's death and resurrection.

2:22, 23 We can guard against man-made religions by asking these questions of any religious group: (1) Does it stress man-made rules and taboos rather than God's grace? (2) Does it foster a critical spirit about others, or does it exercise discipline discreetly and lovingly? (3) Does it stress formulas, secret knowledge, or special visions more than the Word of God? (4) Does it elevate self-righteousness, honoring those who keep the rules, rather than elevating Christ? (5) Does it neglect Christ's universal church, claiming to be an elite group? (6) Does it teach humiliation of the body as a means to spiritual growth rather than focusing on the growth of the whole person? (7) Does it disregard the family rather than holding it in high regard as the Bible does?

2:23 To the Colossians, the discipline demanded by the false teachers seemed good, and legalism still attracts many people today. Following a long list of religious rules requires strong self-discipline and can make a person appear moral, but religious rules cannot change a person's heart. Only the Holy Spirit can do that.

3:1ff In chapter 2, Paul exposed the wrong reasons for self-denial. In chapter 3, he explains true Christian behavior—putting on the new nature by accepting Christ and letting the old nature die. We change our behavior by letting Christ live within us, so that he can shape us into what we *should* be rather than merely what we might want to be in ourselves.

3:2
Phil 3:19,20

3:3
Gal 2:20

3:4
1 Cor 15:43
1 Jn 3:2

3:5
Mk 7:21-23
Rom 8:13
Gal 5:19
Eph 5:3,5
3:7
Eph 2:2

3:8
Eph 4:22,29
Jas 1:21

3:9
Eph 4:22,25

3:10
Rom 8:29; 12:2
Eph 2:10; 4:24

3:11
Rom 10:12
1 Cor 12:13
Gal 3:28

3:12
Gal 5:22
Eph 4:2,24
1 Pet 1:2

3:13
Eph 4:32

beside God in the place of honor and power. 2Let heaven fill your thoughts; don't spend your time worrying about things down here. 3You should have as little desire for this world as a dead person does. Your real life is in heaven with Christ and God. 4And when Christ who is our real life comes back again, you will shine with him and share in all his glories.

5Away then with sinful, earthly things; deaden the evil desires lurking within you; have nothing to do with sexual sin, impurity, lust and shameful desires; don't worship the good things of life, for that is idolatry. 6God's terrible anger is upon those who do such things. 7You used to do them when your life was still part of this world; 8but now is the time to cast off and throw away all these rotten garments of anger, hatred, cursing, and dirty language.

9Don't tell lies to each other; it was your old life with all its wickedness that did that sort of thing; now it is dead and gone. 10You are living a brand new kind of life that is continually learning more and more of what is right, and trying constantly to be more and more like Christ who created this new life within you. 11In this new life one's nationality or race or education or social position is unimportant; such things mean nothing. Whether a person has Christ is what matters, and he is equally available to all.

12Since you have been chosen by God who has given you this new kind of life, and because of his deep love and concern for you, you should practice tenderhearted mercy and kindness to others. Don't worry about making a good impression on them but be ready to suffer quietly and patiently. 13Be gentle and ready to forgive;

SINS VS. SIGNS OF LOVE	*Sins of Sexual Attitude and Behavior*	*Sins of Speech*	*Signs of love*
	Evil desires	Anger expressed	Tender-hearted mercy
	Sexual sin	Cursing	Kindness
	Impurity	Dirty language	Humility
	Lust	Lying	Patience
	Shameful desires		Gentleness
			Forgiveness

In Colossians 3:5 Paul tells us to consider ourselves dead to list 1. In 3:8 he tells us to cast off list 2. In 3:12 we're told to practice list 3. List 1 deals with sins of sexual attitudes and behavior—they are particularly destructive because of what they do to destroy any group or church. List 2 deals with sins of speech—these are the relationship-breakers. List 3 contains the relationship-builders, which we are to express as members of Christ's body.

3:2, 3 The Christian's real home is where Christ lives (John 14:2, 3). This gives us a different perspective on our lives here on earth. To let heaven fill your thoughts means to look at life from God's perspective. This is the antidote to materialism; we gain the proper perspective on material goods when we take God's view of them. The more we see the life around us as God sees it, the more we live in harmony with him. We must not become too attached to what is only temporary.

3:4 Christ gives us power to help us live now, and he gives us hope for the future—he will return again. In the rest of this chapter Paul explains how Christians should live *now* in order to be prepared for Christ's return.

3:5 We should consider ourselves dead and unresponsive to evil desires: sexual sin, impurity, lustful desires, and materialism. This is never easy, so we must make a conscious, daily decision to live according to God's values and to rely on the Holy Spirit's power.

3:8 Paul's words to "cast off and throw away" the rotten garments of sin can also be translated, "lay aside the old self and put on the new." Paul was appealing to the commitment the believers had made in their baptism (see the note on 2:12) and urging them to remain true to their confession of faith. They were to "cast off" the old life and "put on" the new life given by Christ and guided by the Holy Spirit. If you have made such a commitment, are you remaining true to it?

3:10 The Christian is in a continuing education program. The more we know of Christ and his work, the more we are being changed to be like him. Because this process is lifelong, we must never cease learning and obeying. There is no justification for drifting along, but there is an incentive to find the rich treasures of growing in him. It takes practice, review, patience, and concentration to keep in line with his will. For more on this idea, see the note on 2:12–15.

3:11 Barriers of nationality, race, education, social standing, wealth, and power should not apply in the Christian church. Christ breaks down all barriers and accepts all people who come to him. Nothing should keep us from telling others about Christ or accepting into our fellowship any and all believers (Ephesians 2:14, 15). Christians should be in the business of building bridges, not walls.

3:12–17 Paul offers a strategy to help us live for God day by day: (1) imitate Christ's merciful, forgiving spirit (3:12, 13); (2) let love guide your life (3:14); (3) let the peace of Christ rule in your heart (3:15); (4) always be thankful (3:15); (5) keep God's Word in you at all times (3:16); (6) do everything as though you were Jesus Christ's representative (3:17).

3:13 The key to forgiving others is remembering how much God has forgiven you. Realizing God's infinite love and forgiveness can help you love and forgive others.

never hold grudges. Remember, the Lord forgave you, so you must forgive others. | **3:14** Rom 13:8

14Most of all, let love guide your life, for then the whole church will stay together in perfect harmony. 15Let the peace of heart which comes from Christ be always present in your hearts and lives, for this is your responsibility and privilege as members of his body. And always be thankful. | **3:15** Jn 14:27 Eph 2:14-16 Phil 4:7

16Remember what Christ taught and let his words enrich your lives and make you wise; teach them to each other and sing them out in psalms and hymns and spiritual songs, singing to the Lord with thankful hearts. 17And whatever you do or say, let it be as a representative of the Lord Jesus, and come with him into the presence of God the Father to give him your thanks. | **3:16** Jer 15:16 Rom 10:17 Eph 5:19 2 Tim 3:15-17 | **3:17** Eph 5:20 1 Thess 5:18

Principles for relationships

18You wives, submit yourselves to your husbands, for that is what the Lord has planned for you. 19And you husbands must be loving and kind to your wives and not bitter against them, nor harsh. | **3:18** Eph 5:22 | **3:19** Eph 5:25

20You children must always obey your fathers and mothers, for that pleases the Lord. 21Fathers, don't scold your children so much that they become discouraged and quit trying. | **3:20** Eph 6:1 | **3:21** Eph 6:4

22You slaves must always obey your earthly masters, not only trying to please them when they are watching you but all the time; obey them willingly because of your love for the Lord and because you want to please him. 23Work hard and cheerfully at all you do, just as though you were working for the Lord and not merely for your masters, 24remembering that it is the Lord Christ who is going to pay you, giving you your full portion of all he owns. He is the one you are really working for. 25And if you don't do your best for him, he will pay you in a way that | **3:22** Eph 6:5,6 | **3:23** Eph 6:7 | **3:24** Eph 6:8 | **3:25** Acts 10:34

		RULES OF SUBMISSION
Wives, submit to your husbands (3:18).	*Husbands*, be loving and kind toward your wives (3:19).	
Children, obey your parents (3:20).	*Parents*, don't scold your children so much that they become discouraged and quit trying (3:21).	
Slaves, obey your masters (3:22).	*Masters*, be just and fair toward your slaves (4:1).	
(*Employees*, work hard for your employers.)	(*Employers*, be just and fair with your employees.)	

The New Testament includes many instructions concerning relationships. Most people read these instructions for the other person and ignore the ones that apply to themselves. But you can't control another person's behavior, only your own. Start by following your own instructions and not insisting on the obedience of others first.

3:14, 15 Christians should live in perfect harmony. This does not mean there cannot be differences in opinion, but loving Christians will work together despite their differences. Such love is not a feeling, but a decision to meet others' needs (see 1 Corinthians 13). It leads to peace between individuals and among the members of the body of believers. Do problems in your relationship with other Christians cause open conflicts or mutual silence? Consider what you can do to heal those relationships with selfless acts of love.

3:15 Another translation of this verse is, "Let the peace of Christ rule in your hearts." The word *rule* comes from athletics: Paul tells us to let Christ's peace be "umpire" in our hearts. Our hearts are the center of conflict because there our feelings and desires clash—our fears and hopes, our distrust and trust, our jealousy and love. How can we deal with these constant conflicts and live as God wants? Paul explains that we must decide between conflicting elements on the basis of peace—which choice will promote peace in our souls and in our churches?

3:16 Although the early Christians had access to the Old Testament and freely used it, they did not yet have the New Testament or any other Christian books to study. Their stories and

teachings about Christ were memorized and passed on from person to person. Sometimes they were set to music, and so music became an important part of Christian worship and education.

3:17 As a Christian, you represent Christ at all times—wherever you go, whatever you say. What impression do people have of Christ when they see or talk with you?

3:18—4:1 Paul describes three relationships: (1) husbands and wives, (2) parents and children, and (3) masters and slaves. In each case there is mutual responsibility to submit and love, to obey and encourage, to work hard and be fair. Examine your family and work relationships. Do you relate to others as God intended? See Ephesians 5:21—6:9 for similar instructions.

3:22—4:1 Here Paul does not condemn or condone slavery, but explains that Christ transcends all divisions between people. Slaves are told to work hard as though their master were Christ himself (3:22-25); but masters should be just and fair (4:1). Perhaps Paul was thinking specifically of Onesimus and Philemon— the slave and master whose conflict lay behind the letter to Philemon (see the book of Philemon). Philemon was a slave owner in the Colossian church, and Onesimus had been his slave (4:9).

4:1
Lev 19:13
Eph 6:9

4:2
Lk 18:1
Acts 1:14
Eph 6:18
1 Thess 5:17

4:4
Eph 6:20

4:5
Eph 5:15,16

4:6
Eccles 10:12
Eph 4:29
1 Pet 3:15

4:7
Acts 20:4
Eph 6:21,22

4:9
Philem 10

4:10
Acts 12:12; 15:37
19:29; 20:4
27:2
2 Tim 4:11

4:11
Acts 11:2

4:12
Col 1:7,28

4:13
Col 2:1

4:14
2 Tim 4:10,11
Philem 24

4:15
Rom 16:5
1 Cor 16:19
Philem 2

4:16
1 Thess 5:27

you won't like—for he has no special favorites who can get away with shirking.

4 You slave owners must be just and fair to all your slaves. Always remember that you, too, have a Master in heaven who is closely watching you.

2Don't be weary in prayer; keep at it; watch for God's answers and remember to be thankful when they come. 3Don't forget to pray for us too, that God will give us many chances to preach the Good News of Christ for which I am here in jail. 4Pray that I will be bold enough to tell it freely and fully, and make it plain, as, of course, I should.

5Make the most of your chances to tell others the Good News. Be wise in all your contacts with them. 6Let your conversation be gracious as well as sensible, for then you will have the right answer for everyone.

Paul's final greetings

7Tychicus, our much loved brother, will tell you how I am getting along. He is a hard worker and serves the Lord with me. 8I have sent him on this special trip just to see how you are, and to comfort and encourage you. 9I am also sending Onesimus, a faithful and much loved brother, one of your own people. He and Tychicus will give you all the latest news.

10Aristarchus, who is with me here as a prisoner, sends you his love, and so does Mark, a relative of Barnabas. And as I said before, give Mark a hearty welcome if he comes your way. 11Jesus Justus also sends his love. These are the only Jewish Christians working with me here, and what a comfort they have been!

12Epaphras, from your city, a servant of Christ Jesus, sends you his love. He is always earnestly praying for you, asking God to make you strong and perfect and to help you know his will in everything you do. 13I can assure you that he has worked hard for you with his prayers, and also for the Christians in Laodicea and Hierapolis.

14Dear doctor Luke sends his love, and so does Demas.

15Please give my greeting to the Christian friends at Laodicea, and to Nymphas, and to those who meet in his home. 16By the way, after you have read this letter will

4:10 *a hearty welcome,* literally, "receive him."

4:2 Have you ever grown tired of praying for something or someone? Paul says, "Keep at it." Persistence demonstrates our faith that God answers our prayers. Faith shouldn't die if the answers don't come immediately, for the delay may be God's way of working his will in your life. When you feel weary in your prayers, know that God is present, always listening, always acting—maybe not in ways you had hoped, but in ways he knows are best.

4:6 When we tell others about Christ, it is important always to be gracious in what we say. No matter how much sense the message makes, we lose our effectiveness if we are not courteous. Just as we like to be respected, we must respect others if we want them to listen to what we have to say.

4:7 Tychicus was one of Paul's personal respresentatives and probably the bearer of the letters to the Colossians and Ephesians (see also Ephesians 6:21, 22). He accompanied Paul to Jerusalem with the collection for the church (Acts 20:4).

4:10 Mark left with Paul and Barnabas on their first missionary journey (Acts 12:25), but then left in the middle of the trip for unknown reasons (Acts 15:37-39). Barnabas and Mark were relatives, and when Paul refused to take Mark on another journey, Barnabas and Mark journeyed together to preach the Good News (Acts 15:39-41). Mark also worked with Peter (Acts 12:12, 13; 1 Peter 5:13). Later, Mark and Paul were reconciled (Philemon 1:24). Mark wrote the Gospel of Mark.

4:12 Epaphras founded the Colossian church (see the note on 1:7), and his report to Paul in Rome caused Paul to write this letter. Epaphras was a hero of the Colossian church, one of the believers who helped keep the church together in spite of growing troubles. His earnest prayers for the believers show his deep love and concern for them.

4:13 Laodicea was located 11 miles northwest of Colosse; Hierapolis was about five miles north of Laodicea. See the note on 2:1 for more about Laodicea.

4:14 Luke spent much time with Paul, not only accompanying him on most of his third missionary journey, but sitting with him in the prison at Rome. Luke wrote the Gospel of Luke and the book of Acts. Demas was faithful to Paul for a while, but then left him (2 Timothy 4:10).

4:15 The early Christians often met in homes. Church buildings were not common until the third century.

4:16 Some suggest that the letter to Laodicea may be the book of Ephesians. More likely there was a special letter to the Laodiceans, of which we have no record today. Paul wrote several letters that have been lost (see, for example, 2 Corinthians 2:3 and note).

you pass it on to the church at Laodicea? And read the letter I wrote to them. 17And say to Archippus, "Be sure that you do all the Lord has told you to."

18Here is my own greeting in my own handwriting: Remember me here in jail. May God's blessings surround you.

4:17
2 Tim 4:5
Philem 2

4:18
Heb 13:3

Sincerely, Paul

4:17 Paul's letter to Philemon is also addressed to Archippus (Philemon 1:2). Paul called him "a soldier of the cross." He may have been a Roman soldier who had become a member of the Colossian church, or he may have been Philemon's son.

4:18 Paul usually dictated his letters to a scribe, but often ended with a short note in his own handwriting (see also 1 Corinthians 16:21; Galatians 6:11). This prevented false teachers from writing letters in the name of Paul, a problem Paul had previously faced (2 Thessalonians 3:17). It also gave the letters a personal touch.

4:18 To understand the letter to the Colossians, we need to know that the church was facing pressure from a cult-like heresy that promised deeper spiritual life through secret knowledge (an early form of gnosticism). The false teachers destroyed faith in Christ by undermining Christ's humanity and divinity, and attempted to divide the physical and spiritual.

Paul makes it clear in Colossians that Christ alone is the source of our spiritual life, the Head of the Body. He is Lord of both the physical and spiritual worlds. The path to deeper spiritual life is not through religious duties, special knowledge, or secrets; it is only through a clear connection with the Lord Jesus Christ. We must never let anything come between us and our Savior.

1 THESSALONIANS

SLOWLY they walk, scattering the leaves and trampling the grass under measured and heavy steps. The minister's words still echoing in their minds, they hear workmen moving toward the terrible place, preparing to cover the casket of their loved one. Death, the enemy, has torn the bonded relationships of family and friends, leaving only memories and tears.

But like a golden shaft of sun piercing the winter sky, a singular truth shatters the oppressive gloom—death is not the end! Christ is the victor over death and there is hope of the resurrection through him.

Many first-century Christians were persecuted—whether at the hands of zealous Jews (like Paul before his conversion), angry Greeks, or ruthless Roman authorities. Persecution included stonings, beatings, crucifixions, torture, and death. To be a follower of Christ meant to be willing to give up everything in order to follow him.

Paul faced persecution when he established the church in Thessalonica during his second missionary journey (in about A.D. 51). He wrote this letter a short time later to encourage the young believers there. He wanted to assure them of his love, to praise them for their faithfulness in the midst of persecution, and to remind them of their hope—the sure return of their Lord and Savior, Jesus Christ.

Paul begins this letter with a note of affirmation, thanking God for the strong faith and good reputation of the Thessalonians (1:1–10). Then Paul reviews their relationship—how he and his companions brought the gospel to them (2:1–12), how they accepted the message (2:13–16), and how he longed to be with them again (2:17–20). Because of his concern, he sent Timothy to encourage them in their faith (3:1–13).

Paul then presents the central thrust of his message—exhortation and comfort. He challenges the Thessalonians to please God in their daily living by avoiding all sexual sin (4:1–8), to love one another (4:9, 10), and to live as good citizens in a sinful world (4:11, 12).

Paul comforts the Thessalonians by reminding them of the hope of the resurrection (4:13–18). Then he warns them to be prepared at all times, for Jesus Christ could return at any moment. When Christ returns, those Christians who are alive and those who have died will be raised to new life (5:1–11).

Paul then gives the Thessalonians a handful of reminders on how to prepare themselves for the Second Coming—warn the lazy (5:14), comfort the frightened (5:14), care for the weak (5:14), "be patient with everyone" (5:14), do good to everyone (5:15), "always be joyful" (5:16), pray continually (5:17), "be thankful" (5:18), test everything that is taught (5:20, 21), and stay away from evil (5:22). Paul concludes his letter with two benedictions and a request for prayer.

As you read this letter, listen carefully to Paul's practical advice for Christian living. When you feel overwhelmed by sorrow, remember that there is hope in Christ's return, the resurrection, and the promise of eternal life!

VITAL STATISTICS

PURPOSE:
To strengthen the Thessalonian Christians in their faith and give them the assurance of Christ's return

AUTHOR:
Paul

TO WHOM WRITTEN:
The church at Thessalonica and all believers everywhere

DATE WRITTEN:
About A.D. 51 from Corinth; one of Paul's earliest letters

SETTING:
The church at Thessalonica was very young, having been established only two or three years before this letter was written. The Thessalonian Christians needed to mature in their faith. In addition, there was a misunderstanding concerning Christ's Second Coming—some thought he would return immediately, others wondered whether those who had already died would experience a bodily resurrection at his Second Coming.

KEY VERSE:
"For since we believe that Jesus died and then came back to life again, we can also believe that when Jesus returns, God will bring back with him all the Christians who have died" (4:14).

KEY PEOPLE:
Paul, Timothy, Silas

KEY PLACE:
Thessalonica

SPECIAL FEATURES:
Paul received from Timothy a favorable report about the Thessalonians. However, he wrote this letter to correct their misconceptions about the resurrection and the Second Coming of Christ.

THE BLUEPRINT

1. Faithfulness to the Lord (1:1—3:13)
2. Watchfulness for the Lord (4:1—5:28)

Paul and his companions were faithful to bring the gospel to the Thessalonians in the midst of persecution. The Thessalonians had only recently become Christians and yet remained faithful to the Lord, despite the fact that the apostles were not with them. Others have been faithful in bringing God's Word to us. We must remain faithful and live with the expectation that Christ will return at any time.

MEGATHEMES

THEME	EXPLANATION	IMPORTANCE
Persecution	Paul and the new Christians at Thessalonica experienced persecution because of their faith in Christ. We can expect trials and troubles as well. We need to stand firm in our faith in the midst of trials, being strengthened by the Holy Spirit.	The Holy Spirit helps us to remain strong in faith, able to show genuine love to others and maintain our moral character even when we are being persecuted, slandered, or oppressed.
Paul's ministry	Paul expressed his concern for this church even while he was being slandered. Paul's commitment to share the gospel in spite of difficult circumstances is a model we should follow.	Paul not only delivered his message, but gave of himself. In our ministries, we must become like Paul—faithful and bold, yet sensitive and self-sacrificing.
Hope	One day all believers, both those who are alive and those who have died, will be united with Christ. To those Christians who die before Christ's return, there is hope—the hope of the resurrection of the body.	If we believe in Christ, we will live with him forever. All those who belong to Jesus Christ—from throughout history—will be present with him at his Second Coming.
Being prepared	No one knows the time of Christ's return. We are to live moral and holy lives, ever watchful for his coming. Believers must not neglect daily responsibilities, but always work and live as unto the Lord.	The gospel is not only what we believe, but also how we must live. The Holy Spirit leads us in faithfulness, so we can avoid lust and fraud. Live as though you expect Christ's return at any time. Don't be caught unprepared.

1. Faithfulness to the Lord

1 *From:* Paul, Silas and Timothy.
To: The Church at Thessalonica—to you who belong to God the Father and the Lord Jesus Christ: May blessing and peace of heart be your rich gifts from God our Father, and from Jesus Christ our Lord.

1:1
Jn 14:23
Rom 1:7
2 Cor 1:19
2 Thess 1:1
1 Pet 5:12

1:1 Paul and his companions probably arrived in Thessalonica in the early summer of A.D. 50. They planted the first Christian church in that city, but had to leave in a hurry because their lives were threatened (Acts 17:1–10). At the first opportunity, probably when he stopped at Corinth, Paul sent Timothy back to Thessalonica to see how the new believers were doing. Timothy returned to Paul with good news: the Christians in Thessalonica were remaining firm in the faith and were unified. But the Thessalonians did have some questions about their new faith. Paul had not had time to answer all their questions during his brief visit and other questions had arisen in the meantime. So Paul wrote to answer their questions and commend them on their faithfulness to the Good News.

1:1 For more information on Paul, see his Profile in Acts 9. Timothy's Profile is in 1 Timothy. Silas accompanied Paul on his second missionary journey (Acts 15:36—17:15). He helped Paul establish the church in Thessalonica (Acts 17:1–9). He is called Silvanus in 2 Corinthians 1:19 and in 1 Peter 5:12. His Profile is found in Acts 16.

1:1 Thessalonica was the capital and largest city of the Roman province of Macedonia. The most important Roman highway (the Egnatian Way)—extending from Rome all the way to the Orient—went through Thessalonica. This highway, along with the city's thriving seaport, made Thessalonica one of the wealthiest and most flourishing trade centers in the Roman Empire. Recognized as a free city, Thessalonica was allowed self-rule and was exempted from most of the restrictions placed by Rome on other cities in the empire. However, with its international flavor came many pagan religions and cultural influences that challenged the faith of the young Christians there.

Paul commends the faith of the Thessalonian believers

1:2
Rom 1:9
2 Thess 1:3

1:3
Heb 6:10
Jas 2:17

1:4
Col 3:12
2 Thess 2:13
2 Pet 1:10

1:5
1 Cor 2:4
2 Cor 6:6
1 Thess 2:10
2 Thess 3:7

1:6
Acts 17:1-6
1 Cor 4:16

1:8
Rom 1:8; 10:18
2 Thess 3:1

2We always thank God for you and pray for you constantly. 3We never forget your loving deeds as we talk to our God and Father about you, and your strong faith and steady looking forward to the return of our Lord Jesus Christ.

4We know that God has chosen you, dear brothers, much beloved of God. 5For when we brought you the Good News, it was not just meaningless chatter to you; no, you listened with great interest. What we told you produced a powerful effect upon you, for the Holy Spirit gave you great and full assurance that what we said was true. And you know how our very lives were further proof to you of the truth of our message. 6So you became our followers and the Lord's; for you received our message with joy from the Holy Spirit in spite of the trials and sorrows it brought you.

7Then you yourselves became an example to all the other Christians in Greece. 8And now the Word of the Lord has spread out from you to others everywhere, far beyond your boundaries, for wherever we go we find people telling us about your

LOCATION OF THESSALONICA
Paul visited Thessalonica on his second and third missionary journeys. It was a seaport and trade center located on the Egnatian Way, a busy international highway. Paul probably wrote his two letters to the Thessalonians from Corinth.

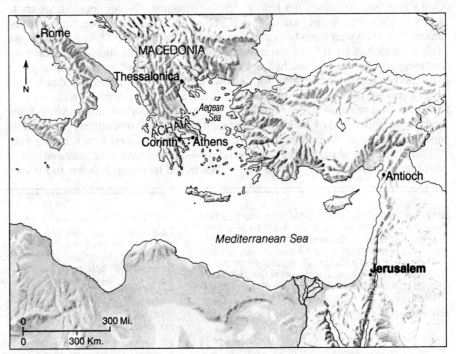

1:3 The Thessalonian believers stood firm when they were persecuted (1:6; 3:1–4, 7, 8). Paul commends these young Christians for their loving deeds, strong faith, and deep commitment to Christ. These characteristics are the marks of an effective Christian.

1:5 The power of the Holy Spirit changes people when they believe the Good News. When we tell others about Christ, we must depend on the Holy Spirit to open their eyes and convince them that they need salvation. His power changes them—not our cleverness or persuasion. Without the work of the Holy Spirit, our words are meaningless. The Holy Spirit not only convicts people of sin but also assures them of the truth of the gospel. (For more information on the Holy Spirit, see John 14:23–26; 15:26, 27; and the notes on John 3:6 and Acts 1:4.)

1:5 The Good News produced a powerful effect upon the Thessalonians. Whenever the Word of God is heard and obeyed, lives are changed! Christianity is more than a collection of interesting facts; it is the power of God for salvation to every one who believes. What has God's power done in your life since you first put your faith in Christ?

1:5 Paul says, "our very lives were further proof." The Thessalonians could see that what Paul, Silas, and Timothy were preaching was true, because they lived it. Does your life confirm or contradict what you say you believe?

1:6 The Thessalonians received the message of salvation with great joy. Even though their new faith led to persecution from both Jews and Gentiles (3:2–4; Acts 17:5), they stood firm in their faith. Many Thessalonians were apparently concerned about the condition of those believers who had already died. What would happen to them when Christ returned? Paul answered these questions by explaining to the Thessalonian Christians what happens when believers die (see 4:13ff).

1:7–10 All of us should respond to the Good News as the Thessalonian believers did: *turn* from sin, *serve* the living and true God, and *look forward* to Jesus' return. We should turn from sin because Christ is coming to judge the earth; we should be fervent in our service because we have little time to further the work of Christ's Kingdom before he returns. We should be prepared for Jesus to return at any time because we don't know when he will come.

remarkable faith in God. We don't need to tell *them* about it, 9for *they* keep telling *us* about the wonderful welcome you gave us, and how you turned away from your idols to God so that now the living and true God only is your Master. 10And they speak of how you are looking forward to the return of God's Son from heaven—Jesus, whom God brought back to life—and he is our only Savior from God's terrible anger against sin.

1:9
1 Cor 12:2

1:10
Rom 2:7; 5:9
Phil 3:20
1 Thess 5:9
Heb 9:28
Rev 1:7

Paul reviews his relationship with the Thessalonians

2 You yourselves know, dear brothers, how worthwhile that visit was. 2You know how badly we had been treated at Philippi just before we came to you, and how much we suffered there. Yet God gave us the courage to boldly repeat the same message to you, even though we were surrounded by enemies. 3So you can see that we were not preaching with any false motives or evil purposes in mind; we were perfectly straightforward and sincere.

4For we speak as messengers from God, trusted by him to tell the truth; we change his message not one bit to suit the taste of those who hear it; for we serve God alone, who examines our hearts' deepest thoughts. 5Never once did we try to win you with flattery, as you very well know, and God knows we were not just pretending to be your friends so that you would give us money! 6As for praise, we have never asked for it from you or anyone else, although as apostles of Christ we certainly had a right to some honor from you. 7But we were as gentle among you as a mother feeding and caring for her own children. 8We loved you dearly—so dearly that we gave you not only God's message, but our own lives too.

9Don't you remember, dear brothers, how hard we worked among you? Night and day we toiled and sweated to earn enough to live on so that our expenses would not be a burden to anyone there, as we preached God's Good News among you. 10You yourselves are our witnesses—as is God—that we have been pure and honest and faultless toward every one of you. 11We talked to you as a father to his own

2:1
1 Thess 1:9

2:2
Acts 16:22; 17:2
Phil 1:30

2:3
2 Cor 4:2
2 Pet 1:16

2:4
Prov 17:3
1 Cor 7:25
Gal 1:10
1 Tim 1:11

2:5
Acts 20:33

2:7
2 Tim 2:24

2:8
Rom 1:11; 15:29
2 Cor 12:15

2:9
Acts 18:3
2 Cor 11:9
2 Thess 3:8

2:10
1 Thess 1:5

2:11
1 Cor 4:14

1:10 Paul emphasizes Christ's Second Coming throughout this book . Because the Thessalonian church was being persecuted, Paul encouraged them to look forward to the deliverance Christ would bring. A believer's hope is in the return of Jesus, "our great God and Savior" (Titus 2:13). Our perspective on life remains incomplete without this hope. Just as surely as Christ was raised from the dead and ascended into heaven, he will return and usher in eternity (Acts 1:11).

2:1 Paul was referring here to his first visit to Thessalonica (see Acts 17:1–9).

2:1–3 The Thessalonians knew that Paul had been imprisoned in Philippi just prior to coming to Thessalonica (see Acts 16:11—17:1). Fear of imprisonment did not keep Paul from preaching the Good News. If God wants us to do something, he will give us the strength and courage to do it in spite of the obstacles that may come our way.

2:3 This pointed statement may be a response to accusations from the Jewish leaders who-had stirred up the crowds (Acts 17:5). Paul demonstrates the sincerity of his motives by showing that he and Silas suffered for sharing the gospel in Philippi. Paul did not seek money, fame, or popularity by sharing the Good News. We must always examine our motives for sharing the Good News.

2:4–8 In trying to persuade people, we often alter our position just enough to make our message more palatable. Paul never changed his *message* to make it more acceptable, but he did tailor his *presentation* to each audience. Although our presentation must be altered to be appropriate to the situation, the truth of the gospel must never be compromised.

2:5 We often feel disgusted when we hear someone "butter up" another person. Flattery is a false cover-up for a person's real intentions, and Christian leaders should not practice it. Christians who proclaim God's truth have a special responsibility to be honest. Can people be sure that you will always be honest and

straightforward in your words and actions?

2:6–8 When Paul was with the Thessalonians, he didn't flatter them, didn't take their money, didn't seek their praise, and wasn't a burden to them. He and Silas completely focused their efforts on presenting God's message of salvation to the Thessalonians. This was important! The Thessalonian believers had their lives changed by God, not Paul; it was Christ's message they believed, not Paul's. When we witness for Christ, our focus should not be on the impression we make. As true ministers of Christ, we should point to him, not to ourselves.

2:7 Gentleness is not often a respected quality. Power and assertiveness gain more respect in our society, even though none of us likes to be bullied. Gentleness is love in action—being considerate, meeting the needs of others, allowing time for the other person to talk, and being willing to learn. It is an essential trait for both men and women. We all need to maintain a gentle attitude in our relationships with others.

2:9 Although Paul had the right to receive financial support from the people he taught, he worked as a tentmaker (Acts 18:3) to support himself and not be a burden to the new Thessalonian believers.

2:11 No loving father would neglect the safety of his children, allowing them to walk into circumstances that might prove fatal or permanently damaging. In the same way, we must take new believers under our wings until they are mature enough to stand firm in their faith. When new Christians are strong enough to influence others for the gospel, rather than be influenced by others to practices contrary to the gospel, they are ready to be out from under our wings.

2:11, 12 By his words and example, Paul encouraged the Thessalonians to live in ways that would bring joy to God. Is there anything about your daily life that would embarrass God? What do people think of God when they examine your life? What does God

2:12
Eph 4:1
Col 1:10
1 Pet 1:15

2:13
Mt 10:40
Heb 4:2,12

2:14
Acts 17:5
1 Thess 1:6
Heb 10:33

2:15
Mt 5:12
Lk 24:20
Acts 7:52

2:16
Lk 11:52
Acts 9:23; 13:50
14:19; 17:5

2:17
1 Cor 5:3
1 Thess 3:10

2:18
Rom 1:13; 15:22

2:19
1 Cor 15:23
Phil 2:16
1 Thess 3:13
Rev 1:7; 22:12

2:20
2 Cor 1:14

3:1
Acts 17:15

3:2
Rom 16:21

3:4
1 Thess 2:14

children—don't you remember?—pleading with you, encouraging you and even demanding 12that your daily lives should not embarrass God, but bring joy to him who invited you into his Kingdom to share his glory.

13And we will never stop thanking God for this: that when we preached to you, you didn't think of the words we spoke as being just our own, but you accepted what we said as the very Word of God—which, of course, it was—and it changed your lives when you believed it.

14And then, dear brothers, you suffered what the churches in Judea did, persecution from your own countrymen, just as they suffered from their own people the Jews. 15After they had killed their own prophets, they even executed the Lord Jesus; and now they have brutally persecuted us and driven us out. They are against both God and man, 16trying to keep us from preaching to the Gentiles for fear some might be saved; and so their sins continue to grow. But the anger of God has caught up with them at last.

17Dear brothers, after we left you and had been away from you but a very little while (though our hearts never left you), we tried hard to come back to see you once more. 18We wanted very much to come and I, Paul, tried again and again, but Satan stopped us. 19For what is it we live for, that gives us hope and joy and is our proud reward and crown? It is you! Yes, you will bring us much joy as we stand together before our Lord Jesus Christ when he comes back again. 20For you are our trophy and joy.

Paul is encouraged by Timothy's good report about the Thessalonians

3 Finally, when I could stand it no longer, I decided to stay alone in Athens 2, 3and send Timothy, our brother and fellow worker, God's minister, to visit you to strengthen your faith and encourage you, and to keep you from becoming fainthearted in all the troubles you were going through. (But of course you know that such troubles are a part of God's plan for us Christians. 4Even while we were

---

think about how you live from day to day?

2:13 In the New Testament the phrase "Word of God" usually refers to the preaching of the gospel, the Old Testament Scriptures, and Jesus Christ himself. Today we often apply it only to the Scriptures. We must remember that Jesus Christ himself is the "Word" (John 1:1), the subject of our preaching and teaching.

2:14 When Paul refers to the Jews, he is talking about certain Jews who opposed his preaching of the gospel. He does not mean all Jews. Many of Paul's converts were Jewish. Paul himself was a Jew (2 Corinthians 11:22).

2:14 Just as the Jewish Christians in Jerusalem were persecuted by their own people, so the Gentile Christians in Thessalonica were persecuted by their fellow Gentiles. It is discouraging to face persecution, especially when it comes from your own people. But when we take a stand for Christ, we may face opposition, disapproval, ridicule, and persecution from our neighbors, friends, and even family members.

2:15, 16 Why were so many Jews opposed to Christianity? First, although the Jewish religion was declared "legal" by the Roman government, it still had a tenuous relationship with the government. At this time, Christianity was viewed as a sect of Judaism. The Jews were afraid that reprisals leveled against the Christians might be stretched to include them. Second, the Jewish leaders thought Jesus was a false prophet and they didn't want his teachings to spread. Third, they feared that if many Jews were drawn away, their own political position might be weakened. Fourth, they were proud of their special status as "God's chosen people" and they resented the fact that Gentiles were full members within the church.

2:18 Paul was not using the word "Satan" here symbolically—he knew that Satan was real. Satan is called "the god of this evil

world" (2 Corinthians 4:4) and "the mighty prince of the power of the air" (Ephesians 2:2). We don't know exactly what hindered Paul from returning to Thessalonica—opposition, illness, travel complications, or a direct attack by Satan—but Satan worked in some way to keep him from Thessalonica. Many of the difficulties which prevent us from accomplishing God's work can be attributed to Satan (see Ephesians 6:12).

2:20 The ultimate reward for Paul's ministry was not money, prestige, or fame, but new believers whose lives had been changed by God through the preaching of the gospel. This should be the motivation of all Christians who seek to further the Kingdom of God.

3:1-4 Because Paul could not return to Thessalonica (2:18), he sent Timothy as his representative. According to Acts 17:10, Paul left Thessalonica and went to Beroea. When trouble broke out in Beroea, some Christians took Paul to Athens while Silas and Timothy stayed behind (Acts 17:13-15). Later Paul sent Timothy to encourage the Thessalonian Christians to be strong in their faith in the face of persecution.

3:1-3 Some think that troubles are always caused by sin or a lack of faith. Here Paul states that troubles may be a part of God's plan for believers. Going through trials can build character (James 1:2-4), patience (Romans 5:3-5), and sensitivity toward others who also face trouble (2 Corinthians 1:3-7). Problems are unavoidable for godly people in an ungodly world. Your troubles may be a sign of effective Christian living.

3:4 Some people turn to God hoping to escape suffering on earth. Rather than promising escape from suffering, God gives us power to grow through our sufferings. The Christian life is marked by obedience to Christ despite temptation and hardship.

still with you we warned you ahead of time that suffering would soon come—and it did.)

5As I was saying, when I could bear the suspense no longer I sent Timothy to find out whether your faith was still strong. I was afraid that perhaps Satan had gotten the best of you and that all our work had been useless. 6And now Timothy has just returned and brings the welcome news that your faith and love are as strong as ever, and that you remember our visit with joy and want to see us just as much as we want to see you. 7So we are greatly comforted, dear brothers, in all of our own crushing troubles and suffering here, now that we know you are standing true to the Lord. 8We can bear anything as long as we know that you remain strong in him.

9How can we thank God enough for you and for the joy and delight you have given us in our praying for you? 10For night and day we pray on and on for you, asking God to let us see you again, to fill up any little cracks there may yet be in your faith.

11May God our Father himself and our Lord Jesus send us back to you again. 12And may the Lord make your love to grow and overflow to each other and to everyone else, just as our love does toward you. 13This will result in your hearts being made strong, sinless and holy by God our Father, so that you may stand before him guiltless on that day when our Lord Jesus Christ returns with all those who belong to him.

2. Watchfulness for the Lord

Live to please God

4 Let me add this, dear brothers: You already know how to please God in your daily living, for you know the commands we gave you from the Lord Jesus himself. Now we beg you—yes, we demand of you in the name of the Lord Jesus—that you live more and more closely to that ideal. 3, 4For God wants you to be holy and pure, and to keep clear of all sexual sin so that each of you will marry in holiness and honor— 5not in lustful passion as the heathen do, in their ignorance of God and his ways.

6And this also is God's will: that you never cheat in this matter by taking another man's wife, because the Lord will punish you terribly for this, as we have solemnly told you before. 7For God has not called us to be dirty-minded and full of lust, but to be holy and clean. 8If anyone refuses to live by these rules he is not disobeying the rules of men but of God who gives his *Holy* Spirit to you.

3:13 *with all those who belong to him,* literally, "with all his saints. Amen."

3:5
Mt 4:3
1 Cor 7:5
2 Cor 11:3

3:6
Phil 1:8

3:8
Phil 4:1

3:10
2 Cor 13:9
1 Thess 1:2,3
2 Tim 1:3

3:11
2 Thess 3:5

3:12
Phil 1:9

3:13
Zech 14:5
1 Cor 1:8
1 Thess 2:19
4:17
Jude 14
Rev 22:12

4:1
Eph 4:1
Col 1:10

4:3,4
1 Cor 6:18; 7:2
Heb 13:4
1 Pet 3:7

4:6
1 Cor 6:8
Heb 13:4

4:7
Lev 11:44
1 Pet 1:15

4:8
Rom 5:5
1 Jn 3:24

3:5 Satan is the most powerful of the evil spirits. His power can affect both the spiritual world (Ephesians 2:1–3; 6:10–12) and the physical world (2 Corinthians 12:7–10). Satan even tempted Jesus (Matthew 4:1–11). But Jesus defeated Satan when he died on the cross for the sins of the world and rose again to bring new life. At the proper time God will overthrow Satan forever (Revelation 20:7–10).

3:8 In the midst of persecution or pressure, believers should encourage each other. Compliments, expressions of thanks, and support for those who are wavering in the faith help to build up fellow believers.

3:9 It is great joy for a Christian to see another person come to faith in Christ and mature in that faith. Paul experienced this joy countless times. He thanked God for those who had come to know Christ and prayed for their continued growth in faith. If there are new Christians who have brought you joy, thank God for them and support them as they continue to grow in the faith.

3:11 We have no record that Paul returned to Thessalonica; but when he was traveling through Asia on his third journey, he was joined by Aristarchus and Secundus, who were from Thessalonica (Acts 20:4, 5).

3:12 If we are full of God's love, it will overflow to others. It's not enough merely to be courteous to others; we must actively and persistently show love to others. Our love should be continually growing. If your capacity to love has remained unchanged for some time, ask God to fill you again with his never-ending supply of love. Then look for opportunities to express his love.

3:11–13 This refers to the Second Coming of Christ, when he will establish his eternal Kingdom. At that time he will gather all believers, those who have died and those who are alive, into one united family under his rule. All believers from all times, including these Thessalonians, will be with Christ in his Kingdom.

4:1–8 Sexual standards were very low in the Roman Empire, and in many societies today they are not any higher. The temptations to engage in sexual intercourse outside the marriage relationship have always been powerful. Giving in to these temptations can have disastrous results. Sexual sins always hurt someone: families, businesses, and even churches. It has not only physical consequences, but spiritual ones as well. For more on why sexual sin is so harmful, see the note on 1 Corinthians 6:18.

4:1–8 Sexual desires and activities must be placed under Christ's control. God created sex for procreation, pleasure, and as an expression of love between a husband and wife. Sexual experience must be limited to the marriage relationship to avoid hurting ourselves, our relationship to God, and our relationship to others.

4:9
Jer 31:34
Jn 6:45; 13:34
1 Jn 2:20,27

4:10
1 Thess 3:12

4:11
Eph 4:28
2 Thess 3:11,12

9But concerning the pure brotherly love that there should be among God's people, I don't need to say very much, I'm sure! For God himself is teaching you to love one another. 10Indeed, your love is already strong toward all the Christian brothers throughout your whole nation. Even so, dear friends, we beg you to love them more and more. 11This should be your ambition: to live a quiet life, minding your own business and doing your own work, just as we told you before. 12As a result, people who are not Christians will trust and respect you, and you will not need to depend on others for enough money to pay your bills.

Remember the hope of the resurrection

4:13
Lev 19:28
Deut 14:1,2
Eph 2:12

4:14
1 Cor 15:18,52

4:15
1 Cor 15:52

4:16
Joel 2:11
Mt 24:30
Acts 1:11
1 Cor 15:52
2 Thess 1:7

4:17
Dan 7:13
Acts 1:9
Rev 11:12
21:3,4

13And now, dear brothers, I want you to know what happens to a Christian when he dies so that when it happens, you will not be full of sorrow, as those are who have no hope. 14For since we believe that Jesus died and then came back to life again, we can also believe that when Jesus returns, God will bring back with him all the Christians who have died.

15I can tell you this directly from the Lord: that we who are still living when the Lord returns will not rise to meet him ahead of those who are in their graves. 16For the Lord himself will come down from heaven with a mighty shout and with the soul-stirring cry of the archangel and the great trumpet-call of God. And the believers who are dead will be the first to rise to meet the Lord. 17Then we who are still alive and remain on the earth will be caught up with them in the clouds to meet the Lord in the air and remain with him forever. 18So comfort and encourage each other with this news.

Be prepared: no one knows when the Lord will return

5:1
Mt 24:3

5:2
2 Pet 3:10

5:3
Isa 26:17

5 When is all this going to happen? I really don't need to say anything about that, dear brothers, 2for you know perfectly well that no one knows. That day of the Lord will come unexpectedly like a thief in the night. 3When people are saying, "All is well, everything is quiet and peaceful"—then, all of a sudden, disaster will

---

**THE EVENTS
OF CHRIST'S
RETURN**

1. Christ will return visibly with a mighty shout.
2. There will be an unmistakable cry from an angel.
3. There will be a trumpet fanfare such as has never been heard.
4. Believers in Christ who are dead will rise from their graves.
5. Believers who are alive will be lifted into the clouds and meet Christ.

While Christians have often disagreed about what events will lead up to the return of Christ, there has been less disagreement about what will happen once Christ does return.

4:11 This is part of what it means to live as a Christian—to be responsible in all areas of your life. You can hardly be effective when you share your faith with others if people don't respect you. Whatever you do, do it faithfully and be a positive force in society.

4:13ff The Thessalonians wondered why many of their fellow believers had died and what would happen to them when Christ returned. Paul wanted the Thessalonians to understand that death is not the end of the story. When Christ returns, all believers—dead and alive—will be reunited, never to suffer or die again.

4:15 What does Paul mean when he says, "I can tell you this directly from the Lord"? This was either something God revealed directly to Paul, or it was a teaching of Jesus which had been passed along orally by the apostles and other Christians.

4:15–18 Exactly when the dead will be raised, in relation to the other events at the Second Coming, is not as important as the purpose for which Paul wrote these words—to challenge believers to comfort and encourage one another when loved ones died. This passage can be a great comfort when any believer dies. The same love that should unite believers in this life (4:9) will unite believers when Christ returns and reigns for eternity.

4:15–18 Because Jesus Christ came back to life, so will all believers. All Christians, including those living when he returns, will live with Jesus forever. Therefore, we need not despair when loved ones die or world events take a tragic turn. For God will turn our tragedies to triumphs, our poverty to riches, our pain to glory, and our defeat to victory. All believers throughout history will stand reunited in God's very presence, safe and secure. As Paul comforted the Thessalonians with the promise of the resurrection, so we should comfort and reassure one another with this great hope.

5:1–3 Efforts to determine the date of Christ's return are foolish. Don't be misled by anyone who claims to know. We are told here that no one knows and that even believers will be surprised. The Lord will return suddenly and unexpectedly, warns Paul, so be ready! Because no one knows when Jesus will come back to earth, we should be ready at all times. Suppose he were to return today. How would he find you living? Are you ready to meet him? Live each day prepared to welcome him.

5:2 The day of the Lord is a future time when God intervenes directly and dramatically in world affairs. Predicted and discussed often in the Old Testament (Isaiah 13:6–12; Joel 2:28–32; Zephaniah 1:14–18), the day of the Lord will include both punishment and blessing. Christ will judge sin and set up his eternal Kingdom.

fall upon them as suddenly as a woman's birth pains begin when her child is born. And these people will not be able to get away anywhere—there will be no place to hide.

4But, dear brothers, you are not in the dark about these things, and you won't be surprised as by a thief when that day of the Lord comes. 5For you are all children of the light and of the day, and do not belong to darkness and night. 6So be on your guard, not asleep like the others. Watch for his return and stay sober. 7Night is the time for sleep and the time when people get drunk. 8But let us who live in the light keep sober, protected by the armor of faith and love, and wearing as our helmet the happy hope of salvation.

9For God has not chosen to pour out his anger upon us, but to save us through our Lord Jesus Christ; 10he died for us so that we can live with him forever, whether we are dead or alive at the time of his return. 11So encourage each other to build each other up, just as you are already doing.

5:4
Lk 21:34
1 Jn 2:8

5:5
Jn 12:36
Acts 26:18
Eph 5:8

5:7
Acts 2:15

5:8
Isa 59:17
Rom 8:24
Eph 6:14,17
1 Pet 1:13

5:9
Rom 5:9
2 Tim 2:19

5:10
Rom 14:9

Paul's final instructions

12Dear brothers, honor the officers of your church who work hard among you and

Reference	Example	Suggested application
5:11	Build each other up.	Point out to someone a quality you appreciate in him or her.
5:12	Give honor to leaders.	Look for ways to cooperate.
5:13	Think highly of leaders.	Withhold your next critical comment about those in positions of responsibility.
5:13	Give wholehearted love.	Say "thank you" to your leaders for their efforts.
5:13	Avoid quarreling.	Search for ways to get along with others.
5:14	Warn the lazy.	Challenge someone to join you in a project.
5:14	Comfort the frightened.	Encourage those who are frightened by reminding them of God's promises.
5:14	Tenderly care for the weak.	Support those who are weak by loving them and praying for them.
5:14	Practice patience.	Think of a situation that tries your patience and plan ahead of time how you can stay calm.
5:15	Resist revenge.	Instead of planning to get even with those who mistreat you, do good to them.
5:16	Be joyful.	Remember that even in the midst of turmoil, God is in control.
5:17	Pray continuously.	God is always with you—talk to him.
5:18	Be thankful.	Make a list of all the gifts God has given you, giving thanks to God for each one.
5:19	Do not smother the Holy Spirit.	Cooperate with the Spirit the next time he prompts you to participate in a Christian meeting.
5:20	Do not scoff at those who prophesy.	Receive God's word from those who speak for him.
5:22	Keep away from evil.	Avoid situations where you will be drawn into temptation.
5:23	Count on God's constant help.	Realize that the Christian life is to be lived not in our own strength, but through God's power.

CHECKLIST FOR ENCOURAGERS
The command to "encourage others" is found throughout the Bible. In 5:11–23, Paul gives many specific examples of how we can encourage others.

5:8 For more about the Christian's armor, see Ephesians 6:13–17

5:9–11 As you near the end of a foot race, your legs ache, your throat burns, and your whole body cries out for you to stop. This is when supporters are most valuable. Their encouragement helps you push through the pain to the finish. In the same way, Christians are to encourage one another. A word of encouragement offered at the right moment can be the difference between finishing well and

collapsing along the way. Look around you. Be sensitive to others' need for encouragement and offer supportive words or actions.

5:12, 13 Think of your pastor and other church leaders. How can you honor them? Express your appreciation, tell them how you have been helped by their leadership and teaching, and thank them for their ministry in your life. If you say nothing, how will they know where you stand? Remember, they need and deserve your

5:14
2 Thess 3:6

5:15
Lev 19:18
Rom 12:17
Gal 6:10

5:19
Eph 4:30
2 Tim 1:6

5:20
1 Cor 14:1

5:21
1 Jn 4:1

5:16
Phil 4:4

5:17
Eph 6:18

5:23
2 Pet 3:14

5:24
1 Cor 1:9

5:27
Col 4:16

5:28
Rom 16:20

warn you against all that is wrong. ¹³Think highly of them and give them your wholehearted love because they are straining to help you. And remember, no quarreling among yourselves.

¹⁴Dear brothers, warn those who are lazy; comfort those who are frightened; take tender care of those who are weak; and be patient with everyone. ¹⁵See that no one pays back evil for evil, but always try to do good to each other and to everyone else. ¹⁶Always be joyful. ¹⁷Always keep on praying. ¹⁸No matter what happens, always be thankful, for this is God's will for you who belong to Christ Jesus.

¹⁹Do not smother the Holy Spirit. ²⁰Do not scoff at those who prophesy, ²¹but test everything that is said to be sure it is true, and if it is, then accept it. ²²Keep away from every kind of evil. ²³May the God of peace himself make you entirely pure and devoted to God; and may your spirit and soul and body be kept strong and blameless until that day when our Lord Jesus Christ comes back again. ²⁴God, who called you to become his child, will do all this for you, just as he promised. ²⁵Dear brothers, pray for us. ²⁶Shake hands for me with all the brothers there. ²⁷I command you in the name of the Lord to read this letter to all the Christians. ²⁸And may rich blessings from our Lord Jesus Christ be with you, every one.

Sincerely, Paul

---

support and love expressed in practical ways.

5:14 Don't lie down with the lazy; warn them. Don't yell at the frightened; comfort them. At times it's difficult to distinguish between laziness and fear. Two people may be doing nothing—one because he is lazy and the other out of fear of doing something wrong. The key to ministry is sensitivity: sensing the condition of each person and offering the appropriate remedy for each situation. You can't effectively help until you know the problem. You can't apply the medicine until you know where the wound is.

5:16–18 Our joy, prayers, and thankfulness to God should not fluctuate with our circumstances or feelings. Obeying these three commands—be joyful, keep praying, and be thankful—often goes against our natural inclinations. When we make a conscious decision to do what God says, however, we will begin to see people in a new perspective. When we do God's will, we will find it easier to be joyful and thankful.

5:17 We cannot spend all our time on our knees, but it is possible to have a prayerful attitude all the time. This attitude is built upon acknowledging our dependence on God, realizing his presence within us, and determining to obey him fully. We then find it natural to pray frequent, spontaneous, short prayers. A prayerful attitude is not a substitute for regular times of prayer, but should be an outgrowth of those times.

5:18 Paul was not teaching that we should thank God *for* everything that happens to us, but *in* everything. Evil does not come from God, so we should not thank him for evil. But when evil strikes, we can still be thankful for who God is and for the good he can bring through the distress.

5:19 By warning us not to "smother the Holy Spirit," Paul means we should not ignore or toss aside the gifts the Holy Spirit gives. Here he mentions prophecy; in 1 Corinthians 14:39, he mentions tongues. Sometimes spiritual gifts are controversial and cause

division in a church. Rather than trying to solve the problems, some Christians prefer to smother the gifts. This impoverishes the church. We should not stifle the Holy Spirit's work in anyone's life but encourage the full expression of these gifts in the body of Christ.

5:20, 21 We shouldn't make fun of those who don't agree with what we believe, but we should always check their words against the Bible. We are on dangerous ground if we scoff at a person who speaks the truth. Instead we should carefully check out what people say, accepting what is true and rejecting what is false.

5:22–24 A Christian can no more avoid all evil than a boat can avoid all water. He can, however, make sure his "boat" has no leaks. Evil should never be allowed into a Christian's heart.

5:23 The spirit, soul, and body are integral parts of a person. This expression is Paul's way of saying that God must be involved in *every* aspect of our lives. It is wrong to think we can separate our spiritual lives from everything else, obeying God only in some ethereal sense or living for him only one day each week. Christ must control *all* of us, not just a "religious" part.

5:27 For every Christian to hear this letter, it had to be read in a public meeting, for there were not enough copies to circulate. Paul wanted to make sure everyone had the opportunity to hear his message because he was answering important questions and offering needed encouragement.

5:28 The Thessalonian church was young, and they needed help and encouragement. Both the persecution they faced and the temptations of their pagan culture were potential problems for these new Christians. Therefore, Paul wrote to strengthen their faith and bolster their resistance to persecution and temptation. We too have a responsibility to help new believers, to make sure they continue in their faith and don't become sidetracked by wrong beliefs or practices. First Thessalonians can better equip us to help our brothers and sisters in Christ.

2 THESSALONIANS

VITAL STATISTICS

PURPOSE:
To clear up the confusion about
the Second Coming of Christ

AUTHOR:
Paul

TO WHOM WRITTEN:
The church at Thessalonica and
all believers everywhere

DATE WRITTEN:
About A.D. 51 or 52, a few
months after 1 Thessalonians,
from Corinth

SETTING:
Many in the church were
confused about the timing of
Christ's return. Because of
mounting persecution, they
thought the day of the Lord
must be imminent, and they
interpreted Paul's first letter to
say that the Second Coming
would be at any moment. In
light of this misunderstanding,
many persisted in being lazy
and disorderly with the excuse
of waiting for Christ's return.

KEY VERSE:
"May the Lord bring you into an
even deeper understanding of
the love of God and of the
patience that comes from Christ"
(3:5).

KEY PEOPLE:
Paul, Silas, Timothy

KEY PLACES:
Thessalonica

SPECIAL FEATURES:
This is a follow-up letter to
1 Thessalonians. In this epistle,
Paul indicates various events
that must precede the Second
Coming of Christ.

EVEN when clearly stated or written, words can
be misinterpreted and misunderstood, especially
when filtered through the sieve of prejudices and
preconceptions.

Paul faced this problem with the Thessalonians.
He had written to help them grow in the faith,
comforting and encouraging them by affirming
the reality of Christ's return. Just a few months
later, however, word came from Thessalonica
that some had misunderstood his teaching about
the Second Coming. His announcement that
Christ could come at any moment had caused some to stop working and
just wait, rationalizing their laziness by pointing to Paul's teaching.
Adding fuel to this fire was the continued persecution of the church.
Many felt that indeed this must be the "day of the Lord."

Responding quickly, Paul sent his second epistle to this young church.
In it he gave further instruction concerning the Second Coming and the
day of the Lord (2:1, 2). Second Thessalonians, therefore, continues the
subject of 1 Thessalonians and is a call to continued courage and consistent
conduct.

The letter begins with Paul's trademark—a personal greeting and a
statement of thanksgiving for their faith (1:1–3). He mentions their
patience in spite of their crushing troubles and hardships (1:4) and uses
this to broach the subject of Christ's return. At that time, Christ will
vindicate the righteous who endure and he will punish the wicked
(1:5–12).

Paul then directly answers the misunderstanding concerning the timing
of the events of the end times. He tells them not to listen to rumors and
reports that the day of the Lord has already begun (2:1, 2) because a
number of events must occur before he returns (2:3–12). Meanwhile,
they should stand firm for Christ's truth (2:13–15), receive God's comfort
and hope (2:16, 17), pray for strength and that the Lord's message will
spread (3:1–5), and warn those who are lazy (3:6–15). Paul ends with
personal greetings and a benediction (3:16–18).

Almost 2,000 years later, we stand much closer to the time of Christ's
return; but we also would be wrong to see his imminent appearance as
an excuse for idle waiting and heavenward gazing. Being prepared for
his coming means spreading the gospel, reaching out to those in need,
and building the church, his body. As you read 2 Thessalonians, then,
see clearly the reality of his return and your responsibility to live for him
until that day.

THE BLUEPRINT

1. The bright hope of Christ's return
   (1:1—2:17)
2. Living in the light of Christ's return
   (3:1–18)

Paul wrote to encourage those who were facing persecution and to correct a misunderstanding about the timing of Christ's return. The teaching about the Lord's return promoted idleness in this young church. The imminent coming of Christ should never make us lazy; we should be even more busy—living purely, using our time well, and working for his Kingdom. We must work not only during easy times when it is convenient, but also during difficult times. Christians must patiently wait, watch, and work for Christ's return.

MEGATHEMES

THEME	EXPLANATION	IMPORTANCE
Persecution	Paul encouraged the church to have patience in spite of troubles and hardships. God will bring victory to his faithful followers and judge those who persecute them.	God promises to reward our faith with his power, helping us bear persecution. Suffering for our faith will strengthen us to serve Christ.
Christ's return	Since Paul had said that the Lord would come at any moment, some of the Thessalonian believers had stopped work in order to wait for Christ.	Christ will return and bring total victory to all who trust in him. If we are ready, we need not be concerned about *when* he will return. We should stand firm, keep working, and wait for Christ.
Great rebellion	Before Christ's return, there will be a great rebellion against God led by the man of rebellion (the Antichrist). God will remove all the restraints on evil before he brings judgment on the rebels. The Antichrist will attempt to deceive many.	We should not be afraid when we see evil increase. God is in control, no matter how evil the world becomes. God guards us from Satanic attack. We can have victory over evil by remaining faithful to him.
Persistence	Because church members had quit working and become disorderly and disobedient, Paul chastised them for their laziness. He called them to show courage and true Christian conduct.	We must never get so tired of doing right that we quit. We can be persistent by making the most of our time and talent. Our endurance will be rewarded.

1. The bright hope of Christ's return

1 *From:* Paul, Silas and Timothy.
To: The church of Thessalonica—kept safe in God our Father and in the Lord Jesus Christ.

1:1
2 Cor 1:19
1 Thess 1:1

²May God the Father and the Lord Jesus Christ give you rich blessings and peace-filled hearts and minds.

1:2
Rom 1:7

Paul encourages those experiencing persecution

³Dear brothers, giving thanks to God for you is not only the right thing to do, but it is our duty to God, because of the really wonderful way your faith has grown, and because of your growing love for each other. ⁴We are happy to tell other churches

1:3
Job 17:9
Ps 84:7
1 Thess 1:2

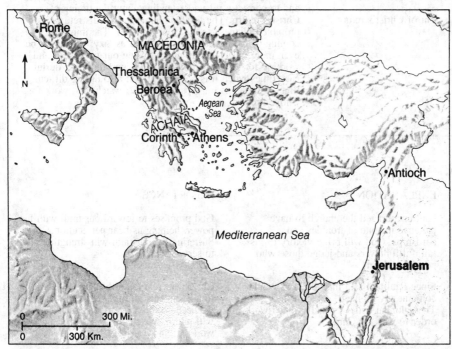

LOCATION OF THESSALONICA
After Paul visited Thessalonica on his second missionary journey, he went on to Beroea, Athens, and Corinth (Acts 17, 18). From Corinth, Paul wrote his two letters to the Thessalonian church.

Map labels: Rome, MACEDONIA, Thessalonica, Beroea, Aegean Sea, ACHAIA, Corinth, Athens, N, Antioch, Mediterranean Sea, Jerusalem

0 — 300 Mi.
0 — 300 Km.

1:1 Paul wrote this letter from Corinth less than a year after he wrote 1 Thessalonians. He and his companions, Timothy and Silas, had visited Thessalonica on Paul's second missionary journey (Acts 17:1–10). They started the first church there, but Paul had to leave suddenly because of persecution. This prompted him to write his first letter (1 Thessalonians), which contains words of comfort and encouragement. Paul then heard how the Thessalonians had responded to this letter. The good news was that they continued to grow in their faith, but the bad news was that false teachings about Christ's return were spreading, leading many to quit their jobs and wait for the end of the world. So Paul wrote to them again. While the purpose of Paul's first letter was to comfort the Thessalonians with the assurance of Christ's Second Coming, his second letter was to correct false teaching about the Second Coming.

1:1 Paul, Silas, and Timothy were together in Corinth (Acts 18:5). Paul wrote this letter on behalf of all three of them. He often included Timothy as a co-sender of his letters (see Philippians 1:1; Colossians 1:1; 1 Thessalonians 1:1). For more information about Paul, see his Profile in Acts 9. Timothy's Profile is found in 1 Timothy, and Silas' is in Acts 16.

1:1 Thessalonica was the capital and largest city of the Roman province of Macedonia. The most important Roman highway—extending from Rome to the Orient—went through Thessalonica. This highway, along with the city's thriving seaport, made

Thessalonica one of the wealthiest and most flourishing trade centers in the Roman Empire. Recognized as a free city, Thessalonica was allowed self-rule and was exempted from most of the restrictions placed by Rome on other cities. Because of this open climate, however, the city had many pagan religions and cultural influences that challenged the Christians' faith.

1:3 Regardless of his letters' contents, Paul's style was affirming. He began most of his letters by stating what he most appreciated about his readers and the joy he felt because of their faith in God.

1:4–6 Paul was persecuted during his first visit to Thessalonica (Acts 17:5–9). No doubt those who responded to his message and became Christians continued to be persecuted by both Jews and Gentiles. In Paul's first letter to the Thessalonians, he said that Christ's return would bring deliverance from persecution and judgment on the persecutors. But this caused the people to expect Christ's return right away to rescue and vindicate them. Thus Paul points out that while waiting for God's Kingdom, believers can learn from their suffering.

1:4, 5 The keys to surviving suffering are patience and faith. When we are faced with crushing troubles and hardships we can have faith that God is using them for our good and for his glory—these troubles will better prepare us for his Kingdom. Knowing that God is fair and just gives us confidence that he has not forgotten us in our troubles, and that, in his timing, he will relieve us of our suffering and will judge those who persecute us.

about your patience and complete faith in God, in spite of all the crushing troubles and hardships you are going through.

5This is only one example of the fair, just way God does things, for he is using your sufferings to make you ready for his Kingdom, 6while at the same time he is preparing judgment and punishment for those who are hurting you.

7And so I would say to you who are suffering, God will give you rest along with us when the Lord Jesus appears suddenly from heaven in flaming fire with his mighty angels, 8bringing judgment on those who do not wish to know God, and who refuse to accept his plan to save them through our Lord Jesus Christ. 9They will be punished in everlasting hell, forever separated from the Lord, never to see the glory of his power, 10when he comes to receive praise and admiration because of all he has done for his people, his saints. And you will be among those praising him, because you have believed what we told you about him.

11And so we keep on praying for you that our God will make you the kind of children he wants to have—will make you as good as you wish you could be!—rewarding your faith with his power. 12Then everyone will be praising the name of the Lord Jesus Christ because of the results they see in you; and your greatest glory will be that you belong to him. The tender mercy of our God and of the Lord Jesus Christ has made all this possible for you.

Paul predicts the coming of the Antichrist

2 And now, what about the coming again of our Lord Jesus Christ, and our being gathered together to meet him? Please don't be upset and excited, dear brothers, by the rumor that this day of the Lord has already begun. If you hear of people having visions and special messages from God about this, or letters that are supposed to have come from me, don't believe them. 3Don't be carried away and deceived regardless of what they say.

For that day will not come until two things happen: first, there will be a time of great rebellion against God, and then the man of rebellion will come—the son of hell. 4He will defy every god there is, and tear down every other object of adoration

---

1:5
2 Tim 2:12

1:6
Ex 23:22
Rev 6:10

1:7
Mk 8:38
1 Thess 4:16
Rev 14:13

1:8
Ps 79:6
Rom 2:8
Heb 10:27

1:9
Deut 33:2
Isa 2:19
1 Thess 5:3
2 Thess 2:8

1:10
Jn 17:10
Eph 3:21

1:11
Eph 4:1
1 Thess 1:3

1:12
Phil 2:9

2:1
Mt 24:31
1 Thess 2:19
4:15-17

2:2
2 Thess 2:15
3:17

2:3
1 Tim 4:1

2:4
Isa 14:13
Mt 24:15
1 Cor 8:5,6

1:5 As we live for Christ, we will experience troubles and hardships. Some say troubles are a result of sin or lack of faith. But Paul teaches that they may be a part of God's plan for believers. Our problems help us look upward and forward, not inward (Mark 13:35, 36); they help build strong character (Romans 5:3, 4); and they help us be sensitive to others who also must struggle (2 Corinthians 1:3–5). In addition, problems are unavoidable because we are trying to be godly people in an ungodly world. Your troubles may well be a sign of effective Christian living.

1:5, 6 There are two dimensions of the comfort mentioned by Paul. We can be comforted in knowing that our sufferings strengthen us, making us ready for Christ's Kingdom. We can also take comfort in the fact that one day everyone will stand before God; then, wrongs will be righted, judgment will be pronounced, and evil will be terminated.

1:7–9 Paul describes hell as eternal separation from God. In hell, people no longer have any hope for salvation. Those doomed to hell don't want to know God and they refuse to accept his salvation. They will be allowed to stay away from him—forever.

1:11 When we truly love God, we are repeatedly disappointed in our performance. We want to be good, and yet we are unable to do so. God's purpose for all believers is to make them the kind of children he wants to have. This would mean becoming as good as we wish we could be. As our faith in God increases, God increases the power available in us to do good. If you want God's power in your life, believe in *his* ability to do good rather than in yours. Then when Christ comes again, he will make you better than you ever thought you could be.

2:1ff Paul launches into a discussion about the end of the world and Christ's Second Coming. He says that great suffering and trouble lie ahead, but evil will not prevail, because Christ will return

to judge all people. Although Paul presents a few signs of the end times, his emphasis, like Jesus' (Mark 13), is not on specific or current events but on each person's need to prepare for Christ's return by living rightly day by day. If we are ready, we won't have to be concerned about what will happen. God is in control of all events. (See 1 Thessalonians 4, 5 for Paul's earlier teaching on this subject.)

2:1, 2 In the Bible, the *day of the Lord* is used in two ways: the end times (which began with Christ and in which we are now living), and the final judgment day (which is yet to come). Paul emphasizes that the judgment day has not yet come.

2:3ff When Paul first wrote to the Thessalonians, they were in danger of losing hope in the Second Coming. Now they have shifted to the opposite extreme—some of them thought Jesus would be coming any minute. Paul tried to restore the balance by describing certain events that would happen before Christ's return.

2:3 Throughout history there have been antichrists— individuals who epitomized evil (see 1 John 2:18; 4:3; 2 John 7). Antichrists have occured in every generation and will continue to occur until a "man of rebellion" arises. Just before the Second Coming, a completely evil individual will arise. He will be Satan's tool with Satan's power—perhaps even Satan himself (2:9). This "son of hell" will be *the* Antichrist.

It is dangerous, however, to label certain individuals *antichrists* and try to predict Christ's coming based on those assumptions. Paul mentions the Antichrist, not necessarily to help us recognize him, but to urge us to ready ourselves for anything that might threaten our faith. If our faith is strong, we don't need to be afraid of what lies ahead. God is in control, and he will be victorious over the Antichrist. Our task is to ready ourselves for Christ and to spread his Good News so even more people will be prepared also.

and worship. He will go in and sit as God in the temple of God, claiming that he himself is God. [5]Don't you remember that I told you this when I was with you? [6]And you know what is keeping him from being here already; for he can come only when his time is ready.

[7]As for the work this man of rebellion and hell will do when he comes, it is already going on, but he himself will not come until the one who is holding him back steps out of the way. [8]Then this wicked one will appear, whom the Lord Jesus will burn up with the breath of his mouth and destroy by his presence when he returns. [9]This man of sin will come as Satan's tool, full of satanic power, and will trick everyone with strange demonstrations, and will do great miracles. [10]He will completely fool those who are on their way to hell because they have said "no" to the Truth; they have refused to believe it and love it, and let it save them, [11]so God will allow them to believe lies with all their hearts, [12]and all of them will be justly judged for believing falsehood, refusing the Truth, and enjoying their sins.

Believers should stand firm

[13]But we must forever give thanks to God for you, our brothers loved by the Lord, because God chose from the very first to give you salvation, cleansing you by the work of the Holy Spirit and by your trusting in the Truth. [14]Through us he told you the Good News. Through us he called you to share in the glory of our Lord Jesus Christ.

[15]With all these things in mind, dear brothers, stand firm and keep a strong grip on the truth that we taught you in our letters and during the time we were with you.

[16]May our Lord Jesus Christ himself and God our Father, who has loved us and given us everlasting comfort and hope which we don't deserve, [17]comfort your hearts with all comfort, and help you in every good thing you say and do.

2. Living in the light of Christ's return
Paul requests prayer

3 Finally, dear brothers, as I come to the end of this letter I ask you to pray for us. Pray first that the Lord's message will spread rapidly and triumph wherever it goes, winning converts everywhere as it did when it came to you. [2]Pray too that

2:7 Gen 6:3
1 Jn 4:3
2:8 Job 4:9
Isa 11:4
Mt 25:31
Heb 10:27
Rev 19:15
2:9 Mt 24:24
Eph 2:2
Rev 13:13
2:10 2 Cor 4:3
2:11 1 Kgs 22:22,23
Mt 24:5
Rom 1:24,28
2:12 Rom 1:32; 2:8
2:13 Eph 1:4
1 Pet 1:2
2:14 Jn 17:22
Rom 8:29,30
1 Thess 2:12
2:15 1 Cor 11:2; 16:13
2:16 Jn 3:16
2:17 1 Thess 3:2; 5:11
3:1 1 Thess 1:8; 5:25
3:2 Rom 15:30,31

2:13 *God chose from the very first to give you salvation,* or, "because God chose you to be among the first to believe."

2:7 "The work . . . is already going on" can also be translated "the mystery of lawlessness is already at work." Paul uses the word *mystery* for something no one can discover, but which God will reveal. The mystery of lawlessness, then, is the hidden, subtle, underlying force from which all sin springs. Civilization has a veneer of decency through law enforcement, education, science, and reason. Although we are horrified by criminal acts, we have yet to see the real horror of complete lawlessness. This will happen when the restraining forces are removed. Why will God allow this to happen? To show men and nations their own sinfulness, and to show them by bitter experience the true alternative to the Lordship of Christ. Men totally without God can act no better than vicious animals. Lawlessness, to a certain extent, is already going on, but the Lawless One has not yet arrived.

2:7 Who holds back the man of rebellion? Three possibilities have been suggested: (1) government and law, which help to curb evil, (2) the ministry and activity of the church and the effects of the gospel, or (3) the Holy Spirit. The Bible is not clear on who this "restrainer" is, only that he will not restrain forever. But we should not fear this—God is far stronger than the man of rebellion, and he will save his people.

2:9 Miracles from God can help strengthen our faith and lead people to Christ, but miracles are not necessarily from God. Christ's miracles were significant not just because of their power, but also because of their purpose—to help, to heal, to point us to God. The man of rebellion will have power to do mighty miracles, but his power will be from Satan. He will use this power to destroy

and to lead people away from God and toward himself. If anyone draws attention only to himself, his work is not from God.

2:10–12 God gives people freedom to turn their backs on him and believe Satan's lies. But if they say no to the Truth, they will experience the consequences of their sin.

2:13 Paul consistently taught that salvation begins and ends with God. We can do nothing to be saved on our own merit—we must accept God's gift of salvation (see the note on Ephesians 1:4). There is no other way to receive forgiveness from sin.

2:14 God worked through Paul and his companions to tell the Good News and to call new believers to share in Christ's glory. It seems strange that God works through us—fallible, unfaithful, untrustworthy human creatures. But he has given us the fantastic privilege of accomplishing his great mission— telling the world how to find salvation.

2:15 Paul knew that the Thessalonians would face pressure from persecutions, false teachers, worldliness, and apathy to waver from the truth and to leave the faith; so he urged them to keep a "grip on the truth" and to stand firm. We are also confronted with temptations to turn away from God. We should hold on to the truth found in Christ's teachings because our lives depend on it. Never forget the reality of his life and love!

3:2, 3 Beneath the surface of the routine of daily life, a fierce struggle among invisible spiritual powers is being waged. Like the wind, the evil powers' force can be devastating. Our main defense is prayer that God will protect us from evil and that he will make us

3:3
Jn 17:15
1 Cor 1:9
2 Pet 2:9

3:4
1 Thess 4:9,10

3:5
1 Jn 4:16

we will be saved out of the clutches of evil men, for not everyone loves the Lord. 3But the Lord is faithful; he will make you strong and guard you from satanic attacks of every kind. 4And we trust the Lord that you are putting into practice the things we taught you, and that you always will. 5May the Lord bring you into an ever deeper understanding of the love of God and of the patience that comes from Christ.

Paul admonishes the church against laziness

3:6
Rom 16:17
1 Cor 5:4; 11:2
1 Thess 5:14

3:8
Acts 18:3
1 Thess 2:9

3:9
Mt 10:10
1 Cor 9:4
1 Tim 5:17
1 Pet 5:3

3:10
1 Thess 4:11

3:11
1 Tim 5:13

3:12
Rom 12:11
1 Thess 4:1,11

3:15
Gal 6:1
1 Thess 5:14

6Now here is a command, dear brothers, given in the name of our Lord Jesus Christ by his authority: Stay away from any Christian who spends his days in laziness and does not follow the ideal of hard work we set up for you. 7For you well know that you ought to follow our example: you never saw us loafing; 8we never accepted food from anyone without buying it; we worked hard day and night for the money we needed to live on, in order that we would not be a burden to any of you. 9It wasn't that we didn't have the right to ask you to feed us, but we wanted to show you, firsthand, how you should work for your living. 10Even while we were still there with you we gave you this rule: "He who does not work shall not eat."

11Yet we hear that some of you are living in laziness, refusing to work, and wasting your time in gossiping. 12In the name of the Lord Jesus Christ we appeal to such people—we command them—to quiet down, get to work, and earn their own living. 13And to the rest of you I say, dear brothers, never be tired of doing right.

14If anyone refuses to obey what we say in this letter, notice who he is and stay away from him, that he may be ashamed of himself. 15Don't think of him as an enemy, but speak to him as you would to a brother who needs to be warned.

Paul's final greetings

3:16
Rom 15:33

3:17
1 Cor 16:21
Gal 6:11
Col 4:18
Philem 19

16May the Lord of peace himself give you his peace no matter what happens. The Lord be with you all.

17Now here is my greeting which I am writing with my own hand, as I do at the end of all my letters, for proof that it really is from me. This is in my own handwriting. 18May the blessing of our Lord Jesus Christ be upon you all.

Sincerely, Paul

---

strong. (See also comments on Ephesians 6:10–19 concerning our armor for spiritual warfare.) The following guidelines can help you prepare for and survive satanic attacks: (1) take the threat of spiritual attack seriously; (2) pray for strength and help from God; (3) study the Bible to recognize Satan's style and tactics, (4) memorize Scripture so it will be a source of help no matter where you are; (5) associate with those who speak the truth; and (6) practice what you are taught by spiritual leaders.

3:6-15 Some people in the Thessalonian church were falsely teaching that since Christ's Second Coming could happen any day, people should set aside their responsibilities, quit work, do no future planning, and just wait for Christ. But their lack of activity only led them into sin. They became a burden to the church, which was supporting them; they wasted time that could have been used for helping others; and they gossiped (3:11). They may have thought they were being more spiritual by not working, but Paul told them to be responsible and get back to work. Being ready for Christ means obeying him in every area of life. Because we know Christ is coming, we must do everything we can to live in a way that will please him when he arrives.

3:6-10 There's a difference between leisure and laziness. Relaxation and recreation provide a necessary and much needed

balance; but when it is time to work, Christians should be responsible. We should make the most of our talent and time, doing all we can to provide for ourselves and our dependents.

3:11, 12 Gossip is tantalizing. It is exciting to hear, and it makes us feel like insiders. But instead of building up, gossip tears down. If you often find your nose in other people's business, you may be underemployed. Look for a task to do for Christ or for your family and get to work.

3:14, 15 Paul counsels the church to stop financially supporting and to stop associating with those who persist in their laziness. Hunger and loneliness could be very effective means in making the idle become productive. Paul was not advising coldness or cruelty, but the kind of tough love one would show a brother.

3:18 The book of 2 Thessalonians is especially meaningful for those who are being persecuted or are under pressure for their faith. In chapter 1 we are told what suffering can do for us. In chapter 2 we are assured of final victory. In chapter 3 we are encouraged to continue living responsibly in spite of difficult circumstances. Christ's return is more than a doctrine; it is a promise. It is not just for the future; it has a vital impact on how we live now.

1 TIMOTHY

VITAL STATISTICS

PURPOSE:
To give encouragement and instruction to Timothy, a young leader

AUTHOR:
Paul

TO WHOM WRITTEN:
Timothy, young church leaders, and all believers everywhere

DATE WRITTEN:
About A.D. 64, from Rome or Macedonia (possibly Philippi), probably just prior to Paul's final imprisonment in Rome

SETTING:
Timothy was one of Paul's closest companions. Paul had sent Timothy to the church at Ephesus to counter the false teaching which had arisen there (1 Timothy 1:3, 4). Timothy probably served for a time as a leader in the church at Ephesus. Paul hoped to visit Timothy (3:14, 15; 4:13), but in the meantime, he wrote this letter to give Timothy practical advice for the ministry.

KEY VERSE:
"Don't let anyone think little of you because you are young. Be their ideal; let them follow the way you teach and live; be a pattern for them in your love, your faith, and your clean thoughts" (4:12).

KEY PEOPLE:
Paul, Timothy

KEY PLACE:
Ephesus

SPECIAL FEATURES:
First Timothy is a personal letter and a handbook of church administration and discipline.

WITHOUT trying, we model our values. Parents in particular demonstrate to their children what they consider important. "Like father, like son" is not just a well-worn cliché; it is a truth often repeated in our homes. And experience proves that children often follow the life-styles of their parents, repeating their successes and mistakes.

Timothy is a prime example of one who was influenced by godly relatives. His mother, Eunice, and grandmother, Lois, were Jewish believers who helped shape his spiritual life (2 Timothy 1:5; 3:15). Timothy is the first "second generation" Christian mentioned in the New Testament.

Timothy became Paul's protegé and was probably a leader of the church at Ephesus for a time. As a young minister, Timothy faced all sorts of pressures, conflicts, and challenges from the church and his surrounding culture. To counsel and encourage Timothy, Paul sent this very personal letter.

Paul wrote 1 Timothy in about A.D. 64, probably just prior to his final Roman imprisonment. Because he had appealed to Caesar, Paul was sent as a prisoner to Rome (see Acts 25—28). Most scholars believe that Paul was released in about A.D. 62 (possibly because the "statute of limitations" had expired), and that during the next few years he was able to travel. During this time, he wrote the letters of 1 Timothy and Titus. Soon, however, the Emperor Nero began his campaign to eliminate Christianity. It is believed that during this time, Paul was imprisoned again and eventually executed. During this second Roman imprisonment, Paul wrote 2 Timothy. Titus and the two letters to Timothy comprise what are called the "pastoral epistles."

Paul's first letter to Timothy affirms their relationship (1:2). He warns Timothy about false teachers (1:3–11), and urges him to cling tightly to his faith in Christ (1:12–20). Next Paul considers public worship, emphasizing the importance of prayer (2:1–7) and order in church meetings (2:8–15). This leads to a discussion of the qualifications of church leaders—pastors (elders) and deacons. Here Paul lists specific criteria for each office (3:1–16).

Paul speaks again about false teachers, telling Timothy how to recognize them and respond to them (4:1–16). Next, he gives practical advice on pastoral care to the young and old (5:1, 2), widows (5:3–16), elders (5:17–25), and slaves (6:1, 2). Paul concludes by exhorting Timothy to guard his motives (6:3–10), to stand firm in his faith (6:11, 12), to live above reproach (6:13–16), and to minister faithfully (6:17–21).

First Timothy holds many lessons. If you are a church leader, take note of Paul's relationship with this young disciple—his careful counsel and guidance. Measure yourself against the qualifications Paul gives for elders and deacons. If you are young in the faith, follow the example of godly Christian leaders, like Timothy, who imitated Paul's life. If you are a parent, remind yourself of the profound effect a Christian home can have on family members—a faithful mother and grandmother led Timothy to Christ and his ministry helped change the world.

THE BLUEPRINT

1. Instructions on right belief (1:1–20)
2. Instructions for the church (2:1—3:16)
3. Instructions for leaders (4:1—6:21)

Paul advised Timothy on such practical topics as qualifications for church leaders, public worship, confronting false teaching, and how to treat various groups of people within the church. Right belief and right behavior are critical for anyone who desires to lead or serve effectively in the church. We should all believe rightly, participate in church actively, and minister to one another lovingly.

MEGATHEMES

THEME	EXPLANATION	IMPORTANCE
Sound doctrine	Paul instructed Timothy to preserve the Christian faith by teaching sound doctrine and modeling right living. Timothy had to oppose false teachers who were leading church members away from belief in salvation by faith in Jesus Christ alone.	We must know the truth in order to defend it. We must cling to the belief that Christ came to save us. We should stay away from those who twist the words of the Bible for their own purposes.
Public worship	Prayer in public worship must be done with a proper attitude toward God and fellow believers.	Christian character must be evident in every aspect of worship. We must rid ourselves of any anger, resentment, or offensive attire that might disrupt worship or damage church unity.
Church leadership	Paul gives specific instructions concerning the qualifications for church leaders so that the church might honor God and run smoothly.	Church leaders must be wholly committed to Christ. If you are a new or young Christian, don't be anxious to become a leader in the church. Seek to develop your Christian character first. Be sure to seek God, not your own ambition.
Personal discipline	It takes discipline to be a leader in the church. Timothy, like all church leaders, had to guard his motives, minister faithfully, and live above reproach. Any pastor must keep morally and spiritually fit.	To stay in good spiritual shape, you must discipline yourself to study God's Word and to live a godly life. Put your spiritual abilities to work!
Caring church	The church has a responsibility to care for the needs of all its members, especially the sick, the poor, and the widowed.	Caring for the family of believers demonstrates our Christ-like attitude and exhibits genuine love to nonbelievers.

1. Instructions on right belief

1 *From:* Paul, a missionary of Jesus Christ, sent out by the direct command of God our Savior and by Jesus Christ our Lord—our only hope. ²*To:* Timothy.

Timothy, you are like a son to me in the things of the Lord. May God our Father and Jesus Christ our Lord show you his kindness and mercy and give you great peace of heart and mind.

Paul warns about false teachers

³, ⁴As I said when I left for Macedonia, please stay there in Ephesus and try to stop the men who are teaching such wrong doctrine. Put an end to their myths and fables, and their idea of being saved by finding favor with an endless chain of angels leading up to God—wild ideas that stir up questions and arguments instead of helping people accept God's plan of faith. ⁵What I am eager for is that all the Christians there will be filled with love that comes from pure hearts, and that their minds will be clean and their faith strong.

⁶But these teachers have missed this whole idea and spend their time arguing and talking foolishness. ⁷They want to become famous as teachers of the laws of Moses when they haven't the slightest idea what those laws really show us. ⁸Those laws are good when used as God intended. ⁹But they were not made for us, whom God has saved; they are for sinners who hate God, have rebellious hearts, curse and swear, attack their fathers and mothers, and murder. ¹⁰, ¹¹Yes, these laws are made

1:1
Gal 1:1,2
Col 1:27
Tit 1:3; 3:4

1:2
Acts 16:1
1 Cor 4:17
2 Tim 1:2
Tit 1:4

1:3,4
Acts 19:1,10
20:1-3
Gal 1:6,7
1 Tim 4:7; 6:3,4
Tit 3:9

1:5
Rom 13:8
Gal 5:14
2 Tim 1:5; 2:22
1 Pet 3:16

1:6
Tit 1:10

1:8
Rom 7:12,16

1:9
Gal 3:19
Rev 21:8

1:1 This letter was written to Timothy in A.D. 64 or 65, after Paul's first imprisonment in Rome (Acts 28:16–31). Paul was apparently released from prison for several years, during which time he revisited many churches in Asia and Macedonia. When Paul and Timothy returned to Ephesus, they found widespread false teaching in the church. Paul had warned the Ephesian elders to be on guard against the false teachers who would inevitably come after he had left (Acts 20:29, 30). Paul sent Timothy to lead the Ephesian church while he moved on to Macedonia. Paul may have written this letter from somewhere within Macedonia. Paul wrote to Timothy to help him deal with the difficult situation in the Ephesian church. Paul was then arrested again and later executed.

1:1 For more information on Paul, see his Profile in Acts 9.

1:1 Paul called himself a missionary or, literally, an *apostle*, "one who is sent." Paul was sent by Jesus Christ to give the message of salvation to the Gentiles (Acts 9:1–20).

1:1 In adventure stories, the hero often rescues defenseless victims at the last possible moment. Within this fictional world, the bold adventurer is the only hope for the victims. Within the reality of the spiritual realm, our only hope is Jesus Christ. Only he can save us. Where have you placed your hope?

1:3, 4 Paul first visited Ephesus on his second missionary journey (Acts 18:19–21). Later, on his third missionary journey, he stayed there for almost three years (Acts 19, 20). Ephesus, along with Rome, Corinth, Antioch, and Alexandria, was one of the major cities in the Roman Empire. It was a center for the commerce, politics, and religions of Asia Minor, and the place where the temple dedicated to the goddess Artemis (Diana) was located.

1:3, 4 The church at Ephesus was probably plagued by the same heresy that threatened the church at Colosse, the false doctrine that to be acceptable to God one had to find favor with angels. To aid in their salvation, some Ephesians constructed lists and biographies of angels. The false teachers mentioned here were motivated by their own interests rather than Christ's. They embroiled the church in endless and irrelevant disputes (1:6, 7). Today we have many opportunities to enter into such worthless and irrelevant discussions. Such disputes crowd out the life-changing message of Christ. Stay away from religious speculation and theological haggling. It may seem harmless at first, but it has a way of sidetracking us from the central message

of the gospel—the person and work of Jesus Christ.

1:3–11 The world is filled with people demanding allegiance, many of whom would have us turn from Christ to follow them. Often their influence is subtle. How can you recognize false teaching before it does irreparable damage? (1) It stirs up questions and arguments instead of helping people come to Jesus (1:4). (2) It is often promoted by teachers whose motivation is to make a name for themselves (1:7). (3) It will be contrary to the true teaching of the Scriptures (1:6, 7; 4:1–3). Instead of listening to false teachers, we should learn what the Bible teaches and remain steadfast in our faith in Christ alone.

1:5 The false teachers were motivated by curiosity, power, and prestige. By contrast, genuine Christian teachers are motivated by love, truth, and faith. It may be exciting to explore esoteric doctrines in order to impress people with our great "knowledge," but position based on falsehood is ultimately empty, a cheap and temporary thrill. Leaders who truly follow Christ will find lasting, eternal reward as they see his truth spread throughout the world and his love transform people everywhere.

1:6 Theological hairsplitting—arguing about tiny details of Scripture—can take us into interesting, but irrelevant bypaths and cause us to miss the intent of God's message. The false teachers at Ephesus constructed vast speculative systems and then argued about the minor details of their wholly imaginary ideas. We should allow nothing to distract us from the Good News of Jesus Christ, the main point of Scripture. We need to know what the Scriptures say, apply them to our lives daily, and teach them to others. When we do this we will be able to evaluate all teachings in light of the central truth about Jesus. Don't spend so much time on the minute details of Scripture that you miss the main point of what God is trying to teach you.

1:7–11 The "whole idea" the false teachers missed (1:6) was the purpose of God's law. The law was not meant to give believers a list of commands for every occasion, but to show nonbelievers their sin and bring them to God. For more of what Paul says about our relationship to law, see Romans 5:20, 21; 13:9, 10; Galatians 3:24–29.

1:10, 11 There are those who attempt to legitimize homosexuality as an acceptable alternative lifestyle. Even some Christians say people have a right to choose how they want to live. But the Bible to identify as sinners all who are immoral and impure: homosexuals, kidnappers, liars, and all others who do things that contradict the glorious Good News of our blessed God, whose messenger I am.

1:11
2 Cor 4:4

God's mercy on Paul

1:12
2 Cor 3:5,6
Phil 4:13
Col 1:25

1:13
Lk 23:34
Acts 8:3; 26:9
1 Cor 15:9

1:14
Lk 7:47
Rom 5:20
2 Tim 1:13

1:15
Lk 19:10
Rom 5:8

1:16
Eph 2:7

1:17
1 Tim 6:15,16

12How thankful I am to Christ Jesus our Lord for choosing me as one of his messengers, and giving me the strength to be faithful to him, 13even though I used to scoff at the name of Christ. I hunted down his people, harming them in every way I could. But God had mercy on me because I didn't know what I was doing, for I didn't know Christ at that time. 14Oh, how kind our Lord was, for he showed me how to trust him and become full of the love of Christ Jesus.

15How true it is, and how I long that everyone should know it, that Christ Jesus came into the world to save sinners—and I was the greatest of them all. 16But God had mercy on me so that Christ Jesus could use me as an example to show everyone how patient he is with even the worst sinners, so that others will realize that they, too, can have everlasting life. 17Glory and honor to God forever and ever. He is the King of the ages, the unseen one who never dies; he alone is God, and full of wisdom. Amen.

Cling tightly to the faith

1:18
2 Cor 10:4

1:19
1 Tim 6:12

1:20
1 Cor 5:5
2 Tim 2:17; 4:14

18Now, Timothy, my son, here is my command to you: Fight well in the Lord's battles, just as the Lord told us through his prophets that you would. 19Cling tightly to your faith in Christ and always keep your conscience clear, doing what you know is right. For some people have disobeyed their consciences and have deliberately done what they knew was wrong. It isn't surprising that soon they lost their faith in Christ after defying God like that. 20Hymenaeus and Alexander are two examples of this. I had to give them over to Satan to punish them until they could learn not to bring shame to the name of Christ.

---

specifically calls homosexual behavior sin (see Leviticus 18:22; Romans 1:18–32; 1 Corinthians 6:9–11). We must be careful, however, to condemn only the practice, not the people. People who commit homosexual acts are not to be feared, ridiculed, or hated. They can be forgiven and their lives can be transformed. The church should be a haven of forgiveness and healing for homosexuals without compromising its stance against homosexual behavior. For more on this subject see the note on Romans 1:27.

1:12–17 People can feel so guilt-ridden by their past that they think God could never forgive and accept them. But consider Paul's past. He had hunted down and murdered God's own people before coming to faith in Christ (Acts 9:1–9). God forgave Paul and he can forgive you.

1:14 When we become Christians, we often feel that our love for Jesus and others is inadequate. But we can be confident that Christ will give us the faith and love we need. Even with our weak faith, we must demonstrate genuine love toward others. Christ will increase both our faith and love as our relationship with him deepens.

1:15 In this verse, often memorized and quoted, Paul summarizes the Good News: Jesus saves sinners, and no sinner is beyond his saving power. Do you believe that? Jesus didn't come just to show us how to live, or to challenge us to be better people. He came to offer us salvation that leads to eternal life. Have you accepted his offer?

1:18 Paul highly valued the gift of prophecy (1 Corinthians 14:1) through which important messages of warning and encouragement came to the church. Just as pastors are set apart for ministry in today's church, Timothy was set apart for ministry when elders laid

their hands on him (see 4:14). Apparently at this ceremony, several believers prophesied about Timothy's gifts and strengths. These words from the Lord must have encouraged him throughout his ministry.

1:19 How can you keep your conscience clear? Treasure your faith in Christ more than anything else and do what you know is right. Each time you deliberately ignore your conscience, you are hardening your heart. Soon your capacity to tell right from wrong will disappear. But when you walk with God, he is able to speak to you through your conscience, letting you know the difference between right and wrong. Be sure to act on those inner tugs to do what is right—then your conscience will remain clear.

1:20 Hymenaeus' error is explained in 2 Timothy 2:17, 18. He weakened people's faith by teaching that the resurrection had already occurred. Paul says in 1 Timothy 1:20, that he gave him "over to Satan," which meant that Paul had removed him from the fellowship of the church. He did this so that Hymenaeus would see his error and repent. The ultimate purpose of this discipline was not punishment, but correction. The church today is too often lax in disciplining Christians who deliberately sin. Deliberate disobedience should be handled quickly and sternly to prevent the entire congregation from being infected. But it must be done in a way that strives to bring the offender back to Christ and into the loving embrace of the church. The definition of discipline includes these words: strengthening, purifying, training, correcting, perfecting. Therefore, condemnation, suspicion, withholding forgiveness, or permanent exile are not to be a part of church discipline.

2. Instructions for the church
Instructions about worship

2 Here are my directions: Pray much for others; plead for God's mercy upon them; give thanks for all he is going to do for them.

²Pray in this way for kings and all others who are in authority over us, or are in places of high responsibility, so that we can live in peace and quietness, spending our time in godly living and thinking much about the Lord. ³This is good and pleases God our Savior, ⁴for he longs for all to be saved and to understand this truth: ⁵*That God is on one side and all the people on the other side, and Christ Jesus, himself man, is between them to bring them together,* ⁶*by giving his life for all mankind.*

This is the message which at the proper time God gave to the world. ⁷And I have been chosen—this is the absolute truth—as God's minister and missionary to teach this truth to the Gentiles, and to show them God's plan of salvation through faith.

⁸So I want men everywhere to pray with holy hands lifted up to God, free from sin and anger and resentment. ⁹, ¹⁰And the women should be the same way, quiet and sensible in manner and clothing. Christian women should be noticed for being kind and good, not for the way they fix their hair or because of their jewels or fancy clothes. ¹¹Women should listen and learn quietly and humbly.

¹²I never let women teach men or lord it over them. Let them be silent in your

2:1 Eph 6:18
2:2 Rom 13:1
2:3 1 Tim 1:1
2:4 1 Tim 4:10; 2 Tim 2:25
2:5 Rom 8:35
2:6 Gal 4:4
2:7 Acts 9:15; 1 Cor 9:1; 2 Tim 1:1
2:8 Ps 24:4; 63:4
2:9 1 Pet 3:3
2:11 1 Cor 14:34
2:12 Tit 2:5

2:2 *in godly living and thinking much about the Lord,* literally, "in gravity."

2:1–6 Although God is all-powerful and all-knowing, he has chosen to let us help him change the world through our prayers. How this works is a mystery to us because of our limited understanding, but it is a reality. Paul urges us to pray for each other and for our leaders in government. Our earnest prayers will have powerful results (James 5:16).

2:2 Paul's command to pray for rulers was remarkable considering that Nero was emperor at this time (A.D. 54–68). Nero was a notoriously cruel emperor. He needed a scapegoat for the great fire that destroyed much of Rome in A.D. 64, so to take the focus off himself he blamed the Roman Christians. Persecution erupted throughout the Roman Empire. Not only were Christians denied certain privileges in society, some were even publicly butchered, burned, or fed to animals. Social ostracism was widespread. When Paul wrote this letter, persecution was a growing threat to believers.

2:4 Both Peter and Paul said that God longs for all to be saved (see 2 Peter 3:9). This does not mean that all *will* be saved, because the Bible makes it clear that many reject him (Matthew 25:31–46; John 12:44–50; Hebrews 10:26–29). These verses indicate that the gospel has a universal scope; it is not limited to people of one race, one sex, or one national background. God loves the whole world and sent his Son to save it, and he is hurt by all who turn away from him.

2:2–6 We human beings are separated from God by sin, and only one person in the universe can stand between us and bring us together again—Jesus, who is both God and man. Jesus' sacrifice brought new life to all mankind. Have you let him bring you to the Father?

2:8 Besides being displeasing to God, it is difficult to pray when we have sinned or when we feel angry and resentful. That is why Jesus told us to interrupt worship, if necessary, to make peace with others (Matthew 5:23, 24). Our goal is to have a right relationship with God and also with others.

2:9–15 To understand these verses, we must understand the situation in which Paul and Timothy worked. In first-century Jewish culture, women were not allowed to study. When Paul said women should learn quietly and humbly, he was offering them new opportunities. Paul did not want the Ephesian women to teach because they didn't yet have enough knowledge or experience. The Ephesian church had a particular problem with false teachers.

Evidently the women were especially susceptible to their teaching (2 Timothy 3:1–9), because they did not yet have enough biblical knowledge to see through the false claims. In addition, some of the women were apparently flaunting their new-found Christian freedom by wearing inappropriate clothing (2:9, 10). Paul was telling Timothy not to put anyone (in this case, women) into positions of leadership who were not yet mature in the faith (see 5:22). The same principle applies to churches today (see note on 3:6).

2:9, 10 Some Christian women were apparently trying to gain respect by looking beautiful rather than becoming Christlike in their characters. Some may have thought they could win unbelieving husbands through their appearance (see Peter's counsel to such women in 1 Peter 3:1–6). It is not unscriptural for a woman to want to be attractive; the holy city itself is described as "a glorious sight, as a bride at her wedding" (Revelation 21:2). Beauty, however, begins inside a person. A gentle, modest, loving character gives a light to the face that cannot be duplicated by the best cosmetics and jewelry in the world. A carefully groomed and well-decorated exterior looks artificial and cold unless inner beauty is present.

2:12 Some interpret this passage to mean that women should never teach in the assembled church. However, other commentators say that Paul's words "I never let" can be more literally translated "I am not allowing." Paul did not believe women should never teach men. Paul's commended coworker, Priscilla, taught Apollos, the great preacher (Acts 18:24–26). In addition, Paul frequently mentions other women who held positions of responsibility in the church. Phoebe was a deaconess (see Romans 16:1 in other translations). Mary, Tryphaena, and Tryphosa were the Lord's workers (Romans 16:6, 12), as were Euodias and Syntyche (Philippians 4:2). Thus, here in 1 Timothy 2:12, Paul would have been prohibiting the Ephesian women from teaching, not all women (see note on 2:9–15).

As to women being silent in church meetings, the word *silence* here is often translated "be in quietness," expressing an attitude of being composed and not unruly. A different Greek word is used to mean "complete silence." In addition, Paul himself acknowledges that women publicly prayed and prophesied (1 Corinthians 11:5). Apparently, however, the women in the Ephesian church were abusing their newly acquired Christian freedom. Because these women were new converts and uneducated, they did not yet have the necessary experience or knowledge to teach those who already had extensive biblical education.

TIMOTHY

Painful lessons are usually doorways to new opportunities. Even the apostle Paul had much to learn. Shortly after his disappointing experience with John Mark, Paul recruited Timothy to be his assistant. Paul's intense personality may have been too much for John Mark to handle. It could easily have been the same for Timothy. But Paul seems to have learned a lesson in patience from his old friend Barnabas. As a result, Timothy became a "son" to Paul.

Timothy probably became a Christian after Paul's first missionary visit to Lystra (Acts 16:1–5). Timothy's mother and grandmother had already taught him a great deal from the Old Testament Scriptures. By the time Paul visted Lystra a second time, Timothy had become a respected disciple of Jesus in his hometown. He did not hesitate to join Paul and Silas on their journey. His willingness to be circumcised as an adult is clearly a mark of his commitment (Timothy's mixed Greek/Jewish background could have created problems on their missionary journeys, since many of their audiences would be made up of Jews who were concerned with the strict keeping of this tradition). The circumcision helped to avoid that potential problem.

Beyond the tensions of his mixed racial background, Timothy seemed to struggle with a naturally timid character. Unfortunately, many who share Timothy's character are quickly written off as too great a risk to deserve much responsibility. By God's grace, Paul saw great potential in Timothy. Paul demonstrated his confidence in Timothy by entrusting him with important responsibilities. Paul sent Timothy as his personal representative to Corinth during a particularly tense time (1 Corinthians 4:14–17). Although Timothy was apparently ineffective in that difficult mission, Paul did not give up on him. He continued to travel with Paul.

Our last pictures of Timothy come from the most personal letters in the New Testament: 1 and 2 Timothy. In them, the aging apostle Paul is near the end of his life, but his burning desire to continue his mission has not dimmed. Paul is writing to one of his closest friends: they have traveled, suffered, cried, and laughed together. Paul left Timothy in Ephesus to oversee the young church there (1 Timothy 1:3, 4). He writes to encourage Timothy and give him needed direction. These letters have provided comfort and help to countless other "Timothys" through the years. When you face a challenge which is beyond your abilities, read 1 and 2 Timothy, and remember that others have shared your experience.

Strengths and accomplishments:
- Became a believer after Paul's first missionary journey and joined him for his other two journeys
- Was a respected Christian in his hometown
- Was Paul's special representative on several occasions
- Received two personal letters from Paul
- Probably knew Paul better than any other person, becoming like a son to him

Weaknesses and mistakes:
- Struggled with a timid and reserved nature
- He allowed others to look down upon his youthfulness
- He was apparently unable to correct some of the problems in the church at Corinth when Paul sent him there

Lessons from his life:
- Youthfulness should not be an excuse for ineffectiveness
- Our inadequacies and inabilities should not keep us from being available to God

Vital statistics:
- Where: Lystra
- Occupation: Missionary-in-training
- Relatives: Mother: Eunice. Grandmother: Lois. Greek father.
- Contemporaries: Paul, Silas, Luke, Mark, Peter, Barnabas

Key verses:
"There is no one like Timothy for having a real interest in you; everyone else seems to be worrying about his own plans and not those of Jesus Christ. But you know Timothy. He has been just like a son to me in helping me preach the Good News" (Philippians 2:20–22).

Timothy's story is told in Acts, starting in chapter 16. He is also mentioned in Romans 16:21; 1 Corinthians 4:17; 16:10, 11; 2 Corinthians 1:1, 19; Philippians 1:1; 2:19–23; Colossians 1:1, 2; 1 Thessalonians 1:1–10; 2:3, 4; 3:2–6; 1 and 2 Timothy; Philemon 1:1; Hebrews 13:23.

church meetings. 13Why? Because God made Adam first, and afterwards he made Eve. 14And it was not Adam who was fooled by Satan, but Eve, and sin was the result. 15So God sent pain and suffering to women when their children are born, but he will save their souls if they trust in him, living quiet, good, and loving lives.

2:13
Gen 2:7,22

2:14,15
Gen 3:6,13,16

Standards for church leaders

3 It is a true saying that if a man wants to be a pastor he has a good ambition. 2For a pastor must be a good man whose life cannot be spoken against. He must have only one wife, and he must be hard working and thoughtful, orderly, and full of good deeds. He must enjoy having guests in his home, and must be a good Bible teacher. 3He must not be a drinker or quarrelsome, but he must be gentle and kind, and not be one who loves money. 4He must have a well-behaved family, with children who obey quickly and quietly. 5For if a man can't make his own little family behave, how can he help the whole church?

3:1
Acts 20:28

3:2
Tit 1:6,8

3:3
Tit 1:7

3:4
1 Tim 3:12

6The pastor must not be a new Christian, because he might be proud of being chosen so soon, and pride comes before a fall. (Satan's downfall is an example.) 7Also, he must be well spoken of by people outside the church—those who aren't Christians—so that Satan can't trap him with many accusations, and leave him without freedom to lead his flock.

3:7
2 Cor 8:21
2 Tim 2:26

8The deacons must be the same sort of good, steady men as the pastors. They must not be heavy drinkers and must not be greedy for money. 9They must be earnest, wholehearted followers of Christ who is the hidden Source of their faith. 10Before they are asked to be deacons they should be given other jobs in the church as a test of their character and ability, and if they do well, then they may be chosen as deacons.

3:8
Phil 1:1

3:9
1 Tim 1:19

11Their wives must be thoughtful, not heavy drinkers, not gossipers, but faithful

3:1 *pastor*, more literally, "church leader," or "presiding elder."

2:13, 14 In previous letters Paul had talked about male/female roles in marriage (Ephesians 5:21–33; Colossians 3:18, 19). Here he talks about male/female roles within the church. Some scholars see these verses about Adam and Eve as an illustration of what was happening in the Ephesian church. Just as Eve had been deceived in the Garden of Eden, so the women in the church were being deceived by false teachers. And just as Adam was the first human created by God, so the men in the church in Ephesus should be the first to speak and teach, because they had had more experience in learning the things of God. This view, then, stresses that Paul's teaching here is not universal, but applies to churches with similar problems. Other scholars, however, contend that the roles Paul points out are God's design for his created order. He established these roles to maintain harmony in both the family and the church.

2:14 Paul was not excusing Adam for his part in the Fall (Genesis 3:6, 7, 17–19). On the contrary, in his letter to the Romans Paul placed the primary blame for mankind's sinful nature on Adam (Romans 5:12–21).

2:15 This verse is literally translated, "But women will be saved through childbirth." There are several interpretations: (1) Man sinned and was condemned to hard labor. Woman sinned and was condemned to pain in childbearing. Both men and women, however, can be saved through trusting Christ and obeying him. (2) Women who fulfill their God-given roles are demonstrating true commitment and obedience to Christ. One of the most important roles for a wife and mother is to care for her family. (3) The childbirth mentioned here refers to the birth of Jesus Christ. Women (and men) are saved spiritually because of the most important birth, that of Christ himself. (4) From the lessons learned through the trials of childbirth, women can develop qualities that teach them about love, trust, submission, and service.

3:1–13 It is good to want to be a spiritual leader, but the standards are high. Paul enumerates some of the qualifications

here. Do you hold a position of spiritual leadership, or would you like to be a leader some day? Check yourself against Paul's standard of excellence. Those with great responsibility must meet high expectations.

3:2 When Paul says elders (see textual note) should have only one wife, he is prohibiting both polygamy and promiscuity. This does not prohibit an unmarried man from becoming an elder or a widowed elder from remarrying.

3:4, 5 Christian workers and volunteers sometimes make the mistake of thinking their work is so important that they are justified in ignoring their families. Spiritual leadership, however, must begin at home. If a man is not willing to care for, discipline, and teach his children, he is not qualified to lead the church.

3:6 New believers should become secure and strong in the faith before taking a leadership role in the church. Too often, when the church is desperate for workers, they place new believers into positions of responsibility for which they are unqualified. New faith needs to pass the test of time in order to mature. New believers should have a place of service, but not be put into leadership positions until they are firmly grounded in the Christian way of life.

3:8–10 *Deacon* means "one who serves." This position was begun by the apostles in the Jerusalem church (Acts 6:1–6) to care for the physical needs of the congregation, especially the needs of the Greek-speaking widows. Deacons were leaders in the church and their qualifications resemble those of elders. In some churches today, the office of deacon has become a catch-all position in which new and young Christians are often asked to serve. That is not the New Testament pattern. Paul says men are to be tested with lesser responsibilities before being made deacons.

3:11 Some have translated *wives* as "women helpers" or "deaconesses." It is unclear whether this verse refers to wives of deacons or female leaders of the church (such as Phoebe, the deacon mentioned in Romans 16:1). In either case, Paul expects

3:12
1 Tim 3:2,4

3:13
Mt 25:21

in everything they do. 12Deacons should have only one wife and they should have happy, obedient families. 13Those who do well as deacons will be well rewarded both by respect from others and also by developing their own confidence and bold trust in the Lord.

14I am writing these things to you now, even though I hope to be with you soon,

3:15
Mt 16:16-18
Eph 2:21

15so that if I don't come for awhile you will know what kind of men you should choose as officers for the church of the living God, which contains and holds high the truth of God.

3:16
Isa 7:14
Mt 4:11
Jn 1:14
Rom 1:3,4
Acts 1:9
1 Jn 4:2,3; 5:6

16It is quite true that the way to live a godly life is not an easy matter. But the answer lies in Christ, who came to earth as a man, was proved spotless and pure in his Spirit, was served by angels, was preached among the nations, was accepted by men everywhere and was received up again to his glory in heaven.

3. Instructions for elders
Paul's warning about false teachers

4:1
Jn 16:13
2 Thess 2:3
2 Pet 2:1
1 Jn 4:6

4 But the Holy Spirit tells us clearly that in the last times some in the church will turn away from Christ and become eager followers of teachers with devil-inspired ideas. 2These teachers will tell lies with straight faces and do it so often that their consciences won't even bother them.

4:2
Eph 4:19

4:3
Prov 18:22
Col 2:16
Heb 13:4

3They will say it is wrong to be married and wrong to eat meat, even though God gave these things to well-taught Christians to enjoy and be thankful for. 4For everything God made is good, and we may eat it gladly if we are thankful for it, 5and if we ask God to bless it, for it is made good by the Word of God and prayer.

4:4
1 Cor 10:26
Tit 1:15

4:6
2 Tim 3:14

6If you explain this to the others you will be doing your duty as a worthy pastor who is fed by faith and by the true teaching you have followed.

4:7
1 Tim 1:4

4:8
Col 2:23

7Don't waste time arguing over foolish ideas and silly myths and legends. Spend your time and energy in the exercise of keeping spiritually fit. 8Bodily exercise is all right, but spiritual exercise is much more important and is a tonic for all you do. So exercise yourself spiritually and practice being a better Christian, because that will help you not only now in this life, but in the next life too. 9, 10This is the truth and everyone should accept it. We work hard and suffer much in order that people

---

the behavior of prominent women in the church to be just as responsible as that of prominent men.

3:14, 15 To be a church leader is a heavy responsibility because the church belongs to the living God. Church leaders are not to be elected because they are popular, nor should they be allowed to push their way to the top. Instead they should be chosen by the church because of their respect for truth, both in doctrine and in their personal lives.

3:15, 16 The lists of qualifications for church office show that living a godly life requires effort and self-discipline. All believers, even if they never plan to be church leaders, should strive to follow these guidelines because they are consistent with what God says is true and right. The strength to do so comes from Christ.

4:1 The "last times" began with Christ's resurrection and will continue until his return, when he will set up his Kingdom and judge all mankind.

4:1, 2 False teachers were and still are a threat to the church. Jesus and the apostles repeatedly warned against them (see, for example, Mark 13:21–23; Acts 20:28–31; 2 Thessalonians 2:1–12; 2 Peter 3:3–7). The danger Timothy faced in Ephesus seems to have come from certain people in the church who followed some Greek philosophers who held that the body is evil and that only the soul matters. They refused to believe that the God of creation was good, because his very contact with the physical world would soil him. Though these Greek-influenced church members honored Jesus, they could not believe he was truly human. Their teachings, if left unchecked, would greatly distort Christian truth.

It is not enough that a teacher appears to know what he is

talking about, is disciplined and moral, and says he is speaking for God. If his words contradict biblical teaching, his teaching is false. Paul was warning Timothy not only of this specific problem, but of any teaching that causes us to dilute or reject parts of our faith. Such false teaching can be very direct or extremely subtle.

4:1–5 Why did Paul say the false teachers were devil- inspired (4:1)? Satan deceives people by offering a clever imitation of the real thing. The false teachers were giving stringent rules and this made them look righteous. Their strict disciplines for the body, however, could not remove sin (see Colossians 2:20–23). We must look beyond a teacher's methods and disciplines to his teaching about Jesus Christ. His attitude toward Christ shows the source of his message.

4:4, 5 In opposition to the false teachers, Paul affirms that everything God made is good (see Genesis 1). We should ask his blessing on his created gifts that give us pleasure and we should thank him for them. This doesn't mean we should abuse what God has made (for example gluttony abuses God's gift of good food, lust abuses God's gift of love, and murder abuses God's gift of life). We should not abuse what God has made, but enjoy these gifts by using them to serve and honor God. Have you thanked God for the good things he has made? Are you using them in a way that is pleasing to you *and* to God?

4:7–10 Are you in shape physically and spiritually? In our society, much emphasis is placed on physical fitness, but Paul declared that spiritual health is even more important than physical health. We must develop our faith through using the abilities God has given us in the service of the church (see 4:14–16).

will believe it, for our hope is in the living God who died for all, and particularly for those who have accepted his salvation.

[11]Teach these things and make sure everyone learns them well. [12]Don't let anyone think little of you because you are young. Be their ideal; let them follow the way you teach and live; be a pattern for them in your love, your faith, and your clean thoughts. [13]Until I get there, read and explain the Scriptures to the church; preach God's Word.

[14]Be sure to use the abilities God has given you through his prophets when the elders of the church laid their hands upon your head. [15]Put these abilities to work; throw yourself into your tasks so that everyone may notice your improvement and progress. [16]Keep a close watch on all you do and think. Stay true to what is right and God will bless you and use you to help others.

Caring for different groups in the church

5 Never speak sharply to an older man, but plead with him respectfully just as though he were your own father. Talk to the younger men as you would to much loved brothers. [2]Treat the older women as mothers, and the girls as your sisters, thinking only pure thoughts about them.

[3]The church should take loving care of women whose husbands have died, if they don't have anyone else to help them. [4]But if they have children or grandchildren, these are the ones who should take the responsibility, for kindness should begin at home, supporting needy parents. This is something that pleases God very much.

[5]The church should care for widows who are poor and alone in the world, if they are looking to God for his help and spending much time in prayer; [6]but not if they are spending their time running around gossiping, seeking only pleasure and thus ruining their souls. [7]This should be your church rule so that the Christians will know and do what is right.

[8]But anyone who won't care for his own relatives when they need help, especially those living in his own family, has no right to say he is a Christian. Such a person is worse than the heathen.

4:10
1 Tim 2:4; 3:15

4:11
1 Tim 5:7

4:12
1 Cor 16:11
Tit 2:7

4:13
1 Tim 3:14

4:14
Acts 6:6
1 Tim 1:8
2 Tim 1:6

5:1
Lev 19:32
Tit 2:2,6

5:4
Mt 15:4
Eph 6:2
1 Tim 2:3

5:5
Lk 2:37
1 Pet 3:5

5:6
Jas 5:5

4:12, 13 Timothy was a young leader. It would be easy for older Christians to look down on him because of his youth. He had to earn the respect of his elders by setting an example in his teaching and living, of love, faith, and purity. Regardless of your age, God can use you. Whether you are young or old, don't think of your age as a handicap. Live so others can see Christ in you.

4:14, 15 As a young leader in a church with a lot of problems, Timothy may have felt intimidated. The elders and prophets encouraged him and charged him to use his spiritual abilities responsibly. Highly skilled and talented athletes will lose their abilities if their muscles aren't toned by constant use, so we will lose our spiritual gifts if we don't put them to work. Our talents are enhanced by exercise, but failing to use them causes them to waste away from lack of practice and nourishment. What gifts and abilities has God given you? Use them regularly in serving God and others (see Romans 12:1–8; 2 Timothy 1:6–8).

5:2 Men in the ministry can avoid improper attitudes toward women by treating them as sisters, not as possessions or objects. If men see women as fellow members in God's family, they will protect them and help them grow spiritually.

5:3 Because there were no pensions, no social security, no life insurance, and few honorable jobs for women, widows were usually unable to support themselves. If a widow had no children or other family members to support her, she was doomed to poverty. From the beginning the church took care of its widows, who in turn gave valuable service to the church.

5:3ff Paul wanted Christian families to be as self-supporting as possible. He insisted that children and grandchildren take care of the widows in their families (5:4); he suggested that younger

widows remarry and start new families (5:14); and he ordered the church not to support lazy members who refused to work (2 Thessalonians 3:10). Nevertheless, when necessary, the believers pooled their resources (Acts 2:44–47); they gave generously to help disaster-ridden churches (1 Corinthians 16:1–4); and they took care of a large number of widows (Acts 6:1–6). The church has always had limited resources, and it has always had to balance financial responsibility with generosity. It only makes sense for members to work as hard as they can and to be as independent as possible so they can adequately care for themselves and for less fortunate members. When church members are both responsible and generous, everyone's needs can be met.

5:4 The responsibility for caring for the helpless naturally falls first on their families, the people whose lives are closely linked with theirs. But families cannot always provide all the necessary care. The church should support those who have no families, and it should also help the others—whether elderly, young, handicapped, ill, or poverty stricken—with their emotional and spiritual needs. Often families who are caring for their own helpless members have heavy burdens. They may need extra money, a listening ear, a helping hand, or a word of encouragement. Interestingly, those who are helped often turn around and help others so that the church turns into a circle of caring.

5:8 Almost everyone has relatives, family of some kind. Family relationships are so important in God's eyes, Paul says, that one who neglects his family responsibilities should not call himself a Christian. Are you doing your part to meet the needs of those included in your family circle?

5:10
Gen 18:3,4
Acts 9:36

9A widow who wants to become one of the special church workers should be at least sixty years old and have been married only once. 10She must be well thought of by everyone because of the good she has done. Has she brought up her children well? Has she been kind to strangers as well as to other Christians? Has she helped those who are sick and hurt? Is she always ready to show kindness?

11The younger widows should not become members of this special group because after awhile they are likely to disregard their vow to Christ and marry again.

5:12
Heb 6:4-6
5:13
2 Thess 3:11
Tit 1:11
5:14
1 Cor 7:9
1 Tim 3:15
Tit 2:5
5:15
1 Tim 1:20
5:16
Ruth 2:18

12And so they will stand condemned because they broke their first promise. 13Besides, they are likely to be lazy and spend their time gossiping around from house to house, getting into other people's business. 14So I think it is better for these younger widows to marry again and have children, and take care of their own homes; then no one will be able to say anything against them. 15For I am afraid that some of them have already turned away from the church and been led astray by Satan.

16Let me remind you again that a widow's relatives must take care of her, and not leave this to the church to do. Then the church can spend its money for the care of widows who are all alone and have nowhere else to turn.

5:17
Rom 12:8
Gal 6:6
1 Thess 5:12
5:18
Deut 25:4
Lk 10:7

17Pastors who do their work well should be paid well and should be highly appreciated, especially those who work hard at both preaching and teaching. 18For the Scriptures say, "Never tie up the mouth of an ox when it is treading out the grain—let him eat as he goes along!" And in another place, "Those who work deserve their pay!"

5:19
Mt 18:16
5:20
Deut 13:11
2 Cor 7:11
Eph 5:11

19Don't listen to complaints against the pastor unless there are two or three witnesses to accuse him. 20If he has really sinned, then he should be rebuked in front of the whole church so that no one else will follow his example.

5:21
1 Tim 6:13
5:22
1 Tim 4:14
5:23
1 Tim 3:8

21I solemnly command you in the presence of God and the Lord Jesus Christ and of the holy angels to do this whether the pastor is a special friend of yours or not. All must be treated exactly the same. 22Never be in a hurry about choosing a pastor; you may overlook his sins and it will look as if you approve of them. Be sure that you yourself stay away from all sin. 23(By the way, this doesn't mean you should completely give up drinking wine. You ought to take a little sometimes as medicine for your stomach because you are sick so often.)

5:24
Rev 14:13

24Remember that some men, even pastors, lead sinful lives and everyone knows it. In such situations you can do something about it. But in other cases only the judgment day will reveal the terrible truth. 25In the same way, everyone knows how much good some pastors do, but sometimes their good deeds aren't known until long afterward.

5:9 one of the special church workers, literally, "enrolled as a widow."

5:9-16 Apparently older widows took a vow by which they committed themselves to work for the church in exchange for financial support. Three out of four women today eventually are widowed, and most of the older women in our churches have lost their husbands. Does your church provide an avenue of service for these women? Could you help match their gifts and abilities with your church's needs?

5:17, 18 Faithful, diligent church leaders should be supported and appreciated. Too often they are targets for criticism because the congregation has unrealistic expectations. How do you treat your church leaders? Do you enjoy finding fault, or do you show your appreciation? Do they receive enough financial support to allow them to live without worry and provide for the needs of their families? Jesus and Paul emphasized the importance of supporting ministers who lead and teach us (see Galatians 6:6 and the notes on Luke 10:7 and 1 Corinthians 9:4–10).

5:17, 18 Preaching and teaching are closely related. Preaching is proclaiming the Word of God and confronting listeners with the truth of Scripture. Teaching is explaining the truth in Scripture, helping learners understand difficult passages, and helping them apply God's Word to daily life.

5:19, 20 Church leaders are not exempt from sin, faults, and mistakes. But they are often criticized for the wrong reasons—minor imperfections, failure to meet someone's expectations, personality clashes. Thus Paul said that complaints should not even be heard unless two or three witnesses will confirm them. Sometimes church leaders should be confronted about their behavior, and sometimes they should be rebuked. But all rebuking must be done fairly, lovingly, and for the purpose of restoration.

5:22 It is a serious responsibility to choose church leaders. They must have strong faith and live upright lives, having the qualities described in 1 Timothy 3:1–7 and Titus 1:5–9. Not everyone who wants to be a church leader is eligible. Be certain of an applicant's qualifications before asking him to lead you spiritually.

6 Christian slaves should work hard for their owners and respect them; never let it be said that Christ's people are poor workers. Don't let the name of God or his teaching be laughed at because of this.

2If their owner is a Christian, that is no excuse for slowing down; rather they should work all the harder because a brother in the faith is being helped by their efforts.

Teach these truths, Timothy, and encourage all to obey them.

Avoid worthless arguments and the longing to be rich

3Some may deny these things, but they are the sound, wholesome teachings of the Lord Jesus Christ and are the foundation for a godly life. 4Anyone who says anything different is both proud and stupid. He is quibbling over the meaning of Christ's words and stirring up arguments ending in jealousy and anger, which only lead to name-calling, accusations, and evil suspicions. 5These arguers—their minds warped by sin—don't know how to tell the truth; to them the Good News is just a means of making money. Keep away from them.

6Do you want to be truly rich? You already are if you are happy and good. 7After all, we didn't bring any money with us when we came into the world, and we can't carry away a single penny when we die. 8So we should be well satisfied without money if we have enough food and clothing. 9But people who long to be rich soon begin to do all kinds of wrong things to get money, things that hurt them and make them evil-minded and finally send them to hell itself. 10For the love of money is the first step toward all kinds of sin. Some people have even turned away from God because of their love for it, and as a result have pierced themselves with many sorrows.

Paul's final instructions

11Oh, Timothy, you are God's man. Run from all these evil things and work instead at what is right and good, learning to trust him and love others, and to be patient and gentle. 12Fight on for God. Hold tightly to the eternal life which God has given you, and which you have confessed with such a ringing confession before many witnesses.

13I command you before God who gives life to all, and before Christ Jesus who gave a fearless testimony before Pontius Pilate, 14that you fulfill all he has told you to do, so that no one can find fault with you from now until our Lord Jesus Christ returns. 15For in due season Christ will be revealed from heaven by the blessed and only Almighty God, the King of kings and Lord of lords, 16who alone can never die, who lives in light so terrible that no human being can approach him. No mere man has ever seen him, nor ever will. Unto him be honor and everlasting power and dominion forever and ever. Amen.

17Tell those who are rich not to be proud and not to trust in their money, which

6:1
Tit 2:9

6:2
1 Tim 4:11

6:3
1 Tim 1:3,10
Tit 1:1

6:4
1 Cor 8:2
1 Tim 1:4
2 Tim 2:14

6:5
Rom 16:17
2 Tim 3:8
Tit 1:11

6:6
Ps 37:16
Phil 4:11
1 Tim 4:8

6:7
Job 1:21

6:8
Prov 30:8
Heb 13:5

6:9
Mt 13:22

6:11
2 Tim 2:22

6:12
1 Tim 1:19
2 Tim 2:2-4; 4:7

6:13
Jn 18:37

6:14
1 Thess 3:13

6:15
1 Tim 1:17
Rev 17:14; 19:16

6:16
Ex 33:20
2 Chron 5:14
Ps 104:2
Jn 1:18; 5:26
1 Tim 1:17

6:17
Lk 12:20

6:1, 2 In Paul's culture there was a great social and legal gulf separating masters and slaves. But as Christians, masters and slaves became spiritual equals, brothers or sisters in the faith (Galatians 3:28). Paul did not speak to the evils in the institution of slavery, but he gave guidelines for Christian slaves and Christian masters. His counsel for the master/slave relationship can be applied to the employer/employee relationship today. Employees should work hard, showing respect for their employers. In turn, employers should be fair (Ephesians 6:5–9; Colossians 3:22–25). Our work should reflect our faithfulness to and love for Christ.

6:3–5 Division within the church often begins with quibblings over minute points of theology. This leads to all sorts of problems. A person's understanding of the finer points of theology should not become the basis for lording it over others or making money. Instead, theology should always unify the church. Stay away from those who just want to argue.

6:6–10 Despite almost overwhelming evidence to the contrary, most people still believe that money brings happiness. Rich people

craving greater riches can be caught in an endless cycle which only ends in ruin and destruction. How can you keep away from the love of money? Paul gives us some principles: (1) realize that one day riches will all be gone (6:7, 17); (2) be content with what you have (6:8); (3) monitor what you are willing to do to get more money (6:9, 10); (4) love people more than money (6:11); (5) love God's work more than money (6:11); (6) freely share what you have with others (6:18). (See Proverbs 30:7–9.)

6:13 Jesus' trial before Pilate is recorded in the Gospels: Matthew 27:11–26; Mark 15:1–15; Luke 23:1–25; John 18:28—19:16.

6:17–19 Ephesus was a wealthy city and the Ephesian church probably had many wealthy members. Paul advised Timothy to deal with that potential problem by teaching that the possession of riches carries great responsibility. Those who have money must be generous, not arrogant because they have a lot to give. They must be careful not to put their trust in money instead of in the living God for their security. Even if we don't have material wealth, we can be rich in good works toward others. No matter how poor

will soon be gone, but their pride and trust should be in the living God who always richly gives us all we need for our enjoyment. [18]Tell them to use their money to do good. They should be rich in good works and should give happily to those in need, always being ready to share with others whatever God has given them. [19]By doing this they will be storing up real treasure for themselves in heaven—it is the only safe investment for eternity! And they will be living a fruitful Christian life down here as well.

  [20]Oh, Timothy, don't fail to do these things that God entrusted to you. Keep out of foolish arguments with those who boast of their "knowledge" and thus prove their lack of it. [21]Some of these people have missed the most important thing in life—they don't know God. May God's mercy be upon you.

                       Sincerely, Paul

6:19
Mt 6:20
1 Tim 6:12

6:20
2 Tim 2:16

6:21
1 Tim 1:19
2 Tim 2:18

---

we are, we have something to share with someone.

6:21 The book of 1 Timothy provides guiding principles for local churches, including rules for public worship and qualifications for elders (pastors), deacons, and special church workers (widows). Paul tells the church leaders to correct unsound doctrine and to deal lovingly and fairly with all people in the church. The church is not organized for the sake of organization, but so Christ can be honored and glorified in its midst. While studying these guidelines, don't lose sight of the most important things in the life of the church—knowing God, working together in loving harmony, and taking God's Good News to the world.

2 TIMOTHY

VITAL STATISTICS

PURPOSE:
To give final instructions and encouragement to Timothy, an elder of the church at Ephesus

AUTHOR:
Paul

TO WHOM WRITTEN:
Timothy

DATE WRITTEN:
About A.D. 66 or 67 from prison in Rome. After a year or two of freedom, Paul was arrested again and executed under Emperor Nero.

SETTING:
Paul is virtually alone in prison; only Luke is with him. He writes this letter to pass the torch to the new generation of church leaders. He also asks for visits from his friends, for his books, and especially the parchments—possibly parts of the Old Testament, the Gospels, and other biblical manuscripts.

KEY VERSE:
"Work hard so God can say to you, 'Well done.' Be a good workman, one who does not need to be ashamed when God examines your work. Know what his Word says and means" (2:15).

KEY PEOPLE:
Paul, Timothy, Luke, Mark, and others

KEY PLACES:
Rome, Ephesus

SPECIAL FEATURES:
Because this is Paul's last letter, it reveals his heart and his priorities—sound doctrine, steadfast faith, confident endurance, and enduring love.

"FAMOUS last words" is more than a cliché. When notable men and women of influence are about to die, many wait to hear their final words of insight and wisdom; and those words are repeated worldwide. This is also true with a dying loved one. Gathered at his or her side, the family strains to hear every whispered syllable of blessing, encouragement, and advice, knowing that this will be the final message.

One of the most knowledgeable, influential, and beloved men of history was the apostle Paul. And we have his famous last words.

Paul was facing death. He was not dying of a disease in a sterile hospital with loved ones gathered near. He was very much alive, but his condition was terminal. Convicted as a follower of Jesus of Nazareth, he lay in a cold Roman prison, cut off from the world, with just a visitor or two and his writing materials. Paul knew that soon he would be executed (4:6), and so he wrote his final thoughts to his "son" Timothy, passing to him the torch of leadership, reminding him of what was truly important, and encouraging him in the faith. Imagine how Timothy must have read and reread every word—this was the last message from his beloved mentor, Christ's great missionary apostle, Paul. Because of the situation and the recipient, this is the most intimate and moving of all Paul's letters, and his last.

Paul's introduction is tender, and the love he has for Timothy seeps from every phrase (1:1–5). He then reminds Timothy of the qualities necessary for a faithful minister of Jesus Christ (1:6—2:13). Timothy should remember his call and use his gifts with boldness (1:6–12), hold tightly to the truth (1:13–18), prepare others to follow him in the ministry (2:1, 2), be disciplined and ready to suffer hardship like a soldier, an athlete, and a farmer (2:3–7), and keep his eyes and mind focused on Christ (2:8–13). Paul challenges Timothy to hold to sound doctrine, reject error and foolish discussions, know the Word (2:14–19), and keep his life pure (2:20–26).

Next, Paul warns Timothy of the opposition he and other believers would face in the last days from self-centered people who use the church for their own gain and who teach new and false doctrines (3:1–9). He tells Timothy to be prepared for them by remembering his example (3:10, 11), understanding the real source of the opposition (3:12, 13), and finding strength and power in the Word of God (3:14–17). Then Paul gives Timothy a stirring charge—to preach the Word (4:1–4) and to fulfill his ministry until the end (4:5–8).

Paul concludes with personal requests and items of information. In these final words, he reveals his loneliness and his strong love for his brothers and sisters in Christ (4:9–22).

There has never been another person like Paul, the missionary apostle. He was a man of deep faith, undying love, constant hope, tenacious conviction, and profound insight. And he was inspired by the Holy Spirit to give us God's message. As you read 2 Timothy, know that you are reading the last words of this great man of God—last words to Timothy and to all who would claim to follow Christ.

THE BLUEPRINT

1. Foundations of Christian service
   (1:1—2:26)
2. Difficult times for Christian service
   (3:1—4:22)

Paul gives helpful advice to Timothy to remain solidly grounded in Christian service and endure suffering during the difficult days to come. It is easy for us to serve Christ for the wrong reasons: because it is exciting, rewarding, or personally enriching. Without a proper foundation, however, we will find it easy to quit during difficult times. All believers need a strong foundation for their service, because Christian service does not get easier as we grow older, and it will become no easier as we near the last days.

MEGATHEMES

THEME	EXPLANATION	IMPORTANCE
Boldness	In the face of opposition and persecution, Timothy was to carry out his ministry unashamed and unafraid. Paul urged him to utilize the gifts of preaching and teaching that the Holy Spirit had given him.	The Holy Spirit helps us to be wise and strong. God honors our confident testimony even when we suffer. To get over our fear of what people might say or do, we must take our eyes off of people and look only to God.
Faithfulness	Christ was faithful to all of us in dying for our sin. Paul was a faithful minister even when he was in prison. Paul urged Timothy not only to maintain sound doctrine, but also loyalty, diligence, and endurance.	We can count on opposition, suffering, and hardship as we serve Christ. But this shows that our faithfulness is having an effect on others. As we trust Christ, he counts us worthy to suffer and will give us the strength we need to be steadfast.
Preaching and Teaching	Paul and Timothy were active in preaching and teaching the Good News about Jesus Christ. Paul encouraged Timothy not only to carry the torch of truth but also to train others, passing on to them sound doctrine and enthusiasm for Christ's mission.	We must prepare people to transmit God's Word to others so that they might pass it on. Does your church carefully train others to teach?
Error	In the final days before Christ returns, there will be false teachers, spiritual dropouts, and heresy. The remedy for error is to have a solid program for teaching Christians.	Because of the deception and false teaching, we must be disciplined and ready to reject error by knowing God's Word. Know the Word of God as your sure defense against error and confusion.

1. Foundations of Christian service

1 *From:* Paul, Jesus Christ's missionary, sent out by God to tell men and women everywhere about the eternal life he has promised them through faith in Jesus Christ.

1:1
Jn 5:24
Tit 1:1,2
1 Jn 5:10,11,20

2*To:* Timothy, my dear son. May God the Father and Christ Jesus our Lord shower you with his kindness, mercy and peace.

1:2
1 Tim 1:2
Tit 1:4

Paul encourages Timothy to be faithful

3How I thank God for you, Timothy. I pray for you every day, and many times during the long nights I beg my God to bless you richly. He is my fathers' God, and mine, and my only purpose in life is to please him.

1:3
Acts 23:1; 24:14
Rom 1:9

4How I long to see you again. How happy I would be, for I remember your tears as we left each other.

1:4
Acts 20:37
2 Tim 4:9

5I know how much you trust the Lord, just as your mother Eunice and your grandmother Lois do; and I feel sure you are still trusting him as much as ever.

1:5
Acts 16:1

6This being so, I want to remind you to stir into flame the strength and boldness that is in you, that entered into you when I laid my hands upon your head and blessed you. **7**For the Holy Spirit, God's gift, does not want you to be afraid of people, but to be wise and strong, and to love them and enjoy being with them.

1:6
Acts 8:18
1 Tim 4:14

1:7
Rom 8:15

8If you will stir up this inner power, you will never be afraid to tell others about our Lord, or to let them know that I am your friend even though I am here in jail for Christ's sake. You will be ready to suffer with me for the Lord, for he will give you strength in suffering.

1:8
Rom 1:16
Eph 3:1
2 Tim 2:3

9It is he who saved us and chose us for his holy work, not because we deserved it but because that was his plan long before the world began—to show his love and kindness to us through Christ. **10**And now he has made all of this plain to us by the

1:9
Rom 8:28-30
11:29
Eph 1:4; 2:9
1 Thess 4:7
Tit 3:5

1:10
1 Cor 15:54

1:6 *stir into flame the strength and boldness,* implied. Literally, "stir up the gift of God."

1:1 This is a somber letter. Paul was imprisoned for the last time, and he knew he would soon die. Unlike his first imprisonment in Rome, when he was in a house (Acts 28:16, 23, 30) and continued to preach and teach, this time he was probably confined to a cold dungeon, awaiting his death (4:6–8). Emperor Nero had begun a major persecution in A.D. 64 as part of his plan to pass the blame for the great fire of Rome from himself to the Christians. This persecution spread across the empire and included social ostracism, public torture, and murder. As Paul waited to die, he wrote a letter to his dear friend Timothy. These are the last words we have from Paul, written in approximately A.D. 66–67.

1:1 For more information on the great missionary, Paul, see his Profile in Acts 9.

1:2 Paul's second letter to Timothy was written about two to four years after his first letter. Timothy had been Paul's traveling companion on the second and third missionary journeys, and Paul had left him in Ephesus to help the church there. For more information on Timothy, see his Profile in 1 Timothy.

1:3 Paul consistently prayed for Timothy, his friend, his fellow traveler, and a strong leader in the Christian church. Although the two men were separated from each other, their prayers provided a source of mutual encouragement. We too should pray consistently for others, especially for those with whom we do God's work.

1:4 We don't know when Paul and Timothy last parted, but it was probably when Paul was arrested and taken to Rome for his second imprisonment. The tears they shed at parting reveal the depth of their relationship.

1:5 Timothy's mother and grandmother, Lois and Eunice, were early Christian converts, possibly through Paul's ministry in their home city, Lystra (Acts 16:1). They communicated their strong Christian faith to Timothy, even though his father was probably not a believer. Don't hide your light at home: our families are fertile fields for planting gospel seeds. Let your parents, children, spouse, brothers, and sisters know of your faith in Jesus, and be

sure they see Christ's love, helpfulness, and joy in you.

1:6 At the time of his ordination, Timothy received special gifts of the Spirit to enable him to serve the church (see 1 Timothy 4:14). In telling Timothy to stir those gifts into flame, Paul was encouraging him to persevere. Timothy did not need new revelations or new gifts; he needed the courage and self- discipline to hang onto the truth and use the gifts he had already received (see 1:13, 14). If he would step out boldly in faith and proclaim the gospel once again, the Holy Spirit would go with him and give him power.

1:6, 7 Timothy was experiencing great opposition to his message and to himself as a leader. His youth, his association with Paul, and his leadership had come under fire. Paul urged him to be bold. When we allow people to intimidate us, we neutralize our effectiveness for God. The power of the Holy Spirit can help us overcome our fear of what some might say or do to us so we can continue to do God's work.

1:7 Paul mentions three characteristics of the effective Christian leader: wisdom, strength, and love. These are available to us because the Holy Spirit lives in us. See Galatians 5:22, 23 for a list of characteristics resulting from the Holy Spirit's control.

1:8 In this time of mounting persecution, Timothy may have been afraid to continue preaching Christ. His fears were based on fact. As Paul warned him, suffering would come: Timothy, like Paul, would be jailed for preaching the gospel (Hebrews 13:23). But Paul promised Timothy that God would give him strength and that he would be ready when it was his turn to suffer. Even when persecution is not a threat, it can be difficult to share our faith in Christ. Fortunately we, like Paul and Timothy, can call on the Holy Spirit's power to give us courage.

1:9, 10 This is a brief synopsis of the gospel. God loves us, chose us, and sent Christ to die for us. We can have eternal life through faith in him because he broke the power of death by his resurrection. We do not deserve to be saved, but God offers us salvation anyway. All we have to do is believe and accept his offer.

coming of our Savior Jesus Christ, who broke the power of death and showed us the way of everlasting life through trusting him. 11And God has chosen me to be his missionary, to preach to the Gentiles and teach them.

12That is why I am suffering here in jail and I am certainly not ashamed of it, for I know the one in whom I trust, and I am sure that he is able to safely guard all that I have given him until the day of his return.

13Hold tightly to the pattern of truth I taught you, especially concerning the faith and love Christ Jesus offers you. 14Guard well the splendid, God-given ability you received as a gift from the Holy Spirit who lives within you.

15As you know, all the Christians who came here from Asia have deserted me; even Phygellus and Hermogenes are gone. 16May the Lord bless Onesiphorus and all his family, because he visited me and encouraged me often. His visits revived me like a breath of fresh air, and he was never ashamed of my being in jail. 17In fact, when he came to Rome he searched everywhere trying to find me, and finally did. 18May the Lord give him a special blessing at the day of Christ's return. And you know better than I can tell you how much he helped me at Ephesus.

Good soldiers are not afraid to suffer

2 Oh, Timothy, my son, be strong with the strength Christ Jesus gives you. 2For you must teach others those things you and many others have heard me speak about. Teach these great truths to trustworthy men who will, in turn, pass them on to others.

3Take your share of suffering as a good soldier of Jesus Christ, just as I do, 4and as Christ's soldier do not let yourself become tied up in worldly affairs, for then you cannot satisfy the one who has enlisted you in his army. 5Follow the Lord's rules for doing his work, just as an athlete either follows the rules or is disqualified and wins no prize. 6Work hard, like a farmer who gets paid well if he raises a large crop. 7Think over these three illustrations, and may the Lord help you to understand how they apply to you.

8Don't ever forget the wonderful fact that Jesus Christ was a Man, born into King David's family; and that he was God, as shown by the fact that he rose again from

1:13 *and love Christ Jesus offers you,* literally, "and love that is in Christ Jesus."

Cross-references (left margin):

1:11
1 Tim 2:7

1:12
1 Tim 6:20
1 Pet 4:19

1:13
Rom 6:17
1 Tim 1:14
2 Tim 3:14
Heb 10:23

1:14
Rom 8:9,11,16
Gal 4:6

1:15
2 Tim 4:10

1:16
2 Tim 4:19
Philem 7

1:18
Heb 6:10

2:1
Eph 3:16; 6:10
Col 1:11

2:2
1 Cor 15:3-7
2 Tim 2:13

2:3
1 Cor 9:7

2:4
2 Pet 2:20

2:5
1 Cor 9:25

2:6
1 Cor 9:7,10

2:8
Acts 2:24
13:33, 34
Rom 1:3,4

1:12 Paul was in prison, but that did not stop his ministry. He carried it on through others like Timothy. Paul had lost all his material possessions, but he would never lose his faith. He trusted God to use him regardless of his circumstances. If your situation looks bleak, give your concerns to Christ. He will guard your faith and find a way to use you even in the midst of suffering.

1:12 The phrase "safely guard all that I have given him" has three main interpretations: (1) Paul knew God would guard the souls of those converted through his preaching; (2) he trusted God to guard his own soul until the Second Coming; or (3) he was confident that, though he was in prison and facing death, God would carry out the gospel ministry through others such as Timothy. Paul may have expressed his confidence to encourage Timothy, who was discouraged by the problems in Ephesus and fearful of persecution. Even in prison, Paul knew God was still in control.

1:13, 14 Timothy was in a time of transition. He had been Paul's bright young helper; soon he would be on his own as leader of a difficult, but critically important, church. Although his responsibilities were changing, Timothy was not without help. He had everything he needed to face the future, if he would hold tightly onto it. When you are facing difficult transitions, it is good to follow Paul's advice to Timothy and look back at your experience. Who is the foundation of your faith? What gifts has the Holy Spirit given you? How can you build on the foundation that has already been laid, using the gifts you have already been given?

2:2 If the church consistently followed this advice, it would

expand geometrically as well-taught believers would teach others and commission them, in turn, to teach still others. Disciples need to be equipped to pass their faith on; our work is not done until new believers are telling others the Good News they have learned (see Ephesians 4:12, 13).

2:3-7 As Timothy preached and taught, he would face suffering, but he should be willing to take it. Christian leaders are not the only ones to suffer. Soldiers, athletes, and farmers all must discipline themselves and be willing to sacrifice to achieve the results they want. Like soldiers, we have to give up worldly security and endure rigorous discipline. Like athletes, we must train hard and follow the rules. Like farmers, we must work extremely hard. We keep going in spite of suffering because of the thought of victory, the vision of winning, and the hope of harvest. All our suffering is made worthwhile by our goal of glorifying God, winning people to Christ, and one day living eternally with him.

2:8 False teachers were a problem in Ephesus (see Acts 20:29, 30; 1 Timothy 1:3–11). At the heart of false teaching is an incorrect view of Christ. In Timothy's day it was popular to assert that he is divine but not human—God but not man. Nowadays we often hear that he is human but not divine—man but not God. Either view destroys the Good News that Jesus Christ has taken our sins on himself and has reconciled God and man. In this verse, Paul firmly states that Jesus is fully God and fully man. This is the only biblical view. For more on this important concept see the note on Philippians 2:5–7.

the dead. 9It is because I have preached these great truths that I am in trouble here and have been put in jail like a criminal. But the Word of God is not chained, even though I am. 10I am more than willing to suffer if that will bring salvation and eternal glory in Christ Jesus to those God has chosen.

2:9
Phil 1:7

2:10
Col 1:24

11I am comforted by this truth, that when we suffer and die for Christ it only means that we will begin living with him in heaven. 12And if we think that our present service for him is hard, just remember that some day we are going to sit with him and rule with him. But if we give up when we suffer, and turn against Christ, then he must turn against us. 13Even when we are too weak to have any faith left, he remains faithful to us and will help us, for he cannot disown us who are part of himself, and he will always carry out his promises to us.

2:11
Rom 6:5,8
1 Thess 5:10

2:12
Mt 10:33
Rom 8:17
1 Pet 4:13

2:13
Num 23:19
1 Cor 1:9

Good workers are not ashamed of their work

14Remind your people of these great facts, and command them in the name of the Lord not to argue over unimportant things. Such arguments are confusing and useless, and even harmful. 15Work hard so God can say to you, "Well done." Be a good workman, one who does not need to be ashamed when God examines your work. Know what his Word says and means. 16Steer clear of foolish discussions which lead people into the sin of anger with each other. 17Things will be said that will burn and hurt for a long time to come. Hymenaeus and Philetus, in their love of argument, are men like that. 18They have left the path of truth, preaching the lie that the resurrection of the dead has already occurred; and they have weakened the faith of some who believe them.

19But God's truth stands firm like a great rock, and nothing can shake it. It is a foundation stone with these words written on it: "The Lord knows those who are

2:14
1 Tim 1:4; 6:4
Tit 3:9

2:17
1 Tim 1:20

2:18
1 Cor 15:12-20

2:19
Num 16:5
Nah 1:7
Jn 10:14

2:9 The truth about Jesus was no more popular in Paul's day than in ours, but that won't stop it from reaching receptive hearts. When Paul said Jesus was God, he angered the Jews who had condemned Jesus for blasphemy, but many Jews became Christians (1 Corinthians 1:24). He angered the Romans who worshiped the emperor as God, but even some in Caesar's palace turned to Jesus (Philippians 4:22). When Paul said Jesus was man, he angered the Greeks who thought divinity was soiled if it had any contact with humanity; still many Greeks accepted the faith (Acts 11:20, 21). The truth that Jesus is one person with two united natures has never been easy to accept, but it *is* being accepted by people every day. Are you one of those who has accepted this life-changing message?

2:10 We are free to choose between life and death, and yet God has chosen us. This is a mystery our finite minds cannot easily grasp. But even if we do not completely understand it, we can still choose Jesus and be grateful that he has chosen us.

2:11-13 God is faithful to his children, and although we may suffer great hardships here, he promises that someday we will live eternally with him. What will this involve? It means believers will live in Christ's Kingdom, and that we will share in the administration of that Kingdom. This was Paul's comfort as he went through suffering and death, and it can be ours, too. Are you facing hardships? Don't turn away from God—he promises you a wonderful future with him. For more information about living eternally with God, see Matthew 16:24–27; 19:28, 29; Luke 22:28–30; Romans 5:17; 6:8; 8:10, 11, 17; 1 Corinthians 15:42–58; Colossians 3:3, 4; 1 Thessalonians 4:13–18; Revelation 3:21; 21:1—22:21.

2:12, 13 Jesus will stay by our side even when we have endured so much that we seem to have no faith left. We may be faithless at times, but Jesus remains faithful to his promise to be with us always, "even to the end of the world" (see Matthew 28:20; Romans 8:38, 39).

2:15 Life on earth is not a script which we meaninglessly act out. It is a time of deciding whether we will live for God or not and then *living out* what we have decided. Because God will examine what kinds of workers we have been for him, we should build our lives on his Word and build his Word into our lives, because it alone tells us how to live for him and serve him. Believers who ignore the Bible will certainly be ashamed at the judgment. Consistent and diligent study of God's Word is vital, or else we will be lulled into neglecting God and our true purpose for living.

2:16 In important areas, we must carefully work through our disagreements. But when we bicker long hours over words and theories that are not central to the Christian faith and life, we only provoke anger and hurt feelings. Even if such "foolish discussions" lead to resolution, they gain little ground for the Kingdom. Learning and discussing are not bad in themselves unless they keep believers constantly focusing on false doctrine or unhelpful trivialities. This, in turn, keeps us from our work and service to God.

2:17 Hymenaeus is also mentioned in 1 Timothy 1:20. Paul had "handed him over to Satan" because of his false teaching.

2:18 The false teachers were denying the resurrection of the body. They believed that when a person became a Christian he was spiritually reborn, and that was the only resurrection there would ever be. To them, resurrection was symbolic and spiritual, not physical. Paul clearly taught, however, that believers will be resurrected after they die, and their bodies as well as their souls will live eternally with Christ (1 Corinthians 15:35ff; 2 Corinthians 5:1–10; 1 Thessalonians 4:15–18). We cannot shape the doctrines of Scripture to match our opinions. If we do, we are putting ourselves above God. We must instead shape our opinions into beliefs that match God's Word.

2:19 False teachers are still spouting lies. Some distort the truth; some dilute it; and some simply delete it by saying it no longer applies. But no matter how many follow the liars, God's truth never changes, is never shaken, and will never fade. When we know and believe God's truth, he will never forsake us.

really his," and "A person who calls himself a Christian should not be doing things that are wrong."

2:20
Rom 9:21

20In a wealthy home there are dishes made of gold and silver as well as some made from wood and clay. The expensive dishes are used for guests, and the cheap

2:21
2 Tim 3:17

ones are used in the kitchen or to put garbage in. 21If you stay away from sin you will be like one of these dishes made of purest gold—the very best in the house—so that Christ himself can use you for his highest purposes.

2:22
1 Tim 6:11

22Run from anything that gives you the evil thoughts that young men often have, but stay close to anything that makes you want to do right. Have faith and love, and

2:23
1 Tim 6:4
Tit 3:9

enjoy the companionship of those who love the Lord and have pure hearts. 23Again I say, don't get involved in foolish arguments which only upset people

2:24
1 Tim 3:2,3
Tit 1:7-9

and make them angry. 24God's people must not be quarrelsome; they must be gentle, patient teachers of those who are wrong. 25Be humble when you are trying

2:25
1 Tim 2:4
Tit 3:2
1 Pet 3:15

to teach those who are mixed up concerning the truth. For if you talk meekly and courteously to them they are more likely, with God's help, to turn away from their wrong ideas and believe what is true. 26Then they will come to their senses and

2:26
Eph 4:27; 6:11
1 Tim 3:7

escape from Satan's trap of slavery to sin which he uses to catch them whenever he likes, and then they can begin doing the will of God.

2. Difficult times for Christian service
The last days characterized by sinfulness

3:1
1 Tim 4:1
Jude 18

3 You may as well know this too, Timothy, that in the last days it is going to be very difficult to be a Christian. 2For people will love only themselves and their

3:2
Lk 16:14
Rom 1:30
1 Tim 1:9

money; they will be proud and boastful, sneering at God, disobedient to their parents, ungrateful to them, and thoroughly bad. 3They will be hardheaded and never give in to others; they will be constant liars and troublemakers and will think

3:3
Rom 1:31

nothing of immorality. They will be rough and cruel, and sneer at those who try to be good. 4They will betray their friends; they will be hotheaded, puffed up with

3:5
1 Tim 5:8

pride, and prefer good times to worshiping God. 5They will go to church, yes, but they won't really believe anything they hear. Don't be taken in by people like that.

3:6
Jude 4

6They are the kind who craftily sneak into other people's homes and make friendships with silly, sin-burdened women and teach them their new doctrines.

3:8
Ex 7:11

7Women of that kind are forever following new teachers, but they never understand the truth. 8And these teachers fight truth just as Jannes and Jambres fought against

---

2:22 Running away is sometimes considered cowardly. But wise people realize that removing oneself physically from temptation is often prudent. Timothy, a young man, was warned to run from anything that produced evil thoughts (1 Timothy 6:11). Perhaps you experience a recurring temptation that is difficult to resist. Remove yourself physically from the situation. Knowing when to run is as important in spiritual battle as knowing when and how to fight.

2:23–26 As a teacher, Timothy helped those who were confused about the truth. Paul's advice to him, and to all who teach God's truth, is to be humble, patiently and courteously explaining the truth. Good teaching never promotes quarrels or foolish arguments. Whether you are teaching Sunday school, leading a Bible study, or preaching in church, remember to listen to people's questions and treat them respectfully. If you do this, they will be willing to hear what you have to say.

3:1 Paul's reference to the *last days* reveals his sense of urgency. The last days began after Jesus' resurrection, when the Holy Spirit came upon the believers at Pentecost, and will continue until his Second Coming.

3:1ff In many parts of the world today it does not seem especially difficult to be a Christian. No one is jailed for reading the Bible or executed for preaching Christ. But when we read Paul's descriptive list of behavior in the last days, we recognize it as a description of our society—even, unfortunately, of many Christians. There is a comfortableness about superficial Christianity that

should cause us to be uncomfortable. Check your life against this list. Don't give in to society's pressures. Stand up against its evil ways by living as God would have his people live.

3:5 "They will go to church" is a paraphrase of "Having a form of godliness." The appearance of godliness includes going to church, knowing Christian doctrine, and following a community's Christian traditions. Such practices can make a person look good, but if the inner attitudes of belief, love, and worship are lacking, the outer appearance doesn't mean a thing. Paul warns us not to be taken in by people who only look like Christians. They can be hard to distinguish from true Christians at first glance, but their lives give them away. The characteristics described in 3:2–4 are unmistakable.

3:6, 7 Because of their cultural background, women in the Ephesian church had had no formal religious training. They enjoyed their new freedom to study Christian truths, but their eagerness to learn made them a target for false teachers. Paul warned Timothy to watch out for men who would take advantage of these women. New believers need to grow in their knowledge of the Word, because ignorance can make them vulnerable to deception.

3:8, 9 Jannes and Jambres, according to tradition, were two of the magicians who counterfeited Moses' miracles before Pharaoh (Exodus 7:11, 12). Moses exposed and defeated them (Exodus 8:18, 19), just as God would overthrow the false teachers plaguing the Ephesian church.

Moses. They have dirty minds, warped and twisted, and have turned against the Christian faith.

9But they won't get away with all this forever. Some day their deceit will be well known to everyone, as was the sin of Jannes and Jambres.

3:9
Ex 8:18; 9:11

Paul's charge to Timothy

10But you know from watching me that I am not that kind of person. You know what I believe and the way I live and what I want. You know my faith in Christ and how I have suffered. You know my love for you, and my patience. 11You know how many troubles I have had as a result of my preaching the Good News. You know about all that was done to me while I was visiting in Antioch, Iconium and Lystra, but the Lord delivered me. 12Yes, and those who decide to please Christ Jesus by living godly lives will suffer at the hands of those who hate him. 13In fact, evil men and false teachers will become worse and worse, deceiving many, they themselves having been deceived by Satan.

3:10
1 Tim 6:11

3:11
Acts 13:14,45, 50; 14:19
2 Cor 1:5
11:23-27
12:10

3:12
Jn 15:20
Acts 14:22
1 Thess 3:3

14But you must keep on believing the things you have been taught. You know they are true for you know that you can trust those of us who have taught you. 15You know how, when you were a small child, you were taught the holy Scriptures; and it is these that make you wise to accept God's salvation by trusting in Christ Jesus. 16The whole Bible was given to us by inspiration from God and is useful to teach us what is true and to make us realize what is wrong in our lives; it straightens us out and helps us do what is right. 17It is God's way of making us well prepared at every point, fully equipped to do good to everyone.

3:14
2 Tim 1:13; 2:2

3:15
Jn 5:47; 20:30, 31
Rom 10:17

3:16
Rom 15:4
2 Pet 1:20,21

3:17
1 Tim 6:11
2 Tim 2:21

4 And so I solemnly urge you before God and before Christ Jesus—who will some day judge the living and the dead when he appears to set up his Kingdom— 2to preach the Word of God urgently at all times, whenever you get the chance, in season and out, when it is convenient and when it is not. Correct and

4:1
Acts 10:42

4:2
1 Tim 5:10
Tit 1:13

3:16 *The whole Bible,* literally, "Every Scripture."

3:9 Sin has consequences, and no one will get away with it forever. Live each day as if your actions will one day be known to all. Now is the time to change anything you would want to hide then.

3:11 In Lystra, Timothy's hometown, Paul was stoned and left for dead (Acts 14:19); and this was only one incident among many. In 2 Corinthians 11:23–33 he summarizes his lifetime of suffering for the sake of the gospel. Paul mentions his suffering here to contrast his experience with that of the false teachers.

3:14 Besieged by false teachers and the inevitable pressures of a growing ministry, Timothy could easily have abandoned his faith or modified his doctrine. Once again Paul counsels him to look to his past, to hold to the basic teachings about Jesus that are eternally true. Like Timothy, we are surrounded by false teachings, and most of us are very busy. But we must not allow our society to distort or crowd out God's eternal truth. Spend time every day thinking about the foundations of your Christian faith, the great truths on which you build your life.

3:15 Timothy was one of the first second-generation Christians: he became a Christian not because an evangelist preached a powerful sermon, but because his mother and grandmother taught him the holy Scriptures when he was a small child. The evangelist's work is important, but the parent's work is just as important. At home and in church, we should realize that teaching small children is both an opportunity and a responsibility. Jesus wanted little children to come to him (Matthew 19:13–15). Like Lois and Eunice, do your part in leading them to Christ.

3:16 The Bible is not a collection of stories, fables, myths, or merely human ideas about God. It is not just a human book. Through the Holy Spirit God revealed his person and plan to godly men, who wrote down God's message for his people (2 Peter 1:20, 21). This process is known as inspiration. The writers wrote from their own personal, historical, and cultural contexts. But even

though they used their own minds, talents, language, and style, they wrote what God wanted them to write. Scripture is completely trustworthy because God was in control of its writing, and its words are entirely authoritative for our faith and lives.

3:16 The whole Bible is God's inspired Word. Because it is inspired and trustworthy, we should *read* it and *apply* it to our lives. The Bible is our standard for testing everything else that claims to be true. It is our safeguard against false teaching and our source of guidance for how we should live. It is our only source of knowledge about how we can be saved. God wants to show you what is true and equip you to live for him. How much time do you spend in God's Word? Read it regularly to discover God's truth and become confident in your life and faith. Develop a plan for reading the whole Bible, not just the same familiar passages.

3:17 In our zeal for the *truth* of Scripture, we must never forget its *purpose*—to equip us to do good to others. We do not study God's Word simply to increase our own knowledge or to prepare us to win arguments. We do not even study it primarily to learn how to save our own souls (most people are saved before they begin intensively studying the Bible). We study Scripture so that we will know how to do Christ's work in the world. Our knowledge of God's Word is not useful unless we use it to do good to others.

4:1, 2 It was important for Timothy to preach the gospel so that the Christian faith could spread throughout the world. We believe in Christ today because people like Timothy were faithful to their mission. It is still vitally important for the church to preach the gospel. Half the people who have ever lived are alive today, and most of them do not know Jesus. He is coming soon, and he wants to find a faithful church waiting for him. It may be inconvenient to take a stand for Christ or to tell others about his love, but preaching the Word of God is the most important responsibility the church has been given. Be prepared, courageous, and sensitive to God-given opportunities to tell the Good News.

4:3
2 Tim 3:1

4:4
2 Thess 2:11
1 Tim 1:4

4:5
Col 4:17
2 Tim 1:8

4:6
Phil 1:23

4:7
1 Cor 9:24-27
Phil 3:12-14
1 Tim 6:12

4:8
1 Cor 9:25
Phil 3:11
Col 1:5
2 Tim 1:12
Rev 2:10

4:9
2 Tim 1:4

4:10
Col 4:14
Philem 24

4:11
Col 4:10,14

4:12
Acts 20:4
Eph 6:21

4:16
Acts 7:60
1 Cor 13:5

4:17
Ps 22:21
Acts 9:15
2 Tim 3:11
Tit 1:3

4:18
Ps 121:7
Rom 11:36

rebuke your people when they need it, encourage them to do right, and all the time be feeding them patiently with God's Word.

³For there is going to come a time when people won't listen to the truth, but will go around looking for teachers who will tell them just what they want to hear. ⁴They won't listen to what the Bible says but will blithely follow their own misguided ideas.

⁵Stand steady, and don't be afraid of suffering for the Lord. Bring others to Christ. Leave nothing undone that you ought to do.

⁶I say this because I won't be around to help you very much longer. My time has almost run out. Very soon now I will be on my way to heaven. ⁷I have fought long and hard for my Lord, and through it all I have kept true to him. And now the time has come for me to stop fighting and rest. ⁸In heaven a crown is waiting for me which the Lord, the righteous Judge, will give me on that great day of his return. And not just to me, but to all those whose lives show that they are eagerly looking forward to his coming back again.

Paul's final words

⁹Please come as soon as you can, ¹⁰for Demas has left me. He loved the good things of this life and went to Thessalonica. Crescens has gone to Galatia, Titus to Dalmatia. ¹¹Only Luke is with me. Bring Mark with you when you come, for I need him. ¹²(Tychicus is gone too, as I sent him to Ephesus.) ¹³When you come, be sure to bring the coat I left at Troas with Brother Carpus, and also the books, but especially the parchments.

¹⁴Alexander the coppersmith has done me much harm. The Lord will punish him, ¹⁵but be careful of him, for he fought against everything we said.

¹⁶The first time I was brought before the judge no one was here to help me. Everyone had run away. I hope that they will not be blamed for it. ¹⁷But the Lord stood with me and gave me the opportunity to boldly preach a whole sermon for all the world to hear. And he saved me from being thrown to the lions. ¹⁸Yes, and the Lord will always deliver me from all evil and will bring me into his heavenly Kingdom. To God be the glory forever and ever. Amen.

4:17 *he saved me from being thrown to the lions*, literally, "I was delivered out of the mouth of the lion."

4:3, 4 It is difficult to accept correction, to be told we have to change. But no matter how much the truth hurts, we must be willing to listen to it so we can more fully obey God.

4:5-8 As he neared the end of his life, Paul could confidently say he had been faithful to his call. Thus he faced death calmly; he knew he would be rewarded at Christ's Second Coming. Is your life preparing you for death? Do you share Paul's confident expectation of meeting Christ? The Good News is that the heavenly reward is not just for giants of the faith, like Paul, but for all who "are eagerly looking forward" to Jesus' Second Coming. Paul gave these words to encourage Timothy, and us, that no matter how difficult the fight seems—keep fighting. We will discover when we are with Jesus Christ that it was all worth it.

4:8 In Roman athletic games, a laurel wreath was given to the winners. A symbol of triumph and honor, it was the most coveted prize in ancient Rome. This is probably what Paul was thinking of when he spoke of the crown. See 2 Corinthians 5:10 and the note on Matthew 19:27 for more on the rewards awaiting us for our faith and deeds.

4:10 Demas had been one of Paul's coworkers (Colossians 4:14; Philemon 1:24), but he deserted Paul because he "loved the good things of this life," or more literally, "loved this present world." There are two ways to love the world. God loves the world as he created it and as it could be if it were rescued from evil. That is why he sacrificed his Son to save it (John 3:16). Others, like Demas, love the world as it is, sin and all. Do you love the world as

it could be if justice were done, the hungry were fed, and people loved one another? Or do you love what the world has to offer—wealth, power, pleasure—even if gaining it means hurting people and neglecting the work God has given you to do?

4:11, 12 Mentioning Demas reminded Paul of other, more faithful coworkers. Only Luke was with him, and Paul was feeling lonely. Tychicus, one of his most trusted companions (Acts 20:4; Ephesians 6:21; Colossians 4:7; Titus 3:12), had already left for Ephesus. He missed his young helpers Timothy and Mark. Mark, also called John and John Mark, had left Paul on his first missionary journey, and this had greatly angered Paul (Acts 13:13; 15:36-41). But Mark later proved himself a worthy helper, and Paul recognized him as a good friend and trusted Christian leader (Colossians 4:10; Philemon 1:24).

4:13 Paul's arrest was probably so sudden that he was not allowed to return home to gather his personal belongings. As a prisoner in a damp and chilly dungeon, Paul asked Timothy to bring him a coat. Paul wanted his parchments. These may have included parts of the Old Testament, the Gospels, copies of his own letters, or other important documents.

4:17 With his mentor in prison and his church in turmoil, Timothy was not feeling at all brave. Paul may have been subtly telling him, "The Lord has called you to preach, and he will give you the courage to do so." God always gives us the strength to do what he has commanded. This strength may not be evident, however, until we step out in faith and actually begin doing the task.

¹⁹Please say "hello" for me to Priscilla and Aquila and those living at the home of Onesiphorus. ²⁰Erastus stayed at Corinth, and I left Trophimus sick at Miletus. ²¹Do try to be here before winter. Eubulus sends you greetings, and so do Pudens, Linus, Claudia, and all the others. ²²May the Lord Jesus Christ be with your spirit.

Farewell, Paul

4:19
Acts 18:2
2 Tim 1:16
4:20
Acts 19:22; 20:4
4:22
Gal 6:18

4:19, 20 Priscilla and Aquila were fellow Christian leaders with whom Paul had lived and worked (Acts 18:2, 3). Onesiphorus visited and encouraged Paul in jail (2 Timothy 1:16–18). Erastus was one of Paul's trusted companions (Acts 19:22), as was Trophimus (Acts 20:4; 21:29).

4:22 As Paul reached the end of his life, he could look back and know he had been faithful to God's call. Now it was time to pass the torch to the next generation, preparing leaders to take his place so that many would continue to hear the life-changing message of Jesus Christ. Timothy was Paul's living legacy, a product of Paul's faithful teaching, discipleship, and example. Because of Paul's work with many believers, including Timothy, the world is full of believers today who are also carrying on the work. What legacy will you leave behind? Whom are you training to carry on your work? It is our responsibility to keep the Word of God alive for the next generation.

TITUS

GREAT speakers and teachers gather a following, and soon a church is flourishing. Lives are being changed and led into the kingdom. But when this catalyst leaves or dies, with him or her goes the drive and the heart of the organization.

People flocked to hear Paul's teaching. Articulate, motivated, and filled with the Holy Spirit, he faithfully proclaimed the Good News throughout the Roman Empire—lives were changed and churches planted. But Paul knew that the church must be built on Christ, not on any other person. He knew that eventually he would not be there to build, encourage, discipline, and teach, so he trained young pastors to assume leadership in the church after he was gone. Paul urged them to center their lives and preaching on the Word of God (2 Timothy 3:16, 17) and to train others to carry on the ministry (2 Timothy 2:2).

Titus was a Greek believer, probably converted to Christ through Paul's ministry. Taught and nurtured by Paul, he stood before the leaders of the church in Jerusalem as a living example of what Christ was doing among the Gentiles (Galatians 2:1–3). He was one of Paul's trusted traveling companions and closest friends. Later he became Paul's special ambassador (2 Corinthians 7:5–16) and eventually the overseer of the churches on Crete (Titus 1:5). Slowly and carefully, Paul developed Titus into a mature Christian leader. The letter to Titus is another step in this discipleship process. As with Timothy, Paul tells Titus how to organize and lead the churches.

Paul begins with a longer than usual greeting and introduction, outlining the leadership progression—Paul's ministry (1:1–3), Titus' responsibilities (1:4, 5), and those leaders whom Titus would appoint and train (1:5). Paul then lists pastoral qualifications (1:6–9), and contrasts them with the false leaders and teachers (1:10–16).

Next, Paul emphasizes the importance of good works in the life of the Christian, telling Titus how to relate to the various age groups in the church (2:2–6). He urges Titus to be a good example of a mature believer (2:7, 8) and to teach with courage and conviction (2:9–15). He then discusses the general responsibilities of Christians in society—Titus should remind the people of these (3:1–8), and he should avoid divisive arguments (3:9–11). Paul concludes with a few matters of itinerary and personal greetings (3:12–15).

As you read this pastoral epistle, you will gain insight into the organization and life of the early church and principles for structuring contemporary churches. But you should also see how to be a responsible Christian leader. Read the Epistle to Titus and determine, like Paul, to train men and women to lead and teach others.

VITAL STATISTICS

PURPOSE:
To advise Titus in his responsibility of supervising the churches on the island of Crete

AUTHOR:
Paul

TO WHOM WRITTEN:
Titus, a Greek convert, who had become Paul's special representative to the island of Crete

DATE WRITTEN:
About A.D. 64, around the same time 1 Timothy was written; probably from Macedonia when Paul traveled in between his Roman imprisonments

SETTING:
Paul sent Titus to organize and oversee the churches on Crete. This letter tells him how to do this job.

KEY VERSE:
"I left you there on the island of Crete so that you could do whatever was needed to help strengthen each of its churches, and I asked you to appoint pastors [elders] in every city who would follow the instructions I gave you" (1:5).

KEY PEOPLE:
Paul, Titus

KEY PLACES:
Crete, Nicopolis

SPECIAL FEATURES:
Titus is very similar to 1 Timothy with its instructions to pastors (elders).

THE BLUEPRINT

1. Leadership in the church (1:1-16)
2. Right living in the church (2:1-15)
3. Right living in society (3:1-15)

Paul calls for church order and right living in an island known for laziness, gluttony, lying, and evil. The Christians are to be disciplined as individuals and orderly as a church. We need to obey this message in our day when discipline is not respected or rewarded by our society. Although others may not regard our efforts, we must live upright lives, obey the government, and control our speech. We should live together peacefully in the church and be living examples of our faith in society.

MEGATHEMES

THEME	EXPLANATION	IMPORTANCE
A Good Life	The good news of salvation is that we can't be saved by living a good life; we are saved only by faith in Jesus Christ. But the gospel transforms people's lives, so that they eventually perform good works. Our service won't save us, but we are saved to serve.	A good life is a witness to the gospel's power. As Christians, we must have commitment and discipline to serve. Are you putting your faith in action by serving others?
Character	Titus' responsibility at Crete was to appoint pastors (elders) on Crete to maintain proper organization and discipline, so Paul listed the qualities needed for the eldership. Their conduct in their homes revealed their fitness for service in the church.	It's not enough to be educated or have a following to be Christ's kind of leader. You must have self-control, spiritual and moral fitness, and Christian character. Who you are is just as important as what you can do.
Church Relationships	Church teaching was to relate to various groups. Older Christians were to teach and to be examples to younger men and women. Every age and group has a lesson to learn and a role to play.	Right living and right relationship go along with right doctrine. Treat relationships with other believers as an outgrowth of your faith.
Citizenship	Christians must be good citizens in society, not just in church. Believers must obey the government and work honestly.	How you fulfill your civic duties is a witness to the watching world. Your community life should reflect Christ's love as much as your church life does.

1. Leadership in the church

1 *From:* Paul, the slave of God and the messenger of Jesus Christ. I have been sent to bring faith to those God has chosen and to teach them to know God's truth—the kind of truth that changes lives—so that they can have eternal life, which God promised them before the world began—and he cannot lie. ³And now in his own good time he has revealed this Good News and permits me to tell it to everyone. By command of God our Savior I have been trusted to do this work for him.

⁴*To:* Titus, who is truly my son in the affairs of the Lord.

1:1
1 Tim 2:4; 6:3
2 Tim 1:9; 2:25

1:2
1 Tim 1:9
Tit 3:7

1:3
Acts 9:15
1 Tim 1:1,11
2 Tim 4:17
Tit 2:10

1:1 Paul wrote this letter between his first and second imprisonments in Rome (before he wrote 2 Timothy) to guide Titus in working with the churches on the island of Crete. Paul had visited Crete with Titus, and he left him there to minister (1:5). Crete was a center for training Roman soldiers. Thus, there was a large pagan influence on this small island. Therefore, the church in Crete needed strong Christian leadership.

1:1 In one short phrase, Paul gives us insight into his reason for living. He calls himself a slave (or servant) of God—that is, he was committed to obeying God. This obedience led him to spend his life telling others about Christ. How would you describe your purpose in life? To what are you devoted? For more information on Paul, see his Profile in Acts 9.

1:1, 2 The foundation of our faith is trust in God's character. Because he *is* truth, he is the *source* of all truth and cannot lie. The eternal life he has promised will be ours because he keeps his promises. Build your faith on the foundation of a trustworthy God who will not lie.

1:3 God is called "our Savior" (1:3), as is Jesus (1:4). Jesus did the work of salvation by dying for our sins and therefore is our Savior. God planned the work of salvation and forgives our sins; thus, he is our Savior as well. Both the Father and the Son are involved in saving us.

1:4 Titus, a Greek, was one of Paul's most trusted and dependable coworkers. Paul sent Titus to Corinth on several

May God the Father and Christ Jesus our Savior give you his blessings and his peace.

Qualifications for church leaders

1:5
Acts 14:23

1:6
1 Tim 3:2-4

5I left you there on the island of Crete so that you could do whatever was needed to help strengthen each of its churches, and I asked you to appoint pastors in every city who would follow the instructions I gave you. 6The men you choose must be well thought of for their good lives; they must have only one wife and their children must love the Lord and not have a reputation for being wild or disobedient to their parents.

1:7
1 Cor 4:1,2
1 Tim 3:2,3

1:8
1 Tim 3:2,3

1:9
2 Thess 2:15

7These pastors must be men of blameless lives because they are God's ministers. They must not be proud or impatient; they must not be drunkards or fighters or greedy for money. 8They must enjoy having guests in their homes and must love all that is good. They must be sensible men, and fair. They must be clean minded and level headed. 9Their belief in the truth which they have been taught must be strong and steadfast, so that they will be able to teach it to others and show those who disagree with them where they are wrong.

1:5 *pastors,* more literally, "elders." Also in vs 7.

TITUS GOES TO CRETE
Tradition says that after Paul was released from prison in Rome, he and Titus traveled together for a while. They stopped in Crete, and when it was time for Paul to go, he left Titus behind to help the churches there.

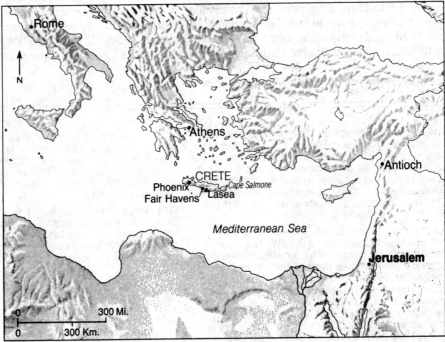

special missions to help the church in its troubles (2 Corinthians 7, 8). Paul and Titus also traveled together to Jerusalem (Galatians 2:3) and Crete (1:5). Paul left Titus there to lead the new churches springing up on the island. Titus is last mentioned by Paul in 2 Timothy 4:10, his last recorded letter. Titus had leadership ability, so Paul gave him leadership responsibility, urging him to use his abilities well.

1:5 Crete, a small island in the Mediterranean Sea, had a large population of Jews. The churches there were probably founded by Cretan Jews who had been in Jerusalem at Pentecost (Acts 2:11) more than 30 years before Paul wrote this letter.

1:5 It was important for each church to have spiritual leaders, and Paul had appointed elders in various churches (Acts 14:23). These

men led the churches by helping believers mature spiritually and equipping them to live for Jesus Christ despite the opposition.

1:5-9 The Greek word for "pastors" here is "elders" (see textual note). Paul briefly describes some qualifications an elder should have. He gave Timothy a similar set of instructions for the church in Ephesus (see 1 Timothy 3:1–7; 5:22). Notice that most of the qualifications involve the elder's character, not his knowledge or skill. A person's lifestyle and relationships provide a window into his or her character. Consider these qualifications as you evaluate a person for a position of leadership. While it is important to have an elder or pastor who can effectively preach God's Word, it is even more important to have one who can live out God's Word and be an example for others to follow.

Warning against false teachers

¹⁰For there are many who refuse to obey; this is especially true among those who say that all Christians must obey the Jewish laws. But this is foolish talk; it blinds people to the truth, ¹¹and it must be stopped. Already whole families have been turned away from the grace of God. Such teachers are only after your money. ¹²One of their own men, a prophet from Crete, has said about them, "These men of Crete are all liars; they are like lazy animals, living only to satisfy their stomachs." ¹³And this is true. So speak to the Christians there as sternly as necessary to make them strong in the faith, ¹⁴and to stop them from listening to Jewish folk tales and the demands of men who have turned their backs on the truth.

¹⁵A person who is pure of heart sees goodness and purity in everything; but a person whose own heart is evil and untrusting finds evil in everything, for his dirty mind and rebellious heart color all he sees and hears. ¹⁶Such persons claim they know God, but from seeing the way they act, one knows they don't. They are rotten and disobedient, worthless so far as doing anything good is concerned.

1:10
Acts 15:1
2 Cor 11:13
1 Tim 1:6
1:11
1 Tim 5:13; 6:5
1:13
2 Cor 13:10
1 Tim 5:20
1:14
Col 2:22
1 Tim 1:4
2 Tim 4:4
1:15
Lk 11:39
Rom 14:14
1:16
Ezek 33:31
1 Tim 5:8
2 Tim 3:8
1 Jn 2:4

2. Right living in the church

2 But as for you, speak up for the right living that goes along with true Christianity. ²Teach the older men to be serious and unruffled; they must be sensible, knowing and believing the truth and doing everything with love and patience.

³Teach the older women to be quiet and respectful in everything they do. They must not go around speaking evil of others and must not be heavy drinkers, but they should be teachers of goodness. ⁴These older women must train the younger women to live quietly, to love their husbands and their children, ⁵and to be sensible and clean minded, spending their time in their own homes, being kind and obedient to their husbands, so that the Christian faith can't be spoken against by those who know them.

⁶In the same way, urge the young men to behave carefully, taking life seriously.

2:1
1 Tim 6:3
Tit 1:9
2:3
1 Pet 3:3,4
2:5
Eph 5:22
Col 3:18
1 Tim 5:14

1:10 *Judaizers* caused problems in many churches where Paul had preached the Good News. These were Jews who taught that the Gentiles had to obey all the Jewish laws before they could become Christians. This confused many new Christians. Paul had to write letters to several churches to help them understand that Gentile believers did not have to become Jews first in order to be Christians—God accepts anyone who comes to him in faith (see Romans 1:17; Galatians 3:2–7).

1:10–14 Paul is warning Titus to be on the lookout for false teachers—those who say they speak God's Word but whose message is not at all consistent with it. Some false teachers are simply confused—they speak their misguided opinions without checking them against the Bible. Others have evil motives—they pretend to be Christians only because they can get more money, additional business, or a feeling of power from being a leader in the church. Jesus and the apostles repeatedly warned against false teachers (see Mark 13:22; Acts 20:29; 2 Thessalonians 2:3–12; 2 Peter 3:3–7), because their teachings attack the foundations of truth and integrity upon which the Christian faith is built. You can recognize false teachers because they will (1) focus more attention on themselves than on Christ; (2) ask you to do something that will compromise or dilute your faith; (3) de-emphasize the divine nature of Christ or the inspiration of the Bible; or (4) urge the church to make decisions based more on human judgment than on prayer and biblical guidelines.

1:12 Paul is quoting a line from a poem by Epimenides, a poet and philosopher who had lived in Crete 600 years earlier. "To play the Cretan" had become a phrase meaning to be a cheat and a liar. Paul used a familiar phrase to make a point.

1:15 Some people see good all around them, while others see nothing but evil. What is the difference? Our souls become filters through which we perceive goodness or evil. The pure of heart (those who have Christ in control of their lives) learn to see good

even in the midst of evil. But evil people learn to see evil even in the midst of good. Turn your thoughts to God and his Word, and you will discover goodness more and more, even in this evil world. Whatever you choose to fill your mind with will affect the way you think and act. Fill your mind with what is good, and then there will be little room for what is evil.

1:16 Many people claim to know God, to be born again. How can we know if they are telling the truth? We will not know for certain in this life, but a glance at their lifestyle will quickly tell us what they value and whether they have ordered their lives around Kingdom priorities. The way we live says much about what we believe (see 1 John 2:4–6).

2:1–8 In most churches there are people of all ages. This makes the church strong, but it also brings potential for problems. So Paul gives Titus counsel on how to help various types of people. The older people should teach the younger, by words *and* by example. All believers should live good lives, resisting the pagan influences of their culture as well as false teaching.

2:3–5 Women who were new Christians were to learn how to have harmony in the home by watching older women who had been Christians for some time. We have the same need today. Younger wives and mothers should learn to live in a Christian manner—loving their husbands and caring for their children—through observing exemplary women of God. If you are of an age or position where people look up to you, can you be confident that your example is motivating younger believers to live in a way that honors God?

2:6 This advice given to young men was very important. In ancient Greek society, the role of the husband/father was not viewed as a nurturing role, but merely a functional one. Many young men today have been raised in families where the father neglected his responsibilities to his wife and children. The few husbands and fathers who are good examples of Christian living in

7And here you yourself must be an example to them of good deeds of every kind. Let everything you do reflect your love of the truth and the fact that you are in dead earnest about it. 8Your conversation should be so sensible and logical that anyone who wants to argue will be ashamed of himself because there won't be anything to criticize in anything you say!

9Urge slaves to obey their masters and to try their best to satisfy them. They must not talk back, 10nor steal, but must show themselves to be entirely trustworthy. In this way they will make people want to believe in our Savior and God.

11For the free gift of eternal salvation is now being offered to everyone; 12and along with this gift comes the realization that God wants us to turn from godless living and sinful pleasures and to live good, God-fearing lives day after day, 13looking forward to that wonderful time we've been expecting, when his glory shall be seen—the glory of our great God and Savior Jesus Christ. 14He died under God's judgment against our sins, so that he could rescue us from constant falling into sin and make us his very own people, with cleansed hearts and real enthusiasm for doing kind things for others. 15You must teach these things and encourage your people to do them, correcting them when necessary as one who has every right to do so. Don't let anyone think that what you say is not important.

3. Right living in society

Obey the government

3 Remind your people to obey the government and its officers, and always to be obedient and ready for any honest work. 2They must not speak evil of anyone, nor quarrel, but be gentle and truly courteous to all.

3Once we, too, were foolish and disobedient; we were misled by others and became slaves to many evil pleasures and wicked desires. Our lives were full of resentment and envy. We hated others and they hated us.

4But when the time came for the kindness and love of God our Savior to appear, 5then he saved us—not because we were good enough to be saved, but because of his kindness and pity—by washing away our sins and giving us the new joy of the indwelling Holy Spirit 6whom he poured out upon us with wonderful fullness—and all because of what Jesus Christ our Savior did 7so that he could declare us good in God's eyes—all because of his great kindness; and now we can share in the wealth of the eternal life he gives us, and we are eagerly looking forward to receiving it. 8These things I have told you are all true. Insist on them so that Christians will be careful to do good deeds all the time, for this is not only right, but it brings results.

---

their families are extremely important role models for young men who need to *see* how it is done more than to be *told* how to do it.

2:6-8 Paul urged Titus to be a good example to those around him so that others might see his good deeds and imitate him. His life would give his words greater impact. If you want someone to act a certain way, be sure that you live that way yourself. Then you will earn the right to be heard.

2:8 Paul counseled Titus to be sensible and logical (reasonable) in his conversation, to avoid criticism. Such conversation comes from careful Bible study and listening before speaking. If we are impulsive, unreasonable, and confusing, we are likely to start arguments rather than to convince people of the truth.

2:9, 10 Slavery was common in Paul's day. Paul did not condemn slavery in any of his letters, but he advised slaves and masters to be loving and responsible in their conduct (see also Ephesians 6:5-9). The standards set by Paul apply to any employee/employer relationship. Employees should always do their best work and be trustworthy, not just when the employer is watching. Businesses in the United States lose millions of dollars a year to employee theft and time-wasting. If all Christian employees followed Paul's advice, what a transformation it would make!

2:11-14 The power to live the Christian life comes from Jesus Christ. Because Christ died and rescued us from sin, we are free from sin's control. He gives us the power and understanding to live according to God's will, to look forward to his return, and to do good.

2:15 Paul told Titus to teach the Scriptures as well as to live them. We must also teach, encourage, and correct others when necessary. Although good teaching occurs in classrooms and small groups, much of the teaching Paul refers to must be done in the "classroom" of personal and family relationships.

3:1, 2 As Christians, our first allegiance is to Jesus as Lord, but we also must obey our government and its leaders. Christians are not above the law, but keeping the civil law is only the beginning of our Christian responsibility. In a democracy, it is also important to be involved and to serve. (See the notes on Acts 5:29 and Romans 13:1ff.)

3:3-8 Paul summarizes what Christ does for us when he saves us. We move from a life full of sin to one led by God's Holy Spirit. *All* our sins, not merely some, are washed away. We gain eternal life with *all* its treasures. We have the *fullness* of the Holy Spirit, and he continually renews our hearts. None of this occurs because we earned or deserved it; it is all a gift of God's grace.

3:4-6 All persons of the Trinity participate in the work of salvation. Based upon the redemptive work of his Son, the Father sends the Holy Spirit to wash away our sins and continually renew us.

Avoid useless arguments

9Don't get involved in arguing over unanswerable questions and controversial theological ideas; keep out of arguments and quarrels about obedience to Jewish laws, for this kind of thing isn't worthwhile; it only does harm. 10If anyone is causing divisions among you, he should be given a first and second warning. After that have nothing more to do with him, 11for such a person has a wrong sense of values. He is sinning, and he knows it.

3:9
1 Tim 1:4
2 Tim 2:14,16,
23
3:10
Mt 18:15-17
Rom 16:2

Paul's final instructions

12I am planning to send either Artemas or Tychicus to you. As soon as one of them arrives, please try to meet me at Nicopolis as quickly as you can, for I have decided to stay there for the winter. 13Do everything you can to help Zenas the lawyer and Apollos with their trip; see that they are given everything they need. 14For our people must learn to help all who need their assistance, that their lives will be fruitful.

15Everybody here sends greetings. Please say "hello" to all of the Christian friends there. May God's blessings be with you all.

Sincerely, Paul

3:12
Acts 20:4
2 Tim 4:12,21
Col 4:9
3:13
Acts 18:24
3:14
Rom 12:13
Phil 1:11
Tit 3:8
2 Pet 1:8
3:15
Col 4:18

3:9–11 Paul warns Titus, as he warned Timothy, not to get involved in arguments over unanswerable questions (2 Timothy 2:14). This does not mean we should refuse to study, discuss, and examine different interpretations of difficult Bible passages. Paul is warning against petty quarrels, not honest discussion that leads to wisdom. When foolish arguments develop, it is best to turn the discussion back to a track that is going somewhere or politely excuse yourself from the discussion.

3:9–11 A person must be warned when he or she is causing division that threatens the unity of the church. This warning should not be a heavy-handed action, but should correct the individual's divisive nature and restore him or her to fellowship. A person who refuses to be corrected has already chosen to be outside the fellowship. As Paul says, "He is sinning and he knows it." (See also Matthew 18:15–18 and 2 Thessalonians 3:14, 15 for help in handling such problems in the church.)

3:12 The city of Nicopolis was on the western coast of Greece. Artemas or Tychicus would take over Titus' work on the island of Crete, so Titus could meet Paul in Nicopolis. Tychicus was one of Paul's trusted companions (Acts 20:4; Ephesians 6:21; Colossians 4:7). Titus would have to leave quickly because sea travel was dangerous in the winter months.

3:13 Apollos was a famous Christian preacher. A native of Alexandria in North Africa, he became a Christian in Ephesus and was trained by Aquila and Priscilla (Acts 18:24–28; 1 Corinthians 1:12).

3:15 The letters of Paul to Titus and Timothy mark the end of Paul's writing and the end of his life and ministry. These letters are rich treasures for us today because they give vital information for church leadership. They provide a strong model for elders, pastors, and other Christian leaders as they develop younger leaders to carry on the work, following Paul's example of preparing Timothy and Titus to carry on his ministry. For practical guidelines on church leadership and problem solving, carefully study the principles found in these letters.

PHILEMON

AT THE FOREMAN'S signal, the giant ball is released, and with dynamite force and a reverberating crash, it meets the wall, snapping bricks like twigs and scattering pieces of mortar. Repeatedly, the powerful pendulum works, and soon the barrier has been reduced to rubble. Then it is carted away so that construction can begin.

Life has many walls and fences which divide, separate, and compartmentalize. Not made of wood or stone, they are personal obstructions, blocking people from each other and from God. But Christ came as the great wall remover, tearing down the sin partition which separates us from God and blasting the barriers which keep us from each other (see Ephesians 2:14–16).

Roman, Greek, and Jewish cultures had many societal barriers—people were assigned to certain social classes and were expected to remain in their place—men and women, enslaved and free, rich and poor, Jews and Gentiles, Greeks and barbarians, pious and heathen. In Christ the walls came down, and Paul could declare, "In this new life one's nationality or race or education or social position is unimportant; such things mean nothing. Whether a person has Christ is what matters, and he is equally available to all" (Colossians 3:11).

This life-changing truth forms the backdrop for the letter to Philemon. The epistle to Philemon is Paul's personal plea on behalf of a slave. Onesimus "belonged" to Paul's friend Philemon, who was probably a member of the Colossian church. But Onesimus, had run away and may have even stolen from his master. He ran to Rome where he met Paul, and there he responded to the Good News and came to faith in Christ (1:10). So Paul writes to Philemon and reintroduces Onesimus to him, explaining that he is sending him back, not just as a slave but also as a brother in Christ (1:11, 12, 15, 16). Tactfully he asks Philemon to forgive Onesimus and to accept his servant back (1:10, 13–16, 20). The social barriers of the past and the new ones erected by Onesimus' desertion and theft should no longer divide them—they are one in Christ.

This small book is a masterpiece of grace and tact and is a profound demonstration of the power of Christ and of true Christian fellowship in action. What separates you from fellow believers—race, status, wealth, education, personality? As with Philemon, God calls you to unity: break down those walls and embrace all brothers and sisters in Christ.

VITAL STATISTICS

PURPOSE:
To convince Philemon to forgive his runaway slave, Onesimus, and to accept him as a brother in the faith

AUTHOR:
Paul

TO WHOM WRITTEN:
Philemon, who was probably a wealthy member of the Colossian church

DATE WRITTEN:
About A.D. 60, during Paul's first imprisonment in Rome, at about the same time Ephesians and Colossians were written

SETTING:
Slavery was very common in the Roman Empire, and evidently some Christians had slaves. Paul does not condemn the institution in his writings, but he makes a radical statement by calling this slave Philemon's brother in Christ.

KEY VERSES:
"Perhaps you could think of it this way: that he ran away from you for a little while so that now he can be yours forever, no longer only a slave, but something much better—a beloved brother, especially to me . . ." (1:15, 16).

KEY PEOPLE:
Paul, Philemon, Onesimus

KEY PLACES:
Colosse, Rome

THE BLUEPRINT

1. Paul's appreciation of Philemon (1:1–7)
2. Paul's appeal for Onesimus (1:8–25)

Paul pleads for Onesimus, a repentant runaway slave. Paul's intercession for him illustrates what Christ has done for us. As Paul interceded for a slave, so Christ intercedes for us, slaves to sin. As Onesimus was reconciled to Philemon, so we are reconciled to God through Christ. As Paul offered to pay the debts of a slave, so Christ paid our debt of sin. Like Onesimus, we must return to God our Master and serve him with glad hearts and transformed lives.

MEGATHEMES

THEME	EXPLANATION	IMPORTANCE
Forgiveness	Philemon was Paul's friend and Onesimus' owner. Paul asked him not to punish Onesimus, but to forgive and restore him as a new Christian brother.	Christian relationships must be full of forgiveness and acceptance. Can you forgive those who have wronged you?
Barriers	Slavery was widespread in the Roman Empire, but no one is beyond God's love. Slavery was a barrier between people, but Christian love and fellowship are to overcome such barriers.	In Christ we are one family. No walls of race, economic status, or political differences should separate believers. Let Christ work through you to remove barriers between Christian brothers and sisters.
Respect	Paul was a friend of both Philemon and Onesimus. He had the authority as an apostle to tell Philemon what to do. Yet Paul chose to appeal to his friend in Christian love rather than to order him.	Tactful persuasion accomplishes a great deal more than commands, when dealing with people. Remember to exhibit courtesy and respect in dealing with people.

1. Paul's appreciation of Philemon

1 *From:* Paul, in jail for preaching the Good News about Jesus Christ, and from Brother Timothy.

To: Philemon, our much loved fellow worker, and to the church that meets in your home, and to Apphia our sister, and to Archippus who like myself is a soldier of the cross.

³May God our Father and the Lord Jesus Christ give you his blessings and his peace.

⁴I always thank God when I am praying for you, dear Philemon, ⁵because I keep hearing of your love and trust in the Lord Jesus and in his people. ⁶And I pray that as you share your faith with others it will grip their lives too, as they see the wealth of good things in you that come from Christ Jesus. ⁷I myself have gained much joy and comfort from your love, my brother, because your kindness has so often refreshed the hearts of God's people.

1:1
Eph 4:1
2 Tim 1:8
Philem 9,23,24
1:2
Rom 16:5
1 Cor 16:29
Phil 2:25
Col 4:17
1:4
Rom 1:8,9
2 Thess 1:3
1:6
Phil 1:9
1:7
2 Cor 7:13
2 Tim 1:16

2. Paul's appeal for Onesimus

⁸,⁹Now I want to ask a favor of you. I could demand it of you in the name of Christ because it is the right thing for you to do, but I love you and prefer just to ask you—I, Paul, an old man now, here in jail for the sake of Jesus Christ. ¹⁰My plea

1:8
1 Thess 2:6

1:1, 2 Paul wrote this letter from Rome in about A.D. 60, when he was under house arrest (see Acts 28:30, 31). Onesimus was a domestic slave who belonged to Philemon, a wealthy man and a member of the church in Colosse. Onesimus had run away from Philemon and made his way to Rome where he met Paul, who apparently led him to Christ (1:10). Paul convinced Onesimus that running away from his problems wouldn't solve them and he persuaded Onesimus to return to his master. Paul wrote this letter to Philemon to ask him to be reconciled to his runaway slave who was now also a Christian brother.

1:1, 2 For more information on Paul's life and ministry, see his Profile in Acts 9. Timothy's name is included with Paul's in 2 Corinthians, 1 Thessalonians, 2 Thessalonians, Philippians, Colossians, and Philemon—the last three of these letters are from a group known as the "prison epistles," (the fourth letter in this group is Ephesians). Timothy was one of Paul's trusted companions; Paul wrote two letters to him— 1 and 2 Timothy.

1:1, 2 Philemon was a Greek landowner living in Colosse. He was converted under Paul's ministry, and the Colossian church met in his home. Onesimus was one of Philemon's slaves.

1:1, 2 Archippus may have been Philemon's son or possibly an elder of the Colossian church. In either case, Paul included him as

a recipient of the letter, possibly so Archippus could read the letter with Philemon and encourage him to follow Paul's advice.

1:1, 2 The early churches often met in people's homes. Because of sporadic persecutions and the great expense involved, church buildings were not constructed at this time.

1:7 Paul reflected on Philemon's kindness, love, and comfort. He had opened his heart and his home to the church. We should do likewise, opening ourselves and our homes to others, offering Christian fellowship to refresh people's spirits.

1:8, 9 Since Paul was an elder and an apostle, he could have used his authority with Philemon, commanding him to deal kindly with his runaway slave. But Paul based his request not on his own authority, but on Philemon's Christian commitment. Paul wanted Philemon's heartfelt, not grudging obedience. When you know something is right and you have the power to demand it, do you appeal to your authority or the other person's commitment? Here Paul provides a good example of how to deal with a possible conflict between Christian friends.

1:10 A master had the legal right to kill a runaway slave. Onesimus feared for his life. So Paul wrote this letter to Philemon to help him understand his new relationship with Onesimus. Onesimus was now a Christian brother, not a mere possession.

is that you show kindness to my child Onesimus, whom I won to the Lord while here in my chains. 11Onesimus (whose name means "Useful") hasn't been of much use to you in the past, but now he is going to be of real use to both of us. 12I am sending him back to you, and with him comes my own heart.

13I really wanted to keep him here with me while I am in these chains for preaching the Good News, and you would have been helping me through him, 14but I didn't want to do it without your consent. I didn't want you to be kind because you had to but because you wanted to. 15Perhaps you could think of it this way: that he ran away from you for a little while so that now he can be yours forever, 16no longer only a slave, but something much better—a beloved brother, especially to me. Now he will mean much more to you too, because he is not only a servant but also your brother in Christ.

17If I am really your friend, give him the same welcome you would give to me if I were the one who was coming. 18If he has harmed you in any way or stolen anything from you, charge me for it. 19I will pay it back (I, Paul, personally guarantee this by writing it here with my own hand) but I won't mention how much you owe me! The fact is, you even owe me your very soul! 20Yes, dear brother, give me joy with this loving act and my weary heart will praise the Lord.

21I've written you this letter because I am positive that you will do what I ask and even more!

22Please keep a guest room ready for me, for I am hoping that God will answer your prayers and let me come to you soon.

23Epaphras my fellow prisoner, who is also here for preaching Christ Jesus, sends you his greetings. 24So do Mark, Aristarchus, Demas and Luke, my fellow workers.

25The blessings of our Lord Jesus Christ be upon your spirit.

Paul

1:13 Phil 1:7; 2:30
1:14 2 Cor 9:7
1:15 Gen 45:5,8 Rom 8:28
1:16 Mt 23:8 1 Cor 7:22 Col 3:22
1:17 2 Cor 8:23
1:19 2 Thess 3:17
1:21 2 Cor 7:16
1:22 Phil 1:24-26 2:24
1:23 Col 1:7; 4:12
1:24 Acts 12:12 19:29; 27:2 Col 4:10,14 Philem 1
1:25 Gal 6:18 2 Tim 4:22

1:10ff Paul asked Philemon to forgive his runaway slave who had become a Christian, and not only to forgive, but to accept him as a brother. As Christians, we should forgive as we have been forgiven (Matthew 6:5–15; Ephesians 4:31, 32). True forgiveness means we treat the one we've forgiven as we would want to be treated. Is there someone you say you have forgiven, but who still needs your kindness?

1:13–16 What a difference Onesimus' status as a Christian made in his relationship to Philemon. He was no longer merely a servant, he was also a brother. Now both Onesimus and Philemon were members of God's family—equals in Christ. A Christian's status as a member of God's family transcends all other distinctions among believers. Do you look down on any fellow Christians? Remember, they are your brothers and sisters, your equals before Christ (Galatians 3:28). How you treat your brothers and sisters in Christ's family reflects your true Christian commitment.

1:15, 16 Slavery was widespread throughout the Roman Empire. In these early days, Christians did not have the political power to change the slavery system. Paul didn't condemn or condone slavery but worked to transform relationships. The gospel begins to change social structures by changing the *people* within those structures. (See 1 Corinthians 7:20–24; Ephesians 6:5–9; Colossians 3:22—4:1.)

1:17–19 Paul genuinely loved Onesimus. Paul showed his love by personally guaranteeing payment for any stolen goods or injuries for which Onesimus might be responsible. Paul's investment in the life of this new believer certainly encouraged and strengthened Onesimus' faith. Are there young believers who need you to demonstrate such self-sacrifice towards them? Be grateful when you can invest in the lives of others.

1:19 When Paul said, "you even owe me your very soul," he was reminding Philemon that it was he who had led him to Christ. Because Paul was Philemon's spiritual father, he hoped Philemon would feel a debt of gratitude that he would repay by accepting Onesimus with a spirit of forgiveness.

1:22 Paul was released from prison soon after writing this letter, but the Bible doesn't say whether he returned to Colosse.

1:23 Epaphras was well known to the Colossians, since he had founded the church there (Colossians 1:7). He was a hero to this church, helping to hold it together in spite of growing persecution and struggles with false doctrine. Epaphras' earnest prayers for the Colossian Christians revealed his deep love for them (Colossians 4:12, 13). He was probably in prison with Paul for preaching the gospel.

1:24 Mark, Aristarchus, Demas, and Luke are also mentioned in Colossians 4:10, 14. Mark had accompanied Paul and Barnabas on their first missionary journey (Acts 12:25ff). John Mark also wrote the Gospel of Mark. Luke had accompanied Paul on his third missionary journey and was the writer of the Gospel of Luke and the book of Acts. Demas was faithful to Paul for a while but then deserted him (see 2 Timothy 4:9, 10).

1:25 Paul urged Philemon to be reconciled to his slave, receiving him as a brother and fellow member of God's family. *Reconciliation* means reestablishing relationship. Christ has reconciled us to God and to others. Many barriers arise between people—race, social status, sex, personality differences—but Christ can break down these barriers. Jesus Christ changed Onesimus' relationship to Philemon from slave to brother. Only in Christ can our most hopeless relationships be transformed into something wonderful.

HEBREWS

VITAL STATISTICS

PURPOSE:
To present the sufficiency and
superiority of Christ

AUTHOR:
Paul, Luke, Barnabas, Apollos,
Silas, Philip, Priscilla, and
others have been suggested
because the name of the author
is not given in the biblical text
itself. Whoever it was speaks of
Timothy as "Brother" (13:23).

TO WHOM WRITTEN:
Hebrew Christians who may
have been considering a return
to Judaism, perhaps because of
immaturity, due to their lack of
understanding of biblical truths.
They seem to be "second-
generation" Christians (2:3).

DATE WRITTEN:
Probably before the destruction
of the Temple in Jerusalem in
A.D. 70, since the religious
sacrifices and ceremonies are
referred to in the book, but no
mention is made of the
Temple's destruction

SETTING:
These Jewish Christians were
probably undergoing fierce
persecution, socially and
physically, both from Jews and
from Romans. Christ had not
returned to establish his
Kingdom, and the people
needed to be reassured that
Christianity was true and that
Jesus was indeed the Messiah.

KEY VERSE:
"God's Son shines out with
God's glory, and all that God's
Son is and does marks him as
God. He regulates the universe
by the mighty power of his
command. He is the one who
died to cleanse us and clear our
record of all sin, and then sat
down in highest honor beside
the great God of heaven" (1:3).

KEY PEOPLE:
Old Testament men and women
of faith (chapter 11)

SPECIAL FEATURES:
Although Hebrews is called a
"letter" (13:22), it has the form
and the content of a sermon.

CONSCIENTIOUS consumers shop for value.
Wise parents desire only the best for their children, nourishing their growing bodies, minds,
and spirits. Individuals with integrity seek the
best investment of time, talents, and treasures.
In every area, to settle for less would be wasteful,
foolish, and irresponsible. Yet that is a natural
pull, to move toward what is convenient, comfortable, and less than ideal.

Judaism was not second-rate or easy. Divinely
designed, it was the best religion, expressing true
worship and devotion to God. The commandments, the rituals, and the
prophets described God's promises and revealed the way to forgiveness
and salvation. Then Christ came, fulfilling the Law and the Prophets,
conquering sin, and freely providing eternal life.

This message was difficult for Jews to accept. Although they had
sought the Messiah for centuries, they were entrenched in thinking and
worshiping in traditional forms. Following Jesus seemed to repudiate
their marvelous heritage and profound Scriptures. With caution and
questions they listened to the gospel, but many rejected it and sought to
eliminate this "heresy." Those who did accept Jesus as the Messiah,
often found themselves slipping back into the old and familiar.

Hebrews is a masterful document written to demonstrate the exclu-
siveness and superiority of the new covenant. The overarching message
of Hebrews is that Christianity is superior to Judaism because Christ is
supreme and is completely sufficient for salvation.

Hebrews begins by emphasizing that the old (Judaism) and the new
(Christianity) are both religions "revealed" by God (1:1–3). In the
doctrinal section which follows (1:4—10:23), the writer shows how Jesus
is greater than angels (1:4—2:18) and Moses (3:1–19), provides a better
rest (4:1–13), and is superior to the Old Testament priesthood (4:14—7:28).
Christianity surpasses Judaism because it has a better covenant (8:1–13),
a better sanctuary (9:1–10), and a more sufficient sacrifice for sins
(9:1—10:18).

Having established the superiority of Christianity, the writer moves on
to the practical implications of following Christ. The readers are exhorted
to hold on to their new faith, encourage each other, and look forward to
Christ's return (10:19–25). They are warned about the consequences of
rejecting Christ's sacrifice for them (10:26–31) and reminded of the
rewards for faithfulness (10:32–39). Then the author explains what it is
to live by faith, giving illustrations of the faithful men and women in the
history of Israel (11:1–40). We are exhorted to pattern our lives after
Christ, allowing God to discipline us (12:1–17). This section ends by
comparing the old covenant with the new (12:18–29). The writer concludes
with moral exhortations (13:1–17), a request for prayer (13:18, 19), and
a benediction followed by greetings (13:20–25).

Jesus Christ is the perfect revelation of God, the final and complete
sacrifice for sin, and the *only* way to eternal life. Read Hebrews and
begin to see history and life from God's perspective. Then give yourself
unreservedly and completely to Christ. Don't settle for anything less.

THE BLUEPRINT

A. THE SUPERIORITY OF CHRIST
(1:1—10:18)
1. Christ is greater than the angels
2. Christ is greater than Moses
3. Christ is greater than the Old Testament priesthood
4. The new covenant is greater than the old

The superiority of Christ over everyone and everything is clearly demonstrated by the author. Christianity supersedes all other religions and can never be surpassed. Where can one find anything better than Christ? Living in Christ is having the best there is in life. All competing religions are deceptions or cheap imitations.

B. THE SUPERIORITY OF FAITH
(10:19—13:25)

Jews who had become Christians in the first century were tempted to fall back into Judaism because of uncertainty, the security of customs, and persecution. Today believers are also tempted to fall back into legalism, fulfilling minimum religious requirements, rather than pressing on in genuine faith. We must strive to live by faith each day.

MEGATHEMES

THEME	EXPLANATION	IMPORTANCE
Christ Is Superior	Hebrews reveals Jesus' true identity as God. He is the ultimate authority. He is greater than any religion or any angel. He is superior to any Jewish leader (such as Abraham, Moses, or Joshua) and superior to any priest. He is the complete revelation of God.	Jesus alone can forgive your sin. He has secured your forgiveness and salvation by his death on the cross. You can find peace with God and real meaning for life by believing in Christ.
High Priest	In the Old Testament, the High Priest represented the Jews before God. Jesus Christ links us with God. There is no other superior way to reach God. Because Jesus Christ lived a sinless life, he is the perfect substitute to die for our sin. He is our perfect representative with God.	Jesus guarantees our access to God the Father. He intercedes for us so we can boldly come to the Father with our needs. When we are weak we can come confidently to God for forgiveness and help.
Sacrifice	Christ's sacrifice was the ultimate fulfillment of all that the Old Testament sacrifices represented—God's forgiveness for sin. Because Christ is the perfect sacrifice for our sin, our sins are completely forgiven—past, present, and future.	Christ removed sin which barred us from God's presence and fellowship. But we must accept his sacrifice for us. By believing in him we are no longer guilty, but cleansed and made whole. His sacrifice makes the way for us to have eternal life.
Maturity	Though we are saved from sin when we believe in Christ, we are given the task to go on and grow in our faith. Through our relationship with Christ we can live blameless lives, be set aside for his special use, and develop maturity.	The process of maturing in our faith takes time. Daily commitment and service produce maturity. When we are mature in our faith, we are not easily swayed or shaken.
Faith	Faith is confident trust in God. God's salvation is in his son Jesus, who is the only one who can save us from sin.	If you trust in Jesus Christ for your complete salvation, he will transform you completely. A life of obedience and complete truth is pleasing to God.
Endurance	Faith enables Christians to face trials. Genuine faith includes the commitment to stay true to God when we are under fire. Endurance builds character and leads to victory.	You can have victory in your trials if you don't give up or turn your back on Christ. Stay true to Christ and pray for endurance.

A. THE SUPERIORITY OF CHRIST (1:1—10:18)

The relationship of Christianity to Judaism was a critical issue in the early church. The author clears up confusion by carefully explaining how Christ is superior to angels, Moses, and High Priests. The new covenant is shown to be far superior to the old. This can be of great encouragement to us and help us avoid drifting away from our faith in Christ.

1. Christ is greater than the angels

Jesus Christ is God's Son

1 Long ago God spoke in many different ways to our fathers through the prophets [in visions, dreams, and even face to face], telling them little by little about his plans.

1:1
Num12:6-8

2But now in these days he has spoken to us through his Son to whom he has given everything, and through whom he made the world and everything there is.

1:2
Ps 2:8
Jn 1:1,3,18; 8:25

3God's Son shines out with God's glory, and all that God's Son is and does marks him as God. He regulates the universe by the mighty power of his command. He is the one who died to cleanse us and clear our record of all sin, and then sat down in highest honor beside the great God of heaven.

1:3
Ps 110:1
Jn 14:9
2 Cor 4:4
Col 1:15

God's Son compared to the angels

4Thus he became far greater than the angels, as proved by the fact that his name "Son of God," which was passed on to him from his Father, is far greater than the names and titles of the angels. 5, 6For God never said to any angel, "You are my Son, and today I have given you the honor that goes with that name." But God said it about Jesus. Another time he said, "I am his Father and he is my Son." And still

1:4
Eph 1:21
Phil 2:9

1:5
a) Ps 2:7
Rev 1:5
b) 2 Sam 7:14

1:1 *in visions, dreams, and even face to face,* implied.   **1:5, 6** *today I have given you the honor that goes with that name,* literally, "this day I have begotten you."

Hebrews passage	Old Testament passage	How Christ is higher than the angels	**CHRIST AND THE ANGELS**
1:5, 6	Psalm 2:7	Christ is called Son of God, a title never given to an angel.	
1:7, 14	Psalm 104:4	Angels are important, but servants.	
1:8, 9	Psalm 45:6	Christ's Kingdom is forever.	
1:10	Psalm 102:25	Christ is the Creator of the world.	
1:13	Psalm 110:1	Christ is given unique honor by God.	

The writer of Hebrews quotes from the Old Testament repeatedly in demonstrating Christ's greatness in comparison to the angels. His audience of first-century Jewish Christians had developed an unbalanced belief in angels and their role. Christ's lordship is affirmed without disrespect to God's valued angelic messengers.

1:1 The book of Hebrews describes in detail how Jesus Christ fulfills the promises and prophecies of the Old Testament. The Jews believed in the Old Testament Scriptures, but most rejected Jesus as the long-awaited Messiah. The recipients of this letter seem to have been Jewish Christians. They were well-versed in Scripture, and they had professed faith in Christ. Whether through doubt, persecution, or false teaching, however, they may have been in danger of giving up their Christian faith and returning to Judaism.

The authorship of this book is uncertain. Several names have been suggested including Luke, Barnabas, Apollos, Priscilla, and Paul. Most scholars do not believe Paul was the author, because the writing style of Hebrews is quite different from that of Paul's epistles. In addition, Paul identified himself in his other letters and appealed to his authority as an apostle, whereas this writer never gives his or her name and appeals to eyewitnesses of Jesus' ministry for authority. Nevertheless, the author of Hebrews evidently knew Paul well. Hebrews was probably written by one of Paul's close associates who often heard him preach.

1:1, 2 God used many approaches to send his messages to people in Old Testament times. He spoke to Isaiah in visions (Isaiah 6), to Jacob in a dream (Genesis 28:10–22), and to Abraham and Moses personally (Genesis 18; Exodus 31:18).

Jewish people familiar with these stories would not have found it hard to believe that God was still revealing his will, but it was astonishing for them to think that God had revealed *himself* by speaking through his Son, Jesus Christ. Jesus is the fulfillment and culmination of God's many revelations through the centuries.

1:2, 3 Not only is Jesus God's spokesman; he is God himself—the very God who spoke in Old Testament times. He is eternal; he worked with the Father in creating the world (John 1:3; Colossians 1:16). He is the full revelation of God. You can have no clearer view of God than by looking at him. Jesus Christ is the complete embodiment of God.

1:3 The book of Hebrews links God's saving power with his creative power. In other words, the power that brought the universe into being and that keeps it operating is the very power that removes our sins. How wrong it is, then, to think that God can't forgive us. No sin is too big for the Ruler of the universe to handle. He can and will forgive us when we come to him through his Son.

1:5, 6 Jesus is God's firstborn (unique) Son. In Jewish families the firstborn son held the place of highest privilege and responsibility. The Jewish Christians reading this message would understand that as God's firstborn, Jesus was superior to any created being.

another time—when his firstborn Son came to earth—God said, "Let all the angels of God worship him."

1:6
Ps 89:27; 97:7

7God speaks of his angels as messengers swift as the wind and as servants made of flaming fire; 8but of his Son he says, "Your Kingdom, O God, will last forever and ever; its commands are always just and right. 9You love right and hate wrong; so God, even your God, has poured out more gladness upon you than on anyone else."

1:7
Ps 104:4

1:8,9
Ps 45:6,7

1:10-12
Ps 102:25-27

10God also called him "Lord" when he said, "Lord, in the beginning you made the earth, and the heavens are the work of your hands. 11They will disappear into nothingness, but you will remain forever. They will become worn out like old clothes, 12and some day you will fold them up and replace them. But you yourself will never change, and your years will never end."

1:13
Ps 110:1
Mt 22:44

13And did God ever say to an angel, as he does to his Son, "Sit here beside me in honor until I crush all your enemies beneath your feet"?

1:14
Ps 34:7; 91:11
Rom 8:17
Heb 2:3

14No, for the angels are only spirit-messengers sent out to help and care for those who are to receive his salvation.

Warning against drifting away

2:2
Deut 5:5; 33:2
Acts 7:38,53
Gal 3:19

2 So we must listen very carefully to the truths we have heard, or we may drift away from them. 2For since the messages from angels have always proved true and people have always been punished for disobeying them, 3what makes us think that we can escape if we are indifferent to this great salvation announced by the Lord Jesus himself, and passed on to us by those who heard him speak?

2:3
Heb 1:1,2; 10:29

2:4
Mk 6:14

4God always has shown us that these messages are true by signs and wonders and

---

LESSONS FROM CHRIST'S HUMANITY

Christ is the perfect human	leader	and he wants to lead you
	model	and he is worth imitating
	sacrifice	and he died for you
	conqueror	and he conquered death to give you eternal life
	High Priest	and he is merciful, loving, and understanding

God, in Christ, became a living, breathing human being. Hebrews points out many reasons why this is so important.

1:11, 12 Because the readers of Hebrews experienced the rejection of their fellow Jews, they often felt isolated. Many were tempted to exchange the changeless Christ for their familiar old faith. The writer of Hebrews warns them not to do this: Christ is the *only* security in a changing world. Whatever may happen in this world, Christ remains forever changeless. A Christian, then, is absolutely secure, because he stands on the firmest foundation in the universe—Jesus Christ.

1:12 What does it mean that Christ is changeless? It means that his character will never change. He is persistent in his love for us, committed to fairness and justice, and absolutely set on being merciful to us who are so undeserving. Rejoice today that Christ is changeless—he will always help you when you need it and offer forgiveness when you fall.

1:13 False teachers in many of the early churches taught that God could be approached only through angels. Instead of worshiping God directly, followers of these heretics bowed to angels. Hebrews clearly denounces such teaching as false. Some thought of Jesus as the highest angel of God. But Jesus is not a superior angel; and, in any case, angels are not to be worshiped (see Colossians 2:18; Revelation 19:1–10). Jesus is God, he alone deserves our worship.

1:14 Angels, God's messengers, were created by God and are under his authority (Colossians 1:16). They have several functions: serving believers (1:14), protecting the helpless (Matthew 18:10,

11), proclaiming God's messages (Revelation 14:6–12), and executing God's judgment (Acts 12:1–23; Revelation 20:1–3).

2:1–3 Listening is hard work. It involves our minds, bodies, and senses. Listening to Christ means not merely hearing, but also responding in obedience (see James 1:22–25). We must persevere in our obedience to Christ.

2:3 Eyewitnesses to Jesus' ministry had handed down his teachings to the readers of this book. These readers were second-generation believers who had not seen Christ in the flesh. They are like us; we have not seen Jesus personally, but we base our belief in Jesus on eyewitness accounts recorded in the Bible.

2:3 A central theme of Hebrews is that Christ is infinitely greater than all other proposed means to God. Your previous faith was good, the author said to his Jewish readers, but Christ is incomparably better. Just as Christ is greater than angels, so his message is more important than theirs. Don't turn your back on Christ in an attempt to escape your troubles.

2:4 In the book of Acts, miracles and gifts of the Spirit authenticated the gospel wherever it was preached (see Acts 9:31–42; 14:1–20). Paul, who discusses spiritual gifts in Romans 12, 1 Corinthians 12—14, and Ephesians 4, says that the purpose of spiritual gifts is to build up the church, making it strong and mature. When we see the gifts of the Spirit in an individual or congregation, we know God is truly present. As we receive his gifts, we should recognize him and thank him for them.

various miracles and by giving certain special abilities from the Holy Spirit to those who believe; yes, God has assigned such gifts to each of us.

Christ came as a human being

5And the future world we are talking about will not be controlled by angels. 6No, for in the book of Psalms David says to God, "What is mere man that you are so concerned about him? And who is this Son of Man you honor so highly? 7For though you made him lower than the angels for a little while, now you have crowned him with glory and honor. 8And you have put him in complete charge of everything there is. Nothing is left out."

2:5
Heb 6:5

2:6
Ps 8:4-6

2:8
1 Cor 15:27

We have not yet seen all of this take place, 9but we do see Jesus—who for awhile was a little lower than the angels—crowned now by God with glory and honor because he suffered death for us. Yes, because of God's great kindness, Jesus tasted death for everyone in all the world.

2:9
Acts 2:33
Phil 2:6-9

10And it was right and proper that God, who made everything for his own glory, should allow Jesus to suffer, for in doing this he was bringing vast multitudes of God's people to heaven; for his suffering made Jesus a perfect Leader, one fit to bring them into their salvation.

2:10
Lk 13:32; 24:46
Acts 3:15
Rom 11:36
Heb 5:9

11We who have been made holy by Jesus, now have the same Father he has. That is why Jesus is not ashamed to call us his brothers. 12For he says in the book of Psalms, "I will talk to my brothers about God my Father, and together we will sing his praises." 13At another time he said, "I will put my trust in God along with my brothers." And at still another time, "See, here am I and the children God gave me."

2:11
Mt 28:10
Jn 20:17
Rom 8:29
Heb 10:10; 13:12

2:12
Ps 22:22

2:13
Isa 8:17,18
Jn 17:6,9
11,12

14Since we, God's children, are human beings—made of flesh and blood—he became flesh and blood too by being born in human form; for only as a human being could he die and in dying break the power of the devil who had the power of death. 15Only in that way could he deliver those who through fear of death have been living all their lives as slaves to constant dread.

2:14
Jn 1:14
Rom 8:3
1 Cor 15:54,55
2 Tim 1:10
1 Jn 3:8

16We all know he did not come as an angel but as a human being—yes, a Jew. 17And it was necessary for Jesus to be like us, his brothers, so that he could be our merciful and faithful High Priest before God, a Priest who would be both merciful to us and faithful to God in dealing with the sins of the people. 18For since he

2:17
Phil 2:7
Heb 3:1; 4:15
5:1
1 Jn 2:2

2:18
Heb 4:15; 5:2

2:9 God has put Jesus in charge of everything and Jesus has revealed himself to us. We do not yet see Jesus reigning on earth, but we can picture him in his heavenly glory. When confused by tomorrow and anxious about the future, strive to keep a clear view of Jesus Christ—who he is, what he has done, and what he is doing for us right now. This will give stability to your decisions day by day.

2:9, 10 God's kindness led Christ to his death—what a startling juxtaposition of ideas! Yet kindness can and often does involve sacrifice and pain. Jesus did not come into the world to gain status or political power, but to suffer and die so that we could truly live. If this is difficult to understand, perhaps it is time to evaluate our own motives. Are we more interested in power or submission, domination or service, getting or giving? If kindness, not selfishness, motivates us, we too may have to suffer.

2:10 Jesus' suffering made him a perfect Leader (see 5:8, 9), and our suffering can make us better servants of God. People who have known pain are able to reach out with sensitivity to their hurting brothers and sisters. When you suffer, ask how your experience can help you serve Christ better.

2:11–13 The Psalms often look forward to Christ and his work in the world. Here a portion of Psalm 22, a messianic psalm, is quoted. Because God has adopted all believers as his children, Jesus calls them his brothers.

2:14 Jesus had to be human so he could die, so he could

overcome the same temptations we face, and so he could mediate between God and human beings. He identified with us so that we could identify with God.

2:14 By dying, Jesus became our sacrifice and delivered us from death. By rising from the dead, he defeated death, the enemy (see Romans 6:5–11; 1 Corinthians 15).

2:14, 15 Christ's death and resurrection free us from the fear of death because death has been defeated. Do some of your loved ones need the freedom from the fear of death which only Christ can give? All who live in dread of death should have the opportunity to know the truth of Christ's victory. How can you share this understanding with those close to you?

2:16, 17 In the Old Testament, the High Priest was the mediator between God and his people. His job was to regularly offer animal sacrifices according to the law and to intercede before God for the people's sins. Jesus Christ is now our High Priest. He has *once and for all* paid the penalty for all our sins by his own sacrificial death, and he continually intercedes on our behalf before God. We are released from sin's domination over us when we commit ourselves fully to Christ, trusting completely in what he has done for us (see note on 4:14 for more about Jesus as the High Priest).

2:18 Knowing that Christ suffered and was tempted helps us go through our own suffering. We know he understands our struggles, and we trust him to help us survive suffering and overcome temptation. When you face trials, go to Jesus. He understands your needs and is able to help (see 4:14–16).

himself has now been through suffering and temptation, he knows what it is like when we suffer and are tempted, and he is wonderfully able to help us.

2. Christ is greater than Moses
Jesus compared to Moses

3:1
Jn 17:3
Heb 2:17; 4:14

3 Therefore, dear brothers whom God has set apart for himself—you who are chosen for heaven—I want you to think now about this Jesus who is God's Messenger and the High Priest of our faith.

3:2
Num 12:7,8

²For Jesus was faithful to God who appointed him High Priest, just as Moses also faithfully served in God's house. ³But Jesus has far more glory than Moses, just as

3:3
2 Cor 3:7-11

a man who builds a fine house gets more praise than his house does. ⁴And many people can build houses, but only God made everything.

3:5
Ex 14:31
Deut 18:15,18

⁵Well, Moses did a fine job working in God's house, but he was only a servant; and his work was mostly to illustrate and suggest those things that would happen

3:6
a) Eph 2:19-22
1 Tim 3:15
1 Pet 2:5
b) Mt 10:22
Rom 11:22

later on. ⁶But Christ, God's faithful Son, is in complete charge of God's house. And we Christians are God's house—he lives in us!—if we keep up our courage firm to the end, and our joy and our trust in the Lord.

Now is the time to listen to God

3:7
2 Sam 23:2
Ps 95:7,8
Acts 1:16

⁷,⁸And since Christ is so much superior, the Holy Spirit warns us to listen to him, to be careful to hear his voice today and not let our hearts become set against him, as the people of Israel did. They steeled themselves against his love and com-

3:9
Ps 95:9
Acts 7:36

plained against him in the desert while he was testing them. ⁹But God was patient with them forty years, though they tried his patience sorely; he kept right on doing

3:10
Ps 95:10

his mighty miracles for them to see. ¹⁰"But," God says, "I was very angry with them, for their hearts were always looking somewhere else instead of up to me, and they never found the paths I wanted them to follow."

3:11
Ps 95:11

¹¹Then God, full of this anger against them, bound himself with an oath that he would never let them come to his place of rest.

¹²Beware then of your own hearts, dear brothers, lest you find that they, too, are

---

3:1 This verse was especially meaningful to Jewish Christians. For Jews, the highest human authority was the High Priest. For Christians, the highest human authorities were God's messengers, his apostles. Jesus, God's Messenger and High Priest, is the ultimate authority in the church.

3:1-6 The author uses different pictures to explain Jesus' relationship to believers: he is (1) the Messenger of God, to whom we should listen; (2) our High Priest, by whom we come to God the Father; (3) our Creator, whom we should praise; and (4) the ruler of God's house, whom we should obey. The Bible is filled with pictures of Jesus Christ, and each one shows a different facet of his character.

3:2, 3 To the Jewish people, Moses was a great hero; he brought their ancestors, the Israelites, from Egyptian bondage to the Promised Land. He also wrote the first five books of the Old Testament and was the prophet through whom God gave the moral and the ceremonial law. But Jesus is superior to Moses, because Moses was merely a human servant of God, while Jesus is God himself (1:3). As Moses led the people of Israel out of Egypt, delivering them from bondage, so Christ leads us out of the slavery to sin. Why settle for Moses, the book of Hebrews asks its readers, when you can have Jesus Christ, who appointed Moses?

3:5 Moses was faithful to God's calling, which was not only to deliver Israel, but also to prepare the way for the Messiah. This is also true of all the Old Testament saints. Thus, knowing the Old Testament is the best foundation for understanding the New Testament. Reading the Old Testament, we see (1) how God used people to accomplish his purposes, (2) how he used events and personalities to illustrate important truths, (3) how, through prophets, he announced the Messiah, and (4) how, through worship, he prepared people to understand the Messiah's work. Include the Old Testament in your regular Bible reading, and the

New Testament will grow clearer and more meaningful to you.

3:6 Since Christ dwells within us as believers, we courageously remain firm to the end. We are not saved by persevering, but perseverance reveals our faithfulness. Without this enduring faithfulness, we could easily be blown away by the winds of persecution.

3:7-15 Many times the Bible warns us not to harden our hearts. "Hardening our hearts" is an expression that means we have set ourselves against God to the point that we are no longer able to turn to him to be saved. Such hardheartedness begins when we refuse to obey God's revealed will. The Israelites became hardhearted when they disobeyed God's command to conquer the Promised Land (see Numbers 13, 14; see also Numbers 20 and Psalm 95). Let us be careful to obey God's Word and not allow our hearts to become hardened.

3:11 God's rest has several meanings in Scripture: (1) the seventh day of creation and the weekly Sabbath commemorating it (Genesis 2:2; Hebrews 4:4-9), (2) the Promised Land of Canaan (Deuteronomy 12:8-12; Psalm 95), (3) peace with God now because of our relationship with him through faith (Hebrews 4:1, 3, 8-11), and (4) our future eternal life with Christ (Hebrews 4:8-11). All of these meanings were probably familiar to the Jewish Christian readers of Hebrews.

3:12-14 Our hearts lead us away from the living God when we stubbornly refuse to believe him. If we persist in our unbelief, he will eventually leave us alone. But God can give us new hearts, new desires, and a new spirit (Ezekiel 36:22-27). One antidote to a wayward heart is steadfast fellowship with other believers, talking daily about our mutual faith and encouraging one another with love and concern.

evil and unbelieving and are leading you away from the living God. 13Speak to each
other about these things every day while there is still time, so that none of you will
become hardened against God, being blinded by the glamor of sin. 14For if we are
faithful to the end, trusting God just as we did when we first became Christians, we
will share in all that belongs to Christ.

15But *now* is the time. Never forget the warning, "*Today* if you hear God's voice
speaking to you, do not harden your hearts against him, as the people of Israel did
when they rebelled against him in the desert."

16And who were those people I speak of, who heard God's voice speaking to
them but then rebelled against him? They were the ones who came out of Egypt
with Moses their leader. 17And who was it who made God angry for all those forty
years? These same people who sinned and as a result died in the wilderness. 18And
to whom was God speaking when he swore with an oath that they could never go
into the land he had promised his people? He was speaking to all those who
disobeyed him. 19And why couldn't they go in? Because they didn't trust him.

A rest for God's people

4 Although God's promise still stands—his promise that all may enter his place
of rest—we ought to tremble with fear because some of you may be on the
verge of failing to get there after all. 2For this wonderful news—the message that
God wants to save us—has been given to us just as it was to those who lived in the
time of Moses. But it didn't do them any good because they didn't believe it. They
didn't mix it with faith. 3For only we who believe God can enter into his place of
rest. He has said, "I have sworn in my anger that those who don't believe me will
never get in," even though he has been ready and waiting for them since the world
began.

4We know he is ready and waiting because it is written that God rested on the
seventh day of creation, having finished all that he had planned to make.

5Even so they didn't get in, for God finally said, "They shall never enter my
rest." 6Yet the promise remains and some get in—but not those who had the first
chance, for they disobeyed God and failed to enter.

7But he has set another time for coming in, and that time is now. He announced
this through King David long years after man's first failure to enter, saying in the
words already quoted, "Today when you hear him calling, do not harden your
hearts against him."

8This new place of rest he is talking about does not mean the land of Israel that
Joshua led them into. If that were what God meant, he would not have spoken long

3:13 *glamor*, literally, "deceitfulness."

Cross references (right margin):

3:13 Eph 4:22
3:14 Heb 3:6
3:15 Ps 95:7
3:16 Deut 1:34,35
3:17 1 Cor 10:5
4:2 1 Thess 2:13
4:3 Ps 95:11
4:4 Gen 2:2 / Ex 31:17
4:6 Num 14:26-30 / Heb 3:18
4:7 Ps 95:7
4:8 Josh 22:4

3:15–19 The Israelites failed to enter the Promised Land because they lacked trust in God. They did not believe God would help them conquer the land (see Numbers 14, 15); and lacking trust, they failed. So God sent them into the wilderness to wander for 40 years, an unhappy alternative to the wonderful gift he had planned for them. Lack of trust in God always prevents us from receiving his best.

4:1–3 Some of the Jewish Christians who received this letter of Hebrews may have been on the verge of turning back from their promised rest in Christ, just as the people in Moses' day turned back from the Promised Land. In both cases, the difficulties of the present moment overshadowed the reality of God's promise, and people stopped believing that God was able to fulfill his promises. When we place our trust in our own efforts instead of in Christ, we too are in danger of turning back. Our own efforts are never adequate; only Christ can see us through.

4:2 The Israelites of Moses' day illustrate a problem facing many who fill our churches today. They know a great deal about Christ, but they do not know him personally. They don't mix their knowledge with faith. Let the Good News about Christ affect your life. Believe in him and respond in obedience to him.

4:4 God rested on the seventh day to celebrate the completion of creation. The world was perfect, and he was well satisfied with it. This rest is a foretaste of our eternal joy when creation is redeemed, when every mark of sin has been destroyed and the world is perfect once again. Our rest in Christ begins when we trust him to do his good and perfect work in us and through us.

4:7 God gave Israel the opportunity to enter Canaan, but they failed because they didn't trust him (Numbers 14, 15). Now God offers "another time" to enter his ultimate place of rest—he gives us the opportunity to come to Christ. *Now* is the time to believe in Christ and enter the place of rest, which is peace with God. Tomorrow may be too late.

4:8–11 God wants us to enter his rest. For the Israelites of Moses' time, this rest was the Promised Land. For Christians, it is peace with God now and eternal life in a new earth later. We do not need to wait for the next life to enjoy God's rest and peace; we may have it daily now! Our daily rest in the Lord will not terminate with death, but will mature into an eternal rest in the home Christ is preparing for us (John 14:1–4).

afterwards about "today" being the time to get in. 9So there is a full complete rest *still waiting* for the people of God. 10Christ has already entered there. He is resting from his work, just as God did after the creation. 11Let us do our best to go into that place of rest, too, being careful not to disobey God as the children of Israel did, thus failing to get in.

12For whatever God says to us is full of living power: it is sharper than the sharpest dagger, cutting swift and deep into our innermost thoughts and desires with all their parts, exposing us for what we really are. 13He knows about everyone, everywhere. Everything about us is bare and wide open to the all-seeing eyes of our living God; nothing can be hidden from him to whom we must explain all that we have done.

3. Christ is greater than the Old Testament priesthood
Jesus Christ is our High Priest

14But Jesus the Son of God is our great High Priest who has gone to heaven itself to help us; therefore let us never stop trusting him. 15This High Priest of ours understands our weaknesses, since he had the same temptations we do, though he never once gave way to them and sinned. 16So let us come boldly to the very throne of God and stay there to receive his mercy and to find grace to help us in our times of need.

5 The Jewish high priest is merely a man like anyone else, but he is chosen to speak for all other men in their dealings with God. He presents their gifts to God and offers to him the blood of animals that are sacrificed to cover the sins of the people and his own sins too. And because he is a man he can deal gently with other men, though they are foolish and ignorant, for he, too, is surrounded with the same temptations and understands their problems very well.

4:10
Rev 14:13
4:11
2 Pet 2:6

4:12
Isa 49:2
Jer 23:29
1 Cor 14:24,25
Eph 6:17
1 Pet 1:23
4:13
2 Chron 16:9
Jn 2:25

4:14
Heb 2:17; 3:1
4:15
2 Cor 5:21
Heb 2:17,18
1 Pet 2:22
1 Jn 3:5
4:16
Heb 7:19; 10:19,22

5:1
Lev 4:3; 9:7
Heb 2:17;
7:27 8:3,4

THE CHOICES OF MATURITY	Mature choices	Versus	Immature choices
One way to evaluate spiritual maturity is by looking at the choices we make. The writer of Hebrews notes many of the ways those choices change with personal growth.	Teaching others	rather than . . .	just being taught.
	Developing depth of understanding	rather than . . .	struggling with the basics.
	Self-evaluation	rather than . . .	self-criticism.
	Seeking unity	rather than . . .	disunity.
	Desiring spiritual challenges	rather than . . .	desiring entertainment.
	Careful study and observation	rather than . . .	opinions and half-hearted efforts.
	Active faith	rather than . . .	cautious apathy and doubt.
	Confidence	rather than . . .	fear.
	Feelings and experiences evaluated in the light of God's Word	rather than . . .	experiences evaluated according to feelings.

4:12 The Word of God is not merely words from God, a vehicle for communicating ideas; it is living, life-changing, and dynamic as it works in us. With the incisiveness of a surgeon's knife, it reveals who we are and what we are not. It discerns what is within us, both good and evil. We must not only listen to the Word; we must let it shape our lives.

4:13 Since nothing can be hidden from God, he sees all we do and knows all we think. Even when we are unaware of his presence, even when we try to hide from him, he knows. We can have no secrets from him. Remarkably, though he knows us intimately, he still loves us.

4:14 To the Jews, the High Priest was the highest religious authority in the land. He alone entered the Holy of Holies once a year to make atonement for the sins of the whole nation (Leviticus 16). Like the High Priest, Jesus mediates between God and us. As man's representative, he intercedes for us before God. As God's

representative, he assures us of God's forgiveness. Jesus has more authority than the Jewish High Priests because he is truly God and truly man. Unlike the High Priest who could go before God only once a year, Christ is always at God's right hand, interceding for us.

4:15 Jesus is like us because he experienced every kind of temptation we experience today. But he is different because, although he was tempted, he never sinned. Jesus is the only human being who has ever lived without committing sin. Now in heaven, he completely understands our weaknesses and temptations and offers forgiveness.

4:16 Prayer is our approach to God. Some Christians do it meekly with heads hung, afraid to ask God to meet their needs. Others pray flippantly with little thought. Come with reverence, for he is your King, but come with bold assurance, for he is your Friend and Counselor.

4Another thing to remember is that no one can be a high priest just because he wants to be. He has to be called by God for this work in the same way God chose Aaron. 5That is why Christ did not elect himself to the honor of being High Priest; no, he was chosen by God. God said to him, "My Son, today I have honored you." 6And another time God said to him, "You have been chosen to be a priest forever, with the same rank as Melchizedek."

7Yet while Christ was here on earth he pleaded with God, praying with tears and agony of soul to the only one who would save him from [premature] death. And God heard his prayers because of his strong desire to obey God at all times.

8And even though Jesus was God's Son, he had to learn from experience what it was like to obey, when obeying meant suffering. 9It was after he had proved himself perfect in this experience that Jesus became the Giver of eternal salvation to all those who obey him. 10For remember that God has chosen him to be a High Priest with the same rank as Melchizedek.

Go beyond elementary principles

11There is much more I would like to say along these lines, but you don't seem to listen, so it's hard to make you understand.

12, 13You have been Christians a long time now, and you ought to be teaching others, but instead you have dropped back to the place where you need someone to teach you all over again the very first principles in God's Word. You are like babies who can drink only milk, not old enough for solid food. And when a person is still living on milk it shows he isn't very far along in the Christian life, and doesn't know much about the difference between right and wrong. He is still a baby-Christian! 14You will never be able to eat solid spiritual food and understand the deeper things of God's Word until you become better Christians and learn right from wrong by practicing doing right.

6 Let us stop going over the same old ground again and again, always teaching those first lessons about Christ. Let us go on instead to other things and become

5:5 *I have honored you,* literally, "begotten you." **5:7** *premature,* implied.

Cross references (right margin):

5:2 Heb 2:18; 7:28
5:3 Heb 7:27; 9:7
5:4 Ex 28:1 Num 16:40
5:5 Ps 2:7 Acts 13:33 Heb 1:5
5:6 Ps 110:4
5:7 Ps 22:1-4 Mt 26:39,53
5:8 Phil 2:8 Heb 1:2
5:10 Heb 2:17; 6:20
5:12 1 Cor 3:1,2
5:13 1 Cor 14:20 Eph 4:13,14
5:14 1 Cor 2:6,14
6:1 Phil 3:13-16 Heb 5:12,16

5:4-6 This chapter stresses both Christ's divine appointment and his humanity. (The writer uses two Old Testament verses to show Christ's divine appointment—Psalms 2:7 and 110:4.) In the days when this book was written, the Romans chose the High Priest in Jerusalem. In the Old Testament, however, God chose Aaron, and only his descendants could be High Priests. Christ, like Aaron, was chosen by God.

5:6 Melchizedek was a priest of Salem (now called Jerusalem). His Profile is found in Genesis 15. Melchizedek's position is explained in Hebrews 7.

5:7 Jesus found no pleasure in suffering and dying, but he chose to endure pain and humiliation in order to obey his Father. At times we will choose to undergo trials, not because we want to suffer, but because we want to obey God. Let Jesus' obedience sustain you and encourage you in times of trial. You can face anything when you know Jesus Christ is with you.

5:7 Have you ever felt that God didn't hear your prayers? Be sure you are praying with an obedient spirit, willing to do what God wants. God responds to his obedient children.

5:8 Jesus' life was not a script that he passively followed. It was a life he chose freely (John 10:17, 18). He chose to obey, even though obedience led to suffering and death. Because he obeyed perfectly even under trial, he can help us obey, no matter how difficult obedience seems to be.

5:9 Christ was always morally perfect. Through obedience he proved his perfection to us, not to God or to himself. In the Bible, *perfection* often means completeness or maturity. By sharing our

experience of suffering, Christ shared our human experience completely. He is now able to offer eternal salvation to those who obey him.

5:12, 13 These Jewish Christians were immature. They were reluctant to move beyond age-old traditions, established doctrines, and discussion of the basics. They wouldn't be able to understand what the writer was teaching about the high-priestly role of Christ unless they moved out of their comfortable position, cut some of their Jewish ties, and stopped trying to blend in with their culture. Commitment to Christ moves people out of the comfort zone.

5:12-14 In order to grow from a "baby" Christian to a "grown-up" Christian, each of us must learn discernment. By practice we must train our consciences, our senses, our minds, and our bodies to distinguish right from wrong. Can you recognize temptation before it controls you? Can you tell correct use of Scripture from mistaken or shallow uses?

5:14 Our capacity to feast on the deeper things of God is determined by our spiritual growth. Too often we want God's banquet before we are spiritually capable of digesting it. As you grow in the Lord, you will find that you will feast even more bountifully at his table.

6:1, 2 Certain basics are essential for all believers. Those principles that all Christians must know include repentance, baptism, faith, etc. We need to move on to a more complete theology, to a more profound understanding of the faith. And this is what the author intends to do (6:3). Christians should be teaching new Christians the basics, and then, acting on what they know, they should be learning even more from God's Word.

6:2
Acts 6:6; 8:17
17:31; 19:4
24:25
Rom 2:16

6:3
1 Cor 4:19

mature in our understanding, as strong Christians ought to be. Surely we don't need to speak further about the foolishness of trying to be saved by being good, or about the necessity of faith in God; 2you don't need further instruction about baptism and spiritual gifts and the resurrection of the dead and eternal judgment.

3The Lord willing, we will go on now to other things."

6:2 *spiritual gifts,* literally, "the laying on of hands."

ABRAHAM IN THE NEW TESTAMENT			
Abraham was an ancestor of Jesus Christ	Matthew 1:1, 2, 17; Luke 3:23–38	Jesus Christ was human; he was born into the line of Abraham, whom God had chosen to be the father of a great nation through which the whole world would be blessed. We are blessed because of what Jesus Christ, Abraham's descendant, did for us.
Abraham was the father of the Jewish nation	Matthew 3:9; Luke 3:8; Acts 13:26; Romans 4:1; 11:1; 2 Corinthians 11:22; Hebrews 6:14	God wanted to set apart a nation for himself, a nation that would tell the world about him. He began with a man of faith who, though old and childless, believed God's promise of innumerable descendants. We can trust God to do the impossible when we have faith.
Abraham was honored by God	Hebrews 7:4	God honors those who trust him. Although the world may disdain us if we trust in God, God promises to honor us.
Abraham, because of his faith, now sits in the Kingdom with Christ	Matthew 8:11; Luke 13:28; 16:23–31	Abraham followed God and now he is enjoying his reward—eternity with God. We will one day meet Abraham, because we have been promised eternity as well.
God *is* Abraham's God, thus Abraham is alive with God	Matthew 22:32; Mark 12:26; Luke 20:37; Acts 7:32	As Abraham lives forever, we will live forever because we, like Abraham, have chosen the life of faith.
Abraham received great promises from God	Luke 1:55, 72, 73; Acts 3:25; 7:17, 18; Galatians 3:6, 14–16; Hebrews 6:13–15	Many of the promises God made to Abraham seemed impossible to be realized, but Abraham trusted God. The promises to believers in God's Word also seem too incredible to believe, but we can trust God to keep all his promises.
Abraham followed God	Acts 7:2–8; Hebrews 11:8, 17–19	Abraham followed God's leading from his homeland to an unknown territory, which became the Jews' Promised Land. When we follow God, even before he makes all his plans clear to us, we will never be disappointed.
God blessed Abraham because of his faith	Romans 4; Galatians 3:6–9, 14–29; Hebrews 11:8, 17–19; James 2:21–24	Abraham showed faith in times of disappointment, trial, and testing. Because of his faith, God counted him righteous, his "friend." God accepts us because of our faith.
Abraham is the father of all those who come to God by faith	Romans 9:6–8; Galatians 3:7–9, 14–29	The Jews are Abraham's children, and Christ was his descendant. We are Christ's brothers and sisters; thus all believers are Abraham's children and God's children. Abraham was righteous because of his faith; we are made righteous by faith in Christ. The promises made to Abraham apply to us because of Christ.

6:3 These Christians needed to go on to understand Christ as the perfect High Priest and fulfillment of all the Old Testament prophecies. Rather than arguing about the respective merits of Judaism and Christianity, they needed to depend on Christ and live effectively for him.

4There is no use trying to bring you back to the Lord again if you have once understood the Good News and tasted for yourself the good things of heaven and shared in the Holy Spirit, 5and know how good the Word of God is, and felt the mighty powers of the world to come, 6and then have turned against God. You cannot bring yourself to repent again if you have nailed the Son of God to the cross again by rejecting him, holding him up to mocking and to public shame.

7When a farmer's land has had many showers upon it and good crops come up, that land has experienced God's blessing upon it. 8But if it keeps on having crops of thistles and thorns, the land is considered no good and is ready for condemnation and burning off.

9Dear friends, even though I am talking like this I really don't believe that what I am saying applies to you. I am confident you are producing the good fruit that comes along with your salvation. 10For God is not unfair. How can he forget your hard work for him, or forget the way you used to show your love for him—and still do—by helping his children? 11And we are anxious that you keep right on loving others as long as life lasts, so that you will get your full reward.

12Then, knowing what lies ahead for you, you won't become bored with being a Christian, nor become spiritually dull and indifferent, but you will be anxious to follow the example of those who receive all that God has promised them because of their strong faith and patience.

God's certain promise gives hope

13For instance, there was God's promise to Abraham: God took an oath in his own name, since there was no one greater to swear by, 14that he would bless Abraham again and again, and give him a son and make him the father of a great nation of people. 15Then Abraham waited patiently until finally God gave him a son, Isaac, just as he had promised.

16When a man takes an oath, he is calling upon someone greater than himself to force him to do what he has promised, or to punish him if he later refuses to do it; the oath ends all argument about it. 17God also bound himself with an oath, so that those he promised to help would be perfectly sure and never need to wonder whether he might change his plans.

18He has given us both his promise and his oath, two things we can completely count on, for it is impossible for God to tell a lie. Now all those who flee to him to save them can take new courage when they hear such assurances from God; now they can know without doubt that he will give them the salvation he has promised them.

19This certain hope of being saved is a strong and trustworthy anchor for our

6:4
Mt 7:22
Jn 4:10; 6:32
Eph 2:8
Heb 10:26,32
2 Pet 2:20
1 Jn 5:16
6:5
Heb 2:5
1 Pet 2:3
6:6
Heb 10:26,29

6:10
Mt 10:42; 25:40
Jn 13:20
1 Thess 1:3
6:11
Col 2:2
Heb 3:6; 10:22
6:12
Heb 1:14; 10:36
13:7

6:13
Gen 22:16
Gal 3:16
6:14
Gen 22:16,17
6:15
Gen 21:5
6:16
Ex 22:11
Gal 3:15
6:17
Ps 110:4
Rom 11:29
Heb 11:9

6:18
Tit 1:2
Heb 3:6; 12:1

6:19
Lev 16:15,16
Ps 130:7
Heb 9:7

6:4-6 In the first century, a pagan who investigated Christianity and then went back to paganism made a clean break with the church. But for Jewish Christians who decided to return to Judaism, the break was less obvious. Their lifestyle remained relatively unchanged. But by deliberately turning away from Christ, they were cutting themselves off from God's forgiveness. Those who persevere in believing are true saints; those who continue to reject Christ are unbelievers, no matter how well they behave.

6:6 Some think this verse refers to believers who turn from their salvation. Others think this refers to unbelievers who come close to salvation, then turn away. Either way, those who reject Christ will not be saved. Christ died once for all. He will not be crucified again. Apart from his cross, there is no other possible way of salvation. But the author does not really believe that his readers are in danger of missing salvation (see 6:9).

6:7, 8 Land that produces good fruit receives loving care, but land that produces thistles and thorns has to be burned off so the farmer can start over. An unproductive Christian life falls under God's condemnation. We are not saved by works or conduct, but what we do is the *evidence* of our faith. Being productive for Christ is serious business.

6:12 Hope keeps the Christian from feeling dull or becoming bored. Like an athlete, train hard and run well, remembering the reward that lies ahead (Philippians 3:14).

6:15 Abraham waited patiently—it was 25 years from the time God promised him a son (Genesis 17:16) to Isaac's birth (Genesis 21:1-3).

6:17 God's promises are unchangeable and trustworthy because God is unchangeable and trustworthy. When God promised Abraham a son, he took an oath in his own name. The oath was as good as his name, and his name was as good as his divine nature.

6:18, 19 God embodies all truth, and he therefore cannot lie. Because God is truth, you can be secure in his promises; you don't need to wonder if he will change his plans. For the true seeker who comes to God in belief, God gives an unconditional promise of acceptance. When you ask God in all openness, honesty, and sincerity of heart to save you from your sins, *he will do it.* This assurance should give you courage and hope.

6:19, 20 The veil (the curtain) referred to in the text hung across the entrance from the Holy Place to the Holy of Holies, the two innermost chambers of the Tabernacle. This curtain prevented anyone from entering, gazing into, or even getting a fleeting

souls, connecting us with God himself behind the sacred curtains of heaven, [20]where Christ has gone ahead to plead for us from his position as our High Priest, with the honor and rank of Melchizedek.

6:20
Heb 4:14; 5:6
9:24

Melchizedek compared to Abraham

7:1
Gen 14:17-20
Ps 110:4
Heb 5:6,10

7 This Melchizedek was king of the city of Salem, and also a priest of the Most High God. When Abraham was returning home after winning a great battle against many kings, Melchizedek met him and blessed him; [2]then Abraham took a tenth of all he had won in the battle and gave it to Melchizedek.

Melchizedek's name means "Justice," so he is the King of Justice; and he is also the King of Peace because of the name of his city, Salem, which means "Peace." [3]Melchizedek had no father or mother and there is no record of any of his ancestors. He was never born and he never died but his life is like that of the Son of God—a priest forever.

7:4
Gen 14:20

[4]See then how great this Melchizedek is:

(a)]Even Abraham, the first and most honored of all God's chosen people, gave Melchizedek a tenth of the spoils he took from the kings he had been fighting. [5]One could understand why Abraham would do this if Melchizedek had been a Jewish priest, for later on God's people were required by law to give gifts to help their priests because the priests were their relatives. [6]But Melchizedek was not a relative, and yet Abraham paid him.

7:5
Num 18:21,26

7:6
Rom 4:13
Gal 3:16

(b)]Melchizedek placed a blessing upon mighty Abraham, [7]and as everyone knows, a person who has the power to bless is always greater than the person he blesses.

7:8
Heb 5:6

[8]*(c)]The Jewish priests, though mortal, received tithes; but we are told that Melchizedek lives on.*

[9]*(d)]One might even say that Levi himself (the ancestor of all Jewish priests, of all who receive tithes), paid tithes to Melchizedek through Abraham.* [10]For although Levi wasn't born yet, the seed from which he came was in Abraham when Abraham paid the tithes to Melchizedek.

7:11
Gal 2:21
Heb 7:17,18

[11]*(e)]If the Jewish priests and their laws had been able to save us, why then did God need to send Christ as a priest with the rank of Melchizedek, instead of sending someone with the rank of Aaron—the same rank all other priests had?*

7:14
Gen 49:10
Isa 11:1
Mt 1:3
Lk 3:33
Rom 1:3
Rev 5:5

[12, 13, 14]And when God sends a new kind of priest, his law must be changed to permit it. As we all know, Christ did not belong to the priest-tribe of Levi, but came from the tribe of Judah, which had not been chosen for priesthood; Moses had never given them that work.

Christ is like Melchizedek

[15]So we can plainly see that God's method changed, for Christ, the new High Priest who came with the rank of Melchizedek, [16]did not become a priest by meeting the old requirement of belonging to the tribe of Levi, but on the basis of power flowing from a life that cannot end. [17]And the Psalmist points this out when

7:17
Ps 110:4

6:20 *from his position as our High Priest,* literally, "having become our high priest." **7:3** *Melchizedek had no father or mother.* No one can be sure whether this means that Melchizedek was Christ appearing to Abraham in human form or simply that there is no *record* of who Melchizedek's father and mother were, no *record* of his birth or death.

---

glimpse of the interior of the Holy of Holies (see also 9:1–8). The High Priest could enter the Holy of Holies only once a year to stand before God's presence and atone for the sins of the entire nation. But Christ is in God's presence at all times, not just once a year, as the High Priest who can continually plead for us.

7:1 *Melchizedek* means "king of righteousness," and *Salem* means "peace."

7:2 The writer of Hebrews uses this story to show that there is someone greater even than Abraham, father of the Jewish nation, and Levi (Abraham's descendant). Therefore, the Jewish priesthood (made up of Levi's descendants) was inferior to Melchizedek's priesthood (a type of Christ's priesthood).

7:3–10 Melchizedek was a priest of the most high God (see note on Genesis 14:18 and his Profile in Genesis 15). He is said to be a priest forever (Psalm 110:4) because his priesthood has no record of beginning or end—he was a priest of God in Salem (Jerusalem) long before the nation of Israel and the levitical system began.

7:11–16 Jesus' high-priestly role was superior to that of any priest of Levi, because the Messiah was a priest of a higher rank (Psalm 110:4). The animal sacrifices had to be repeated, and they offered only temporary forgiveness; Christ's sacrifice was offered once, and it offers total and permanent forgiveness. Under the new covenant, the levitical priesthood was canceled in favor of Christ's role as High Priest.

he says of Christ, "You are a priest forever with the rank of Melchizedek." **18**Yes, the old system of priesthood based on family lines was canceled because it didn't work. It was weak and useless for saving people. **19**It never made anyone really right with God. But now we have a far better hope, for Christ makes us acceptable to God, and now we may draw near to him.

20God took an oath that Christ would always be a Priest, **21**although he never said that of other priests. Only to Christ he said, "The Lord has sworn and will never change his mind: You are a Priest forever, with the rank of Melchizedek." **22**Because of God's oath, Christ can guarantee forever the success of this new and better arrangement.

23Under the old arrangement there had to be many priests, so that when the older ones died off, the system could still be carried on by others who took their places. **24**But Jesus lives forever and continues to be a Priest so that no one else is needed. **25**He is able to save completely all who come to God through him. Since he will live forever, he will always be there to remind God that he has paid for their sins with his blood.

26He is, therefore, exactly the kind of High Priest we need; for he is holy and blameless, unstained by sin, undefiled by sinners, and to him has been given the place of honor in heaven. **27**He never needs the daily blood of animal sacrifices, as other priests did, to cover over first their own sins and then the sins of the people; for he finished all sacrifices, once and for all, when he sacrificed himself on the cross. **28**Under the old system, even the high priests were weak and sinful men who could not keep from doing wrong, but later God appointed by his oath his Son who is perfect forever.

4. The new covenant is greater than the old

Christ is the High Priest of the new covenant

8 What we are saying is this: Christ, whose priesthood we have just described, is our High Priest, and is in heaven at the place of greatest honor next to God himself. **2**He ministers in the temple in heaven, the true place of worship built by the Lord and not by human hands.

3And since every high priest is appointed to offer gifts and sacrifices, Christ must make an offering too. **4**The sacrifice he offers is far better than those offered by the

7:18
Rom 8:3
Gal 4:9
Heb 7:11

7:19
Acts 13:39
Rom 3:20; 5:2
Gal 2:16
Heb 6:18; 9:9
10:19-22

7:21
Num 23:19
Ps 110:4
Heb 7:28

7:22
Heb 8:6

7:24
Isa 9:6,7
Jn 12:34
Rev 1:18

7:25
Rom 8:34
1 Tim 2:5
1 Jn 2:1

7:26
2 Cor 5:21
1 Pet 2:22

7:27
Lev 9:7
16:6,11,15
Rom 6:10
Eph 5:2
Heb 5:3; 9:7,12

7:28
Heb 2:10; 5:1,2

8:1
Col 3:1
Heb 1:3; 2:17

8:2
Ex 33:7
Heb 9:11; 10:11

8:3
Eph 5:2
Heb 5:1

7:18, 19 The law was not intended to save people, but to point out sin (see Romans 3:20; 5:20) and to point toward Christ (see Galatians 3:24, 25). Salvation comes through Christ, whose sacrifice brings forgiveness for our sins.

7:22-24 This new arrangement is also called the new covenant or new testament. It is new in allowing us to go directly to God through Christ, no longer having to rely on sacrificed animals and priests to gain God's forgiveness. This new arrangement is better because, while priests died, Christ lives forever. Priests and sacrifices could not save people, but Christ truly saves.

7:25 What does it mean that Jesus is able to save completely? No one else can add to what Jesus did to save us; our past, present, and future sins are all forgiven, and Jesus is with the Father as a sign that our sins are forgiven. If you are a Christian, remember that Christ has paid the price for your sins once and for all. (See also 9:25, 26.)

7:25 As our High Priest, Christ is our advocate, the mediator between us and God. The Old Testament High Priest went before God once a year to plead for the forgiveness of the nation's sins; Christ makes perpetual intercession before God for us. Christ's presence in heaven with the Father assures us that our sins have been paid for and forgiven (see Romans 8:33, 34; Hebrews 2:17, 18; 4:15, 16).

7:27 In Old Testament times when animals were sacrificed, they were cut into pieces, the parts were washed, the fat was burned, the blood was sprinkled, and the meat was boiled. Blood was

demanded as atonement for sins, and God accepted animal blood to cover the people's sins (Leviticus 17:11). Because of the sacrificial system, the Israelites were generally aware that sin costs and that they themselves were sinful. One problem with the world today is that most people don't realize how costly it was for Jesus to secure our forgiveness—it cost him his blood (1 Peter 1:18, 19).

7:27 Because Christ died *once* and *for all*, he finished all sacrifices. He forgave sins—past, present, and future. The Jews did not need to go back to the old system because Christ, the perfect sacrifice, completed the work of redemption. You need not look for another way to have your sins forgiven—Christ was the final sacrifice for you.

7:28 These verses help explain why Jesus had to die. As we better understand the Jewish sacrificial system, we see that Jesus' death served as the perfect atonement for our sins. His death brings us eternal life. How callous, how cold, how stubborn are those who refuse to accept this death, God's greatest gift.

8:4 Under the old Jewish system, priests were chosen only from the tribe of Levi, and sacrifices were offered daily on the altar for forgiveness of sins (see 7:12-14). This system would not have allowed Jesus to be a priest because he was from the tribe of Judah. But his perfect sacrifice ended all need for further priests and sacrifices.

The use of the present tense, "the priests *still follow* the old Jewish system," seems to indicate that this book was written before A.D. 70 when the Temple in Jerusalem was destroyed, ending the sacrifices.

earthly priests. (But even so, if he were here on earth he wouldn't even be permitted to be a priest, because down here the priests still follow the old Jewish system of sacrifices.) 5Their work is connected with a mere earthly model of the real tabernacle in heaven; for when Moses was getting ready to build the tabernacle, God warned him to follow exactly the pattern of the heavenly tabernacle as shown to him on Mount Sinai. 6But Christ, as a Minister in heaven, has been rewarded with a far more important work than those who serve under the old laws, because the new agreement which he passes on to us from God contains far more wonderful promises.

7The old agreement didn't even work. If it had, there would have been no need for another to replace it. 8But God himself found fault with the old one, for he said, "The day will come when I will make a new agreement with the people of Israel and the people of Judah. 9This new agreement will not be like the old one I gave to their fathers on the day when I took them by the hand to lead them out of the land of Egypt; they did not keep their part in that agreement, so I had to cancel it. 10But this is the new agreement I will make with the people of Israel, says the Lord: I will write my laws in their minds so that they will know what I want them to do without my even telling them, and these laws will be in their hearts so that they will want to obey them, and I will be their God and they shall be my people. 11And no one then will need to speak to his friend or neighbor or brother, saying, 'You, too, should know the Lord,' because everyone, great and small, will know me already. 12And I will be merciful to them in their wrongdoings, and I will remember their sins no more."

13God speaks of these new promises, of this new agreement, as taking the place of the old one; for the old one is out of date now and has been put aside forever.

Marginal references:

8:5
Ex 25:40
Col 2:17
Heb 9:23

8:6
2 Cor 3:6
Heb 7:22

8:7
Heb 7:11

8:8-11
Jer 31:31-34

8:11
Jn 6:45
1 Jn 2:27

8:13
Heb 12:24

THE OLD AND NEW COVENANTS

Like pointing out the similarities and differences between the photograph of a person and the actual person, the writer of Hebrews shows the connection between the old Mosaic covenant and the new Messianic covenant. He proves that the old covenant was a shadow of a real Christ.

The Old Covenant under Moses	The New Covenant in Christ	Application
Gifts and sacrifices by those guilty of sin	Self-sacrifice by the guiltless Christ	Christ died for you
Focused on a physical building where one goes to worship	Focuses on the reign of Christ in the hearts of believers	God is directly involved in your life
A model	A reality	Not temporal, but eternal
Limited promises	Limitless promises	We can trust God's promises to us
Failed agreement by people	Faithful agreement by Christ	Christ has kept the agreement where people couldn't
External standards and rules	Internal standards—a new heart	God sees both actions and motives—we are accountable to God, not rules
Limited access to God	Unlimited access to God	God is personally available
Based on fear	Based on love and forgiveness	Forgiveness keeps our failures from destroying the agreement
Legal cleansing	Personal cleansing	God's cleansing is complete
Continual sacrifice	Conclusive sacrifice	Christ's sacrifice was perfect and final
Obey the rules	Serve the living God	We have a relationship, not regulations
Forgiveness earned	Forgiveness freely given	We have true and complete forgiveness
Repeated yearly	Completed by Christ's death	Christ's death can be applied to your sin
Man's effort	God's grace	Initiated by God's love for you
Available to some	Available to all	Available to you

8:7-12 This passage quotes Jeremiah 31:31-34 and compares the new agreement with the old. The old agreement was the covenant of law between God and Israel. The new and better way is the covenant of grace—Christ's offer to forgive our sins and bring us to God through his sacrificial death. This agreement is new in extent—it goes beyond Israel and Judah to all the Gentile nations. It is new in application, since it is written in our hearts and minds. It offers a new way to forgiveness, not through animal sacrifice but through faith. Have you entered into this new agreement and begun walking in the better way?

8:10, 11 Under God's new agreement, God's law is inside us. The Holy Spirit reminds us of Christ's words, quickens our consciences, influences our motives and desires, and makes us want to obey.

Rules for worship under the old covenant

9 Now in that first agreement between God and his people there were rules for worship and there was a sacred tent down here on earth. Inside this place of worship there were two rooms. The first one contained the golden candlestick and a table with special loaves of holy bread upon it; this part was called the Holy Place. ³Then there was a curtain and behind the curtain was a room called the Holy of Holies. ⁴In that room there were a golden incense-altar and the golden chest, called the ark of the covenant, completely covered on all sides with pure gold. Inside the ark were the tablets of stone with the Ten Commandments written on them, and a golden jar with some manna in it, and Aaron's wooden cane that budded. ⁵Above the golden chest were statues of angels called the cherubim—the guardians of God's glory—with their wings stretched out over the ark's golden cover, called the mercy seat. But enough of such details.

⁶Well, when all was ready the priests went in and out of the first room whenever they wanted to, doing their work. ⁷But only the high priest went into the inner room, and then only once a year, all alone, and always with blood which he sprinkled on the mercy seat as an offering to God to cover his own mistakes and sins, and the mistakes and sins of all the people.

⁸And the Holy Spirit uses all this to point out to us that under the old system the common people could not go into the Holy of Holies as long as the outer room and the entire system it represents were still in use.

⁹This has an important lesson for us today. For under the old system, gifts and sacrifices were offered, but these failed to cleanse the hearts of the people who brought them. ¹⁰For the old system dealt only with certain rituals—what foods to eat and drink, rules for washing themselves, and rules about this and that. The people had to keep these rules to tide them over until Christ came with God's new and better way.

Christ is the perfect offering for sin

¹¹He came as High Priest of this better system which we now have. He went into that greater, perfect tabernacle in heaven, not made by men nor part of this world, ¹²and once for all took blood into that inner room, the Holy of Holies, and sprinkled it on the mercy seat; but it was not the blood of goats and calves. No, he took his own blood, and with it he, by himself, made sure of our eternal salvation.

¹³And if under the old system the blood of bulls and goats and the ashes of young cows could cleanse men's bodies from sin, ¹⁴just think how much more surely the blood of Christ will transform our lives and hearts. His sacrifice frees us from the worry of having to obey the old rules, and makes us want to serve the living God.

9:1
Ex 25:8

9:2
Ex 25:23,31
26:1
Lev 24:5

9:3
Ex 26:31,33
40:3

9:4
Ex 16:33
25:10,16
30:1; 31:18
Num 17:10
Deut 10:2
2 Chron 5:10

9:5
Ex 25:18-20
Lev 16:2

9:7
Ex 30:10
Lev 16:11
Num 15:25
Heb 5:3

9:8
Jn 14:6
Heb 10:20

9:9
Gal 3:21,22
Heb 5:1

9:10
Lev 11:2,25
Num 6:3; 19:7
Rom 14:17
Eph 2:15

9:11
Mk 14:58;
Heb 8:2; 9:24 10:1

9:12
Lev 4:3
Heb 7:27

9:13
Lev 16:14,15
Num 19:2,9

9:14
Heb 1:3; 6:1
1 Pet 3:18
1 Jn 1:7

9:1 The "sacred tent" refers to the Tabernacle that God instructed Moses to set up (see Exodus 36–40).

9:6–8 The High Priest could enter the Holy of Holies, the innermost room of the Tabernacle, one day each year, the Day of Atonement, to atone for the nation's sins. The Holy of Holies was a small room that contained the ark of the covenant (a gold-covered chest containing the original stone tablets on which the Ten Commandments were written, a pot of manna, and Aaron's rod). The top of the chest served as the "mercy seat" (the altar) on which the blood was sprinkled by the High Priest on the Day of Atonement. The Holy of Holies was the most sacred spot on earth for the Jews. Only the High Priest could enter—the other priests and the common people were forbidden to come into the room. Their only access to God was through the High Priest who offered a sacrifice and used its blood to atone first for his own sins and then for the people's sins (see also 10:19).

9:9–14 Though you know Christ, you may still be trying to make yourself good enough for God. But rules and rituals have never cleansed people's hearts. By Jesus' blood alone (1) our consciences are cleared, (2) we are freed from death and can live to serve God, and (3) we are freed from sin's power. If you are carrying a load of guilt because you can't be good enough for God, take another look at Jesus' death and what it means for you.

9:12 This imagery comes from the Day of Atonement rituals described in Leviticus 16.

9:13, 14 Through the blood of sacrificed animals, God cleansed people from sin, making them *ceremonially* acceptable according to Old Testament law. But Christ's sacrifice transforms our lives and hearts and makes us clean on the inside. His sacrifice is infinitely more effective than animal sacrifices.

9:14 God required the people to bring perfect animals for sacrifices. Their sins cost them something; they could not dump them on the heads of useless or damaged animals. This pointed to Christ, the unblemished Lamb of God. Because he was sinless, his sacrifice was infinitely valuable.

9:14 If our hearts are not changed, following God's rules is unpleasant and difficult. We rebel against being told how to live. The Holy Spirit, however, gives us new desires. He helps us want to obey God (see Philippians 2:12, 13). With new hearts, we find that serving God is our greatest joy.

9:15
Rom 3:25
1 Tim 2:5
Heb 3:1
1 Pet 3:18

For by the help of the eternal Holy Spirit, Christ willingly gave himself to God to die for our sins—he being perfect, without a single sin or fault. 15Christ came with this new agreement so that all who are invited may come and have forever all the wonders God has promised them. For Christ died to rescue them from the penalty of the sins they had committed while still under that old system.

16Now, if someone dies and leaves a will—a list of things to be given away to certain people when he dies—no one gets anything until it is proved that the person who wrote the will is dead. 17The will goes into effect only after the death of the person who wrote it. While he is still alive no one can use it to get any of those things he has promised them.

9:17
Gal 3:15

9:18
Ex 24:6

9:19
Ex 24:5-8
Lev 14:4
Heb 1:1

9:20
Ex 24:8
Mt 26:28

9:21
Ex 29:12
Lev 8:15

9:22
Lev 17:11

9:23
Heb 8:5

18That is why blood was sprinkled [as proof of Christ's death] before even the first agreement could go into effect. 19For after Moses had given the people all of God's laws, he took the blood of calves and goats, along with water, and sprinkled the blood over the book of God's laws and over all the people, using branches of hyssop bushes and scarlet wool to sprinkle with. 20Then he said, "This is the blood that marks the beginning of the agreement between you and God, the agreement God commanded me to make with you." 21And in the same way he sprinkled blood on the sacred tent and on whatever instruments were used for worship. 22In fact we can say that under the old agreement almost everything was cleansed by sprinkling it with blood, and without the shedding of blood there is no forgiveness of sins.

23That is why the sacred tent down here on earth, and everything in it—all copied from things in heaven—all had to be made pure by Moses in this way, by being sprinkled with the blood of animals. But the real things in heaven, of which these down here are copies, were made pure with far more precious offerings.

9:24
Rom 8:34
Heb 6:20; 7:25
8:2; 9:12
1 Jn 2:1

9:25
Heb 9:2,7

9:26
1 Cor 10:11
Eph 1:10
Heb 7:27; 10:10
1 Pet 3:18

24For Christ has entered into heaven itself, to appear now before God as our Friend. It was not in the earthly place of worship that he did this, for that was merely a copy of the real temple in heaven. 25Nor has he offered himself again and again, as the high priest down here on earth offers animal blood in the Holy of Holies each year. 26If that had been necessary, then he would have had to die again and again, ever since the world began. But no! He came once for all, at the end of the age, to put away the power of sin forever by dying for us.

9:27
Gen 3:19
Eccles 3:20

9:28
Mt 25:34; 26:28
Acts 1:11
Rom 5:15; 6:10
Tit 2:13
Heb 4:15; 5:19
7:27
1 Pet 2:24

27And just as it is destined that men die only once, and after that comes judgment, 28so also Christ died only once as an offering for the sins of many people; and he will come again, but not to deal again with our sins.

This time he will come bringing salvation to all those who are eagerly and patiently waiting for him.

9:18 *as proof of Christ's death*, implied.

9:15 Value, in our human way of thinking, is not measured by how *many* can have something good, but by how *few* can have something good. "Limited edition" means "valuable" because only a few can have it. God's great plan of redemption, however, stands in sharp contrast to this. It is the most valuable of all treasures, yet it is available to all. The more who have it, and the more they use it, the greater its value! Exercise your faith by sharing it and using it to serve God, and so increase its value.

9:15 People in Old Testament times were saved through Christ's sacrifice, although it had not yet happened. In offering unblemished animal sacrifices, they were looking forward to Christ's coming. There was no point in returning to the sacrificial system now that Christ had come and died for sins. Why continue to look toward something that has already happened?

9:22 Why does forgiveness require the shedding of blood? This is no arbitrary decree on the part of a bloodthirsty God, as some have supposed. There is no greater symbol of life than blood; blood keeps us alive. Jesus shed his blood—gave his life—for our sins so that we wouldn't have to experience spiritual death, which is eternal separation from God. Jesus is the source of life, not death, and he offered his own life so that we might live. After

shedding his blood for us, he rose victorious from the grave and proclaimed victory over sin and death.

9:23 In a way we don't fully understand, the earthly Tabernacle was a reflection and symbol of heavenly realities.

9:24 Amidst references to priests, tabernacles, sacrifices, and other ideas unfamiliar to us, we come to this description of Christ as our Friend. We can relate to this role and be encouraged by it. A friend stands with and stands for; Christ is on our side at God's side. He is our Lord and Savior, but do you also know him as your friend?

9:26 The "end of the age" refers to the time of Christ's coming to earth in fulfillment of the Old Testament prophecies. He ushered in the new era of grace and forgiveness. We are still living in the "last days." The day of the Lord has begun and will be completed at Christ's return.

9:27 All people die physically, but Christ died so that we would not have to die spiritually. His death affects our past, present, and future. He has forgiven our past sin; he has given us the Holy Spirit to help us deal with present sin; and he promises to return and raise us to eternal life in a world from which sin is banished.

A sacrifice once for all

10 The old system of Jewish laws gave only a dim foretaste of the good things Christ would do for us. The sacrifices under the old system were repeated again and again, year after year, but even so they could never save those who lived under their rules. 2If they could have, one offering would have been enough; the worshipers would have been cleansed once for all, and their feeling of guilt would be gone.

3But just the opposite happened: those yearly sacrifices reminded them of their disobedience and guilt instead of relieving their minds. 4For it is not possible for the blood of bulls and goats really to take away sins.

5That is why Christ said, as he came into the world, "O God, the blood of bulls and goats cannot satisfy you, so you have made ready this body of mine for me to lay as a sacrifice upon your altar. 6You were not satisfied with the animal sacrifices, slain and burnt before you as offerings for sin. 7Then I said, 'See, I have come to do your will, to lay down my life, just as the Scriptures said that I would.'"

8After Christ said this, about not being satisfied with the various sacrifices and offerings required under the old system, 9he then added, "Here I am. I have come to give my life."

He cancels the first system in favor of a far better one. 10Under this new plan we have been forgiven and made clean by Christ's dying for us once and for all.

11Under the old agreement the priests stood before the altar day after day offering sacrifices that could never take away our sins. 12But Christ gave himself to God for our sins as one sacrifice for all time, and then sat down in the place of highest honor at God's right hand, 13waiting for his enemies to be laid under his feet. 14For by that one offering he made forever perfect in the sight of God all those whom he is making holy.

15And the Holy Spirit testifies that this is so, for he has said, 16"This is the agreement I will make with the people of Israel, though they broke their first agreement: I will write my laws into their minds so that they will always know my will, and I will put my laws in their hearts so that they will want to obey them." 17And then he adds, "I will never again remember their sins and lawless deeds."

10:1
Col 2:17
Heb 7:19; 8:5
9:11

10:3
Lev 16:21
Heb 9:7

10:4
Mic 6:6
Heb 9:12

10:7
Ps 40:6-8; 50:8
Isa 1:11
Jer 6:20
Amos 5:21

10:10
Jn 17:19
Eph 5:26
Heb 7:27; 9:14,28
1 Pet 2:24

10:11
Num 28:3
Heb 5:1

10:12
Col 3:1
Heb 1:3

10:13
Ps 110:1

10:15
Heb 3:7
2 Pet 1:21

10:16,17
Jer 31:33,34

10:3 When people gathered for sacrifice on the Day of Atonement, they were reminded of their sins and felt guilty all over again. What they needed was forgiveness—the permanent, powerful, sin-destroying forgiveness we have from Christ. Once we have confessed a sin to him, we need never think of it again. He has forgiven it, and it no longer exists.

10:4 Animal blood could not take away sin; it could only take it out of sight until Jesus came to deal with it permanently. How, then, were people forgiven in Old Testament times? Just as they are forgiven today—through God's grace, which they accepted through faith.

10:5-10 This quotation is not cited in any other New Testament book. The writer of Hebrews applied to Christ the words of the psalmist in Psalm 40:6–8. But all of Psalm 40 does not apply to Christ (for example, verse 12, where the psalmist speaks of his own sins). Christ came to offer his body upon the cross for us as a sacrifice completely acceptable to God.

10:5-10 The costly sacrifice of a valued animal's life impressed upon the sinner the seriousness of his sin before God. Because Jesus shed his own blood for us, his sacrifice is infinitely bigger than any Old Testament offering. Looking at the immeasurable gift he has given us, we should be overwhelmed with desire to obey him.

10:9 Canceling the first system in favor of a far better one means doing away with the system of sacrifices contained in the ceremonial law; it doesn't mean eliminating God's *moral* law. The ceremonial law prepared people for Christ's coming. With Christ's death and resurrection it was no longer needed. Through Christ we

can fulfill the moral law as we let him live in us.

10:11, 12 It was customary for the priests to stand while offering sacrifices. Christ's act of sitting down at God's right hand symbolizes the end of the sacrificial system.

10:12 The Jewish readers of this book were in danger of returning to the old Jewish system, which would be saying that Christ's sacrifice wasn't enough to forgive their sins. But adding anything to his sacrifice or taking anything from it denies its validity. Any system to win God's approval through good works is essentially rejecting the significance of Christ's death and spurning the Holy Spirit's work. Beware of anyone who tells you that Christ's sacrifice was incomplete or that something else is needed to make you acceptable to God, because this can lead you away from right faith and right living.

10:14 We have been made perfect (complete in Christ), but we are being made holy. Through his death and resurrection, Christ once for all made his believers perfect in God's sight. At the same time, he is making them holy in their daily pilgrimage here. We should not be surprised, ashamed, or shocked that we still need perfection. God is not finished with us. We can encourage this growth process by obeying Christ, by appropriating the values of Scripture in all areas of our lives, and by accepting the forgiveness Christ provides.

10:17 The writer concludes his argument with this powerful statement that God will never remember our sins. If, in Christ, forgiveness is complete, there is no need to continue the former sacrificial system. As believers, we can be confident that our sins—past, present, and future—have been forgiven and forgotten.

18Now, when sins have once been forever forgiven and forgotten, there is no need to offer more sacrifices to get rid of them.

B. THE SUPERIORITY OF FAITH (10:19—13:25)

Moving from argument to instruction, the author cites many examples of those who have demonstrated faith throughout history. Living by faith is far better than merely fulfilling rituals and rules. This can challenge us to grow in faith and to live in obedience to God each day.

Living by faith

19And so, dear brothers, now we may walk right into the very Holy of Holies where God is, because of the blood of Jesus. 20This is the fresh, new, life-giving way which Christ has opened up for us by tearing the curtain—his human body—to let us into the holy presence of God.

21And since this great High Priest of ours rules over God's household, 22let us go right in, to God himself, with true hearts fully trusting him to receive us, because we have been sprinkled with Christ's blood to make us clean, and because our bodies have been washed with pure water.

23Now we can look forward to the salvation God has promised us. There is no longer any room for doubt, and we can tell others that salvation is ours, for there is no question that he will do what he says.

24In response to all he has done for us, let us outdo each other in being helpful and kind to each other and in doing good.

25Let us not neglect our church meetings, as some people do, but encourage and warn each other, especially now that the day of his coming back again is drawing near.

26If anyone sins deliberately by rejecting the Savior after knowing the truth of forgiveness, this sin is not covered by Christ's death; there is no way to get rid of it. 27There will be nothing to look forward to but the terrible punishment of God's awful anger which will consume all his enemies. 28A man who refused to obey the laws given by Moses was killed without mercy if there were two or three witnesses to his sin. 29Think how much more terrible the punishment will be for those who have trampled underfoot the Son of God and treated his cleansing blood as though it were common and unhallowed, and insulted and outraged the Holy Spirit who brings God's mercy to his people.

30For we know him who said, "Justice belongs to me; I will repay them"; who also said, "The Lord himself will handle these cases." 31It is a fearful thing to fall into the hands of the living God.

32Don't ever forget those wonderful days when you first learned about Christ. Remember how you kept right on with the Lord even though it meant terrible suffering. 33Sometimes you were laughed at and beaten, and sometimes you

---

10:19
Heb 9:25

10:20
Jn 10:9; 14:6
Heb 6:19; 9:8

10:21
1 Tim 3:15
Heb 2:17; 3:6

10:22
Ezek 36:25
2 Cor 7:1
Eph 3:12
Jas 1:6
1 Jn 3:21

10:23
1 Cor 1:9; 10:13
Heb 3:6

10:25
Acts 2:42
Heb 3:13
2 Pet 3:9

10:26
Num 15:30
1 Tim 2:4
2 Pet 2:20
1 Jn 5:16

10:27
Ezek 36:5

10:28
Deut 17:2-5

10:29
Mt 12:31
1 Cor 11:29

10:30
Deut 32:35,36
Ps 50:4; 135:14

10:31
2 Cor 5:11

10:32
Gal 3:4

10:33
1 Cor 4:9
Phil 1:7
1 Thess 2:14

10:19 The Holy of Holies in the Temple was sealed from view by a curtain. Only the High Priest could enter this holy room, and he did so only once a year on the Day of Atonement when he atoned for the nation's sins. But now, Jesus' death has removed the curtain, and all believers may walk into God's presence at any time (see also 6:19, 20).

10:22-25 These are some of the privileges that come with our new life in Christ: (1) we have personal access to God through Christ and can approach him without an elaborate system (10:22); (2) we may grow in faith, overcome doubts and questions, and deepen our relationship with God (10:23); (3) we may enjoy encouragement from each other (10:24); (4) we may worship together (10:25).

10:25 To neglect Christian meetings is to give up the encouragement and help of other Christians. We gather together to share our faith and strengthen each other in the Lord. As we near the end of the age and as we get closer to the day when Christ will return, we may face many spiritual struggles, tribulations, and even persecution. Anti-Christian forces will grow in strength. Difficulties should never be excuses for missing church services. Rather, as

difficulties arise, we should make an even greater effort to be faithful in attendance.

10:26 When people deliberately reject Christ's offer of salvation, they reject God's most precious gift. They push away the work of the Holy Spirit, the one who communicates to us God's saving love. This warning was given to Jewish Christians who were tempted to reject Christ for Judaism, but it applies to anyone who rejects Christ for another religion or, having understood Christ's atoning work, deliberately turns away from it (see also Numbers 15:30, 31 and Mark 3:28–30). The point is that there is no other acceptable sacrifice for sin than the death of Christ on the cross. If someone deliberately, intentionally, purposely rejects the sacrifice of Christ after clearly understanding the gospel teaching about it, then there is no other hope of salvation for that person, for God has not provided any other name under heaven by whom we could be saved (see Acts 4:12).

10:31 This judgment is for those who have rejected God's mercy. For those who accept Christ's love and accept his salvation, the coming judgment is no cause for worry. Being saved through his grace, they have nothing to fear (see 1 John 4:18).

watched and sympathized with others suffering the same things. ³⁴You suffered with those thrown into jail, and you were actually joyful when all you owned was taken from you, knowing that better things were awaiting you in heaven, things that would be yours forever.

³⁵Do not let this happy trust in the Lord die away, no matter what happens. Remember your reward! ³⁶You need to keep on patiently doing God's will if you want him to do for you all that he has promised. ³⁷His coming will not be delayed much longer. ³⁸And those whose faith has made them good in God's sight must live by faith, trusting him in everything. Otherwise, if they shrink back, God will have no pleasure in them.

³⁹But we have never turned our backs on God and sealed our fate. No, our faith in him assures our souls' salvation.

Great heroes of faith

11 What is faith? It is the confident assurance that something we want is going to happen. It is the certainty that what we hope for is waiting for us, even though we cannot see it up ahead. ²Men of God in days of old were famous for their faith.

³By faith—by believing God—we know that the world and the stars—in fact, all things—were made at God's command; and that they were all made from things that can't be seen.

⁴It was by faith that Abel obeyed God and brought an offering that pleased God more than Cain's offering did. God accepted Abel and proved it by accepting his gift; and though Abel is long dead, we can still learn lessons from him about trusting God.

⁵Enoch trusted God too, and that is why God took him away to heaven without dying; suddenly he was gone because God took him. Before this happened God had said how pleased he was with Enoch. ⁶You can never please God without faith, without depending on him. Anyone who wants to come to God must believe that there is a God and that he rewards those who sincerely look for him.

⁷Noah was another who trusted God. When he heard God's warning about the

11:5 *God had said,* implied.

10:34	Mt 5:12 / Heb 13:3
10:36	Col 3:24 / Heb 9:15
10:37,38	Lk 18:8 / Hab 2:3,4
11:1	Rom 8:24 / Heb 3:6,14
11:2	Heb 11:3
11:3	Gen 1:1-31 / John 1:3 / Rom 1:19,20 / 4:20 / Heb 1:2
11:4	Gen 4:3-5
11:5	Gen 5:22-24
11:6	Jn 3:18,36 / Heb 7:19 / 10:19-22
11:7	Gen 6:13-22 / Rom 3:22 / Phil 3:9

10:34–37 Hebrews encourages believers, though in the midst of persecution and pressures, to persevere in their Christian lives. We don't usually think of suffering as good, but it can be a positive experience. During times of great stress, we may feel God's presence clearly. Knowing that Jesus is with us in our suffering, and expecting him to return soon to put an end to all pain, we grow in our faith and our relationship with him (see Romans 5:3–5).

10:35–38 The writer encouraged his readers not to shrink back from their faith in times of persecution, but to show by their endurance that their faith was real. Faith means resting in what Christ has done for us in the past, but it also means hoping for what he will do for us in the future (see Romans 8:12–25; Galatians 3:10–13).

11:1 Do you remember how you felt when you were younger and your birthday approached? You were excited and anxious. You knew you would certainly receive gifts and other special treats. But some things would be a surprise. Birthdays combined assurance and anticipation, and so does faith! Faith is the conviction based on past experience that God's new and fresh surprises will surely be ours.

11:1 Two words describe our faith: confidence and certainty. These two qualities need a secure beginning and ending point. The beginning point of faith is believing in God's character—he *is* who he says. The end point is believing in God's promises—he will *do* what he says. We believe that God will fulfill his promises even though we don't see those promises materializing *now*—this is true faith (see John 20:24–31).

11:3 God called the universe into being out of nothing; he

declared that it was to be, and it was. Our faith is in the God who created the entire universe by his Word. God's Word has awesome power. When he speaks, do you listen and respond? How can you better prepare yourself to respond to his Word?

11:4 Cain and Abel were Adam and Eve's first two sons. Abel offered a sacrifice that pleased God, while Cain's sacrifice was unacceptable. Abel's Profile is found in Genesis 5. Cain's Profile is in Genesis 6. Abel's sacrifice (a substitutionary animal) was more acceptable to God, both because it was a blood sacrifice, and because of the attitude in which Abel offered it.

11:6 Believing that God exists is only the beginning, even the demons believe that much (James 2:19, 20). God will not settle for your mere acknowledgment of his existence. He wants a personal, dynamic, life-transforming relationship with you. Those who "sincerely look for him," will find that they are rewarded with God's intimate presence.

11:6 Sometimes we wonder about the fate of those who haven't heard of Christ and have not even had a Bible to read. God assures us that all who honestly seek him—who act in faith on the knowledge of God that they possess—will be rewarded. When you tell others about God's Good News, encourage them to be honest and diligent in their search for truth. Those who hear the gospel are responsible for what they have heard (see 2 Corinthians 6:1, 2).

11:7 Noah experienced what it meant to be different from his neighbors. God commanded him to build a huge boat in the middle of dry land, and although God's command seemed foolish, Noah obeyed. Noah's obedience made him appear strange to his neighbors, just as the new beliefs of Jewish Christians made them

future, Noah believed him even though there was then no sign of a flood, and wasting no time, he built the ark and saved his family. Noah's belief in God was in direct contrast to the sin and disbelief of the rest of the world—which refused to obey—and because of his faith he became one of those whom God has accepted.

11:8
Gen 12:1-4

8Abraham trusted God, and when God told him to leave home and go far away to another land which he promised to give him, Abraham obeyed. Away he went, not even knowing where he was going. 9And even when he reached God's promised land, he lived in tents like a mere visitor, as did Isaac and Jacob, to whom God gave the same promise. 10Abraham did this because he was confidently waiting for God to bring him to that strong heavenly city whose designer and builder is God.

11:9
Gen 12:8

11:10
Heb 11:16; 12:22
Rev 21:2

11:11
Gen 17:19
21:1-3

11Sarah, too, had faith, and because of this she was able to become a mother in spite of her old age, for she realized that God, who gave her his promise, would certainly do what he said. 12And so a whole nation came from Abraham, who was too old to have even one child—a nation with so many millions of people that, like the stars of the sky and the sand on the ocean shores, there is no way to count them.

11:12
Gen 15:5
Rom 4:19

11:13
Gen 23:4
Mt 13:17
Jn 8:56
Heb 11:39

13These men of faith I have mentioned died without ever receiving all that God had promised them; but they saw it all awaiting them on ahead and were glad, for they agreed that this earth was not their real home but that they were just strangers visiting down here. 14And quite obviously when they talked like that, they were looking forward to their real home in heaven.

11:14
Heb 13:14

11:15
Gen 24:6

15If they had wanted to, they could have gone back to the good things of this world. 16But they didn't want to. They were living for heaven. And now God is not ashamed to be called their God, for he has made a heavenly city for them.

11:16
Gen 26:24
Ex 3:6,15
Phil 3:20

17While God was testing him, Abraham still trusted in God and his promises, and so he offered up his son Isaac, and was ready to slay him on the altar of sacrifice; 18yes, to slay even Isaac, through whom God had promised to give Abraham a whole nation of descendants!

11:17
Gen 22:1,2
Jas 2:21

11:18
Gen 21:12

11:19
Rom 4:21

19He believed that if Isaac died God would bring him back to life again; and that is just about what happened, for as far as Abraham was concerned, Isaac was doomed to death, but he came back again alive! 20It was by faith that Isaac knew God would give future blessings to his two sons, Jacob and Esau.

11:20
Gen 27:27-29

11:21
Gen 47:31; 48:5

21By faith Jacob, when he was old and dying, blessed each of Joseph's two sons as he stood and prayed, leaning on the top of his cane.

---

stand out. As you obey God, don't be surprised if others consider you different. Your obedience makes their disobedience stand out. Remember, if God asks you to do something, he will give you the necessary strength to carry out that task. For more information on Noah, see his Profile in Genesis 8.

11:8-10 Abraham's life was filled with faith. At God's command, he left home and went to another land—obeying without question (Genesis 12:1ff). He believed the covenant that God made with him (Genesis 12:2, 3; 13:14-16; 15:1-6). In obedience to God, Abraham was even willing to sacrifice his son Isaac (Genesis 22:1-19). Do not be surprised if God asks you to give up the security of the familiar to obey him. For further information on Abraham, see his Profile in Genesis 17.

11:11, 12 Sarah was Abraham's wife. They were unable to have children through many years of their marriage. God promised Abraham a son, but Sarah doubted that she could become pregnant in her old age. At first she laughed, but afterwards, she believed (Genesis 18). For more information on Sarah, see her Profile in Genesis 19.

11:13-16 The people of faith listed here died without receiving all that God had promised, but they never lost their vision of heaven. Many Christians become frustrated and defeated because their needs, wants, expectations, and demands are not immediately met when they believe in Christ. They become impatient and want to quit. Are you discouraged because your goal seems far away? Take courage from these heroes of faith who lived and died without

seeing the fruit of their faith on earth, and yet continued to believe.

11:17-19 Abraham was willing to give up his son when God commanded him to do so (Genesis 22:1-19). God did not let Abraham take Isaac's life, because God gave the command to test Abraham's faith. Instead of taking Abraham's son, God gave him a whole nation of descendants through Isaac. If you are afraid to trust God with your most prized possession, dream, or person, pay attention to Abraham's example. Because Abraham was willing to give up everything for God, he received back more than he could have imagined. What we receive, however, is not always immediate, or in the form of material possessions. After all, material possessions should be among the least satisfying of rewards. Our best and greatest rewards await us in eternity.

11:20 Isaac was the son promised to Abraham and Sarah in their old age. It was through Isaac that God fulfilled his promise to give Abraham countless descendants. Isaac had twin sons, Jacob and Esau. God chose the younger son, Jacob, through whom to continue his promise to Abraham. For more information on Isaac, see his Profile in Genesis 22.

11:21 Jacob was Isaac's son and Abraham's grandson. Jacob's sons became the fathers of Israel's 12 tribes. Even when Jacob (also called "Israel") was dying in a strange land, he believed the promise that Abraham's descendants would be like the sand on the seashore and that Israel would become a great nation (Genesis 48:1-22). True faith helps us see beyond the grave. For more information on Jacob and Esau, see their Profiles in Genesis.

22And it was by faith that Joseph, as he neared the end of his life, confidently spoke of God bringing the people of Israel out of Egypt; and he was so sure of it that he made them promise to carry his bones with them when they left!

23Moses' parents had faith too. When they saw that God had given them an unusual child, they trusted that God would save him from the death the king commanded, and they hid him for three months, and were not afraid.

24, 25It was by faith that Moses, when he grew up, refused to be treated as the grandson of the king, but chose to share ill-treatment with God's people instead of enjoying the fleeting pleasures of sin. 26He thought that it was better to suffer for the promised Christ than to own all the treasures of Egypt, for he was looking forward to the great reward that God would give him. 27And it was because he trusted God that he left the land of Egypt and wasn't afraid of the king's anger. Moses kept right on going; it seemed as though he could see God right there with him. 28And it was because he believed God would save his people that he commanded them to kill a lamb as God had told them to and sprinkle the blood on the doorposts of their homes, so that God's terrible Angel of Death could not touch the oldest child in those homes, as he did among the Egyptians.

29The people of Israel trusted God and went right through the Red Sea as though they were on dry ground. But when the Egyptians chasing them tried it, they all were drowned.

30It was faith that brought the walls of Jericho tumbling down after the people of Israel had walked around them seven days, as God had commanded them. 31By faith—because she believed in God and his power—Rahab the harlot did not die with all the others in her city when they refused to obey God, for she gave a friendly welcome to the spies.

32Well, how much more do I need to say? It would take too long to recount the stories of the faith of Gideon and Barak and Samson and Jephthah and David and Samuel and all the other prophets. 33These people all trusted God and as a result

11:22
Gen 50:24,25
Ex 13:19

11:23
Ex 1:16; 2:2

11:25
Ex 2:10-12
Ps 84:10

11:27
Ex 10:28; 12:37
Heb 11:1

11:28
Ex 12:1-13,21-30

11:29
Ex 14:13-31

11:30
Josh 6:20

11:31
Josh 2:9; 6:23
Jas 2:25

11:32
Judg 4:6; 6:11
11:1; 13:24
1 Sam 1:20
16:1

11:33
1 Sam 17:34
Dan 6:22

11:22 Joseph, one of Jacob's sons, was sold into slavery by his jealous brothers (Genesis 37). Eventually, Joseph was sold again, this time to an officer of the Pharaoh of Egypt. Because of his faithfulness to God, however, Joseph was given a top-ranking position in Egypt. Although Joseph could have used that position to build a personal empire, he remembered God's promise to Abraham. After he had been reconciled to his brothers, he brought his family to be near him, and requested that his bones be taken to the Promised Land when the Jews eventually left Egypt (Genesis 50:24, 25). Faith means trusting in God and doing what he wants, regardless of the circumstances. For more information on Joseph, see his Profile in Genesis 37.

11:23 Moses' parents trusted God for their son's life. They were not merely proud parents, they were believers who had faith that God would care for him. As a parent, have you trusted God enough to take care of your children? God has a plan for every person, and your important task is to pray for and prepare your children to do the work God has planned for them to do. Faith allows us to entrust even our children to God.

11:24-28 Moses became one of Israel's greatest leaders, a prophet and a lawgiver. But when he was born, his people were slaves in Egypt and the Egyptian officials had ordered that all Hebrew baby boys were to be killed. Moses was spared, however, and Pharaoh's daughter raised Moses in Pharaoh's own household (Exodus 1, 2)! It took faith for Moses to give up his place in the palace, but he could do it because he saw the fleeting nature of great wealth and prestige. It is easy to be deceived by the temporary benefits of wealth, popularity, status, and achievement, and to be blind to the long-range benefits of God's Kingdom. Faith helps us look beyond the world's value system to see the eternal values of God's Kingdom. For more information on Moses, see his Profile in Exodus 16.

11:31 When Joshua planned the conquest of Jericho, he sent

spies to investigate the fortifications of the city. The spies met Rahab, who had two strikes against her—she was a Gentile and a prostitute. But she showed that she had faith in God by welcoming the spies and by trusting God to spare her and her family when the city was destroyed. Faith helps us to change and do what is right regardless of our past or the disapproval of others. For more information on Rahab, see her Profile in Joshua 2.

11:32-40 These verses summarize the lives of other great men and women of faith. Some experienced outstanding victories, even over death. But others were severely mistreated, tortured, and even killed. Having a steadfast faith in God does not guarantee a happy, carefree life. On the contrary, our faith almost guarantees us some form of abuse from the world. While we are on earth, we may never see the purpose of our suffering. But we know that God will keep his promises to us. Is your faith based on the assurance that God will keep his promises to you?

11:33-35 The Old Testament records the lives of various people who experienced these great victories. Deborah won battles (Judges 4, 5). Joshua overthrew kingdoms (the book of Joshua). Nehemiah ruled God's people well (the book of Nehemiah). Daniel was kept from harm in the den of lions (Daniel 6). Shadrach, Meshach, and Abednego were kept from harm in the fiery furnace (Daniel 3). Elijah escaped the swords of evil queen Jezebel's henchmen (1 Kings 19:2ff). Hezekiah became strong after sickness (2 Kings 20). Gideon had great power in battle (Judges 7). A widow's son was brought back to life by the prophet Elisha (2 Kings 4:8-37).

We, too, can experience victory through faith in Christ. Our victories may be similar to those experienced by the Old Testament saints, but more likely, each of our victories will be directly related to our unique circumstances in life. Ultimately our most important victory will not be that we are saved from physical torture or death. Those experiences happen to some, but they only

won battles, overthrew kingdoms, ruled their people well, and received what God had promised them; they were kept from harm in a den of lions, 34and in a fiery furnace. Some, through their faith, escaped death by the sword. Some were made strong again after they had been weak or sick. Others were given great power in battle; they made whole armies turn and run away. 35And some women, through faith, received their loved ones back again from death. But others trusted God and were beaten to death, preferring to die rather than turn from God and be free—trusting that they would rise to a better life afterwards.

36Some were laughed at and their backs cut open with whips, and others were chained in dungeons. 37, 38Some died by stoning and some by being sawed in two; others were promised freedom if they would renounce their faith, then were killed with the sword. Some went about in skins of sheep and goats, wandering over deserts and mountains, hiding in dens and caves. They were hungry and sick and ill-treated—too good for this world. 39And these men of faith, though they trusted God and won his approval, none of them received all that God had promised them; 40for God wanted them to wait and share the even better rewards that were prepared for us.

God's discipline proves his love

12 Since we have such a huge crowd of men of faith watching us from the grandstands, let us strip off anything that slows us down or holds us back, and especially those sins that wrap themselves so tightly around our feet and trip us up; and let us run with patience the particular race that God has set before us.

2Keep your eyes on Jesus, our leader and instructor. He was willing to die a shameful death on the cross because of the joy he knew would be his afterwards; and now he sits in the place of honor by the throne of God.

3If you want to keep from becoming fainthearted and weary, think about his patience as sinful men did such terrible things to him. 4After all, you have never yet struggled against sin and temptation until you sweat great drops of blood.

5And have you quite forgotten the encouraging words God spoke to you, his child? He said, "My son, don't be angry when the Lord punishes you. Don't be

---

symbolize the real victory that God has promised. Even though we may physically die, we will live forever because of Christ. In the promised resurrection, even physical death will be defeated and Christ's victory will be made complete.

11:35–38 Many think that pain is the exception in the Christian life. When suffering occurs they say, "Why me?" They feel that God has deserted them, or perhaps he was not as dependable as they thought. In reality, however, we live in an evil world, and life includes much suffering even for believers. But God is still in control. He allows some Christians to become martyrs for the faith, and he allows others to survive persecution. Rather than asking, "Why me?" it is much more helpful to ask, "Why not me?" Your faith and the values of this world are on a collision course. Expect pain and suffering to come, and you will not be shocked when it hits. But we can also take comfort in knowing that Jesus suffered too. He understands our fears, our weaknesses, our disappointments (see 2:16–18; 4:14–16). He has promised never to leave us (Matthew 28:18–20), and he intercedes on our behalf (7:24, 25). In times of pain, persecution, or suffering we should trust confidently in Christ and in him alone.

11:39, 40 Hebrews 11 has been called faith's hall of fame. No doubt the author surprised his readers by this conclusion: these mighty Jewish heroes did not receive God's total reward, because they died before Christ came. In God's plan, they and the Christian believers (who were also enduring much testing) would be rewarded together. Once again Hebrews shows that Christianity supersedes Judaism.

12:1 This "huge crowd" is composed of the people described in chapter 11. Their faithfulness is a constant encouragement to us.

We do not struggle alone and we are not the first to struggle with problems in our lives. Others have run the race and won and their witness stirs us to run and win also. What an inspiring heritage we have!

12:1–4 The Christian life involves hard work. It requires us to give up whatever endangers our relationship with God, to run patiently, and to struggle against sin with the power of the Holy Spirit. To live this life effectively, we must keep our eyes on Jesus. We stumble when we look away from him and at ourselves or the circumstances surrounding us. We are running Christ's race, not our own, and we must always keep him in sight.

12:3 When we face hardship and discouragement, it is easy to lose sight of the big picture. But we're not alone, there is help. Many have already made it through life enduring far more difficult circumstances than we have experienced. Suffering is the training ground for Christian maturity. It develops our patience and makes our final victory sweet.

12:4 This verse can also be translated, "You have not yet resisted to the point of shedding blood." These readers were facing difficult times of persecution, but none of them had yet died for their faith. Because they were still alive, the writer urged them to continue to run their race. Just as Christ did not give up, neither should they.

12:5–11 Who loves his child more—the father who allows the child to do what will harm him, or the one who corrects, trains, and even punishes the child to help him learn what is right? It's never pleasant to be corrected and disciplined by God, but his discipline is a sign of his deep love for you. When God corrects you, see it as proof of his love and ask him what he is trying to teach you.

discouraged when he has to show you where you are wrong. 6For when he punishes you, it proves that he loves you. When he whips you it proves you are really his child."

7Let God train you, for he is doing what any loving father does for his children. Whoever heard of a son who was never corrected? 8If God doesn't punish you when you need it, as other fathers punish their sons, then it means that you aren't really God's son at all—that you don't really belong in his family. 9Since we respect our fathers here on earth, though they punish us, should we not all the more cheerfully submit to God's training so that we can begin really to live?

10Our earthly fathers trained us for a few brief years, doing the best for us that they knew how, but God's correction is always right and for our best good, that we may share his holiness. 11Being punished isn't enjoyable while it is happening—it hurts! But afterwards we can see the result, a quiet growth in grace and character.

12So take a new grip with your tired hands, stand firm on your shaky legs, 13and mark out a straight, smooth path for your feet so that those who follow you, though weak and lame, will not fall and hurt themselves, but become strong.

Warning against refusing to listen

14Try to stay out of all quarrels and seek to live a clean and holy life, for one who is not holy will not see the Lord. 15Look after each other so that not one of you will fail to find God's best blessings. Watch out that no bitterness takes root among you, for as it springs up it causes deep trouble, hurting many in their spiritual lives. 16Watch out that no one becomes involved in sexual sin or becomes careless about God as Esau did: he traded his rights as the oldest son for a single meal. 17And afterwards, when he wanted those rights back again, it was too late, even though he wept bitter tears of repentance. So remember, and be careful.

18You have not had to stand face to face with terror, flaming fire, gloom, darkness and a terrible storm, as the Israelites did at Mount Sinai when God gave them his laws. 19For there was an awesome trumpet blast, and a voice with a message so terrible that the people begged God to stop speaking. 20They staggered back under God's command that if even an animal touched the mountain it must die. 21Moses himself was so frightened at the sight that he shook with terrible fear.

22But you have come right up into Mount Zion, to the city of the living God, the heavenly Jerusalem, and to the gathering of countless happy angels; 23and to the church, composed of all those registered in heaven; and to God who is Judge of all;

12:6
Prov 3:12
Ps 94:12
Jas 1:12
Rev 3:19

12:7
Deut 8:5

12:8
1 Pet 5:9

12:9
Isa 38:16

12:10
2 Pet 1:4

12:11
1 Pet 1:6

12:12
Isa 35:3

12:13
Prov 4:26
Gal 6:1

12:14
Rom 6:22; 14:19

12:15
Deut 29:18
Heb 4:1

12:16
Gen 25:33

12:17
Gen 27:34

12:18
Ex 19:12,16

12:19
Ex 20:19

12:20
Ex 19:12

12:22
Ps 68:17
Gal 4:26
Rev 3:12; 14:1
21:2

12:23
Phil 3:12
Heb 2:12

12:11 We may respond to discipline in several ways: (1) we can accept it with resignation; (2) we can accept it with self-pity, thinking we really don't deserve it; (3) we can be angry and resent God for it; or (4) we can accept it gratefully as the appropriate response towards a loving Father.

12:12, 13 God is not only a disciplining parent, but also a demanding coach who pushes us to our limits and requires of us a disciplined life. Although we may not feel strong enough to push on to victory, we will be able to continue as we follow Christ and draw upon his strength. Then we can use our growing strength to help those around us who are weak and struggling.

12:12, 13 The word "so" is a clue that what follows is important! We must not live with only our own survival in mind. Others will follow our example, and we have a responsibility to them if we claim to live for Christ. Does your example make it easier for others to believe, follow, and mature in Christ? Or would those who follow you end up confused and misled?

12:14 The readers were familiar with the ceremonial cleansing ritual that prepared them for worship, and they knew they had to be "holy" or "clean" in order to enter the Temple. Sin always blocks our vision of God, so if we want to see God, we must remove it from our lives (see Psalm 24:3, 4). Holiness is coupled with peace—staying out of quarrels. A right relationship with God leads to right relationships with fellow believers. Although we will not always feel love toward all other believers, we must pursue peace as we become more Christlike.

12:15 Like a small root that grows into a great tree, bitterness springs up in our hearts and overshadows even our deepest Christian relationships. Bitterness brings with it jealousy, dissension, and immorality. When the Holy Spirit fills our lives, however, he leaves no room for bitterness.

12:16, 17 Esau's story shows us that mistakes and sins sometimes have long-lasting consequences (Genesis 25:29–34; 27:36). Even repentance and forgiveness do not always eliminate sins's consequences. How often do you make decisions based on what you want now, rather than on what you need long-term? Evaluate the long-range effects of your decisions and actions.

12:18–24 What a contrast between the people's terrified approach to God at Mount Sinai and their joyful approach at Mount Zion! What a difference Jesus has made! Before he came, God seemed distant and threatening. After he came, God welcomes us through Christ into his presence. Don't neglect to accept his invitation.

12:22 Christians are partakers in the heavenly Jerusalem right now because Christ rules our lives, the Holy Spirit is always with us, and we experience sweet fellowship with other believers. The full and ultimate rewards and reality of the heavenly Jerusalem are depicted in Revelation 21.

12:24
Gen 4:10
Ex 24:8
Heb 9:19; 10:19

and to the spirits of the redeemed in heaven, already made perfect; 24and to Jesus himself, who has brought us his wonderful new agreement; and to the sprinkled blood which graciously forgives instead of crying out for vengeance as the blood of Abel did.

12:25
Num 16
Heb 1:1; 2:2

25So see to it that you obey him who is speaking to you. For if the people of Israel did not escape when they refused to listen to Moses, the earthly messenger, how terrible our danger if we refuse to listen to God who speaks to us from heaven!

12:26
Ex 19:18

12:27
Ps 102:26
Mt 24:35
2 Pet 3:10

26When he spoke from Mount Sinai his voice shook the earth, but, "Next time," he says, "I will not only shake the earth, but the heavens too." 27By this he means that he will sift out everything without solid foundations, so that only unshakable things will be left.

12:28
Dan 2:44

12:29
Ex 24:17
Deut 9:3
Isa 66:15

28Since we have a Kingdom nothing can destroy, let us please God by serving him with thankful hearts, and with holy fear and awe. 29For our God is a consuming fire.

Holy and obedient lives

13:1
Rom 12:10

13:2
Gen 18:1-3
Mt 25:35

13:3
Mt 25:36
Col 4:18
Heb 10:34

13 Continue to love each other with true brotherly love. 2Don't forget to be kind to strangers, for some who have done this have entertained angels without realizing it! 3Don't forget about those in jail. Suffer with them as though you were there yourself. Share the sorrow of those being mistreated, for you know what they are going through.

13:4
1 Cor 7:38

4Honor your marriage and its vows, and be pure; for God will surely punish all those who are immoral or commit adultery.

13:5
Gen 28:15
Ps 37:25

13:6
Ps 118:6

5Stay away from the love of money; be satisfied with what you have. For God has said, "I will never, *never* fail you nor forsake you." 6That is why we can say without any doubt or fear, "The Lord is my Helper and I am not afraid of anything that mere man can do to me."

13:7
Heb 6:12

7Remember your leaders who have taught you the Word of God. Think of all the good that has come from their lives, and try to trust the Lord as they do.

13:8
Jn 8:58

13:9
Eph 4:14
Col 2:16

8Jesus Christ is the same yesterday, today, and forever. 9So do not be attracted by strange, new ideas. Your spiritual strength comes as a gift from God, not from ceremonial rules about eating certain foods—a method which, by the way, hasn't helped those who have tried it!

13:10
1 Cor 10:18

10We have an altar—the cross where Christ was sacrificed—where those who

---

12:27-29 Eventually the world will crumble, and only God's Kingdom will last. Those who follow Christ are part of this Kingdom, and they will withstand the shaking, sifting, and burning. When we feel unsure about the future, we can take confidence from these verses. Whatever happens here, our future is built on a solid foundation that cannot be destroyed. Don't put your confidence in that which will be destroyed; instead, build your life on Christ and his unshakable Kingdom. (See Matthew 7:24-29 for the importance of building on a solid foundation.)

13:1-5 Real love toward others produces tangible actions; (1) kindness to strangers (13:2); (2) sympathy for those who are in prison and those who have been mistreated (13:3); (3) respect for one's marriage vows (13:4); and (4) satisfaction with what you have (13:5). Make sure your love runs deep enough to affect your hospitality, sympathy, fidelity, and contentment.

13:2 Three Bible characters entertained angels without realizing it: (1) Abraham (Genesis 18:1ff), (2) Gideon (Judges 6:11ff), and (3) Manoah (Judges 13:2ff). Some people say they cannot be hospitable because their homes are not large enough or nice enough. But even if you have no more than a table and two chairs in a rented room, there are people who would be grateful to spend time in your home. Are there visitors to your church who would like to share a meal with you? Do you know single people who would enjoy an evening of tea and talk? Is there any way your home could meet the needs of traveling missionaries? Hospitality simply means making other people feel comfortable and at home.

13:3 We are to have sympathy for those in prison, especially for Christians imprisoned for their faith. Jesus said his true followers would visit those in prison as his representatives (Matthew 25:36).

13:5, 6 We are contented when we realize God's sufficiency for our needs. Christians today who become materialistic are saying with their lives that God can't take care of them—or at least won't take care of them the way they want. Insecurity can lead to the love of money, whether we are rich or poor. The only antidote is to trust God to meet all our needs.

13:7 If you are a Christian, you owe much to others who have taught you and modeled for you what you needed to know about the gospel and living the Christian life. Continue following the good examples of those who have invested a part of themselves in you. A part of following their example is to pass on the faith to others—to invest your life through evangelism, service, and Christian education.

13:8 We must keep our eyes on Christ, our ultimate leader, who, unlike human leaders, will never change. He has been and will be the same forever. In a changing world we can trust our unchanging Lord.

13:9 Apparently some were teaching that keeping the Old Testament ceremonial laws and rituals was important to salvation. But these laws were useless for conquering a person's evil thoughts and desires (Colossians 2:23). The laws could influence conduct, but they could not change the heart. Lasting changes in conduct begin when the Holy Spirit comes to live in the heart.

continue to seek salvation by obeying Jewish laws can never be helped. [11]Under the system of Jewish laws the high priest brought the blood of the slain animals into the sanctuary as a sacrifice for sin, and then the bodies of the animals were burned outside the city. [12]That is why Jesus suffered and died outside the city, where his blood washed our sins away.

[13]So let us go out to him beyond the city walls [that is, outside the interests of this world, being willing to be despised] to suffer with him there, bearing his shame. [14]For this world is not our home; we are looking forward to our everlasting home in heaven.

[15]With Jesus' help we will continually offer our sacrifice of praise to God by telling others of the glory of his name. [16]Don't forget to do good and to share what you have with those in need, for such sacrifices are very pleasing to him. [17]Obey your spiritual leaders and be willing to do what they say. For their work is to watch over your souls, and God will judge them on how well they do this. Give them reason to report joyfully about you to the Lord and not with sorrow, for then you will suffer for it too.

Final words

[18]Pray for us, for our conscience is clear and we want to keep it that way. [19]I especially need your prayers right now so that I can come back to you sooner.

[20, 21]And now may the God of peace, who brought again from the dead our Lord Jesus, equip you with all you need for doing his will. May he who became the great Shepherd of the sheep by an everlasting agreement between God and you, signed with his blood, produce in you through the power of Christ all that is pleasing to him. To him be glory forever and ever. Amen.

[22]Brethren, please listen patiently to what I have said in this letter, for it is a short one. [23]I want you to know that Brother Timothy is now out of jail; if he comes here soon, I will come with him to see you. [24, 25]Give my greetings to all your leaders and to the other believers there. The Christians from Italy who are here with me send you their love. God's grace be with you all.

Good-bye.

13:13 *willing to be despised*, implied.

13:11
Lev 4:12,21

13:12
Jn 19:17
Heb 9:12

13:13
1 Pet 4:14

13:14
Heb 10:34; 11:10

13:15
Lev 7:12
Ps 50:14
1 Pet 2:5

13:17
Ezek 3:17
33:2,7
Acts 20:28

13:18
Acts 24:16

13:19
Philem 22

13:20
Isa 40:11
Ezek 31:23
37:24
Zech 9:11
Jn 10:11

13:21
Rom 11:36
Phil 2:13
1 Pet 5:10

13:23
Acts 16:1
1 Thess 3:2

13:13 This verse can also be translated, "Let us go to him outside the camp, and bear the disgrace he endured." The Jewish Christians were being ridiculed and persecuted by Jews who didn't believe in Jesus the Messiah. Most of the book of Hebrews tells them how much greater Christ is than the sacrificial system. Now the writer makes the point of his lengthy argument: It may be necessary to leave the "camp" and suffer with Christ. To be outside the camp meant to be unclean. But Jesus suffered humiliation and uncleanness outside the Jerusalem gates on their behalf. The time had come for Jewish Christians to declare their loyalty to Christ above any other loyalty, to choose to follow the Messiah whatever suffering that might entail. Is there anything holding us back from complete loyalty to Jesus Christ?

13:14 We should not be attached to this world, because all that we are and have here is temporary. Only our relationship with God and our service to him will last. Don't store up your treasures here, store them in heaven (Matthew 6:19–21).

13:15, 16 If these Jewish Christians, because of their witness to the Messiah, could no longer worship with other Jews, they could consider praise their sacrifice—one they could offer anywhere, anytime. This must have reminded them of the prophet Hosea's words, "O Lord, take away our sins; be gracious to us and receive us, and we will offer you the sacrifice of praise" (Hosea 14:2). A sacrifice of praise today would include thanking Christ for his sacrifice on the cross and telling others about it.

13:17 The task of church leaders is to help people mature in Christ. Cooperative followers greatly ease the burden of leadership. Does your conduct give your leaders reason to report joyfully about you?

13:18, 19 The writer recognized the need for prayer. Christian leaders are especially vulnerable to criticism from others, pride if they succeed, depression if they fail, and Satan's constant efforts to nullify their work for God. They desperately need our prayers! For whom should you regularly pray?

13:20, 21 These verses include two significant results of Christ's action in our lives. The writer prayed that God would (1) work in the Christians to produce the kind of *persons* that would please him, and (2) equip the Christians to do the kind of *work* that would please him. Let God change you, then use you.

13:23 We have no record of Timothy's imprisonment, but we learn here that he had been released. For more about Timothy, see his Profile in 1 Timothy.

13:24, 25 Hebrews is a call to Christian maturity. It was addressed to first-century Jewish Christians, but it applies to Christians of any age or background. Christian maturity means making Christ the beginning and end of our faith. To mature, we must center our lives on him, not depending on religious ritual, not falling back into sin, not trusting in ourselves, and not letting anything come between us and Christ.

JAMES

"MIRACULOUS!" . . . "Revolutionary!" . . . "Greatest ever!" We are inundated with a flood of extravagant claims as we flip the television dial or magazine pages. We are assured that these products are "new," "improved," "fantastic," and will change lives. For only a few dollars we can have "cleaner clothes," "whiter teeth," "glamorous hair," "tastier food," happiness, friends, and the good life. And just before an election, no one can match the politicians' promises. But talk is cheap, and we soon realize that the boasts were hollow, quite far from the truth.

Christians also make great claims, and are often guilty of belying them with their actions. Professing to trust God and to be his people, they cling tightly to the world and its values. Possessing all the right answers, they contradict the gospel with their lives.

With energetic style and pointed, well-chosen words, James confronts the unethical practices of his readers head-on. Christianity must not only be *believed*, it must be *lived*. "What's the use of saying that you have faith and are Christians if you aren't proving it by helping others? Will *that* kind of faith save anyone?" (2:14). The proof that our faith is real is a *changed life*.

Genuine faith will inevitably produce good works. This is the central theme of James' epistle, around which he supplies practical advice on living the Christian life.

James begins his epistle outlining some general characteristics of the Christian life (1:1–27). Next, he exhorts Christians to act justly in society (2:1–13). He follows this practical advice with a theological discourse on the relationship between faith and action (2:14–26). Then James shows the importance of controlling one's speech (3:1–12). In 3:13–18, James distinguishes two kinds of wisdom, earthly and heavenly. Then he encourages his readers to turn from evil desires and obey God (4:1–12). James reproves those who trust in their own plans and possessions (4:13—5:6). Finally, James exhorts his readers to be patient with each other (5:7–11), to be straightforward in their promises (5:12), to pray for each other (5:13–18), and to help one another remain faithful to God (5:19, 20).

This epistle could be considered a how-to book on Christian living. Confrontation, challenge, and commitment await you in its pages. Read James and become a *doer* of the Word (1:22–25).

VITAL STATISTICS

PURPOSE:
To expose unethical practices and to teach right Christian behavior

AUTHOR:
James, Jesus' brother, a leader in the Jerusalem church

TO WHOM WRITTEN:
First century Jewish Christians residing in Gentile communities outside Palestine, and to all Christians everywhere

DATE WRITTEN:
Probably A.D. 49, prior to the Jerusalem council held in A.D. 50

SETTING:
This letter expresses James' concern for persecuted Christians who were once part of the Jerusalem church

KEY VERSE:
". . . You say the way to God is by faith alone, plus nothing; well, I say that good works are important too, for without good works you can't prove whether you have faith or not . . ." (2:18).

THE BLUEPRINT

1. Genuine religion (1:1–27)
2. Genuine faith (2:1—3:12)
3. Genuine wisdom (3:13—5:20)

James wrote to Jewish Christians who had been scattered throughout the Mediterranean world because of persecution. In their hostile surroundings they were tempted to let intellectual agreement pass for true faith. This letter can have rich meaning for us as we are reminded that genuine faith transforms lives. We are encouraged to put our faith into action. It is easy to say we have faith, but true faith will produce loving actions toward others.

MEGATHEMES

THEME	EXPLANATION	IMPORTANCE
Living Faith	James wants believers not only to hear the truth, but also to do it. He contrasts empty faith ("claims without conduct") with faith that works. Commitment to love and to serve is evidence of true faith.	Living faith makes a difference. Make sure your faith is more than just a statement— it should also result in action. Be alert to ways of putting your faith to work.
Trials	In the Christian life there are trials and temptations. Successfully overcoming these adversities produces maturity and strong character.	Don't resent troubles when they come. Pray for wisdom; God will supply all that you will need to face persecution or adversity. He will give you patience and keep you strong in times of trial.
Law of Love	We are saved by God's gracious mercy, not by keeping the law. But Christ gave us a special command, "love your neighbor as yourself" (Matthew 19:19). We are to love and serve those around us.	Keeping the law of love shows that our faith is vital and real. To show love to others, we must root out our own selfishness.
Wise Speech	Wisdom shows itself in speech. We are responsible for the destructive results of our talk. The wisdom of God that helps control the tongue can help control all our actions.	Accepting God's wisdom will affect your speech because your words will reveal their godly source. Think before you speak and allow God to give you self-control.
Wealth	James taught Christians not to compromise with worldly attitudes about wealth. Because the glory of wealth fades, Christians should store up God's treasures through sincere service. Christians must not show partiality to the wealthy, nor be prejudiced against the poor.	All of us are accountable for how we use what we have. We should not hoard wealth, but be generous towards others. In addition, we should not be impressed by the wealthy nor look down on those who are poor.

1. Genuine religion

1 *From:* James, a servant of God and of the Lord Jesus Christ.
To: Jewish Christians scattered everywhere. Greetings!

Enduring trials and temptations

²Dear brothers, is your life full of difficulties and temptations? Then be happy, ³for when the way is rough, your patience has a chance to grow. ⁴So let it grow, and don't try to squirm out of your problems. For when your patience is finally in full bloom, then you will be ready for anything, strong in character, full and complete.
⁵If you want to know what God wants you to do, ask him, and he will gladly tell you, for he is always ready to give a bountiful supply of wisdom to all who ask him;

1:2
1 Pet 1:6-8
1:3
Rom 2:7; 5:3-5
1:5
Prov 2:3-13
Mt 7:7-11
Jas 3:17

1:1 The writer of this letter, a leader of the church in Jerusalem (see Acts 12:17; 15:13), was not James the apostle, but James, Jesus' brother. The book of James was one of the earliest epistles, probably written before A.D. 50. After Stephen was martyred (Acts 8:1–3), Christians in Jerusalem were scattered throughout the Roman world. Persecution increased. Because these early believers did not have the support of established Christian churches, James wrote to them as a concerned leader, to encourage them in their faith during that difficult time.

1:2 The word *temptation* as used here refers to trials or testing. It does not mean an enticement to do evil. While God tests us, he never provokes us to commit sin (see 1:12–16).

1:2, 3 James doesn't say *if* the way is rough, but *when* it is rough. He assumes we will have trials and that it is possible to profit from them. James tells us to turn our hardships into times of learning. Rough times can teach us patience. For other passages dealing with patience (also called perseverance and steadfastness), see Romans 2:7; 5:3–5; 8:24, 25; 2 Corinthians 6:3–7; 2 Peter 1:2–9.

1:2–4 We can't really know the depth of our character until we see how we react under pressure. It is easy to be kind when everything is going well, but can we still be kind when others are treating us unfairly? Instead of complaining about our struggles, we should see them as opportunities for growth. Thank God for promising to be with you in rough times. Ask him to help you solve your problems or give you the strength to endure them. Then be patient. God will not leave you alone with your problems; he will stay close by and help you grow.

1:5 The statement, "If you want to know what God wants you to do" can also be translated, "If any of you lacks wisdom." James is not only talking about knowledge, but the ability to make wise decisions in difficult circumstances. If we need wisdom, we can pray to God and he will supply what we need. Christians never need to grope about in the dark, hoping to stumble upon answers. God's wisdom is available to guide our choices.

1:5 When James speaks of wisdom, he means practical discernment. Wisdom begins with respect for God, leads to right

1:6
Mt 21:22
Mk 11:22-24

1:9
Deut 15:7-11
Prov 17:5
Lk 14:11

1:10,11
Isa 40:7
1 Pet 1:24

1:12
Job 5:17-19
Prov 3:11,12
2 Tim 4:8
Heb 10:32-34
Jas 5:11
Rev 2:10; 3:11

1:13
Gen 22:1
Rom 9:19,20

1:16
1 Cor 6:9

1:17
Gen 1:1-5,
14-16
Ps 19:1-8; 136:7
Heb 13:8

he will not resent it. 6But when you ask him, be sure that you really expect him to tell you, for a doubtful mind will be as unsettled as a wave of the sea that is driven and tossed by the wind; 7, 8and every decision you then make will be uncertain, as you turn first this way, and then that. If you don't ask with faith, don't expect the Lord to give you any solid answer.

9A Christian who doesn't amount to much in this world should be glad, for he is great in the Lord's sight. 10, 11But a rich man should be glad that his riches mean nothing to the Lord, for he will soon be gone, like a flower that has lost its beauty and fades away, withered—killed by the scorching summer sun. So it is with rich men. They will soon die and leave behind all their busy activities.

12Happy is the man who doesn't give in and do wrong when he is tempted, for afterwards he will get as his reward the crown of life that God has promised those who love him. 13And remember, when someone wants to do wrong it is never God who is tempting him, for God never wants to do wrong and never tempts anyone else to do it. 14Temptation is the pull of man's own evil thoughts and wishes. 15These evil thoughts lead to evil actions and afterwards to the death penalty from God. 16So don't be misled, dear brothers.

17But whatever is good and perfect comes to us from God, the Creator of all light, and he shines forever without change or shadow. 18And it was a happy day

1:18 *happy day for him,* literally, "Of his own free will he gave us," etc.

CHAPTER SUMMARY

Chapter 1	Confident Stand	What a Christian has
Chapter 2	Compassionate Service	What a Christian does
Chapter 3	Careful Speech	What a Christian says
Chapter 4	Contrite Submission	What a Christian feels
Chapter 5	Concerned Sharing	What a Christian gives

---

living, and results in increased ability to tell right from wrong. God is willing to give us this wisdom. To learn God's will, we need to ask him to reveal it to us, and then we must be willing to do what he tells us to do.

1:5–8 If you have ever seen the constant rolling of huge waves at sea, you know how restless they are—subject to the forces of wind, gravity, and tide. Doubt leaves one as unsettled as the restless waves, tossed to-and-fro. If you want to stop being tossed about, believe that God knows what is best for you. Ask him for wisdom, and trust that he will give it to you. Then your decisions will be sure and solid.

1:6 What is a doubtful mind? It is a mind that is not completely convinced that God's way is best. It treats God's Word like any human advice, retaining the option of disobedience. It vacillates between feelings, the world's ideas, and God's commands. The cure for a doubtful mind is wholehearted commitment to God's reliable way. See the note on James 1:5.

1:7, 8 To "ask with faith" is to ask with confidence that God will align our desires with his purposes. For more on this concept, read the note on Matthew 21:22.

1:9 This verse refers to a person of humble circumstances, without status or wealth. Such people are often overlooked, even in our churches today.

1:9–11 If wealth, power, and status mean nothing to God, why do we attribute so much importance to them and honor those who possess them? Do your material possessions give you a sense of purpose and a reason for living? If they were gone, what would be left? What you have in your heart, not your bank account, matters to God and endures for eternity.

1:10, 11 The rich should be glad that wealth means nothing to God, because wealth is easily lost. The poor should be glad riches mean nothing to God, otherwise they would be considered unworthy. True wealth is found in an individual's spiritual life, not his financial assets. God is interested in what is lasting (our souls), not in what is temporary (our money and possessions). See Mark

4:19 for Jesus' words on this subject.

1:12 The world says happiness comes from pleasure, money, location, job, image, and success. These cannot provide lasting happiness, however, because they are temporary and provide no eternal benefits.

1:12–15 Temptation comes from evil desire within, not from God. It begins with an evil thought. It becomes sin when we dwell on the thought and allow it to become an action. Like a snowball rolling downhill, sin's destruction grows the more we let sin have its way. The best time to stop a snowball is before it is too big or moving too fast to control. See Matthew 4:1–11; 1 Corinthians 10:13; and 2 Timothy 2:22 for more about escaping temptation.

1:13–15 It is easy to blame others and make excuses for evil thoughts and wrong actions. Excuses include (1) it's the other person's fault; (2) I couldn't help it; (3) everybody's doing it; (4) it was just a mistake; (5) nobody's perfect; (6) the devil made me do it; (7) I was pressured into it; (8) I didn't know it was wrong. A person who makes excuses is trying to shift the blame from himself to something or someone else. A Christian, on the other hand, accepts responsibility for his wrongs, confesses them, and asks God for forgiveness.

1:13, 14 People who live for God often wonder why they still have temptations. Does God tempt them? God *tests* people, but he does not *tempt* them by trying to seduce them into sin. He allows Satan to tempt them, however, in order to refine their faith and to grow in their dependence upon Christ. We can endure the temptation to sin by turning to God for strength and choosing to act in obedience to his Word.

1:17 Scripture often compares goodness with light and evil with darkness. For other passages where God is pictured as light, see Psalm 27:1, Isaiah 60:19–22, John 1:1–14.

1:18 First-century Christians were the first generation to believe in Jesus Christ as Messiah. James calls them "the first children in his God's new family."

for him when he gave us our new lives, through the truth of his Word, and we became, as it were, the first children in his new family.

Listening and doing

19Dear brothers, don't ever forget that it is best to listen much, speak little, and not become angry; 20for anger doesn't make us good, as God demands that we must be.

21So get rid of all that is wrong in your life, both inside and outside, and humbly be glad for the wonderful message we have received, for it is able to save our souls as it takes hold of our hearts.

22And remember, it is a message to obey, not just to listen to. So don't fool yourselves. 23For if a person just listens and doesn't obey, he is like a man looking at his face in a mirror; 24as soon as he walks away, he can't see himself anymore or remember what he looks like. 25But if anyone keeps looking steadily into God's law for free men, he will not only remember it but he will do what it says, and God will greatly bless him in everything he does.

26Anyone who says he is a Christian but doesn't control his sharp tongue is just fooling himself, and his religion isn't worth much. 27The Christian who is pure and without fault, from God the Father's point of view, is the one who takes care of orphans and widows, and who remains true to the Lord—not soiled and dirtied by his contacts with the world.

2. Genuine faith

Do not favor the rich

2 Dear brothers, how can you claim that you belong to the Lord Jesus Christ, the Lord of glory, if you show favoritism to rich people and look down on poor people?

2If a man comes into your church dressed in expensive clothes and with valuable

1:19 Prov 10:19; 15:18; 17:27,28; Eph 4:26,31
1:21 Rom 13:12,13; Eph 4:22; 1 Pet 1:23
1:22 Mt 7:24; 12:50 28:20; Lk 6:46-49; Jn 13:17
1:25 2 Cor 3:17,18; Gal 5:1; Jas 2:12; 1 Pet 2:16
1:26 Prov 13:3; 21:23
1:27 Deut 14:29 24:17-20; Col 3:1-3; Jas 4:4; 1 Jn 2:15-17
2:1 Lev 19:15; Deut 16:19; Prov 24:23 28:21; 1 Cor 2:8

1:19 When we talk too much and listen too little, we communicate to others that we think our ideas are much more important than theirs. James wisely advises us to reverse this process. Put a mental stopwatch on your conversations and keep track of how much you talk and how much you listen. In your conversations, do others feel that their viewpoints and ideas have value?

1:19, 20 This verse speaks of anger that erupts when our egos are bruised—"*I* am hurt"; "*My* opinions are not being heard." When injustice and sin occur, we *should* become angry because others are being hurt. But we should not become angry when we fail to win an argument, or when we feel neglected. Selfish anger never helps anybody.

1:22–25 It is important to know what God's Word says, but it is much more important to obey it. The effectiveness of our Bible study time can be measured by the effect it has on our behavior and attitudes.

1:25 "God's law for free men" is also called the "law of liberty," or the "perfect law that gives freedom." It seems paradoxical that a law could give us freedom. But God's law points out sin in our lives and gives us opportunity to ask God's forgiveness (see Romans 7:7, 8). As Christians, we are saved by God's grace. Salvation includes freedom from sin's control. We can live a holy life that we could not live otherwise. As believers, we are free to live as we should (as God created us to live). Of course, this does not mean that we are free to do as we please (see 1 Peter 2:14–16).

1:27 In the first century, orphans and widows had very few means of economic support. Unless a family member was willing to care for them, they were reduced to begging, selling themselves as slaves, or starving. By caring for these powerless people, the church put God's Word into practice. Giving with no hope of receiving in return, they showed what it means to serve others. This is what Jesus expects of all true believers.

2:1ff In this chapter James argues for the necessity of good works. He sets forth three truths: (1) Commitment is an essential part of faith. You cannot be a Christian simply by affirming the right doctrines or agreeing with biblical facts. You must commit your mind and heart to Christ (2:19). (2) Good works are the evidence of true faith. A genuine Christian will have a changed life (2:18). (3) Faith without good works doesn't do anybody any good—it is useless (2:14–17). These statements are consistent with Paul's teaching that salvation is by faith alone. Paul emphasizes the purpose of faith—to bring salvation. James emphasizes the results of faith—a changed life.

2:1ff Often we treat a well-dressed, impressive-looking person better than someone who looks poor. We do this because we would rather identify with successful people than with apparent failures. We feel better about ourselves when we associate with people we admire. The irony, as James reminds us, is that the supposed winners may have gained their impressive lifestyle at our expense. In addition, the rich find it hard to identify with the Lord Jesus who came as a humble servant. Are you easily impressed by status, wealth, or fame? Are you partial to the "haves" while ignoring the "have nots"? This prejudice is sin. God views all people as equals, and if he favors anyone, it is the poor and the powerless who cannot help themselves. We should follow his example.

2:2–4 Why is it wrong to judge a person by his economic status? Wealth may indicate intelligence, wise decisions, and hard work. On the other hand, it may mean only that a person had the good fortune of being born into a wealthy family. Or it can even be the sign of greed, dishonesty, and selfishness. By honoring someone just because he dresses well, we are making his appearance more important than his character. We sometimes do this because (1) poverty makes us uncomfortable; we don't want to face our responsibilities to those who have less than we do; (2) we too want to be wealthy, and we hope to use the rich person as a means to

gold rings on his fingers, and at the same moment another man comes in who is poor and dressed in threadbare clothes, 3and you make a lot of fuss over the rich man and give him the best seat in the house and say to the poor man, "You can stand over there if you like, or else sit on the floor"—well, 4judging a man by his wealth shows that you are guided by wrong motives.

5Listen to me, dear brothers: God has chosen poor people to be rich in faith, and the Kingdom of Heaven is theirs, for that is the gift God has promised to all those who love him. 6And yet, of the two strangers, you have despised the poor man. Don't you realize that it is usually the rich men who pick on you and drag you into court? 7And all too often they are the ones who laugh at Jesus Christ, whose noble name you bear.

8Yes indeed, it is good when you truly obey our Lord's command, "You must love and help your neighbors just as much as you love and take care of yourself." 9But you are breaking this law of our Lord's when you favor the rich and fawn over them; it is sin.

10And the person who keeps every law of God, but makes one little slip, is just as guilty as the person who has broken every law there is. 11For the God who said you must not marry a woman who already has a husband, also said you must not murder, so even though you have not broken the marriage laws by committing adultery, but have murdered someone, you have entirely broken God's laws and stand utterly guilty before him.

12You will be judged on whether or not you are doing what Christ wants you to. So watch what you do and what you think; 13for there will be no mercy to those who have shown no mercy. But if you have been merciful, then God's mercy toward you will win out over his judgment against you.

Faith results in good works

14Dear brothers, what's the use of saying that you have faith and are Christians

2:4
Jn 7:24

2:5
Prov 8:17-21
Mt 5:3; 11:6
Lk 6:20; 12:21
1 Cor 1:27
2 Cor 6:10

2:7
Acts 11:26
1 Pet 4:16

2:8
Lev 19:18
Mt 7:12
Rom 13:8

2:10
Deut 27:26
Mt 5:18,19
Gal 5:3

2:11
Ex 20:13,14
Deut 5:17,18
Mt 19:18

2:12
Jas 1:25

2:13
Mt 18:32-35

SHOWING FAVORITISM

Why it is wrong to show favoritism to the wealthy:

1. It is inconsistent with Christ's teachings.
2. It results from evil thoughts.
3. It belittles people made in God's image.
4. It is a by-product of selfish motives.
5. It goes against the biblical definition of love.
6. It shows a lack of mercy to those less fortunate.
7. It is hypocritical.
8. It is sin.

---

that end; (3) we want the rich person to join our church and help support it financially. All these motives are selfish; none of them sees the rich man or the poor man as a human being in need of fellowship. If we say Christ is Lord of our lives, then we must live as he lived, showing no favoritism and loving all people regardless of their circumstances.

2:2-4 We are often partial to the rich because we mistakenly assume they are rich because they have been blessed by God. But God does not promise earthly rewards or riches; in fact, Christ calls us to be ready to suffer for him and give up everything in order to hold on to eternal life (Matthew 6:19-21; 19:28-30; Luke 12:14-34; Romans 8:15-21; 1 Timothy 6:17-19).

2:5 When James speaks about the poor, he is talking about those who have no money, and also those whose simple values are despised by much of our affluent society. Perhaps they prefer serving to managing, human relationships to financial security, peace to power. This does not mean that the poor will automatically go to heaven and the rich to hell. Poor people, however, are usually more aware of their powerlessness, and thus it is usually easier for them to acknowledge their need for salvation. One of the greatest barriers to salvation for the rich is pride. For the poor, it is bitterness.

2:8, 9 We must treat all people as we would want to be treated. We should not ignore the rich, because then we would be withholding our love. But we must not favor them for what they can do for us, while ignoring the poor because they can offer us little in return. (See also Leviticus 19:18; Matthew 22:37-40; Romans 13:8.)

2:10, 11 It is easy to spot the sins in others while we overlook or rationalize our own. James reminds us that if we've broken just one law, we are sinners. You can't break the law a little bit; if you have broken it at all, you need Christ to pay for your sin. Measure yourself, not someone else, against God's standards. Ask for forgiveness where you need it, and then renew your effort to show your faith by your actions.

2:13 Our sins are forgiven by God's mercy alone. We can't earn forgiveness by forgiving others. But when we withhold forgiveness from others after having received it ourselves, it shows we don't understand or appreciate God's mercy toward us (see Matthew 6:14, 15; Ephesians 4:31, 32).

2:14 Intellectual assent—agreement with a set of Christian teachings—is incomplete faith. True faith transforms our lives. If our lives remain unchanged, we don't truly believe the truths we claim to believe.

if you aren't proving it by helping others? Will *that* kind of faith save anyone? [15]If you have a friend who is in need of food and clothing, [16]and you say to him, "Well, good-bye and God bless you; stay warm and eat hearty," and then don't give him clothes or food, what good does that do?

[17]So you see, it isn't enough just to have faith. You must also do good to prove that you have it. Faith that doesn't show itself by good works is no faith at all—it is dead and useless.

[18]But someone may well argue, "You say the way to God is by faith alone, plus nothing; well, I say that good works are important too, for without good works you can't prove whether you have faith or not; but anyone can see that I have faith by the way I act."

[19]Are there still some among you who hold that "only believing" is enough? Believing in one God? Well, remember that the demons believe this too—so strongly that they tremble in terror! [20]Fool! When will you ever learn that "believing" is useless without *doing* what God wants you to? Faith that does not result in good deeds is not real faith.

[21]Don't you remember that even our father Abraham was declared good because of what he *did,* when he was willing to obey God, even if it meant offering his son Isaac to die on the altar? [22]You see, he was trusting God so much that he was willing to do whatever God told him to; his faith was made complete by what he did, by his actions, his good deeds. [23]And so it happened just as the Scriptures say, that Abraham trusted God, and the Lord declared him good in God's sight, and he was even called "the friend of God." [24]So you see, a man is saved by what he does, as well as by what he believes.

[25]Rahab, the prostitute, is another example of this. She was saved because of what she did when she hid those messengers and sent them safely away by a different road. [26]Just as the body is dead when there is no spirit in it, so faith is dead if it is not the kind that results in good deeds.

Controlling the tongue

3 Dear brothers, don't be too eager to tell others their faults, for we all make many mistakes; and when we teachers of religion, who should know better, do wrong, our punishment will be greater than it would be for others.

If anyone can control his tongue, it proves that he has perfect control over himself in every other way. [3]We can make a large horse turn around and go wherever we want by means of a small bit in his mouth. [4]And a tiny rudder makes a huge ship turn wherever the pilot wants it to go, even though the winds are strong.

[5]So also the tongue is a small thing, but what enormous damage it can do. A great

3:1 *don't be too eager to tell others their faults,* literally, "not many (of you) should become masters (teachers)."

2:15
Mt 25:35,36

2:16
1 Jn 3:17

2:17
Gal 5:6
Jas 2:14-16,
20,26
1 Pet 1:5-9

2:18
Mt 7:16
Rom 3:28

2:19
Deut 6:4
Isa 43:10
44:6,8
Mt 8:28,29

2:20
Gal 5:6
Jas 2:14,17,26

2:21
Gen 22:16-18

2:22
Heb 11:17

2:23
Gen 15:6
Isa 41:8
Jn 15:13-15
Rom 4:3-5

2:25
Josh 2:4,6,15
Heb 11:31

2:26
Gal 5:6
Jas 2:14,17,20

3:1
Mt 23:8-10
Rom 2:17-24
Jas 1:26

3:2
Jas 1:4

3:3
Ps 32:9

3:5
Prov 26:20

2:17 Living the way God wants us to live does not earn our way into heaven, but it shows that our commitment to God is real. Godly conduct is not a substitute for, but a verification of our faith in Christ.

2:18 At first glance, this verse seems to contradict Romans 3:28, "we are saved by faith in Christ and not by the good things we do." Deeper investigation, however, shows that the teachings of James and Paul are not at odds. While it is true that our good works can never earn salvation, true faith always results in a changed life and good works. Paul speaks against those who try to be saved by works instead of true faith; James speaks against those who confuse mere intellectual assent with true faith. After all, even demons know who Jesus is, but they don't obey him (2:19). True faith involves a commitment of your whole self to God.

2:21-24 James says Abraham was declared good (righteous) because of what he *did,* and Paul says he was declared good (righteous) because of what he *believed* (Romans 4:1-5). James and Paul are not contradicting, but complementing each other. Belief brings us salvation; active obedience demonstrates that our belief is genuine.

2:25 Rahab lived in Jericho, a city the Israelites conquered as they entered the Promised Land (Joshua 2). When Israel's spies came to the city, she hid them and helped them escape. In this way she demonstrated faith in God's purpose for Israel. As a result, she and her family were saved when the city was destroyed (Joshua 2). Hebrews 11:31, 32 lists Rahab among the heroes of faith.

3:1, 2 Teaching was a highly valued and respected profession in Jewish culture. Many Jews who embraced Christianity wanted to become teachers. James warned that although it is good to aspire to teach, the teachers' responsibility is great because their words affect others' spiritual lives. If you are in a teaching or leadership role, how is your example affecting those you lead?

3:2, 3 What you say and what you *don't* say are both important. Proper speech is not only saying the right words at the right time, but controlling your desire to say what you shouldn't. Examples of wrongly using the tongue include gossiping, putting others down, bragging, manipulating, false teaching, exaggerating, complaining, flattering, and lying. Before you speak, ask, "Is it true, is it necessary, and is it kind?"

3:6
Ps 120:3
Prov 6:12-19
10:11; 16:27
Mt 15:11
Mk 7:15,16

3:8
Ps 140:3
Rom 3:13

3:9
Gen 1:26,27; 5:1
1 Cor 11:7

3:12
Mt 7:16

forest can be set on fire by one tiny spark. 6And the tongue is a flame of fire. It is full of wickedness, and poisons every part of the body. And the tongue is set on fire by hell itself, and can turn our whole lives into a blazing flame of destruction and disaster.

7Men have trained, or can train, every kind of animal or bird that lives and every kind of reptile and fish, 8but no human being can tame the tongue. It is always ready to pour out its deadly poison. 9Sometimes it praises our heavenly Father, and sometimes it breaks out into curses against men who are made like God. 10And so blessing and cursing come pouring out of the same mouth. Dear brothers, surely this is not right! 11Does a spring of water bubble out first with fresh water and then with bitter water? 12Can you pick olives from a fig tree, or figs from a grape vine? No, and you can't draw fresh water from a salty pool.

3. Genuine wisdom
Wisdom from heaven

3:14
Rom 13:13
3:15
Jas 1:17
3:16
1 Cor 3:3
3:17
Lk 6:36
Rom 12:9-11,18
2 Cor 6:6
Phil 1:11
Heb 12:10,11
Jas 2:13; 4:8
1 Jn 3:18-20

3:18
Prov 11:18
Mt 5:9

13If you are wise, live a life of steady goodness, so that only good deeds will pour forth. And if you don't brag about them, then you will be truly wise! 14And by all means don't brag about being wise and good if you are bitter and jealous and selfish; that is the worst sort of lie. 15For jealousy and selfishness are not God's kind of wisdom. Such things are earthly, unspiritual, inspired by the devil. 16For wherever there is jealousy or selfish ambition, there will be disorder and every other kind of evil.

17But the wisdom that comes from heaven is first of all pure and full of quiet gentleness. Then it is peace-loving and courteous. It allows discussion and is willing to yield to others; it is full of mercy and good deeds. It is wholehearted and straightforward and sincere. 18And those who are peacemakers will plant seeds of peace and reap a harvest of goodness.

SPEECH	When our speech is motivated by:	It is full of:
	Satan	Jealousy
		Selfishness
		Earthly concerns and desires
		Unspiritual thoughts and ideas
		Disorder
		Evil
	God and his wisdom	Mercy
		Love for others
		Peace
		Courtesy
		Yielding to others
		Sincerity, straightforwardness
		Quiet gentleness
		Goodness

3:6 James compares the damage the tongue can do to a raging fire—the tongue's wickedness has its source in hell itself. The uncontrolled tongue can do terrible damage. Satan uses the tongue to divide people and pit them against one another. Idle words are damaging because they spread destruction quickly, and no one can stop the results once they are spoken. A few words spoken in anger can destroy a relationship that took years to build. Before you speak, remember that words are like fire—you can neither control nor reverse the damage they can do.

3:7–12 If no human being can control the tongue, why bother trying? Because even if we do not achieve perfect control of it in this life, we can still learn enough control to reduce the damage it can do. It is better to fight a fire than to go around setting new ones! Remember that we are not fighting the tongue's fire in our own strength. The Holy Spirit will give us increasing power to monitor and control what we say. As Christians we are not perfect, but we should never stop growing.

3:9–12 Our contradictory speech often puzzles us. At times it is right and pleasing to God, but at other times it is violent and destructive. Which of these reflects our true identity? The tongue gives us a picture of our basic human nature. We are good—made in God's image; but we are also bad—fallen and sinful. God works to change us from the inside out. As the Holy Spirit purifies our hearts, he also gives us self-control so that we will speak words that please God.

3:13–18 Have you ever known anyone who claimed to be wise, but acted foolishly? True wisdom can be measured by the depth of one's character. As you can identify a tree by the type of fruit it produces, you can evaluate your wisdom by the way you act. Foolishness leads to disorder, but wisdom leads to peace and goodness.

Drawing near to God

4 What is causing the quarrels and fights among you? Isn't it because there is a whole army of evil desires within you? ²You want what you don't have, so you kill to get it. You long for what others have, and can't afford it, so you start a fight to take it away from them. And yet the reason you don't have what you want is that you don't ask God for it. ³And even when you do ask you don't get it because your whole aim is wrong—you want only what will give *you* pleasure.

⁴You are like an unfaithful wife who loves her husband's enemies. Don't you realize that making friends with God's enemies—the evil pleasures of this world—makes you an enemy of God? I say it again, that if your aim is to enjoy the evil pleasure of the unsaved world, you cannot also be a friend of God. ⁵Or what do you think the Scripture means when it says that the Holy Spirit, whom God has placed within us, watches over us with tender jealousy? ⁶But he gives us more and more strength to stand against all such evil longings. As the Scripture says, God gives strength to the humble, but sets himself against the proud and haughty.

⁷So give yourselves humbly to God. Resist the devil and he will flee from you. ⁸And when you draw close to God, God will draw close to you. Wash your hands, you sinners, and let your hearts be filled with God alone to make them pure and true to him. ⁹Let there be tears for the wrong things you have done. Let there be sorrow and sincere grief. Let there be sadness instead of laughter, and gloom instead of joy. ¹⁰Then when you realize your worthlessness before the Lord, he will lift you up, encourage and help you.

¹¹Don't criticize and speak evil about each other, dear brothers. If you do, you will be fighting against God's law of loving one another, declaring it is wrong. But your job is not to decide whether this law is right or wrong, but to obey it. ¹²Only he who made the law can rightly judge among us. He alone decides to save us or destroy. So what right do you have to judge or criticize others?

Trust God in making future plans

¹³Look here, you people who say, "Today or tomorrow we are going to such and

4:2
1 Jn 3:15

4:3
1 Jn 3:22; 5:14

4:4
Jn 15:19
1 Jn 2:15

4:5
1 Cor 6:19
2 Cor 6:16

4:6
Ps 138:6
Prov 3:34; 29:23
Mt 23:12
1 Pet 5:5

4:7
Rom 14:11
Eph 5:21
6:11,12
1 Pet 5:6,8,9

4:8
Ps 73:28
Isa 1:16; 55:6,7
Mt 15:2
1 Pet 3:21

4:9
Lk 6:25

4:11
Mt 7:1
2 Cor 12:20
Eph 4:31
2 Tim 3:3
1 Pet 2:1

4:12
Mt 10:28
Rom 2:1
14:4,13
Jas 5:9

4:1–3 Quarrels among believers are always harmful. James tells us that these quarrels result from evil desires within us—we want more possessions, more money, higher status, more recognition. When we want badly enough to fulfill these desires, we fight in order to do so. Instead of aggressively grabbing what we want, we should ask God to help us get rid of our selfish desires and trust him to give us what we really need.

4:2, 3 James mentions the most common problems in prayer: not asking, asking for the wrong things, asking for the wrong reasons. Do you talk to God at all? When you do, what do you talk about? Do you ask only to satisfy your desires? Do you seek God's approval for what you already plan to do? Our prayers will become powerful when we allow God to change our desires so that they perfectly correspond to his will for us (1 John 3:21, 22).

4:3, 4 There is nothing wrong with wanting a pleasurable life. God gives us good gifts that he wants us to enjoy (1:17; Ephesians 4:7; 1 Timothy 4:4, 5). But it is wrong to seek pleasure at others' expense or at the expense of obeying God. Pleasure that keeps us from pleasing God is sinful; pleasure in God's rich bounty is good.

4:4–6 The cure for evil desires is humility (see Proverbs 16:18, 19; 1 Peter 5:5, 6). Pride makes us self-centered and leads us to conclude we deserve all we can see, touch, or imagine. It creates greedy appetites for far more than we need. The antidote to self-centered desires is to humble ourselves before God, realizing that we need nothing except his approval. When his Holy Spirit fills us, we realize that the things we have coveted are only cheap substitutes for what God has to offer.

4:7 Although God and Satan are at war, we don't need to wait until the end to see who will win. God has *already* defeated Satan (Colossians 2:13–15; Revelation 12:10–12), and when Christ returns, Satan and all he stands for will be eliminated forever

(Revelation 20:10–15). Satan is here now, however, and he is trying to win us over to his evil cause. With the Holy Spirit in our lives, we can resist Satan and he will flee from us.

4:8 How can you draw close to God? James gives five suggestions: (1) "Give yourselves humbly to God" (4:7). Realize that you need his forgiveness, and be willing to follow him. (2) "Resist the devil" (4:7). Don't allow him to entice and tempt you. (3) "Wash your hands" (that is, lead a pure life) and "let your hearts be filled with God" (4:8). Be cleansed from sin, replacing it with God's purity. (4) Let there be tears, sorrow, and sincere grief for your sins (4:9). Don't be afraid to express deep heartfelt sorrow for them. (5) "Realize your worthlessness" (4:10). Humble yourself before God, and he will lift you up (1 Peter 5:6).

4:10 "Realize your worthlessness" can also be translated, "Humble yourselves before the Lord." Humbling ourselves means recognizing that our worth comes from God alone. We do not deserve his favor, but he reaches out to us in love and gives us worth and dignity, despite our human shortcomings.

4:11, 12 Jesus summarized the law as love to God and neighbor (Matthew 22:37–40), and Paul said love demonstrated towards a neighbor fully satisfies the law (Romans 13:6–10). When we fail to love, we are actually breaking God's law. Examine your attitudes and actions toward others. Do you build people up or tear them down? When you're ready to criticize someone, remember God's law of love and say something good about him or her instead. If you make this a habit, your tendency to find fault with others will diminish and your ability to obey God's law will increase.

4:13–16 It is good to have goals, but goals can disappoint us if we leave God out of them. There is no point in making plans as though God does not exist, because the future is in his hands. What would you like to be doing ten years from now? One year

4:14
Ps 102:3

4:16
1 Cor 4:7,8; 5:6

4:17
Lk 12:47,48
Rom 2:17-23

such a town, stay there a year, and open up a profitable business." ¹⁴How do you know what is going to happen tomorrow? For the length of your lives is as uncertain as the morning fog—now you see it; soon it is gone. ¹⁵What you ought to say is, "If the Lord wants us to, we shall live and do this or that." ¹⁶Otherwise you will be bragging about your own plans, and such self-confidence never pleases God.

¹⁷Remember, too, that knowing what is right to do and then not doing it is sin.

Warning to the rich

5:1
Prov 11:4,28
Isa 13:6
Zeph 1:18
Mt 19:23,24
Lk 6:24

5:4
Ex 2:23,24
Lev 19:13
Deut 24:14,15
Ps 9:12
Jer 22:13

5 Look here, you rich men, now is the time to cry and groan with anguished grief because of all the terrible troubles ahead of you. ²Your wealth is even now rotting away, and your fine clothes are becoming mere moth-eaten rags. ³The value of your gold and silver is dropping fast, yet it will stand as evidence against you, and eat your flesh like fire. That is what you have stored up for yourselves, to receive on that coming day of judgment. ⁴For listen! Hear the cries of the field workers whom you have cheated of their pay. Their cries have reached the ears of the Lord of Hosts.

FAITH THAT WORKS

James offers a larger number of similarities to the Sermon on the Mount than any other book in the New Testament. James relied heavily on Jesus' teachings.

Lesson	Reference
When your life is full of difficulties and persecutions, be happy. A reward awaits you.	James 1:2 Matthew 5:10–12
You are to be perfect, strong in character, full and complete.	James 1:4 Matthew 5:48
Ask God and he will answer.	James 1:5; 5:15 Matthew 7:7–12
Those who are humble, who don't amount to much by the world's standards, should be very glad.	James 1:9 Matthew 5:3
Watch out for your anger . . . it can be dangerous.	James 1:20 Matthew 5:22
Be merciful to others, as God is merciful to you.	James 2:13 Matthew 5:7; 6:14
Your faith must prove itself by helping others.	James 2:14–16 Matthew 7:21–23
Happy are those who strive for peace; peacemakers plant seeds of peace and reap a harvest of goodness.	James 3:17, 18 Matthew 5:9
You cannot serve God *and* money, pleasures, or evil. Friendship with evil makes you an enemy of God.	James 4:4 Matthew 6:24
When we humble ourselves and realize our need for God, he will come to us and encourage us.	James 4:10 Matthew 5:3, 4
Don't criticize or speak evil of others; it works against God's command to love one another.	James 4:11 Matthew 7:1, 2
Treasures on earth will only erode and disappear—we must store eternal treasures in heaven.	James 5:2 Matthew 6:19
Be patient in suffering, as God's prophets were patient.	James 5:10 Matthew 5:12
Be honest in your speech so you can say a simple "yes" or "no" and always be trusted.	James 5:12 Matthew 5:33–37

---

from now? Tomorrow? How will you react if God steps in and rearranges your plans? Plan ahead, but hang on to your plans lightly. If you put God's desires at the center of your planning, you will not be disappointed.

4:14 Life is short no matter how long we live. Don't be deceived into thinking you have lots of remaining time to live for Christ, to enjoy your loved ones, or to do what you know you should. Live for God today! Then, no matter when your life ends, you will have fulfilled God's plan for you.

4:17 We tend to think that *doing* wrong is sin. But James tells us that sin is also *not* doing right. (These two kinds of sin are sometimes called sins of commission and sins of omission.) It is a sin to lie; it can also be a sin to know the truth and not tell it. It is a sin to speak evil of someone; it is also a sin to avoid him when you

know he needs your friendship. We should be willing to help as the Holy Spirit guides us. We should also pray that we do not sin by neglecting to do what is good and right.

5:1–6 James proclaims the worthlessness of riches, not the worthlessness of the rich. Today's money will be worthless when Christ returns, so we should spend our time accumulating treasures that will be worthwhile in God's eternal Kingdom. Money itself is not the problem; Christian leaders need money to live and support their families; missionaries need money to help them spread the gospel; churches need money to do their work effectively. It is the *love* of money that leads to evil (1 Timothy 6:10). This is a warning to all Christians who are tempted to adopt worldly standards rather than God's standards (Romans 12:1, 2). Also read Matthew 6:19–21 to see what Jesus says about riches.

[5]You have spent your years here on earth having fun, satisfying your every whim, and now your fat hearts are ready for the slaughter. [6]You have condemned and killed good men who had no power to defend themselves against you.

Patience in suffering

[7]Now as for you, dear brothers who are waiting for the Lord's return, be patient, like a farmer who waits until the autumn for his precious harvest to ripen. [8]Yes, be patient. And take courage, for the coming of the Lord is near.

[9]Don't grumble about each other, brothers. Are you yourselves above criticism? For see! The great Judge is coming. He is almost here. [Let him do whatever criticizing must be done.]

[10]For examples of patience in suffering, look at the Lord's prophets. [11]We know how happy they are now because they stayed true to him then, even though they suffered greatly for it. Job is an example of a man who continued to trust the Lord in sorrow; from his experiences we can see how the Lord's plan finally ended in good, for he is full of tenderness and mercy.

[12]But most of all, dear brothers, do not swear either by heaven or earth or anything else; just say a simple yes or no, so that you will not sin and be condemned for it.

Faithful prayer

[13]Is anyone among you suffering? He should keep on praying about it. And those who have reason to be thankful should continually be singing praises to the Lord. [14]Is anyone sick? He should call for the elders of the church and they should pray over him and pour a little oil upon him, calling on the Lord to heal him. [15]And their prayer, if offered in faith, will heal him, for the Lord will make him well; and if his sickness was caused by some sin, the Lord will forgive him.

[16]Admit your faults to one another and pray for each other so that you may be

5:9 *Let him do whatever criticizing must be done,* implied.

5:5
Lk 16:19
5:6
Jas 4:2
5:7
2 Pet 3:4-13
5:8
Rom 8:25; 13:11
Heb 10:25-37
5:9
1 Cor 4:5
Jas 4:12
5:10
Jer 2:30
Mt 5:11,12
5:11
Job 1:20-22
2:7-10
Rom 2:4
5:12
Mt 5:33-37
23:16-22
5:13
Lk 22:44
Col 3:16,17
5:14
Mk 6:13
Tit 1:5
5:15
Mt 21:22
Mk 16:18
Jas 1:6
5:16
Mt 18:15-18
1Jn 1:9

5:6 The defenseless people James mentions here are probably poor laborers. The poor who could not pay their debts were thrown in prison or forced to sell all their possessions, and at times, even sell their family members into slavery. With no opportunity to work off their debts, poor people often died of starvation. God called this murder.

5:7, 8 The farmer must wait patiently for his crops to grow, he cannot hurry the process. But he does not take the summer off and hope that all goes well in the fields. There is much work to do to ensure a good harvest. In the same way, we must wait patiently for Christ's return. We cannot make Christ return any sooner, but while we wait there is much work we can do to advance God's Kingdom. Both the farmer and the Christian must live by faith, looking toward the future reward for their labors. Don't live as if Christ will never come. Work faithfully to build his Kingdom, for the King *will* come when the time is ripe.

5:9 When things go wrong, we tend to blame others for our miseries (see the note on Genesis 3:12, 13). Blaming others is easier than owning our share of the responsibility, but it is both destructive and sinful. Before you judge others for their shortcomings, remember that Christ the Judge will come to evaluate each of us (Matthew 7:1–5). He will not let us get away with shifting the blame to others.

5:10, 11 For more on the topic of suffering, see the notes on Job 1:1ff; 2:10; 3:23–26; 4:7, 8; 23:14; 42:17; and Job's Profile in Job 2.

5:12 A person with a reputation for exaggeration or lying often can't get anyone to believe him on his word alone. Christians should never become like that. Always be honest so that others will believe your simple yes or no. By avoiding lies, half-truths, and omissions of the truth, you will become known as a trustworthy person.

5:14, 15 Here James is talking about someone who is

incapacitated physically. In Scripture, oil was both a medicine (see the parable of the Good Samaritan in Luke 10:30–37) and a symbol of the Spirit of God (as used in anointing kings, see 1 Samuel 16:1–13). Thus oil can represent both the medical and the spiritual spheres of life. Christians should not separate the physical and the spiritual—Jesus Christ is Lord over both the body and the spirit.

5:14, 15 People in the church are not alone. Members of Christ's body should be able to count on others for support and prayer, especially when they are sick or suffering. The elders should be on call to respond to the weakness of any member, and the church should stay alert to pray for the needs of all its members. Prayer, especially corporate prayer, is essential to the life of the church.

5:15 "And their prayer, if offered in faith," does not refer to the faith of the sick person, but to the faith of the church. God heals, faith doesn't, and all prayers are subject to God's will. But our prayers are part of God's healing process. That is why God often waits for our prayers of faith before intervening to heal a person.

5:16 "Admit your faults" can be translated "Confess your sins." Christ has made it possible for us to go directly to God for forgiveness, but confessing our sins to one another still has an important place in the life of the church. (1) If we have sinned against an individual, we must ask him or her to forgive us. (2) If our sin has affected the church, we must confess it publicly. (3) If we need loving support as we struggle with a sin, we should confess it to those who are able to provide that support. (4) If, after confessing a private sin to God, we still don't feel his forgiveness, we may wish to confess that sin to a fellow believer and hear him or her assure us of God's pardon. In Christ's Kingdom, every believer is a priest to other believers (1 Peter 2:9). This means we are charged with helping others come to Christ and telling other's of Christ's words of forgiveness.

healed. The earnest prayer of a righteous man has great power and wonderful results. [17]Elijah was as completely human as we are, and yet when he prayed earnestly that no rain would fall, none fell for the next three and one half years! [18]Then he prayed again, this time that it *would* rain, and down it poured and the grass turned green and the gardens began to grow again.

5:17
1 Kgs 17:1-7
18:36-39
Lk 4:25

Restore wandering believers

[19]Dear brothers, if anyone has slipped away from God and no longer trusts the Lord and someone helps him understand the Truth again, [20]that person who brings him back to God will have saved a wandering soul from death, bringing about the forgiveness of his many sins.

Sincerely, James

5:19
Prov 19:27
Mt 18:15
1 Tim 6:10
2 Pet 3:17

5:16–18 The Christian's most powerful resource is communion with God through prayer. The results are often greater than we thought were possible. Some people see prayer as a last resort to be tried when all else fails. This is backwards. Prayer should come first. Since God's power is infinitely greater than our own, it only makes sense to rely on it—especially because he encourages us to do so.

5:17 For more about the great prophet Elijah, read his Profile in 1 Kings 18.

5:19, 20 Clearly the person who has slipped away is a believer who has fallen into sin—one who is no longer living a life consistent with his beliefs. Christians disagree over whether or not it is possible for people to lose their salvation, but all agree that those who move away from their faith are in serious trouble and need to repent. James urges Christians to help backsliders return to God. We can do this by taking the initiative, praying for the person, and acting in love to meet the person where he is and bring him back to God.

5:20 The book of James emphasizes faith in action. Right living is the evidence and result of faith. The church must serve with compassion, speak lovingly and truthfully, live in obedience to God's commands, and love one another. The body of believers ought to be an example of heaven on earth, drawing people to Christ through love for God and one another. If we truly believe God's Word, we will *live* it day by day. God's Word is not merely something we read or think about, but something we do. Belief, faith, and trust must have hands and feet—ours!

1 PETER

VITAL STATISTICS

PURPOSE:
To offer encouragement to suffering Christians

AUTHOR:
Peter

TO WHOM WRITTEN:
Jewish Christians who had been driven out of Jerusalem and scattered throughout Asia Minor, and to all believers everywhere

DATE WRITTEN:
About A.D. 62–64 from Rome

SETTING:
Peter was probably in Rome when the great persecution under Emperor Nero began. (Peter was eventually executed during this persecution.) Throughout the Roman Empire, Christians were being tortured and killed for their faith, and the church in Jerusalem was being scattered throughout the Mediterranean world.

KEY VERSE:
"These trials are only to test your faith, to see whether or not it is strong and pure . . ." (1:7).

KEY PEOPLE:
Peter, Silvanus, Mark

KEY PLACES:
Jerusalem, Rome, and the regions of Pontus, Galatia, Cappadocia, Asia Minor, and Bithynia

SPECIAL FEATURES:
Peter used several images that were very special to him because Jesus had used them when he revealed certain truths to Peter. Peter's name (which means "stone") had been given to him by Jesus. Peter's conception of the church—a spiritual house composed of living stones built upon Christ as the foundation—came from Christ. Jesus encouraged Peter to care for the church as a shepherd tending the flock. Thus, it is not surprising to see Peter using living stones (2:5–9) and shepherds and sheep (2:25; 5:2, 4) to describe the church.

CRUSHED, overwhelmed, devastated, torn— these feelings wash over those who suffer, blinding all vision of hope, threatening to destroy them. Suffering has many forms—physical abuse, debilitating disease, social ostracism, persecution. The pain and anguish tempt one to surrender and give in.

Many first-century Christians suffered because they believed in Jesus Christ. Christians were beaten (Acts 16:16–40), stoned to death (Acts 8:54–60), put in jail and executed (Acts 12:1–5), and many were fed to lions. Apostles were not immune from such suffering. Peter was put in jail and beaten several times (see Acts 4:1–22; 5:12–42).

Peter wrote this epistle to the Jewish Christians scattered throughout Asia Minor who were suffering for their faith in Christ. He comforts them and urges them to remain faithful to Christ in the midst of their trials.

Peter begins by thanking God for salvation (1:2–6). He explains to his readers that trials will refine their faith (1:7–9). They should believe in spite of their circumstances; for many in past ages believed in God's plan of salvation—even the prophets of old who wrote about it, but didn't understand it. But now salvation has been revealed in Christ (1:10–13).

In response to such a great salvation, Peter commands his readers to live holy lives (1:14–16), to reverently fear and trust God (1:17–21), to be honest and loving in their relationships with others (2:1–3a), and to become like Christ (2:3b–4).

Jesus Christ, the "precious Cornerstone" upon whom the church is to be built (2:5, 6), is also the "Stone that was rejected," causing those who "will not listen to God's Word" to fall (2:7, 8). But the church, built upon this Stone, is to be God's holy priesthood (2:9, 10).

Peter then explains how believers should live during difficult times (2:11—4:11). Christians should be above reproach (2:12–17), imitating Christ in all their social roles—masters and servants, husbands and wives, church members and neighbors (2:18—3:17). Jesus Christ should be our model for obedience to God in the midst of great suffering (3:18—4:11).

Peter then outlines the right attitude to have when persecution comes: expect it (4:12), be thankful for the privilege of suffering for Christ (4:13–18), and trust God for deliverance (4:19).

Next, Peter gives some special instructions—elders should feed God's flock (5:1–4), younger men should follow the leadership of the elders (5:5, 6), and everyone should trust God and resist Satan (5:7–11).

Peter concludes by introducing Silvanus and by giving personal greetings from himself, the church in Rome, and Mark (5:12–14).

When you suffer for doing what is right, remember that following Christ is a costly commitment. When you are persecuted for your faith, rejoice that you have been counted worthy to suffer for Christ. He suffered for us; as his followers, we should expect nothing less. As you read 1 Peter, remember that trials will come to refine your faith. When they come, remain faithful to God.

THE BLUEPRINT

1. God's great blessings to his people (1:1—2:10)
2. The conduct of God's people in the midst of suffering (2:11—4:19)
3. The shepherding of God's people in the midst of suffering (5:1–14)

Peter wrote to Jewish Christians who were experiencing persecution for their faith. He wrote to comfort them with the hope of eternal life and to challenge them to continue living holy lives. Those who suffer for being Christians become partners with Christ in his suffering. As we suffer, we must remember that Christ is both our hope in the midst of suffering and our example of how to endure suffering faithfully.

MEGATHEMES

THEME	EXPLANATION	IMPORTANCE
Salvation	Our salvation is a gracious gift from God. God chose us out of his love for us, Jesus died to pay the penalty for our sin, and the Holy Spirit cleansed us from sin when we believed. Eternal life is a wonderful privilege for those who trust in Christ.	Our safety and security are in God. If we experience joy in relationship with Christ now, how much greater will our joy be when he returns and we see him face to face. Such a hope should motivate us to serve Christ with greater commitment.
Persecution	Peter offers faithful believers comfort and hope. We should expect ridicule, rejection, and suffering because we are Christians. Persecution makes us stronger because it refines our faith. We can face persecution victoriously as Christ did, if we rely on him.	Christians still suffer for what they believe. We should expect persecution, but we don't have to be terrified by it. The fact that we will live eternally with Christ should give us the confidence, patience, and hope to stand firm even when we are persecuted.
God's Family	We are privileged to belong to God's family, a community with Christ as the Founder and Foundation. Everyone in this community is related—we are all brothers and sisters, loved equally by God.	Because Christ is the foundation of our family, we must be devoted, loyal, and faithful to him. By obeying him, we show that we are his children. We must accept the challenge to live differently from the society around us.
Family Life	Peter encouraged the wives of unbelievers to submit to their husbands' authority as a means to winning them to Christ. He urged all family members to treat others with sympathy, love, tenderness, and humility.	We must treat our families lovingly. Though it's never easy, willing service is the best way to influence loved ones. To gain the strength we need for self-discipline and submission, pray for God's help.
Judgment	God will judge everyone with perfect justice. We all will face God. He will punish evildoers and those who persecute God's people. Those who love him will be rewarded with life forever in his presence.	Because all are accountable to God, we can leave judgment of others to him. We must not hate or resent those who persecute us. We should realize that we will be held responsible for how we live each day.

1. God's great blessings to his people

1 *From:* Peter, Jesus Christ's missionary.

To: The Jewish Christians driven out of Jerusalem and scattered throughout Pontus, Galatia, Cappadocia, Asia Minor, and Bithynia.

1:1
Acts 2:9,10
6:9; 16:6,7
Gal 1:2

The hope of eternal life

²Dear friends, God the Father chose you long ago and knew you would become

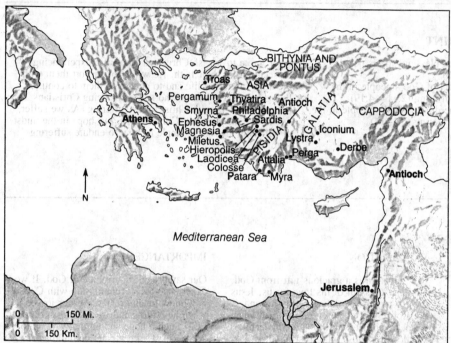

THE CHURCHES OF PETER'S LETTER Peter addressed his letter to the churches located through Bithynia, Pontus, Asia, Galatia, and Cappadocia. Paul had evangelized many of these areas; others had churches that were begun by the Jews who were in Jerusalem on the day of Pentecost and heard Peter's powerful sermon (see Acts 2:9–11).

1:1 Peter wrote this letter to encourage and strengthen believers who were facing trials and persecution. During most of the first century, persecution was not the rule throughout the Roman Empire. Soldiers were not searching for Christians and torturing them. Christians, however, could expect trials. All would be misunderstood; some would be harassed; a few would be tortured and even put to death. Christians faced persecution from three sources: the Romans, the Jews, and their own families.

The legal status of Christians in the Roman Empire was unclear. Many Romans still thought of Christians as a Jewish sect; and since the Jewish religion was legal, they considered Christianity legal also—as long as Christians went along with the empire's laws. However, if Christians refused to worship the emperor or join the army, or if they were involved in civil disturbances (such as the one in Ephesus recorded in Acts 19:23ff), they might be punished by the civil authorities.

Many Jews did not appreciate being legally associated with Christians. As the book of Acts frequently records, they harmed Christians physically, drove them out of town, or attempted to turn Roman officials against them. Saul, later the great apostle Paul, was an early Jewish persecutor of Christians.

Another source of persecution was the Christian's own family. Under Roman law, the head of the household had absolute authority over all its members. Unless the ruling male became a Christian, the wife, children and servants who were believers might well face extreme hardship. If they were sent away, they would have no place to turn but the church; if they were beaten, no court of law would uphold their interests.

The book of 1 Peter may have been written especially for new Christians and those planning to be baptized. They needed to be warned about what lay ahead, and they needed Peter's

encouraging words to help them face it. This letter is still helpful for new Christians or any Christians facing trials. Many Christians around the world are living under secular governments more repressive than the Roman Empire of the first century. Christians everywhere are subject to misunderstanding, ridicule, and even harassment by unbelieving friends, employers, and family members. And none of us is exempt from catastrophe, pain, illness, and death—trials that, like persecution, make us draw heavily on God's grace. For today's readers, as well as for Peter's original audience, the theme of this letter is *hope.*

1:1 Peter was one of the 12 disciples chosen by Jesus (Mark 1:16–18; John 1:42) and, with James and John, was part of the inner group Jesus singled out for special training and fellowship. Peter was one of the first to recognize Jesus as the Messiah, God's Son; and Jesus gave him a special leadership role in the church (Matthew 16:16–19; Luke 22:31, 32; John 21:15–19). Although during Jesus' trial Peter denied knowing Jesus, he repented and became a great apostle. For more information on Peter, see his Profile in Matthew 27.

1:1 The first believers and leaders of the early church were Jews. When they became Christians, they didn't give up their Jewish heritage, just as we didn't give up our nationalities when we became Christians. Because of persecution, these believers had been scattered throughout the Roman world (this scattering is mentioned in Acts 8:1–4). Persecution didn't quench the gospel; instead, it introduced it to the whole empire. Thus the churches to which Peter wrote probably included Gentile Christians as well.

1:2 Peter encouraged his readers by this strong declaration that they were *chosen* by God the Father and were his children. At one

1:3
Tit 3:5
Jas 1:18
1 Pet 1:13,23
1 Jn 3:3

1:4
Acts 20:32
Col 3:24
2 Tim 4:8
Heb 11:16

1:5
Jn 10:28
Phil 4:7
2 Thess 2:13
1 Pet 4:13

1:6
Mt 5:12
Rom 5:2
Jas 1:2
1 Pet 3:17; 4:12

1:7
Job 23:10
Prov 17:3
Isa 48:10
Jas 1:3

1:8
Jn 20:29
Eph 3:19
1 Jn 4:2

1:10
Gen 49:10
Hag 2:7
Mt 13:17; 26:24
Col 3:4

1:11
Ps 22:6
Mt 26:24
Rom 8:9
2 Pet 1:21

1:12
Acts 2:2-4
Eph 3:10
Heb 11:39

his children. And the Holy Spirit has been at work in your hearts, cleansing you with the blood of Jesus Christ and making you to please him. May God bless you richly and grant you increasing freedom from all anxiety and fear.

³All honor to God, the God and Father of our Lord Jesus Christ; for it is his boundless mercy that has given us the privilege of being born again, so that we are now members of God's own family. Now we live in the hope of eternal life because Christ rose again from the dead. ⁴And God has reserved for his children the priceless gift of eternal life; it is kept in heaven for you, pure and undefiled, beyond the reach of change and decay. ⁵And God, in his mighty power, will make sure that you get there safely to receive it, because you are trusting him. It will be yours in that coming last day for all to see. ⁶So be truly glad! There is wonderful joy ahead, even though the going is rough for a while down here.

⁷These trials are only to test your faith, to see whether or not it is strong and pure. It is being tested as fire tests gold and purifies it—and your faith is far more precious to God than mere gold; so if your faith remains strong after being tried in the test tube of fiery trials, it will bring you much praise and glory and honor on the day of his return.

⁸You love him even though you have never seen him; though not seeing him, you trust him; and even now you are happy with the inexpressible joy that comes from heaven itself. ⁹And your further reward for trusting him will be the salvation of your souls.

¹⁰This salvation was something the prophets did not fully understand. Though they wrote about it, they had many questions as to what it all could mean. ¹¹They wondered what the Spirit of Christ within them was talking about, for he told them to write down the events which, since then, have happened to Christ: his suffering, and his great glory afterwards. And they wondered when and to whom all this would happen.

¹²They were finally told that these things would not occur during their lifetime,

---

time, only the nation of Israel could claim to be God's chosen people; but through Christ, all believers—Jews, former Jews, and Gentiles—belong to God. Our salvation and security rest in the free and merciful choice of the almighty God; no trials or persecutions can rob us of the eternal life he gives to those who believe in him.

1:2 This verse mentions all three members of the Godhead—God the Father, God the Son, and God the Holy Spirit. All three work as one to bring about our salvation. The Father chose us before we chose him (Ephesians 1:4). The Son died for us while we were still sinners (Romans 5:6–10). The Holy Spirit works in our lives to bring us salvation and to set us apart for God's pleasure.

1:3 The term *born again* refers to spiritual birth—the Holy Spirit's act of bringing believers into God's family. Jesus used this term when he explained salvation to Nicodemus (see John 3).

1:3–6 Do you need encouragement? Peter's words offer joy and hope in times of trouble, and he bases his confidence on what God has done for us in Christ Jesus. We're called to *live* in the hope of eternal life (1:3). Our hope is not only for the future: eternal life begins when we believe in God and join his family. The eternal life we now have gives us hope and enables us to live with confidence in God.

1:5 God will help us remain true to our faith, whatever difficult times we must face. The "coming last day" is the Judgment Day of Christ described in Romans 14:10 and Revelation 20:11–15. We may have to endure trials, persecution, or violent death, but our souls cannot be harmed if we have accepted Christ's gift of salvation. We know we will receive the promised rewards.

1:7 Why were Christians the target of persecution? (1) They refused to worship the emperor as a god and thus were viewed as atheists and traitors. (2) They refused to worship at pagan temples, so business for these money-making enterprises dropped wherever Christianity took hold. (3) They didn't support the Roman

ideals of self, power, and conquest; and the Romans scorned the Christian ideal of self-sacrificing service. (4) They exposed and rejected the horrible immorality of pagan culture.

1:7 Peter mentions suffering several times in this letter: 1:6, 7; 3:13–17; 4:12–19; 5:9. When he speaks of trials, he is not talking about natural disasters or God's punishments, but the response of an unbelieving world to people of faith. All believers face such trials when they let their light shine into the darkness. We must accept trials as part of the refining process that burns away impurities, preparing us to meet Christ. Trials teach us patience (Romans 5:3, 4; James 1:2, 3) and help us grow to be the kind of people God wants us to be.

1:7 As gold is heated, impurities float to the top and can be skimmed off. Steel is tempered or strengthened by heating it in fire. Likewise, our trials, struggles, and persecutions strengthen our faith and make us useful to God.

1:10–13 Although the plan of salvation was a mystery to the Old Testament prophets, they still suffered persecution and some died for God. Some Jewish Christians reading Peter's letter, by contrast, had seen Jesus for themselves and knew why he came. They based their assurance on Jesus' death and resurrection. With their firsthand knowledge and personal experience of Jesus, their faith should have been even stronger than that of the Old Testament prophets.

1:11 The Spirit of Christ is another name for the Holy Spirit. Before Jesus left his ministry on earth to return to heaven, he promised to send his Holy Spirit, the Comforter, to teach, help, and guide his followers (John 14:15–17, 26; 16:7). The Holy Spirit would tell them all about Jesus and reveal his glory (John 15:26; 16:14). The Old Testament prophets, writing under the Holy Spirit's inspiration (2 Peter 1:20, 21), described the coming Messiah; the New Testament apostles, through the inspiration of the same Spirit, preached the crucified and risen Lord.

but long years later, during yours. And now at last this Good News has been plainly announced to all of us. It was preached to us in the power of the same heaven-sent Holy Spirit who spoke to them; and it is all so strange and wonderful that even the angels in heaven would give a great deal to know more about it.

13So now you can look forward soberly and intelligently to more of God's kindness to you when Jesus Christ returns.

1:13
1 Cor 1:7
1 Thess 5:6

A call to holy living

14Obey God because you are his children; don't slip back into your old ways—doing evil because you knew no better. 15But be holy now in everything you do, just as the Lord is holy, who invited you to be his child. 16He himself has said, "You must be holy, for I am holy."

1:14
Rom 12:2
Eph 4:18
1 Pet 1:2; 4:2

1:15
2 Cor 7:1
1 Thess 4:7
1 Jn 3:3

17And remember that your heavenly Father to whom you pray has no favorites when he judges. He will judge you with perfect justice for everything you do; so act in reverent fear of him from now on until you get to heaven. 18God paid a ransom to save you from the impossible road to heaven which your fathers tried to take, and the ransom he paid was not mere gold or silver, as you very well know. 19But he paid for you with the precious lifeblood of Christ, the sinless, spotless Lamb of God. 20God chose him for this purpose long before the world began, but only recently was he brought into public view, in these last days, as a blessing to you.

1:16
Lev 11:44,45

1:17
Deut 10:17
Ps 89:26

1:18
Isa 52:3

1:19
Ex 12:5
Jn 1:29
Heb 9:14

21Because of this, your trust can be in God who raised Christ from the dead and gave him great glory. Now your faith and hope can rest in him alone. 22Now you can have real love for everyone because your souls have been cleansed from selfishness and hatred when you trusted Christ to save you; so see to it that you really do love each other warmly, with all your hearts.

1:20
Gal 4:4
2 Tim 1:9,10

1:21
Rom 4:24

1:22
Jn 13:34
Rom 12:10

23For you have a new life. It was not passed on to you from your parents, for the life they gave you will fade away. This new one will last forever, for it comes from Christ, God's ever-living Message to men. 24Yes, our natural lives will fade as grass does when it becomes all brown and dry. All our greatness is like a flower that droops and falls; 25but the Word of the Lord will last forever. And his message is the Good News that was preached to you.

1:23
Jn 1:13; 3:3

1:24
Isa 40:6-8

1:25
Isa 40:8

2 So get rid of your feelings of hatred. Don't just pretend to be good! Be done with dishonesty and jealousy and talking about others behind their backs.

2:1
Eph 4:22,25,31

1:14–16 The God of Israel and of the Christian church is holy—he sets the standard for morality. Unlike the Roman gods, he is not warlike, adulterous, or spiteful. Unlike the gods of the pagan cults popular in the first century, he is not bloodthirsty or promiscuous. He is a God of mercy and justice who cares personally for each of his followers. Our holy God expects us to imitate him by having high moral standards for ourselves. Like him, we should be both merciful and just; like him, we should sacrifice ourselves for others.

1:15, 16 After people commit their lives to Christ, they still feel a pull back to their old ways. Peter tells us to be like our heavenly Father—holy in everything we do. Holiness means being totally devoted or dedicated to God, set aside for his special use, and set apart from sin and its influence. We're to be set apart and different, not blending in with the crowd, yet not being different just for the sake of being different. What makes us different are God's qualities in our lives. Our focus and priorities must be his. All this is in direct contrast to our old ways (1:14). We cannot become holy on our own, but God gives us his Holy Spirit to help us obey and to give us power to overcome sin. Don't use the excuse that you can't help slipping into sin. Call on God's power to free you from sin's grip.

1:17 Reverent fear is not the fear of a slave for a ruthless master, but the healthy respect of a believer for the all-powerful God. Because God is the judge of all the earth, we dare not ignore him or treat him casually. We should not assume that our privileged status as God's children gives us freedom to do whatever we want. We should not be spoiled children, but grateful children who love to show respect for our heavenly Father.

1:18, 19 A ransom is money paid to buy freedom for a slave. God paid a ransom to free us from the tyranny of sin (Romans 6:6, 7; 1 Corinthians 6:20; Colossians 2:13, 14; Hebrews 9:12). We could not escape from sin on our own; only the life of God's Son could free us. In Mark 10:45, Jesus says that he is our ransom.

1:20 Christ's sacrifice for our sins was not an afterthought, not something God decided to do when the world got out of control. This plan was set in motion by the all-knowing, eternal God long before the world was created. What a blessing it must have been to Jewish believers to know that Christ's coming and his work of salvation were planned by God long before the world began. This assured them that the law was not being scrapped because it didn't work, but that both the law and the coming of Christ were part of God's eternal plan.

1:22 Real love involves selfless giving; therefore, a self-centered person can't truly love. God's love and forgiveness free us to take our eyes off ourselves and to meet others' needs. By sacrificing his life, Christ showed that he truly loved you. Now you can love others by following his example and giving of yourself sacrificially.

1:24, 25 Quoting Isaiah 40:6–8, Peter reminds the believers that everything in this life—possessions, accomplishments, people—will eventually fade away and disappear. Only God's will, Word, and work are permanent. We must stop grasping the temporary and focus our time, money, and energy on the permanent—the Word of God and our new, eternal life in Christ.

2:2
Mt 18:3; 19:14
Eph 4:15
Heb 6:5

2, 3Now that you realize how kind the Lord has been to you, put away all evil, deception, envy, and fraud. Long to grow up into the fullness of your salvation; cry for this as a baby cries for his milk.

Living building stones for God's house

2:4
1 Pet 2:7

4Come to Christ, who is the living Foundation of Rock upon which God builds; though men have spurned him, he is very precious to God who has chosen him above all others.

2:5
Isa 61:6; 66:21
Eph 2:21
1 Tim 3:15
Heb 13:12
Rev 1:6

5And now you have become living building-stones for God's use in building his house. What's more, you are his holy priests; so come to him—[you who are acceptable to him because of Jesus Christ]—and offer to God those things that please him. 6As the Scriptures express it, "See, I am sending Christ to be the carefully chosen, precious Cornerstone of my church, and I will never disappoint those who trust in him."

2:6
Isa 28:16
Rom 9:32,33
Eph 2:20

2:7
Ps 118:22
Mt 21:42

7Yes, he is very precious to you who believe; and to those who reject him, well—"The same Stone that was rejected by the builders has become the Cornerstone, the most honored and important part of the building." 8And the Scriptures also say, "He is the Stone that some will stumble over, and the Rock that will make them fall." They will stumble because they will not listen to God's Word, nor obey it, and so this punishment must follow—that they will fall.

2:8
Isa 8:14
Lk 2:34,35
1 Cor 1:23
Gal 5:11

2:9
Ex 19:6
Deut 7:6; 10:15
Isa 43:20
Acts 26:18
1 Pet 2:5
Rev 1:6

9But you are not like that, for you have been chosen by God himself—you are priests of the King, you are holy and pure, you are God's very own—all this so that you may show to others how God called you out of the darkness into his wonderful light. 10Once you were less than nothing; now you are God's own. Once you knew very little of God's kindness; now your very lives have been changed by it.

2:10
Hos 1:10; 2:23
Rom 9:25; 10:19

2:2, 3 An alternative paraphrase of these verses could read: "If you have tasted the Lord's goodness and kindness, cry for more, as a baby cries for milk. Eat God's Word—read it, think about it—and grow strong in the Lord and be saved." **2:5** *because of Jesus Christ,* implied.

2:2, 3 One characteristic all children share is that they want to grow up, to be like the big kids or their parents. When we are born again, we are spiritual babies. If we are healthy, we will yearn to grow. How sad when we are satisfied to stay where we are as months and years roll by. Crying for milk is a natural instinct for a baby; an adult may have to learn to long for spiritual nourishment. Once we see our need and begin to find comfort and fulfillment in Christ, however, our spiritual appetite will increase and we will start to mature. How strong is your desire to grow spiritually? What spiritual food can you take today?

2:4-8 In describing the church as God's building, Peter draws on several Old Testament texts familiar to his Jewish Christian readers: Psalm 118:22; Isaiah 8:14; 28:16. Peter's readers would have understood the chief stone to be Israel; now Peter applies the image to Christ. Once again Peter shows that the church does not cancel the Jewish heritage, but fulfills it.

2:4-8 Peter portrays the church as a living Temple: Christ is the foundation, and each believer is a stone. Paul portrays it as a body: Christ is the head, and each believer is a member (see, for example, Ephesians 4:15, 16). Both pictures emphasize *community*. One stone is not a temple or even a wall; one body part is useless without the others. In our individualistic society, it is easy to forget our interdependence with other Christians. When God calls you to a task, remember that he is also calling others to work with you. Together your individual efforts will be multiplied. Look for those people and join with them to build a beautiful house for God.

2:6 Christians will sometimes face disappointment in this life, but their trust in God is never misplaced. God will not let them down. We can safely put our confidence in him, for the eternal life he promises is certain.

2:6-8 No doubt Peter often thought of Jesus' words to him right after he confessed that Jesus was "the Christ, the Messiah, the Son of the living God": "You are Peter, a stone; and upon this rock

I will build my church; and all the powers of hell shall not prevail against it" (Matthew 16:16–18). What is the stone that really counts in the building of the church? Peter answers: Christ himself. What are the characteristics of Christ, the Cornerstone? (1) He is completely trustworthy; (2) he is precious to believers; (3) and, though rejected by some, he is the most important part of the church.

2:8 Jesus Christ is called "the Stone that some will stumble over." They stumble because they reject him or refuse to believe he is who he says he is. But Psalm 118:22 says that "the stone that was rejected has become the capstone of the arch," the most important part of God's building, the church. In the same way today, people who refuse to believe in Christ have made the greatest mistake of their lives—they have stumbled over the one person who could save them and give meaning to their lives, and they have fallen into God's hands for judgment.

2:9 Christians sometimes speak of "the priesthood of all believers." In Old Testament times, people did not approach God directly. A priest acted as intermediary between God and sinful man. With Christ's victory on the cross, that changed. Now we can come directly into God's presence without fear (Hebrews 4:16), and we are given the responsibility of bringing others to him also (2 Corinthians 5:18–21). When we are united with Christ as members of his body, we join in his work of reconciling God and man. This is what it means to be a priest of the King.

2:9, 10 People often base their self-concept on their accomplishments, but who we are in Christ is far more important than our jobs, our successes, our wealth, or our knowledge. We have been chosen by God as his very own, and we have been called to represent him to others. Remember that your value comes from being one of God's children, not from what you can achieve. You have worth because of what God does, not because of what you do.

2. The conduct of God's people in the midst of suffering
Obey those in authority

11Dear brothers, you are only visitors here. Since your real home is in heaven I beg you to keep away from the evil pleasures of this world; they are not for you, for they fight against your very souls.

12Be careful how you behave among your unsaved neighbors; for then, even if they are suspicious of you and talk against you, they will end up praising God for your good works when Christ returns.

13For the Lord's sake, obey every law of your government: those of the king as head of the state, 14and those of the king's officers, for he has sent them to punish all who do wrong, and to honor those who do right.

15It is God's will that your good lives should silence those who foolishly condemn the Gospel without knowing what it can do for them, having never experienced its power. 16You are free from the law, but that doesn't mean you are free to do wrong. Live as those who are free to do only God's will at all times.

17Show respect for everyone. Love Christians everywhere. Fear God and honor the government.

18Servants, you must respect your masters and do whatever they tell you—not only if they are kind and reasonable, but even if they are tough and cruel. 19Praise the Lord if you are punished for doing right! 20Of course, you get no credit for being patient if you are beaten for doing wrong; but if you do right and suffer for it, and are patient beneath the blows, God is well pleased.

21This suffering is all part of the work God has given you. Christ, who suffered for you, is your example. Follow in his steps: 22He never sinned, never told a lie,

2:11
Rom 12:1; 13:14
Gal 5:16
Jas 4:1

2:12
Phil 2:15
Tit 2:8

2:13
Rom 13:1

2:14
Rom 13:3,4

2:15
1 Pet 2:12; 3:17

2:16
Jn 8:32
1 Cor 7:22
Jas 1:25

2:17
Rom 12:10; 13:7
1 Pet 1:22

2:18
Eph 6:5
Jas 3:17

2:20
1 Pet 3:14,17

2:21
Mt 11:29; 16:24
Acts 14:22
1 Pet 3:9,18

2:22
Isa 53:9
2 Cor 5:21

2:11 Heaven is an important concept in the Bible, but it is not the pink-cloud-and-harp existence popular in cartoons. In Scripture, heaven is where God dwells. It operates according to God's principles and values, and it is eternal and unshakable. Heaven came to earth in the Jewish sanctuary (the Temple and Tabernacle) where God's presence dwelt. It came in a fuller way in the person of Jesus Christ, "God with us." It permeated the entire world as the Holy Spirit came to dwell in the heart of every believer.

Someday, after God judges and destroys all sin, the Kingdom of Heaven will rule every corner of this earth. We will be with Christ in a way not possible in this life. John saw this day in a vision, and he cried out, "Look, the home of God is now among men, and he will live with them and they will be his people; yes, God himself will be among them" (Revelation 21:3). Our real home, our true loyalty, is not to the things of this earth that will be destroyed. It is to God's truth, his way of life, his perfect creation. Because of this, we often feel like strangers in a world that would prefer to ignore God. In reality, however, we are citizens of the growing Kingdom of Heaven that, at Christ's Second Coming, will last forever.

2:12 Peter's advice sounds like Jesus' in Matthew 5:16: If your actions are above reproach, even hostile people will end up praising God. Peter's readers were scattered among Gentiles who were inclined to believe vicious lies about Christians. Attractive, gracious, upright behavior on the part of Christians could show these rumors to be false and could even win some of the unsaved critics to the Lord's side. Don't write off people because they misunderstand Christianity; instead, show them Christ in your life. The day may come when they will praise him with you.

2:12–17 When Peter told his readers to respect the civil government, he was speaking of the Roman Empire under Nero, a notoriously cruel tyrant. Obviously he was not telling believers to compromise their consciences; as Peter had told the High Priest years before, "We must obey God rather than men" (Acts 5:29). But in most aspects of their daily lives, it was possible and desirable for Christians to live according to the law of their land. Today, some Christians live in freedom while others live under repressive governments. All are commanded to cooperate with the rulers as far as conscience will allow. We are to do this "for the Lord's sake"—so that his Good News and his people will be respected. If we are to be persecuted, it should be for standing for God, and not for breaking moral or civil laws. For more about the Christian and government, see the note on Romans 13:1ff.

2:16 We are free from the law as a means to earning God's approval, but we are still to live, out of gratitude for our free salvation, the kind of moral life required by the Ten Commandments.

2:18–23 Many Christians were household servants. It would be easy for them to submit to masters who were gentle and kind, but Peter encouraged loyalty and persistence even in the face of unjust treatment. In the same way, we should submit to our employers whether they are kind or harsh. By so doing, we may win them to Christ by our good example. Paul gave similar advice in his letters (see Ephesians 6:5–9; Colossians 3:22–25), as did Jesus (Matthew 5:46; Luke 6:32–36).

2:21 There are many reasons for human suffering. Some is the direct result of sin in our lives; some happens because of our foolishness; and some seems to be the result of chance. Peter is writing about yet another category of suffering: that which is part of the work God has given us to do. Christ never sinned, yet he suffered so that we could be set free. When we follow Christ's example and live for others, we too may suffer. Our goal should be to live as Christ lived and to face suffering as he did—with patience, calmness, and confidence that God is in control of the future.

2:21–25 Peter had learned about suffering from Jesus. He knew that Jesus' suffering was part of God's plan (Matthew 16:21- 23; Luke 24:25–27, 44–47) and was intended to save us (Matthew 20:28; 26:28). He also knew that all who follow Jesus must be prepared to suffer (Mark 8:34, 35). Having learned and experienced these truths with Jesus, Peter passes them on to the Jewish Christians and to us.

2:23
Isa 53:7
1 Pet 3:9

2:24
Isa 53:4,5,11

2:25
Heb 13:20
1 Pet 5:4

23never answered back when insulted; when he suffered he did not threaten to get even; he left his case in the hands of God who always judges fairly. 24He personally carried the load of our sins in his own body when he died on the cross, so that we can be finished with sin and live a good life from now on. For his wounds have healed ours! 25Like sheep you wandered away from God, but now you have returned to your Shepherd, the Guardian of your souls who keeps you safe from all attacks.

Wives and husbands

3:1
1 Cor 7:16; 9:19
Eph 5:22
1 Pet 2:18; 3:7

3:3
Isa 3:16-24
1 Tim 2:9

3:4
Ps 45:13
Rom 2:29; 7:22

3:5
1 Tim 5:5
1 Pet 1:3

3:6
Gen 18:12

3:7
Mt 5:23,24
18:19
Eph 5:25
Col 3:19

3 Wives, fit in with your husbands' plans; for then if they refuse to listen when you talk to them about the Lord, they will be won by your respectful, pure behavior. Your godly lives will speak to them better than any words.

3Don't be concerned about the outward beauty that depends on jewelry, or beautiful clothes, or hair arrangement. 4Be beautiful inside, in your hearts, with the lasting charm of a gentle and quiet spirit which is so precious to God. 5That kind of deep beauty was seen in the saintly women of old, who trusted God and fitted in with their husbands' plans.

6Sarah, for instance, obeyed her husband Abraham, honoring him as head of the house. And if you do the same, you will be following in her steps like good daughters and doing what is right; then you will not need to fear [offending your husbands].

7You husbands must be careful of your wives, being thoughtful of their needs and honoring them as the weaker sex. Remember that you and your wife are partners in receiving God's blessings, and if you don't treat her as you should, your prayers will not get ready answers.

3:6 *offending your husbands,* implied.

2:24 Christ died for *our* sins, in *our* place, so we would not have to suffer the punishment we deserve. This is called *substitutionary atonement.*

3:1ff If a man became a Christian, he usually brought his whole family into the church (see, for example, the story of the conversion of the Philippian jailer, Acts 16:29–33). By contrast, a woman who became a Christian usually came into the church alone. Under Roman law, the husband and father had absolute authority over all members of his household, including his wife. If he disapproved of her new beliefs, she could endanger her marriage by demanding her rights as a free woman in Christ. Peter reassured Christian women married to unbelievers that they did not need to preach to their husbands. Under the circumstances, their best approach would be loving service: they should show their husbands the kind of self-giving love that Christ showed the church. By being exemplary wives, they would please their husbands. At the very least, the men would then allow them to continue practicing their "strange" religion. At best, their husbands would join them and become Christians too.

3:1–7 A changed life speaks loudly and clearly, and it is often the most effective way to influence a family member. Peter instructed Christian wives to develop inner beauty rather than being overly concerned about their appearance. Their husbands would be won by their love rather than by their looks. Live your Christian faith quietly and consistently in your home, and your family will see Christ in you.

3:3 We should not be obsessed by fashion, but neither should we be so unconcerned that we do not bother to care for ourselves. Hygiene, neatness, and grooming are important, but even more important are a person's attitude and spirit. True beauty begins inside.

3:6 Submission is voluntarily cooperating with someone else out

of love and respect for God and for that person. Ideally, submission is mutual ("Honor Christ by submitting to each other"—Ephesians 5:21). Even when it is one-sided, however, it can be an effective Christian tool. Jesus Christ submitted to death so that we could be saved; we may sometimes have to submit to unpleasant circumstances so that others will see Christ in us. (Christian submission never requires us to violate our principles, however; we should never submit to evil.) One-sided submission requires tremendous strength. We could not do it without the power of the Holy Spirit working in us.

3:7 When Peter calls women the "weaker sex" he does not imply moral or intellectual inferiority, but he is recognizing women's physical limitations. Women in his day, if unprotected by men, were vulnerable to attack, abuse, and financial disaster. Women's lives may be easier today, but they are still more vulnerable to criminal attack and family abuse. And in spite of increased opportunities in the workplace, most women still earn considerably less than most men, and the vast majority of the nations' poor are single mothers and their children. A man who honors his wife as a member of the weaker sex will protect, respect, help, and stay with her. He will not expect her to work full-time outside and full-time at home; he will lighten her load wherever he can. He will be sensitive to her needs, and he will relate to her with courtesy, consideration, insight, and tact.

3:7 If a man does not treat his wife kindly, his prayers become ineffective, because a living relationship with God depends on right relationships with others. Jesus said that if you have a problem with a fellow believer, you must make things right with that person before coming to worship (Matthew 5:23, 24). This principle carries over into family relationships. If men use their position to mistreat their wives, their relationship with God will suffer.

Suffering for doing good

8And now this word to all of you: You should be like one big happy family, full of sympathy toward each other, loving one another with tender hearts and humble minds. 9Don't repay evil for evil. Don't snap back at those who say unkind things about you. Instead, pray for God's help for them, for we are to be kind to others, and God will bless us for it.

10If you want a happy, good life, keep control of your tongue, and guard your lips from telling lies. 11Turn away from evil and do good. Try to live in peace even if you must run after it to catch and hold it! 12For the Lord is watching his children, listening to their prayers; but the Lord's face is hard against those who do evil.

13Usually no one will hurt you for wanting to do good. 14But even if they should, you are to be envied, for God will reward you for it. 15Quietly trust yourself to Christ your Lord and if anybody asks why you believe as you do, be ready to tell him, and do it in a gentle and respectful way.

16Do what is right; then if men speak against you, calling you evil names, they will become ashamed of themselves for falsely accusing you when you have only done what is good. 17Remember, if God wants you to suffer, it is better to suffer for doing good than for doing wrong!

We are partners with Christ in our suffering

18Christ also suffered. He died once for the sins of all us guilty sinners, although

3:8
Rom 12:16
Eph 4:32

3:9
Lk 6:28
Rom 12:14,17
Heb 6:14; 12:17

3:10-12
Ps 34:12–16

3:13
Prov 16:7

3:14
Isa 8:12,13

3:15
Col 4:6
2 Tim 2:25
1 Pet 1:3,17

3:16
1 Pet 2:12; 3:21

3:17
1 Pet 2:20,21
4:15,19

		SUBMISSION
Functional	a distinguishing of our roles and the work we do	
Relational	a loving acknowledgement of another's value as a person	
Reciprocal	a mutual, humble cooperation with one another	
Universal	an acknowledgement by the church of the all-encompassing lordship of Jesus Christ	

Submission is voluntarily cooperating with anyone out of love and respect for God first, then secondly, love and respect for that person. Submitting to nonbelievers is difficult, but it is a vital part of leading them to Jesus Christ. We are not called to submit to nonbelievers to the point that we compromise our relationship with God, but we must look for every opportunity to humbly serve in the power of God's Spirit.

3:8 Peter lists five key elements that should characterize any group of believers: (1) harmony—pursuing the same goals; (2) sympathy—being responsive to others' needs; (3) love—seeing one another as brothers and sisters; (4) tender hearts—being affectionately sensitive; and (5) humble minds—being willing to encourage one another and rejoice in each other's successes. These five qualities go a long way toward helping believers serve God effectively.

3:8, 9 Peter developed the qualities of tenderness and humility the hard way. In his early days with Christ, these attitudes did not come naturally to his impulsive, strong personality (see Mark 8:31–33; John 13:6–9 for examples of Peter's blustering). But the Holy Spirit changed Peter, turning his strong personality to God's use, and teaching him tenderness and humility.

3:9 In our fallen world, it is often acceptable to tear people down verbally or get back at them if we feel hurt. Peter, remembering Jesus' teaching to turn the other cheek (Matthew 5:39), encourages his readers to pay back wrongs by praying for the offenders. In God's Kingdom, revenge is unacceptable behavior. So is insulting a person, no matter how indirectly it is done. Rise above getting back at those who hurt you. Instead of reacting angrily to these people, pray for them.

3:10 For more about controlling your tongue, see the notes in James 3.

3:11 Too often we see peace as merely the absence of conflict, and we think peacemaking is a passive role. But an effective peacemaker actively pursues peace. He builds good relationships, knowing that peace is a by-product of commitment. He anticipates problems and deals with them before they occur. When conflicts

arise, he brings them into the open and deals with them before they grow unmanageable. Making peace can be harder work than waging war, but it results not in death but in life and happiness.

3:15 Some Christians believe faith is a personal matter that should be kept to oneself. It is true that we shouldn't be boisterous or obnoxious in sharing our faith, but we should always be ready to answer, gently and respectfully, when asked about our faith, our lifestyle, or our Christian perspective. Is your hope in Christ readily observable to others? Are you prepared to tell others what Christ has done in your life?

3:16 You may not be able to keep people from attacking you, but you can at least stop supplying them with ammunition. As long as you do what is right, their accusations will be empty and will only embarrass them. Keep your conduct above criticism!

3:18–20 The meaning of these verses is not completely clear, and commentators have explained them many different ways. The traditional interpretation is that Christ, between his death and resurrection, announced salvation to God's faithful followers who had been waiting for their salvation during the whole Old Testament era. Matthew records that when Jesus died, "many godly men and women who had died came back to life again" (see Matthew 27:52, 53). Other commentators think this passage says that Christ's spirit was in Noah as he preached to those imprisoned by sin. Still others hold that Christ went to Hades to proclaim his victory to the fallen angels imprisoned there since Noah's day (see 2 Peter 2:4). In any case, the passage shows that Christ's Good News is not limited. It has been preached in the past as well as in the present; it has gone to the dead as well as to the living. God has given everyone the opportunity to come to him, but this does

3:19
1 Pet 4:6

3:20
Gen 6:3; 7:1
8:18
Heb 11:7
1 Pet 1:9,22
2:25; 4:19

3:21
Heb 9:14
10:22; 13:18

3:22
Mk 16:19
Rom 8:38
Heb 1:6; 4:14
6:20

4:1
Rom 6:7
Gal 2:20
Col 3:5
1 Pet 2:21

4:2
Rom 6:2,11

4:3
Rom 13:13
Eph 2:2; 4:17

4:4
Eph 5:18
1 Pet 3:16

4:5
Acts 10:42
17:31
Rom 14:10

4:7
Rom 13:11-13

4:8
1 Pet 1:22

4:10
Rom 12:6-8

he himself was innocent of any sin at any time, that he might bring us safely home to God. But though his body died, his spirit lived on, 19and it was in the spirit that he visited the spirits in prison, and preached to them— 20spirits of those who, long before in the days of Noah, had refused to listen to God, though he waited patiently for them while Noah was building the ark. Yet only eight persons were saved from drowning in that terrible flood. 21(That, by the way, is what baptism pictures for us: In baptism we show that we have been saved from death and doom by the resurrection of Christ; not because our bodies are washed clean by the water, but because in being baptized we are turning to God and asking him to cleanse our *hearts* from sin.) 22And now Christ is in heaven, sitting in the place of honor next to God the Father, with all the angels and powers of heaven bowing before him and obeying him.

4 Since Christ suffered and underwent pain, you must have the same attitude he did; you must be ready to suffer, too. For remember, when your body suffers, sin loses its power, 2and you won't be spending the rest of your life chasing after evil desires, but will be anxious to do the will of God. 3You have had enough in the past of the evil things the godless enjoy—sex, sin, lust, getting drunk, wild parties, drinking bouts, and the worship of idols, and other terrible sins.

4Of course, your former friends will be very surprised when you don't eagerly join them any more in the wicked things they do, and they will laugh at you in contempt and scorn. 5But just remember that they must face the Judge of all, living and dead; they will be punished for the way they have lived. 6That is why the Good News was preached even to those who were dead—killed by the flood—so that although their bodies were punished with death, they could still live in their spirits as God lives.

Continue to love each other in the midst of suffering

7The end of the world is coming soon. Therefore be earnest, thoughtful men of prayer. 8Most important of all, continue to show deep love for each other, for love makes up for many of your faults. 9Cheerfully share your home with those who need a meal or a place to stay for the night.

10God has given each of you some special abilities; be sure to use them to help

3:21 *In baptism we show that we have been saved from death and doom by the resurrection of Christ,* or "Baptism, which corresponds to this, now saves you through the resurrection." **4:3** *and other terrible sins,* literally, "lawless idolatries." **4:6** *killed by the flood,* implied. See 3:19, 20. **4:8** *for love makes up for many of your faults,* or "love overlooks each other's many faults."

not mean a second chance for those who reject Christ in this life.

3:21 In baptism we identify with Jesus Christ, who separates us from the lost and gives us new life. It is not the ceremony by itself that saves us, but faith in Christ's death and resurrection. Baptism is the symbol of the transformation that happens in the hearts of those who believe (Romans 6:3-5; Galatians 3:27; Colossians 2:12). By identifying themselves with Christ through baptism, Peter's readers could never turn back, even under the pressure of persecution. Public baptism would keep them from the temptation to renounce their faith.

4:1, 2 Some people will do anything to avoid pain. As followers of Christ, however, we should be willing and prepared to do God's will and to suffer for it if necessary. When our bodies are in pain or our lives in jeopardy, our real values show up clearly, and sinful pleasures seem less important.

4:4 A person whose life changes radically at conversion may experience contempt from his old friends. He may be scorned not only because he refuses to participate in certain activities, but also because his priorities have changed and he is now heading in the opposite direction. His very life incriminates their sinful activities.

4:5 The basis of salvation is whether we have believed in Jesus (Acts 16:31), but the basis for judgment is how we have lived. Those who inflict persecution are marked for punishment when they stand before God. Believers have nothing to fear, however, because Jesus will be the final Judge over all (John 5:22).

4:5, 6 Many people in the early church had an unclear idea of life after death. In Thessalonica, Christians worried that loved ones who died before Christ's return might never see him (1 Thessalonians 4:13-18). Peter's readers needed to be reminded that the dead will be judged. The judgment will be perfectly fair, he points out, because even the dead have heard the gospel (see also 3:18, 19). The Good News was first announced when Jesus Christ preached on the earth, but it has been operating since before the creation of the world (Ephesians 1:4), and it affects all mankind, the dead as well as the living.

4:7-9 Live expectantly, for Christ is coming. Getting ready to meet him involves continually growing in love for God and for others (see Jesus' summary of the law in Matthew 22:37-40). It is important to pray regularly, and it is also important to reach out to needy people. Your possessions, status, and power will mean nothing in God's Kingdom, but you will spend eternity with other people. Invest your time and talents where they will make an eternal difference.

4:10, 11 Some people, well aware of their abilities, believe they have the right to use them as they please. Others feel they have no special talents at all. To both groups Peter addresses these verses. Everyone has some abilities, he says; find yours and use them. All our abilities should be dedicated to others, he points out; none are for our own exclusive enjoyment. Peter mentions preaching and helping. Paul lists these and other abilities in Romans 12:6-8; 1 Corinthians 12:8-11; Ephesians 4:11.

each other, passing on to others God's many kinds of blessings. ¹¹Are you called to preach? Then preach as though God himself were speaking through you. Are you called to help others? Do it with all the strength and energy that God supplies, so that God will be glorified through Jesus Christ—to him be glory and power forever and ever. Amen.

¹²Dear friends, don't be bewildered or surprised when you go through the fiery trials ahead, for this is no strange, unusual thing that is going to happen to you. ¹³Instead, be really glad—because these trials will make you partners with Christ in his suffering, and afterwards you will have the wonderful joy of sharing his glory in that coming day when it will be displayed.

¹⁴Be happy if you are cursed and insulted for being a Christian, for when that happens the Spirit of God will come upon you with great glory. ¹⁵Don't let me hear of your suffering for murdering or stealing or making trouble or being a busybody and prying into other people's affairs. ¹⁶But it is no shame to suffer for being a Christian. Praise God for the privilege of being in Christ's family and being called by his wonderful name! ¹⁷For the time has come for judgment, and it must begin first among God's own children. And if even we who are Christians must be judged, what terrible fate awaits those who have never believed in the Lord? ¹⁸If the righteous are barely saved, what chance will the godless have?

¹⁹So if you are suffering according to God's will, keep on doing what is right and trust yourself to the God who made you, for he will never fail you.

3. The shepherding of God's people in the midst of suffering

5 And now, a word to you elders of the church. I, too, am an elder; with my own eyes I saw Christ dying on the cross; and I, too, will share his glory and his honor when he returns. Fellow elders, this is my plea to you: ²Feed the flock of God; care for it willingly, not grudgingly; not for what you will get out of it, but because you are eager to serve the Lord. ³Don't be tyrants, but lead them by your

4:14 *the Spirit of God will come upon you with great glory,* or "the glory of the Spirit of God is being seen in you."

4:12
1 Pet 1:6

4:13
Rom 8:17
2 Cor 1:5
Phil 3:10
2 Tim 2:12

4:14
Mt 5:11
Jn 15:21
2 Cor 4:10
Heb 11:26

4:15
1 Thess 4:11
2 Thess 3:11
1 Tim 5:13

4:16
Acts 5:41; 28:22

4:17
Jer 25:29
Mal 3:5
Rom 2:9
2 Thess 1:8

4:18
Lk 23:31

4:19
Ps 31:5,6

5:1
Lk 24:48
Rev 1:9

5:2
Jn 21:16
Acts 20:28

4:11 How is God glorified when we use our abilities? When we use them as he directs, to help others, they will see Jesus in us and praise him for the help they have received. Peter may have been thinking of Jesus' words, "Let your good deeds glow for all to see, so that they will praise your heavenly Father" (Matthew 5:16).

4:14–16 Again Peter brings to mind Jesus' words: "When you are reviled and persecuted and lied about because you are my followers—wonderful!" (Matthew 5:11). It is never shameful to suffer for Christ, and he will send his Spirit to strengthen those who are persecuted for their faith. This does not mean that all suffering is good, however. Sometimes a person will grumble, "He's just picking on me because I'm a Christian," when it's obvious to everyone else that the person's own unpleasant behavior is the cause of his problems. It may take careful thought or wise counsel to determine the real cause of our suffering. We can be assured, however, that whenever we suffer because of our loyalty to Christ, he will be with us all the way.

4:16 It is not shameful to suffer for being a Christian. When Peter and John were persecuted for preaching the Good News, they rejoiced because such persecution was a mark of God's approval of their work (Acts 5:41). Don't seek out suffering, and don't try to avoid it. Instead, keep on doing what is right regardless of the suffering it might bring.

4:17, 18 This is not final judgment but God's refining discipline (Hebrews 12:7). God often allows the consequences of sin to take their course, even with believers. He does this for several reasons: (1) to show us our potential for sinning, (2) to encourage us to turn from sin and more constantly depend on him, (3) to prepare us to face other, even stronger temptations in the future, and (4) to help us stay faithful and keep on trusting him. If believers need earthly discipline (judgment) from God, how much more will unbelievers receive it? If believers are "barely saved" (only because of God's

mercy, or as some say, barely saved through persecution), what chance do those have who reject Christ?

4:19 God created the world, and he has faithfully ordered it and kept it since the creation. Because we know he is faithful, we can count on him to fulfill his promises to us. If he can oversee the forces of nature, surely he can see us through the trials we face.

5:1 Elders were church officers providing supervision, protection, discipline, instruction, and direction for the other believers. *Elder* simply means "older." Both Greeks and Jews gave positions of great honor to wise older men, and the Christian church continued this pattern of leadership. Elders carried great responsibility, and they were expected to live exemplary lives.

5:1, 2 Peter, one of Jesus' 12 disciples, was one of the three who saw Christ's glory at the transfiguration (Mark 9:1–13; 2 Peter 1:16–18). Often the spokesman for the apostles, he witnessed Jesus' death and resurrection, preached at Pentecost, and became a pillar of the Jerusalem church. But writing to the elders, he identifies himself as a fellow elder, not a superior. He asks them to "feed the flock of God," exactly what Jesus had told him to do (John 21:15–17). Peter was taking his own advice as he worked along with the other elders in caring for God's faithful people. His identification with the elders is a powerful example of Christian leadership, where authority is based on service, not power (Mark 10:42–45).

5:2–5 Peter describes several characteristics of good leaders in the church: (1) they realize they are caring for God's flock, not their own; (2) they lead out of eagerness to serve, not out of obligation; (3) they are concerned for what they can give, not for what they can get; (4) they lead by example, not force. All of us lead others in some way. Whatever your role, your leadership should be in line with these characteristics.

5:4
1 Cor 9:25
Heb 13:20,21

5:5
Prov 3:34
Jas 4:6

5:6
Jas 4:10

5:7
Mt 6:25
Heb 13:5

5:8
Job 1:7
Jas 4:7
1 Pet 1:13

5:9
Acts 14:22
Heb 12:8

5:10
Rom 16:25
2 Thess 2:17
2 Tim 2:10
1 Pet 1:6; 4:10

5:12
Acts 11:23
2 Cor 1:19
Heb 13:22

5:13
Acts 12:12

5:14
Rom 16:16
Eph 6:23

good example, 4and when the Head Shepherd comes, your reward will be a never-ending share in his glory and honor.

5You younger men, follow the leadership of those who are older. And all of you serve each other with humble spirits, for God gives special blessings to those who are humble, but sets himself against those who are proud. 6If you will humble yourselves under the mighty hand of God, in his good time he will lift you up.

7Let him have all your worries and cares, for he is always thinking about you and watching everything that concerns you.

8Be careful—watch out for attacks from Satan, your great enemy. He prowls around like a hungry, roaring lion, looking for some victim to tear apart. 9Stand firm when he attacks. Trust the Lord; and remember that other Christians all around the world are going through these sufferings too.

10After you have suffered a little while, our God, who is full of kindness through Christ, will give you his eternal glory. He personally will come and pick you up, and set you firmly in place, and make you stronger than ever. 11To him be all power over all things, forever and ever. Amen.

Peter's final greetings

12I am sending this note to you through the courtesy of Silvanus who is, in my opinion, a very faithful brother. I hope I have encouraged you by this letter for I have given you a true statement of the way God blesses. What I have told you here should help you to stand firmly in his love.

13The church here in Rome—she is your sister in the Lord—sends you her greetings; so does my son Mark. 14Give each other the handshake of Christian love. Peace be to all of you who are in Christ.

Peter

5:13 *The church here in Rome,* literally, "She who is at Babylon is likewise chosen"; but Babylon was the Christian nickname for Rome, and the "she" is thought by many to be Peter's wife to whom reference is made in Mt 8:14; 1 Cor 9:5, etc. Others believe this should read: "Your sister church here in Babylon salutes you, and so does my son Mark."

5:4 The Head Shepherd is Jesus Christ. This refers to his Second Coming, when he will judge all people.

5:5 Both young and old can benefit from Peter's instructions. Pride often keeps elders from trying to understand young people and young people from listening to their elders. Peter told both young and old to be humble and serve each other. Young men should follow the leadership of older men, who should lead by example. Respect your elders, listen to those younger than you, and be humble enough to admit you can learn from each other.

5:6 We often worry about our position and status, hoping we'll get proper recognition for what we do. But Peter advises us to remember that God's recognition counts more than human praise. God is able and willing to bless us according to his own timing. Obey God regardless of present circumstances, and in his good time—either in this life or in the next—he will lift you up.

5:7 Carrying your worries, stress, and daily struggles by yourself shows that you have not trusted God fully with your life. It takes humility, however, to recognize that God cares, to admit your need, and to let others in his family help you. Sometimes we think that struggles caused by our own sin and foolishness are not God's concern. But when we turn to him in repentance, he will bear the weight even of those struggles. Letting God have your worries is active, not passive. Don't submit to circumstances, but to the Lord who controls circumstances.

5:8, 9 Lions attack sick, young, or straggling animals; they choose victims who are alone or not alert. Peter warns us to watch out for Satan when we are suffering or persecuted. Feeling alone, weak, helpless, and cut off from other believers, so focused on our troubles that we forget to watch for danger, we are especially vulnerable to Satan's attacks. During times of suffering, seek other Christians for support. Keep your eyes on Christ, and resist the devil. Then, says James, "he will flee from you" (James 4:7).

5:10 When we are suffering, we feel as though our pain will never end. Peter shows these faithful Christians the wider perspective. In comparison with eternity, their suffering would last only "a little while." Some of Peter's readers would be picked up, set in place, and strengthened in their own lifetimes. Others would be released from their suffering through death. All of God's faithful followers, however, are assured of Christ's eternal glory—endless, joyful life in which suffering plays no part at all (Revelation 21:4).

5:12 Silvanus, also called Silas, was one of the men chosen to deliver the letter from the Jerusalem council to the church in Antioch (Acts 15:22). He accompanied Paul on his second missionary journey (Acts 15:40—18:11), helped Paul write his letters to the Thessalonians (1 Thessalonians 1:1; 2 Thessalonians 1:1), and ministered with Timothy in Corinth (2 Corinthians 1:19).

5:13 Mark, also called John or John Mark, was known to many of this letter's readers because he had traveled widely (Acts 12:25—13:13; 15:36—51) and was recognized as a leader in the church (Colossians 4:10; Philemon 1:24). Mark was probably with the disciples at the time of Jesus' arrest (Mark 14:51, 52). Tradition holds that Peter was Mark's main source of information when he wrote the Gospel of Mark.

5:14 Peter wrote this letter just before the cruel emperor Nero began persecuting Christians in Rome and throughout the empire. Afraid for his life, Peter had three times denied even knowing Jesus (John 18:15—27); now, having learned how to stand firm in an evil world, he encourages other Christians who are facing persecution for their faith. Peter himself lived by the words he wrote, for he was martyred for his faith. Those who stand for Christ will be persecuted, because the world is ruled by Christ's greatest enemy. But just as the small group of early believers stood against persecution, so we must be willing to stand for our faith with the patience, endurance, and courage that Peter exhibited.

2 PETER

VITAL STATISTICS

PURPOSE:
To warn Christians about false teachers and to exhort them to grow in their faith and knowledge of Christ

AUTHOR:
Peter

TO WHOM WRITTEN:
The church at large

DATE WRITTEN:
About A.D. 67, three years after 1 Peter was written, possibly from Rome

SETTING:
Peter knows that his time on earth is limited (1:13, 14), so he is writing about what is on his heart, warning believers of what will happen when he is gone—especially about false teachers. He reminds them of the unchanging truth of the gospel.

KEY VERSES:
"For as you know him better, he will give you, through his great power, everything you need for living a truly good life: he even shares his own glory and his own goodness with us!" (1:3).

KEY PEOPLE:
Peter, Paul

SPECIAL FEATURES:
The date and destination are uncertain, and the authorship has been disputed. Because of this, 2 Peter was the last book admitted to the canon of the New Testament Scripture. Also, there are similarities between 2 Peter and Jude.

WARNINGS have many forms—lights, signs, sights, sounds, smells, feelings, and written words. With varied focus, their purpose is the same—to warn one of imminent danger. Responses to these warnings will also vary, from disregard and neglect to evasive or corrective action. How a person reacts to a warning is usually determined by the situation and the source of the warning. An impending storm is treated differently than an oncoming automobile, and the counsel of a friend is heeded much more than the flippant remark of a stranger.

Second Peter is a letter of warning—from an authority none other than the courageous, experienced, and faithful apostle. It is the last communication from this great warrior of Christ. Soon thereafter he would die, martyred for the faith.

Previously Peter had written to comfort and encourage believers in the midst of suffering and persecution—an external onslaught. But three years later, in this epistle containing his written message, he wrote to warn them of an internal attack—complacency and heresy. He speaks of holding fast to the nonnegotiable facts of the faith, of growing and maturing in the faith, and of rejecting all who would twist the truth. If his readers heeded Peter's warnings, their lives would be honoring to Christ and their churches would be Christ-centered.

After a brief greeting (1:1), Peter gives the antidote for stagnancy and shortsightedness in the Christian life (1:2–11). He explains that his days are numbered (1:12–15) and that the believers should listen to his messages and the words of Scripture (1:16–21).

Peter then gives a blunt warning about false teachers (2:1–22). They will become prevalent in the last days (2:1, 2), they will do or say anything for money (2:3), they will laugh at the things of God (2:2, 10, 11), they will do whatever they feel like doing (2:12–17), they will be proud and boastful (2:18, 19), and they will be judged and punished by God (2:3–10, 20–22).

Peter concludes his brief letter by explaining why he has written it (3:1–18). He reminds them that God predicted the coming of false teachers, and gives the reasons for the delay in Christ's return (3:1–13), encouraging them to beware of heresies, and to grow in their faith (3:14–18).

Addressed to "all of you who have our kind of faith," 2 Peter could have been written to us. Our world is filled with false prophets and teachers claiming to have the truth and clamoring for attention and allegiance. Listen carefully to Peter's message and heed his warning. Determine to grow in your knowledge of Christ and to reject all those who preach anything but that which is consistent with the revealed Word of God.

THE BLUEPRINT

1. Guidance for growing Christians (1:1–21)
2. Danger to growing Christians (2:1–22)
3. Hope for growing Christians (3:1–18)

While Peter wrote his first letter to teach about handling persecution (trials from without), he wrote this letter to teach about handling heresy (trials from within). False teachers are often subtly deceitful. Believers today must still be vigilant against falling into false doctrine, heresy, and cults. This letter gives us clues to help detect false teaching.

MEGATHEMES

THEME	EXPLANATION	IMPORTANCE
Diligence	If our faith is real, it will be evident in our faithful behavior. If people are diligent in Christian growth, they won't backslide or be deceived by false teachers.	Growth is essential. It begins with faith and culminates in love for others. To keep growing we need to know God, keep on following him, and remember what he taught us. We must remain diligent in faithful obedience and Christian growth.
False Teachers	Peter warns the church to beware of false teachers. These teachers were proud of their position, promoted sexual sin, and advised against keeping the Ten Commandments. Peter countered them by pointing to the Spirit-inspired Scriptures as our authority.	Christians need discernment to be able to resist false teachers. God can rescue us from their lies if we stay true to his Word, the Bible, and reject those who twist the truth.
Christ's Return	One day Christ will create a new heaven and earth where we will live forever. As Christians, our hope is in this promise. But with Christ's return comes his judgment on all who refuse to believe.	The cure for complacency, lawlessness, and heresy is found in the confident assurance that Christ will return. God is still giving unbelievers time to repent. To be ready, Christians must keep on trusting and resist the pressure to give up waiting for Christ's return.

1. Guidance for growing Christians

1 *From:* Simon Peter, a servant and missionary of Jesus Christ.
To: all of you who have our kind of faith. The faith I speak of is the kind that Jesus Christ our God and Savior gives to us. How precious it is, and how just and good he is to give this same faith to each of us.

1:1
Rom 1:1,12
2 Cor 4:13
Eph 4:5
Tit 2:13
1 Pet 1:1,7; 2:7

1:1 First Peter was written around the time that the Roman Emperor Nero began his heavy persecution of Christians. Second Peter was written two or three years later (between A.D. 66–68), after intense persecution had begun. First Peter was a letter of encouragement to the Christians who suffered, but 2 Peter focuses on the church's internal problems, especially the false teachers who were causing people to doubt and turn away from Christianity. Second Peter combats their heresies by denouncing the evil motives of the false teachers and reaffirming Christianity's truths—the authority of Scripture, the primacy of faith, and the certainty of Christ's return.

Character qualities to develop in life

2Do you want more and more of God's kindness and peace? Then learn to know him better and better. 3For as you know him better, he will give you, through his great power, everything you need for living a truly good life: he even shares his own glory and his own goodness with us! 4And by that same mighty power he has given us all the other rich and wonderful blessings he promised; for instance, the promise to save us from the lust and rottenness all around us, and to give us his own character.

5But to obtain these gifts, you need more than faith; you must also work hard to be good, and even that is not enough. For then you must learn to know God better and discover what he wants you to do. 6Next, learn to put aside your own desires so that you will become patient and godly, gladly letting God have his way with you. 7This will make possible the next step, which is for you to enjoy other people and to like them, and finally you will grow to love them deeply. 8The more you go on in this way, the more you will grow strong spiritually and become fruitful and useful to our Lord Jesus Christ. 9But anyone who fails to go after these additions to faith is blind indeed, or at least very shortsighted, and has forgotten that God delivered him from the old life of sin so that now he can live a strong, good life for the Lord.

10So, dear brothers, work hard to prove that you really are among those God has called and chosen, and then you will never stumble or fall away. 11And God will open wide the gates of heaven for you to enter into the eternal kingdom of our Lord and Savior Jesus Christ.

Paying attention to Scripture

12I plan to keep on reminding you of these things even though you already know them and are really getting along quite well! 13, 14But the Lord Jesus Christ has showed me that my days here on earth are numbered, and I am soon to die. As long as I am still here I intend to keep sending these reminders to you, 15hoping to impress them so clearly upon you that you will remember them long after I have gone.

16For we have not been telling you fairy tales when we explained to you the

1:2
2 Pet 3:18
1:3
2 Thess 2:14
1:4
Jas 1:27
1 Jn 2:15,16
1:5
Col 2:3
1:6
1 Cor 9:25
Gal 5:22
1:7
Jn 13:34,35
Rom 12:10
1 Pet 1:22
1:8
Jn 15:1-6
Col 1:10
2 Pet 1:3
1:9
2 Cor 4:3,4
1 Jn 2:11
1:10
Mt 22:14
Rom 8:28-31
11:29
1 Thess 1:4
Jude 24
1:11
2 Tim 4:18
2 Pet 2:20
Rev 3:21
1:13,14
Jn 13:36; 21:18
2 Tim 4:6
2 Pet 1:12; 3:1
1:16
Mt 17:1-5; 28:18
Mk 13:26
Lk 9:28-32
Eph 4:14
1 Thess 2:19
1 Tim 1:4

1:2 Many believers want more of God's kindness and peace, but they are unwilling to put forth the effort to get to know him better. To enjoy the privileges God offers us freely, we have to combine hard work with complete trust.

1:3, 4 The expression "God's goodness" is literally translated "divine nature." The power to grow doesn't come from within us, but from God. Since we don't have the resources to live a "truly good life," God gives us his nature to keep us from sin and help us live for him.

1:5-9 Faith is more than belief in certain facts; it must result in action, or it dies away because it does not demonstrate a truly transformed life (James 2:14-17). Peter lists several of faith's actions: learning to know God better, developing patience, doing God's will, loving others. These actions do not come automatically; they require hard work. They are not optional. All of them must be a continual part of the Christian life. We don't finish one and start on the next, but we work on them all together.

1:6 False teachers were saying that self-control is not needed because works do not help the believer anyway (2:19). It is true that works cannot save us, but it is absolutely false to think they are unimportant. We are saved so that we can grow to resemble Christ and so that we can serve others. God wants to produce his character of active love in us. But to do this, he demands effort from us. To grow spiritually, we must develop self-control.

1:9 Our faith must go beyond what we believe; it must become a dynamic part of our lives, resulting in good works and spiritual maturity. Salvation does not depend on good works, but it results

in good works. A person who claims to be saved while remaining unchanged may not understand faith at all.

1:10 Peter wants to rouse the complacent believers who have listened to the false teachers and believe that because salvation is not based on good works they can live as they want. If you truly belong to the Lord, he says, your hard work will prove it. If you're not working for God, maybe you don't belong to him. If you are the Lord's—and your hard work backs up your claim—you will never be led astray by false teaching or glamorous sin.

1:12-15 Outstanding coaches constantly review the basics of the sport with their teams, and good athletes can execute the fundamentals consistently well. In our spiritual lives we must not neglect the basics of our faith when we go on to study deeper truths. Just as an athlete needs constant practice, we need constant reminders of the fundamentals of our faith and of how we came to believe in the first place. Don't allow yourself to be bored or impatient with messages on the basics of the Christian life. Instead, take the attitude of an athlete who continues to practice and refine the basics even as he learns more advanced skills.

1:13, 14 Many years before, Christ had prepared Peter for the kind of death he would face (see John 21:18, 19). Now Peter knew his death was at hand. Peter was martyred for the faith in about A.D. 68. One tradition says he was crucified upside down, at his own request, because he did not feel worthy to die in the same manner as his Master.

1:16-18 Peter is referring to the transfiguration where Jesus' divine identity was revealed to him and two other disciples (see Matthew 17:1-8; Mark 9:2-8; Luke 9:28-36).

power of our Lord Jesus Christ and his coming again. My own eyes have seen his splendor and his glory: [17, 18]was there on the holy mountain when he shone out with honor given him by God his Father; I heard that glorious, majestic voice calling down from heaven, saying, "This is my much-loved Son; I am well pleased with him."

[19]So we have seen and proved that what the prophets said came true. You will do well to pay close attention to everything they have written, for, like lights shining into dark corners, their words help us to understand many things that otherwise would be dark and difficult. But when you consider the wonderful truth of the prophets' words, the light will dawn in your souls and Christ the Morning Star will shine in your hearts. [20, 21]For no prophecy recorded in Scripture was ever thought up by the prophet himself. It was the Holy Spirit within these godly men who gave them true messages from God.

2. Danger to growing Christians

2 But there were false prophets, too, in those days, just as there will be false teachers among you. They will cleverly tell their lies about God, turning against even their Master who bought them; but theirs will be a swift and terrible end. [2]Many will follow their evil teaching that there is nothing wrong with sexual sin. And because of them Christ and his way will be scoffed at.

[3]These teachers in their greed will tell you anything to get hold of your money. But God condemned them long ago and their destruction is on the way. [4]For God did not spare even the angels who sinned, but threw them into hell, chained in gloomy caves and darkness until the judgment day. [5]And he did not spare any of the people who lived in ancient times before the flood except Noah, the one man who spoke up for God, and his family of seven. At that time God completely destroyed the whole world of ungodly men with the vast flood. [6]Later, he turned the cities of Sodom and Gomorrah into heaps of ashes and blotted them off the face of the earth, making them an example for all the ungodly in the future to look back upon and fear.

[7, 8]But at the same time the Lord rescued Lot out of Sodom because he was a good man, sick of the terrible wickedness he saw everywhere around him day after day. [9]So also the Lord can rescue you and me from the temptations that surround us, and continue to punish the ungodly until the day of final judgment comes. [10]He is especially hard on those who follow their own evil, lustful thoughts, and those who are proud and willful, daring even to scoff at the Glorious Ones without so much as trembling, [11]although the angels in heaven who stand in the very presence of the Lord, and are far greater in power and strength than these false teachers, never speak out disrespectfully against these evil Mighty Ones.

1:17
Mt 17:5
Heb 1:3

1:19
Ps 119:105
Prov 6:23
Lk 1:78,79
2 Cor 4:6
1 Pet 1:10-12
Rev 22:16

1:20
Rom 12:6
2 Pet 3:3

1:21
Jn 14:26
1 Cor 2:13
2 Tim 3:16

2:1
Deut 13:1-3
Mt 7:15
2 Cor 11:13
1 Tim 4:1
Jude 4

2:3
1 Tim 6:5
Jude 16

2:4
Jude 6
Rev 20:1-3

2:5
Gen 6:13-22
1 Pet 3:20
2 Pet 3:6

2:6
Gen 19:24,25
Mt 10:15; 11:23
Rom 9:29
Jude 7

2:7
Gen 19:5,16,29
2 Pet 3:17

2:9
Jude 6

2:10
Ex 22:28
2 Pet 3:3
Jude 8,16,18

2:11
Jude 9

1:16–21 This section is a strong statement on the inspiration of Scripture. Peter affirms that the Old Testament prophets wrote God's messages, and he puts himself and the other apostles in the same category since they also proclaim God's truth. The Bible is not a collection of fables or of human ideas about God. It is God's very words given *through* people *to* people. Peter emphasizes his authority as an eyewitness as well as the God-inspired authority of Scripture to prepare for his attack on the false teachers. If these wicked men contradict the apostles and the Bible, their message cannot come from God.

2:1 Jesus had told the disciples that false teachers would come (Matthew 24:11; Mark 13:22, 23). Peter had heard these words, and now he was seeing them come true. Just as false prophets had contradicted the true prophets in Old Testament times (see, for example, Jeremiah 23:16–40; 28:1–17), telling people only what they wanted to hear, so false teachers twisted Christ's teachings and the words of his apostles. These teachers belittled the significance of Jesus' life, death, and resurrection. Some claimed he couldn't be God; others claimed he couldn't have been a real man. They allowed and even encouraged all kinds of wrong and immoral acts, especially sexual sin. Though these false teachers were popular, Peter warned that they would be destroyed.

2:3 Teachers should be paid by the people they teach, but these false teachers were attempting to make more money by distorting the truth and saying what people wanted to hear. They were more interested in making money than in teaching truth. Peter and Paul both condemned greedy, lying teachers (see 1 Timothy 6:5).

2:4–6 If God did not spare angels, or people who lived before the flood, or the citizens of Sodom and Gomorrah, he would not spare these false teachers. Some would have us believe that God will save all people because he is so loving. But we are foolish if we think he will cancel the last judgment. These three examples should warn us clearly that God judges sin and that unrepentant sinners cannot escape.

2:7–9 Just as God rescued Lot from Sodom, so he will rescue us from the temptations of a wicked world. Lot was not sinless, but he put his trust in God and was spared when Sodom was destroyed. For more information on Lot, see his Profile in Genesis 14.

¹²But false teachers are fools—no better than animals. They do whatever they feel like; born only to be caught and killed, they laugh at the terrifying powers of the underworld which they know so little about; and they will be destroyed along with all the demons and powers of hell.

¹³That is the pay these teachers will have for their sin. For they live in evil pleasures day after day. They are a disgrace and a stain among you, deceiving you by living in foul sin on the side while they join your love feasts as though they were honest men. ¹⁴No woman can escape their sinful stare, and of adultery they never have enough. They make a game of luring unstable women. They train themselves to be greedy; and are doomed and cursed. ¹⁵They have gone off the road and become lost like Balaam, the son of Beor, who fell in love with the money he could make by doing wrong; ¹⁶but Balaam was stopped from his mad course when his donkey spoke to him with a human voice, scolding and rebuking him.

¹⁷These men are as useless as dried-up springs of water, promising much and delivering nothing; they are as unstable as clouds driven by the storm winds. They are doomed to the eternal pits of darkness. ¹⁸They proudly boast about their sins and conquests, and, using lust as their bait, they lure back into sin those who have just escaped from such wicked living.

¹⁹"You aren't saved by being good," they say, "so you might as well be bad. Do what you like, be free."

But these very teachers who offer this "freedom" from law are themselves slaves to sin and destruction. For a man is a slave to whatever controls him. ²⁰And when a person has escaped from the wicked ways of the world by learning about our Lord and Savior Jesus Christ, and then gets tangled up with sin and becomes its slave again, he is worse off than he was before. ²¹It would be better if he had never known about Christ at all than to learn of him and then afterwards turn his back on the holy commandments that were given to him. ²²There is an old saying that "A dog comes back to what he has vomited, and a pig is washed only to come back and wallow in the mud again." That is the way it is with those who turn again to their sin.

2:10 *at the Glorious Ones,* or "the glories of the unseen world." **2:12** *the terrifying powers of the underworld,* literally, "the things they do not understand." **2:12** *all the demons and powers of hell,* implied. Literally, "will be destroyed in the same destruction with them."

2:12
Jude 10

2:13
Rom 13:13
1 Cor 11:21
Phil 3:19
2 Pet 2:15

2:14
Eph 2:3
2 Pet 2:18; 3:16

2:15
Num 22:5-7,17
Deut 23:4
Acts 13:10
2 Pet 2:13
Jude 11
Rev 2:14

2:16
Num 22:21-28

2:17
Jude 12,13

2:18
Acts 2:40
Eph 4:17-19
2 Pet 2:2,14,20
Jude 16

2:19
Jn 8:34
Rom 6:16
Gal 5:13

2:20
Mt 12:43-45
Lk 11:26
2 Tim 2:4
2 Pet 1:2; 2:18

2:21
Ezek 18:24
1 Tim 6:14
Heb 6:4; 10:26
Jas 4:17

2:22
Prov 26:11

2:10–12 The "Glorious Ones" may be angels, all the glories of the unseen world, or, more probably, fallen angels. A similar passage is found in Jude 1:8–10. Whichever they are, the false teachers scoffed at the spiritual realities they did not understand, taking Satan's power lightly and thinking they had the ability to judge evil. Many in our world today mock the supernatural. They deny the reality of the spiritual world and claim that only what can be seen and felt is real. Like the false teachers of Peter's day, they are fools who will be proven wrong in the end. Don't take Satan and his supernatural powers of evil lightly or feel arrogant about how defeated he will be. Although he will be destroyed completely, he is at work now trying to lure complacent or arrogant Christians over to his side.

2:13, 14 The love feast was part of the celebration of the Lord's Supper. It was a full meal, ending with communion. The false teachers, though living openly sinful lives, took part in the love feasts with everyone else in the church. In one of the greatest of hypocritical acts, they attended a sacred feast designed to promote love and unity among believers, while at the same time they gossiped and slandered those who disagreed with their opinions. As Paul told the Corinthians, "If anyone eats this bread and drinks from this cup of the Lord in an unworthy manner, he is guilty of sin against the body and blood of the Lord" (1 Corinthians 11:27). These men were guilty of more than false teaching and evil pleasures; they were guilty of leading others away from God's Son, Jesus.

2:15 Balaam was hired by a pagan king to curse Israel. He did what God told him for a while (Numbers 22—24), but eventually his evil motives and desire for money won out (Numbers 25:1–3; 31:16). Like the false teachers of Peter's day, Balaam used religion for personal advancement, a sin God does not take lightly.

2:19 Many believe freedom means doing anything you want. But no one is ever completely free in that sense. If we refuse to follow God, we will follow our own sinful desires and become enslaved to what our bodies want. If we submit our lives to Christ, he will free us from slavery to sin. Christ frees us to serve him, which always results in our ultimate good.

2:20–22 Peter is speaking of a person who has learned about Christ and how to be saved, and has perhaps even been positively influenced by the lives of Christians, but then rejects the truth and returns to his sin. He is worse off than before, because he has rejected the only way out of his sin, the only way of salvation. Like a man sinking in quicksand who refuses to grab the rope thrown to him, the person who turns away from Christ casts aside his only means of escape (see the note on Luke 11:24-26).

3. Hope for growing Christians

3:1
Acts 3:21
Eph 3:5
2 Pet 1:13

3 This is my second letter to you, dear brothers, and in both of them I have tried to remind you—if you will let me—about facts you already know: facts you learned from the holy prophets and from us apostles who brought you the words of our Lord and Savior.

3:3
1 Tim 4:1
2 Pet 2:10
Jude 18

3First, I want to remind you that in the last days there will come scoffers who will do every wrong they can think of, and laugh at the truth. 4This will be their line of argument: "So Jesus promised to come back, did he? Then where is he? He'll never come! Why, as far back as anyone can remember everything has remained exactly as it was since the first day of creation."

3:4
Isa 5:19
Jer 17:15

3:5,6
Gen 1:6,9,10
7:10-12
Ps 24:2; 136:6
Col 1:17
Heb 11:3

5, 6They deliberately forget this fact: that God did destroy the world with a mighty flood, long after he had made the heavens by the word of his command, and had used the waters to form the earth and surround it. 7And God has commanded that the earth and the heavens be stored away for a great bonfire at the judgment day, when all ungodly men will perish.

3:7
Isa 66:15
Mt 10:15
1 Cor 3:13
2 Thess 1:8
Heb 12:29

8But don't forget this, dear friends, that a day or a thousand years from now is like tomorrow to the Lord. 9He isn't really being slow about his promised return, even though it sometimes seems that way. But he is waiting, for the good reason that he is not willing that any should perish, and he is giving more time for sinners to repent. 10The day of the Lord is surely coming, as unexpectedly as a thief, and then the heavens will pass away with a terrible noise and the heavenly bodies will disappear in fire, and the earth and everything on it will be burned up.

3:9
Isa 30:18
Rom 2:4; 13:11
1 Tim 2:4
Rev 2:21

3:10
Mt 24:43
1 Cor 1:8
1 Thess 5:2
Rev 3:3

11And so since everything around us is going to melt away, what holy, godly lives we should be living! 12You should look forward to that day and hurry it along—the day when God will set the heavens on fire, and the heavenly bodies will melt and disappear in flames. 13But we are looking forward to God's promise of new heavens and a new earth afterwards, where there will be only goodness.

3:12
Ps 50:3
Isa 24:19; 34:4
1 Cor 1:7

3:13
Isa 60:21
65:17,25
Rev 21:1,27

14Dear friends, while you are waiting for these things to happen and for him to come, try hard to live without sinning; and be at peace with everyone so that he will be pleased with you when he returns.

3:14
1 Pet 1:7

3:15
Acts 9:17
Rom 2:4;
Col 1:25-27
Heb 5:11

15, 16And remember why he is waiting. He is giving us time to get his message of salvation out to others. Our wise and beloved brother Paul has talked about these same things in many of his letters. Some of his comments are not easy to understand, and there are people who are deliberately stupid, and always demand some unusual interpretation—they have twisted his letters around to mean something

3:16
Isa 28:13
Heb 5:11
2 Pet 3:2

3:13 *where there will be only goodness,* literally, "wherein righteousness dwells."

3:3, 4 Scoffers in the last days would say Jesus was never coming back, but Peter refutes their argument by explaining God's mastery over time. The "last days" are the time between Christ's first and second comings; thus we, like Peter, live in the last days. We must do the work to which God has called us and believe he will return as he promised.

3:7 In Noah's day the earth was judged by water; at the Second Coming it will be judged by fire. This fire is described in Revelation 19:20; 20:10–15.

3:8 God may have seemed slow to these believers as they faced persecution every day and longed to be delivered. But God is not slow; he just is not on our timetable (Psalm 90:4). Jesus is waiting so that more sinners will repent and turn to him. We must not sit and wait for him, but live in the realization that time is short and we have important work to do. Be ready to meet him any time, even today; yet plan your course of service as if he may not return for many years.

3:10, 11 Christ's Second Coming will be sudden and terrible for those who do not believe in him. For other prophetic pictures of the day of the Lord, see Isaiah 34:4; Joel 3:15, 16; Matthew 24; Mark 13; Luke 21; Revelation 6:12–17. Realizing that the earth is going to be burned up, we should put our confidence in what is lasting

and eternal. Do you spend more of your time piling up possessions, or striving to develop Christlike character?

3:12 How can we "hurry" Christ's return? We really can't. He is waiting so more people can repent; thus we should work hard to share the Good News and bring more people to faith in him (see Matthew 24:14).

3:13 God's purpose for mankind is not destruction but re-creation (see Isaiah 6:17; 66:22; Revelation 21, 22). He will purify the heavens and earth with fire, and he will then create them anew. We can joyously look forward to the restoration of God's good world.

3:14 We should not become lazy and complacent because Christ has not yet returned. Instead, our lives should express our eager expectation of his coming. What would you like to be doing when Christ returns? Is that the way you are living each day?

3:15, 16 By the time of Peter's writing, Paul's letters already had a widespread reputation. Notice that Peter speaks of Paul's letters as if they are on a level with "other parts of Scripture." Already the early church was thinking of them as inspired by God.

quite different from what he meant, just as they do the other parts of the Scripture—and the result is disaster for them.

17I am warning you ahead of time, dear brothers, so that you can watch out and not be carried away by the mistakes of these wicked men, lest you yourselves become mixed up too. 18But grow in spiritual strength and become better acquainted with our Lord and Savior Jesus Christ. To him be all glory and splendid honor, both now and forevermore.

3:17
1 Cor 10:12
Eph 4:14
2 Pet 2:18
Rev 2:5

3:18
Rom 11:36
2 Tim 4:18
2 Pet 1:2,8
Rev 1:6

Good-bye, Peter

3:15–18 Peter and Paul had very different backgrounds and personalities, and they preached from different viewpoints. Paul emphasized salvation by grace, not law; while Peter preferred to talk about Christian life and service. The two men did not contradict each other, however; and they always held each other in high respect. The false teachers intentionally misused Paul's writings by twisting them to condone lawlessness. No doubt this made them popular, because people always like to have their favorite sins justified, but it totally destroyed Paul's message. Paul may have been thinking of teachers like these when he wrote Romans 6:15: "Does this mean that now we can go ahead and sin and not worry about it? . . . Of course not!" Peter warns his readers to avoid the mistakes of these wicked teachers by growing in the knowledge of Jesus. The better we know Jesus, the less attractive false teaching will be.

3:18 Peter concludes this brief letter as he began, by urging his readers to get to know God better and better. This is the most important step in refuting false teachers. No matter where we are in our spiritual journey, no matter how mature we are in our faith, the sinful world always challenges our faith in one way or another. We still have much room for growth. If every day we find some way to draw closer to Christ, we will be prepared to stand for truth in all circumstances.

1 JOHN

"A GOOD MAN . . . yes . . . perhaps one of the best who ever lived . . . but just a man,'' say many. Others disagree, claiming that he suffered from delusions of grandeur—a "messiah complex.'' And the argument continues to rage over Jesus' true identity. Whoever he was, they all agree that Jesus left his mark on history.

Hearing these discussions, even Christians can begin to wonder and doubt. Is Jesus really God? Did he come to save sinners like us?

First John was written to dispel doubts and to build assurance by presenting a clear picture of Christ. Entering into human history through the incarnation, the Son of God became the very embodiment of God in the flesh—seen, heard, and touched by the author of this epistle, John the apostle. John walked and talked with Jesus, saw him heal, heard him teach, watched him die, met him arisen, and saw him ascend. John knew God—he had lived with him and had seen him work.

As the elder statesman in the church, he wrote this letter to his "little children." In it he presents God as light, as love, and as life. He explains in simple and practical terms what it means to have fellowship with God.

At the same time, false teachers had entered the church, denying the incarnation of Christ. John wrote to correct their serious errors. So, John's letter is a model for us to follow as we combat modern heresies.

John opens this letter by giving his credentials as an eyewitness of the incarnation and by stating his reason for writing (1:1–4). He then presents God as "light," symbolizing absolute purity and holiness (1:5–7), and explains how believers can walk in God's light and have fellowship with him (1:8–10) because they have Christ as their advocate (2:1, 2). He urges them to obey Christ fully and to love all the members of God's family (2:3–17). He warns his readers of "antichrists" and the Antichrist who will try to lead them away from the truth (2:18–29).

In the next section, John presents God as love (3:1—4:21). Because God loves us, he calls us his children and makes us like Christ (3:1, 2). This truth should motivate us to live in union with Christ (3:3–6). We can be sure that our fellowship with God is genuine when our lives are filled with good works and love for others (3:7–24). Again, John warns of false teachers who twist the truth. We should reject these false teachers (4:1–6) as we continue to live in God's love (4:7–21).

In the last section, John presents God as "life" (5:1–21). God's life is in his Son. To have life in his Son is to have eternal life.

First John was written to help you know the reality of God in your life, to assure you that you have eternal life through Christ, and to encourage you to have continual fellowship with the God who is light and love. Read of God's love in this letter and with renewed confidence, pass on his love to others.

VITAL STATISTICS

PURPOSE:
To reassure Christians in their faith and to counter false teachings

AUTHOR:
The apostle John

TO WHOM WRITTEN:
The letter is untitled and was written to no particular church. It was sent as a pastoral letter to several Gentile congregations. It was also written to all believers everywhere.

DATE WRITTEN:
Probably between A.D. 85 and 90 from Ephesus

SETTING:
John was an older man and perhaps the only surviving apostle at this time. He had not yet been banished to the island of Patmos where he would live in exile. As an eyewitness of Christ, he wrote authoritatively to give this new generation of believers assurance and confidence in God and in their faith.

KEY VERSE:
"I have written this to you who believe in the Son of God so that you may know you have eternal life" (5:13).

KEY PEOPLE:
John, Jesus

SPECIAL FEATURES:
John is the apostle of love, and love is mentioned throughout this letter. There are a number of similarities between this letter and John's Gospel—in vocabulary, style, and main ideas. John uses brief statements and simple words, and he features sharp contrasts—light and darkness, truth and error, God and Satan, life and death, love and hate.

THE BLUEPRINT

1. God is light (1:1—2:29)
2. God is love (3:1—4:21)
3. God is life (5:1–21)

John wrote about the most vital aspects of faith so readers would know Christian truth from error. He emphasizes the basics of faith so we can be confident in our faith. In our dark world, God is light. In our cold world, God brings the warmth of love. In our dying world, God brings life. When we feel a lack of confidence, these truths bring us certainty.

MEGATHEMES

THEME	EXPLANATION	IMPORTANCE
Sin	Even Christians sin. Sin requires God's forgiveness and Christ's death provides it for us. Determining to live according to God's standards in the Bible shows our lives are being transformed.	We cannot deny our sin nature, maintain that we are "above" sinning, or minimize the consequences of sin in our relationship with God. We must resist the attraction of sin, yet we must confess when we do sin.
Love	Christ commands us to love others as he did. This love is evidence that we are truly saved. God is the Creator of love; he cares that his children love each other.	Love means putting others first, being unselfish. Love is action—showing others we care—not just saying it. To show love we must give sacrificially of our time and money to meet the needs of others.
Family of God	We become God's children by believing in Christ. God's life in us enables us to love our fellow family members.	How we treat others shows who our Father is. Live as a faithful, loving family member.
Truth and Error	Teaching that the body does not matter, false teachers encouraged believers to throw off moral restraints. They also taught that Christ wasn't really a man and that we must be saved by having some special mystical knowledge. The result was that people became indifferent to sin.	God is truth and light, so the more we get to know him the better we can keep focused on the truth. Don't be led astray by any teaching that denies Christ's deity or humanity. Check the message; test the claims.
Assurance	God is in control of heaven and earth. Because his Word is true, we can have assurance of eternal life and victory over sin. By faith we can be certain of our eternal destiny with him.	Assurance of our relationship with God is a promise, but it is also a way of life. We build our confidence by trusting in God's Word and in Christ's provision for our sin.

1. God is light

Jesus Christ is God's Son

1 Christ was alive when the world began, yet I myself have seen him with my own eyes and listened to him speak. I have touched him with my own hands. He is God's message of life. ²This one who is life from God has been shown to us and we guarantee that we have seen him; I am speaking of Christ, who is eternal Life. He was with the Father and then was shown to us. ³Again I say, we are telling

1:1
Jn 1:1,4,14
1 Jn 4:14

1:2
Jn 1:1-4
19:35; 20:30,31
1 Jn 5:11,13,20

1:1 First John was written by John, one of Jesus' original 12 disciples. He was the "disciple Jesus loved" (John 21:20) and, along with Peter and James, had a special relationship with Jesus. This letter was probably written between A.D. 85–90 from Ephesus, before John's exile to the island of Patmos (see Revelation 1:9). Jerusalem had been destroyed in A.D. 70, and Christians were scattered throughout the empire. By the time John wrote this epistle, Christianity had been around for more than a generation. It had faced and survived severe persecution. The main problem confronting the church at this time was seduction: many believers were conforming to the world's standards, failing to stand up for Christ, and compromising their faith. False teachers were plentiful, and they accelerated the church's downward slide away from the Christian faith.

John wrote this letter to put believers back on track, to show the difference between light and darkness, and to encourage the church to grow in genuine love for God and for each other. He also wrote to assure true believers that they possessed eternal life and to help them know their faith was genuine—so they could enjoy all the benefits of being God's children. For more about John, see his Profile in John 13.

1:1–5 John opens his first letter to the churches much as he opened his Gospel, emphasizing that Christ is eternal, that God came into the world as a man, that he, John, was an eyewitness to Jesus' life, and that Jesus brings light and life.

1:3 As an eyewitness to Jesus' ministry, John was qualified to teach the truth about him. The readers of this letter had not seen and heard Jesus themselves, but they could trust that what John wrote was accurate. We are like those second- and third-generation Christians. Though we have not personally seen, heard, or touched Jesus, we have the New Testament record of his eyewitnesses, and we can trust that they spoke the truth about him.

you about what we ourselves have actually seen and heard, so that you may share the fellowship and the joys we have with the Father and with Jesus Christ his son. 4And if you do as I say in this letter, then you, too, will be full of joy, and so will we.

1:4
Jn 15:11

Living in the light of God

1:5
Jn 1:9; 8:12
1 Tim 6:16
1 Jn 3:11
1:6
2 Cor 6:14
1:7
Heb 9:14
1:8
Prov 20:9
1:9
Heb 9:14
1:10
Prov 20:9

5This is the message God has given us to pass on to you: that God is Light and in him is no darkness at all. 6So if we say we are his friends, but go on living in spiritual darkness and sin, we are lying. 7But if we are living in the light of God's presence, just as Christ does, then we have wonderful fellowship and joy with each other, and the blood of Jesus his Son cleanses us from every sin.

8If we say that we have no sin, we are only fooling ourselves, and refusing to accept the truth. 9But if we confess our sins to him, he can be depended on to forgive us and to cleanse us from every wrong. [And it is perfectly proper for God to do this for us because Christ died to wash away our sins.] 10If we claim we have not sinned, we are lying and calling God a liar, *for he says we have sinned.*

1:9 *Confess our sins to him,* implied. Literally, "if we confess our sins."

1:3, 4 There are three steps to true Christian fellowship. First, it is grounded in the testimony of the Word of God. Without this underlying strength, togetherness is impossible. Second, it is mutual, depending on the unity of believers. Third, it is daily renewed through the Holy Spirit. True fellowship combines the social and the spiritual, and it is made possible only by a living relationship with Christ.

1:5, 6 Light represents what is good, pure, true, holy, and reliable. Darkness represents sin and evil. To say "God is light" means that God is perfectly holy and true, and that he alone can guide us out of the darkness of sin. Light is also related to truth, in that it exposes whatever exists, whether it is good or bad. In the dark, good and evil look alike; in the light, they can be clearly distinguished. Just as darkness cannot exist in the presence of light, sin cannot exist in the presence of a holy God. If we want to have a relationship with God, we must put aside our sinful ways of living. To claim that relationship but live for ourselves is hypocrisy. Christ will expose and judge such deceit.

1:6 False teachers who thought the body was evil or worthless had one of two approaches to behavior: either they insisted on denying bodily desires through rigid discipline, or they approved of gratifying every physical lust because the body was going to be destroyed anyway. Obviously the second approach was more popular! Here John exposes the error in both these approaches. Faith is not real unless it results in changed lives and good works, and people cannot be true believers if they continue living in sin. And the body itself is not evil, for Jesus himself had a human body.

1:7 How does Jesus' blood cleanse us from every sin? In Old Testament times, believers symbolically transferred their sins to the head of an animal, which they then sacrificed (see a description of this ceremony in Leviticus 4). The animal died in their place, ridding them of sin and allowing them to continue living in God's favor. This ceremony taught important truths about sin and forgiveness, but it did not actually remove sin. Real cleansing from sin came with Jesus, the "Lamb of God who takes away the world's sin" (John 1:29). Sin, by its very nature, brings death—that is a fact as certain as the law of gravity. Jesus did not die for his own sins; he had none. Instead, by a transaction we may never fully understand, he died for the sins of the world. When we identify ourselves with him, his death becomes ours. We discover that he has already paid the penalty for our sins; his blood has cleansed us. Just as he rose from the grave, we rise to a new life of fellowship with him (Romans 6:4).

1:8 John here attacks more false teaching. Some were saying they had no natural tendency toward sin, that their sinful nature had been eliminated, and that they were now incapable of sinning. This is at best self-deception, at worst a lie. They refused to take sin seriously. They wanted to be considered Christians, but they saw no need to confess their sins and repent. The blood of Jesus did not mean much to them, because they didn't think they needed it. Instead of repenting and being cleansed by Christ's blood, they were introducing impurity into the circle of believers. In this life, no Christian will ever be beyond sinning, so no one should dare let down his guard.

1:8–10 The false teachers taught not only that they had no sin in them (1:8), but also that no matter what they did they would not sin (1:10). This is a lie. They forgot one basic truth: we are sinners by nature and by practice. At conversion all our sins are forgiven—past, present, and future. Yet even after we become Christians, we still sin and must confess. This kind of confession is not to gain God's acceptance, but to remove the barrier to fellowship that our sin has put between us and him. It is difficult, however, for many people to admit their faults and shortcomings, even to God. It takes humility and honesty to recognize our weaknesses, and most of us would rather pretend we are strong. But we need not fear revealing our sins to God—he knows them already. He will not push us away, no matter what we've done. Instead he will push away the sins and draw us to himself.

1:9 Confession is supposed to free us to enjoy fellowship with Christ. It should ease our consciences and lighten our cares. But some Christians do not understand how it works. They feel so guilty that they confess the same sins over and over, and then wonder if they might have forgotten something. Other Christians believe God forgives them when they confess, but if they died with unconfessed sins, they would be forever lost. These Christians do not understand that *God wants to forgive us.* He allowed his beloved Son to die just so he could pardon us. When we come to Christ, he forgives all the sins we have committed or will ever commit. We don't need to confess the same sins all over again, and we don't need to fear that he will cast us out if we don't keep our slate perfectly clear at all moments. Of course we want to continue to confess our sins, but not because we think failure to do so will make us lose our salvation. Our hope in Christ is secure. Instead, we confess our sins so we can enjoy maximum fellowship and joy with him.

True confession also involves a commitment not to continue in sin. We are not genuinely confessing our sins before God if we plan to commit the sin again and just want temporary forgiveness. We must pray for strength to defeat the temptation the next time it appears.

2 My little children, I am telling you this so that you will stay away from sin. But if you sin, there is someone to plead for you before the Father. His name is Jesus Christ, the one who is all that is good and who pleases God completely. 2He is the one who took God's wrath against our sins upon himself, and brought us into fellowship with God; and he is the forgiveness for our sins, and not only ours but all the world's.

3And how can we be sure that we belong to him? By looking within ourselves: are we really trying to do what he wants us to?

4Someone may say, "I am a Christian; I am on my way to heaven; I belong to Christ." But if he doesn't do what Christ tells him to, he is a liar. 5But those who do what Christ tells them to will learn to love God more and more. That is the way to know whether or not you are a Christian. 6Anyone who says he is a Christian should live as Christ did.

7Dear brothers, I am not writing out a new rule for you to obey, for it is an old one you have always had, right from the start. You have heard it all before. 8Yet it is always new, and works for you just as it did for Christ; and as we obey this commandment, *to love one another*, the darkness in our lives disappears and the new light of life in Christ shines in.

9Anyone who says he is walking in the light of Christ but dislikes his fellow man,

2:1
Rom 8:34
1 Tim 2:5
Heb 7:25; 9:24

2:2
Jn 1:29; 4:42
Rom 3:25
Heb 2:17
1 Jn 4:10

2:3
1 Jn 3:22,24

2:5
Jn 14:23
1 Jn 2:3; 3:24
4:12; 5:2

2:6
Mt 11:29
Jn 6:56,57; 15:4
1 Pet 2:21

2:7
Heb 6:9
1 Jn 3:2,11,23
2 Jn 5,6

2:8
Jn 1:9; 13:34
Eph 5:8
1 Thess 5:4

2:2 *he is the forgiveness for our sins,* or "he is the atoning sacrifice for our sins."

Contrast between:	Passage
Light and darkness	1:5
The new rule and the old commandment	2:7, 8
Loving God and loving the world	2:15, 16
Christ and Antichrist	2:18
Truth and falsehood	2:20, 21
Child of God and child of Satan	3:1–10
Eternal life and eternal death	3:14
Love and hatred	3:15, 16
True teaching and false teaching	4:1–3
Love and fear	4:18, 19
Having life and not having life	5:11, 12

A BOOK OF CONTRASTS
One of the distinct features of John's writing style was his habit of noting both sides of a conflict. He wrote to show the difference between real Christianity and anything else. Here are some of his favorite contrasts.

2:1 John uses the address "little children" in a warm, fatherly way. He is not talking down to his readers but is showing affection for them. John, by now a very old man, had spent almost all his life in ministry, and many of his readers were indeed his spiritual children.

2:1, 2 To people who are feeling guilty and condemned, John offers reassurance. They know they have sinned, and Satan (called "the Accuser of our brothers" in Revelation 12:10) is demanding the death penalty. When you feel this way, don't give up hope—the best defense attorney in the universe is pleading your case. Jesus Christ, your advocate, is the Judge's Son. He has already suffered your penalty in your place. You can't be tried again for a case that is no longer on the docket. United with Jesus, you are as safe as he is. Don't be afraid to ask him to plead your case—he has already won it (see Romans 8:33, 34; Hebrews 7:24, 25).

2:2 We sometimes have a difficult time forgiving someone who wrongs us. Imagine how hard it would be to tell everyone we are willing to forgive no matter what they do! This is what God has done in Jesus. No one, no matter what they have done, is beyond hope of forgiveness. All we have to do is turn to Jesus and commit our hearts to him.

2:3–6 How can you be sure you belong to Christ? This passage gives two ways to know: a Christian should do what Christ tells him to do and live as Christ wants him to live. And what does Christ tell us to do? John answers in 3:23: "Believe on the name of his Son

Jesus Christ, and love one another." True Christian faith results in loving behavior; that is why John says our behavior can assure us that we are Christ's.

2:6 Living as Christ did doesn't mean choosing 12 disciples, performing great miracles, or being crucified. We cannot merely copy Christ's life, because much of it had to do with his identity as God's Son, his special role in dying for sin, and the cultural context of the first-century Roman world. To live today as Christ did in the first century, we must follow his example of complete obedience to God and loving service to people.

2:7, 8 The commandment to love is both old and new. It is old because it comes from the Old Testament (Leviticus 19:18), but it is new because Jesus interpreted it in a radically new way (John 13:34, 35). In the Christian church, love goes beyond respect to self-sacrifice and servanthood (John 15:13). In fact, it can be defined as "selfless giving." It reaches beyond friends to enemies and persecutors (Matthew 5:43–48). Love should be the unifying force and the identifying mark of the Christian community. It is the key to walking in the light, because we cannot grow spiritually while we hate others. A growing relationship with God results in growing relationships with others.

2:9–11 Does this mean if you dislike anyone you aren't a Christian? These verses are not talking about disliking a disagreeable Christian brother. There will always be people we will not like as well as others. John's words focus on the attitude that

2:11
Jn 12:35
2 Cor 4:4
2 Pet 1:9
1 Jn 2:9; 3:15

is still in darkness. 10But whoever loves his fellow man is "walking in the light" and can see his way without stumbling around in darkness and sin. 11For he who dislikes his brother is wandering in spiritual darkness and doesn't know where he is going, for the darkness has made him blind so that he cannot see the way.

Do not love this evil world

2:12
Lk 24:27
Acts 4:12
1 Cor 6:11
1 Jn 2:1

2:13
1 Jn 1:1; 4:4

12I am writing these things to all of you, my little children, because your sins have been forgiven in the name of Jesus our Savior. 13I am saying these things to you older men because you really know Christ, the one who has been alive from the beginning. And you young men, I am talking to you because you have won your battle with Satan. And I am writing to you younger boys and girls because you, too, have learned to know God our Father.

2:14
Jer 31:33
Eph 6:10
1 Jn 1:1; 1:10
2:13

2:15
Mt 6:24
Rom 12:2
Jas 1:27; 4:4

2:16
Prov 27:20
Rom 13:14

2:17
1 Cor 7:31

14And so I say to you fathers who know the eternal God, and to you young men who are strong, with God's Word in your hearts, and have won your struggle against Satan: 15Stop loving this evil world and all that it offers you, for when you love these things you show that you do not really love God; 16for all these worldly things, these evil desires—the craze for sex, the ambition to buy everything that appeals to you, and the pride that comes from wealth and importance—these are not from God. They are from this evil world itself. 17And this world is fading away, and these evil, forbidden things will go with it, but whoever keeps doing the will of God will live forever.

Warning against antichrists

18Dear children, this world's last hour has come. You have heard about the

---

JOHN COUNTERS FALSE TEACHINGS		John counters two major strands in the false teachings of the heretics in this epistle:
	1:6, 8	They denied the reality of sin. John says that if we continue in sin, we can't claim to belong to God. If we say we have no sin, we are only fooling ourselves and refusing to accept the truth.
	2:22; 4:1–3	They denied that Jesus was the Messiah—God in the flesh. John said that if we believe that Jesus was God incarnate and trust him for our salvation, we are children of God.

---

causes us to ignore or despise others, to treat them as irritants, competitors, or enemies. Fortunately, Christian love is not a feeling but a choice. We can choose to be concerned with people's well-being and treat them with respect, whether or not we feel affection toward them. If we choose to love others, God will give us the necessary strength and will show us how to express our love.

2:12, 13 John was writing to believers of all ages, his "little children," who had experienced forgiveness through Jesus. The older men were mature in the faith and had a long-standing relationship with Christ. The younger men had struggled with Satan's temptations and had won. The boys and girls had learned about Christ and were just beginning their spiritual journey. In each stage of life, God's Word is relevant. Each stage of life builds upon the other. As children learn about Christ, they grow in their ability to win battles with temptation. As young adults move from victory to victory, they grow in their relationship with Christ. Older adults, having known Christ for years, have developed the wisdom needed to teach young people and start the cycle all over again. Is your Christian growth appropriate for your stage in life?

2:15, 16 Some people think worldliness has to do with external behavior—the people we associate with, the places we go, the activities in which we participate. This is not entirely accurate, for worldliness begins in the heart. It is characterized by these three attitudes: (1) lust—preoccupation with gratifying physical desires; (2) materialism—craving and accumulating things, and (3) pride—obsession with one's status or importance. When the serpent tempted Eve (Genesis 3:6), he tempted her in these areas. Also, when the devil tempted Jesus in the wilderness, these were

his three areas of attack (see Matthew 4:1–11). By contrast, God values self-control, a spirit of generosity, and humble service. It is possible to avoid "worldly pleasures" while still harboring worldly attitudes in one's heart. It is also possible, like Jesus, to love sinners and spend time with them while maintaining the values of God's Kingdom. What values are most important to you? Do your actions reflect the world's values or God's values? Will you fail like Eve did or be victorious like Jesus was?

2:17 When our attachment to things is strong, it's hard to believe that the things we want will one day pass away. It may be even harder to believe that the person who does the will of God will live forever. But this was John's conviction based on the facts of Jesus' life, death, resurrection, and the promises he made. Knowing that this evil world and its sin will end gives us courage to continue doing God's will.

2:18–21 John is talking about the "last days," the time between Christ's first and second comings. The first-century readers of 1 John lived in the last days, and so do we. During this time, "antichrists" (false teachers who pretend to be Christians and lure weak members away from Christ) will appear. Finally, just before the world ends, one great Antichrist will arise (Revelation 13; 19:20; 20:10). We do not need to fear these evil people, however. The Holy Spirit shows us their errors, so we are not deceived. However, we must teach the Word of God clearly and carefully to the peripheral, weak members among us so they won't fall prey to these teachers "who come disguised as harmless sheep, but are wolves" (Matthew 7:15).

Antichrist who is coming—the one who is against Christ—and already many such persons have appeared. This makes us all the more certain that the end of the world is near. [19]These "against-Christ" people used to be members of our churches, but they never really belonged with us or else they would have stayed. When they left us it proved that they were not of us at all.

[20]But you are not like that, for the Holy Spirit has come upon you, and you know the truth. [21]So I am not writing to you as to those who need to know the truth, but I warn you as those who can discern the difference between true and false.

[22]And who is the greatest liar? The one who says that Jesus is not Christ. Such a person is antichrist, for he does not believe in God the Father and in his Son. [23]For a person who doesn't believe in Christ, God's Son, can't have God the Father either. But he who has Christ, God's Son, has God the Father also.

[24]So keep on believing what you have been taught from the beginning. If you do, you will always be in close fellowship with both God the Father and his Son. [25]And he himself has promised us this: *eternal life*.

[26]These remarks of mine about the Antichrist are pointed at those who would dearly love to blindfold you and lead you astray. [27]But you have received the Holy Spirit and he lives within you, in your hearts, so that you don't need anyone to teach you what is right. For he teaches you all things, and he is the Truth, and no liar; and so, just as he has said, you must live in Christ, never to depart from him.

[28]And now, my little children, stay in happy fellowship with the Lord so that when he comes you will be sure that all is well, and will not have to be ashamed and shrink back from meeting him. [29]Since we know that God is always good and does only right, we may rightly assume that all those who do right are his children.

2:19
Mt 24:24
2 Tim 2:19

2:20
Jn 14:26
1 Jn 2:27

2:23
Jn 8:19; 16:3
17:3
1 Jn 4:15; 5:1

2:24
1 Jn 1:3; 2:7
2 Jn 9

2:25
Jn 3:15; 6:40
17:3

2:26
1 Jn 3:7
2 Jn 7

2:27
Jer 31:33
Jn 14:16,26
16:13
1 Cor 2:10-12
1 Thess 4:9
1 Jn 2:20

2:28
Mk 8:38
Lk 17:30
Col 3:4
1 Thess 2:19
1 Jn 3:2,21

2:29
1 Jn 3:7,9; 4:7
5:1,4,18

2:19 The antichrists were not total strangers to the church; they once belonged to it, but they did not continue. John does not say why they left; it is clear that their reasons for joining in the first place were wrong. Today many people are "Christians" for less than the best reasons. Perhaps going to church is a family tradition. Maybe they like the social and business contacts they make there. Or possibly going to church is a long-standing habit, and they have never stopped to ask themselves why they do it. What is your main reason for being a Christian? Unless it is a Christ-centered reason, you may not really belong. You don't have to settle for less than the best. You can become personally acquainted with Jesus Christ and become a loyal, trustworthy follower.

2:20 When you become a Christian you receive the Holy Spirit. One way the Holy Spirit helps the believer and the church is by communicating truth. Jesus is the Truth (John 14:6), and the Holy Spirit guides believers to him (John 16:13). People who are against Christ are also against truth, and the Holy Spirit is not working in their lives. But people who are led by the Spirit are continually growing in their experience of Jesus' truth (see 2:27).

2:23 Apparently the "antichrists" in John's day were attempting to be loyal to God while denying and opposing Christ. This, John firmly said, is impossible. Since Jesus is God's Son and his Messiah, to deny him is to reject God's way of revealing himself to the world. A person who accepts Christ as God's Son, however, accepts God the Father at the same time. The two are one and cannot be separated. Many cultists today call themselves "Christians" but deny that Jesus is divine. We must expose these heresies and oppose such teachings so the weak believers among us do not succumb to their teachings.

2:24 These Christians had heard the gospel, very likely from John himself. They knew that Christ was God's Son, that he died for our sins and was raised to give us new life, and that he would return

and establish his Kingdom in its fullness. But now they were being infiltrated by teachers who denied these basic doctrines of the Christian faith, and some of the believers were in danger of succumbing to false arguments. John encouraged them to hold on to the Christian truth they heard at the beginning of their walk with Christ. It is important to grow in our knowledge of the Lord, to deepen our understanding through careful study, and to teach these truths to others. But no matter how much we learn, we must never abandon the basic truths about Jesus. Jesus will always be God's Son, and his sacrifice for our sins is permanent. No truth will ever contradict these teachings in the Bible.

2:26, 27 Christ promised to send the Holy Spirit to teach his followers and remind them of all that Jesus had taught (John 14:26). As a result, Christians have the Holy Spirit within them to keep them from going astray. In addition, they have the God-inspired Scriptures, against which they can test questionable teachings. Let the Holy Spirit help you discern truth from error. For more about who the Holy Spirit is and what he does, see the notes on John 3:6; Acts 1:5; and Ephesians 1:14.

2:27 Christ lives in us, and we also live in Christ. This means we place our total trust in him and live as he wants us to live. It implies a personal, life-giving relationship. John uses the same idea in John 15:5, where he speaks of Christ as the Vine and his followers as the branches (see also 3:24; 4:15).

2:28, 29 The visible proof of being a Christian is right behavior. Many people do some good things but don't have faith in Jesus Christ. Others claim to have faith but rarely produce good works. A deficit in either faith or right behavior is cause for shame when Christ returns. Because true faith always results in good works, those who claim to have faith *and* who consistently live rightly are true believers. Good works cannot produce salvation (see Ephesians 2:8, 9), but they are necessary proof that true faith has actually occurred (James 2:14–17).

2. God is love

We are God's children

3:1
Jn 1:11,12
17:26
Rom 8:16
Eph 1:4,5

3:2
Ps 17:15
Jn 17:24
Rom 8:19,29
1 Cor 15:49

3:3
1 Thess 5:25
1 Pet 1:7-9

3:5
Isa 53:1-12
Jn 1:29
2 Cor 5:21

3:6
1 Jn 3:9

3:7
1 Jn 2:1,26,29

3:8
Mt 13:38
Jn 8:44; 16:11
1 Jn 3:10

3:9
Jas 1:18
1 Pet 1:3
1 Jn 2:29; 3:6
4:7; 5:1,4,18

3:10
Rom 13:8-14
1 Jn 2:9; 4:8

3:11
Jn 13:34; 15:12
1 Jn 1:5; 2:7
2 John 5,6

3:12
Gen 4:3-8

3 See how very much our heavenly Father loves us, for he allows us to be called his children—think of it—and we really *are!* But since most people don't know God, naturally they don't understand that we are his children. ²Yes, dear friends, we are already God's children, right now, and we can't even imagine what it is going to be like later on. But we do know this, that when he comes we will be like him, as a result of seeing him as he really is. ³And everyone who really believes this will try to stay pure because Christ is pure.

⁴But those who keep on sinning are against God, for every sin is done against the will of God. ⁵And you know that he became a man so that he could take away our sins, and that there is no sin in him, no missing of God's will at any time in any way. ⁶So if we stay close to him, obedient to him, we won't be sinning either; but as for those who keep on sinning, they should realize this: They sin because they have never really known him or become his.

⁷Oh, dear children, don't let anyone deceive you about this: if you are constantly doing what is good, it is because you *are* good, even as he is. ⁸But if you keep on sinning, it shows that you belong to Satan, who since he first began to sin has kept steadily at it. But the Son of God came to destroy these works of the devil. ⁹The person who has been born into God's family does not make a practice of sinning, because now God's life is in him; so he can't keep on sinning, for this new life has been born into him and controls him—he has been *born again.*

We must love other Christians

¹⁰So now we can tell who is a child of God and who belongs to Satan. Whoever is living a life of sin and doesn't love his brother shows that he is not in God's family; ¹¹for the message to us from the beginning has been that we should love one another.

¹²We are not to be like Cain, who belonged to Satan and killed his brother. Why did he kill him? Because Cain had been doing wrong and he knew very well that his

---

3:1ff Verse 1 tells us who we are—members of God's family. Verse 2 tells us who we are becoming—reflections of God. The rest of the chapter tells us what we take with us as we grow to resemble God: (1) victory over sin (3:4–9); (2) love for the brothers (3:10–18); and (3) confidence before God (3:19–24).

3:1 As believers, our self-worth is based on the fact that God loves us and calls us his children. We are his children *now*, not just sometime in the distant future. Knowing that we are his children encourages us to live as Jesus did. For other references on being part of God's family, see Romans 8:14–17; Galatians 3:26,27; 4:6,7.

3:2 The Christian life is a process of becoming more and more Christlike (see Romans 8:29). This process will not be complete until we see him face to face (1 Corinthians 13:12; Philippians 3:21), but knowing that it is our ultimate goal should motivate us to live more and more like Christ each day.

3:4ff There is a difference between committing a sin and remaining in sin. Even the most faithful believers sometimes commit sins, but they do not cherish a particular sin and choose to commit it. A believer who commits a sin repents, confesses, and is forgiven. A person who remains in sin, by contrast, is not sorry for what he is doing. Thus he never confesses and never receives forgiveness. Such a person is against God, no matter what religious claims he makes.

3:5 Under the Old Testament sacrificial system, a lamb without blemish was offered as a sacrifice for sin. Jesus is "the Lamb of God who takes away the world's sin" (John 1:29). Because he lived a perfect life and sacrificed himself for our sins, we can be completely forgiven (1 John 2:2). We can look back to his death for

us and know we need never suffer eternal death (1 Peter 1:18–20).

3:8, 9 We all have areas where temptation is strong and habits are hard to conquer. These weaknesses give Satan a foothold, so we must deal with them. If we are struggling with a particular sin, however, these verses are not directed at us, even if for the time we seem to "keep on sinning." John is not talking about people whose victories are still incomplete; he is talking about people who make a practice of sinning and look for ways to justify it.

Three steps are necessary to find victory over prevailing sin: (1) one must seek the power of the Holy Spirit and the Word of God on a daily basis; (2) one must flee lustful desires; and (3) one needs the help of the body of Christ—accountability to others and the prayers of others.

3:9 We are born again when the Holy Spirit lives in us and gives us Jesus' new life. Being born again is more than a fresh start; it is a rebirth, receiving a new family name based on Christ's death for us. God forgives us and totally accepts us. The Holy Spirit gives us new minds and hearts, lives in us, and begins helping us be like Christ. Our perspective changes too. We have a new mind which is to be renewed day by day by the Holy Spirit (see Romans 12:2; Ephesians 4:22–24). So we must begin to think and act differently. See John 3:1–21 for more on being born again.

3:12, 13 Cain killed his brother, Abel, when God accepted Abel's offering and not Cain's (Genesis 4:1–16). Abel's offering showed that Cain was not giving his best to God, and Cain's jealous anger drove him to murder. People who live good lives expose and shame those who don't. If we live for God, the world will often hate us because we make them painfully aware of their immoral way of living.

brother's life was better than his. [13]So don't be surprised, dear friends, if the world hates you.

[14]If we love other Christians it proves that we have been delivered from hell and given eternal life. But a person who doesn't have love for others is headed for eternal death. [15]Anyone who hates his Christian brother is really a murderer at heart; and you know that no one wanting to murder has eternal life within. [16]We know what real love is from Christ's example in dying for us. And so we also ought to lay down our lives for our Christian brothers.

[17]But if someone who is supposed to be a Christian has money enough to live well, and sees a brother in need, and won't help him—how can God's love be within *him*? [18]Little children, let us stop just *saying* we love people; let us *really* love them, and *show it* by our *actions*. [19]Then we will know for sure, by our actions, that we are on God's side, and our consciences will be clear, even when we stand before the Lord. [20]But if we have bad consciences and feel that we have done wrong, the Lord will surely feel it even more, for he knows everything we do.

[21]But, dearly loved friends, if our consciences are clear, we can come to the Lord with perfect assurance and trust, [22]and get whatever we ask for because we are obeying him and doing the things that please him. [23]And this is what God says we must do: Believe on the name of his Son Jesus Christ, and love one another. [24]Those who do what God says—they are living with God and he with them. We know this is true because the Holy Spirit he has given us tells us so.

Distinguish truth from false teaching

4 Dearly loved friends, don't always believe everything you hear just because someone says it is a message from God: test it first to see if it really is. For there are many false teachers around, [2]and the way to find out if their message is from the Holy Spirit is to ask: Does it really agree that Jesus Christ, God's Son, actually became man with a human body? If so, then the message is from God. [3]If not, the

3:13
Jn 15:18; 17:14

3:14
Jn 5:24; 13:35

3:15
Mt 5:21,22
Jn 8:44
Gal 5:21

3:16
Jn 3:16; 15:13
Rom 5:8
Eph 5:2,25

3:17
Lk 3:11
Jas 2:15
1 Jn 4:20

3:18
Rom 12:9
1 Jn 3:7

3:19
Jn 18:37
1 Jn 2:21

3:22
Mt 21:22
Jn 8:29; 9:31
Jas 5:16

3:24
Rom 8:9
1 Jn 2:3,5,27

4:1
1 Thess 5:20

4:2
1 Cor 12:3
1 Jn 1:2; 2:23
5:1

3:20 *the Lord will surely feel it even more,* or, perhaps, "the Lord will be merciful anyway." Literally, "If our heart condemns us God is greater than our heart."

3:15 John echoes Jesus' words that one who hates another person is a murderer at heart (Matthew 5:21, 22). Christianity is a religion of the heart; outward compliance alone is not enough. Bitterness against someone who has wronged you is an evil cancer within you and will eventually destroy you. Don't let a "root of bitterness" (Hebrews 12:15) grow in you or your church.

3:16 Real love is an action, not a feeling. It produces selfless, sacrificial giving. The greatest act of love anyone can do is to give himself or herself for others. How can we lay down our lives? Sometimes it is easier to say we'll die for others than to truly live for them, which involves putting others' desires first. Jesus taught this same principle of love in John 15:13.

3:17, 18 These verses give an example of how to lay down our lives for others. Christians must show their love, and one way to do that is to provide money to help meet others' needs. This is strikingly similar to James' teaching (James 2:14–17). How clearly do your actions say you really love others? Are you as generous as you should be with your money, possessions, and time?

3:19, 20 Many are afraid they don't love others as they should. They feel guilty because they think they are not ready or they are unable to show proper love. Their conscience bothers them. John had these people in mind when he wrote this letter. How do we escape the gnawing accusations of our conscience? Not by ignoring them or rationalizing our behavior, but by right actions, says John. If we still feel guilty, we should remind ourselves that God knows our hearts as well as our actions. If we are in Christ, he will not condemn us (Romans 8:1; Hebrews 9:14, 15). So if you are living for the Lord but feel you are not "good enough," remind yourself that God is greater than your conscience. He knows you belong to him, so you can know it too.

3:21, 22 If your conscience is genuinely clear, you can come to God without fear, confident that your requests will be heard. John reaffirms Jesus' promise, "Ask, and you will be given what you ask for" (Matthew 7:7; see also Matthew 21:22; John 9:31; 15:7). You will receive if you obey, because when you obey, you ask in line with God's will. Of course this does not mean you can have anything you want, like instant riches. If you are truly seeking God's will, there are some things you do not request.

3:23 In the Bible, a person's name stands for his character. It represents who he really is. We are to believe not only in Jesus' words, but also in his very person as the Son of God. Moreover, to believe "in his name" means to pattern your life after Christ's, to become more like him by uniting yourself with him.

4:1, 2 There are many ways to test teachers to see if their message is truly from God. One is to check their words with what God says in the Bible. Other tests include their commitment to the body of believers (2:19), their lifestyle (3:23, 24), and the fruit of their ministry (4:6). But the most important test of all, says John, is what they believe about Christ. Do they teach that Jesus is fully God and fully man? Our world is filled with voices claiming to speak for God. Give them these tests to see if they are indeed speaking God's truth.

4:1–3 Some people believe everything they read or hear. Unfortunately, many things printed and taught are not true. Christians should have faith, but they should not be gullible. Verify every message you hear, even if the person who brings it says it's from God. If the message is truly from God, it will be consistent with Christ's teachings.

4:3 The Antichrist will be a person who epitomizes all that is evil, and he will be readily received by an evil world. He is more fully described in 2 Thessalonians 2:3–12 and Revelation 13.

message is not from God but from one who is against Christ, like the "Antichrist" you have heard about who is going to come, and his attitude of enmity against Christ is already abroad in the world.

4Dear young friends, you belong to God and have already won your fight with those who are against Christ, because there is someone in your hearts who is stronger than any evil teacher in this wicked world. 5These men belong to this world, so, quite naturally, they are concerned about worldly affairs and the world pays attention to them. 6But we are children of God; that is why only those who have walked and talked with God will listen to us. Others won't. That is another way to know whether a message is really from God; for if it is, the world won't listen to it.

Love comes from God

7Dear friends, let us practice loving each other, for love comes from God and those who are loving and kind show that they are the children of God, and that they are getting to know him better. 8But if a person isn't loving and kind, it shows that he doesn't know God—for God is love.

9God showed how much he loved us by sending his only Son into this wicked

4:4
Jn 12:31; 14:30
Rom 8:31
1 Jn 2:1,13
3:20
4:5
Jn 15:19
17:14,16
4:6
Jn 8:47; 10:27
14:17
1 Cor 14:37
1 Tim 4:1

4:7
1 Jn 2:3,29
3:11; 5:1
4:8
Ex 34:4,5
Mic 7:18
1 Jn 4:7,16

HERESIES Most of the eyewitnesses to Jesus' ministry had died by the time John composed this epistle. Some of the second- or third-generation Christians began to have doubts about what they had been taught about Jesus. Some Christians with a Greek background had a hard time believing that Jesus was human as well as divine, because in Platonic thought, the spirit was all-important. The body was only a prison from which one desired to escape. Heresies developed from a uniting of this kind of Platonic thought and Christianity.

A particularly widespread false teaching, later called *Docetism* (from a Greek word meaning "to seem"), held that Jesus was actually a spirit who only appeared to have a body. In reality he cast no shadow and left no footprints; he was God, but not man. Another heretical teaching, related to *Gnosticism* (from a Greek word meaning "knowledge"), held that all physical matter was evil, the spirit was good, and only the intellectually enlightened could enjoy the benefits of religion. Both groups found it hard to believe in a Savior who was fully human.

John answers these false teachers as an eyewitness to Jesus' life on earth. He saw Jesus, talked with him, touched him—he knew that Jesus was more than a mere spirit. In the very first sentence of his letter, John establishes that Jesus had been alive before the world began and also that he lived as a man among men. In other words, he was both divine and human.

Through the centuries, many heretics have denied that Jesus was both God and man. In John's day people had trouble believing he was man; today more people have problems seeing him as God. But Jesus' divine-human nature is the pivotal issue of Christianity. Before you accept what religious teachers say about any topic, listen carefully to what they believe about Jesus. To deny either his divinity or his humanity is to consider him less than Christ, the Savior.

4:4 It is easy to be frightened by the wickedness we see all around us. Evil is obviously much stronger than we are. John assures us, however, that God is stronger yet. He will conquer all evil—and his Spirit lives in our hearts!

4:6 False teachers are popular with the world because, like the false prophets of the Old Testament, they tell people what they want to hear. John warns that Christians who faithfully teach God's Word will not win any popularity contests in the world. People don't want to hear their sins denounced; they don't want to listen to demands that they change their lives. Where do you want to be popular?

4:7ff Everyone believes love is important, but we usually think of it as a feeling. In reality, love is a choice and an action, as 1 Corinthians 13:4–7 shows. God is the source of our love: he loved us enough to sacrifice his son for us. Jesus is our example of what it means to love; everything he did in life and death was supremely loving. The Holy Spirit gives us the power to love. God's love always involves a choice and an action, and our love should be like his.

How well is your love for God displayed, in the choices you make and the actions you take?

4:8 John said, "God is love," not "Love is God." Our world, with its shallow and selfish view of love, has turned these words around and contaminated our understanding of love. The world thinks love is what makes you feel good, and it is willing to sacrifice moral principles and others' rights in order to obtain such "love." But that isn't real love; it is love's exact opposite—selfishness. We cannot apply to God the view of love propagated by an evil world. Our definition of love must come from God who is holy, just, and perfect. We must learn to love like God does.

4:9, 10 Love explains (1) why God creates—because he loves, he creates people to love; (2) why God cares—because he loves them, he cares for sinful people; (3) why we are free to choose—he wants a loving response from us; (4) why Christ died—his love for us caused him to seek a solution to the problem of sin; and (5) why we receive eternal life—his love expresses itself to us forever.

world to bring to us eternal life through his death. ¹⁰In this act we see what real love is: it is not our love for God, but his love for us when he sent his Son to satisfy God's anger against our sins.

4:10
Jn 15:16
Rom 5:8,10
Tit 3:4,5
1 Jn 2:2

¹¹Dear friends, since God loved us as much as that, we surely ought to love each other too. ¹²For though we have never yet seen God, when we love each other God lives in us and his love within us grows ever stronger. ¹³And he has put his own Holy Spirit into our hearts as a proof to us that we are living with him and he with us. ¹⁴And furthermore, we have seen with our own eyes and now tell all the world that God sent his Son to be their Savior. ¹⁵Anyone who believes and says that Jesus is the Son of God has God living in him, and he is living with God.

4:12
Jn 1:18; 14:23
1 Tim 6:16

4:13
Jn 14:20
Rom 8:9
1 Jn 3:24

4:14
Jn 1:14; 3:17
4:42
1 Jn 1:2; 2:2

¹⁶We know how much God loves us because we have felt his love and because we believe him when he tells us that he loves us dearly. God is love, and anyone who lives in love is living with God and God is living in him. ¹⁷And as we live with Christ, our love grows more perfect and complete; so we will not be ashamed and embarrassed at the day of judgment, but can face him with confidence and joy, because he loves us and we love him too.

4:15
Mt 16:16
Jn 6:69
Rom 10:9

4:17
Mt 10:15
Jas 2:13

4:18
Rom 8:15

¹⁸We need have no fear of someone who loves us perfectly; his perfect love for us eliminates all dread of what he might do to us. If we are afraid, it is for fear of what he might do to us, and shows that we are not fully convinced that he really loves us. ¹⁹So you see, our love for him comes as a result of his loving us first.

²⁰If anyone says "I love God," but keeps on hating his brother, he is a liar; for if he doesn't love his brother who is right there in front of him, how can he love God whom he has never seen? ²¹And God himself has said that one must love not only God, but his brother too.

4:21
Lev 19:18
Mt 5:43; 22:37
Jn 13:34
1 Jn 3:11

3. God is life

5 If you believe that Jesus is the Christ—that he is God's Son and your Savior—then you are a child of God. And all who love the Father love his children too. ²So you can find out how much you love God's children—your brothers and sisters in the Lord—by how much you love and obey God. ³Loving God means doing what he tells us to do, and really, that isn't hard at all; ⁴for every child of God

5:1
Jn 1:11
8:41,42

5:3
Mic 6:8
Mt 11:30
1 Jn 2:3

4:10 Nothing sinful or evil can exist in God's presence. He is absolute goodness. He cannot overlook, condone, or excuse sin as if it never happened. He loves us, but his love does not make him morally lax. If we trust in Jesus, however, we do not have to bear the penalty for our sins (1 Peter 2:24). We can be acquitted (Romans 5:18).

4:12 Some people love to be with others. They befriend strangers easily and always are surrounded by many friends. Other people are shy or reserved. They have a few friends, but they are uncomfortable talking with people they don't know or mingling in crowds. Shy people don't need to become extroverts in order to love others. John isn't telling us *how many* people to love, but *how much* to love the people we already know. Our job is to faithfully love the people God has given us to love, whether there are two or two hundred of them. If God sees we are ready to love others, he will bring them to us. No matter how shy we are, we don't need to be afraid of the love commandment. God never leads us beyond the sufficiency of his strength.

4:13 When we become Christians, we receive the Holy Spirit. God's presence in our lives is a proof that we really belong to him and gives us the power to love (Romans 5:5; 8:9; 2 Corinthians 1:22). Rely on that power as you reach out to others. If you lack assurance of your salvation, listen to the Holy Spirit within you (see also Romans 8:16).

4:17 The day of judgment is that final day when we will appear before Christ and be held accountable for our lives. With God living in us through Christ, we have no reason to fear this day, because we have been saved from punishment. Instead, we can look forward to the judgment, because it will mean the end of sin

and the beginning of a face-to-face relationship with Jesus Christ.

4:18 If we ever fall prey to fear of eternity, heaven, or God's judgment, we can remind ourselves of God's love. We know he loves us perfectly (Romans 8:38, 39). We can resolve our fears first by focusing on his immeasurable love for us, then by allowing him to love others through us. We can be confident if in this life we have learned to be more like Jesus.

4:19 God's love is the source of all human love, and it spreads like fire. In loving his children, he kindles a flame in their hearts. In turn, they love others, who are warmed by God's love through them.

4:20, 21 It is easy to say we love God when it doesn't cost us anything more than weekly attendance at religious services. But the real test of our love for God is how we treat the people right in front of us—our family members and fellow believers. We cannot truly love God while neglecting to love those who are created in his image.

5:1, 2 When we become Christians, we become part of God's family, with fellow believers as our brothers and sisters. It is God who determines who the other family members are, not us. We are simply called to accept and love them. How well do you treat your fellow members in the family of God?

5:3, 4 Jesus never promised that obeying him would be easy. Hard work, however, can be rewarding if we value its results. Another way of translating the last half of verse 3 is this: "His commands are not burdensome." The hard work and self-discipline of serving Christ is no burden to those who love him. And if our load starts to feel heavy, we can always trust Christ to help us bear it.

5:5
1 Cor 15:57

5:6
Hag 2:5
Mt 18:16
Jn 15:26; 19:34
Rev 19:11,13

5:9
Mt 3:16,17
Jn 5:31-38; 8:18

5:10
Jn 3:18,33
Rom 8:16
Gal 4:6
1 Jn 1:10

5:11
Jn 1:4
1 Jn 2:25; 4:9
5:13,20

5:12
Jn 3:15,36; 5:24
14:6; 17:2,3

5:13
Jn 20:31
1 Jn 3:23

5:14
Mt 7:7
Jn 14:13
15:7
1 Jn 3:21,22

5:16
Num 15:30
Jer 7:16; 14:11
Mk 3:29
Heb 6:4; 10:26
Jas 5:15

5:17
1 Jn 2:1; 3:4

5:18
Jn 10:28,29
1 Jn 2:13; 3:9

can obey him, defeating sin and evil pleasure by trusting Christ to help him.
5But who could possibly fight and win this battle except by believing that Jesus is truly the Son of God? 6, 7, 8And we know he is, because God said so with a voice from heaven when Jesus was baptized, and again as he was facing death—yes, not only at his baptism but also as he faced death. And the Holy Spirit, forever truthful, says it too. So we have these three witnesses: the voice of the Holy Spirit in our hearts, the voice from heaven at Christ's baptism, and the voice before he died. And they all say the same thing: that Jesus Christ is the Son of God. 9We believe men who witness in our courts, and so surely we can believe whatever God declares. And God declares that Jesus is his Son. 10All who believe this know in their hearts that it is true. If anyone doesn't believe this, he is actually calling God a liar, because he doesn't believe what God has said about his Son.

11And what is it that God has said? That he has given us eternal life, and that this life is in his Son. 12So whoever has God's Son has life; whoever does not have his Son, does not have life.

13I have written this to you who believe in the Son of God so that you may know you have eternal life. 14And we are sure of this, that he will listen to us whenever we ask him for anything in line with his will. 15And if we really know he is listening when we talk to him and make our requests, then we can be sure that he will answer us.

16If you see a Christian sinning in a way that does not end in death, you should ask God to forgive him and God will give him life, unless he has sinned that one fatal sin. But there is that one sin which ends in death and if he has done that, there is no use praying for him. 17Every wrong is a sin, of course. I'm not talking about these ordinary sins; I am speaking of that one that ends in death.

18No one who has become part of God's family makes a practice of sinning, for Christ, God's Son, holds him securely and the devil cannot get his hands on him. 19We know that we are children of God and that all the rest of the world around us

5:6-8 *as he was facing death,* literally, "This is he who came by water and blood." See Mt 3:16, 17; Lk 9:31, 35; Jn 12:27, 28, 32, 33. Other interpretations of this verse are equally possible. *as he faced death,* literally, "not by water only, but by water and blood." *and the voice before he died,* literally, "the Spirit, and the water, and the blood." *Jesus Christ is the Son of God,* implied.

5:6–8 The phrase, "a voice from heaven" is a paraphrase of "he . . . came by water and blood" (see textual note). This expression may refer to Jesus' baptism and Jesus' crucifixion. At this time, there was a false teaching in circulation which said that Jesus was God only between his baptism and his death—that is, he was born merely human until he was baptized, at which time "the Christ" then descended upon him, but then later left him before his death on the cross. But if Jesus died only as a man, he could not have taken upon himself the sins of the world, and Christianity would be an empty religion. Only an act of God could take away the punishment we deserve for our sins.

5:9 In the Gospels, God twice clearly declared that Jesus is his Son, once at Jesus' baptism (Matthew 3:16, 17), and once at his transfiguration (Matthew 17:5).

5:12 Whoever believes in God's Son has eternal life. He is all you need. You don't need to *wait,* because eternal life begins today. You don't need to *work* for it, because it is already yours. You don't need to *worry,* because you have been given eternal life by God himself, and it is guaranteed.

5:13 Some people *hope* they will be given eternal life. John says we can *know* we have it. Our certainty is based on God's promise that he has given us eternal life through his Son. This is true whether you feel close to God or distant from him. Eternal life is not based on feelings, but on facts. You can know you have eternal life if you believe God's truth. If you lack assurance as to whether you are a Christian, ask yourself if you have honestly committed your life to him as your Savior and Lord. If so, you know by faith that you are indeed a child of God.

5:14, 15 The emphasis here is on God's will, not our will. When we communicate with God, we don't demand what we want, rather we

discuss with him what *he* wants for us. If we align our prayers to his will, he will listen; and we can be certain that if he listens, he will give us a definite answer. Start praying with confidence!

5:16, 17 Commentators differ widely in their thoughts about what this sin is, and whether the death it causes is physical or spiritual. Paul wrote that some Christians had died because they took communion "in an unworthy manner" (1 Corinthians 11:27–30), and Ananias and Sapphira were struck dead when they lied to God (Acts 5:1–11). Blasphemy against the Holy Spirit results in spiritual death (Mark 3:29), and the book of Hebrews describes the spiritual death of the person who turns against Christ (Hebrews 6:4–6). John was probably thinking of the people who had left the Christian fellowship and joined the "antichrists." By rejecting the only way of salvation, these people were putting themselves out of reach of prayer. In most cases, however, even if we know what the "sin which ends in death" is, we have no sure way of knowing if a certain person has committed it. Therefore we should continue praying for our loved ones and Christian brothers and sisters, leaving the judging up to God. Note that John says, "there is no use praying for him," rather than "You cannot pray about that." He recognized the lack of certainty.

5:18, 19 Christians commit sins, of course, but they ask God to forgive them and then they continue serving him. God has freed them from their slavery to Satan, and he keeps them safe from Satan's continued attacks. The rest of the world does not have the Christian's freedom to obey God. Unless they come to Christ in faith, they have no choice but to obey Satan. There is no middle ground; people either belong to God and obey him, or they live under Satan's control.

is under Satan's power and control. **20**And we know that Christ, God's Son, has come to help us understand and find the true God. And now we are in God because we are in Jesus Christ his Son, who is the only true God; and he is eternal Life.

21Dear children, keep away from anything that might take God's place in your hearts. Amen.

Sincerely, John

5:20
Lk 24:45
Jn 1:1,18; 14:20
15:5; 17:3,21,23
1 Jn 5:5,10
Rev 3:7

5:21
1 Cor 10:7
1 Thess 1:9

5:21 This verse is also translated, "Keep yourself from idols." An idol is anything that substitutes for the true faith, anything that robs Christ of his full deity and humanity, any human idea that claims to be more authoritative than the Bible, anything that replaces God as the center of our lives.

5:21 What we think about Jesus Christ is central to our teaching, preaching, and living. Jesus is the God-man, fully God and fully human at the same time. He came to earth to die in our place for our sins. Through faith in him, we can have eternal life and the power to do his will. What is your answer to the most important question you could ever be asked—who is Jesus Christ?

2 JOHN

TRUTH and *love* are frequently discussed in our world, but seldom practiced.

From politicians to salesmen, people conveniently ignore or conceal facts and use words to enhance positions or sell products. Perjury is common, and integrity and credibility are endangered species. It is not surprising that we have to "swear" to tell the truth.

And what about love? Our world is filled with its words—popular songs, greeting cards, media counselors, and romantic novels shower us with notions and dreams of ethereal, idyllic relationships and feelings. Real love, however, is scarce—selfless giving, caring, sharing, and even dying if need be. We yearn to love and be loved, but see few living examples of real love.

Christ is the antithesis of society's prevailing values— falsehood, and self-centeredness—for *he is truth and love* in person. Therefore, all who claim loyalty to him must be committed to these ideals, following and living the truth, and acting with love toward one another.

The apostle John had seen truth and love firsthand—he had been with Jesus. So affected was this disciple that all of his writings (the Gospel of John, the letters of 1, 2, and 3 John, and the book of Revelation) are filled with this theme—truth and love are vital to the Christian and are inseparable in the Christian life. Second John, his brief letter to a dear friend, is no different. John says to follow the truth and obey God (1:4), watch out for false leaders (1:7), and love God and each other (1:6).

Second John will take just a few minutes to read, but its message should last a lifetime. As you reflect on these few paragraphs penned by the wise and aged follower of Christ, recommit yourself to being a person of truth, of love, and of obedience to the Lord.

VITAL STATISTICS

PURPOSE:
To emphasize the basics of following Christ—truth and love—and to warn against false teachers

AUTHOR:
The apostle John

TO WHOM WRITTEN:
To a woman called "Cyria" or "the elect lady" and her household— some think that the greeting refers instead to a local church

DATE WRITTEN:
About the same time as 1 John, around A.D. 90, from Ephesus

SETTING:
Evidently this woman and her family were involved in one of the churches which John was overseeing—they had developed a strong friendship. John was warning her of the false teachers which were becoming prevalent in some of the churches.

KEY VERSE:
"If we love God, we will do what he tells us to. And he has told us from the very first to love each other" (1:6).

KEY PEOPLE:
John, Cyria and her children

THE BLUEPRINT

1. Watch out for false teachers (1:1–11)
2. John's final words (1:12, 13)

False teachers were a dangerous problem for the church to which John was writing. His warning against giving hospitality to false teachers may sound harsh and unloving to many today. Yet these men were teaching heresy that could seriously harm many believers—for eternity.

MEGATHEMES

THEME	EXPLANATION	IMPORTANCE
Truth	Following God's Word, the Bible, is essential to Christian living because God is truth. Christ's true followers consistently obey his truth.	To be loyal to Christ's teaching we must seek to know the Bible, but never twist its message to our own needs or purposes, nor encourage others who misuse it.
Love	Christ's command is for Christians to love one another. This is the basic ingredient of true Christianity.	To obey Christ fully, we must believe his command to love others. Helping, giving, and meeting needs put love into practice.
False Leaders	We must be wary of religious leaders who are not true to Christ's teaching. We should not give them a platform to spread false teaching.	Don't encourage those who are contrary to Christ. Politely remove yourself from association with false leaders. Be aware of what's being taught in the church.

1. Watch out for false teachers

1 *From:* John, the old Elder of the church.

To: That dear woman Cyria, one of God's very own, and to her children whom I love so much, as does everyone else in the church. ²Since the Truth is in our hearts forever, ³God the Father and Jesus Christ his Son will bless us with great mercy and much peace, and with truth and love.

⁴How happy I am to find some of your children here, and to see that they are living as they should, following the Truth, obeying God's command.

⁵And now I want to urgently remind you, dear friends, of the old rule God gave us right from the beginning, that Christians should love one another. ⁶If we love God, we will do whatever he tells us to. And he has told us from the very first to love each other.

⁷Watch out for the false leaders—and there are many of them around—who don't believe that Jesus Christ came to earth as a human being with a body like ours. Such people are against the truth and against Christ. ⁸Beware of being like them, and losing the prize that you and I have been working so hard to get. See to it that you win your full reward from the Lord. ⁹For if you wander beyond the teaching of Christ, you will leave God behind; while if you are loyal to Christ's teachings, you will have God too. Then you will have both the Father and the Son.

¹⁰If anyone comes to teach you, and he doesn't believe what Christ taught, don't even invite him into your home. Don't encourage him in any way. ¹¹If you do you will be a partner with him in his wickedness.

2. John's final words

¹²Well, I would like to say much more, but I don't want to say it in this letter, for I hope to come to see you soon and then we can talk over these things together and have a joyous time.

¹³Greetings from the children of your sister—another choice child of God.

Sincerely, John

1:2
Jn 8:32
14:16,17
2 Cor 4:7,10
1 Jn 1:8; 3:18

1:5
Jn 13:34; 15:12
Eph 5:2
1 Pet 1:22

1:6
Jn 14:15
15:10,14
Rom 13:8
1 Jn 2:7; 4:7-12

1:7
1 Tim 4:1-5
2 Pet 2:1-3
1 Jn 2:18,26
4:1-3

1:8
Phil 3:14; 4:1

1:9
Jn 8:31; 15:7
1 Jn 2:23,24

1:10
Rom 16:17
1 Cor 5:11
Tit 3:10

1:11
1 Tim 5:22
Jude 23

1:1 John was one of Jesus' 12 disciples and the writer of the Gospel of John, three epistles, and the book of Revelation. For more information about him, see his Profile in John 13. This letter was written shortly after 1 John to warn about false teachers. The salutation is literally translated, "To the chosen lady and her children." Although some think this letter was written to a specific woman, it may also refer to a church whose identity is no longer known.

1:2 The "Truth" is the truth about Jesus Christ, as opposed to the lies of the false teachers (see 1 John 2:21-23).

1:5, 6 The love Christians should have for one another is a recurrent New Testament theme. Yet love for one's neighbor is an old command first appearing in the third book of Moses (Leviticus 19:18). We can show love in many ways: by avoiding prejudice and discrimination, by accepting people, by listening, helping, giving, serving, and refusing to judge. But just knowing God's command is not enough. We must put it into practice. (See also Matthew 22:37-39 and 1 John 2:7, 8.)

1:7 In John's day, many false teachers taught that spirit was good and matter was evil; therefore, they reasoned that Jesus could not have been both God and man. In strong terms, John warned against this kind of teaching. There are still many false teachers who promote an understanding of Jesus that is not biblical. They are dangerous because they twist the truth and undermine the foundations of Christian faith. They may use the right words but

change the meanings. The way your teachers live shows a lot about what they believe about Christ. For more on testing teachers, see 1 John 4:1.

1:8 The prize and full reward to which John refers is not salvation but the rewards of loyal service. All who value the truth and persistently hold to it will win their "full reward from the Lord." Those who live for themselves and justify it by teaching false doctrines will lose that reward (see Matthew 7:21-23).

1:10 John instructed the believers not to give hospitality to false teachers. They were to do nothing that would encourage the heretics in their propogation of falsehood. In addition, if believers invited them in, it would show they were approving of what the false teachers said and did. It may seem rude to turn people away, even if they are teaching heresy, but how much better to be faithful to God than merely courteous to people! John is not condemning hospitality to unbelievers, but rather the supporting of those who are dedicated to opposing the true teachings of God. Note that John adds that a person who supports a false teacher in any way shares that teacher's wicked work.

1:13 False teaching is serious business, and we dare not overlook it. It is so serious that John wrote this letter especially to warn against it. There are so many false teachings in our world today that we might be tempted to take them lightly. Instead, we should realize the dangers they pose and actively refuse to give heresies any foothold.

3 JOHN

WHEN company arrives at the door, with them comes the promise of soiled floors, dirty dishes, altered schedules, personal expense, and inconvenience. From sharing a meal to providing a bed, *hospitality* costs . . . in time, energy, and money. But how we treat others reflects our true values. Do we see people as objects or inconveniences, or as unique creations of a loving God? And which is more important to God, a person or a carpet? Perhaps the most effective way to demonstrate God's values and Christ's love to others is to invite and welcome guests into our homes.

For Gaius, hospitality was a habit, and his reputation for friendship and generosity, especially to "traveling teachers and missionaries" (1:5) had spread. To affirm and thank him for his Christian lifestyle, and to encourage him in his faith, John wrote this personal note.

John's format for this epistle centers around three men— Gaius, the example of one who follows Christ and loves others (1:1–8); Diotrephes, the self-proclaimed church leader who does not reflect God's values (1:9–11); and Demetrius, who also follows the truth (1:12). John encouraged Gaius to practice hospitality, cling to the truth, and do what is right.

Although this is a personal letter, we can apply its lessons to our lives. As you read 3 John, with which man do you identify? Are you a Gaius, generously giving to others? A Demetrius, loving the truth? Or a Diotrephes, looking out for yourself? Determine to reflect Christ's values in your relationships, opening your home and touching others with his love.

VITAL STATISTICS

PURPOSE:
To commend Gaius for his hospitality and to encourage him in his Christian life

AUTHOR:
The apostle John

TO WHOM WRITTEN:
Gaius, a prominent Christian in one of the churches known to John

DATE WRITTEN:
About A.D. 90, from Ephesus

SETTING:
Church leaders traveled from town to town helping to establish new congregations. They depended on the hospitality of fellow believers. Gaius was one who welcomed them into his home.

KEY VERSE:
"Dear friend, you are doing a good work for God in taking care of the traveling teachers and missionaries who are passing through" (1:5).

KEY PEOPLE:
John, Gaius, Diotrephes, Demetrius

THE BLUEPRINT

1. God's children live by the standards of the gospel (1:1–12)
2. John's final words (1:13–15)

John wrote to commend Gaius who was taking care of traveling teachers and missionaries and to warn against people like Diotrephes, who are proud and refuse to listen to spiritual leaders in authority. If we are to live in the truth of the gospel, we must look for ways to support pastors, Christian workers, and missionaries today. All Christians should work together to support God's work, both at home and around the world.

MEGATHEMES

THEME	EXPLANATION	IMPORTANCE
Hospitality	John wrote to encourage those who were kind to others. Genuine hospitality for traveling Christian workers was needed then and is still important.	Faithful Christian teachers and missionaries need our support. Whenever you can extend hospitality to others, it will make you a partner in their ministry.
Pride	Diotrephes not only refused to offer hospitality, but he set himself up as a church boss. Pride disqualified him as a real leader.	Christian leaders must shun pride and its effects on them. Be careful not to misuse your position of leadership.
Faithfulness	Gaius and Demetrius were commended for their faithful work in the church. They were held up as examples of faithful, selfless servants.	Don't take for granted Christian workers who serve faithfully. Be sure to encourage them so they won't grow weary of serving.

1. God's children live by the standards of the gospel

1 *From:* John, the Elder.

To: Dear Gaius, whom I truly love.

1:1
2 Jn 1

²Dear friend, I am praying that all is well with you and that your body is as healthy as I know your soul is. ³Some of the brothers traveling by have made me very happy by telling me that your life stays clean and true, and that you are living by the standards of the Gospel. ⁴I could have no greater joy than to hear such things about my children.

1:3
2 Jn 4

1:4
1 Cor 4:15
Gal 4:19
1 Jn 2:1

⁵Dear friend, you are doing a good work for God in taking care of the traveling teachers and missionaries who are passing through. ⁶They have told the church here of your friendship and your loving deeds. I am glad when you send them on their way with a generous gift. ⁷For they are traveling for the Lord, and take neither food, clothing, shelter, nor money from those who are not Christians, even though they have preached to them. ⁸So we ourselves should take care of them in order that we may become partners with them in the Lord's work.

1:5
Rom 12:13
Heb 13:2
1 Pet 4:10,11

1:6
Col 1:10
1 Thess 1:12

1:7
Mt 10:9-14
Mk 6:8-13
Lk 9:3-5
10:4-11
Acts 20:33

⁹I sent a brief letter to the church about this, but proud Diotrephes, who loves to push himself forward as the leader of the Christians there, does not admit my authority over him and refuses to listen to me. ¹⁰When I come I will tell you some of the things he is doing and what wicked things he is saying about me and what insulting language he is using. He not only refuses to welcome the missionary travelers himself, but tells others not to, and when they do he tries to put them out of the church.

1:9
Mt 19:30; 20:16
Mk 10:31
Lk 13:30
Phil 2:3

1:10
3 Jn 5

¹¹Dear friend, don't let this bad example influence you. Follow only what is good. Remember that those who do what is right prove that they are God's children; and those who continue in evil prove that they are far from God. ¹²But

1:11
Ps 34:14
1 Cor 4:16; 11:1
1 Jn 2:29; 3:6,9

1:1 This letter gives us an important glimpse into the life of the early church. Third John, addressed to Gaius, is about the need for hospitality to traveling preachers and other believers. It also warns against a would-be church dictator.

1:1 John was one of Jesus' 12 disciples and the writer of the Gospel of John, three epistles, and the book of Revelation. For more information about him, see his Profile in John 13. We have no further information about Gaius, but he is someone John loved dearly. Perhaps he had shared his home and hospitality with John at some time during John's travels. If so, John would have appreciated his actions, because traveling preachers depended on hospitality to survive (see Matthew 10:11–16).

1:2 John was concerned for Gaius' physical *and* spiritual well-being. This was in direct contrast to the popular heresy of the day that taught the separation of spirit and matter and despised the physical side of life. Still today, many people fall into this way of thinking. This non-Christian attitude logically leads to one of two responses: neglect of the body and physical health, or indulgence of the body's sinful desires. God is concerned for both your body and your soul. As responsible Christians, we should neither neglect nor indulge ourselves, but care for our physical needs and discipline our bodies so we are at our best for God's service.

1:4 John says "my children" because, as a result of his preaching, he was the spiritual father of many, including Gaius.

1:5 In the church's early days, traveling prophets, evangelists, and teachers were helped on their way by people like Gaius who housed and fed them. Hospitality is a lost art in many churches today. We would do well to invite more people for meals—fellow church members, young people, traveling missionaries, those in need, visitors. This is an active and much-appreciated way to show your love. In fact it is probably more important today. Because of our individualistic, self-centered society, there are many lonely people who wonder if anyone cares whether they live or die. If you find such a lonely person, show him or her that *you* care!

1:7 The traveling missionaries neither asked for nor accepted anything from non-Christians, because they didn't want anyone

questioning their motives for preaching. God's true preachers did not preach in order to make money, but out of love for God. It is the church's responsibility to care for Christian workers; this should never be left to nonbelievers (see 2 Corinthians 12:13).

1:7 When you help someone who is spreading the gospel, you are in a very real way a partner in the ministry. This is the other side of the principle in 2 John 1:10 (see the note there). Not everyone should go to the mission field; those who work for Christ at home are vital to the ministry of those who go and need support. We can support missionaries by praying for them and by giving them our money, hospitality, and time.

1:9 This letter to which John refers was neither 1 or 2 John, but another letter that no longer exists.

1:9, 10 All we know about Diotrephes is that he wanted to control the church. John denounces (1) his refusal to listen to other spiritual leaders, (2) his slander of the leaders, (3) his bad example in refusing to welcome any gospel teachers, and (4) his attempt to excommunicate those who opposed his leadership. Sins such as pride, jealousy, and slander are still present in the church, and when a leader makes a habit of encouraging sin and discouraging godly actions, he must be stopped. If no one speaks up, great harm can come to the church. We must confront sin in the church; if we try to avoid it, it will continue to grow. Some leaders misuse the Old Testament idea of "opposing God's anointed"; but such use is false because that injunction applied to the prophet, not to every church leader. A true Christian leader is a servant, not an autocrat!

1:12 We know nothing about Demetrius except that he probably carried this letter from John to Gaius. The book of Acts mentions an Ephesian silversmith named Demetrius who opposed Paul (Acts 19:24ff), but this is probably another man. In contrast to the corrupt Diotrephes, Demetrius had a high regard for truth. John personified truth as a witness to Demetrius' character and teaching. In other words, if truth itself could speak, it would speak on Demetrius' behalf. When Demetrius arrived, Gaius would have certainly opened his home to him.

everyone, including Truth itself, speaks highly of Demetrius. I myself can say the
same for him, and you know I speak the truth.

2. John's final words

1:13
2 Jn 12
1:14
2 Jn 12

¹³I have much to say but I don't want to write it, ¹⁴for I hope to see you soon and
then we will have much to talk about together. ¹⁵So good-bye for now. Friends here
send their love, and please give each of the folks there a special greeting from me.

Sincerely, John

1:15 Whereas 2 John emphasized the need to refuse hospitality
to false teachers, 3 John urges continued hospitality to those who
teach the truth. Hospitality is a strong sign of support for people
and their work. It means giving them of your means so their stay
will be comfortable and their work and travel easier. Actively look
for creative ways to show hospitality to God's workers. It may be in
the form of a letter of encouragement, a "care" package, financial
support, an open home, or prayer.

JUDE

VITAL STATISTICS

PURPOSE:
To remind the church of the need for constant vigilance—to keep strong in the faith and to defend it against heresy

AUTHOR:
Jude, James' brother and Jesus' half-brother

TO WHOM WRITTEN:
Jewish Christians and all believers everywhere

DATE WRITTEN:
About A.D. 65

SETTING:
From the first century on, the church has been threatened by heresy and false teaching—we must always be on our guard.

KEY VERSE:
"Dearly loved friends, I had been planning to write you some thoughts about the salvation God has given us, but now I find I must write of something else instead, urging you to stoutly defend the truth which God gave, once for all, to his people to keep without change through the years" (1:3).

KEY PEOPLE:
Jude, James, Jesus

TO protect from harm—to guard from attack—to repulse enemies, for centuries rugged defenders have built walls and waged wars, expending material and human resources in battle to save nations and cities. And with total commitment and courageous abandon, individuals have fought for their families. It is a rule of life that we fight for survival, defending with all our strength what is most precious to us, from every real or imagined attack.

God's Word and the gift of eternal life have infinite value. They have been entrusted to Christ's faithful followers. There are many people who live in opposition to God and his followers. They twist God's truth, seeking to deceive and destroy the unwary. But God's truth stands, carried and defended by those who have committed their lives to God's Son. It is an important task, an awesome responsibility, and a profound privilege to have this commission.

This was Jude's message to Christians everywhere. Opposition would come and godless teachers would arise, but Christians should "stoutly defend the truth" (1:3) by rejecting all falsehood and immorality (1:4–19), remembering God's mighty acts of rescue and punishment (1:5–11, 14–16) and the warnings of the apostles (1:17–19). His readers are to build up their own faith through prayer (1:20), keeping close to Christ (1:21), helping others (1:22, 23), and hating sin (1:23). Then Jude concludes with a glorious benediction of praise to God (1:24, 25).

How much do you value God's Word, the fellowship of the church, and obedience to Jesus Christ? There are many false teachers waiting to destroy your Christ-centered life, the credibility of God's Word, and the unity of the body of Christ. Read Jude and determine to stand firm in your faith and defend God's truth at all costs.

THE BLUEPRINT

1. The danger of false teachers (1:1–16)
2. The duty to fight for God's truth (1:17–25)

Jude wrote to motivate Christians everywhere to action. He wanted them to recognize the dangers of false teaching, to protect themselves and other believers, and to win back those who had already been deceived. Jude was writing against godless teachers who were saying that Christians could do as they pleased without fear of God's punishment. While few teach this heresy openly in the church today, many in the church act as though this were true. This letter contains a warning against living a nominal Christian life.

MEGATHEMES

THEME	EXPLANATION	IMPORTANCE
False teachers	Jude warns against false teachers and leaders who reject the lordship of Christ, undermine the faith of others, and lead them astray. These leaders and any who follow them will be punished.	We must stoutly defend Christian truth. Make sure that you avoid leaders and teachers who change the Bible to suit their own purposes. Genuine servants of God will faithfully portray Christ in their words and conduct.
Apostasy	Jude also warns against apostasy—turning away from Christ. We are to remember that God punishes rebellion against him. We must be careful not to drift away from a firm commitment to Christ.	Those who do not seek to know the truth in God's Word are susceptible to apostasy. Christians must guard against any false teachings that would distract them from the truth preached by the apostles and written in God's Word.

1. The danger of false teachers

1:1
Mt 13:55
1:3
Acts 20:27
1 Cor 15:3-9
1 Tim 6:12
Tit 1:4
2 Pet 3:1,2
Jude 20
1:4
Rom 6:1-4
Gal 6:13
2 Tim 3:6
1 Pet 2:16
2 Pet 2:1-4,10,
18-22
2 Jn 7

1 *From:* Jude, a servant of Jesus Christ, and a brother of James.
To: Christians everywhere—beloved of God and chosen by him. ²May you be given more and more of God's kindness, peace, and love.

³Dearly loved friends, I had been planning to write you some thoughts about the salvation God has given us, but now I find I must write of something else instead, urging you to stoutly defend the truth which God gave, once for all, to his people to keep without change through the years. ⁴I say this because some godless teachers have wormed their way in among you, saying that after we become Christians we can do just as we like without fear of God's punishment. The fate of such people was written long ago, for they have turned against our only Master and Lord, Jesus Christ.

1:1 The letter of Jude focuses on *apostasy*—when people turn away from God's truth and embrace false teachings. Jude reminds his readers of God's judgment on those who apostasized in the past. This letter is a warning against false teachers—in this case, probably Gnostic teachers (see the note on Colossians 2:4ff, for a description of the Gnostic heresy). Gnostics opposed two of the basic foundations of Christianity—the incarnation of Christ and Christian ethics. Jude wrote to combat these false teachings and to encourage true doctrine and right conduct.

1:1 Jude was a brother of James, who was one of the leaders in the early church. Both of these men were Jesus' half-brothers. Mary was their mother. Joseph was the father of James and Jude, and although Mary was Jesus' true mother, God was Jesus' true Father.

1:3 Jude emphasizes the important relationship between correct doctrine and true faith. The truth of the Bible must not be compromised because it gives us the real facts about Jesus and salvation. Scripture is inspired by God and should never be twisted or changed; when it is, we become confused over right and wrong and lose sight of the only path that leads to eternal life. Before writing about salvation, then, Jude felt he had to set his readers back on the right track, calling them back to the basics of their

faith. Then the way to salvation would be clearer.

1:4 Even some of our churches today have godless (or false) teachers who twist the Bible's teachings to justify their own opinions, lifestyle, or wrong behavior. This may give them temporary freedom to do as they wish, but they will discover that in twisting Scripture they are playing with fire. God will judge them for excusing, tolerating, and promoting sin.

1:4 Because people think theology is dry, they avoid studying the Bible. Those who refuse to learn correct doctrine, however, are susceptible to false teaching because they are not fully grounded in God's truth. We must understand the basic doctrines of our faith so that we can recognize false doctrines and prevent them from hurting us and others.

1:4 Many first-century false teachers taught that Christians could do whatever they liked without fear of God's punishment. They took a light view of God's holiness and his justice. Paul refutes this same kind of false teaching in Romans 6:1–23. Even today, some Christians minimize the sinfulness of sin, believing that how they live has little to do with their faith. They may do well to ask, "Does the way I live show that I am sincere about my faith?" Those who truly have faith will show it by their deep respect for God and their sincere desire to live according to the principles in his Word.

5My answer to them is: Remember this fact—which you know already—that the Lord saved a whole nation of people out of the land of Egypt, and then killed every one of them who did not trust and obey him. 6And I remind you of those angels who were once pure and holy, but turned to a life of sin. Now God has them chained up in prisons of darkness, waiting for the judgment day. 7And don't forget the cities of Sodom and Gomorrah and their neighboring towns, all full of lust of every kind including lust of men for other men. Those cities were destroyed by fire and continue to be a warning to us that there is a hell in which sinners are punished.

8Yet these false teachers carelessly go right on living their evil, immoral lives, degrading their bodies and laughing at those in authority over them, even scoffing at the Glorious Ones. 9Yet Michael, one of the mightiest of the angels, when he was arguing with Satan about Moses' body, did not dare to accuse even Satan, or jeer at him, but simply said, "The Lord rebuke you." 10But these men mock and curse at anything they do not understand, and, like animals, they do whatever they feel like, thereby ruining their souls.

11Woe upon them! For they follow the example of Cain who killed his brother; and, like Balaam, they will do anything for money; and like Korah, they have disobeyed God and will die under his curse.

12When these men join you at the love feasts of the church, they are evil smears among you, laughing and carrying on, gorging and stuffing themselves without a thought for others. They are like clouds blowing over dry land without giving rain, promising much, but producing nothing. They are like fruit trees without any fruit at picking time. They are not only dead, but doubly dead, for they have been pulled out, roots and all, to be burned.

13All they leave behind them is shame and disgrace like the dirty foam left along the beach by the wild waves. They wander around looking as bright as stars, but ahead of them is the everlasting gloom and darkness that God has prepared for them.

14Enoch, who lived seven generations after Adam, knew about these men and

1:6 Or, "who abandoned their original rank and left their proper home."

1:5
Ex 14:21-31
Num 14:20-24
Deut 2:14,15
1 Cor 10:5-10
1:6
2 Pet 2:4,9
Rev 12:9
1:8
2 Pet 2:10
1:9
Deut 34:6
Dan 10:13,20,
21; 12:1
Zech 3:2
Rev 12:7
1:11
Gen 4:3-16
Num 16:1-35
22:20-33
26:5-11; 31:16
Hab 2:6-19
Mt 11:21
23:13-33
2 Pet 2:15-16
1 Jn 3:12
Rev 2:14
1:12
Mt 15:13
1 Cor 11:20-22
Phil 3:19
1 Thess 5:6,7
Jas 5:5
1:13
Isa 57:20
Phil 3:19
2 Pet 2:17
Jude 6
Rev 20:10; 21:8
1:14
Gen 5:18-24
Deut 33:2
1 Chron 1:1-4

1:5-7 Jude gives three examples of rebellion: (1) the children of Israel—who, although they were delivered from Egypt, refused to trust God and enter the Promised Land (Numbers 14:26- 39); (2) the angels—who, although they were once pure and holy, and living in God's presence, gave in to pride and rebelled against God (2 Peter 2:4); and (3) the cities of Sodom and Gomorrah—which were so full of sin that God wiped them off the face of the earth (Genesis 19:1–29). If the chosen people, angels, and sinful cities were punished, how much more would these false teachers be severely judged?

1:7 Many people don't want to believe that God sentences people to hell (literally, "eternal fire") for rejecting him, but this is clearly taught in Scripture. Sinners who don't seek forgiveness from God will face eternal separation from him. Jude gave this warning to all who rebel against, ignore, or reject God.

1:8 The "Glorious Ones" here probably refer to angels. Just as the men of Sodom insulted angels (Genesis 19), these false teachers whom Jude refers to, scoff at any authority. For more information on the danger of insulting Glorious Ones, see the note on 2 Peter 2:10.

1:9 This incident is not recorded any other place in Scripture. Moses' death is recorded in Deuteronomy 34. Here Jude is making use of an apocryphal book called The Assumption of Moses. The book demonstrated that Moses was taken immediately into God's presence after his death. Two other saints in the Old Testament were also taken into God's presence (only they were taken before they died)—Enoch (Genesis 5:21–24) and Elijah (2 Kings 2:1–15). Moses and Elijah appeared with Jesus at the Transfiguration (Matthew 17:1–9).

1:10 False teachers claimed that they possessed secret knowledge which gave them authority. Their "knowledge" of God was esoteric—mystical and beyond human understanding. In reality, the nature of God is beyond our understanding. But God, in his grace, has chosen to reveal himself to us—in his Word, and supremely in Jesus Christ. Therefore, we must seek to know all we can about what he has revealed, even though we cannot fully comprehend God with our finite human minds. Beware of those who claim to have all the answers and who belittle what they do not understand.

1:11 Jude offers three examples of men who did whatever they wanted (1:10)—Cain, who murdered his brother out of vengeful jealousy (Genesis 4:1–16); Balaam, who prophesied to get money, not out of obedience to God's command (Numbers 22—24); and Korah, who rebelled against God's divinely appointed leaders, wanting the power for himself (Numbers 16:1–35). These stories illustrate attitudes that are typical of false teachers—pride, selfishness, jealousy, greed, lust for power, and disregard of God's will.

1:12 When the Lord's Supper was celebrated in the early church, believers ate a full meal before taking part in the communion with the bread and wine. The meal was called a love feast; it was designed to be a sacred time of fellowship to prepare one's heart for communion. In several of the churches, however, this meal had turned into a time of gluttony and drunken revelry. In Corinth, for example, some people hastily gobbled food while others went hungry (1 Corinthians 11:20–22). No church function should be an occasion for selfishness, gluttony, greed, disorder, or other sins which destroy unity or take one's mind away from the real purpose for assembling together.

1:12 The false teachers were "doubly dead." They were useless because they weren't producing fruit; and they weren't even believers, so they were rooted up and burned.

said this about them: "See, the Lord is coming with millions of his holy ones. [15]He will bring the people of the world before him in judgment, to receive just punishment, and to prove the terrible things they have done in rebellion against God, revealing all they have said against him." [16]These men are constant gripers, never satisfied, doing whatever evil they feel like; they are loudmouthed "show-offs," and when they show respect for others, it is only to get something from them in return.

1:16
Num 14:36-38
Deut 1:27,28
1 Thess 4:3-8
Jas 1:14,15
1 Pet 2:3,10,18
Jude 18

2. The duty to fight for God's truth

1:17
Heb 2:3
2 Pet 3:2

[17]Dear friends, remember what the apostles of our Lord Jesus Christ told you, [18]that in the last times there would come these scoffers whose whole purpose in life is to enjoy themselves in every evil way imaginable. [19]They stir up arguments; they love the evil things of the world; they do not have the Holy Spirit living in them.

1:18
2 Pet 3:3
Jude 16

1:19
Prov 18:1
1 Cor 2:14

[20]But you, dear friends, must build up your lives ever more strongly upon the foundation of our holy faith, learning to pray in the power and strength of the Holy Spirit.

1:20
Acts 9:31
Rom 8:15,26,27
Col 2:7
Jude 3

[21]Stay always within the boundaries where God's love can reach and bless you. Wait patiently for the eternal life that our Lord Jesus Christ in his mercy is going to give you. [22]Try to help those who argue against you. Be merciful to those who doubt. [23]Save some by snatching them as from the very flames of hell itself. And as for others, help them to find the Lord by being kind to them, but be careful that you yourselves aren't pulled along into their sins. Hate every trace of their sin while being merciful to them as sinners.

1:21
2 Tim 4:8
Tit 2:13
Heb 9:28

1:23
Rom 11:14
1 Cor 5:5
Rev 3:4

1:24,25
Jn 10:28,29
Rom 14:4; 16:25
2 Cor 4:14
Eph 3:20
1 Pet 4:13

[24,25]And now—all glory to him who alone is God, who saves us through Jesus Christ our Lord; yes, splendor and majesty, all power and authority are his from the beginning; his they are and his they evermore shall be. And he is able to keep you from slipping and falling away, and to bring you, sinless and perfect, into his glorious presence with mighty shouts of everlasting joy. Amen.

1:14 Enoch is mentioned briefly in Genesis 5:21–24. This quotation is from a book of the Apocrypha called 1 Enoch.

1:14 Other places where Jesus is mentioned as coming with angels are Matthew 16:27 and 24:31. Daniel 7:10 speaks of God judging mankind in the presence of millions of angels.

1:17 Other apostles also warned about false teachers—see Acts 20:29; 1 Timothy 4:1; 2 Timothy 3:1–5; 2 Peter 2:1–3; 2 John 7.

1:18 The "last times" is a common phrase referring to the time between Jesus' first and second comings. We live in the last times.

1:20 To pray in the power and strength of the Holy Spirit means to be guided by the Holy Spirit who prays for us (Romans 8:26, 27), opens our minds to Jesus (John 14:26), and teaches us about him (John 15:26).

1:21 To stay within the boundaries of God's love means to live close to him and his people, not listening to false teachers who would pull us away from him (John 15:9, 10).

1:22, 23 Effective witnessing saves people from God's judgment. Unbelievers, no matter how successful they seem by worldly standards, are lost and in need of salvation. We should not take witnessing lightly—it is a matter of life and death.

1:23 In trying to find common ground with those to whom we witness, we must be careful not to fall into the quicksand of compromise. When reaching out to others, we must be sure our own footing is safe and secure. Be careful not to become so much like non-Christians that no one can tell who you are or what you believe. Influence them for Christ—don't allow them to influence you to sin!

1:24, 25 As the epistle begins, so it ends—with assurance. God's power enables believers to keep from falling prey to false teachers. Although false teachers are widespread and dangerous, we don't have to be afraid if we trust God and are rooted and grounded in him.

1:24, 25 To be sinless and perfect (literally, "without blemish") will be the ultimate condition of the believer when he or she finally sees Christ face to face. When we are given our new bodies, we will be like Christ (1 John 3:2). Coming into Christ's presence will be more wonderful than we could ever imagine!

1:24, 25 The audience to whom Jude wrote was susceptible to heresies and to temptations toward immoral living. He encouraged the believers to remain firm in their faith and trust in God's promises for their future. This was all the more important because they were living in a time of increased apostasy. We too are living in the last days, much closer to the end than were the original readers of this letter. We too are susceptible to doctrinal error. We too are tempted to give in to sin. Although there is much false teaching around us, we need not fear or give up in despair—God can keep us from falling, and if we remain faithful, he guarantees that he will bring us into his presence and give us everlasting joy.

THE REVELATION

VITAL STATISTICS

PURPOSE:
To reveal the full identity of Christ and to give warning and hope to believers

AUTHOR:
The apostle John

TO WHOM WRITTEN:
The seven churches in Asia and all believers everywhere

DATE WRITTEN:
About A.D. 95, from Patmos

SETTING:
Most scholars believe that the seven churches of Asia to whom John writes were experiencing the persecution which took place under Emperor Domitian (A.D. 90–95). It seems that the Roman authorities had exiled John to the island of Patmos (off the coast of Asia). John, who had been an eyewitness of the incarnate Christ, has a vision of the glorified Christ. God also reveals to him what is to take place in the future—judgment and the ultimate triumph of God over evil.

KEY VERSE:
"If you read this prophecy aloud to the church, you will receive a special blessing from the Lord. Those who listen to it being read and do what it says will also be blessed. For the time is near when these things will all come true" (1:3).

KEY PEOPLE:
John, Jesus

KEY PLACES:
Patmos, the seven churches, the new Jerusalem

SPECIAL FEATURES:
Revelation is written in "apocalyptic" form—a type of Jewish literature which uses symbolic imagery to communicate hope (the ultimate triumph of God) to those in the midst of persecution. The events are ordered according to literary, rather than strictly chronological patterns.

WITH TINY wrinkles and cries, he entered the world and, wrapped in strips of cloth, took his first nap on a bed of straw. Subject to time and parents, he grew to manhood in Roman-occupied Palestine, his gentle hands becoming strong and calloused in Joseph's woodworking shop. As a man, he walked through the countryside and city, touching individuals, preaching to crowds, and training 12 men to carry on his work. At every step he was hounded by those seeking to rid the world of his influence. Finally, falsely accused and tried, he was condemned to a disgraceful execution by foreign hands. And he died—spat upon, cursed, pierced, and hung heavenward for all to deride. Jesus, the God-man, gave his life completely so that all might live.

At God's appointed time, the risen and ascended Lord Jesus will burst onto the world scene. Then everyone will know that Jesus is Lord of the universe! Those who love him will rejoice, greeting their Savior with hearts overflowing into songs of praise. But his enemies will be filled with fear. Allied with Satan, the enemies of Christ will marshal their legions against Christ and his armies. But who can withstand God's wrath? Christ will win the battle and reign victorious forever! Jesus, the humble suffering Servant, is also the powerful, conquering King and Judge.

Revelation is a book of hope. John, the beloved apostle and eyewitness of Jesus, proclaims that their victorious Lord will surely return to vindicate the righteous and judge the wicked. But Revelation is also a book of warning. Things are not as they should be in the churches, so Christ calls them to commit themselves to live in righteousness.

Although Jesus gave this revelation of himself to John nearly 2,000 years ago, it still stands as a warning to God's people today. We can take heart as we understand John's vision of hope—Christ will return to rescue his people and settle accounts with all who defy him.

John begins this book by explaining how he received this revelation from God (1:1–20). He then records specific messages from Jesus to the seven churches in Asia (2:1—3:22). Suddenly the scene shifts, as a mosaic of dramatic and majestic images burst into view before John's eyes. This series of visions portray the future rise of evil, culminating in the Antichrist (4:1—18:24). This is followed by the triumph of the King of kings, the marriage of the Lamb, the final judgment, and the coming of the new Jerusalem (19:1—22:5). Revelation concludes with the promise of Christ's soon return (22:6–21), and John breathes a prayer which has been echoed by Christians through the centuries, "Amen! Come, Lord Jesus!" (22:20).

As you read the book of Revelation, marvel with John at the wondrous panorama of God's revealed plan. Listen as Christ warns the churches, and root out any sin that blocks your relationship with him. Have hope, knowing that God is in control, Christ's victory is assured, and all who trust him will be saved.

THE BLUEPRINT

A. LETTERS TO THE CHURCHES
(1:1—3:22)

The vision John received opens with instructions for him to write to seven churches. He both commends them for their strength and warns them about their flaws. Each letter was directed to a church then in existence, but also represents conditions in the church throughout history. Both in the church and in our individual lives, we must constantly fight against the temptation to become loveless, immoral, lenient, compromising, lifeless, or casual about our faith. The letters make it clear how our Lord feels about these qualities.

B. MESSAGE FOR THE CHURCH
(4:1—22:21)
1. Worshiping God in heaven
2. Breaking the seven seals
3. Sounding the seven trumpets
4. Observing the great conflict
5. Pouring out the seven plagues
6. Seizing the final victory
7. Making all things new

This revelation is both a warning to Christians who have grown apathetic and an encouragement to those who are faithfully enduring the struggles in this world. It reassures us that good will triumph over evil, gives us hope in difficult times, and direction when we are wavering in our faith. Christ's message to the church is a message of hope for all believers in every generation.

MEGATHEMES

THEME	EXPLANATION	IMPORTANCE
God's sovereignty	God is sovereign. He is greater than any power in the universe. God is not to be compared with any leader, government, or religion. He controls history for the purpose of uniting true believers in loving fellowship with him.	Though Satan's power may temporarily increase, we are not to be led astray. God is all-powerful. He is in control. He will safely bring his true family into eternal life. Because he cares for us, we can trust him with our very lives.
Christ's return	Christ came to earth as a "Lamb," the symbol of his perfect sacrifice for our sin. He will return as the triumphant "Lion," the rightful ruler and conqueror. He will defeat Satan, settle accounts with all those who reject him, and bring his faithful people into eternity.	Assurance of Christ's return gives suffering Christians the strength to endure. We can look forward to his return as King and Judge. Since no one knows the time when he will appear, we must be ready at all times by keeping our faith strong.
God's faithful people	John wrote to encourage the church to resist the demands to worship the Roman emperor. He warns all God's faithful people to be devoted only to Christ. Revelation identifies who the faithful people are and what they should be doing until Christ returns.	You can take your place in the ranks of God's faithful people by believing in Christ. Victory is sure for those who resist temptation and make loyalty to Christ their top priority.
Judgment	One day God's anger toward sin will be fully and completely unleashed. Satan will be defeated with all of his agents. False religion will be destroyed. God will reward the faithful with eternal life, but all who refuse to believe in him will face eternal punishment.	Evil and injustice will not prevail forever. God's final judgment will put an end to these. We need to be certain of our commitment to Jesus if we want to escape this great final judgment. No one who is uncommitted to Christ will escape God's punishment.
Hope	One day God will create a new heaven and a new earth. All believers will live with him forever in perfect peace and security. Those who have already died will be raised to life. These promises for the future bring us hope.	Our great hope is that what Christ promises will be true. When we have confidence in our final destination, we can follow Christ with unwavering dedication no matter what we must face. Those facing oppression can be encouraged by hoping in Christ's return.

A. LETTERS TO THE CHURCHES (1:1—3:22)

Near the end of his life, John received a vision from Christ which he recorded for the benefit of the seven churches in Asia and for Christians throughout history. This is the only book in the Bible that promises a blessing to those who listen to its words and do what it says.

1 This book unveils some of the future activities soon to occur in the life of Jesus Christ. God permitted him to reveal these things to his servant John in a vision; and then an angel was sent from heaven to explain the vision's meaning. 2John wrote it all down—the words of God and Jesus Christ and everything he heard and saw.

3If you read this prophecy aloud to the church, you will receive a special blessing from the Lord. Those who listen to it being read and do what it says will also be blessed. For the time is near when these things will all come true.

John's greetings and praise to God

4*From:* John

To: The seven churches in Turkey.

Dear Friends:

May you have grace and peace from God who is, and was, and is to come! and from the seven-fold Spirit before his throne; 5and from Jesus Christ who faithfully

1:1
Dan 2:28-45
Jn 12:49; 17:8
Rev 1:9; 5:7
17:1
22:6,8,16

1:2
Rev 1:9; 12:17

1:3
Rev 3:11
22:7,10

1:4
Ex 3:14
Zech 3:9; 4:2-6
Rev 3:14; 17:14

1:5
Rev 3:14; 17:14

1:1 *the life of Jesus Christ,* literally, "the revelation of *(concerning,* or *from)* Jesus Christ." **1:4** *in Turkey,* literally, "in Asia." *the seven-fold Spirit,* literally, "the seven Spirits." But see Isa 11:2, where various aspects of the Holy Spirit are described, and Zech 4:2-6, giving probability to the paraphrase; see also 2:7.

1:1 Revelation is a book about the future *and* about the present. It offers future hope to all believers, especially those who have suffered for their faith, by proclaiming Christ's final victory over evil and the reality of eternal life with him. It also gives present guidance as it teaches us about Jesus Christ and how we should live for him now. With graphic pictures we learn that (1) Jesus Christ is coming again, (2) evil will be judged, and (3) the dead will be raised for judgment, resulting in eternal life or eternal destruction.

1:1 According to tradition, John, the author, was the only one of Jesus' original 12 disciples who was not killed for the faith. He also wrote the Gospel of John and the letters of 1, 2, and 3 John. When he wrote Revelation, John was in exile on the island of Patmos in the Aegean Sea, sent there by the Romans for his witness about Jesus Christ. For more information on John, see his Profile in John 13.

1:1 This verse is also translated, "the revelation *of, concerning,* or *from* Jesus Christ." The book of Revelation unveils Christ's full identity and God's plan for the end of the world; it focuses on Jesus Christ, his Second Coming, his victory over evil, and the establishment of his Kingdom. Don't focus so much on the timetable of these events or the details of John's imagery that you miss the main message—the infinite love, power, and justice of the Lord Jesus Christ.

1:1 The book of Revelation is *apocalyptic* (meaning "uncovered," "unveiled," or "revealed") in style. This is a type of ancient literature that usually featured spectacular and mysterious imagery and was written in the name of an ancient hero. John was acquainted with Jewish apocalyptic works, but his book is different in several ways: (1) he uses his own name rather than the name of an ancient hero; (2) he denounces evil and exhorts people to high Christian standards; (3) he offers hope rather than gloom. John was not a psychic attempting to predict the future; he was a prophet of God describing what God showed him.

1:1 For more about angels, see the note on 5:11.

1:1 Jesus gave his message to John in a vision, allowing him to see and record certain future events so they could be an encouragement to all believers. The vision includes many signs and symbols, because they well convey the essence of what is to happen. What John saw, in most cases, was indescribable, so he was given illustrations to show what it was *like.* When reading this symbolic language, don't think you have to understand every detail—John didn't. Instead, realize that John's imagery is used to show us that Christ is indeed the glorious and victorious Lord of all.

1:1-3 The book of Revelation reveals future events, but there is not the gloomy pessimism we might expect. The drama of these unfolding events is spectacular, but there is nothing to fear if you are on the winning side. When you think about the future, walk with confidence because Christ, the victor, walks with you.

1:3 Revelation is a book of prophecy that is both *prediction* (foretelling future events) and *proclamation* (preaching about who God is and what he will do). Prophecy is more than telling the future. Behind the predictions are important principles about God's character and promises. Each prophecy in this book has present implications—the reader is urged to trust God more and "conquer" sin (see 2:7, 11, 17, 29, 3:5, 12, 21).

1:3 The usual news reports—filled with violence, scandal, and political haggling—are depressing, and many wonder where the world is heading. God's plan for the future, however, provides inspiration and encouragement, because we know he will intervene in history to conquer evil. John encourages churches to read this book aloud so everyone can hear it and be assured of the fact that God will triumph, and that even though they may experience terrible persecution, God will vindicate them.

1:3 When John says, "the time is near when these things will all come true," he is urging his readers to be ready at all times for the last judgment and the establishment of God's Kingdom. We do not know when these events will occur, but we must always be prepared. They will happen quickly, and there will be no second chance to change sides.

1:4 Jesus told John to write to seven churches who knew and trusted him and who had read his earlier letters. The letters were addressed so that they could be read and passed on in a systematic fashion, following the main Roman road clockwise around the province of Asia (now called Turkey).

1:4 The seven-fold Spirit is another name for the Holy Spirit. The number seven is used throughout the Revelation to symbolize completeness and perfection. For more about the Holy Spirit, see the notes on John 3:6 and Acts 1:5.

1:5 The Trinity—the Father, the Son, and the Holy Spirit—is the source of all truth (John 14:6, 17; 1 John 2:27; Revelation 19:11). Thus we can be assured that God's Word is reliable.

1:6
Ex 19:6
Dan 4:34
Rom 11:36
1 Tim 6:16
1 Pet 2:5,9
Jude 24,25

reveals all truth to us. He was the first to rise from death, to die no more. He is far greater than any king in all the earth. All praise to him who always loves us and who set us free from our sins by pouring out his lifeblood for us. 6He has gathered us into his Kingdom and made us priests of God his Father. Give to him everlasting glory! He rules forever! Amen!

A JOURNEY THROUGH THE BOOK OF REVELATION
Revelation is a complex book which has baffled interpreters for centuries. We can avoid a great deal of confusion by understanding the literary structure of this book. This will allow us to understand the individual scenes within the overall structure of Revelation and keep us from getting unnecessarily bogged down in the details of each vision. John gives hints throughout the book which indicate a change of scene, a change of subject, or a flashback to an earlier scene.

In chapter one, John relates the circumstances which led to the writing of this book (1:1–20). In chapters two and three, Jesus gives special messages to the seven churches of Asia Minor (2:1—3:22).

Suddenly John is caught up into heaven where he sees a vision of God Almighty on his throne. All of Christ's followers and the heavenly angels are worshiping him (4:1–11). John watches as God gives a scroll with seven seals to the Worthy Lamb, Jesus Christ, (5:1–14). The Lamb begins to break the seals one by one. As each seal is broken, a new vision appears.

As the first four seals are broken, riders appear on different color horses—war, famine, disease, and death are in their path (6:1–8). As the fifth seal is broken, John sees those in heaven who have been martyred for their faithfulness to Jesus Christ (6:9–11).

A set of contrasting images appears at the breaking of the sixth seal. On one side, there is a huge earthquake, stars falling from the sky, and the heavens rolling up like a scroll (6:12–17). On the other side, multitudes are before the great throne, worshiping and praising God and the Lamb (7:1–17).

Finally, the seventh seal is broken (8:1–5), unveiling a series of God's judgments announced by seven angels with seven trumpets. The first four angels bring hail, fire, a volcano, and a poisonous star—the sun and moon are darkened (8:6–13). The fifth trumpet announces the coming of locusts with the power to sting (9:1–12). The sixth trumpet heralds the coming of an army of warriors on horses (9:13–21). In chapter 10:1–11, John is given a small scroll to eat. Following this, John is commanded to measure the Temple of God (11:1–3). He sees two prophets who proclaim God's judgment on the earth for three and a half years (11:4–13).

Finally the seventh trumpet blasts, calling the rival forces of good and evil to the final battle. On one side is Satan and his forces, on the other side stands Jesus Christ with his forces (11:14—13:18). In the midst of this call to battle, John sees three angels announcing the final judgment (14:1–13). Two angels begin to reap this harvest of judgment upon the earth (14:14–20). Following upon the heels of these two angels are seven more angels who pour out God's judgment upon the earth from seven bowls (15:1—16:21). One of these angels from the group of seven reveals to John a vision of a Prostitute called Babylon (symbolizing the Roman Empire) riding a scarlet animal (17:1–18). After the defeat of Babylon (18:1–24), "a vast crowd in heaven" shout choruses of praise to God for his mighty victory (19:1–21).

The final three chapters of the book of Revelation catalogue the events which finalize Christ's victory over the enemy: Satan's thousand-year imprisonment (20:1–10), the final judgment (20:11–15), the creation of a new earth and a new Jerusalem (21:1—22:5). An angel then gives John final instructions concerning the visions he has seen and what to do once he has written them all down (22:6–11).

Revelation concludes with the promise of Christ's soon return, an offer to drink of the Water of Life which runs through the main street of the new Jerusalem, and a warning to those who read the book (22:12–21). May we pray with John, "Amen! Come, Lord Jesus!" (22:20).

The Bible ends with a message of warning and hope for men and women of every generation. Christ is victorious and all evil has been done away with. As you read the book of Revelation, marvel at God's grace in the salvation of the saints, his power over the evil forces of Satan, and remember the hope of this victory to come.

1:5 Others had risen from the dead—people whom the prophets, Jesus, and the apostles had brought back to life during their ministries—but later these people died again. Jesus was the first who rose from death *to die no more.*

1:5, 6 Many hesitate to share what Christ has done in their lives because they don't feel the change has been spectacular enough. But you qualify as a witness for Jesus because of what he has done for you, not because of what you have done for him. John assures us that Christ has done specific things for each person that can be shared with others. For example, Christ demonstrated

his great love by "setting us free from our sins" through his death on the cross, guaranteeing us a place in his Kingdom, and making us priests to administer God's love to others. The fact that the all-powerful God has offered eternal life to you is nothing short of spectacular.

1:5-9 Jesus is portrayed as an all-powerful King, victorious in battle, glorious in peace. He is not just a humble earthly teacher, but the glorious God. When you read John's description of his vision, keep in mind it is not just good advice, but truth from the King of Kings. Let it penetrate your life.

⁷See! He is arriving, surrounded by clouds; and every eye shall see him—yes, and those who pierced him. And the nations will weep in sorrow and in terror when he comes. Yes! Amen! Let it be so!

1:7
Dan 7:13
Zech 12:10
Jn 19:36,37

⁸"I am the A and the Z, the Beginning and the Ending of all things," says God, who is the Lord, the All Powerful One who is, and was, and is coming again!

1:8
Isa 41:4; 48:12
Rev 21:6; 22:13

The vision of Christ

⁹It is I, your brother John, a fellow sufferer for the Lord's sake, who am writing this letter to you. I, too, have shared the patience Jesus gives, and we shall share his Kingdom!

1:9
Rom 8:17
2 Thess 3:5
Rev 1:6; 3:10

I was on the island of Patmos, exiled there for preaching the Word of God, and

1:8 *I am the A and the Z,* literally, "I am Alpha and Omega." *is coming again,* literally, "who comes" or "who is to come."

Approach	Description	Challenge	Caution	INTERPRETING THE BOOK OF REVELATION
PRETERIST VIEW	John is writing to encourage Christians in his own day who are experiencing persecution from the Roman Empire.	To gain the same kind of encouragement John's first readers gained from the vivid images of God's sovereignty.	Do not forget that most biblical prophecy has both an immediate and future application.	Over the centuries, four main approaches to interpreting the book of Revelation have developed. Each approach has had capable supporters, but none has proved itself the only way to read this book. However, the most basic application question for each approach can be summarized by asking yourself, "Will this help me become a better follower of Jesus Christ today?"
FUTURIST VIEW	Except for the first three chapters, John is describing events which will occur at the end of history.	To see in contemporary events many of the characteristics John describes and realize the end could come at any time.	Do not assume that we have "figured out" the future, since Jesus said no man will know the day of his return before it happens.	
HISTORICIST VIEW	The book of Revelation is a presentation of history from John's day until the Second Coming of Christ and beyond.	To note the consistency of man's evil throughout history and recognize that names may change but the rebellion against God has not.	Be careful before identifying current events or leaders as fulfilling aspects of the book of Revelation.	
IDEALIST VIEW	The book of Revelation is a symbolic representation of the continual struggle of good and evil. It does not refer to any particular historical events. It is applicable at any point in history.	Read the book to gain insight into the past, prepare for the future, and to live obediently and confidently in the present.	Do not avoid the book because it is difficult. Try to understand Revelation within its broader literary context.	

1:7 John is announcing the return of Jesus to earth (see also Matthew 24; Mark 13; 1 Thessalonians 4:15–18). Jesus' Second Coming will be *visible* and *victorious*. All people will see him arrive (Mark 13:26), and they will *know* it is Jesus. When he comes, he will conquer evil and judge all people according to their deeds (20:11–15).

1:7 "Those who pierced him" could refer to the Roman soldiers who pierced Jesus' side as he hung on the cross or to the Jews who were responsible for his death. John saw this event with his own eyes, and he never forgot the horror of it (see John 19:34, 35; Zechariah 12:10).

1:8 Jesus is the A and the Z (also translated, "the Alpha and Omega," the first and last letters of the Greek alphabet)—the beginning and the end. Jesus is the eternal Lord and Ruler of the past, present, and future (see also 4:8; Isaiah 44:6; 48:12–15). Without him you have nothing that is eternal, nothing that can change your life, nothing that can save you from sin. Is Christ your reason for living, the "first and last" of your life? Honor the One who is the beginning and the end of all existence.

1:9 Patmos was a small rocky island in the Aegean Sea, about 50 miles offshore from the city of Ephesus on the Asia Minor seacoast (see map).

1:9 John describes himself as a "fellow sufferer for the Lord's sake," indicating that the church was undergoing intense persecution as he was writing this letter. The whole church, as the body of Christ, should experience joy and suffering together. Follow John's example in your relationships with other Christians: identify with them, encourage them to be steadfast and faithful, and remind them of their future reward with God (see also Romans 5:2–4).

1:9 The Christian church was facing severe persecution— almost all believers were victims of suffering in some way because of this empire-wide persecution. Some were even being killed for their faith. John was exiled to Patmos because he refused to stop preaching the Word of God. We may not face such persecution for our faith in Jesus, but few of us have the courage even now to share God's Word with others. If we are afraid to share our faith during easy times, how will we do during times of persecution?

1:10
Rev 4:1,2
21:10

1:11
Rev 1:2,19
2:1,18,24
3:1,4,7,14

1:12
Zech 4:2-6

1:13
Dan 10:5,6
Rev 2:1; 14:14

1:14
Dan 7:9,10
Rev 2:18; 19:12

1:15
Dan 10:6

1:16
Rev 1:20; 2:12
10:1; 19:15

for telling what I knew about Jesus Christ. [10]It was the Lord's Day and I was worshiping, when suddenly I heard a loud voice behind me, a voice that sounded like a trumpet blast, [11]saying, "I am A and Z, the First and Last!" And then I heard him say, "Write down everything you see, and send your letter to the seven churches in Turkey: to the church in Ephesus, the one in Smyrna, and those in Pergamos, Thyatira, Sardis, Philadelphia, and Laodicea."

[12]When I turned to see who was speaking, there behind me were seven candlesticks of gold. [13]And standing among them was one who looked like Jesus who called himself the Son of Man, wearing a long robe circled with a golden band across his chest. [14]His hair was white as wool or snow, and his eyes penetrated like flames of fire. [15]His feet gleamed like burnished bronze, and his voice thundered like the waves against the shore. [16]He held seven stars in his right hand and a sharp, double-bladed sword in his mouth, and his face shone like the power of the sun in unclouded brilliance.

1:11 *in Turkey,* "in Asia." **1:13** *like Jesus who called himself the Son of Man,* literally, "like unto a Son of Man." **1:14** *His hair,* literally, "His head—the hair—was white like wool." **1:16** *in his mouth,* literally, "coming out from his mouth."

THE SEVEN CHURCHES
The seven churches were located on a major Roman road. A letter carrier would leave the island of Patmos (where John was exiled), arriving first at Ephesus. He would travel north to Smyrna and Pergamum (Pergamos), turn southeast to Thyatira, and continue on to Sardis, Philadelphia, and Laodicea—in the exact order in which the letters were dictated.

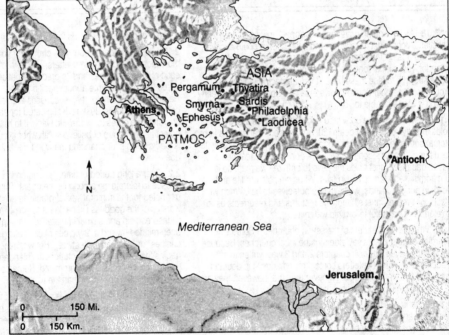

1:13 This man who "looked like Jesus" is Jesus himself. The title *Son of Man* occurs many times in the New Testament in reference to Jesus as the Messiah. John recognized Jesus because he lived with him for three years and had seen him both as the Galilean preacher and as the glorified Son of God at the transfiguration (Matthew 17:1–8). Here Jesus appears as the mighty Son of Man. His white hair indicates his wisdom and divine nature (see Daniel 7:9); his piercing eyes symbolize judgment of all evil; the golden band reveals him as the High Priest who goes into God's presence to plead forgiveness for those who have believed in him.

1:13ff Many of the details in this vision of the Son of Man recur throughout the remainder of the book (especially in the letters to the seven churches, Revelation 2—3). The repetition of these details reminds the reader that the Son of Man is directly involved in judgment and deliverance.

1:13, 14 The seven candlesticks are the seven churches in Turkey (1:20), and Jesus stands among them. No matter what the churches face, Jesus walks among them with reassuring love and fearsome power. Through his Spirit, Jesus Christ is still among the churches today. When a church faces persecution, it should remember his deep love and care. When a church is wracked by internal strife and conflict, it should remember his concern for purity and his intolerance of sin.

1:16 The sword in Jesus' mouth symbolizes the power and force of his message. His words of judgment are sharp as swords (Isaiah 49:2; Hebrews 4:12).

17, 18When I saw him, I fell at his feet as dead; but he laid his right hand on me and said, "Don't be afraid! Though I am the First and Last, the Living One who died, who is now alive forevermore, who has the keys of hell and death—don't be afraid! 19Write down what you have just seen, and what will soon be shown to you. 20This is the meaning of the seven stars you saw in my right hand, and the seven golden candlesticks: The seven stars are the leaders of the seven churches, and the seven candlesticks are the churches themselves.

The loveless church

2 "Write a letter to the leader of the church at Ephesus and tell him this:
"I write to inform you of a message from him who walks among the churches and holds their leaders in his right hand.

"He says to you: 2I know how many good things you are doing. I have watched your hard work and your patience; I know you don't tolerate sin among your members, and you have carefully examined the claims of those who say they are apostles but aren't. You have found out how they lie. 3You have patiently suffered for me without quitting.

4"Yet there is one thing wrong; you don't love me as at first! 5Think about those

1:17,18
Isa 41:4
Ezek 1:27,28
Dan 8:17,18
10:8,9,17-19
Lk 24:5
Rev 2:8
1:20
Zech 4:2
Rev 1:4,11,16
2:1; 3:1
2:1
Rev 1:11-16
2:2
2 Cor 11:13
1 Jn 4:1
Rev 2:19
2:3
Jn 15:21
Heb 12:1-13
2:4
Jer 2:2
2:5
Hos 14:1
Rev 1:20; 3:3,19

1:20 *leaders,* literally, "angels." **2:1** *leader,* literally, "angel" and so also in 2:8; 2:12; 2:18; 3:1; 3:7; 3:14. *from him who walks among the churches,* literally, "from him who holds the seven stars in his right hand and walks among the golden candlesticks."

1:17, 18 As the Roman government stepped up its persecution of Christians, John must have wondered if the church could survive and stand against the opposition. But Jesus appeared in glory and splendor, reassuring John that he and his fellow believers had God's strength to face these trials. If you are facing difficult problems, remember that the power available to John and the early church is also available to you.

1:17, 18 Our sins have convicted and sentenced us, but Jesus holds the keys of hell and death (20:14). He alone can free us from eternal bondage to Satan. He alone has the power and authority to set us free from sin's control. Believers don't have to fear hell or death, because Christ holds the keys to both. All we must do is turn from sin and turn to him in faith. When we hold our life and death in our own hands, we sentence ourselves to hell. When we place our lives in Christ's hands, he restores and resurrects us to an eternity of peaceful fellowship with him.

1:20 Who are the "leaders of the seven churches"? Some say guardian angels; others say elders of the local churches. Because each of the seven letters in chapters 2 and 3 was written to a leader and because the letters contain reprimands, it is doubtful that these leaders are angels. Whoever they are, however, they are accountable to God for the churches they lead.

2:1 Ephesus was the capital of Asia Minor, a center of land and sea trade, and, along with Alexandria and Antioch in Syria, one of the three most influential cities in the eastern part of the Roman Empire. The Temple to Diana, one of the ancient wonders of the world, was located in this city, and a major industry was the manufacture of idols of this goddess (see Acts 19:21–41). Paul had ministered in Ephesus for three years and had warned the Ephesians that false teachers would come and try to draw people away from the faith (see Acts 20:29–31). False teachers did indeed cause problems in the Ephesian church (see Ephesians 4:14; 1 Timothy 1:3,4), but the church resisted them as we can see from Paul's letter to them. John spent much of his ministry in this city and knew they had resisted false teaching (2:2).

2:1 The one who "walks among the churches" is Jesus (1:11–13). He holds the leaders of the churches "in his right hand," indicating his power and authority over the churches and their leaders. Ephesus had become a large, proud church, and Jesus' message reminds them that he is the head of the body of believers.

2:1ff Each of the letters to the seven churches basically follows a set form: salutation, evaluation (commendation and/or condemnation), exhortation, and a declaration of Christ's

return with promised rewards for the faithful.

2:1ff Does God care about your church? If you don't think so, look more closely at these seven letters. The Lord of the universe knew each of these churches and its precise situation. In each letter, Jesus tells John to write about specific people, places, and events. He praises believers for their successes and tells them how to correct their failures. Just as Jesus cared for each of these churches, he cares for yours. He wants it to reach its greatest potential. The group of believers with whom you worship and pray is God's vehicle for changing the world. Take it seriously—God does.

2:2 Over a long period of time, the church in Ephesus had refused to tolerate sin among its members. This was not easy in a city noted for the immoral sexual practices associated with the worship of the goddess Diana. We also are living in times of widespread sin and sexual immorality. It is popular to be open-minded toward many types of sin, calling them "personal choices" or "alternative lifestyles." But when the body of believers begins to tolerate sin in the church, the standards are lowered and the church's witness is compromised. Remember, God's approval is infinitely more important than the world's.

2:2, 3 The church at Ephesus is commended for (1) working hard, (2) being patient, (3) resisting sin, (4) critically examining the claims of false apostles, and (5) suffering patiently without quitting. Every church should have these characteristics. But these good things should spring from our love for Jesus Christ. The Ephesians had lost their first love, and they may have been in danger of falling into legalism. The spiritual life of the Ephesian church had become sterile. They had lost their "first love." Jesus describes this "first love" in his summary of the law in Matthew 22:37–40, "'Love the Lord your God with all your heart, soul, and mind.' This is the first and greatest commandment." Because the Ephesian Christians had failed to love God above all else, they were under God's condemnation (2:5).

2:4 The church at Ephesus was once commended for its love for God and others (Ephesians 3:17–19), but many of the church founders had died, and the second-generation believers had lost their zeal for God. They were a busy church—they did much to benefit the church and the community—but they were acting for the wrong reasons. Work for God is not lasting unless it is based on love for God and others.

2:4, 5 As when a man and woman fall in love, new believers experience enthusiasm when they realize how important it is to be

times of your first love (how different now!) and turn back to me again and work as you did before; or else I will come and remove your candlestick from its place among the churches.

2:6
Num 31:15,16
Rev 2:15

2:7
Gen 2:9
3:22-24
Prov 3:18
11:30; 13:12
Rev 22:2,14

6"But there is this about you that is good: You hate the deeds of the licentious Nicolaitans, just as I do.

7"Let this message sink into the ears of anyone who listens to what the Spirit is saying to the churches: To everyone who is victorious, I will give fruit from the Tree of Life in the Paradise of God.

The persecuted church

2:8
Rev 1:8,11,
17,18

2:9
Rev 1:9
2:13,24

8*"To the leader of the church in Smyrna write this letter:*

"This message is from him who is the First and Last, who was dead and then came back to life.

9"I know how much you suffer for the Lord, and I know all about your poverty

THE NAMES OF JESUS	Reference	Jesus' name	Reference	Jesus' name
	1:8	A to Z, Beginning to End	5:5	Root of David
	1:8	Lord	5:6	Lamb
	1:8	All-Powerful One	7:17	Shepherd
	1:13	Son of Man	12:10	Christ
	1:18	First and Last	19:11	Faithful and True
	1:18	The Living One	19:13	Word of God
	2:18	Son of God	19:16	King of Kings
	3:14	Witness	19:16	Lord of Lords
	4:11	Creator	22:16	The Morning Star
	5:5	Lion of Judah		

Scattered among the vivid images of the book of Revelation is a large collection of names for Jesus. Each one tells something of his character and highlights a particular aspect of his role within God's plan of redemption.

forgiven. But when we lose sight of the seriousness of sin, we begin to lose the thrill of our forgiveness (see 2 Peter 1:9). In the first steps of your Christian life, you may have had enthusiasm without knowledge. Do you now have knowledge without enthusiasm? Both are necessary if we are to keep love for God and others intense and untarnished (see Hebrews 10:32, 35). Do you love God with the same fervor as when you were a new Christian?

2:5 To have the "candlestick" removed from its place among the churches means to cease (1) to be an effective church or (2) to be a church at all. Just as the seven-branched candlestick in the Temple gave light for the priests to see by, the churches were to give light to their surrounding communities. But Jesus warned them that their lights could go out. In fact, Jesus himself would extinguish any light that did not fulfill its purpose.

2:6 The Nicolaitans were believers who compromised their faith in order to enjoy some of the sinful practices of Ephesian society. They falsely called themselves "apostles" (2:2). The name *Nicolaitans,* may have come from the Hebrew word for "Balaamites." Balaam was a prophet who induced the Israelites to carry out their lustful desires (see 2:14 and Numbers 31:15, 16). When we want to take part in something we know is wrong, we often make excuses to justify our behavior, saying that it isn't as bad as it seems or it won't hurt our faith. Are you tempted to compromise your faith in order to be accepted by non-Christians? Christ has strong words for those who look for excuses to sin.

2:6 Through John, Jesus commends the church at Ephesus for hating the wicked deeds of the Nicolaitans. Note that they didn't hate the people, just their sinful actions. Accept and love all people, and refuse to tolerate all evil. God cannot tolerate sin, and he expects us to stand against it. The world needs Christians who will stand for God's truth and point people toward right living.

2:7 To be victorious means to believe, persevere, remain faithful, and live as one who follows Christ. Doing so brings great rewards (21:7).

2:7 In the Garden of Eden were two trees—the Tree of Life and the Tree of Conscience (see Genesis 2:9). Eating from the Tree of Life brought eternal life with God; eating from the Tree of Conscience brought knowledge of good and evil. Adam and Eve ate from the Tree of Conscience, which God had forbidden them to do, so they were excluded from Eden and barred from eating from the Tree of Life. Eventually, evil will be destroyed and believers will be brought into a restored paradise. In the new earth, no Tree of Conscience will tempt people to sin. Instead, everyone will eat from the Tree of Life and will live eternally.

2:8 The city of Smyrna was about 25 miles north of Ephesus. It was nicknamed "Port of Asia" because it had an excellent harbor on the Aegean Sea. The church in this city struggled against two hostile forces: a Jewish population strongly opposed to Christianity, and a non-Jewish population that was loyal to Rome and supported emperor worship. Persecution and suffering were inevitable in an environment like this.

2:9-11 Everyone would like to feel good and live comfortably, but pain is part of life—and it is not easy to suffer, no matter what the cause. Jesus commended the church at Smyrna for their faith in the midst of suffering. He then encouraged them that they need not fear the future if they remained faithful. In fact, Smyrna and Philadelphia were the only churches among the seven to receive completely positive messages. If you are experiencing difficult times, don't let them turn you away from God. Instead let them draw you toward greater faithfulness. Trust him and remember your heavenly reward (see also 22:12–14). God is especially near to those who suffer for him.

(but you have heavenly riches!). I know the slander of those opposing you, who say that they are Jews—the children of God—but they aren't, for they support the cause of Satan. [10]Stop being afraid of what you are about to suffer—for the devil will soon throw some of you into prison to test you. You will be persecuted for 'ten days.' Remain faithful even when facing death and I will give you the crown of life—an unending, glorious future. [11]Let everyone who can hear, listen to what the Spirit is saying to the churches: He who is victorious shall not be hurt by the Second Death.

2:10
Dan 1:12,14
3:16-18
1 Cor 9:25
Jas 1:12
Rev 3:10; 12:11
17:14

2:11
Rev 2:7,29
20:6,14

The lenient church

[12]*"Write this letter to the leader of the church in Pergamos:*

"This message is from him who wields the sharp and double-bladed sword. [13]I am fully aware that you live in the city where Satan's throne is, at the center of satanic worship; and yet you have remained loyal to me, and refused to deny me, even when Antipas, my faithful witness, was martyred among you by Satan's devotees.

[14]"And yet I have a few things against you. You tolerate some among you who do as Balaam did when he taught Balak how to ruin the people of Israel by involving them in sexual sin and encouraging them to go to idol feasts. [15]Yes, you have some of these very same followers of Balaam among you!

[16]"Change your mind and attitude, or else I will come to you suddenly and fight against them with the sword of my mouth.

[17]"Let everyone who can hear, listen to what the Spirit is saying to the churches:

2:12
Rev 1:16; 2:16

2:13
Rev 14:12

2:14
Num 31:16
1 Cor 6:13-20
2 Pet 2:15
Rev 2:20

2:15
Rev 2:6

2:16
2 Thess 2:8
Rev 1:16; 2:5
22:7

2:17
Jn 6:49-58
Rev 2:7; 14:3
19:12

2:10 *an unending, glorious future,* implied.   **2:15** *Balaam,* literally, "Nicolaitans," Greek form of "Balaamites."

2:10 Persecution comes from Satan, not from God. Satan, the devil, will cause believers to be thrown into prison and even killed. But believers need not fear death, because it will only result in their receiving the crown of life. Satan may harm their earthly bodies, but he can do them no spiritual harm. "Ten days" means that although persecution will be intense, it will be relatively short. It has a definite beginning and end, and God remains in complete control.

2:10 The message to the church of Smyrna is to remain faithful throughout their suffering because God is in control and his promises are reliable. Jesus never says that by being faithful to him we will avoid troubles, suffering, and persecution. Rather, we must be faithful to him *in* our sufferings. Only then will our faith prove itself genuine. We remain faithful by keeping our eyes on Christ and on what he promises for us now and in the future (see Philippians 3:13, 14; 2 Timothy 4:8).

2:11 Believers and unbelievers alike experience physical death. All people will be resurrected, but believers will be resurrected to eternal life with God while unbelievers will be resurrected to be punished with a Second Death and eternal separation from God (see also 20:14; 21:8, 27; 22:15).

2:12 The city of Pergamos was built on a hill 1,000 feet above the surrounding countryside, creating a natural fortress. It was a sophisticated city, a center of Greek culture and education, with a 200,000-volume library. But it was also the center of four cults, and it rivaled Ephesus in its worship of idols. The city's chief god was a serpent, who was considered the god of healing. People came to Pergamos from all over the world to seek healing from this god.

2:12 Just as the Romans used their swords for authority and judgment, Jesus' sharp, double-bladed sword (1:16) represents God's ultimate authority and judgment. It may also represent God's future separation of believers from unbelievers. Unbelievers cannot experience the eternal rewards of living in God's Kingdom.

2:13 As the center for four idolatrous cults, Pergamos is called "the city where Satan's throne is." Surrounded by Satan worship, the church at Pergamos refused to deny Christ even when Satan's worshipers martyred one of their members. Perhaps the

Nicolaitans taught that it was alright for Christians to participate in these idolatrous rituals on the grounds that "no one believes in it anyway and it is just good citizenship." We, like Pergamos, must "remain loyal" to Christ against similar attempts to rationalize sin. Standing firm against Satan's attractive temptations is never easy, but the alternative is deadly (2:11).

2:14 There is room for differences of opinion among Christians in some areas, but there is no room for heresy and moral impurity. Your town may not participate in idol feasts, but it probably has pornography, sexual sin, cheating, gossiping, and lying. Don't tolerate sin under the pressure to be open-minded.

2:14, 15 It was not easy to be a Christian in Pergamos. Believers experienced great pressure to compromise or leave the faith. Nothing is known about Antipas except that he did *not* compromise. He was faithful, and he died for his faith. Apparently, however, some in the church were tolerating those who taught or practiced what Christ opposed. Compromise can be defined as "blending qualities of two different things," or "a concession of principles." When evil is mixed with good, the good is no longer pure. Don't allow compromise to taint your faith.

2:14–16 Balak was a king who feared the large number of Israelites traveling through his country, so he hired Balaam to pronounce a curse on them. Balaam refused at first, but an offer of money changed his mind (Numbers 22—24). Later he influenced the Israelites to turn to idol worship (Numbers 31:16; also see 2 Peter 2:15; Jude 1:11). Here Christ rebukes the church for tolerating those who, like Balaam, lead people away from God.

2:16 This sword is God's judgment against rebellious nations (19:15, 21) and all forms of sin. See also the note on 2:12.

2:17 "Hidden manna" suggests the spiritual nourishment the faithful believers will receive. As the Israelites traveled toward the Promised Land, God provided manna from heaven for their physical nourishment (Exodus 16:14–18). Jesus, as "the Bread of Life" (John 6:51), provides spiritual nourishment that satisfies our deepest hunger.

2:17 It is unclear what the white stones are or exactly what the names on each will be, but since they are probably related to the

Every one who is victorious shall eat of the hidden manna, the secret nourishment from heaven; and I will give to each a white stone, and on the stone will be engraved a new name that no one else knows except the one receiving it.

The compromising church

18 *"Write this letter to the leader of the church in Thyatira:*

"This is a message from the Son of God, whose eyes penetrate like flames of fire, whose feet are like glowing brass.

19"I am aware of all your good deeds—your kindness to the poor, your gifts and service to them; also I know your love and faith and patience, and I can see your constant improvement in all these things.

20"Yet I have this against you: You are permitting that woman Jezebel, who calls herself a prophetess, to teach my servants that sex sin is not a serious matter; she urges them to practice immorality and to eat meat that has been sacrificed to idols. 21I gave her time to change her mind and attitude, but she refused. 22Pay attention now to what I am saying: I will lay her upon a sickbed of intense affliction, along with all her immoral followers, unless they turn again to me, repenting of their sin with her; 23and I will strike her children dead. And all the churches shall know that I am he who searches deep within men's hearts, and minds; I will give to each of you whatever you deserve.

24, 25"As for the rest of you in Thyatira who have not followed this false teaching ('deeper truths,' as they call them—depths of Satan, really), I will ask nothing further of you; only hold tightly to what you have until I come.

26"To every one who overcomes—who to the very end keeps on doing things that please me—I will give power over the nations. 27You will rule them with a rod of iron just as my Father gave me the authority to rule them; they will be shattered like

2:18
Rev 1:11,14
2:24

2:19
Rev 2:2
2:20
1 Kgs 16:31
2 Kgs 9:7
2:21
Rev 9:20
2:22
Rev 17:2
2:23
Mt 16:27
Lk 16:15
2:24
Rev 2:18; 3:11
2:25
Rev 3:11
2:26
Dan 7:22
Mt 10:22; 19:28
Lk 22:29,30
1 Cor 6:3,4
Rev 2:7; 3:21
20:4
2:27
Ps 2:8,9
Rev 12:5

2:22 *along with all her immoral followers,* literally, "together with all those who commit adultery with her."

---

hidden manna, they may indicate that the individual believer receives eternal "nourishment," or eternal life. In Roman times, stones were given to people to designate a person's right to enter a banquet (similar to our engraved invitations today). The imagery here calls to mind the messianic banquet (19:7). The stones are significant because each will bear the new name of every person who truly believes in Christ. They are the evidence that a person has been accepted by God and declared worthy to receive eternal life. A person's name represented his character. God will give us new names and new hearts.

2:18 Thyatira was a working man's town, with many trade guilds for cloth-making, dyeing, and pottery. Lydia, Paul's first convert in Philippi, was a merchant from Thyatira (Acts 16:14). The city was basically secular, with no focus on any particular religion.

2:19 The believers in Thyatira were commended for growing in good deeds. We should not feel satisfied when we have done one good work, but continue to do more. These are the last days, and there is no time to rest on our laurels.

2:20 A woman in the church in Thyatira was teaching that immorality was not a serious matter for believers. Her name may have been Jezebel, or John may have used the name Jezebel to symbolize the kind of wrong she was doing. Jezebel, a heathen queen of Israel, was considered the most evil woman who had ever lived (see 1 Kings 19:1, 2; 21:1–15; 2 Kings 9:7–10, 30–37; and her Profile in 1 Kings 21).

2:20 Why is sex sin serious? Sex outside marriage always hurts someone. It hurts God because it shows we prefer to follow our own desires instead of God's Word. It hurts others because it violates the commitment so necessary to a relationship. It hurts us because it often brings disease to our bodies and adversely affects our personalities (see 1 Corinthians 6:12–20). Sex sin has tremendous power to destroy families, communities, and even nations, because it destroys the relationships upon which these institutions are built. God wants to protect us from hurting

ourselves and others; thus we are to have no part in sex sin, even if our culture accepts it.

2:20 In heathen temples, meat was often offered to idols. Then the meat that wasn't burned was sold to shoppers in the temple marketplace. Taking meat offered to idols wasn't wrong in itself, but it could violate the principle of sensitivity toward weaker Christian brothers and sisters who would be bothered by it (see 1 Corinthians 8 and the note on Romans 14:2). Jezebel was obviously more concerned about her own selfish pleasure and freedom than about the needs and concerns of fellow believers.

2:21 Obedience to Christ always involves a change of attitudes. When we are converted, a battle begins inside us as Satan tries to keep us from changing. John records this example from Jezebel's life to show the importance of changes in attitude. Our attitudes powerfully influence our behavior. Which of your attitudes would Jesus highlight as needing change? If you're having trouble doing right in an area of your life, perhaps you need a change of attitude.

2:23 The very things we try to hide from God are the sins that need to be confessed to him instead. We cannot hide from Christ, because he knows what is in our hearts. Jesus will judge both our motives and actions.

2:24, 25 Christ told the believers in Thyatira to hold on to their faith and let God's Word be their guide. Likewise, we should hold tightly to the Bible to avoid the many errors set forth as "deeper truths." We can do this by listening carefully to teaching and preaching in church and by reading the Bible daily.

2:26, 27 Christ says that the victorious ones (those who remain faithful until the end and continue to please him) will rule over his enemies and reign with him as he judges evil. We will participate in God's judgment of evil when his enemies are "shattered like a clay pot when it is dashed to the ground" (see also Psalm 2:8, 9; Isaiah 30:14; Jeremiah 19:11; 1 Corinthians 6:2, 3; 12:5; 19:15; 20:3, 4 for more about God's judgment).

a pot of clay that is broken into tiny pieces. ²⁸And I will give you the Morning Star! ²⁹"Let all who can hear, listen to what the Spirit says to the churches.

2:28
2 Pet 1:19
Rev 22:16

The lifeless church

3 "To the leader of the church in Sardis write this letter:

"This message is sent to you by the one who has the seven-fold Spirit of God and the seven stars.

3:1
Rev 1:4,11,16
3:8,15

"I know your reputation as a live and active church, but you are dead. ²Now wake up! Strengthen what little remains—for even what is left is at the point of death. Your deeds are far from right in the sight of God. ³Go back to what you heard and believed at first; hold to it firmly and turn to me again. Unless you do, I will come suddenly upon you, unexpected as a thief, and punish you.

3:3
Mt 24:42,43
1 Thess 5:2-6
1 Pet 3:10
Rev 2:5; 16:15

3:4
Rev 3:5; 4:4
6:11; 19:14

⁴"Yet even there in Sardis some haven't soiled their garments with the world's filth; they shall walk with me in white, for they are worthy. ⁵Everyone who conquers will be clothed in white, and I will not erase his name from the Book of Life, but I will announce before my Father and his angels that he is mine.

3:5
Ps 49:28
Mt 10:32
Lk 10:20; 12:8
Rev 13:8; 17:8
20:12

⁶"Let all who can hear, listen to what the Spirit is saying to the churches.

3:6
Rev 2:7

The obedient church

⁷"Write this letter to the leader of the church in Philadelphia.

"This message is sent to you by the one who is holy and true, and has the key of David to open what no one can shut and to shut what no one can open.

3:7
Isa 6:3; 22:22
Mt 16:19

⁸"I know you well; you aren't strong, but you have tried to obey and have not denied my Name. Therefore I have opened a door to you that no one can shut.

3:8
Acts 14:27
Rev 2:13

⁹"Note this: I will force those supporting the causes of Satan while claiming to be mine (but they aren't—they are lying) to fall at your feet and acknowledge that you are the ones I love.

3:9
Rev 2:9

¹⁰"Because you have patiently obeyed me despite the persecution, therefore I will protect you from the time of Great Tribulation and temptation, which will come upon the world to test everyone alive. ¹¹Look, I am coming soon! Hold

3:10
2 Tim 2:12
2 Pet 2:9
Rev 2:10; 3:8

3:11
Rev 2:10,25
22:7,12,20

3:8 *you have tried to obey*, literally, "you have kept my word." **3:9** *while claiming to be mine*, literally, "say they are Jews but are not." **3:11** *soon*, or, "suddenly," "unexpectedly."

2:28 Christ is called the Morning Star in 2 Peter 1:19 and Revelation 2:28 and 22:16. A morning star appears just before dawn, when things are coldest and darkest. When the world is at its bleakest point, Christ will burst onto the scene, exposing evil with his light of truth and bringing his promised reward.

3:1 The wealthy city of Sardis was actually in two locations. The older section of the city was on the mountain, and, when its population outgrew it, a newer section was built in the valley below.

3:1 The seven-fold Spirit of God is another name for the Holy Spirit (see the note on 1:4).

3:1 The problem in the church of Sardis was not heresy, but spiritual death. In spite of its reputation for being active, Sardis was infested with sin. Its deeds were evil and its garments soiled. The Spirit has no words of commendation for this church that looks good on the outside but is corrupt on the inside.

3:3 The church at Sardis was urged to hold on to the Christian truth they had heard when they first believed in Christ, but get back to the basics of the faith. It is important to grow in our knowledge of the Lord, to deepen our understanding through careful study. But no matter how much we learn, we must never abandon the basic truths about Jesus. Jesus will always be God's Son, and his sacrifice for our sins is permanent. No new truth from God will ever contradict these biblical teachings.

3:5 The Book of Life is where the names of all believers are registered. It symbolizes God's knowledge of who belongs to him. "Clothed in white" means set apart for God and made pure. Christ promises future honor and eternal life to those who stand firm in their faith. They will be guaranteed a listing in the Book of Life and

introduced to the hosts of heaven as ones who belong to Christ.

3:7 Philadelphia was founded by the citizens of Pergamos. The community was built in a frontier area as a gateway to the central plateau of Asia Minor. Philadelphia kept barbarians out of the region and brought in Greek culture and language. The city was destroyed by an earthquake in A.D. 17, and aftershocks kept the people so worried that most of them lived outside the city limits.

3:7 The key of David represents Christ's authority to open the door of invitation into his future Kingdom. After it is open, no one can close it—salvation is assured. Once it is closed, no one can open it—judgment is certain.

3:8 Philadelphia was a small church with little status or influence. However, the Philadelphian church was faithful to God, and he was pleased with them (Smyrna and Philadelphia were the only churches to receive completely positive messages from Christ). God would vindicate them for their faithfulness. If we feel insignificant, we should remember that God wants faithfulness more than worldly success. It isn't what we *accomplish* but what we *are* that really counts with God.

3:10 "I will protect you from the time of Great Tribulation" can also be translated, "I will keep you from failing in the hour of testing." Some believe there will be a future time of great tribulation from which true believers will be spared. Others interpret this to mean that the church will go through the time of tribulation and that God will keep them strong in spite of it. Still others believe this refers to "times of great tribulation" in general, the church's suffering through the ages. Whatever the case, the emphasis is on patiently obeying God through suffering.

tightly to the little strength you have—so that no one will take away your crown.

12"As for the one who conquers, I will make him a pillar in the temple of my God; he will be secure, and will go out no more; and I will write my God's Name on him, and he will be a citizen in the city of my God—the New Jerusalem, coming down from heaven from my God; and he will have my new Name inscribed upon him.

13"Let all who can hear, listen to what the Spirit is saying to the churches.

The lukewarm church

14"Write this letter to the leader of the church in Laodicea:

"This message is from the one who stands firm, the faithful and true Witness [of all that is or was or evermore shall be], the primeval source of God's creation:

15"I know you well—you are neither hot nor cold; I wish you were one or the other! 16But since you are merely lukewarm, I will spit you out of my mouth!

17"You say, 'I am rich, with everything I want; I don't need a thing!' And you don't realize that spiritually you are wretched and miserable and poor and blind and naked.

18"My advice to you is to buy pure gold from me, gold purified by fire—only then will you truly be rich. And to purchase from me white garments, clean and pure, so you won't be naked and ashamed; and to get medicine from me to heal your eyes and give you back your sight. 19I continually discipline and punish everyone I love; so I must punish you, unless you turn from your indifference and become enthusiastic about the things of God.

20"Look! I have been standing at the door and I am constantly knocking. If

3:12
1 Kgs 7:21
Jer 1:18
Ezek 48:35
Gal 4:26,27
Eph 3:15
Heb 12:22
Rev 14:1,21
21:2; 22:4

3:14
Jn 1:3
2 Cor 1:20
Col 1:15-18
Rev 1:5; 21:6
3:15
Rom 12:11
Rev 3:1
3:17
Hos 12:8
Zech 11:5
Mt 5:3
1 Cor 4:8
3:18
1 Cor 3:12,13
1 Pet 1:7
Rev 3:4; 16:15

3:19
Job 5:17
1 Cor 11:32
Heb 12:6
Rev 2:5

3:14 from the one who stands firm, literally, "from the Amen." of all that is evermore shall be, implied.

3:11 Christians have differing gifts, abilities, experience, and maturity. God doesn't expect us all to be the same, but he does expect us to persevere in using our assets for him. The Philadelphians are commended for their effort to obey (3:8) and encouraged to hold tightly to whatever strength they have. You may be a new believer and feel that your faith and spiritual strength are small. Use what you have to live for Christ, and God will commend you.

3:12 The New Jerusalem is the future dwelling of the people of God (21:22). Jesus will make us citizens of his holy city, giving us a new identity. We will have a new citizenship in God's future Kingdom. Everything will be new, pure, and secure.

3:14 Laodicea was the wealthiest of the seven cities of Asia, known for its banking industry, manufacture of wool, and a medical school that produced eye salve. But the city always had a problem with its water supply. At one time an aqueduct was built to bring water to the city from hot springs. But by the time the water reached the city, it was neither hot nor refreshingly cool—only lukewarm. The church had become as bland as the tepid water that came into the city.

3:15 Lukewarm water is unpalatable. The church in Laodicea had become lukewarm and thus distasteful and repugnant. The believers didn't stand for anything. Indifference had led them to idleness. By neglecting to do anything for Christ, the church had become hardened and self-satisfied. The church was destroying itself.

3:17 Some believers falsely assume that lots of material possessions are a sign of God's spiritual blessing. Laodicea was a wealthy city, and the church was also wealthy. But what the Laodiceans could see and buy had become more valuable to them than what is unseen and eternal. Wealth, luxury, and ease can make people feel confident, satisfied, and complacent. But no matter how much you possess or how much money you make, you have nothing if you don't have a vital relationship with Christ.

3:18 Laodicea was known for its great wealth—but Christ told the Laodiceans to buy their gold from him. The city was proud of its

cloth and dyeing industries—but Christ told them that they were naked and must purchase white garments from him. Laodicea prided itself on its precious eye salve that healed many eye problems—but Christ told them to get medicine from him to heal their eyes so they could see the truth. Christ was showing the Laodiceans that true value was not in material possessions, but in a right relationship with God. Their possessions and achievements were valueless compared with the everlasting future of Christ's Kingdom.

3:19 God would discipline this lukewarm church unless they turned from their indifference toward him. His purpose in discipline is not to punish, but to bring people back to him. Are you lukewarm in your devotion to God? God may discipline you to help you out of your indifference; but he uses only loving discipline. You can avoid God's discipline by drawing near to him again through confession, prayer, worship, and studying his Word. Just as the spark of love can be rekindled in marriage, so the Holy Spirit can reignite our zeal for God when we allow him to work in our hearts.

3:20 The Laodicean church was complacent and rich. They felt fulfilled, but they didn't have Christ's presence among them. He knocked at the door of their hearts, but they were so busy enjoying worldly pleasures that they didn't notice he was trying to enter. The pleasures of this world—money, security, material possessions—can be dangerous, because their temporary satisfaction makes us indifferent to God's offer of lasting satisfaction. If you find yourself feeling indifferent to church, to God, or to the Bible, you have begun to shut God out of your life. Leave the door of your heart constantly open to God and you won't need to worry about missing his knock. Letting him in is your only hope of lasting fulfillment.

3:20 Jesus is knocking on the door of our hearts every time we sense we should turn to him. He wants to have fellowship with us, and he wants us to open up to him. He is patient and persistent in trying to get through to us—not breaking and entering, but knocking. He allows us to decide whether or not to open our lives to him. Do you intentionally keep his life-changing presence and power on the other side of the door?

anyone hears me calling him and opens the door, I will come in and fellowship with him and he with me. 21I will let every one who conquers sit beside me on my throne, just as I took my place with my Father on his throne when I had conquered. 22Let those who can hear, listen to what the Spirit is saying to the churches."

3:21
Mt 19:28
Rev 5:5; 6:2
17:14; 20:4

3:22
Rev 2:7

B. MESSAGE FOR THE CHURCH (4:1—22:21)

Moving from the conditions within the churches in Asia to the future of the universal church, John sees the course of coming events in a way similar to Daniel and Ezekiel. Many of these passages contain clear spiritual teachings, but others seem beyond our ability to understand. The clear teaching of this book is that God will defeat all evil in the end. We must live in obedience to Jesus Christ, the coming Conqueror and Judge.

1. Worshiping God in heaven

The glorious throne

4 Then as I looked, I saw a door standing open in heaven, and the same voice I had heard before, that sounded like a mighty trumpet blast, spoke to me and said, "Come up here and I will show you what must happen in the future!" 2And instantly I was, in spirit, there in heaven and saw—oh, the glory of it!—a throne and someone sitting on it! 3Great bursts of light flashed forth from him as from a glittering diamond, or from a shining ruby, and a rainbow glowing like an emerald encircled his throne. 4Twenty-four smaller thrones surrounded his, with twenty-four Elders sitting on them; all were clothed in white, with golden crowns upon their heads. 5Lightning and thunder issued from the throne, and there were voices in the thunder. Directly in front of his throne were seven lighted lamps representing the seven-fold Spirit of God. 6Spread out before it was a shiny crystal sea. Four Living Beings, dotted front and back with eyes, stood at the throne's four sides. 7The first of these Living Beings was in the form of a lion; the second looked like an ox; the third had the face of a man; and the fourth, the form of an eagle, with wings spread out as though in flight. 8Each of these Living Beings had six wings, and the central sections of their wings were covered with eyes. Day after day and night after night they kept on saying, "Holy, holy, holy, Lord God Almighty—the one who was, and is, and is to come."

9And when the Living Beings gave glory and honor and thanks to the one sitting on the throne, who lives forever and ever, 10the twenty-four Elders fell down before him and worshiped him, the Eternal Living One, and cast their crowns before the throne, singing, 11"O Lord, you are worthy to receive the glory and the honor and

4:1
Ezek 1:1
Rev 1:10,19
11:12; 19:11

4:2
Isa 6:1
Rev 1:10; 4:9

4:3
Ezek 1:28; 28:13
Rev 10:1
21:11,19,20

4:4
Mt 19:28
2 Tim 2:12
Rev 11:16; 20:4

4:5
Ex 25:31-39
Zech 4:2-6
Rev 1:4; 5:6

4:6
Ezek 1:5-14
10:12,14
Rev 15:7; 19:4

4:7
Ezek 1:10; 10:21

4:9
Dan 4:34; 12:7
Rev 4:2; 10:6

4:10
Rev 4:4
5:8,14; 10:6

4:11
Rev 10:6

3:22 At the end of each letter to these churches, the believers are urged to listen to and take to heart what is written to them. Although a different message is addressed to each church, all the messages contain warnings and principles for everyone. Which letter speaks most directly to your church? Which has the greatest bearing upon your own spiritual condition at this time? How will you respond?

4:1 Chapters 4 and 5 are a glimpse into Christ's glory. Here we see into the throne room of heaven. God is orchestrating all the events that John will record. The world is not spinning out of control; the God of creation will carry out his plans as Christ initiates the final battle with the forces of evil. John shows us heaven before showing us earth so we will not be frightened by future events.

4:1 The "same voice [John] had heard before" was Christ (see 1:10, 11).

4:2 John says he was "in the Spirit" (alternate translation) four times in the book of Revelation (1:10; 4:2; 17:3; 21:10). This expression means the Holy Spirit was giving him a vision—showing him situations and events he could not see with mere human eyesight. All true prophecy comes from God through the Holy Spirit (2 Peter 1:20, 21).

4:4 Who are these 24 elders? Since there were 12 tribes of Israel in the Old Testament and 12 apostles in the New Testament, the 24

elders in this vision probably represent all the redeemed of God for all time (both before and after Christ's death and resurrection). They symbolize all those—both Jews and Gentiles—who are now part of God's family. The 24 elders show us that *all* the redeemed of the Lord are worshiping him.

4:5 In Revelation, lightning and thunder are connected with significant events in heaven. They remind us of the lightning and thunder at Mount Sinai when God gave the people his laws (Exodus 19:16). The Old Testament often uses such imagery to evoke God's power and majesty (Psalm 77:18).

4:5 The "seven-fold Spirit of God" is another name for the Holy Spirit (see the note on 1:4). See also Zechariah 4:2–6, where the seven lamps are equated with the one Spirit.

4:6 Just as the Holy Spirit is seen symbolically in the seven lighted lamps, so the four Living Beings represent the attributes (the qualities and character) of God. These Beings, probably not real animals, guard God's throne, lead others in worship, and proclaim God's holiness. God's attributes symbolized in the animal-like appearance of these four Beings are faithfulness (the ox), majesty and power (the lion), intelligence (the man), and sovereignty (the eagle). The Old Testament prophet Ezekiel saw four similar beings in one of his visions (Ezekiel 1:5–10).

4:11 The point of this chapter is summed up in this verse: all beings in heaven and earth will praise and honor God because he is the Creator and Sustainer of everything.

the power, for you have created all things. They were created and called into being by your act of will."

The scroll and the Lamb

5:1
Isa 29:11
Ezek 2:9
Dan 12:4
Rev 5:7

5 And I saw a scroll in the right hand of the one who was sitting on the throne, a scroll with writing on the inside and on the back, and sealed with seven seals. ²A mighty angel with a loud voice was shouting out this question: "Who is worthy to break the seals on this scroll, and to unroll it?" ³But no one in all heaven or earth or from among the dead was permitted to open and read it.

5:2
Rev 10:1; 18:21

5:3
Phil 2:10

⁴Then I wept with disappointment because no one anywhere was worthy; no one could tell us what it said.

5:4 *Then I wept with disappointment,* implied.

EVENTS IN REVELATION DESCRIBED ELSEWHERE IN THE BIBLE	Other Reference	Revelation Reference	Event
	Ezekiel 1:22–28	4:2, 3; 10:1–3	Glowing rainbow around God's throne
	Isaiah 53:7	5:68	Christ is pictured as a Lamb
	Psalms 96	5:9–14	New song
	Zechariah 1:7–11; 6:1–8	6:1–8	Horses and horsemen
	Isaiah 2:19–22	6:12; 8:5; 11:13	Earthquake
	Joel 2:28–32; Acts 2:14–21	6:12	Moon turns blood-red
	Mark 13:21–25	6:13	Stars falling from the heavens
	Isaiah 34:1–4	6:14	Heavens rolled up like a scroll
	Zephaniah 1:14–18; 1 Thessalonians 5:1–3	6:15–17	God's inescapable anger
	Jeremiah 49:35–39	7:1	Four winds of judgment
	Luke 8:26–34	9:1, 2; 17:3–8	Bottomless pit
	Joel 1:2—2:11	9:3–11	Plague of locusts
	Luke 21:20–24	11:1–3	Trampling of the holy city of Jerusalem
	Zechariah 4:1–14	11:4–6	Two olive trees as prophets
	Daniel 7	13:1–10	A Creature rising out of the sea
	2 Thessalonians 2:7–14	13:11–15	Wondrous signs and miracles done by evil beings
	Jeremiah 25:15–29	14:9–12	Drinking the cup of God's wrath
	Isaiah 21:1–10	18:2, 3	"Babylon" falls
	Matthew 22:1–14	19:5–8	Wedding banquet of the Lamb
	Ezekiel 38, 39	20:7–10	Conflict with Gog and Magog
	John 5:19–30	20:11–15	Judging of all people
	Ezekiel 37:21–28	21:3	God lives among mankind
	Isaiah 25:1–8	21:4	Our tears will be wiped away forever
	Genesis 2:8–14	22:1, 2	Trees of life
	1 Corinthians 13:11, 12	22:3–5	We will see God face to face
	Daniel 7:18–28	22:5	Believers shall reign with God forever

5:1ff Chapter 5 continues the glimpse into heaven begun in chapter 4.

5:1 In John's day, writing was done on scrolls—pieces of papyrus or vellum up to 30 feet long, rolled up and sealed with clay or wax. The scroll John sees contains the full account of what God has in store for the world, and only Christ can open it (5:3–5). The seven seals indicate the importance of its contents. They are placed throughout the scroll so that as each one is broken, more of the scroll can be read to reveal another phase of God's plan for the end of the world.

⁵But one of the twenty-four Elders said to me, "Stop crying, for look! The Lion of the tribe of Judah, the Root of David, has conquered, and proved himself worthy to open the scroll and to break its seven seals."

⁶I looked and saw a Lamb standing there before the twenty-four Elders, in front of the throne and the Living Beings, and on the Lamb were wounds that once had caused his death. He had seven horns and seven eyes, which represent the seven-fold Spirit of God, sent out into every part of the world. ⁷He stepped forward and took the scroll from the right hand of the one sitting upon the throne. ⁸And as he took the scroll, the twenty-four Elders fell down before the Lamb, each with a harp and golden vials filled with incense—the prayers of God's people!

⁹They were singing him a new song with these words: "You are worthy to take the scroll and break its seals and open it; for you were slain, and your blood has bought people from every nation as gifts for God. ¹⁰And you have gathered them into a kingdom and made them priests of our God; they shall reign upon the earth."

¹¹Then in my vision I heard the singing of millions of angels surrounding the throne and the Living Beings and the Elders: ¹²"The Lamb is worthy" (loudly they sang it!) "—the Lamb who was slain. He is worthy to receive the power, and the riches, and the wisdom, and the strength, and the honor, and the glory, and the blessing."

¹³And then I heard everyone in heaven and earth, and from the dead beneath the earth and in the sea, exclaiming, "The blessing and the honor and the glory and the power belong to the one sitting on the throne, and to the Lamb forever and ever." ¹⁴And the four Living Beings kept saying, "Amen!" And the twenty-four Elders fell down and worshiped him.

5:9 *singing,* literally, "saying," or "said." Also in vss 11, 12.

5:5
Gen 49:9
Isa 11:1,10
Heb 2:10
7:14,25
Rev 22:16

5:6
Isa 53:7
Zech 3:9; 4:10
Dan 8:3
1 Pet 1:19
Rev 1:4; 4:5

5:8
Rev 4:4,10; 5:6,11
8:3,4; 14:2
15:2

5:9
1 Pet 2:6
Rev 4:11; 7:9
14:3; 15:3,4

5:10
Ex 19:6
1 Pet 2:5-9
Rev 1:6; 3:21
20:4

5:11
Deut 33:2
Ps 68:17
Heb 12:22
Rev 4:4,6

5:12
Zech 13:7
Rev 1:6; 4:11

5:13
Phil 2:10,11

5:14
Rev 4:6,10

5:5 The Lion, Jesus, has proved himself worthy to break the seals and open the scroll by living a perfect life of obedience to God, dying on the cross for the sins of the world, and rising from the dead to show his power and authority over evil and death. Only Christ conquered sin, death, hell, and Satan himself; so only he can be trusted with the world's future.

5:5, 6 Jesus Christ is pictured as both a Lion (symbolizing his authority and power) and a Lamb (symbolizing his humble submission to God's will). One of the Elders calls John to look at the Lion, but when John looks he sees a Lamb. It is the Lamb, not the Lion, that becomes the focus in this vision. Christ the Lamb was the perfect sacrifice for the sins of all mankind; therefore, only he can save us from the terrible events revealed by the scroll. Christ the Lamb won the greatest battle of all—defeating all the forces of evil and death by submitting humbly to God's will and dying on the cross, the perfect sacrifice for mankind's sins. Christ the Lion is victorious in battle against Satan (19:19–21). Christ the Lion is victorious because of what Christ the Lamb has already done. We will enjoy the rewards of victory not because of our power and might but through our humble submission to God's will.

5:6 The Lamb's wounds are those inflicted on Jesus' body during his trial and crucifixion (see John 20:24–31). Jesus was called the Lamb of God by John the Baptist (John 1:29). In the Old Testament, lambs were sacrificed to cover sins. The Lamb of God died as the final sacrifice for all sins (see Isaiah 53:7; Hebrews 10:1–12, 18).

5:6 The horns symbolize strength and power (see 1 Kings 22:11; Zechariah 1:18). Although Christ is a sacrificial lamb, he is in no way weak. He was killed, but now he lives in God's strength and power. In Zechariah 4:2–10, the eyes are equated with the seven lamps and the one Spirit.

5:9, 10 People from every nation are praising God before his throne. The gospel is not limited to a specific culture, race, or country. Anyone who comes in repentance and faith is accepted by God and will be part of his Kingdom. Don't allow prejudice or bias to stop you from sharing Christ with others. Christ welcomes all people into his Kingdom.

5:9, 10 The song of the Living Beings and Elders recounts the work of Christ, for which they praise him. He (1) was slain, (2) bought them with his blood, (3) gathered them into a kingdom, (4) made them priests, and (5) appointed them to reign upon the earth. Jesus has already died and paid the penalty for sin. He is now gathering us into his Kingdom and making us priests, and in the future we will reign with him. Worship God and praise him for what he has done, what he is doing, and what he will do for all who trust in him. When we realize the glorious future that awaits us, we will find the strength to face present difficulties.

5:10 The believers' song praises Christ for bringing them into the Kingdom and making them "priests." Christ's death made all believers priests of God—the channels of blessing between God and mankind (1 Peter 2:5–9). While now we are sometimes depised and mocked for our faith, in the future we will reign over all the earth (John 15:17–27).

5:11 Angels are spiritual beings created by God, who help carry out his work on earth. They bring messages (Luke 1:26), protect God's people (Daniel 6:22), offer encouragement (Genesis 16:7ff), give guidance (Exodus 14:19), bring punishment (2 Samuel 24:16), patrol the earth (Ezekiel 1:9–14), and fight the forces of evil (2 Kings 6:16–18; Revelation 20:1). There are both good and evil angels (12:7), but because evil angels are allied with Satan, they have considerably less power and authority. Eventually, the main role of the good angels will be to offer continuous praise to God (see also 19:1–3).

5:14 The scene in chapter 5 shows us that only the Lamb, Jesus Christ, is worthy to open the scroll (the events of history). He holds it, not Satan. Jesus Christ is in control, and he alone is worthy to set into motion the events of the last days of history.

2. Breaking the seven seals

The seals

6:1
Rev 5:1,6

6 As I watched, the Lamb broke the first seal and began to unroll the scroll. Then one of the four Living Beings, with a voice that sounded like thunder, said, "Come!"

6:2
Zech 6:1-3
Rev 10:3,4
14:14; 19:11

²I looked, and there in front of me was a white horse. Its rider carried a bow, and a crown was placed upon his head; he rode out to conquer in many battles and win the war.

6:3
Rev 4:7

³Then he unrolled the scroll to the second seal, and broke it open too. And I heard the second Living Being say, "Come!"

6:4
Zech 1:8; 6:2
Mt 10:34
Jn 19:11

⁴This time a red horse rode out. Its rider was given a long sword and the authority to banish peace and bring anarchy to the earth; war and killing broke out everywhere.

6:5
Ezek 4:16
Zech 6:2

⁵When he had broken the third seal, I heard the third Living Being say, "Come!" And I saw a black horse, with its rider holding a pair of balances in his hand. ⁶And

6:8
Prov 5:5
Jer 15:2
Hos 13:14
Zech 6:3
Mt 11:23
Rev 1:18; 20:14

a voice from among the four Living Beings said, "A loaf of bread for $20, or three pounds of barley flour, but there is no olive oil or wine."

⁷And when the fourth seal was broken, I heard the fourth Living Being say, "Come!" ⁸And now I saw a pale horse, and its rider's name was Death. And there followed after him another horse whose rider's name was Hell. They were given control of one-fourth of the earth, to kill with war and famine and disease and wild animals.

6:9
Ex 29:12
Lev 4:7
Jn 16:2
Phil 2:17
2 Tim 4:6
Rev 12:17; 20:4

⁹And when he broke open the fifth seal, I saw an altar, and underneath it all the souls of those who had been martyred for preaching the Word of God and for being faithful in their witnessing. ¹⁰They called loudly to the Lord and said, "O Sovereign Lord, holy and true, how long will it be before you judge the people of the earth for what they've done to us? When will you avenge our blood against those living on the earth?" ¹¹White robes were given to each of them, and they were told to rest a little longer until their other brothers, fellow servants of Jesus, had been martyred on the earth and joined them.

6:10
Ps 79:10
Zech 1:12
Lk 18:7
Rev 3:7,10; 19:2

6:11
Dan 12:13
2 Thess 1:7
Heb 4:9; 11:40
Rev 3:5; 14:13

6:6 *A loaf of bread for $20, or three pounds of barley flour,* literally, "A choenix of wheat for a denarius, and three choenix of barley for a denarius. . . ." *there is no olive oil or wine,* literally, "do not damage the oil and wine."

6:1ff This is the first of three seven-part judgments. The trumpets (chapters 8, 9) and the flasks (chapter 16) are the other two. As each seal is broken, Christ the Lamb sets in motion events which will bring about the end of human history. This scroll is not completely opened until the seventh seal is broken (8:1). The contents of the scroll reveal the guilt and depravity of human beings and portray God's authority over the events of human history.

6:2ff Four horses appear as the first four seals are broken. The horses represent God's judgment of peoples' sin and rebellion. God is directing human history—even using his enemies to unknowingly accomplish his purposes. The four horses are a foretaste of the final judgments yet to come. Some view this chapter as a parallel to the Olivet Discourse (see Matthew 24). The imagery of four horses is also found in Zechariah 6:1–8.

6:2–8 Each of the four horses is a different color. Some say the white horse represents victory, and its rider is Christ (because Christ later rides to victory on a white horse—19:11). But since the other three horses relate to judgment and destruction, this white horse and rider may be the Antichrist who rules the world by deception for a short time. The other colored horses represent different kinds of judgment: red for warfare and bloodshed; black for famine and death; pale for disease and wild animal attacks.

6:8 "And there followed after him another horse whose rider's name was Hell," can also be translated, "and hell followed him." It is not clear whether Hell was on a separate horse or merely went along with Death, but the horsemen described in verses 2–8 are commonly referred to as the four horsemen of the apocalypse.

6:8 The four horsemen are given control of one-fourth of the earth,

indicating that God is still limiting his judgment—it is not yet complete. With these judgments there is still time for believers to turn to Christ and away from their sin. In this case, the limited punishment not only demonstrates God's wrath on sin, but also his merciful love in giving people yet another opportunity to turn to him before he brings final judgment.

6:9 The altar represents the altar of sacrifice in the Temple, where animals were sacrificed to atone for sins. Instead of the animals' blood at the foot of the altar, John saw the souls of martyrs who had died for preaching God's Word. These martyrs were told that still more would lose their lives for their belief in Christ (6:11). In the face of warfare, famine, persecution, and death, Christians will be called on to stand firmly for what they believe. Only those who endure to the end will be rewarded by God (Mark 13:13).

6:9–11 The martyrs are eager for God to bring justice to the earth, but they are told to wait. Those who suffer and die for their faith will not be forgotten, nor do they die in vain. Rather, they will be singled out by God for special honor. We may wish for justice immediately, as these martyrs did, but we must be patient. God works on his own timetable, and he promises justice. No suffering for the sake of God's Kingdom, however, is wasted effort.

6:10 Romans 12:19 says, "Dear friends, never avenge yourselves. Leave that to God, for he has said that he will repay those who deserve it." The prayer of the saints here is in keeping with the "imprecatory psalms" which call for God's judgment upon the psalmists' enemies. In both cases, the concern is for God to vindicate his name and his suffering people. Here, and in 8:4, 5, the judgments of God are revealed (in the seals, trumpets, and bowls) in answer to the prayers of the saints.

12I watched as he broke the sixth seal, and there was a vast earthquake; and the sun became dark like black cloth, and the moon was blood-red. 13Then the stars of heaven appeared to be falling to earth—like green fruit from fig trees buffeted by mighty winds. 14And the starry heavens disappeared as though rolled up like a scroll and taken away; and every mountain and island shook and shifted. 15The kings of the earth, and world leaders and rich men, and high-ranking military officers, and all men great and small, slave and free, hid themselves in the caves and rocks of the mountains, 16and cried to the mountains to crush them. "Fall on us," they pleaded, "and hide us from the face of the one sitting on the throne, and from the anger of the Lamb, 17because the great day of their anger has come, and who can survive it?"

6:12
Joel 2:10
Mt 24:29
Rev 16:18
6:13
Rev 8:10; 9:1
6:14
Ps 102:26
Heb 1:10-12
2 Pet 3:10
Rev 16:20; 21:1
6:16
2 Thess 1:7-9
6:17
Isa 13:6; 63:4
Mal 3:2

The 144,000 marked by God

7 Then I saw four angels standing at the four corners of the earth, holding back the four winds from blowing, so that not a leaf rustled in the trees, and the ocean became as smooth as glass. 2And I saw another angel coming from the east, carrying the Great Seal of the Living God. And he shouted out to those four angels who had been given power to injure earth and sea, 3"Wait! Don't do anything yet—hurt neither earth nor sea nor trees—until we have placed the Seal of God upon the foreheads of his servants."

4-8How many were given this mark? I heard the number—it was 144,000; out of all twelve tribes of Israel, as listed here:

7:1
Jer 49:36
Zech 6:5
Mt 24:31
7:2
Rev 9:14
7:3
Ezek 9:4,6
Dan 6:16
Eph 4:30
2 Tim 2:19
Rev 14:1; 22:4
7:4
Rev 9:16
14:1,3

Judah	12,000	Simeon	12,000
Reuben	12,000	Levi	12,000
Gad	12,000	Issachar	12,000
Asher	12,000	Zebulun	12,000
Naphatali	12,000	Joseph	12,000
Manasseh	12,000	Benjamin	12,000

6:13 *appeared to be falling to earth,* literally, "fell to the earth." **6:14** *the starry heavens disappeared,* literally, "the sky departed."

6:12 The sixth seal changes the scene back to the physical world. The first five judgments were directed toward specific areas, but this judgment is universal. Everyone will be afraid when the earth itself trembles.

6:15–17 At the sight of God sitting on the throne, all human beings great and small, will be terrified, calling for the mountains to fall on them so they will not have to face the judgment of the Lamb. This picture was not intended to frighten believers. For them, the Lamb is a gentle Savior. But those who previously showed no fear of God and proudly flaunted their unbelief will find they were wrong, and in that day they will have to face his wrath. No one who has rejected God can survive the day of his wrath, but those who belong to Christ will receive a reward rather than punishment. Do you belong to Christ? If so, you need not fear these final days.

7:1ff The sixth seal has been opened, and the people of the earth have tried to hide from God, saying, "Who can survive?" (6:12–17). Just when all hope seems lost, four angels hold back the four winds of judgment until God's people are marked as his. Only then will God break the seventh seal (8:1).

7:2 A seal on a scroll or document identified and protected its contents. God places his Great Seal on his followers, identifying them as his own and guaranteeing his protection over their souls. This shows how valuable we are to him. Our physical bodies may be beaten, maimed, or even destroyed, but *nothing* can harm the souls of those marked by God.

7:3 This Seal of God placed on the foreheads of his servants is the exact opposite of the mark of the beast explained in 13:16. These two marks place the people in two distinct categories—those owned by God and those owned by Satan. This

portrays a theme running throughout Revelation—Satan's attempt to imitate the great works of God.

7:4–8 The number 144,000 is 12 x 12 x 1,000, symbolizing completeness—*all* God's followers will be brought safely to him; not one will be overlooked or forgotten. God seals these believers either by withdrawing them from the earth (this is called the Rapture) or by giving them special power to make it through this time of great persecution. If they are to endure persecution, the seal does not necessarily guarantee protection from physical harm—many will die (see 6:11)—but God protects them from spiritual harm. No matter what happens, they will receive their reward in heaven. Their destiny is secure. These believers will not fall away from God even in intense persecution.

This is not saying that 144,000 individuals must be sealed before the persecution comes, but that when it begins, we can know the faithful have already been sealed (marked by God) and will remain true to him until the end.

7:4–8 This is a different list from the usual listing of the 12 tribes in the Old Testament, because it is a symbolic list of God's true followers. (1) Judah is mentioned first because Judah is both the tribe of David and of Jesus the Messiah (Genesis 49:8–12; Matthew 1:1). (2) Levi had no tribal allotment because of the Levites' work for God in the Temple (Deuteronomy 18:1), but here the tribe is given a place as a reward for faithfulness. (3) Dan and Ephraim are not mentioned, because they were known for rebellion and idolatry, traits unacceptable in God's followers (Genesis 49:17). (4) The two tribes representing Joseph (usually called Ephraim and Manasseh, after Joseph's sons) are here called Joseph and Manasseh, because of Ephraim's rebellion. See Genesis 49 for the story of the beginning of these 12 tribes.

The great crowd

7:9
Rev 3:5; 6:11; 5:9

9After this I saw a vast crowd, too great to count, from all nations and provinces and languages, standing in front of the throne and before the Lamb, clothed in white, with palm branches in their hands. 10And they were shouting with a mighty shout, "Salvation comes from our God upon the throne, and from the Lamb."

7:10
Rev 5:13;
12:10; 19:1; 22:3

7:11
Rev 4:4,6,10

11And now all the angels were crowding around the throne and around the Elders and the four Living Beings, and falling face down before the throne and worshiping God. 12"Amen!" they said. "Blessing, and glory, and wisdom, and thanksgiving, and honor, and power, and might, be to our God forever and forever. Amen!"

7:12
Rev 5:12,14

7:13
Rev 7:9

13Then one of the twenty-four Elders asked me, "Do you know who these are, who are clothed in white, and where they come from?"

7:14
Rev 6:11; 22:14

14"No, sir," I replied. "Please tell me."

7:15
Rev 4:9; 11:19
22:3

"These are the ones coming out of the Great Tribulation," he said; "they washed their robes and whitened them by the blood of the Lamb. 15That is why they are here before the throne of God, serving him day and night in his temple. The one sitting on the throne will shelter them; 16they will never be hungry again, nor thirsty, and they will be fully protected from the scorching noontime heat. 17For the Lamb standing in front of the throne will feed them and be their Shepherd and lead them to the springs of the Water of Life. And God will wipe their tears away."

7:16
Isa 49:10

7:17
Ps 23:1-5
Isa 25:8; 35:10
Jn 4:14; 10:11
Acts 20:28
1 Pet 5:2
Rev 21:4,6
22:1

The seventh seal

8:1
Rev 5:1,9
6:1-17

8 When the Lamb had broken the seventh seal, there was silence throughout all heaven for what seemed like half an hour. 2And I saw the seven angels that stand before God, and they were given seven trumpets.

8:3
Eph 5:2
Heb 9:4
Rev 5:8; 6:9

3Then another angel with a golden censer came and stood at the altar; and a great quantity of incense was given to him to mix with the prayers of God's people, to offer upon the golden altar before the throne. 4And the perfume of the incense mixed with prayers ascended up to God from the altar where the angel had poured them out.

8:4
Ps 141:2

8:5
Lev 16:12
1 Kgs 19:11
Ezek 10:2
Lk 12:49
Rev 16:18

5Then the angel filled the censer with fire from the altar and threw it down upon the earth; and thunder crashed and rumbled, lightning flashed, and there was a terrible earthquake.

7:17 *in front of,* literally, "in the center of the throne"; i.e., directly in front, not to one side. An alternate rendering might be, "at the heart of the throne."

7:9 Who is the crowd too numerous to count? While some say it is the martyrs described in 6:9, it may also be the same group as the 144,000 just mentioned (7:4–8). The 144,000 were sealed by God before the great time of persecution; the vast crowd was spared, as God had promised. Before, they were being prepared; now they are victorious. This crowd in heaven is composed of those who remained faithful to God throughout the generations.

7:10 People try many methods to remove the guilt of sin— good works, intellectual pursuits, and even casting blame. The crowd in heaven however, praises God, saying, "Salvation comes from our God upon the throne, and from the Lamb." Salvation from sin's penalty can come only through Jesus Christ. Have you had the guilt of sin removed in the only way possible?

7:11 More information about the Elders is found in the note on 4:4. The four Living Beings are explained further in the note on 4:6.

7:14 It is difficult to imagine how blood could whiten any cloth, but the blood of Jesus Christ is the world's greatest purifier because it removes the stain of sin. White symbolizes sinless perfection or holiness, which can be given to people only by the sacrifice and shed blood of the the sinless Lamb of God. This is a picture of how we are saved by faith (see Isaiah 1:18; Romans 3:21–26).

7:14 The Great Tribulation has been explained in several ways. Some believe it refers to the suffering of believers through the ages; others believe there will be a specific time of intense

tribulation. In either case, these believers come through their times of suffering by remaining loyal to God. If they are faithful, God will give them eternal life with him (7:17).

7:16, 17 God will provide for his children's needs in their eternal home, where there will be no hunger, thirst, or pain, and he will wipe away all tears. When you are suffering or torn apart by sorrow, take comfort in this truth.

7:17 In verses 1–8 we see the believers receiving a seal to protect them through a time of great tribulation and suffering; in verses 9–17 we see the believers finally with God in heaven. All who have been faithful through the ages are singing before God's throne. Their tribulations and sorrows are over: no more tears for sin, for all sins are forgiven; no more tears for suffering, for all suffering is over; no more tears for death, for all believers have been resurrected to die no more.

8:1, 2 When the seventh seal is opened, the seven trumpet judgments are revealed. In the same way, the seventh trumpet will announce the seven flask (bowl) judgments in 11:15 and 16:1–21. The trumpet judgments, like the seal judgments, are only partial. God's final and complete judgment has not yet come.

8:3 A censer filled with live coals was used in Temple worship. Incense was poured on the coals, and the sweet-smelling smoke drifted upwards, symbolizing believers' prayers ascending to God (see Exodus 30:7–9).

3. Sounding the seven trumpets

The trumpets

[6]Then the seven angels with the seven trumpets prepared to blow their mighty blasts.

[7]The first angel blew his trumpet, and hail and fire mixed with blood were thrown down upon the earth. One-third of the earth was set on fire so that one-third of the trees were burned, and all the green grass.

[8, 9]Then the second angel blew his trumpet, and what appeared to be a huge burning mountain was thrown into the sea, destroying a third of all the ships; and a third of the sea turned red as blood; and a third of the fish were killed.

[10]The third angel blew, and a great flaming star fell from heaven upon a third of the rivers and springs. [11]The star was called "Bitterness" because it poisoned a third of all the water on the earth and many people died.

[12]The fourth angel blew his trumpet and immediately a third of the sun was blighted and darkened, and a third of the moon and the stars, so that the daylight was dimmed by a third, and the nighttime darkness deepened. [13]As I watched, I saw a solitary eagle flying through the heavens crying loudly, "Woe, woe, woe to the people of the earth because of the terrible things that will soon happen when the three remaining angels blow their trumpets."

9 Then the fifth angel blew his trumpet and I saw one who was fallen to earth from heaven, and to him was given the key to the bottomless pit. [2]When he opened it, smoke poured out as though from some huge furnace, and the sun and air were darkened by the smoke.

[3]Then locusts came from the smoke and descended onto the earth and were given power to sting like scorpions. [4]They were told not to hurt the grass or plants or trees, but to attack those people who did not have the mark of God on their foreheads. [5]They were not to kill them, but to torture them for five months with agony like the pain of scorpion stings. [6]In those days men will try to kill themselves but won't be able to—death will not come. They will long to die—but death will flee away!

[7]The locusts looked like horses armored for battle. They had what looked like golden crowns on their heads, and their faces looked like men's. [8]Their hair was long like women's, and their teeth were those of lions. [9]They wore breastplates that seemed to be of iron, and their wings roared like an army of chariots rushing into

8:9 *turned red as blood,* literally, "became blood." **8:11** *"Bitterness,"* literally, "Wormwood." **9:1** *one who has fallen to earth from heaven.*

8:7
Joel 2:30
Zech 13:8,9
Mt 7:25-27
8:8
Ex 7:17
Zech 13:8,9
Rev 16:2
8:9
Rev 8:7-12
9:15,18
8:10
Isa 14:12
Rev 6:13; 9:1
12:4; 16:4
8:11
Ex 15:23
Heb 12:15
Rev 9:15
8:12
Ex 10:21
Zech 13:8
Rev 16:8
8:13
Rev 3:10; 9:12
9:1
Isa 14:12
Lk 8:31; 10:18
Rev 3:10;
8:10; 17:8; 20:1
9:2
Joel 2:2,30
9:3
Ex 10:4,5,12-15
Rev 9:5,7,10
9:4
Ex 12:23
Rev 6:6; 7:2,3
9:6
Job 3:21
Rev 6:16
9:7
Joel 2:4
9:8
Joel 1:6
9:9
Joel 2:5

8:6 The trumpet blasts have three purposes: (1) to warn that judgment is certain, (2) to call the forces of God and evil to battle, and (3) to announce the return of the King, the Messiah. These warnings urge us to make sure our faith is firmly fixed on Christ.

8:7–12 Since only one-third of the earth is destroyed by these trumpet judgments, this is only a partial judgment from God. His full wrath is yet to be unleashed.

8:13 Habakkuk used the image of an eagle to symbolize swiftness and destruction (see Habakkuk 1:8). The picture here is of a strong, powerful bird flying over all the earth, warning of the terrors yet to come. While both believers and unbelievers experience the terrors described in verses 7–12, the "people of the earth" are the unbelievers who will meet spiritual harm with the next three trumpet judgments. God has guaranteed believers protection from spiritual harm (7:2, 3).

8:13 In 6:10, the martyrs call out to God, "How long will it be before you judge the people of the earth?" As we see the world's wickedness, we too may cry out to God, "How long?" In the following chapters, the judgment comes at last. We may be distressed and impatient, but God has his plan and his timing, and we must learn to trust him to know what is best. Judgment is coming—be sure of that. Thank God for the time he gives you to turn from sin, and work to help others turn as well.

9:1 It is not known whether this "one" who fell from heaven is Satan, a fallen angel, Christ, or a good angel. Most likely it is Satan or an angel, because the key to the bottomless pit is held by Christ (1:17, 18), and it was temporarily given to this other being who fell from heaven. This being, whoever he may be, is still under God's control and authority. The bottomless pit represents the place of the demons and of Satan, the Prince of demons (9:11). See also Luke 8:31 for another reference to the bottomless pit.

9:3 The prophet Joel described a locust plague as a foreshadowing of the "Day of the Lord," meaning God's coming judgment (Joel 2:1–10). In the Old Testament, locusts were symbols of destruction because they destroyed vegetation. Here, however, they symbolize an invasion of demons called to torture people who do not believe in God. The limitations placed on the demons show that they are under God's authority.

9:3ff Some interpreters think these locusts are demons— evil spirits ruled by Satan who tempt people to sin. They were not created by Satan, because God is the Creator of all; rather, they are fallen angels who joined Satan in his rebellion. God limits what they can do; they can do nothing without his permission. Demons' main purpose on earth is to destroy, prevent, or distort people's relationship with God. While it is important to recognize their evil activity so we can stay away from them, we must avoid any curiosity about or involvement with demonic forces or the occult.

9:11
Job 26:6
Prov 15:11
Lk 8:31
Jn 12:31; 14:30
Rev 9:1

9:12
Rev 8:13; 11:14

9:13
Ex 30:2-10
Heb 9:24; 10:21
Rev 8:3

9:14
Gen 2:14; 15:18
Rev 7:1; 16:12

9:15
Rev 9:18; 20:7

9:16
Dan 7:10; 11:40
Rev 5:11; 7:4

9:17
Dan 8:2; 9:21

9:20
Deut 4:28
Ps 115:4-7
Dan 5:23
Mic 5:13
Acts 7:41
1 Cor 10:20
Rev 2:21

9:21
Rev 7:2

10:1
Mt 17:2
Rev 1:15,16;
4:3; 5:2; 18:1

10:3
Ps 29:3-9
Rev 4:5

10:4
Dan 8:26; 12:4
Rev 1:10; 22:10

10:6
Rev 4:9,11; 16:17
21:6

battle. 10They had stinging tails like scorpions, and their power to hurt, given to them for five months, was in their tails. 11Their king is the Prince of the bottomless pit whose name in Hebrew is Abaddon, and in Greek, Apollyon [and in English, the Destroyer].

12One terror now ends, but there are two more coming!

13The sixth angel blew his trumpet and I heard a voice speaking from the four horns of the golden altar that stands before the throne of God, 14saying to the sixth angel, "Release the four mighty demons held bound at the great River Euphrates." 15They had been kept in readiness for that year and month and day and hour, and now they were turned loose to kill a third of all mankind. 16They led an army of 200,000,000 warriors—I heard an announcement of how many there were.

17, 18I saw their horses spread out before me in my vision; their riders wore fiery-red breastplates, though some were sky-blue and others yellow. The horses' heads looked much like lions', and smoke and fire and flaming sulphur billowed from their mouths, killing one-third of all mankind. 19Their power of death was not only in their mouths, but in their tails as well, for their tails were similar to serpents' heads that struck and bit with fatal wounds.

20But the men left alive after these plagues *still refused to worship God!* They would not renounce their demon-worship, nor their idols made of gold and silver, brass, stone, and wood—which neither see nor hear nor walk! 21Neither did they change their mind and attitude about all their murders and witchcraft, their immorality and theft.

The angel with the small scroll

10 Then I saw another mighty angel coming down from heaven, surrounded by a cloud, with a rainbow over his head; his face shone like the sun and his feet flashed with fire. 2And he held open in his hand a small scroll. He set his right foot on the sea and his left foot on the earth, 3and gave a great shout—it was like the roar of a lion—and the seven thunders crashed their reply.

4I was about to write what the thunders said when a voice from heaven called to me, "Don't do it. Their words are not to be revealed."

5Then the mighty angel standing on the sea and land lifted his right hand to heaven, 6and swore by him who lives forever and ever, who created heaven and

9:11 and in English, the Destroyer, implied.   **9:14** four mighty demons, literally, "(fallen) angels."

9:13 The altar in the Temple had four projections, one at each corner, and these were called "the horns of the altar" (see Exodus 27:2).

9:14 These four unidentified demons will be exceedingly evil and destructive. But note that they do not have the power to release themselves and do their evil work on earth. Instead, they are held back by God and will be released by him at a specific time, doing only what he allows them to do.

9:15 Here one-third of all people are killed. In 6:7, 8, one-fourth of mankind is killed. Thus, over one-half of the people in the world will have been killed by God's great judgments. Even more would have been killed if God had not set limits on the destruction.

9:16 In John's day this number of warriors in an army was inconceivable, but today there are countries and alliances that could easily amass this many soldiers. This huge army, led by the four demons, will be sent out to destroy one-third of the earth's population. But the judgment is still not complete.

9:20, 21 These men were so hardhearted that even plagues did not drive them to God. People don't usually fall into immorality and evil suddenly—they slip into it a little at a time until, hardly realizing what has happened, they are irrevocably mired in their wicked ways. Any person who allows sin to take root in his life can find himself in this predicament. Temptation entertained today becomes sin tomorrow, then a habit the next day, then death and separation from God forever (see James 1:15). To think you could never become this evil is the first step toward a hard heart.

10:1-6 The purpose of this mighty angel is clear—to announce the final judgments on the earth. His right foot on the sea and left foot on the earth (10:2) indicate that his words deal with all creation, not just a limited part as with the seal and trumpet judgments. The seventh trumpet (11:15) will usher in the seven flask judgments, which will bring an end to the present world. When this universal judgment comes, God's truth will prevail.

10:2 We see two scrolls in Revelation. The first contains a revelation of judgments against evil (5:1ff). The contents of the second scroll are not indicated, but it also may contain a revelation of judgment. The prophet Ezekiel had a vision in which he was told to swallow a scroll filled with judgments against the nation of Israel (Ezekiel 3:1ff). It was sweet in his mouth, but its contents brought destruction—just like the scroll John was told to eat (10:9, 10). God's Word is sweet to believers, but bitter to unbelievers who are judged by it.

10:4 Throughout history people have wanted to know what would happen in the future, and God reveals some of it in this book. But John was stopped from revealing certain parts of his vision. An angel also told the prophet Daniel that some things he saw were not to be revealed yet to everyone (Daniel 12:9), and Jesus told his disciples that the time of the end is known by no one but God (Mark 13:32, 33). God has revealed all we need to know to live for him now. In our desire to be ready for the end, we must not place more emphasis on speculation about the last days than on living godly lives while waiting.

everything in it and the earth and all that it contains and the sea and its inhabitants, that there should be no more delay, 7but that when the seventh angel blew his trumpet, then God's veiled plan—mysterious through the ages ever since it was announced by his servants the prophets—would be fulfilled.

10:7
Amos 3:7
Rev 11:15

8Then the voice from heaven spoke to me again, "Go and get the unrolled scroll from the mighty angel standing there upon the sea and land."

10:8
Rev 10:2

9So I approached him and asked him to give me the scroll. "Yes, take it and eat it," he said. "At first it will taste like honey, but when you swallow it, it will make your stomach sour!" 10So I took it from his hand, and ate it! And just as he had said, it was sweet in my mouth but it gave me a stomach ache when I swallowed it.

10:9
Jer 15:16
Ezek 2:8; 3:1-3

11Then he told me, "You must prophesy further about many peoples, nations, tribes, and kings."

10:11
Rev 5:9

The two prophets

11 Now I was given a measuring stick and told to go and measure the temple of God, including the inner court where the altar stands, and to count the number of worshipers. 2"But do not measure the outer court," I was told, "for it has been turned over to the nations. They will trample the Holy City for forty-two months. 3And I will give power to my two witnesses to prophesy 1,260 days clothed in sackcloth."

11:1
Zech 2:1
Rev 21:15
11:2
Ezek 40:17-20
Lk 21:24
Rev 12:6; 13:5
11:3
Rev 2:13; 12:6

4These two prophets are the two olive trees, and two candlesticks standing before the God of all the earth. 5Anyone trying to harm them will be killed by bursts of fire shooting from their mouths. 6They have power to shut the skies so that no rain will fall during the three and a half years they prophesy, and to turn rivers and oceans to blood, and to send every kind of plague upon the earth as often as they wish.

11:4
Zech 4:3,11,14
11:5
2 Kgs 1:10-12
11:6
Ex 7:19

7When they complete the three and a half years of their solemn testimony, the tyrant who comes out of the bottomless pit will declare war against them and conquer and kill them; 8, 9and for three and a half days their bodies will be exposed in the streets of Jerusalem (the city fittingly described as "Sodom" or "Egypt")—the very place where their Lord was crucified. No one will be allowed to bury them, and people from many nations will crowd around to gaze at them. 10And there will be a worldwide holiday—people everywhere will rejoice and give presents to each

11:7
Rev 13:1,7
11:8
Rev 14:8; 16:9
17:5,18; 18:24
11:9
Ps 79:2
11:10
Neh 8:10
Mt 10:22

11:1 *a measuring stick . . . and to count the number of worshipers,* literally, "Rise and measure the temple of God, and the altar, and them that worship therein." **11:2** *forty-two months,* 3½ years, as in Dan 12:7. Also for *1260 days* in vs 3. **11:4** *two olive trees,* Zech 4:3, 4, 11. **11:7** *the bottomless pit,* Rev 9:11.

10:7 When God's plan for human history is completely revealed, all prophecy will be fulfilled. The end of the age will have arrived (see 11:15).

11:1ff This temple is most likely a symbol of the church (all true believers), because there will be no temple in the New Jerusalem (21:22). John measured the temple to show that God is building walls of protection around his people to spare them from spiritual harm, and that there is a place reserved for all believers who remain faithful to God.

11:2 Those worshiping inside the temple (inner court) will be protected spiritually, but those outside (outer court) will face great suffering. This is a way of saying that true believers will be protected through persecution, but those who refuse to believe will be destroyed.

11:3 In the book of Revelation, numbers are likely to have symbolic rather than literal meanings. The 42 months or 1,260 days equal 3 1/2 years. As half of the perfect number, 7, 3 1/2 can indicate incompletion, imperfection, or even evil. Notice the events predicted for this time period: trouble (Daniel 12:7), the Holy City is trampled (11:2), the woman takes refuge in the wilderness (12:6), and the devil-inspired creature controls the earth (13:5). Some commentators link the 3 1/2 years with the period of famine in the days of Elijah (Luke 4:25; James 5:17). Since Malachi predicted the return of Elijah before the last judgment (Malachi 4:5), and since the events in Daniel and Revelation pave the way for the

Second Coming, perhaps John was making this connection. It is possible, of course, that the 3 1/2 years are literal. If so, we will clearly recognize them when they are over! Whether symbolic or literal, however, they indicate that evil's reign will have a definite end.

11:4 These two prophets (witnesses) bear strong resemblance to Moses and Elijah, two of God's mighty prophets. With God's power, Moses called plagues down upon the nation of Egypt (see Exodus 8—11). Elijah prayed for the rain to cease (1 Kings 17). Both of these men appeared with Christ at his transfiguration (see Matthew 17:1-7).

11:7 This tyrant is also called the "beast" and could refer to Satan or an agent of Satan.

11:8, 9 Jerusalem, once the Holy City and the capital of Israel, is now enemy territory. It is compared with Sodom and with Egypt, both well-known for their evil.

11:10 The whole world rejoices at the deaths of these two prophets, who have caused trouble by saying what the people didn't want to hear—words about their sin, their need for repentance, and the coming punishment. Sinful people hate those who call attention to their sin and who urge them to repent. They hated Christ, and they hate his followers (1 John 3:13). When you obey Christ and take a stand against sin, be prepared to draw the world's hatred. But remember that the great reward awaiting you in heaven far outweighs any suffering you face now.

other and throw parties to celebrate the death of the two prophets who had tormented them so much!

11:11
Ezek 37:5,9-14

11But after three and a half days, the spirit of life from God will enter them and they will stand up! And great fear will fall on everyone. **12**Then a loud voice will shout from heaven, "Come up!" And they will rise to heaven in a cloud as their enemies watch.

11:12
2 Kgs 2:11
Mt 17:1-9
Acts 1:9
Rev 4:1

13The same hour there will be a terrible earthquake that levels a tenth of the city, leaving 7,000 dead. Then everyone left will, in their terror, give glory to the God of heaven.

11:13
Jn 9:24
Rev 6:12;
16:9,11,18,19

14The second woe is past, but the third quickly follows:

11:14
Rev 8:13; 9:12

The seventh trumpet

11:15
Dan 2:44
7:14,27
Acts 4:26
Rev 8:2; 10:7
12:10; 16:17

15For just then the seventh angel blew his trumpet, and there were loud voices shouting down from heaven, "The Kingdom of this world now belongs to our Lord, and to his Christ; and he shall reign forever and ever."

11:16
Mt 19:28
Rev 4:4,10

16And the twenty-four Elders sitting on their thrones before God threw themselves down in worship, saying, **17**"We give thanks, Lord God Almighty, who is and was, for now you have assumed your great power and have begun to reign. **18**The nations were angry with you, but now it is your turn to be angry with them. It is time to judge the dead, and reward your servants—prophets and people alike, all who fear your Name, both great and small—and to destroy those who have caused destruction upon the earth."

11:17
Rev 1:8; 19:6

11:18
Ps 2:1
Dan 7:10
Acts 10:42
Rev 10:7; 13:16
19:5; 20:12

19Then, in heaven, the temple of God was opened and the ark of his covenant could be seen inside. Lightning flashed and thunder crashed and roared, and there was a great hailstorm and the world was shaken by a mighty earthquake.

11:19
Rev 4:5; 15:5

4. Observing the great conflict
The woman and the Dragon

12:2
Isa 26:17
66:6-9
Mic 4:9,10

12:3
Isa 27:1
Rev 13:1,2
17:3,9,12,16

12 Then a great pageant appeared in heaven, portraying things to come. I saw a woman clothed with the sun, with the moon beneath her feet, and a crown of twelve stars on her head. **2**She was pregnant and screamed in the pain of her labor, awaiting her delivery.

3Suddenly a red Dragon appeared, with seven heads and ten horns, and seven crowns on his heads. **4**His tail drew along behind him a third of the stars, which he

11:15 *he shall reign forever and ever,* or "The Lord and his Anointed shall now rule the world from this day to eternity."

11:15 The seventh trumpet is blown, announcing the arrival of the King. There is now no turning back. The coming judgments are no longer partial, but complete in their destruction. God is in control, and he unleashes his full wrath upon the evil world that refuses to turn to him (9:20). When the wrath begins, there will be no escape.

11:16 For more on the 24 Elders, see the note on 4:4.

11:18 In the Bible, God gives rewards to his people according to what they deserve. Throughout the Old Testament, obedience often brought reward in this life (Deuteronomy 28), but obedience and immediate reward are not always linked. If they were, good people would always be rich, and suffering would always be a sign of sin. If we were quickly rewarded for every faithful deed, we would soon think we were pretty good. Before long, we would be doing many good deeds for purely selfish reasons. While it is true that God will reward us for our earthly deeds (see 20:12), our greatest reward is eternal life in his presence.

11:19 In Old Testament days, the ark of the covenant was the most sacred treasure of the Israelite nation. For more information about the ark, see the note on Exodus 37:1.

12:1—14:20 The seventh trumpet (11:15) ushers in the flask judgments (15:1—16:21), but in the intervening chapters (12—14), John sees the conflict between God and Satan. He sees the source of all sin, evil, persecution, and suffering on the earth, and he understands why the great battle between the forces of God and Satan must soon take place. In these chapters the nature of evil is exposed, and Satan is seen in all his wickedness.

12:1–6 The woman represents God's faithful people who have been awaiting the Messiah; the 12 stars on her head represent the 12 tribes of Israel. God set apart the Jews for himself (Romans 9:4, 5), and that nation gave birth to the Messiah. The boy (12:5) is Jesus, born to a devout Jew, Mary (Luke 1:26–33). Evil King Herod immediately tried to destroy the infant Jesus (Matthew 2:13–20). Herod's desire to kill this newborn "king," whom he saw as a threat to his throne, was motivated by Satan (the red Dragon), who wanted to kill the world's Savior. The heavenly pageant of Revelation 12 shows that Christ's quiet birth in the town of Bethlehem had cosmic significance.

12:3, 4 The red Dragon, Satan, has seven heads, ten horns, and seven crowns, representing his power and the kingdoms of the world over which he rules. The stars that plunged to earth with him are usually considered to be the angels who fell with Satan and became his demons. According to Hebrew tradition, one-third of all the angels in heaven fell with Satan. For more on demons, see the note on 9:3ff and Mark 5:1–20.

plunged to the earth. He stood before the woman as she was about to give birth to her child, ready to eat the baby as soon as it was born.

5She gave birth to a boy who was to rule all nations with a heavy hand, and he was caught up to God and to his throne. 6The woman fled into the wilderness, where God had prepared a place for her, to take care of her for 1,260 days. 7Then there was war in heaven; Michael and the angels under his command fought the Dragon and his hosts of fallen angels. 8And the Dragon lost the battle and was forced from heaven. 9This great Dragon—the ancient serpent called the devil, or Satan, the one deceiving the whole world—was thrown down onto the earth with all his army.

10Then I heard a loud voice shouting across the heavens, "It has happened at last! God's salvation and the power and the rule, and the authority of his Christ are finally here; for the Accuser of our brothers has been thrown down from heaven onto earth—he accused them day and night before our God. 11They defeated him by the blood of the Lamb, and by their testimony; for they did not love their lives but laid them down for him. 12Rejoice, O heavens! You citizens of heaven, rejoice! Be glad! But woe to you people of the world, for the devil has come down to you in great anger, knowing that he has little time."

13And when the Dragon found himself cast down to earth, he persecuted the woman who had given birth to the child. 14But she was given two wings like those of a great eagle, to fly into the wilderness to the place prepared for her, where she was cared for and protected from the Serpent, the Dragon, for three and a half years.

15And from the Serpent's mouth a vast flood of water gushed out and swept toward the woman in an effort to get rid of her; 16but the earth helped her by

12:5
Ps 2:9
Rev 2:27; 19:15
12:6
Rev 11:3; 13:5
17:18
12:7
Dan 10:13; 12:1
Jude 9
Rev 12:3
12:9
Gen 3:1
Zech 3:1,2
Mt 4:10
Lk 10:18
Rev 12:3,15
20:2-10
12:10
Rev 7:10; 11:15
12:11
Rev 2:10; 6:9
7:14; 15:2
12:12
Rev 8:13
10:6; 12:9; 13:6
18:20
12:14
Ex 19:4
Dan 7:25; 12:7
Rev 17:3,18
12:15
Hos 5:10

12:14 *for three and a half years,* literally, "a time and times and half a time."

12:6 The wilderness represents a place of spiritual refuge and protection from Satan. By aiding the woman's escape into the wilderness, God offers security to all true believers. Satan always attacks God's people, but God keeps them spiritually secure. Some will experience physical harm, but all will be protected from spiritual harm. God will not let Satan take the souls of his true followers.

12:6 The 1,260 days (3 1/2 years) is the same length of time that the Dragon was allowed to control the earth (13:5) and that the , Holy City was trampled (see the note on 11:3).

12:7 This event fulfills Daniel 12:1ff. Michael is a high- ranking angel. One of his responsibilities is to guard God's community of believers. For instance, it was Michael who fought Satan for the body of Moses (Jude 1:9).

12:7ff Much more happened at Christ's birth, death, and resurrection than most people realize. A battle between the forces of good and evil was under way. With Christ's resurrection, Satan's ultimate defeat was assured. Some believe that Satan's fall to earth took place at Jesus' resurrection or ascension and that the 1,260 days (3 1/2 years) is a symbolic way of referring to the time between Christ's first and second comings. Others say that Satan's defeat occurs at the midpoint of a literal seven-year tribulation period, following the rapture of the church and preceding the Second Coming of Christ and the beginning of his thousand-year reign. Whatever the case, we must remember that Christ is victorious—Satan has already been defeated by Christ's death on the cross (12:10–12).

12:9 Satan is not just a symbol or legend, he is very real. Originally he was an angel of God, but through his pride, he became corrupt. Satan is God's enemy and he constantly tries to hinder God's work, but he is limited by God's power and can do only what he is permitted to do (Job 1:6—2:8). The name *Satan*

means "Adversary" or "Accuser" (12:10). He actively looks for people to attack (1 Peter 5:8, 9). He likes to seek out believers who are vulnerable in their faith, who are spiritually weak.

Even though God permits Satan to do his work in this world, God is still in control. And Jesus has complete power over Satan—he defeated Satan when he died and rose again for the sins of mankind. One day Satan will be bound forever, never again to do his evil work (see 20:10).

12:10 Many believe that until this time, Satan still had access to God (see the note on Job 1:7ff). But here his access is forever barred (see also 9:1). He can no longer accuse people before God (see how Satan made accusations about Job before God in Job 1:6ff).

12:11 The critical blow to Satan came when the Lamb, Jesus Christ, shed his blood for our sins. The victory is won by sacrifice—Christ's sacrifice for sin, and the sacrifices we make because of our faith in him. As we face the battle with Satan, we should not fear it or try to escape from it, but loyally serve Christ who alone brings victory (see Romans 8:34–39).

12:12 The devil begins to step up his persecution because he knows that he "has little time." We are living in the last days, and Satan's work has become more intense. Even though Satan is very powerful, as we can see by the condition of our world, he is always under God's control. One of the reasons God allows Satan to work evil and bring temptation is so that those who pretend to be Christ's followers will be weeded out from his true believers. Satan knows that the great confrontation with Jesus is near. He is desperately trying to recruit as great an enemy force as possible for this final battle.

12:17 While the woman (12:1) represents faithful Jews, and the child (12:5) represents Christ, the "rest of her children" could be either Jewish believers or all believers. Most likely it refers to all believers. He who stands waiting on the beach is the Dragon, Satan.

12:17
Rev 1:2; 11:7
13:7; 14:1

opening its mouth and swallowing the flood! 17Then the furious Dragon set out to attack the rest of her children—all who were keeping God's commandments and confessing that they belong to Jesus. He stood waiting on an ocean beach.

The two Creatures

13:1
Dan 7:2-8
Rev 13:4,12
17:12

13:2
Dan 7:4-6
Rev 2:13; 12:3

13:3
2 Thess 2:9-12
Rev 13:12,14
17:8

13:4
Rev 13:2,12

13:5
Dan 7:8,11,20,
25; 11:36
2 Thess 2:3
Rev 11:2

13:6
Rev 7:15; 12:12

13:7
Rev 5:9; 11:7

13:8
Dan 12:1
1 Pet 1:19,20

13 And now, in my vision, I saw a strange Creature rising up out of the sea. It had seven heads and ten horns, and ten crowns upon its horns. And written on each head were blasphemous names, each one defying and insulting God. 2This Creature looked like a leopard but had bear's feet and a lion's mouth! And the Dragon gave him his own power and throne and great authority.

3I saw that one of his heads seemed wounded beyond recovery—but the fatal wound was healed! All the world marveled at this miracle and followed the Creature in awe. 4They worshiped the Dragon for giving him such power, and they worshiped the strange Creature. "Where is there anyone as great as he?" they exclaimed. "Who is able to fight against him?"

5Then the Dragon encouraged the Creature to speak great blasphemies against the Lord; and gave him authority to control the earth for forty-two months. 6All that time he blasphemed God's Name and his temple and all those living in heaven. 7The Dragon gave him power to fight against God's people and to overcome them, and to rule over all nations and language groups throughout the world. 8And all mankind—whose names were not written down before the founding of the world in the slain Lamb's Book of Life—worshiped the evil Creature.

13:7 *The Dragon gave him power to fight against God's people,* literally, "It was permitted to fight against God's people." **13:8** *whose names were not written down before the founding of the world in the slain Lamb's Book of Life,* or "those whose names were not written in the Book of Life of the Lamb slain before the founding of the world." That is, regarded as slain in the eternal plan and knowledge of God.

12:17 The apostle Paul tells us we are in a spiritual battle (Ephesians 6:10–12). John says the war is still being waged, but the outcome is already determined. Satan and his followers have been defeated and will be destroyed. Nevertheless, Satan is battling daily to bring more into his ranks and to keep his own from defecting to God's side. Those who belong to Christ have gone into battle on God's side, and he has guaranteed them victory. God will not lose the war, but we must make certain not to lose the battle for our own souls. Don't waver in your commitment to Christ. A great spiritual battle is being fought, and there is no time for indecision.

13:1ff Chapter 13 introduces Satan's two evil accomplices: (1) the Creature that comes out of the sea (13:1ff) and (2) the strange animal that comes out of the earth (13:11ff). Together, the three evil beings form an unholy trinity in direct opposition to the holy Trinity of God the Father, the Son, and the Holy Spirit (see especially 16:13, 14).

When Satan tempted Jesus in the wilderness, he wanted Jesus to show his power by turning stones into bread, to do miracles by jumping from a high place, and to gain political power by worshiping Satan (see Matthew 4:1–11). Satan's plan was to rule the world through Jesus, but Jesus refused to do Satan's bidding. Thus Satan turns to the fearsome creatures described in Revelation. To the Creature from the sea he gives political power. To the strange animal from the earth he gives power to do miracles. And the Creature and the animal work together to capture the control of the whole world. This unholy trinity—the Dragon, the evil Creature, and the false prophet—unite in a desperate attempt to overthrow God, but their efforts are doomed to failure. To find out what becomes of them, read Revelation 19:19–21 and 20:10.

13:1 This Creature was initially identified with Rome because the Roman Empire, in its early days, had an evil lifestyle, persecuted believers, and opposed God and his followers. But the Creature also symbolizes the Antichrist—not Satan, but someone under Satan's power and control. This Antichrist looks like a combination of the four beasts which Daniel saw centuries earlier in a vision (Daniel 7). As the Dragon is in opposition to God, so the Creature is against Christ and may be seen as Satan's false messiah. The early Roman Empire was strong and also anti-Christ (or against Christ's standards); many other individual powers throughout history have been anti-Christ. Many Christians believe that Satan's evil will culminate in a final Antichrist, one who will focus all the powers of evil against Jesus Christ and his followers.

13:3ff The Antichrist will be a counterfeit of Christ and will even stage a false resurrection (13:14). People will follow and worship him because they are awed by his power and miracles (13:3, 4). He will unite the world under his leadership (13:7, 8), and he will control the world economy (13:16, 17). People are impressed by power and will follow those who display it forcefully or offer it to their followers. But in following the Creature, they are only fooling themselves: he uses his power to manipulate others, to point to himself, and to promote evil plans. God, by contrast, uses his infinitely greater power to love and serve. Don't be misled by claims of great miracles or reports about a resurrection or reincarnation of someone claiming to be Christ. When Jesus returns, he will reveal himself to all believers (Matthew 24:23–28).

13:5 The power given to the Creature is limited by God. He allows the Creature to have it only for a short time. Even while the Creature is in power, God is still in control (11:15; 12:10–12).

13:5–7 The Creature will conquer God's people and rule over them, but he cannot harm them spiritually. He will establish worldwide dominance and demand that everyone worship him. And many *will* worship him—everyone except true believers (see 2 Thessalonians 2:3, 4). This will result in temporary suffering for God's people, but they will be rewarded with an eternal reward in the end.

13:8 See the note on 3:5 for more information on the Book of Life.

[9]Anyone who can hear, listen carefully: [10]The people of God who are destined for prison will be arrested and taken away; those destined for death will be killed. But do not be dismayed, for here is your opportunity for endurance and confidence.

13:10
Mt 26:52
Heb 6:12

[11]Then I saw another strange animal, this one coming up out of the earth, with two little horns like those of a lamb but a fearsome voice like the Dragon's. [12]He exercised all the authority of the Creature whose death-wound had been healed, whom he required all the world to worship. [13]He did unbelievable miracles such as making fire flame down to earth from the skies while everyone was watching. [14]By doing these miracles, he was deceiving people everywhere. He could do these marvelous things whenever the first Creature was there to watch him. And he ordered the people of the world to make a great statue of the first Creature, who was fatally wounded and then came back to life. [15]He was permitted to give breath to this statue and even make it speak! Then the statue ordered that anyone refusing to worship it must die!

13:11
Rev 13:1,4

13:12
2 Thess 2:4
Rev 14:9; 19:20

13:13
Ex 7:11; 19:9-11
Mt 24:24
2 Thess 2:9
2 Tim 3:8
Rev 11:15
16:14; 19:20

13:14
2 Thess 2:9
Rev 12:9
13:3,8,12

[16]He required everyone—great and small, rich and poor, slave and free—to be tattooed with a certain mark on the right hand or on the forehead. [17]And no one could get a job or even buy in any store without the permit of that mark, which was either the name of the Creature or the code number of his name. [18]Here is a puzzle that calls for careful thought to solve it. Let those who are able, interpret this code: the numerical values of the letters in his name add to 666!

13:15
Dan 3:3
7:20,25
Rev 20:4

13:16
Ps 49:2
Rev 14:9
19:17,18

The Lamb and the 144,000

14 Then I saw a Lamb standing on Mount Zion in Jerusalem, and with him were 144,000 who had his Name and his Father's Name written on their foreheads. [2]And I heard a sound from heaven like the roaring of a great waterfall or the rolling of mighty thunder. It was the singing of a choir accompanied by harps.

14:1
Dan 12:5
Heb 12:22
Rev 3:12; 5:6
7:4

13:10 *those destined for death will be killed,* or, "If anyone imprisons you, he will be imprisoned! If anyone kills you, he will be killed." **13:18** *666,* some manuscripts read "616."

13:10 In this time of persecution, being faithful to Christ could bring imprisonment and even execution. But all that the Creature and his followers can do to believers is harm them physically; no spiritual harm can come to those whose faith in God is sincere.

13:10 "Destined for prison" and "destined for death" are simply other ways of saying that some believers will be hurt and some killed in this great persecution. But all believers will enter God's presence perfected and purified by the blood of the Lamb (7:9–17).

13:10 The times of great persecution which John saw will be an opportunity for believers to endure and grow. The tough times we face right now are also opportunities for spiritual growth. Don't fall into Satan's trap and turn away from God when hard times come. Instead, use these tough times as opportunities for growth.

13:11ff The first Creature came out of the sea (13:1), but this animal comes out of the earth. Later identified as the False Prophet (16:13; 19:20), he is a counterfeit of the Holy Spirit. He seems to do good, but the purpose of his miracles is to deceive.

13:14 Throughout the Bible we see miracles performed as proofs of God's power, love, and authority. But here we see counterfeit miracles performed to deceive. This is a reminder of Pharaoh's magicians, who duplicated Moses' signs in Egypt (Exodus 7–12). True signs and miracles point us to Jesus Christ, but miracles alone can be deceptive. That is why we must ask of each miracle we see, "Is this consistent with what God says in the Bible?" The Creature here gains influence through the signs and then orders the people to worship a statue (see note on Matthew 24:15, 16)—a direct flouting of the second commandment (Exodus 20:4–6). Allowing the Scriptures to guide our faith and practice will keep us from being deceived by false signs, however convincing they appear. Any teaching that contradicts God's Word is false.

13:16–18 This mark, sometimes translated, "the mark of the beast," is designed to mock the mark God places on his followers (7:2, 3). Just as God marks his people to save them, so Satan's Creature marks his people to save them from the persecution that Satan will inflict upon God's followers. Identifying this mark is not as important as identifying the purpose of the mark. Those who accept it are showing their allegiance to Satan, their willingness to operate within the economic system he promotes, and their rebellion against God. To refuse the mark means committing oneself entirely to God, preferring death to compromising one's faith in Christ.

13:18 The meaning of this number has been discussed more than that of any other part of the book of Revelation. The three sixes have been said to represent many things, including the number of man or the unholy trinity of Satan, the Creature, and the False Prophet (16:13). If the number seven is looked upon as the "perfect number" in the Bible, and if three sevens represent complete perfection, then the number 666 falls completely short of perfection. The first readers of this book probably applied the number to the emperor Nero, who symbolized all the evils of the Roman Empire. (The Greek letters of Nero's name represent numbers which total 666.) Whatever specific application the number is given, it symbolizes the worldwide dominion and complete evil of this unholy trinity designed to undo Christ's work and overthrow him.

14:1ff Chapter 13 described the onslaught of evil that will occur when Satan and his helpers control the world. Chapter 14 gives a glimpse of eternity to show believers what awaits them if they endure. The Lamb is the Messiah. Mount Zion, often another name for Jerusalem, the capital of Israel, is contrasted with the worldly empire. The 144,000 represent believers who have endured persecutions on earth and now are ready to enjoy the eternal benefits and blessings of life with God forever. The three angels contrast the destiny of believers with that of unbelievers.

14:3
Rev 2:17; 4:4,6

14:4
Mt 19:12
2 Cor 11:2
Rev 5:9; 7:13-17

14:5
Heb 9:14
1 Pet 2:22
Jude 24

3This tremendous choir—144,000 strong—sang a wonderful new song in front of the throne of God and before the four Living Beings and the twenty-four Elders; and no one could sing this song except those 144,000 who had been redeemed from the earth. 4For they are spiritually undefiled, pure as virgins, following the Lamb wherever he goes. They have been purchased from among the men on the earth as a consecrated offering to God and the Lamb. 5No falsehood can be charged against them; they are blameless.

The three angels

14:6
Rev 5:9

14:7
Ps 124:8
Dan 8:19
Acts 14:15
Rev 4:11

14:8
Jer 51:7,8
Nah 3:19
Rev 16:19
17:2-5
18:2,3,10

14:9
Rev 13:14,16

14:10
Ps 75:8
Ezek 38:22
Mk 8:38
2 Thess 1:7
Rev 16:19
19:20; 20:15
21:8

14:11
Rev 13:17

14:12
Rev 2:13
12:17; 13:10

6And I saw another angel flying through the heavens, carrying the everlasting Good News to preach to those on earth—to every nation, tribe, language and people.

7"Fear God," he shouted, "and extol his greatness. For the time has come when he will sit as Judge. Worship him who made the heaven and the earth, the sea and all its sources."

8Then another angel followed him through the skies, saying, "Babylon is fallen, is fallen—that great city—because she seduced the nations of the world and made them share the wine of her intense impurity and sin."

9Then a third angel followed them shouting, "Anyone worshiping the Creature from the sea and his statue and accepting his mark on the forehead or the hand, 10must drink the wine of the anger of God; it is poured out undiluted into God's cup of wrath. And they will be tormented with fire and burning sulphur in the presence of the holy angels and the Lamb. 11The smoke of their torture rises forever and ever, and they will have no relief day or night, for they have worshiped the Creature and his statue, and have been tattooed with the code of his name. 12Let this encourage God's people to endure patiently every trial and persecution, for they are his saints who remain firm to the end in obedience to his commands and trust in Jesus."

The harvest of the earth

13And I heard a voice in the heavens above me saying, "Write this down: At last

14:4 *For they are spiritually undefiled, pure as virgins,* literally, "They have not defiled themselves with women, for they are virgins." **14:9** *anyone worshiping the Creature from the sea,* implied. **14:13** *his martyrs,* literally, "those who die in the faith of Jesus." Vs 12 implies death from persecution for Christ's sake.

14:4 These people are "spiritually undefiled" because they are true believers, whose robes have been washed and purified by Christ's blood through his death (see the first note on 7:14). In the Old Testament, idolatry was often portrayed as spiritual adultery (see the book of Hosea). These believers are spiritually pure; they have remained faithful to Christ and they have received God's reward for staying committed to him.

14:6, 7 Some believe this is a final, worldwide appeal to all people to recognize the one true God. No one will have the excuse of never hearing God's truth. Others, however, see this as an announcement of judgment rather than an appeal. The people of the world have had their chance to proclaim their allegiance to God, and now God's great judgment is about to begin. If you are reading this, you have already heard God's truth. You know that God's final judgment will not be put off forever. Have you joyfully received the everlasting Good News? If so, you have nothing to fear from God's judgment. The Judge of all the earth is your Savior!

14:8 Babylon was both an evil city and an immoral empire, a world center for idol worship. Babylon ransacked Jerusalem and carried off the kingdom of Judah into captivity (see 2 Kings 24 and 2 Chronicles 36). Just as Babylon was the Jews' worst enemy, the early Roman Empire was the worst enemy of the early Christians. John, who did not dare speak against Rome openly, applied the name *Babylon* to this enemy of God's people (see also 1 Peter 5:13)—and, by extension, to all God's enemies of all times.

14:9-11 Those who worship the Creature, accept his mark on their foreheads, and operate according to the Creature's world

economic system will ultimately face God's judgment. Our world values money, power, and pleasure over God's leadership. To get what the world values, many people deny God and violate Christian principles. Thus they must drink the cup of God's wrath.

14:11 The ultimate result of sin is unending separation from God. Because human beings were created in God's image with an inborn thirst for fellowship with him, separation from God will be the ultimate torment and misery. Sin always brings misery, but in this life we can choose to repent and restore our relationship with God. In eternity there will no longer be opportunity for repentance. If in this life we choose to be independent of God, in the next life we will be separated from him forever. Nobody is forced to choose eternal separation from God and nobody suffers this fate by accident. Jesus invites all of us to open the door of our hearts to him (3:20). If we do this, we will enjoy everlasting fellowship with him.

14:12 This news about God's ultimate triumph should encourage God's people to remain firm through every trial and persecution. They can do this, God promises, by trusting in Jesus and obeying the commands in his Word. The secret to enduring, therefore, is trust and obedience. Trust God to give you patience to endure even the small trials you face daily; obey him, even when obedience is unattractive or dangerous.

14:13 The old saying, "You can't take it with you," is certainly true of money, fame, and belongings. But God's people can produce fruit that survives even death. God will remember our love, kindness, and faithfulness, and those who accept Christ through our witness will join us in the new earth.

the time has come for his martyrs to enter into their full reward. Yes, says the Spirit, they are blest indeed, for now they shall rest from all their toils and trials; for their good deeds follow them to heaven!" [14]Then the scene changed and I saw a white cloud, and someone sitting on it who looked like Jesus, who was called "The Son of Man," with a crown of solid gold upon his head and a sharp sickle in his hand.

[15]Then an angel came from the temple and called out to him, "Begin to use the sickle, for the time has come for you to reap; the harvest is ripe on the earth." [16]So the one sitting on the cloud swung his sickle over the earth, and the harvest was gathered in. [17]After that another angel came from the temple in heaven, and he also had a sharp sickle.

[18]Just then the angel who has power to destroy the world with fire, shouted to the angel with the sickle, "Use your sickle now to cut off the clusters of grapes from the vines of the earth, for they are fully ripe for judgment." [19]So the angel swung his sickle on the earth and loaded the grapes into the great winepress of God's wrath. [20]And the grapes were trodden in the winepress outside the city, and blood flowed out in a stream 200 miles long and as high as a horse's bridle.

5. Pouring out the seven plagues
The angels with the last plagues

15 And I saw in heaven another mighty pageant showing things to come: Seven angels were assigned to carry down to earth the seven last plagues—and then at last God's anger will be finished.

[2]Spread out before me was what seemed to be an ocean of fire and glass, and on it stood all those who had been victorious over the Evil Creature and his statue and his mark and number. All were holding harps of God, [3,] [4]and they were singing the song of Moses, the servant of God, and the song of the Lamb:

> "Great and marvelous
> Are your doings,
> Lord God Almighty.
> Just and true
> Are your ways,
> O King of Ages. .
> Who shall not fear,
> O Lord,
> And glorify your Name?
> For you alone are holy.
> All nations will come
> And worship before you,
> For your righteous deeds
> Have been disclosed."

14:14 *"The Son of Man,"* literally, "one like a Son of Man." **14:18** *who has power to destroy the world with fire,* literally, "who has power over fire." **15:3, 4** *O King of Ages.* Some manuscripts read, "King of the Nations."

Cross references (margin)

14:14
Ezek 1:26
Dan 7:13
Rev 1:13; 6:2

14:15
Jer 51:33
Joel 3:13
Mt 13:39-41
Mk 4:29
Rev 14:17
15:6; 16:17

14:18
Joel 3:13
Rev 6:9; 8:3
14:15

14:19
Deut 32:32,33
Isa 62:2,3
Rev 16:8; 19:15

14:20
Gen 49:11
Lam 1:15
Ezek 39:17-21
Heb 13:11,12

15:1
Lev 26:21
Dan 4:2,3
6:27; 12:6-12
Rev 14:10; 15:6
16:1; 21:9

15:2
Rev 4:6; 5:8
12:11

15:3,4
Ex 15:1
Deut 32:3
Ps 86:9
Jer 10:7
Dan 9:11
Rev 5:9; 14:7

14:14–17 This is an image of judgment: Christ is separating the faithful from the unfaithful like a farmer harvesting his crops. This is a time of joy for the Christians who have been persecuted and martyred—they will receive their long-awaited reward. Christians should not fear the last judgment. Jesus said, "I say emphatically that anyone who listens to my message and believes in God who sent me has eternal life, and will never be damned for his sins, but has already passed out of death into life" (John 5:24).

14:19 A winepress was a large vat or trough where grapes were collected and then smashed. The juice flowed out of a duct that led into a large holding vat. The winepress is often used in the Bible as a symbol of God's wrath and judgment against sin (Isaiah 63:3–6; Lamentations 1:15; Joel 3:12, 13).

15:1 The seven last plagues are also called the seven flask judgments. They actually begin in chapter 16. Unlike the previous plagues, these are universal and will culminate in the abolition of all evil and the end of the world.

15:2 This is probably the "crystal sea" described in 4:6, located before the throne of God. Those who stand on it are victorious over Satan and his evil Creature. They are pure because they have been faithful to God to the end.

15:3, 4 The song of Moses celebrated Israel's deliverance from Egypt (Exodus 15). The song of the Lamb celebrates the ultimate deliverance of God's people from the power of Satan.

⁵Then I looked and saw that the Holy of Holies of the temple in heaven was thrown wide open!

⁶The seven angels who were assigned to pour out the seven plagues then came from the temple, clothed in spotlessly white linen, with golden belts across their chests. ⁷And one of the four Living Beings handed each of them a golden flask filled with the terrible wrath of the Living God who lives forever and forever. ⁸The temple was filled with smoke from his glory and power; and no one could enter until the seven angels had completed pouring out the seven plagues.

The flasks of God's wrath

16 And I heard a mighty voice shouting from the temple to the seven angels, "Now go your ways and empty out the seven flasks of the wrath of God upon the earth."

²So the first angel left the temple and poured out his flask over the earth, and horrible, malignant sores broke out on everyone who had the mark of the Creature and was worshiping his statue.

³The second angel poured out his flask upon the oceans, and they became like the watery blood of a dead man; and everything in all the oceans died.

⁴The third angel poured out his flask upon the rivers and springs and they became blood. ⁵And I heard this angel of the waters declaring, "You are just in sending this judgment, O Holy One, who is and was, ⁶for your saints and prophets have been martyred and their blood poured out upon the earth; and now, in turn, you have poured out the blood of those who murdered them; it is their just reward."

⁷And I heard the angel of the altar say, "Yes, Lord God Almighty, your punishments are just and true."

⁸Then the fourth angel poured out his flask upon the sun, causing it to scorch all men with its fire. ⁹Everyone was burned by this blast of heat, and they cursed the name of God who sent the plagues—they did not change their mind and attitude to give him glory.

¹⁰Then the fifth angel poured out his flask upon the throne of the Creature from the sea, and his kingdom was plunged into darkness. And his subjects gnawed their tongues in anguish, ¹¹and cursed the God of heaven for their pains and sores, but they refused to repent of all their evil deeds.

¹²The sixth angel poured out his flask upon the great River Euphrates and it dried up so that the kings from the east could march their armies westward without

16:10 the Creature from the sea, implied.

15:5-8 The Holy of Holies was the innermost room in the Temple (see Hebrews 9:1-17), where the ark of the covenant resided, (a symbol of God's presence among his people). This room was closed off from view by a great curtain. Only the High Priest could enter there, and only once a year on the Day of Atonement. The Holy of Holies was thrown open once before—at Christ's crucifixion, when the curtain was ripped from top to bottom (Matthew 27:50-53). The wide open entrance into the Holy of Holies symbolizes the open access to God's very presence which Christians have on the basis of Jesus' shed blood. Those of us who are united with the sinless Christ, our High Priest, can approach God boldly (Hebrews 4:14-16), but unrepentant sinners will be destroyed by his presence (Nahum 1:2-6).

The angels coming out of the temple are clothed in white with golden belts across their chests. Their garments, reminiscent of the High Priest's clothing, show that they are free from corruption, immorality, and injustice. The smoke that fills the Temple is the manifestation of God's glory and wrath. There is no escape from this judgment.

15:8 Our eternal reign with Christ won't begin until all evil is destroyed by his judgment.

16:1ff The flask judgments are God's final and complete

judgments upon the earth. The end has come. There are many similarities between the flask judgments and the trumpet judgments (8:6—11:19), but there are three main differences: (1) these judgments are complete where the trumpet judgments are partial; (2) the trumpet judgments still give unbelievers the opportunity to repent, but the flask judgments do not; and (3) mankind is indirectly affected by several of the trumpet judgments but directly attacked by all the flask judgments.

16:7 This verse can be translated, "I heard the altar cry." The significance of the altar itself crying out is that everyone and everything will be praising God, acknowledging his righteousness and perfect justice.

16:9-21 People knew that these judgments had come from God, because they cursed him for sending them. But they still refused to recognize God's authority and repent of their sins. If you find yourself ignoring God more and more, turn back to him now before your heart becomes too hard to repent (see the note on 9:20, 21 for more on hard hearts).

16:12 The Euphrates River was a natural protective boundary against the empires to the east (Babylon, Assyria, Persia). If it dried up, nothing could hold back invading armies. The armies of the east symbolize unhindered judgment.

hindrance. 13And I saw three evil spirits disguised as frogs leap from the mouth of the Dragon, the Creature, and his False Prophet. 14These miracle-working demons conferred with all the rulers of the world to gather them for battle against the Lord on that great coming Judgment Day of God Almighty.

15"Take note: I will come as unexpectedly as a thief! Blessed are all who are awaiting me, who keep their robes in readiness and will not need to walk naked and ashamed."

16And they gathered all the armies of the world near a place called, in Hebrew, Armageddon—the Mountain of Megiddo.

17Then the seventh angel poured out his flask into the air; and a mighty shout came from the throne of the temple in heaven, saying, "It is finished!" 18Then the thunder crashed and rolled, and lightning flashed; and there was a great earthquake of a magnitude unprecedented in human history. 19The great city of "Babylon" split into three sections, and cities around the world fell in heaps of rubble; and so all of "Babylon's" sins were remembered in God's thoughts, and she was punished to the last drop of anger in the cup of the wine of the fierceness of his wrath. 20And islands vanished, and mountains flattened out, 21and there was an incredible hailstorm from heaven; hailstones weighing a hundred pounds fell from the sky onto the people below, and they cursed God because of the terrible hail.

16:13
Rev 12:3
13:1,11,14

16:14
Rev 6:17;
17:14; 19:19

16:15
1 Thess 5:2
Rev 3:3,18

16:16
Judg 5:19
Zech 12:10,11
Rev 19:19

16:17
Dan 12:7-13
Rev 11:15; 21:6

16:18
Mt 24:21
Rev 4:5; 6:12

16:19
Rev 14:8,10

16:20
Rev 6:14; 20:11

16:21
Ex 9:18-25
Rev 11:19; 16:9

6. Seizing the final victory

The Prostitute and the scarlet animal

17 One of the seven angels who had poured out the plagues came over and talked with me. "Come with me," he said, "and I will show you what is going to happen to the Notorious Prostitute, who sits upon the many waters of the world. 2The kings of the world have had immoral relations with her, and the people of the earth have been made drunk by the wine of her immorality."

3So the angel took me in spirit into the wilderness. There I saw a woman sitting on a scarlet animal that had seven heads and ten horns, written all over with blasphemies against God. 4The woman wore purple and scarlet clothing and beautiful jewelry made of gold and precious gems and pearls, and held in her hand a golden goblet full of obscenities:

5A mysterious caption was written on her forehead: "Babylon the Great, Mother of Prostitutes and of Idol Worship Everywhere around the World."

6I could see that she was drunk—drunk with the blood of the martyrs of Jesus she had killed. I stared at her in horror.

17:1
Jer 51:13
Rev 17:5,15
19:2; 21:9

17:2
Jer 51:7-9
Rev 14:8; 17:8
18:3,9

17:3
Rev 1:10; 12:3,6
13:1

17:5
2 Thess 2:7
Rev 16:19
17:2,7

17:6
Dan 7:21,25
Rev 6:9; 16:6
12:11

16:13 *his False Prophet,* described in 13:11-15 and 19:20.   **16:17** *It is finished,* literally, "It has happened."

16:13, 14 These miracle-working demons that come from the unholy trinity unite the rulers of the world for battle against God. The demons which come from the mouths of the three evil rulers signify the verbal enticements and propaganda that will draw many people to their evil causes. For more about demons, see the note on 9:3ff.

16:15 Christ will return unexpectedly (1 Thessalonians 5:1–6), so we must be ready when he returns. We can prepare ourselves by standing firm in the midst of temptation and by being committed to God's moral standards. In what ways does your life show both your readiness and your lack of preparation for Christ's return?

16:16 This battlefield is near the city of Meggido (southeast of the modern port of Haifa) which guarded a large plain in northern Israel. It is a strategic location near a prominent international highway leading north from Egypt through Israel, along the coast, and on to Babylon. Megiddo overlooked the entire plain southward toward Galilee and westward toward Mount Gilboa.

16:16 Sinful men will unite to fight against God in a final display of rebellion. Many are already united against Christ and his people who stand for truth, peace, justice, and morality. Your personal battle with evil foreshadows the great battle pictured here, where God will meet evil and destroy it once and for all. Be strong and courageous as you battle against sin and evil: you are fighting on the winning side.

16:17–21 For more information on Babylon and what it represents in Revelation, see the note on 14:8. The city's division into three sections is a symbol of its complete destruction.

17:1ff The destruction of Babylon mentioned in 16:17–21 is now described in greater detail. The Notorious Prostitute, called Babylon, represented the early Roman Empire with its many gods and the blood of Christian martyrs on its hands. The Prostitute represents the seductiveness of the governmental system as it used immoral means to gain its own pleasure, prosperity, and advantage. In contrast to the Prostitute, Christ's bride, the church is pure and obedient (19:6–9). The wicked city of Babylon stands in contrast to the heavenly city of Jerusalem (21:10—22:5). The original readers easily identified Babylon with Rome, but it also symbolizes any system that is hostile to God (see 17:5).

17:3 The scarlet animal is either the Dragon of 12:3, or the Creature from the sea described in 13:1.

17:6 Throughout history people have been killed for their faith. Over the last century, millions have been killed by oppressive governments, and many of these were believers. The woman's drunkenness shows her pleasure in her evil accomplishments and

17:8
Rev 11:7; 13:1-8,
12,14

17:9
Rev 17:3

17:11
Rev 18:19

17:12
Dan 7:20-22
Rev 17:16
18:10,17,19

17:14
Mt 22:14
1 Tim 6:15
1 Pet 2:9
Rev 3:21; 16:14

17:15
Isa 8:7
Jer 47:2
Rev 13:7; 17:1

17:16
Jer 50:41,42
Ezek 16:37
Dan 7:5
Rev 18:8,19

17:17
Rev 10:7; 17:13

17:18
Rev 11:8; 16:19

7"Why are you so surprised?" the angel asked. "I'll tell you who she is and what the animal she is riding represents. 8He was alive but isn't now. And yet, soon he will come up out of the bottomless pit and go to eternal destruction; and the people of earth, whose names have not been written in the Book of Life before the world began, will be dumbfounded at his reappearance after being dead.

9"And now think hard: his seven heads represent a certain city built on seven hills where this woman has her residence. 10They also represent seven kings. Five have already fallen, the sixth now reigns, and the seventh is yet to come, but his reign will be brief. 11The scarlet animal that died is the eighth king, having reigned before as one of the seven; after his second reign, he too, will go to his doom. 12His ten horns are ten kings who have not yet risen to power; they will be appointed to their kingdoms for one brief moment, to reign with him. 13They will all sign a treaty giving their power and strength to him. 14Together they will wage war against the Lamb, and the Lamb will conquer them; for he is Lord over all lords, and King of kings, and his people are the called and chosen and faithful ones.

15"The oceans, lakes and rivers that the woman is sitting on represent masses of people of every race and nation.

16"The scarlet animal and his ten horns—which represent ten kings who will reign with him—all hate the woman, and will attack her and leave her naked and ravaged by fire. 17For God will put a plan into their minds, a plan that will carry out his purposes: They will mutually agree to give their authority to the scarlet animal, so that the words of God will be fulfilled. 18And this woman you saw in your vision represents the great city that rules over the kings of the earth."

The fall of Babylon

18:1
Ezek 43:2
Rev 10:1

18 After all this I saw another angel come down from heaven with great authority, and the earth grew bright with his splendor.

17:8 *go to eternal destruction,* literally, "go to perdition." *dumbfounded at his reappearance after being dead,* literally, "dumbfounded at the ruler who was, and is not, and will be present."   **17:9** *represent a certain city,* implied in vs 18.

**HOW CAN A
PERSON KEEP
AWAY FROM
THE EVIL
SYSTEM?**
Here
are some
suggestions:

1. People must always be more important than products.
2. Keep away from pride in your own programs, plans, and successes.
3. Remember that God's will and Word must never be compromised.
4. People must always be considered above the making of money.
5. Do what is right, no matter what the cost.
6. Be involved in businesses that provide worthwhile products or services—not just things that feed the world's desires.

---

her false feeling of triumph over the church. But every martyr who fell before her sword only strengthened the church.

17:8 In chapter 12 we met the Dragon (Satan). In chapter 13 we saw the Creature from the sea and the power he received from Satan. In chapters 14—16 we see God's great judgments. In this chapter, a scarlet animal similar to the Creature and the Dragon appears as an ally of the Notorious Prostitute. The animal's resurrection symbolizes the persistence of evil. This resurgence of evil power will convince many to join forces with him, but those who choose the side of evil condemn themselves to the devil's fate—eternal torment.

17:8 For more information on the Book of Life, see the note on 3:5.

17:9-14 Here John was almost certainly referring to Rome, the city famous for its seven hills. Many say this city also symbolizes all evil in the world—any person, religion, group, government, or structure that is against Christ. Whatever view is taken of the seven hills and seven kings, this section indicates the climax of Satan's struggle against God. Evil's power is limited and its destruction is on the horizon.

17:12 The ten horns represent kings of nations yet to arise. Rome

will be followed by other powers. Rome is a good example of how the Antichrist's system will work, demanding complete allegiance, and ruling by raw power, oppression, and slavery. Whoever the ten kings are, they will give their power to the Antichrist and will wage war against the Lamb.

17:16 In a dramatic turn of events, the woman's allies turn on her and destroy her. This is how evil operates. Destructive by its very nature, it discards its own adherents when they cease to serve its purposes. An unholy alliance is an uneasy alliance, because each partner puts its own interests first.

17:17 No matter what happens, we must trust that God is still in charge, and his plans will happen just as he says. He even uses people opposed to him to execute his will. Although he allows evil to permeate this present world, the new earth will never know sin.

18:1ff This chapter shows the complete destruction of Babylon, John's metaphorical name for the evil world power, and all it represents. Everything that tries to block God's purposes will come to a violent end. For more information on how the book of Revelation uses the name *Babylon,* see the note on 14:8.

²He gave a mighty shout, "Babylon the Great is fallen, is fallen; she has become a den of demons, a haunt of devils and every kind of evil spirit. ³For all the nations have drunk the fatal wine of her intense immorality. The rulers of earth have enjoyed themselves with her, and businessmen throughout the world have grown rich from all her luxurious living."

⁴Then I heard another voice calling from heaven, "Come away from her, my people; do not take part in her sins, or you will be punished with her. ⁵For her sins are piled as high as heaven and God is ready to judge her for her crimes. ⁶Do to her as she has done to you, and more—give double penalty for all her evil deeds. She brewed many a cup of woe for others—give twice as much to her. ⁷She has lived in luxury and pleasure—match it now with torments and with sorrows. She boasts, 'I am queen upon my throne. I am no helpless widow. I will not experience sorrow.' ⁸Therefore the sorrows of death and mourning and famine shall overtake her in a single day, and she shall be utterly consumed by fire; for mighty is the Lord who judges her."

⁹And the world leaders, who took part in her immoral acts and enjoyed her favors, will mourn for her as they see the smoke rising from her charred remains. ¹⁰They stand far off, trembling with fear and crying out, "Alas, Babylon, that mighty city! In one moment her judgment fell."

¹¹The merchants of the earth will weep and mourn for her, for there is no one left to buy their goods. ¹²She was their biggest customer for gold and silver, precious stones, pearls, finest linens, purple silks, and scarlet; and every kind of perfumed wood, and ivory goods and most expensive wooden carvings, and brass and iron and marble; ¹³and spices and perfumes and incense, ointment and frankincense, wine, olive oil, and fine flour; wheat, cattle, sheep, horses, chariots, and slaves—and even the souls of men.

¹⁴"All the fancy things you loved so much are gone," they cry. "The dainty luxuries and splendor that you prized so much will never be yours again. They are gone forever."

¹⁵And so the merchants who have become wealthy by selling her these things shall stand at a distance, fearing danger to themselves, weeping and crying, ¹⁶"Alas, that great city, so beautiful—like a woman clothed in finest purple and scarlet linens, decked out with gold and precious stones and pearls! ¹⁷In one moment, all the wealth of the city is gone!"

And all the shipowners and captains of the merchant ships and crews will stand

18:2
Isa 13:19-22
14:23; 21:8,9
Jer 50:39
Rev 14:8

18:3
Ezek 27:9-25
1 Tim 5:11
Rev 17:2

18:4
Gen 19:12,13
Isa 52:11
Jer 51:6,9,45
2 Cor 6:17

18:5
Jer 51:9
Jonah 1:2
Rev 16:19

18:6
Ps 137:8
Jer 51:24
Rev 17:4

18:7
Isa 47:7,8

18:8
Isa 47:9
Jer 50:31,34
Rev 17:16

18:9
Ps 58:10
Jer 50:46
Ezek 26:16
Dan 4:14
Rev 17:2

18:10
Num 16:34
Amos 5:16
Rev 14:8

18:11
Ezek 27:27
Rev 18:3

18:13
1 Tim 1:10

18:16
Lk 16:19
Rev 17:4

18:17
Isa 47:9
Ezek 27:27-36
Jonah 1:6
Rev 17:16

18:2 *of evil spirit,* literally, "of every foul and hateful bird." | **18:3** *have enjoyed themselves with her,* literally, "have committed fornication with her."

18:2, 3 Businessmen in the Roman Empire grew rich by exploiting the sinful pleasures of their society. Many business people today do the same thing. Businesses and governments are often based on greed, money, and power. Many bright individuals are tempted to take advantage of an evil system to enrich themselves. Christians are warned to stay free from the enchantment of money, status, and the "good life." We are to live according to the values Christ lived by: service, giving, self-sacrifice, obedience, and truth.

18:4–8 Babylon "lived in luxury and pleasure." She boasted, "I am queen upon my throne. . . . I will not experience sorrow." The powerful, wealthy people of this world are susceptible to this same attitude. A person who is financially comfortable often feels invulnerable, secure, and in control, not in need of God or anyone else. This kind of attitude defies God, and his judgment against it is harsh. We are told to avoid "her sins" (18:4). If you are financially secure, don't become complacent and deluded by the myth of self-sufficiency. Use your resources to help others and advance God's Kingdom.

18:9, 10 Those who are tied to the world's system will lose everything when it is taken away. Those who work only for material rewards will have nothing when they die or when their possessions are destroyed. What can we take with us to the new earth? Our faith, our characters, and our good deeds toward others. These are more important than any amount of money, power, or pleasure.

18:9–19 Those who are in control of various parts of the economic system will mourn at Babylon's fall. The leaders will mourn because they were the overseers of Babylon's wealth and were in a position to enrich themselves greatly. The merchants mourn because Babylon, the greatest customer for their goods, is gone. The sailors will no longer have anywhere to bring their goods because the merchants have nowhere to sell them. The fall of the evil world system affects all who enjoyed and depended on it. No one remains unaffected by Babylon's fall.

18:11–13 This list of various merchandise illustrates the extreme materialism of this society. Few of these goods are necessities—most are luxuries. The society had become so self-indulgent that people were willing to use evil means to gratify their desires. Even people had become commodities—the "souls of men," slaves, were sold to Babylon. It is amazing to realize that many of these goods, associated with unbelievable luxury in the ancient world, can be found in our homes. In our affluent society it is very easy to leave God out of this part of our lives.

18:11–19 God's people should not live for money. Instead, they should keep on guard constantly against greed, which is always ready to take over their lives. Money will be worthless in eternity, and God calls greed sinful.

18:18
Ezek 27:30,32
Rev 13:4

18:19
Ezek 27:30

18:20
Jer 51:48
Lk 11:49,50
Rev 6:10
12:12; 19:2

18:21
Jer 51:63,64
Dan 11:19

18:22
Ezek 26:13

18:23
Prov 4:18,19
24:20
Jer 7:34; 16:9
Nah 3:4

18:24
Mt 23:35-36
Rev 16:6; 17:6

19:1
Jer 51:48
Jonah 2:9
Mt 6:13
Rev 4:11;
7:10; 12:10

19:2
Rev 6:10;
16:7; 17:1; 18:20

19:3
Isa 34:10
Rev 4:4; 14:11

19:4
Rev 4:10; 5:14

19:5
Rev 11:18

19:6
Rev 11:15

19:7
Ps 45:10-16
Mt 25:1-10
Eph 5:25-32
Rev 21:2

19:8
Ps 45:13; 132:9
Rev 15:4,6
19:14

19:9
Lk 14:15; 22:16
Rev 21:5; 22:6

19:10
Rev 22:8,9

a long way off, 18crying as they watch the smoke ascend, and saying, "Where in all the world is there another city such as this?" 19And they will throw dust on their heads in their sorrow and say, "Alas, alas, for that great city! She made us all rich from her great wealth. And now in a single hour all is gone. . . ."

20But you, O heaven, rejoice over her fate; and you, O children of God and the prophets and the apostles! For at last God has given judgment against her for you.

21Then a mighty angel picked up a boulder shaped like a millstone and threw it into the ocean and shouted, "Babylon, that great city, shall be thrown away as I have thrown away this stone, and she shall disappear forever. 22Never again will the sound of music be there—no more pianos, saxophones, and trumpets. No industry of any kind will ever again exist there, and there will be no more milling of the grain. 23Dark, dark will be her nights; not even a lamp in a window will ever be seen again. No more joyous wedding bells and happy voices of the bridegrooms and the brides. Her businessmen were known around the world and she deceived all nations with her sorceries. 24And she was responsible for the blood of all the martyred prophets and the saints."

19 After this I heard the shouting of a vast crowd in heaven, "Hallelujah! Praise the Lord! Salvation is from our God. Honor and authority belong to him alone; 2for his judgments are just and true. He has punished the Great Prostitute who corrupted the earth with her sin; and he has avenged the murder of his servants."

3Again and again their voices rang, "Praise the Lord! The smoke from her burning ascends forever and forever!"

4Then the twenty-four Elders and four Living Beings fell down and worshiped God, who was sitting upon the throne, and said, "Amen! Hallelujah! Praise the Lord!"

5And out of the throne came a voice that said, "Praise our God, all you his servants, small and great, who fear him."

The wedding banquet of the Lamb

6Then I heard again what sounded like the shouting of a huge crowd, or like the waves of a hundred oceans crashing on the shore, or like the mighty rolling of great thunder, "Praise the Lord. For the Lord our God, the Almighty, reigns. 7Let us be glad and rejoice and honor him; for the time has come for the wedding banquet of the Lamb, and his bride has prepared herself. 8She is permitted to wear the cleanest and whitest and finest of linens." (Fine linen represents the good deeds done by the people of God.)

9And the angel dictated this sentence to me: "Blessed are those who are invited to the wedding feast of the Lamb." And he added, "God himself has stated this."

10Then I fell down at his feet to worship him, but he said, "No! Don't! For I am a servant of God just as you are, and as your brother Christians are, who testify of

---

18:22 *no more pianos, saxophones, and trumpets,* literally, "harpers . . . pipers . . . and trumpeters." **19:2** *sin,* literally, "fornication," the word used symbolically throughout the prophets for the worship of false gods. **19:9** *the angel,* literally, "he"; the exact antecedent is unclear. *God himself has stated this,* literally, "These are the true words of God." **19:10** *The purpose of all prophecy and of all I have shown you is to tell about Jesus,* literally, "The testimony of Jesus is the spirit of prophecy."

19:1, 2 The identity of this Great (or Notorious) Prostitute is explained in the note on 17:1.

19:1–8 A "vast crowd in heaven" initiates the chorus of praise to God for his victory (19:1–3). Then the 24 elders (identified in the note on 4:4), join the chorus (19:4). Finally, the great choir of heaven once again praises God—the wedding banquet of the Lamb has come (19:6–8).

19:1–10 Praise is the heartfelt response to God by those who love him. The more you get to know him and realize what he has done, the more you will respond with praise. Praise is at the heart of true worship. Let your praise of God flow out of your realization of who he is and how much he loves you.

19:7 This is the culmination of human history—the judgment of

the wicked and the marriage feast of the Lamb and his bride, the church. The church consists of all faithful believers from all time. The bride's purity stands in stark contrast to the filth of the Notorious Prostitute of chapter 17.

19:7–9 Here the church is pictured as both the bride (19:7, 8) and the guests invited to the wedding feast (19:9). As those given to Christ, we are the bride; as those called to be part of God's Kingdom, we are the invited guests.

19:9, 10 Jesus is the central focus of God's revelation and his redemptive plan (as announced by the prophets). As you read the book of Revelation, don't get bogged down in all the details of the awesome visions; remember that the overarching theme in all the visions is the ultimate victory of Jesus Christ over evil.

their faith in Jesus. The purpose of all prophecy and of all I have shown you is to tell about Jesus."

The rider on the white horse

11Then I saw heaven opened and a white horse standing there; and the one sitting on the horse was named "Faithful and True"—the one who justly punishes and makes war. 12His eyes were like flames, and on his head were many crowns. A name was written on his forehead, and only he knew its meaning. 13He was clothed with garments dipped in blood, and his title was "The Word of God." 14The armies of heaven, dressed in finest linen, white and clean, followed him on white horses.

15In his mouth he held a sharp sword to strike down the nations; he ruled them with an iron grip; and he trod the winepress of the fierceness of the wrath of Almighty God. 16On his robe and thigh was written this title: "King of Kings and Lord of Lords."

17Then I saw an angel standing in the sunshine, shouting loudly to the birds, "Come! Gather together for the supper of the Great God! 18Come and eat the flesh of kings, and captains, and great generals; of horses and riders; and of all humanity, both great and small, slave and free."

19Then I saw the Evil Creature gathering the governments of the earth and their armies to fight against the one sitting on the horse and his army. 20And the Evil Creature was captured, and with him the False Prophet, who could do mighty miracles when the Evil Creature was present—miracles that deceived all who had accepted the Evil Creature's mark, and who worshiped his statue. Both of them—the Evil Creature and his False Prophet—were thrown alive into the Lake of Fire that burns with sulphur. 21And their entire army was killed with the sharp sword in the mouth of the one riding the white horse, and all the birds of heaven were gorged with their flesh.

The 1,000 years

20 Then I saw an angel come down from heaven with the key to the bottomless pit and a heavy chain in his hand. 2He seized the Dragon—that old Serpent, the devil, Satan—and bound him in chains for 1,000 years, 3and threw him into the

Cross references (right margin):

19:11 Isa 11:4 / Rev 1:14; 3:14 / 6:2

19:12 Rev 2:17

19:13 Isa 63:1-3 / Jn 1:1,14

19:14 Mt 28:3 / Rev 3:4; 4:4

19:15 Isa 11:4; 63:3 / 2 Thess 2:8 / Rev 1:16; 2:27 / 14:19,20

19:16 Rev 2:17; 17:14

19:17 Isa 56:9 / Jer 12:9 / Ezek 39:17-20

19:19 Rev 13:1 / 16:14,16; 18:9

19:20 Dan 2:40-45 / 7:7,11-14 / 2 Thess 2:8-11 / Rev 13:11-16 / 20:10,14,15 / 21:8

20:1 Rev 1:18; 9:1

20:2 Rev 12:9

19:12 *A name was written on his forehead,* implied.   **19:13** *The Word of God,* literally, "The Logos," as in Jn 1:1—the ultimate method of God's revealing himself to man.   **19:20** *the False Prophet.* See ch 13, vss 11-16.

19:11 The name "Faithful and True" contrasts with the faithless and deceitful Babylon described in chapter 18.

19:11–21 John's vision shifts again. Heaven opens and Jesus appears, this time not as a Lamb, but as a warrior on a white horse (symbolizing victory). Jesus came first as a Lamb to be a sacrifice for sin, but he will return as a Conqueror and King to execute judgment (2 Thessalonians 1:7–10). His first coming brought forgiveness, his second will bring judgment. The battle lines have now been drawn between God and evil, and the world is waiting for the King to ride onto the field.

19:12 Although Jesus is called the "Faithful and True" (19:11), the "Word of God" (19:13), and the "King of Kings and Lord of Lords" (19:16), this verse implies that no name can do him justice. He is greater than any description or expression the human mind can devise for him.

19:13 For more about the symbolism of Jesus' garments being dipped in blood, see the first note on 7:14.

19:16 This title indicates our God's sovereignty. Most of the world is worshiping the Antichrist, who they believe has all power and authority. But suddenly out of heaven rides Christ and his army of angels—the "King of Kings and Lord of Lords." His entrance signals the end of the false powers.

19:17 This "supper of the Great God" is a grim contrast to the wedding banquet of the Lamb (19:7). One is a celebration; the other, devastation.

19:19 The Evil Creature is identified in the note on 13:1.

19:19–21 The battle lines are drawn, and the greatest confrontation in the history of the world is about to begin. The Antichrist and the False Prophet have gathered the governments and armies of the earth under the Antichrist's rule (see 16:14). They believe they have come of their own volition; in reality, God has summoned them to battle in order to defeat them. There really is no fight, however, because the victory was won when Jesus died on the cross for sin and rose from the dead. Thus the evil leaders are immediately captured and sent to their punishment, and the forces of evil are all annihilated.

19:20 The Lake of Fire is the final destination of the wicked. It is different from the bottomless pit referred to in 9:1. The Evil Creature and the False Prophet are thrown into the Lake of Fire. Then their leader, Satan himself, is cast there (20:10). Finally Death and Hell are also cast there (20:14). Afterward, everyone whose name is not recorded in the Book of Life will be sent to the same fate (20:15).

20:1 The bottomless pit is explained in the notes on 9:1 and 19:20.

20:2 The Dragon, Satan, is discussed in more detail in the notes on 12:3, 4 and 12:9. The Dragon is not bound in chains for punishment—that occurs in 20:10—but so that he cannot deceive the nations.

20:3 John doesn't say why God once again releases Satan, but it is part of his plan for judging the world. Perhaps it is to expose those who rebel against God in their hearts and confirm those who are truly faithful to God. Whatever the reason, Satan's release

20:4
Dan 7:9,18,
22,27
Mt 19:28
2 Tim 2:12
Rev 3:21
6:9,13

20:5
Ezek 37:2-14
Lk 14:14
Jn 5:28,29
Rom 11:15

20:6
1 Pet 2:9
Rev 1:6; 5:10
20:14; 21:8

20:7
Rev 20:2

20:8
Ezek 38:2
Rev 16:14

20:9
Ps 87:2
Ezek 38:9,22
Lk 9:54; 17:29

20:10
Mt 25:41,46
Rev 14:10; 19:20
20:14,15

20:12
Rom 14:10-12

bottomless pit, which he then shut and locked, so that he could not fool the nations any more until the thousand years were finished. Afterwards he would be released again for a little while.

4Then I saw thrones, and sitting on them were those who had been given the right to judge. And I saw the souls of those who had been beheaded for their testimony about Jesus, for proclaiming the Word of God, and who had not worshiped the Creature or his statue, nor accepted his mark on their foreheads or their hands. They had come to life again and now they reigned with Christ for a thousand years.

5This is the First Resurrection. (The rest of the dead did not come back to life until the thousand years had ended.) 6Blessed and holy are those who share in the First Resurrection. For them the Second Death holds no terrors, for they will be priests of God and of Christ, and shall reign with him a thousand years.

The destruction of Satan

7When the thousand years end, Satan will be let out of his prison. 8He will go out to deceive the nations of the world and gather them together, with Gog and Magog, for battle—a mighty host, numberless as sand along the shore. 9They will go up across the broad plain of the earth and surround God's people and the beloved city of Jerusalem on every side. But fire from God in heaven will flash down on the attacking armies and consume them.

10Then the devil who had betrayed them will again be thrown into the Lake of Fire burning with sulphur where the Creature and False Prophet are, and they will be tormented day and night forever and ever.

The final judgment

11And I saw a great white throne and the one who sat upon it, from whose face the earth and sky fled away, but they found no place to hide. 12I saw the dead, great

20:9 *of Jerusalem,* implied.   **20:11** *they found no place to hide,* literally, "There was no longer any place for them."

---

results in the final destruction of all evil (20:12–15).

20:2–4 The thousand years are often referred to as the *millennium,* (Latin for "one thousand"). Just how and when this thousand years takes place is understood differently among Christian scholars. The three major positions on this issue are called postmillennialism, premillennialism, and amillennialism.

(1) *Postmillennialism* looks for a literal thousand-year period of peace on earth brought in by the church. At the end of the thousand years, Satan will be unleashed once more, but then Christ will return to defeat him and reign forever. Christ's Second Coming does not occur until after the thousand-year period.

(2) *Premillennialism* also views the thousand years as a literal time period, but holds that Christ's Second Coming initiates his thousand-year reign and this reign occurs before the final removal of Satan.

(3) *Amillennialism* understands the thousand-year period to be symbolic of the time between Christ's ascension and his return. This millennium is the reign of Christ in the hearts of believers and in his church; thus it is the same as the church age. This period will end with the Second Coming of Christ.

These different views about the millennium need not cause division and controversy in the church, because each one acknowledges what is most crucial to Christianity—Christ will return, defeat Satan, and reign forever! Whatever and whenever the millennium is, Jesus Christ will unite all believers. We should not let this issue divide us.

20:4 The Creature's mark is explained in the note on 13:16–18.

20:5, 6 Christians hold two basic views concerning this First Resurrection. (1) Some believe the First Resurrection is spiritual, and that the millennium is our spiritual reign with Christ between his first and second comings. During this time, we are priests of God because Christ reigns in our hearts. In this view, the Second Resurrection is the bodily resurrection of all people for judgment.

(2) Others believe the First Resurrection occurs after Satan has been set aside. It is a physical resurrection of believers who then reign with Christ on the earth for a literal 1,000 years. The Second Resurrection occurs at the end of this millennium in order to judge unbelievers who have died.

20:6 The Second Death is spiritual death—everlasting separation from God (see 21:8).

20:7–9 Gog and Magog symbolize all the forces of evil who band together to battle God. Noah's son, Japheth, had a son named Magog (Genesis 10:2). Ezekiel presents Gog as a leader of forces against Israel (Ezekiel 38, 39).

20:9 This is not a typical battle where the outcome is in doubt during the heat of the conflict. Here there is no contest. Two mighty forces of evil—those of the Creature (19:19) and of Satan (20:8)—unite to do battle against God. The Bible uses just two verses to describe each battle—the evil Creature and his forces are captured and thrown into the Lake of Fire (19:20, 21), and fire from God consumes Satan and his attacking armies (20:9, 10). For God, it is as easy as that. There will be no doubt, no worry, no second thoughts for believers about whether they have chosen the right side. If you have chosen God, you will experience this tremendous victory with Christ.

20:10 Satan's power is not eternal—he will meet his doom. He began his evil work in mankind at the beginning (Genesis 3:1–6) and continues it today, but he will be destroyed when he is thrown into the Lake of Fire. Satan was released from the bottomless pit (20:7), but he will never be released from the Lake of Fire. He will never be a threat to anyone again.

20:11–15 At the judgment, the Books are opened. They represent God's judgment, and in them are recorded the deeds of everyone, good or evil. The Book of Life contains the names of those who have put their trust in Christ to save them.

and small, standing before God; and The Books were opened, including the Book of Life. And the dead were judged according to the things written in The Books, each according to the deeds he had done. ¹³The oceans surrendered the bodies buried in them; and the earth and the underworld gave up the dead in them. Each was judged according to his deeds. ¹⁴And Death and Hell were thrown into the Lake of Fire. This is the Second Death—the Lake of Fire. ¹⁵And if anyone's name was not found recorded in the Book of Life, he was thrown into the Lake of Fire.

20:13
Mt 16:27

20:14
1 Cor 15:26; 53
Rev 20:6,10,15

20:15
Rev 3:5; 20:12

7. Making all things new
The new earth

21 Then I saw a new earth (with no oceans!) and a new sky, for the present earth and sky had disappeared. ²And I, John, saw the Holy City, the new Jerusalem, coming down from God out of heaven. It was a glorious sight, beautiful as a bride at her wedding.

³I heard a loud shout from the throne saying, "Look, the home of God is now among men, and he will live with them and they will be his people; yes, God himself will be among them. ⁴He will wipe away all tears from their eyes, and there shall be no more death, nor sorrow, nor crying, nor pain. All of that has gone forever."

⁵And the one sitting on the throne said, "See, I am making all things new!" And then he said to me, "Write this down, for what I tell you is trustworthy and true: ⁶It is finished! I am the A and the Z—the Beginning and the End. I will give to the

21:1
Isa 65:17; 66:22
2 Pet 3:10,13

21:2
Jer 31:23
Heb 11:10; 12:22

21:3
2 Cor 6:16

21:4
Isa 25:8; 35:10
61:3
Rev 7:17

21:5
Isa 43:19
2 Cor 5:17

21:6
Rev 1:8; 22:17

21:3 *be among them;* some manuscripts add, "and be their God."

Genesis	Revelation	THE BEGINNING AND THE END
The sun is created	The sun is not needed	The Bible records for us the beginning of the world and the end of the world. The story of mankind, from beginning to end—from the fall into sin to the redemption of Christ and God's ultimate victory over evil—is found in the pages of the Bible.
Satan is victorious	Satan is defeated	
Sin enters the human race	Sin is banished	
People run and hide from God	People are invited to live with God forever	
People are cursed	The curse is removed	
Tears are shed, with sorrow for sin	No more sin, no more tears or sorrow	
The Garden and earth are cursed	God's city is glorified, the earth is made new	
The fruit from the Tree of Life is not to be eaten	God's people may eat from the Tree of Life	
Paradise is lost	Paradise is regained	
People are doomed to death	Death is defeated, believers live forever with God	

20:14 Death and Hell are thrown into the Lake of Fire— when God's judgment is finished. The Lake of Fire is the ultimate destination of everything wicked—Satan, the Creature, the False Prophet, the demons, Death, Hell, and all those whose names are not recorded in the Book of Life because they have not placed their faith in Jesus Christ.

21:1 The earth as we know it will not last forever, but after God's great judgment, he will create a new earth (see Romans 8:18–21; 2 Peter 3:7–13). God had also promised Isaiah that he would create a new and eternal earth (Isaiah 65:17; 66:22). We don't know how it will look or where it will be, but God and his followers—those whose names are written in the Book of Life—will be united to live there forever. Will you be there?

21:2, 3 The new Jerusalem is where God dwells among his people. Instead of our going up to meet him, he comes down to be with us, just as God became man in Jesus Christ and lived among us (John 1:14). Wherever God reigns, there is peace, security, and love.

21:3, 4 Have you ever wondered what eternity will be like? The

"Holy City, the new Jerusalem" is described as the place where God "will wipe away all tears." Forevermore, there will be no death, pain, sorrow, or crying. What a wonderful truth! No matter what you are going through, it's not the last word—God has written the final chapter, and it is about true fulfillment and eternal joy for those who love him. We do not know as much as we would like, but it is enough to know that eternity with God will be more wonderful than we can imagine.

21:5 God is the Creator. The Bible begins with the majestic story of his creation of the universe, and it concludes with his creation of a new heaven and earth. This is a tremendous hope and encouragement for the believer. When we are with him, with our sins forgiven and our future secure, we will be like Christ. We will be made perfect like him.

21:6 Just as God finished the work of creation (Genesis 2:1–3) and Jesus finished the work of redemption (John 19:30), so the Trinity will finish the entire plan of salvation by inviting the redeemed into a new creation.

21:6 For more about the Water of Life, see the note on 22:1.

21:7
Rom 8:17,32

21:8
Deut 20:8
Mal 3:5
1 Cor 6:9,10
Gal 5:19-21
Eph 5:5
Rev 2:11

thirsty the springs of the Water of Life—as a gift! 7Everyone who conquers will inherit all these blessings, and I will be his God and he will be my son. 8But cowards who turn back from following me, and those who are unfaithful to me, and the corrupt, and murderers, and the immoral, and those conversing with demons, and idol worshipers and all liars—their doom is in the Lake that burns with fire and sulphur. This is the Second Death."

The new Jerusalem

21:9
Rev 21:2

21:10
Ezek 40:1,2
2 Cor 12:2-4
Rev 1:10; 17:3

21:11
Job 28:17
Isa 60:1
Ezek 48:35
Rev 4:3

21:12
Ezek 48:31-34
Rev 22:14

21:14
Eph 2:20
Heb 11:10

21:15
Ezek 40:3
Zech 2:1,3
Rev 11:1

9Then one of the seven angels, who had emptied the flasks containing the seven last plagues, came and said to me, "Come with me and I will show you the bride, the Lamb's wife."

10In a vision he took me to a towering mountain peak and from there I watched that wondrous city, the holy Jerusalem, descending out of the skies from God. 11It was filled with the glory of God, and flashed and glowed like a precious gem, crystal clear like jasper. 12Its walls were broad and high, with twelve gates guarded by twelve angels. And the names of the twelve tribes of Israel were written on the gates. 13There were three gates on each side—north, south, east, and west. 14The walls had twelve foundation stones, and on them were written the names of the twelve apostles of the Lamb.

15The angel held in his hand a golden measuring stick to measure the city and its gates and walls. 16When he measured it, he found it was a square as wide as it was long; in fact it was in the form of a cube, for its height was exactly the same as its

---

WHAT WE KNOW ABOUT ETERNITY

Reference	Description
John 14:2–3	A place prepared for us
John 20:19, 26	Unlimited by physical properties (1 Corinthians 15:23)
1 John 3:2	We shall be like Jesus
1 Corinthians 15:1–58	We will have new bodies
1 Corinthians 2:9	Our experience will be wonderful
Revelation 21:1	A new environment
Revelation 21:3	A new experience of God's presence (1 Corinthians 13:12)
Revelation 21:4	New emotions
Revelation 21:4	There will be no more death

The Bible devotes much less space to describing eternity than it does to convincing people that eternal life is available as a free gift from God. Most of the brief descriptions of eternity would be more accurately called hints, since they use terms and ideas from present experience to describe what we cannot fully grasp until we are there ourselves. These references hint at aspects of what our future will be like if we have accepted Christ's gift of eternal life.

21:7,8 *Cowards* are not those who are fainthearted in their faith or who sometimes doubt or question. Rather, they are those who turn away from God and refuse to follow him further. They are not brave enough to stand up for Christ; they are not humble enough to accept his authority over their lives. They are put in the same list with the corrupt, murderers, liars, idolators, the immoral, and those practicing demonic arts.

Conquerors are those who "endure to the end without renouncing" Christ (Mark 13:13). They will receive the blessings God promised: (1) eating from the Tree of Life (2:7), (2) escaping from the Lake of Fire (2:11), (3) having a special name (2:17), (4) having power over the nations (2:26), (5) being included in the Book of Life (3:5), (6) being a pillar in God's spiritual temple (3:12), and (7) sitting with Christ on his throne (3:21). Those who can endure the testing of evil and remain faithful are those whom God will reward.

21:8 The Lake of fire is explained in the notes on 19:20 and 20:14. The Second Death is spiritual death, meaning either eternal torment or destruction. In either case, it is permanent separation from God.

21:10ff The rest of this section (21:9—22:5) is the final vision of

the book, a stunning description of the new city of God. The vision is symbolic and shows us that our new home with God will defy description. We will not be disappointed by it in any way.

21:12–14 The new Jerusalem is a picture of God's place for God's people. The 12 tribes of Israel (21:12) probably represent all the faithful in the Old Testament; the 12 apostles (21:14) represent the church. Thus, both believing Gentiles and Jews who have been faithful to God will live together on the new earth.

21:15–17 The city's measurements are symbolic of a place that will hold all God's people. Given in cubits, these measurements are all multiples of 12. Twelve is the number for God's people—there were 12 tribes in Israel, and 12 apostles who started the church. The walls are 144 cubits across (translated "216 feet across"); there are 12 layers in the walls, and 12 gates in the city; and the height, length, and breadth are all the same, 12,000 stadia (translated "1,500 miles"). The new Jerusalem is a perfect cube, the same shape as the Holy of Holies in the Temple (1 Kings 6:20). These measurements illustrate that this new home will be perfect for us, and the image portrays God as our Holy of Holies—we will live in him forever.

other dimensions—1,500 miles each way. [17]Then he measured the thickness of the walls and found them to be 216 feet across (the angel called out these measurements to me, using standard units).

[18, 19, 20]The city itself was pure, transparent gold like glass! The wall was made of jasper, and was built on twelve layers of foundation stones inlaid with gems: The first layer with jasper; the second with sapphire; the third with chalcedony; the fourth with emerald; the fifth with sardonyx; the sixth layer with sardus; the seventh with chrysolite; the eighth with beryl; the ninth with topaz; the tenth with chrysoprase; the eleventh with jacinth; the twelfth with amethyst. [21]The twelve gates were made of pearls—each gate from a single pearl! And the main street was pure, transparent gold, like glass.

[22]No temple could be seen in the city, for the Lord God Almighty and the Lamb are worshiped in it everywhere. [23]And the city has no need of sun or moon to light it, for the glory of God and of the Lamb illuminate it. [24]Its light will light the nations of the earth, and the rulers of the world will come and bring their glory to it. [25]Its gates never close; they stay open all day long—and there is no night! [26]And the glory and honor of all the nations shall be brought into it. [27]Nothing evil will be permitted in it—no one immoral or dishonest—but only those whose names are written in the Lamb's Book of Life.

21:17 Rev 13:18

21:18-20 Isa 54:11,12 Rev 4:3,6

21:22 Ps 90:1 Jn 4:21-24 17:23,24

21:23 Isa 60:19,20 Rev 21:25

21:24 Ps 72:10 Isa 60:3 66:10-14

21:25 Isa 60:11,20 Rev 22:5

21:26 Ps 72:10 Isa 49:23

21:27 Isa 52:1 Rev 3:5 22:14,15

The river of Life

22 And he pointed out to me a river of pure Water of Life, clear as crystal, flowing from the throne of God and the Lamb, [2]coursing down the center of the main street. On each side of the river grew Trees of Life, bearing twelve crops of fruit, with a fresh crop each month; the leaves were used for medicine to heal the nations.

[3]There shall be nothing in the city which is evil; for the throne of God and of the Lamb will be there, and his servants will worship him. [4]And they shall see his face; and his name shall be written on their foreheads. [5]And there will be no night there—no need for lamps or sun—for the Lord God will be their light; and they shall reign forever and ever.

22:1 Ezek 47:1,2 Jn 7:37-39 Rev 7:17

22:2 Gen 2:9 Ezek 47:12 Rev 2:7,22:14

22:3 Rev 7:15

22:4 1 Cor 13:12 Rev 7:3; 14:1

22:5 Rev 21:23,25

The promise of Jesus' return

[6, 7]Then the angel said to me, "These words are trustworthy and true: 'I am coming soon!' God, who tells his prophets what the future holds, has sent his angel

22:6,7 Rev 1:3; 21:5

21:17 *216 feet across . . . using standard units*, literally, "144 cubits by human measurements." A cubit was the average length of a man's arm—not an angel's! The angel used normal units of measurement that John could understand. **21:18-20** *The first layer*, implied. **21:22** *are worshiped in it everywhere*, literally, "are its temple." **22:2** *Trees of life*, literally, "the tree of life"—used here as a collective noun, implying plurality. **22:20** *soon*, or, "suddenly," "unexpectedly."

21:18–21 The picture of walls made of jewels reveals that the new Jerusalem will be a place of purity and durability—it will last forever. The ornate breastplate of the High Priest had twelve precious stones, representing the twelve tribes of Israel (see Exodus 28:15–21).

21:22–24 The Temple, center of God's presence among his people, was the primary place of worship. No temple is needed in the new city because God's presence will be everywhere. He will be worshiped throughout the city, and nothing will hinder us from being with him.

21:25–27 Not everyone will be allowed into the new Jerusalem, "only those whose names are written in the Lamb's Book of Life." (The Book of Life is explained in the notes on 3:5 and 20:11–15.) Don't think you'll get in because of your background, personality, or good behavior. Eternal life is available to you only because of what Jesus, the Lamb, has done. Trust him today to secure your citizenship in his new creation.

22:1 The Water of Life is a symbol of eternal life. Jesus used this same image with the Samaritan woman (John 4:7–14). It pictures the fullness of life with God and the eternal blessings that come when we believe in him and satisfy our spiritual thirst (see 22:17).

22:2 This Tree of Life (see textual note) is like the Tree of Life in the Garden of Eden (Genesis 2:9). After Adam and Eve sinned, they were forbidden to eat from the Tree of Life because they could not have eternal life as long as they were under sin's control. But because of the forgiveness of sin through the blood of Jesus, there will be no evil or sin in this city. We will be able to eat freely from the Tree of Life when sin's control over us is destroyed and our eternity with God is secure. Moreover, this "Tree of Life" bears twelve kinds of fruit so that fruit is available each month. Life in the new Jerusalem will be abundant and never-ending.

22:2 Why would the nations need to be healed if all evil is gone? John is quoting from Ezekiel 47:12, where water flowing from the Temple produces trees with healing leaves. He is not implying that there will be illness in the new earth; he is emphasizing that the Water of Life produces health and strength wherever it goes.

22:8
Rev 1:1-4
22:9
Rev 19:10
22:10
Rev 1:3
22:11
Ezek 3:27
Dan 12:10
22:12
Mt 16:27
Rev 22:7
22:13
Rev 1:8,17; 21:6
22:14
Rev 21:2,12,27
22:15
Gal 5:19-21
Rev 21:8
22:16
Isa 11:1
Mt 1:1; 2:2
Rev 1:1; 2:28
22:17
Jn 7:37-39
Rev 2:7,7:17
21:2,6,9
22:18
Deut 4:2; 12:32
Prov 30:5,6
Rev 15:6-16
22:19
Ex 32:33
Deut 4:2
Rev 3:5
21:10 22:5

to tell you this will happen soon. Blessed are those who believe it and all else written in the scroll."

8I, John, saw and heard all these things, and fell down to worship the angel who showed them to me; 9but again he said, "No, don't do anything like that. I, too, am a servant of Jesus as you are, and as your brothers the prophets are, as well as all those who heed the truth stated in this Book. Worship God alone."

10Then he instructed me, "Do not seal up what you have written, for the time of fulfillment is near. 11And when that time comes, all doing wrong will do it more and more; the vile will become more vile; good men will be better; those who are holy will continue on in greater holiness."

12"See, I am coming soon, and my reward is with me, to repay everyone according to the deeds he has done. 13I am the A and the Z, the Beginning and the End, the First and Last. 14Blessed forever are all who are washing their robes, to have the right to enter in through the gates of the city, and to eat the fruit from the Tree of Life.

15"Outside the city are those who have strayed away from God, and the sorcerers and the immoral and murderers and idolaters, and all who love to lie, and do so.

16"I, Jesus, have sent my angel to you to tell the churches all these things. I am both David's Root and his Descendant. I am the bright Morning Star. 17The Spirit and the bride say, 'Come.' Let each one who hears them say the same, 'Come.' Let the thirsty one come—anyone who wants to; let him come and drink the Water of Life without charge. 18And I solemnly declare to everyone who reads this book: If anyone adds anything to what is written here, God shall add to him the plagues described in this book. 19And if anyone subtracts any part of these prophecies, God

---

22:8, 9 Hearing or reading an eyewitness account is the next best thing to seeing the event yourself. John witnessed the events reported in Revelation and wrote them down so we could "see" and believe as he did. If you have read this far, you have "seen." Have you also believed?

22:8, 9 The first of the Ten Commandments is "You may worship no other god than me" (Exodus 20:3). Jesus said that the greatest command of Moses' laws was "Love the Lord your God with all your heart, soul, and mind" (Matthew 22:37). Here, at the end of the Bible, this truth is reiterated. The angel instructs John to "worship God alone." God alone is worthy of our worship and adoration. He is above all creation, even the angels. Are there people, ideas, goals, or possessions that occupy the central place in your life, crowding God out? Worship only God by allowing nothing to distract you from your devotion to him.

22:10, 11 The angel tells John what to do after his vision is over. Instead of sealing up what he has written, as Daniel was commanded to do (Daniel 12:4–12), the scroll is left open to let others see it so that all can read and understand. Daniel's message was sealed because it was not a message for Daniel's time. But the book of Revelation was a message for John's time, and it is equally relevant today. As Christ's return gets closer, there is a greater polarization between God's followers and Satan's followers. We must read the book of Revelation, hear its message, and be prepared for Christ's imminent return.

22:12–14 Those who are washing their robes are those who are seeking to purify themselves from a sinful way of life. They are daily striving to remain faithful and ready for Christ's return. This concept is also explained in the second note on 7:14.

22:14 In Eden, Adam and Eve were barred from the Tree of Life because of their sin (Genesis 3:22–24). In the new earth, God's people will eat from the Tree of Life because their sins have been

removed by Christ's death and resurrection. Those who eat the fruit of this tree will live forever. If Jesus has forgiven your sins, you will have the right to eat from this tree. For more on this concept, see the first note on 22:2.

22:16 Jesus is both David's Root and his Descendant. As the Creator of all, he existed long before David's day. As a human, however, he was one of David's direct descendants (see Isaiah 11:1–5; Matthew 1:1–17). As the Messiah, he is the Morning Star, the light of salvation to all.

22:17 Both the Holy Spirit and the bride, the church, extend the invitation to all the world to come to Jesus and experience the joys of salvation in Christ.

22:17 When Jesus met the Samaritan woman at the well, he told her of the Living Water that he could supply (John 4:10–15). This image is used again as Christ invites anyone to come and drink of the Water of Life. The gospel is unlimited in scope—all people, everywhere, may come. Salvation cannot be earned, but God gives it freely. We live in a world desperately thirsty for Living Water, and many are dying of thirst. But it's still not too late. Let us invite everyone to come and drink.

22:18, 19 This warning is given to those who might purposefully distort the message in this book. Moses gave a similar warning in Deuteronomy 4:1–4. We too must handle the Bible with care and great respect so that we do not distort its message, even unintentionally. We should be quick to put its principles into practice in our lives. No human explanation or interpretation of God's Word should be elevated to the same authority as the text itself.

shall take away his share in the Tree of Life, and in the Holy City just described.

²⁰"He who has said all these things declares: Yes, I am coming soon!"Amen! Come, Lord Jesus!

²¹The grace of our Lord Jesus Christ be with you all. Amen!

22:20
1 Thess 1:10
Heb 9:28
Rev 1:2; 22:7,16
22:21
Rom 16:20

22:20 We don't know the day or the hour, but Jesus is coming soon and at a time when no one will expect him. This is good news to those who trust him, but a terrible message for those who have rejected him and stand under judgment. *Soon* means at any moment, and we must be ready for him, always prepared for his return. Would Jesus' sudden appearance catch you off guard?

22:21 Revelation closes human history as Genesis opened it—in Paradise. But there is one distinct difference in Revelation—evil is gone forever. Genesis describes Adam and Eve walking and talking with God; Revelation describes people worshiping him face to face. Genesis describes a Garden with an evil serpent; Revelation describes a perfect city with no evil. The Garden of Eden was destroyed by sin; but Paradise is re-created in the new Jerusalem.

The book of Revelation ends with an urgent request: "Come, Lord Jesus!" In a world of problems, persecution, evil, and immorality, Christ calls us to endure in our faith (13:10, 11; 14:12). Our efforts to better our world are important, but their results cannot compare with the transformation Jesus will bring about when he returns. He alone controls human history, forgives sin, and will re-create the earth and bring lasting peace.

Revelation is above all a book of hope. It shows that no matter what happens on earth, God is in control. It promises that evil will not last forever. And it depicts the wonderful reward that is waiting for all those who believe in Jesus Christ as Savior and Lord.

Order extra COPIES of Living Letters' Life Application Edition to share with family and friends. This exciting new study Bible will be an invaluable tool as they look into God's living and life-giving Word. $6.95 (paper)

You may also order this Bible resource in other editions from Tyndale:

The Life Application Bible (cloth).
Suggested retail price $34.95. Your price $29.95.

The Life Application New Testament (cover).
Suggested retail price $12.95. Your price $10.95.

cut along dotted line and mail to:
Tyndale, Box 1240, Minneapolis, Minnesota 55440

☐ Please bill me for the following order. (I understand a postage and handling charge will be added.)

☐ Enclosed is my check (or money order) of $_____ for the following order. (I understand there is no postage or handling charge when my check accompanies my order). (Minnesota residents add 6% sales tax.

Please send me the following:

_____ additional copies of Living Letters' Life Application Edition (#LA6C)

_____ copies of the Life Application Bible (#LA6C)

_____ copies of The Life Application New Testament (#LA6)

Name _____

Address _____

City _____ State _____ Zip _____

OX

Order extra copies of *Living Letters: Life Application Edition* to
share with family and friends! This exciting new study Bible will be an invaluable tool as they look into God's living and life-giving Word. **$6.95 (paper)**

You may also order this Bible resource in other editions from Grason:

The Life Application Bible (cloth)
Suggested retail price $34.95 **Your price $29.95**

The Life Application New Testament (kivar)
Suggested retail price $12.95 **Your price $10.95**

cut along dotted line and mail to:
Grason, Box 1240, Minneapolis, Minnesota 55440

- -

❏ Please bill me for the following order (I understand a postage and handling charge will be added).

❏ Enclosed is my check (or money order) of $_____ for the following order (I understand there is no postage or handling charge when my check accompanies my order). Minnesota residents add 6% sales tax.

Please send me the following:

___ additional copies of *Living Letters: Life Application Edition* (41462)

___ copies of *The Life Application Bible* (41460)

___ copies of *The Life Application New Testament* (41461)

Name _____

Address _____

City _____
                                              State   ZIP

XQ